# Disclaimer

The publisher of this book is by no way associated with the National Institute of Standards and Technology (NIST). The NIST did not publish this book. It was published by 50 page publications under the public domain license.

50 Page Publications.

**Book Title:** 2010 Proceedings of the Performance Metrics for Intelligent Systems (PerMIS'10) Workshop

**Book Author:** Rajmohan Madhavan; Elena R. Messina; Brian A. Weiss

**Book Abstract:** The 2010 Performance Metrics for Intelligent Systems workshop is the tenth in a series dedicated to defining measures and methodologies of evaluating performance of intelligent systems. Started in 2000, the PerMIS series focuses on applications of performance measures to applied problems in commercial, industrial, homeland security, and military applications. The main theme of PerMIS'10 is the key role of performance assessment in developing intelligent systems that can co-exist with humans towards improving the quality of our lives intertwined with automation.

**Citation:** NIST SP - 1113

**Keyword:** Performance Evaluation; Performance Assessment; Performance Metrics; Co-X; Testing and Evaluation; Technology Readiness Measures; Benchmarks; Applied Performance Measures

# PERFORMANCE METRICS
## for
# INTELLIGENT SYSTEMS (PerMIS)
# WORKSHOP
### Hyatt Regency, Baltimore, Maryland USA
### September 28 - 30, 2010

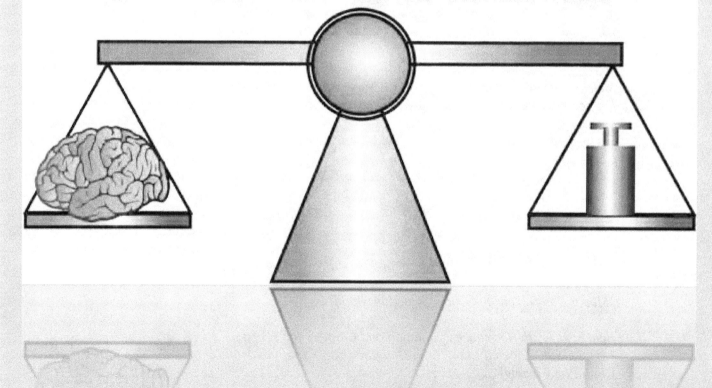

# Table of Contents

Foreword . . . . . . . . . . . . . . . . . . . . . . . . . . . . . . . . . . . . . . . . . . . . . . . . . . . . . . . . . . . . . . vii

Sponsors . . . . . . . . . . . . . . . . . . . . . . . . . . . . . . . . . . . . . . . . . . . . . . . . . . . . . . . . . . . . . . ix

Program Committee . . . . . . . . . . . . . . . . . . . . . . . . . . . . . . . . . . . . . . . . . . . . . . . . . . . . . x

Plenary Speakers . . . . . . . . . . . . . . . . . . . . . . . . . . . . . . . . . . . . . . . . . . . . . . . . . . . . . . . xi

Workshop Program at a Glance . . . . . . . . . . . . . . . . . . . . . . . . . . . . . . . . . . . . . . . . . . . xiv

Workshop Program . . . . . . . . . . . . . . . . . . . . . . . . . . . . . . . . . . . . . . . . . . . . . . . . . . . . . . xv

Author Index . . . . . . . . . . . . . . . . . . . . . . . . . . . . . . . . . . . . . . . . . . . . . . . . . . . . . . . . . . xxi

Acknowledgements . . . . . . . . . . . . . . . . . . . . . . . . . . . . . . . . . . . . . . . . . . . . . . . . . . . . xxiii

# Technical Sessions

### TUE-AM1 Measures & Metrics

*Visual Metrics for the Evaluation of Sensor Data Quality in Outdoor Perception*
*[Christopher Brunner, Thierry Peynot]* . . . . . . . . . . . . . . . . . . . . . . . . . . . . . . . . . . . . . *1*

*Proposals for New UGV, UMV, UAV, and HRI Standards for Rescue Robots*
*[Robin Murphy]* . . . . . . . . . . . . . . . . . . . . . . . . . . . . . . . . . . . . . . . . . . . . . . . . . . . . . . *9*

*Metric Selection for Evaluating Human Supervisory Control of Unmanned Vehicles*
*[Birsen Donmez, M. L. Cummings]* . . . . . . . . . . . . . . . . . . . . . . . . . . . . . . . . . . . . . . *14*

*Performance Measures Framework for Unmanned Systems (PerMFUS): Models for*
*Contextual Metrics*
*[Hui-Min Huang, Elena Messina, Adam Jacoff, Robert Wade, Michael McNair]* . . . . . *22*

*Towards Standardization of Metrics for Evaluation of Artificial Visual Attention*
*[M. Zaheer Aziz, Bärbel Mertsching]* . . . . . . . . . . . . . . . . . . . . . . . . . . . . . . . . . . . . . *29*

*Performance Evaluation Procedure for Vision Based Object Feature Extraction*
*Algorithms*
*[Minku Kang, Wonkook Choo, Seungbin Moon]* . . . . . . . . . . . . . . . . . . . . . . . . . . . . . *37*

*Benchmarks, Performance Evaluation and Contests for 3D Shape Retrieval*
*[Afzal Godil, Zhouhui Lian, Helin Dutagaci, Rui Fang, Vanamali ThiruvadandamPorethi,*
*Chun Pan Cheung]* . . . . . . . . . . . . . . . . . . . . . . . . . . . . . . . . . . . . . . . . . . . . . . . . . . . *42*

*TUE-AM2 Special Session I: Performance Metrics for Mixed Palletizing Operations*

*Mixed Palletizing in Transformed Supply Chains: Operational
Requirements and Technical Challenges [Larry Sweet]\**

*Industrial Robots in Warehousing and Distribution Operations
[Don Faulkner and Sean Murphy]* . . . . . . . . . . . . . . . . . . . . . . . . . . . . . . . . . . . . . . . . . 48

*Planning in Logistics: A Survey
[Pushkar Kolhe, Henrik Christensen]* . . . . . . . . . . . . . . . . . . . . . . . . . . . . . . . . . . . . . . 53

*Metrics for Mixed Pallet Stacking
[Stephen Balakirsky, Tom Kramer, Fred Proctor]* . . . . . . . . . . . . . . . . . . . . . . . . . . . 59

*Mixed Pallet Stacking: An Overview and Summary of the 2010 PerMIS Special Session
[Stephen Balakirsky, Henrik Christensen, Tom Kramer, Pushkar Kolhe,
Fred Proctor* . . . . . . . . . . . . . . . . . . . . . . . . . . . . . . . . . . . . . . . . . . . . . . . . . . . . . . . . . . . 67

*TUE-PM1 Interoperability & Sustainability*

*Modeling and Simulation Analysis Types for Sustainable Manufacturing
[Deogratias Kibira, Guodong Shao, Tina Lee]* . . . . . . . . . . . . . . . . . . . . . . . . . . . . . . 74

*Metrics for the Cost of Proprietary Information Exchange Languages in Intelligent
Systems
[John Horst, Nathan Hartman, George Wong]* . . . . . . . . . . . . . . . . . . . . . . . . . . . . . . 82

*Component Models in Robotics Software
[Azamat Shakhimardanov, Nico Hochgeschwender, Gerhard Kraetzschmar]* . . . . . . . 87

*Benchmarking Production System, Process Energy, and Facility Energy Performance
Using a Systems Approach
[Jorge Arinez, Stephan Biller, Kevin Lyons, Swee Leong, Goudong Shao, B.E. Lee,
John Michaloski]* . . . . . . . . . . . . . . . . . . . . . . . . . . . . . . . . . . . . . . . . . . . . . . . . . . . . . . . 93

*Complexity Measures for Distributed Assembly Tasks
[Ani Hsieh, Joshua Rogoff]* . . . . . . . . . . . . . . . . . . . . . . . . . . . . . . . . . . . . . . . . . . . . . . 102

*Advanced Sensing Towards Improved Forklift Safety
[Roger Bostelman, Will Shackleford]*. . . . . . . . . . . . . . . . . . . . . . . . . . . . . . . . . . . . . . 106

*TUE-PM2 Special Session II: Unmanned and Autonomous System Test Technology*

*Unmanned and Autonomous Systems Test Technology
[Rob Heilman]\**

*A Multi-Vehicle Testbed for Underwater Motion Coordination*
*[Nitin Sydney, Seth Napora, Derek Paley]* . . . . . . . . . . . . . . . . . . . . . . . . . . . . . . . *112*

*Measurement of Autonomous Operation*
*[Bill Hamel]* . . . . . . . . . . . . . . . . . . . . . . . . . . . . . . . . . . . . . . . . . . . *117*

*DCF® – A JAUS and TENA Compliant Agent-based Framework for UAS Performance Evaluation*
*[Nicholas Lenzi, Benjamin Bachrach, Vikram Manikonda]* . . . . . . . . . . . . . . . . . . . *124*

*Testing and Evaluation Aspects of Integration of Unmanned Air Systems into the National Air Space*
*[Mauricio Castillo-Effen, Nikita Visnevski]* . . . . . . . . . . . . . . . . . . . . . . . . . . . *132*

**WED-AM1 Testing & Evaluation of Intelligent Systems**

*Evaluating Intelligent Systems with Performance Uncertainty in Large Test Spaces*
*[Miles Thompson]* . . . . . . . . . . . . . . . . . . . . . . . . . . . . . . . . . . . . . . . . . . *138*

*The Multi-Relationship Evaluation Design Framework: Creating Evaluation Blueprints to Assess Advanced and Intelligent Technologies*
*[Brian Weiss, Linda Schmidt]* . . . . . . . . . . . . . . . . . . . . . . . . . . . . . . . . . . . . *141*

*Implementation and Application of Maximum Likelihood Reliability Estimation from Subsystem and Full System Tests*
*[Coire Maranzano, James Spall]* . . . . . . . . . . . . . . . . . . . . . . . . . . . . . . . . . . *151*

*"What do you do with a drunken robot?" In Situ Performance Measurements of Intelligent Mobile Robots*
*[James Gunderson, Louise Gunderson]* . . . . . . . . . . . . . . . . . . . . . . . . . . . . . . . *159*

*Comprehensive Standard Test Suites for the Performance Evaluation of Mobile Robots*
*[Adam Jacoff, Hui-Min Huang, Elena Messina, Ann Virts, Tony Downs]* . . . . . . . . . . *166*

*Towards a Standardized Test for Intelligent Wheelchairs*
*[Joelle Pineau, Robert West, Amin Atrash, Julien Villemure, Francois Routhier]* . . . *174*

*Evaluation of Ultra-Wideband Technology for Use in 3D Locating Systems*
*[Adam Kopp, Kamel Saidi, Hiam Khoury]* . . . . . . . . . . . . . . . . . . . . . . . . . . . . *180*

**WED-AM2 Special Session III: Evaluation of Human Detection and Tracking for Robot Safety, Collaboration and Interaction**

*An Overview of Human and Machine Performance on Face Recognition*
*[Jonathon Phillips]\**

*Detecting Humans under Partial Occlusion using Markov Logic Networks*
*[Raghuraman Gopalan, William Schwartz]* . . . . . . . . . . . . . . . . . . . . . . . . . . . . *187*

*Transitional or Partnership Human and Robot Collaboration for Automotive Assembly*
*[Jane Shi, Roland Menassa]* . . . . . . . . . . . . . . . . . . . . . . . . . . . . . . . . . . . . . *192*

*Performance Assessment of Face Recognition Using Super-Resolution*
*[Shuowen Hu, Robert Maschal, Susan Young, Tsai Hong, Jonathon Phillips]* . . . . . . *200*

*Inexpensive Ground Truth and Performance Evaluation for Human Tracking using*
*Multiple Laser Measurement Sensors*
*[William Shackleford, Tsai Hong, Tommy Chang]* . . . . . . . . . . . . . . . . . . . . . . . . *206*

*Development of Performance Metrics and Test Methods for First Responder Location*
*and Tracking Systems*
*[Francine Amon, Camillo Gentile, Kate Remley]* . . . . . . . . . . . . . . . . . . . . . . . . *212*

*Automated Gross and Sub-pixel Registration Accuracy of Visible and Thermal Imagery*
*[Stephen Won, Susan Young, Gunasekaran Seetharaman]* . . . . . . . . . . . . . . . . . . *214*

**WED-PM Co-X Panel Discussion**

**THU-AM1 Human-Machine Interaction and Collaboration**

*An Indoor Study to Evaluate a Mixed-Reality Interface For Unmanned Aerial Vehicle*
*Operations in Near Earth Environments*
*[James Hing, Justin Menda, Kurtulus Izzetoglu, Paul Oh]* . . . . . . . . . . . . . . . . . . *219*

*A Network-based Approach for Assessing Co-Operating Manned and Unmanned*
*Systems (MUMS)*
*[Lora Weiss]* . . . . . . . . . . . . . . . . . . . . . . . . . . . . . . . . . . . . . . . . . . . . . . *227*

*Lessons Learned in Evaluating DARPA Advanced Military Technologies*
*[Craig Schlenoff, Brian Weiss, Michelle Steves]* . . . . . . . . . . . . . . . . . . . . . . . . *232*

*Modified Cooper Harper Scales for Assessing Unmanned Vehicle Displays*
*[Birsen Donmez, M. L. Cummings, Amy Brzezinski, Hudson Graham]* . . . . . . . . . . . *240*

*Using the "Negative Attitude Towards Robots Scale" with Telepresence Robots*
*[Katherine Tsui, Munjal Desai, Holly Yanco, Henriette Cramer, Nicander Kemper]* . *248*

*Teams Organization and Performance Analysis in Autonomous Human-Robot Teams*
*[Huadong Wang, Michael Lewis, Shih-Yi Chien]* . . . . . . . . . . . . . . . . . . . . . . . . *256*

*Intentions and Intention Recognition in Intelligent Agents*
*[Gary Berg-Cross, Christopher Crick]* . . . . . . . . . . . . . . . . . . . . . . . . . . . . . . *263*

***THU-AM2 Special Session IV: Evaluation of Sensors for Object Pose Estimation in Manufacturing Applications***

    *6-DOF Pose Estimation: The Need for Standardization in Industrial Applications*
    *[Shaun Edwards, William Flannigan, Paul Evans]* . . . . . . . . . . . . . . . . . . . . . . . . . . . 272

    *Flexible Robotic Assembly in Dynamic Environments*
    *[Jane Shi, Roland Menassa]* . . . . . . . . . . . . . . . . . . . . . . . . . . . . . . . . . . . . . . . . . 276

    *Smart Sensing for Real-Time Pose Estimation, Assembly and Inspection Using 3D Laser Scanning Systems*
    *[Chad English]* . . . . . . . . . . . . . . . . . . . . . . . . . . . . . . . . . . . . . . . . . . . . . . . . . 282

    *Dynamic Performance Evaluation of 6D Laser Tracker Sensor*
    *[Kam Lau, Yubing Yang, Yuangun Liu, Henry Song]* . . . . . . . . . . . . . . . . . . . . . 290

    *Methodology for Evaluating Static Six-Degree-of-Freedom (6DoF) Perception Systems*
    *[Tommy Chang, Tsai Hong, Joe Falco, Mike Shneier, Mili Shah, Roger Eastman]* . . . 295

***THU-PM1 Special Session V: Integrated Performance Assessment Through Experimentation***

    *Evaluating Hierarchical Planner Performance through Field Experiments and Simulation*
    *[Juan Gonzalez, Marshal Childers, Barry Bodt]* . . . . . . . . . . . . . . . . . . . . . . . . . . 303

    *Evaluating the Performance of Unmanned Ground Vehicle Water Detection*
    *[Arturo Rankin, Tonislav Ivanov, Shane Brennan]* . . . . . . . . . . . . . . . . . . . . . . . . 310

    *Autonomous Mobility for Areas with Large Number of Pedestrians*
    *[Alberto Lacaze, Karl Murphy, Nenad Uzunovic, Joseph Putney]* . . . . . . . . . . . . . . 317

    *Observations on Single Operator Performance Controlling Two UGVs in a Field Assessment*
    *[Susan Hill]* . . . . . . . . . . . . . . . . . . . . . . . . . . . . . . . . . . . . . . . . . . . . . . . . . . 323

    *Assessing Unmanned Ground Vehicle Tactical Behaviors Performance*
    *[Marshal Childers, Barry Bodt, Richard Camden]* . . . . . . . . . . . . . . . . . . . . . . . . 330

***THU-PM2 Special Session VI: Performance Evaluation for Mapping & Navigation in Unstructured Environments***

    *Evaluation Criteria for Appearance Based Maps*
    *[Gorkem Erinc, Stefano Carpin]* . . . . . . . . . . . . . . . . . . . . . . . . . . . . . . . . . . . . . 337

    *Evaluation of Maps using Fixed Shapes: The Fiducial Map Metric*
    *[Sören Schwertfeger, Adam Jacoff, Chris Scrapper, Johannes Pellenz, Alexander Kleiner]* . . . . . . . . . . . . . . . . . . . . . . . . . . . . . . . . . . . . . . . . . . . . 344

*The Platform- and Hardware-in-the-loop Simulator for Multi-Robot Cooperation*
*[Tomonari Furukawa, Lin Chi Mak, Kunjin Ryu, Xianqiao Tong]* . . . . . . . . . . . . . . . *352*

*Towards Evaluating World Modeling for Autonomous Navigation in Unstructured and
Dynamic Environments*
*[Rolf Lakaemper, Raj Madhavan]* . . . . . . . . . . . . . . . . . . . . . . . . . . . . . . . *360*

## *Appendix*

*Co-X Panel Discussion*
*[Elena Messina, Brian Weiss, Raj Madhavan]* . . . . . . . . . . . . . . . . . . . . . . . . . . . *366*

*Note: * Presentation Only*

# FOREWORD

"It is both in a spirit of scientific enquiry and for pragmatic motivations that we embark on the quest for metrics for intelligence of constructed systems."

From the White Paper explaining the goals of the Workshop: "Measuring Performance and Intelligence of Systems with Autonomy: Metrics for Intelligence of Constructed Systems," Messina, E. and Meystel, A., Editors, Measuring the Performance and Intelligence of Systems: *Proceedings of the 2000 PerMIS Workshop*, Gaithersburg, MD, August 14-16, 2000, NIST Special Publication 970.

As the new millennium was upon us in 2000, a group of researchers gathered for the first time seeking to address several issues pertaining to intelligent systems:
- How can we measure the current state of the science and assess progress in the field?
- How can users select among different candidate systems and decide which system will be most suited to their application?
- How can we break the cycle of re-invention and constant initiation of project with blank slates and find ways to reuse existing components?

The first Performance Metrics for Intelligent Systems brought together researchers, developers, and users from disparate academic disciplines and domains of application to share ideas about how to tackle the multifaceted challenges of defining and measuring intelligence in artificial systems. The intelligent systems could take numerous forms: robots, factory or enterprise control systems, smart homes, decision support systems, etc. A community was formed, which evolved over the years. The workshop series carried on and became an annual event (with the exception of 2005).

Intelligent systems are becoming more of a reality with each passing year and the questions raised in the first workshop are still relevant. Additional questions have been raised, such as "how does one specify the requirements for the performance of an intelligent system?" and "how can concrete performance goals and good measures of performance help spur and focus innovation?" Over the years, the center of gravity of the program shifted more towards applied measures, rather than theoretical discussions about the general nature of intelligence. Many communities have availed themselves of the special sessions to focus on their particular interests and create mini-workshops. The concept of performance evaluation being an integral part of any research and acquisition program has become accepted. Many of the papers published in the PerMIS proceedings have been highly referenced and provide the communities with good starting points for establishing measurements for new projects and programs. We are extremely grateful to the numerous colleagues who have supported PerMIS throughout the years. Without their dedication and hard work, this series would not have survived for a decade.

In this 10th workshop, we focus our attention to systems which are designed to work closely with humans. The theme of PerMIS'10 is *key role of performance assessment in developing intelligent systems that can co-exist with humans* towards improving the quality of our lives intertwined with automation. Adaptability to human-centered collaboration, the ability to cope with unstructured, dynamic environments, and keeping humans out of harm's way have been widely accepted as critical prerequisites. Designing such flexible, smart, and safe systems requires that their performance be quantifiable thereby facilitating emerging technologies and societal acceptance.

PerMIS'10 is sponsored by NIST, DARPA and NSF, with technical co-sponsorship of the IEEE Washington Section Sensors Council Chapter, and in cooperation with the Association for Computing Machinery (ACM) Special Interest Group on Artificial Intelligence (SIGART). The Defense Advanced Research Projects Agency Information Processing Technology Office graciously provided funding to help support the workshop. Special thanks are due to the National Science Foundation for providing funding to allow undergraduate and graduate students to participate in a special poster session this year. We also thank Professor Holly Yanco of the University of Massachussetts – Lowell for organizing the student poster grants program. We gratefully acknowledge the support of our sponsors.

We thank the special session organizers for proposing interesting topics and assembling researchers related to their sessions. These focused sessions provide an opportunity to delve deeper into specialized topics and to hear from experts in the field. Our thanks are also due to the Program Committee members for publicizing the workshop and the reviewers for providing feedback to the authors, and for helping us to put together an exciting program.

The proceedings of PerMIS will be indexed by INSPEC and Compendex and will be available through ACM's Digital Library, as well as being released as a NIST Special Publication. Outstanding papers from this year's proceedings will be considered for inclusion, in an expanded form, in a special issue of the *International Journal of Intelligent Control and Systems*.

It is our sincere hope that you will enjoy the presentations, the social programs, renew old relationships, and forge new ones at PerMIS'10!

Elena Messina      Raj Madhavan
*General Chair*      *Program Chair*

# SPONSORS

# PROGRAM COMMITTEE

**General Chair:**

Elena Messina (Intelligent Systems Division, NIST, USA)

**Program Chair:**

Raj Madhavan (UMD-CP/ISD-NIST, USA)

**Publications Chair:**

B. Weiss (Intelligent Systems Division, NIST, USA)

**Publicity Chair:**

B. Grabowski (MITRE, USA)

**Poster Session Chair:**

H. Yanco (U. of Mass-Lowell, USA)

S. Balakirsky (NIST, USA)

G. Berg-Cross (EM & I, USA)

G. Blankenship (UMD-CP, USA)

F. Bonsignorio (UC3M, Spain)

R. Bostelman (NIST, USA)

M. Childers (ARL, USA)

M. Fields (ARL, USA)

A. Godil (NIST, USA)

J. Gunderson (GammaTwo, USA)

L. Gunderson (GammaTwo, USA)

S. K. Gupta (UMD-CP, USA)

A. Kleiner (UFreiburg, Germany)

R. Lakaemper (Temple, USA)

M. Lewis (UPitt, USA)

A. del Pobil (UJaume-I, Spain)

E. Prassler (UAppSci-BRS, Germany)

F. Proctor (NIST, USA)

D. Prokhorov (Toyota, USA)

C. Schlenoff (NIST, USA)

C. Scrapper (MITRE, USA)

J. Shi (GM, USA)

M. Shneier (NIST, USA)

E. Tunstel (JHU-APL, USA)

# PLENARY SPEAKERS

## Prof. Gregory Dudek, McGill University, Canada

**Building Interfaces for Robotic Data Collection and Human-Robot Collaboration Underwater and Outdoors**

## Tue. 8:30 am

### ABSTRACT

In outdoor environments robots are ready to serve as tools for scientific data collection as well as assistants for human operators. Typically, however, a robotic system is subservient to a human operator and needs to respond to commands and constraints that may be issued in the field. On the other hand, keyboard entry and reprogramming are not appropriate user-interface mechanisms, even for technical users, when they are on a field expedition. Our lab has been developing human-robot interaction methods that allow a scuba diver to interact with a robotic assistant while underwater. This has entailed both the development of an amphibious robotic device with emphasis on gait selection, locomotion modes and software infrastructure, and on a communication language based on optical sensing of fiducial markers. A key part of this has been measuring the performance of the vehicle underwater and, more significantly, attempting to develop a communication paradigm for use underwater that is at once both expressive and manageable. Due to the substantial logistic overheads in doing work underwater, developing terrestrial surrogate tests to evaluate our work has also been an important requirement. Finally, we are working towards integrating the activities of our underwater vehicles with an amphibious mode of operation, a robotic boat, and a fixed-wing robotic aircraft. While we have made some progress towards our objectives, several challenges remain.

### BIOGRAPHY

Gregory Dudek is a Professor with the School of Computer Science and a member of the McGill Research Centre for Intelligent Machines (CIM) and an Associate member of the Dept. of Electrical Engineering at McGill University. In 9/2008 he became the Director of the McGill School of Computer Science. He is the former Director of McGill's Research Center for Intelligent Machines, a 25 year old inter-faculty research facility. In 2002 he was named a William Dawson Scholar. In 2008 he was made James McGill Chair. In 2010 he was awarded the Fessenden Professorship in Science Innovation. In 2010 he was also awarded the Canadian Image Processing and Pattern Recognition Award for Research Excellence and also for Service to the Research Community. He directs the McGill Mobile Robotics Laboratory. He has been on the organizing and/or program committees of Robotics: Systems and Science, the IEEE International Conference on Robotics and Automation (ICRA), the IEEE/RSJ International Conference on Intelligent Robotics and Systems (IROS), the International Joint Conference on Artificial Intelligence (IJCAI), Computer and Robot Vision, IEEE International Conference on Mechatronics and International Conference on Hands-on Intelligent Mechatronics and Automation among other bodies. He is president of CIPPRS, the Canadian Information Processing and Pattern Recognition Society, an ICPR national affiliate. He was on leave in 2000-2001 as Visiting Associate Professor at the Department of Computer Science at Stanford University and at Xerox Palo Alto Research Center (PARC). During his sabbatical in 2007-2008 he visited the Massachusetts Institute of Technology and co-founded the company Independent Robotics Inc. He obtained his Ph.D. in computer science (computational vision) from the University of Toronto, his MSc in computer science (systems) at the University of Toronto and his BSc in computer science and physics at Queen's University. He has published over 170 research papers on subjects including visual object description and recognition, robotic navigation and map construction, distributed system design and biological perception. This includes a book entitled "Computational Principles of Mobile Robotics" co-authored with Michael Jenkin and published by Cambridge University Press. He has chaired and been otherwise involved in numerous national and international conferences and professional activities concerned with robotics, machine sensing and computer vision. He research interests include perception for mobile robotics, navigation and position estimation, environment and shape modeling, computational vision and collaborative filtering. He grew up in Montreal and favors light food. With his children he is rediscovering model rocketry, rollerblading, and has discovered he's not good at surfing but loves it.

# Prof. Herman Bruyninckx, Katholieke Universiteit Leuven, Belgium

## Benchmarking Reusability and Composability in Complex Software Systems–The Open Source Opportunity

### Tue. 2:00 pm

**ABSTRACT**

Designers of current and future robot systems are confronted with an increasing amount of complexity, not only with respect to the richness of the desired end-user functionalities in these systems, but also with respect to the hardware and software infrastructure required to realise these functionalities. The domain of robotics has passed the tipping point beyond which it is not possible anymore for one single organization or company to develop robot systems completely in house.

Hence, system designers must find ways to integrate third-party components into their designs, reliably, predictably and effectively. This talk defines the concepts of reusability and composability on this context of complex systems design in a multi-sourcing world and discusses a dozen or so aspects that system designers can use to benchmark reusability and composability of components, their own as well as those from third-party providers. Throughout the presentation, the role and importance of free and open source software will be motivated and illustrated via a number of (un)successful real-world examples.

**BIOGRAPHY**

Dr. Bruyninckx obtained the Masters degrees in Mathematics (Licentiate, 1984), Computer Science (Burgerlijk Ingenieur, 1987) and Mechatronics (1988), all from the Katholieke Universiteit Leuven, Belgium. In 1995 he obtained his Doctoral Degree in Engineering from the same university, where he is now professor with research interests in online Bayesian estimation of model uncertainties in sensor-based robot tasks, kinematics and dynamics of robots and humans, and the software engineering of large-scale robot control systems. In 2001, he started the Free Software ("open source") project Orocos, to support his research interests and to facilitate their industrial exploitation.

# Prof. Ken Goldberg, University of California, Berkeley, USA

## Putting the Turing into Manufacturing: Recent Developments in Algorithmic Automation

### Wed. 8:30 am

**ABSTRACT**

Automation for manufacturing today is where computer technology was in the early 1960s, a patchwork of ad-hoc solutions lacking a rigorous scientific methodology. CAD provides detailed models of part geometry. What's missing is formal models of part behavior, frameworks for the systematic design of automated systems that handle (e.g. assemble, inspect, sort, feed) parts, and tools for rigorous specification, analysis, and synthesis.

In 1937, Alan Turing introduced an elegant model of computing with precise vocabulary and operations that formalized concepts of equivalence, correctness, completeness, and complexity. Can we develop similar models for manufacturing?

"Algorithmic Automation" introduces abstractions that allow the functionality of automation to be designed independent of the underlying implementation and can provide the foundation for formal specification and analysis, algorithmic design, and consistency checking. Algorithmic Automation can facilitate integrity, reliability, interoperability, and maintainability and upgrading of automation. Researchers are developing a variety of algorithmic models. I'll present results from my lab and others on specific problems in part feeding and fixturing, including a framework for fixturing deformable parts and new geometric primitives for vibratory bowl feeders, and propose open problems for future research.

**BIOGRAPHY**

Ken Goldberg is Professor of IEOR, EECS, and the iSchool at UC Berkeley, and craigslist Distinguished Professor of New Media. He served two terms as Vice-President of Technical Activities for the IEEE Robotics and Automation Society. His research addresses robot manipulation, geometric algorithms for automation, and networked robots. More information on his work is available at http://goldberg.berkeley.edu/.

# Dr. Jonathan A. Bornstein, Army Research Laboratory, USA

## ARL Autonomous Systems Enterprise

### Wed. 2:00 pm

**BIOGRAPHY**

Dr. Bornstein has been intimately involved in robotics for over a decade. He has served as Chief of the Autonomous Systems Division, Vehicle Technology Directorate, Army Research Laboratory since January 2010. He has responsibility for a group of approximately 30 Government and contractor personnel conducting research in perception and intelligence research for unmanned vehicle systems and a micromechanics group. He is the Collaborative Alliance Manager for the new Robotics CTA and has responsibility for coordination of autonomous systems research throughout ARL. He previously served as Chief of the Army Research Laboratory Robotics Program Office (RPO) and Collaborative Alliance Manager for the Robotics Collaborative Technology Alliance (CTA) (since April 2006) and as an engineer in the RPO since 1997. From 1995 through 1996 he served as a Program Manager at the Defense Advanced Research Projects Agency (DARPA) with responsibility for the Demo II Unmanned Ground Vehicle Program.

Dr. Bornstein received his Ph.D. in Aeronautics & Astronautics from the Polytechnic Institute of New York in 1976. From 1975 through 1985 he was a member of the Fluid Mechanics Group at the Corporate Research Labs of Brown, Boveri & Cie, AG in Baden, Switzerland. In 1985, he joined the Fluid Physics Branch of the U.S. Army Ballistics Research Laboratory conducting research in projectile launch dynamics. With the formation of the Army Research Laboratory in 1992, his technical focus shifted from dynamics to weapons systems and ultimately robotics technology. He received a U.S. Army Research & Development Achievement Award in 1989 and Army Superior Civilian Service Award in 1997. He is a registered Professional Engineer in Maryland.

# Ms. Helen Greiner, CEO of CyPhy Works and Founder of iRobot, USA

### Thur. 8:30 am

**BIOGRAPHY**

Helen Greiner is CEO of CyPhy Works, Inc, a startup company whose mission is to be a "SkunkWorks" for robotics. She is a co-founder of iRobot, a ~$300 million business and the global leader of practical robots. Ms Greiner served as President of iRobot until 2004, Chairman until October 2008, and currently serves on the iRobot Board. While at iRobot, she developed the strategy for and led iRobot's entry into the military market place. She served as the Principal Investigator on the DARPA program that created the original PackBot Tactical Mobile Robot, of which over 3,000 have now been deployed. At iRobot, she helped create a culture of practical innovation and performance that led to the creation of the iRobot Warrior, PackBot EOD, SUGV, and successful participation in many other DARPA, Army and Navy research programs. Ms. Greiner also ran iRobot's financing projects which included raising $35 million venture capital and a $70 million initial public offering. Before starting her new venture, she led iRobot's investment in a deployable Flash LADAR and acquisition of Nekton, an Unmanned Underwater Vehicle (UUV) company. Greiner holds a bachelor's degree in mechanical engineering and a master's degree in computer science, both from MIT. She was presented with an honorary Ph.D. by WPI in 2009.

Ms. Greiner is highly decorated for her contributions in technology innovation and business leadership. She was named by the Kennedy School at Harvard in conjunction with the U.S. News and World Report as one of America's Best Leaders and was honored by the Association for Unmanned Vehicle Systems International (AUVSI) with the prestigious Pioneer Award. She has also been honored as a Technology Review Magazine "Innovator for the Next Century," invited to the World Economic Forum as a Global Leader of Tomorrow, and has been awarded the DEMO God Award at the DEMO Conference. In 2003, she was named one of the Ernst and Young New England Entrepreneurs of the Year and has been inducted in the Women in Technology International (WITI) Hall of Fame. Her 20+ years of experience in robotic technology includes work at NASA's Jet Propulsion Laboratory and MIT's Artificial Intelligence Laboratory. Ms. Greiner is a Trustee of the Boston Museum Science, Massachusetts Institute of Technology (MIT), National Defense Industrial Association (NDIA), Autonomous Unmanned Systems Vehicle International (AUVSI), the Massachusetts Technology Leadership Council (MTLC), and the US Army War College Board of Visitors. Ms. Greiner serves as the elected President and Board Member of the Robotics Technology Consortium (RTC)—a 180 member industrial/academic group.

| Time | Tuesday September 28 | Wednesday September 29 | Thursday September 30 |
|---|---|---|---|
| 8:00-8:30 | Welcome/Opening Remarks | Overview | Overview |
| 8:30-9:30 | Plenary 1: Gregory Dudek | Plenary 3: Ken Goldberg | Plenary 5: Helen Greiner |
| 9:30-10:00 | Coffee Break | Coffee Break | Coffee Break |
| 10:00 -12:30 | TUE-AM1: Measures and Metrics / TUE-AM2: Performance Metrics for Mixed Palletizing Operations | WED-AM1: Testing and Evaluation of Intelligent Systems / WED-AM2: Evaluation of Human Detection and Tracking for Robot Safety, Collaboration and Interaction | THU-AM1: Human-Machine Interaction and Collaboration / THU-AM2: Evaluation of Sensors for Object Pose Estimation in Manufacturing Applications |
| 12:30-14:00 | Lunch | Lunch | Lunch |
| 14:00 - 15:00 | Plenary 2: Herman Bruyninckx | Plenary 4: Jon Bornstein | (14:00-16:00) THU-PM1: Integrated Performance Assessment Through Experimentation / (14:00-16:00) THU-PM2: Performance Evaluation for Mapping & Navigation in Unstructured Environments |
| 15:00-15:30 | Coffee Break | Coffee Break | |
| 15:30-17:30 | TUE-PM1: Interoperability and Sustainability / TUE-PM2: Unmanned and Autonomous System Test Technology | WED-PM: Co-X Panel Discussion | Coffee Break 16:00-16:30 / Adjourn 16:30 |
| | (18:30-20:30) Reception & Poster Session | (18:30 – 22:00) Banquet (Dinner Cruise) | |

## TUESDAY 28

**08:00** Welcome & Opening Remarks – Howard Harary, Acting Director MEL, NIST

**08:30** *Plenary Presentation:*
*Gregory Dudek*
*Building Interfaces for Robotic Data Collection and Human-Robot Collaboration Underwater and Outdoors*

**09:30** Coffee Break

**10:00** **TUE-AM1 Measures & Metrics**
*Chairs: Hui-Min Huang and Seungbin Moon*
- Visual Metrics for the Evaluation of Sensor Data Quality in Outdoor Perception [Christopher Brunner, Thierry Peynot]
- Proposals for New UGV, UMV, UAV, and HRI Standards for Rescue Robots [Robin Murphy]
- Metric Selection for Evaluating Human Supervisory Control of Unmanned Vehicles [Birsen Donmez, M. L. Cummings]
- Performance Measures Framework for Unmanned Systems (PerMFUS): Models for Contextual Metrics [Hui-Min Huang, Elena Messina, Adam Jacoff, Robert Wade, Michael McNair]
- Towards Standardization of Metrics for Evaluation of Artificial Visual Attention [M. Zaheer Aziz, Bärbel Mertsching]
- Performance Evaluation Procedure for Vision Based Object Feature Extraction Algorithms [Minku Kang, Wonkook Choo, Seungbin Moon]
- Benchmarks, Performance Evaluation and Contests for 3D Shape Retrieval [Afzal Godil, Zhouhui Lian, Helin Dutagaci, Rui Fang, Vanamali ThiruvadandamPorethi, Chun Pan Cheung]

**12:30** Lunch

**14:00** *Plenary Presentation:*
*Herman Bruyninckx*
*Benchmarking Reusability and Composability in Complex Software Systems–The Open Source Opportunity*

**15:00** Coffee Break

**15:30** **TUE-PM1 Interoperability & Sustainability**
*Chairs: John Horst and Ani Hsieh*
- Modeling and Simulation Analysis Types for Sustainable Manufacturing [Deogratias Kibira, Guodong Shao, Tina Lee]
- Metrics for the Cost of Proprietary Information Exchange Languages in Intelligent Systems [John Horst, Nathan Hartman, George Wong]
- Component Models in Robotics Software [Azamat Shakhimardanov, Nico Hochgeschwender, Gerhard Kraetzschmar]
- Benchmarking Production System, Process Energy, and Facility Energy Performance Using a Systems Approach [Jorge Arinez, Stephan Biller, Kevin Lyons, Swee Leong, Goudong Shao, B.E. Lee, John Michaloski]
- Complexity Measures for Distributed Assembly Tasks [Ani Hsieh, Joshua Rogoff]
- Advanced Sensing Towards Improved Forklift Safety [Roger Bostelman, Will Shackleford]

**18:30** PRE-dinner Social Gathering Session

# PERMIS

## PROGRAM

| 08:00 | Welcome & Opening Remarks – Howard Harary, Acting Director, MEL, NIST |
|---|---|
| 08:30 | **Plenary Presentation:**<br>**Gregory Dudek**<br>**Building Interfaces for Robotic Data Collection and Human-Robot Collaboration Underwater and Outdoors** |
| 09:30 | Coffee Break |
| 10:00 | **TUE-AM2 Special Session I: Performance Metrics for Mixed Palletizing Operations**<br>*Organizers: Stephen Balakirsky and Henrik Christensen*<br>• Mixed Palletizing in Transformed Supply Chains: Operational Requirements and Technical Challenges [Larry Sweet]<br>• Industrial Robots in Warehousing and Distribution Operations [Don Faulkner and Sean Murphy]<br>• Planning in Logistics: A Survey [Pushkar Kolhe, Henrik Christensen]<br>• Metrics for Mixed Pallet Stacking [Stephen Balakirsky, Tom Kramer, Fred Proctor]<br>• Mixed Pallet Stacking: An Overview and Summary of the 2010 PerMIS Special Session [Stephen Balakirsky, Henrik Christensen, Tom Kramer, Pushkar Kolhe, Fred Proctor] |
| 12:30 | Lunch |
| 14:00 | **Plenary Presentation:**<br>**Herman Bruyninckx**<br>**Benchmarking Reusability and Composability in Complex Software Systems–The Open Source Opportunity** |
| 15:00 | Coffee Break |
| 15:30 | **TUE-PM2 Special Session II: Unmanned and Autonomous System Test Technology**<br>*Organizer: Robert Heilman*<br>• Unmanned and Autonomous Systems Test Technology [Rob Heilman]<br>• A Multi-Vehicle Testbed for Underwater Motion Coordination [Nitin Sydney, Seth Napora, Derek Paley]<br>• Measurement of Autonomous Operation [Bill Hamel]<br>• DCF® – A JAUS and TENA Compliant Agent-based Framework for UAS Performance Evaluation [Nicholas Lenzi, Benjamin Bachrach, Vikram Manikonda]<br>• Testing and Evaluation Aspects of Integration of Unmanned Air Systems into the National Air Space [Mauricio Castillo-Effen, Nikita Visnevski] |
| 18:30 | Reception & Student Poster Session |

**September**

**29**

# WEDNESDAY

## PROGRAM

| | |
|---|---|
| **08:15** | Overview |
| **08:30** | *Plenary Presentation:*<br>*Ken Goldberg*<br>*Putting the Turing into Manufacturing: Recent*<br>*Developments in Algorithmic Automation* |
| **09:30** | Coffee Break |
| **10:00** | **WED-AM1 Testing & Evaluation of Intelligent Systems**<br>*Chairs: Brian Weiss and James Gunderson*<br>• Evaluating Intelligent Systems with Performance Uncertainty in Large Test Spaces [Miles Thompson]<br>• The Multi-Relationship Evaluation Design Framework: Creating Evaluation Blueprints to Assess Advanced and Intelligent Technologies [Brian Weiss, Linda Schmidt]<br>• Implementation and Application of Maximum Likelihood Reliability Estimation from Subsystem and Full System Tests [Coire Maranzano, James Spall]<br>• "What do you do with a drunken robot?" In Situ Performance Measurements of Intelligent Mobile Robots [James Gunderson, Louise Gunderson]<br>• Comprehensive Standard Test Suites for the Performance Evaluation of Mobile Robots [Adam Jacoff, Hui-Min Huang, Elena Messina, Ann Virts, Tony Downs]<br>• Towards a Standardized Test for Intelligent Wheelchairs [Joelle Pineau, Robert West, Amin Atrash, Julien Villemure, Francois Routhier]<br>• Evaluation of Ultra-Wideband Technology for Use in 3-D Locating Systems [Adam Kopp, Kamel Saidi, Hiam Khoury] |
| **12:30** | Lunch |
| **14:00** | *Plenary Presentation:*<br>*Jon Bornstein*<br>**ARL Autonomous Systems Enterprise** |
| **15:00** | Coffee Break |
| **15:30** | WED-PM Co-X Panel Discussion |
| **18:30** | Banquet<br>Dinner Cruise |

**WEDNESDAY 29**

| 08:15 | Overview |
|---|---|

**08:30** *Plenary Presentation:*
*Ken Goldberg*
*Putting the Turing into Manufacturing: Recent*
*Developments in Algorithmic Automation*

| 09:30 | Coffee Break |
|---|---|

**10:00 WED-AM2 Special Session III: Evaluation of Human Detection and Tracking for Robot Safety, Collaboration and Interaction**
*Organizers: Tsai Hong and Roger Eastman*
- An Overview of Human and Machine Performance on Face Recognition [Jonathon Phillips]
- Detecting Humans under Partial Occlusion using Markov Logic Networks [Raghuraman Gopalan, William Schwartz]
- Transitional or Partnership Human and Robot Collaboration for Automotive Assembly [Jane Shi, Roland Menassa]
- Performance Assessment of Face Recognition Using Super-Resolution [Shuowen Hu, Robert Maschal, Susan Young, Tsai Hong, Jonathon Phillips]
- Inexpensive Ground Truth and Performance Evaluation for Human Tracking using Multiple Laser Measurement Sensors [William Shackleford, Tsai Hong, Tommy Chang]
- Development of Performance Metrics and Test Methods for First Responder Location and Tracking Systems [Francine Amon, Camillo Gentile, Kate Remley]
- Automated Gross and Sub-pixel Registration Accuracy of Visible and Thermal Imagery [Stephen Won, S. Susan Young, Gunasekaran Seetharaman]

| 12:30 | Lunch |
|---|---|

**14:00** *Plenary Presentation:*
*Jon Bornstein*
*ARL Autonomous Systems Enterprise*

| 15:00 | Coffee Break |
|---|---|
| 15:30 | WED-PM Co-X Panel Discussion |
| 18:30 | Banquet<br>Dinner Cruise |

**THURSDAY 30**

| | |
|---|---|
| 08:15 | Overview |
| 08:30 | **_Plenary Presentation:_**<br>**_Helen Greiner_** |
| 09:30 | Coffee Break |

**10:00 THU-AM1 Human-Machine Interaction and Collaboration**
*Chairs: Craig Schlenoff and Paul Oh*
- An Indoor Study to Evaluate a Mixed-Reality Interface For Unmanned Aerial Vehicle Operations in Near Earth Environments [James Hing, Justin Menda, Kurtulus Izzetoglu, Paul Oh]
- A Network-based Approach for Assessing Co-Operating Manned and Unmanned Systems (MUMS) [Lora Weiss]
- Lessons Learned in Evaluating DARPA Advanced Military Technologies [Craig Schlenoff, Brian Weiss, Michelle Steves]
- Modified Cooper Harper Scales for Assessing Unmanned Vehicle Displays [Birsen Donmez, M. L. Cummings, Amy Brzezinski, Hudson Graham]
- Using the "Negative Attitude Towards Robots Scale" with Telepresence Robots [Katherine Tsui, Munjal Desai, Holly Yanco, Henriette Cramer, Nicander Kemp]
- Teams Organization and Performance Analysis in Autonomous Human-Robot Teams [Huadong Wang, Michael Lewis, Shih-Yi Chien]
- Intentions and Intention Recognition in Intelligent Agents [Gary Berg-Cross, Christopher Crick]

**12:30 Lunch**

**14:00 THU-PM1 Special Session V: Integrated Performance Assessment Through Experimentation**
*Organizer: Marshal Childers*
- Evaluating Hierarchical Planner Performance through Field Experiments and Simulation [Juan Pablo Gonzalez, Marshal Childers, Barry Bodt]
- Evaluating the Performance of Unmanned Ground Vehicle Water Detection [Arturo Rankin, Tonislav Ivanov, Shane Brennan]
- Autonomous Mobility for Areas with Large Number of Pedestrians [Alberto Lacaze, Karl Murphy, Nenad Uzunovic, Joseph Putney]
- Observations on Single Operator Performance Controlling Two UGVs in a Field Assessment [Susan Hill]
- Assessing Unmanned Ground Vehicle Tactical Behaviors Performance [Marshal Childers, Barry Bodt, Richard Camden]

**16:00 Coffee Break**

**16:30 Adjourn**

# PERMIS

## PROGRAM

| 08:15 | Overview |

| 08:30 | **Plenary Presentation:**<br>**Helen Greiner** |

| 09:30 | Coffee Break |

| 10:00 | **THU-AM2 Special Session IV: Evaluation of Sensors for Object Pose Estimation in Manufacturing Applications**<br>*Organizers: Roger Eastman, Tsai Hong, and Hui-Min Huang* |

- 6-DOF Pose Estimation – The Need for Pose Estimation Evaluation Standardization in Industrial Automation Applications
  [Shaun Edwards. Clay Flannigan, Eric Huber]
- Flexible Robotic Assembly in Dynamic Environments
  [Jane Shi, Roland Menassa]
- Smart Sensing for Real-Time Pose Estimation, Assembly and Inspection using 3D Laser Scanning Systems
  [Chad English]
- Dynamic Performance Evaluation of 6D Laser Tracker Sensor
  [Kam Lau, Yubing Yang, Yuangun Liu,  Henry Song]
- Methodology for Evaluating Static Six-degree-of-freedom (6DoF) Perception Systems
  [Tommy Chang, Tsai Hong, Mili Shih, Roger Eastman, Mike Shneier]
- Panel Discussion: Jane Shi, Edward Roney, Joice Guthrie, Chad English, Shaun Edwards, Bala Muralikrishnan, Roger Eastman

| 12:30 | Lunch |

| 14:00 | **THU-PM2 Special Session VI: Performance Evaluation for Mapping & Navigation in Unstructured Environments**<br>*Organizers: Rolf Lakaemper and Raj Madhavan* |

- Evaluation Criteria for Appearance Based Maps [Gorkem Erinc, Stefano Carpin]
- Evaluation of Maps using Fixed Shapes: The Fiducial Map Metric
  [Sören Schwertfeger, Adam Jacoff, Chris Scrapper, Johannes Pellenz, Alexander Kleiner]
- The Platform- and Hardware-in-the-loop Simulator for Multi-Robot Cooperation [Tomonari Furukawa, Lin Chi Mak, Kunjin Ryu, Xianqiao Tong]
- Towards Evaluating World Modeling for Autonomous Navigation in Unstructured and Dynamic Environments [Rolf Lakaemper, Raj Madhavan]

| 16:00 | Coffee Break |

| 16:30 | Adjourn |

# AUTHOR INDEX

Amon, F. ...............WED-AM2
Arinez, J. ...............TUE-PM1
Atrash, A. ...............WED-AM1
Aziz, M.Z. ...............TUE-AM1
Bachrach, B. ...........TUE-PM2
Balakirsky, S. ...........TUE-AM2
Balakirsky, S. ...........TUE-AM2
Berg-Cross, G. ........THU-AM1
Biller, S. ...................TUE-PM1
Bostelman, R. ..........TUE-PM1
Bodt, B. ...................THU-PM1
Bodt, B. ...................THU-PM1
Brennan, S. .............THU-PM1
Brunner, C. ..............TUE-AM1
Brzezinski, A. ...........THU-AM1
Camden, R. ..............THU-PM1
Carpin, S. ................THU-PM2
Castillo-Effen, M. .....TUE-PM2
Chang, T. ................WED-AM2
Chang, T. ................THU-AM2
Cheung, C.P. ...........TUE-AM1
Chien, S.Y. ..............THU-AM1
Childers, M. .............THU-PM1
Childers, M. .............THU-PM1
Choo, W. .................TUE-AM1
Christensen, H. .......TUE-AM2
Christensen, H. .......TUE-AM2
Cramer, H. ...............THU-AM1
Crick, C. ..................THU-AM1
Cummings, M.L. ......TUE-AM1
Cummings, M.L. .....THU-AM1
Desai, M. .................THU-AM1
Donmez, B. ..............TUE-AM1
Donmez, B. ..............THU-AM1
Downs, T. ................WED-AM1
Dutagaci, H. ............TUE-AM1
Eastman, R. .............THU-AM2
Edwards, S. .............THU-AM2
English, C. ...............THU-AM2
Erinc, G. .................THU-PM2
Evans, P. .................THU-AM2
Falco, J. ..................THU-AM2
Fang, R. ..................TUE-AM1
Faulkner, D. .............TUE-AM2
Flannigan, W. ..........THU-AM2

Furukawa, T. ...........THU-PM2
Gentile, C. ..............WED-AM2
Godil, A. .................TUE-AM1
Gonzalez, J.P. .........THU-PM1
Gopalan, R. .............WED-AM2
Graham, H. ..............THU-AM1
Gunderson, J. .........WED-AM1
Gunderson, L. .........WED-AM1
Hamel, B. ................TUE-PM2
Hartman, N. .............TUE-PM1
Heilman, R. ..............TUE-PM2
Hill, S. ....................THU-PM1
Hing, J. ...................THU-AM1
Hochgeschwender,
N. ...........................TUE-PM1
Hong, T. ..................WED-AM2
Hong, T. ..................WED-AM2
Hong, T. ..................THU-AM2
Horst, J. ..................TUE-PM1
Hsieh, A. .................TUE-PM1
Hu, S. .....................WED-AM2
Huang, H.M. ............TUE-AM1
Huang, H.M. ............WED-AM1
Ivanov, T. ................THU-PM1
Izzetoglu, K. ............THU-AM1
Jacoff, A. ................TUE-AM1
Jacoff, A. ................WED-AM1
Jacoff, A. ................THU-PM2
Kang, M. .................TUE-AM1
Kemper, N. ..............THU-AM1
Khoury, H. ...............WED-AM1
Kibira, D. ................TUE-PM1
Kleiner, A. ...............THU-PM2
Kolhe, P. .................TUE-AM2
Kolhe, P. .................TUE-AM2
Kopp, A. .................WED-AM1
Kraetzschmar, G. .....TUE-PM1
Kramer, T. ...............TUE-AM2
Kramer, T. ...............TUE-AM2
Lacaze, A. ...............THU-PM1
Lakaemper, R. ..........THU-PM2
Lau, K. ....................THU-AM2
Lee, B.E. .................TUE-PM1
Lee, T. ....................TUE-PM1
Leong, S. ................TUE-PM1
Lenzi, N. ..................TUE-PM2
Lewis, M. .................THU-AM1
Lian, Z. ....................TUE-AM1

Liu, Y. .....................THU-AM2
Lyons, K. .................TUE-PM1
Madhavan, R. ..........THU-PM2
Mak, L.C. ................THU-PM2
Manikonda, V. ..........TUE-PM2
Maranzano, C. ........WED-AM1
Maschal, R. .............WED-AM2
McNair, M. ...............TUE-AM1
Menassa, R. ............WED-AM2
Menassa, R. ............THU-AM2
Menda, J. ................THU-AM1
Mertsching, B. .........TUE-AM1
Messina, E. ..............TUE-AM1
Messina, E. .............WED-AM1
Michaloski, J. ..........TUE-PM1
Moon, S. .................TUE-AM1
Murphy, K. ...............THU-PM1
Murphy, R. ...............TUE-AM1
Murphy, S. ...............TUE-AM2
Napora, S. ...............TUE-PM2
Oh, P. .....................THU-AM1
Paley, D. .................TUE-PM2
Pellenz, P. ...............THU-PM2
Peynot, T. ................TUE-AM1
Phillips, J. ...............WED-AM2
Phillips, J. ...............WED-AM2
Pineau, J. ................WED-AM1
Proctor, F. ...............TUE-AM2
Proctor, F. ...............TUE-AM2
Putney, J. ................THU-PM1
Rankin, A. ...............THU-PM1
Remley, K. ...............WED-AM2
Rogoff, J. ................TUE-PM1
Routhier, F. .............WED-AM1
Ryu, K. ....................THU-PM2
Saidi, K. ..................WED-AM1
Schmidt, L. .............WED-AM1
Schwartz, W. ...........WED-AM2
Schwertfeger, S. .....THU-PM2
Schlenoff, C. ...........THU-AM1
Scrapper, C. ............THU-PM2
Seetharaman, G. ....WED-AM2
Shackleford, W. .......TUE-PM1
Shackleford, W. ......WED-AM2
Shakhimardanov, A. TUE-PM1
Shao, G. .................TUE-PM1
Shao, G. .................TUE-PM1
Shi, J. .....................WED-AM2

Shi, J. .....................THU-AM2
Shah, M. ................THU-AM2
Shneier, M. .............THU-AM2
Song, H. .................THU-AM2
Spall, J. .................WED-AM1
Steves, M. ..............THU-AM1
Sweet, L. .................TUE-AM2
Sydney, N. ..............TUE-PM2
ThiruvadandamPorethi,
V. ...............................TUE-AM1
Thompson, M. ........WED-AM1
Tsui, K. ...................THU-AM1
Tong, X. ..................THU-PM2
Uzunovic, N. ...........THU-PM1
Villemure, J. ............WED-AM1
Visnevski, N. ............TUE-PM2
Virts, A. ..................WED-AM1
Wade, R. .................TUE-AM1
Wang, H. ................THU-AM1
Weiss, B. ...............WED-AM1
Weiss, B. ................THU-AM1
Weiss, L. .................THU-AM1
West, R. .................WED-AM1
Won, S. ..................WED-AM2
Wong, G. ................TUE-PM1
Yanco, H. ...............THU-AM1
Yang, Y. .................THU-AM2
Young, S. ...............WED-AM2
Young, S. ...............WED-AM2

# ACKNOWLEDGMENTS

These people provided essential support to make this event happen. Their ideas and efforts are very much appreciated.

### Website and Proceedings
Debbie Russell

### Local Arrangements
Jennifer Peyton

### Conference and Registration
Mary Lou Norris

Angela Ellis

Kathy Kilmer

Intelligent Systems Division
Manufacturing Engineering Laboratory
## National Institute of Standards and Technology
100 Bureau Drive,  MS 8230
Gaithersburg, MD 20899-8230
http://www.nist.gov/mel/isd/permis2010.cfm

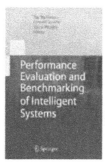

# Visual Metrics for the Evaluation of Sensor Data Quality in Outdoor Perception

Christopher Brunner
ARC Centre of Excellence for Autonomous
Systems
Australian Centre for Field Robotics (ACFR)
The University of Sydney, NSW 2006, Australia
c.brunner@cas.edu.au

Thierry Peynot
ARC Centre of Excellence for Autonomous
Systems
Australian Centre for Field Robotics (ACFR)
The University of Sydney, NSW 2006, Australia
t.peynot@cas.edu.au

## ABSTRACT

This paper proposes an experimental study of quality metrics that can be applied to visual and infrared images acquired from cameras onboard an unmanned ground vehicle (UGV). The relevance of existing metrics in this context is discussed and a novel metric is introduced. Selected metrics are evaluated on data collected by a UGV in clear and challenging environmental conditions, represented in this paper by the presence of airborne dust or smoke.

## Keywords

Perception, Computer Vision, Visual/Infrared Camera, Unmanned Ground Vehicle, Quality Metrics

## 1. INTRODUCTION

### 1.1 Problem Statement

The purpose of this work is to promote integrity and reliability in perceptual systems, with a focus on perception for unmanned ground vehicles (UGVs). Perception is arguably one of the most critical components of an autonomous vehicle as this is the first element in contact with the environment and its output is fundamental for all other components needed to ensure autonomy. Considerable progress has been achieved over the last decades to obtain perception algorithms that can handle the uncertainty in sensor data. By rigorously modelling these uncertainties accurate solutions can be obtained in most regular cases [8]. Nevertheless, the main difficulty remains the interpretation of sensing data. The most significant perception errors are often caused by aspects that cannot be modelled systematically like uncertainty (e.g. interpretation errors due to the presence of a dust cloud obscuring the environment).

This paper proposes an experimental study of quality metrics that can be applied to visual and infrared images acquired from cameras onboard a UGV. Numerous visual metrics can be found in the literature of the television and video

industry. Their relevance in the context of a UGV is discussed in this paper, which leads to a selection of potentially appropriate metrics. Following previous work from the authors [1], which considered information-based metrics, namely: Shannon Information (ShI), Spatial Information (SI) and Temporal Information (TI), the selected metrics were evaluated on data collected by a UGV in clear and challenging environmental conditions, represented in this paper by the presence of airborne dust or smoke. This includes an analysis of the power of discrimination of situations obtained when using these metrics individually or in some combination. Additionally, further discussion of the Spatial Information metric is proposed and a novel metric is introduced to overcome some identified limitations of SI.

The paper is organised as follows. The following Section 1.2 discusses existing metrics in the literature and Section 1.3 discusses the concept of image quality in the context of UGV perception. Section 2 describes the experiments used to analyse the various metrics in Section 3. Finally, Section 4 further discusses the interpretation of the metrics and Section 5 proposes conclusions.

### 1.2 Related Work

The television and video industry has been developing "quality metrics" to attempt to quantify objectively how a human viewer would evaluate the quality of a video stream or image [11, 12]. While the metrics are generally developed to capture the errors caused by compression and transmission and are frequently tailored to the human vision system (HVS), there are many metrics that can still be relevant to the evaluation of UGV perception quality. For example, pictures that are colourful, well-lit, sharp with high contrasts are considered attractive to humans given the choice of dark, low contrast, blurry pictures. Most of these characteristics are also positive for perception applications on a UGV.

The TV transmission infrastructure allows for metrics that compare the output to a known reference input (Full-Reference and Reduced-Reference metrics). However, fidelity of a transmitted image rarely correlates to the perceived quality of the output and, in robotic systems, a reference ground truth is rarely known. Therefore, the subset of metrics known as No-Reference are usually more appropriate to the context of this work. These metrics deal strictly with the quality of an image without relying on any knowledge of what the image should look like.

Video Quality metrics can be further classified into three groups [11, 12]. Data Metrics or "the Fidelity Approach" are purely Full-Reference metrics as they compare images directly. Feature Extraction Based (FEB) metrics or "the Engineering Approach" evaluate specific distortions in an image that are already known to occur and to degrade quality. Vision Model Based metrics (VMB) or "the Psychophysical Approach" model the HVS and evaluate human physical and/or psychological responses to aspects in an image.

FEB and VMB metrics provide the richest area of potential quality metrics for perception systems. Ironically, recent developments in the field are less likely to be suitable for robotic perception as their metrics are strongly tailored to the HVS or specific artefacts due to transmission or compression. For example, metrics designed to react to phenomena such as blocking [9, 10, 7] and ringing [4] are not particularly relevant to robotic perception. Similarly, high-level metrics modelled on physical aspects of the HVS [11, 12] were excluded. In the context of UGV perception systems, the proposed selection of metrics include FEB and VMB metrics evaluating brightness, contrast, blur, sharpness and spatial information.

## 1.3 On Image Quality

Colour and infrared cameras are common sensors on autonomous outdoor robots. Acquired images are used in various crucial high level applications such as localisation, terrain modelling, motion detection, tracking or recognition/classification. Many of the fundamental techniques employed in these applications rely on low-level operations that are often quite similar and can be broken into two families: feature-based methods (FBM) and area-based methods (ABM). FBMs need to actively identify features such as edges, corners, ridges, blobs or shapes/segments. They are typically used in applications such as recognition (e.g. path extraction), sparse stereovision and SLAM. Instead, ABMs directly analyse the intensity in the images without exploiting the saliency of objects. They use criteria similar to a correlation, a Fourier transform or Mutual Information. Examples of applications are dense stereovision and motion estimation using optical flow.

A good quality image for a UGV perception system is one that captures sufficient required information about the environment and can be used by the application to perform the task without failure. In this context, quality is degraded when the image data does not match the environmental ground truth and/or the environment itself does not contain enough information to perform the task. As quality is application-dependent, metrics should be analysed considering their relation with the performance of the two categories of applications: FBM and ABM. The experimental setup used for this analysis is detailed in the next section.

## 2. EXPERIMENTAL SETUP

In previous work [6], synchronised multi-sensor data were collected from a stationary vehicle observing a 'reference' scene (see Fig. 1) in controlled and variable environmental conditions. These included challenging environmental conditions, represented by the presence of airborne dust, smoke or rain. The list of sensors included a Prosilica mono-CCD colour camera acquiring images of resolution $1360 \times 1024$ at 15 frames per second ($fps$) and a Raytheon infrared camera with a frame grabber to acquire an average of $12.5 fps$. The same (static) scene was observed with these cameras in clear conditions and (separately) in the presence of airborne dust, smoke, and rain, all at different times of the day. Other data sets also figure a moving UGV, experiencing the same type

Figure 1: The Argo UGV sensing the *static* trial area

of conditions in an open an unknown environment. Accurate time-stamping of all these visual and infrared images allowed to synchronise the data a posteriori for this experimental study.

Although the metrics were evaluated on various data sets, for this paper, two particular sequences of images were chosen to illustrate the utility of the metrics. The first sequence (70s long, i.e. 700 images) features the presence of variable amounts of airborne dust. The second one (90s, i.e. 900 images) features variable presence of smoke. Figs. 2 and 3 show four representative images from both the colour and infrared cameras for the *Dust* and *Smoke* sequences respectively, to demonstrate the characteristic changes in the environment over the course of data collection.

Figure 2: Representative pairs of colour (top) and infrared (bottom) images for the *Dust* data set. From left to right; Clear conditions at $t = 6s$; Very light dust covering most of image at $t = 11s$; Thick dust cloud at $t = 24s$; Thin dust cloud at $t = 36.2s$.

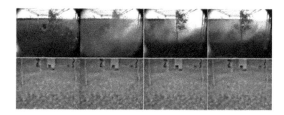

Figure 3: Representative pairs of colour (top) and infrared (bottom) images for the *Smoke* data set. From left to right; Clear conditions at $t = 1s$; Smoke covering most of image at $t = 50.7s$; Thick smoke cloud at $t = 33.9s$; Thin dust cloud at $t = 28.6s$. Note that smoke is not visible in the infrared images.

Although the actual correlation of the signals is not tackled in this paper, using common areas of images from different cameras allows to illustrate the reaction of metrics when applied to data from different sources of information about the same environment. Therefore, a smaller section of the visual camera images has been obtained by trimming the images to manually register with the field of view of the infrared camera. The resolution of the visual image has then been adjusted to match the resolution of the infrared image. A demonstration of the resulting pair of images is shown in Fig. 4. Because the sensors are mounted in different physical positions on the vehicle, the positions of objects in the field of view do not necessarily precisely match. However, the information content of the two images is comparable. Thus, metrics computed on the trimmed images from both cameras will be comparable. In future work, calibration between the sensors may be used to further compensate for this perspective difference.

Figure 4: Representative IR (left) and visual (right) images after the visual image has been trimmed and resized.

# 3. VISUAL QUALITY METRICS

This section proposes to evaluate a selection of metrics that have been considered potentially relevant for our application. They are applied to the situation of perception in challenging condition, as defined above.

Most of these metrics are designed to provide one global value representing the quality of the full image. However, they can be adapted for a local approach where the same aspect is evaluated on sub-images of the original image. For example, this could be particularly relevant for cases when challenging conditions are present but not covering the whole image.

## 3.1 Brightness

Brightness is a measure of the average luminosity of all the pixels in an image.

### 3.1.1 Contribution to Quality

It is often considered that a bright environment is preferable to a dark environment as objects can be observed more clearly. However, brightness also needs to be limited to avoid saturation. In general, extremely dark or bright conditions are not desirable for perception applications. Changes in brightness can strongly affect all area-based methods. The effect on feature-based methods is much more limited but not necessarily absent if it causes some 'weak' features to be lost. The main problem with metrics measuring brightness in the context of outdoor robotics is that they are directly effected by the lighting conditions of the environment. Challenging conditions such as dust and smoke can also influence the brightness of parts of the image depending on the background environment and the refraction of light.

### 3.1.2 Discussion

A minimum and a maximum threshold can be set on Brightness to identify extreme situations when an image is not useful for the considered application. Out of these extreme cases this metric is usually not a relevant indicator of image quality in its own, but it could be used in combination with other metrics for the discrimination of situations where apparent variations of "quality" are in fact only due to a change in lighting conditions.

## 3.2 Contrast

Contrast is a measure of the relative luminance in an image or region. It can be defined as the difference in brightness of objects within the same field of view. Higher contrast of an image is often associated with better quality as it makes features in the image easier to extract.

### 3.2.1 Definition

Although various contrast methods can be found in the literature, this experimental study focuses on the $RMS^1$ contrast [5]. Both a global (i.e. on the whole image) and a local (on patches in the images) method are considered.

By assuming that the histogram of intensities of the pixels in an image can be modelled by a Gaussian distribution, the first standard deviation of this distribution provides a measure of the contrast of the whole image:

$$C^{RMS} = \sqrt{\frac{1}{MN} \sum_{i=0}^{N-1} \sum_{i=0}^{M-1} (L_{ij} - \overline{L})^2} \qquad (1)$$

where $L_{ij}$ is the $i^{th}$ and $j^{th}$ element of the two dimensional image of size $M \times N$ and $\overline{L}$ is the average luminance in the image.

In a more local analysis of Contrast using the same RMS method, for each pixel of the image a local contrast is computed using a patch of $10 \times 10$ neighbouring pixels. The contrast value for the image is then calculated by averaging all the local contrast values across the whole image.

### 3.2.2 Contribution to Quality

Good contrast is crucial for many feature-based methods, as corners, ridges or edges are identified using the relative intensity of neighbouring pixels. A higher contrast is also preferable for area-based methods, to have a better signal-to-noise ratio. A minimum of contrast is usually needed in both cases. Therefore a corresponding threshold (for a minimum quality) can be defined.

Challenging conditions such as dust and smoke partially obscure areas in the image, and therefore affect its global contrast. Whether it increases or decreases as a result depends on the relative intensity of the dust and smoke compared to the background environment. However, locally, within the smoke/dust cloud, the contrast is consistently diminished, reducing the quality of corresponding portions of the image.

### 3.2.3 Experimental Results

Fig. 5 shows the evolution of RMS Contrast for the whole image for the *Dust* and *Smoke* data sets. In these data sets, there is a clear sudden increase in the global RMS Contrast with the appearance of dust and smoke. However, this effect is very strongly dependent on the *relative* intensity of the

---

[1]Root Mean Square

background and the smoke or dust, and the effect of sunlight scattering from the dust and smoke clouds.

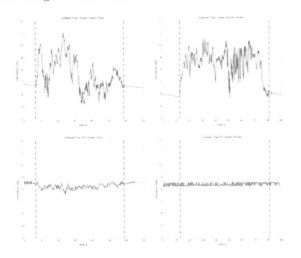

Figure 5: RMS Contrast measurement of the whole image, for *Dust* (left) and *Smoke* (right). Top line: visual camera, bottom line: IR camera. Note that hereafter the times of appearance and then disappearance of dust/smoke will be indicated by dashed vertical lines.

Fig. 6 shows the evolution of contrast using the local method for the *Dust* and *Smoke* data sets. The average contrast of the image drops in both *Dust* and *Smoke* data sets as dust or smoke begin to obscure the background of the scene.

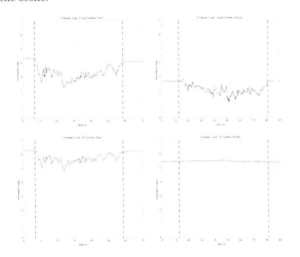

Figure 6: *Local* RMS Contrast measurement for *Dust* (left) and *Smoke* (right). Top line: visual camera, bottom line: IR camera.

### 3.2.4 Discussion

Without utilising further information, the RMS Contrast of the whole image is a poor method of evaluating the quality of an image, due to the dependence on the background

characteristics and the Gaussian assumption. The Gaussian approximation for the distribution of intensity values of the pixels means that a few very bright or very dark pixels can cause a large standard deviation when Contrast in much of the image is in fact very low. This metric can only be used by itself if the background is known or the contrasts drops to a critically low value. In the latter case, the image can be judged as poor quality and unlikely to provide any useful data for the perception algorithms considered in our context.

Calculating the RMS contrast at a pixel-by-pixel level using the method described above has a very high computational cost. Thus, a more appropriate method for real-time applications would use regions of interests (ROI) defined by specifying an appropriate size for a sub-image or by focussing on areas where challenging conditions are expected to appear (if such information is available) and checking the evolution of contrast in them.

## 3.3 Blur

Blurred features are harder to differentiate as the boundaries become smeared. This may lead to difficulties in image analysis and scene interpretation.

### 3.3.1 Definition

Among the different techniques in the literature, *Marziliano Blur* [4] was identified as a method of measuring blur that is quick to compute and quite intuitive. The method is as follows: first, a Sobel filter is applied to the image to extract vertical edges and the edge-filtered-image is thresholded. Then, for each location of non-zero pixel, the local maximum and minimum of luminosity values are found along the horizontal rows of the original image. The distance between these local extrema, expressed in number of pixels, is considered the local blur value. The global blur value (measured in pixels) is then found by averaging the local blur measurements over all suitable edge locations:

$$Blur = \frac{1}{N} \sum_{i=1}^{N} (d_i) \qquad (2)$$

where $N$ is the number of pixels used to calculate the blur and $d_i$ is the distance between the two local extrema of luminosity around pixel $i$.

### 3.3.2 Contribution to Quality

The blurriness of the image can strongly effect feature-based methods, as it reduces the saliency of objects. On the contrary, the effect of blurriness on area-based methods is limited, unless a sudden change in blur occurs.

In normal conditions, the blur from a sensor remains relatively constant regardless of the background environment and changes to lighting conditions.

### 3.3.3 Experimental Results

For the results presented in this paper, the edge image was thresholded to an intensity value of 50 (out of 255) in the Blur calculation. Fig. 7 shows the evolution of Blur for the images in the *Dust* and *Smoke* data sets. In both *Dust* and *Smoke* data sets there is a characteristic increase in Blur for the visual images in the presence of dust and smoke. The most significant troughs in the Blur signal that can be observed in the visual images in the presence of smoke can be attributed to a significant drop in the number of edges that Blur is calculated on (e.g. see at time $t = 51s$ in Fig. 7). Note that there is a decrease in Blur in the infrared images

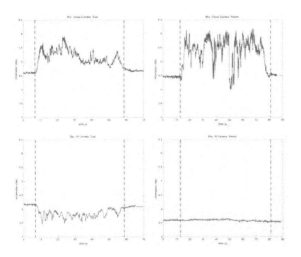

**Figure 7: Blur measurement (in pixels) for *Dust* (left) and *Smoke* (right). Top line: visual camera, bottom line: IR camera.**

in the presence of dust. The difference between the blur in visual and infrared sensors is likely to be related to the intensity threshold that is used to choose edges for the Blur calculation.

### 3.3.4 Discussion

In challenging conditions such as dust and smoke, the overall blur of the visual images is seen to increase significantly. By setting an upper threshold on the blur, challenging conditions could be identified. However, as mentioned above, the value of Blur highly depends on the threshold applied to the edge image, and on the number of edges considered in the calculation of the metric, as a result. In the case of the IR images, the signal-to-noise ratio is much lower. When the background is obscured by challenging conditions strong edges are dimmed or lost, and small edges essentially due to the noise become dominant in the calculation of Blur, resulting in an increase of the metric. This makes this Blur metric difficult to use for the IR camera in its current form.

## 3.4 Sharpness

Sharpness (or acutance) [2] describes the rate of change of luminosity with respect to spatial position.

### 3.4.1 Definition

The sharpness of an image is found by averaging the gradient between neighbouring cells [2].

$$Gx^2 = \sum(\frac{\Delta I^2}{n}) \qquad (3)$$

$$Acutance = (Gx^2/I_0) \times C \qquad (4)$$

where $\Delta I$ is the difference in the grey scale value between a pixel and each of the 8 surrounding pixels; $n$ is the total number of contributing values, that is, the number of pixels multiplied by 8; $I_0$ is the mean luminosity value of the image; and C is a scaling factor.

### 3.4.2 Contribution to Quality

Sharpness highly effects feature-based methods, in particular those using features such as edge or corner detectors.

Area-based methods are not much effected by images that are not sharp. However, both categories of methods (FBM and ABM) experience difficulties with images whose sharpness changes rapidly. Note that Sharpness is dependent on the focus of the sensor being used.

The appearance of challenging conditions are shown to decrease the sharpness of images as the background edges are dulled.

### 3.4.3 Experimental Results

Fig. 8 shows the evolution of sharpness for the images in the *Dust* and *Smoke* data sets.

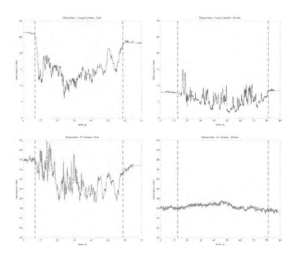

**Figure 8: Sharpness for *Dust* (left) and *Smoke* (right). Top line: visual camera, bottom line: IR camera.**

### 3.4.4 Discussion

The Sharpness method is essentially using an edge detector and averaging the intensities of the edges over the whole image. Indeed, the response of the Sharpness metric (Fig. 8) to both the *Dust* and *Smoke* data sets is very similar to the SI metric (see below). Averaging the intensities of an edge-filtered image provides no more information than can be found using Spatial Information and Spatial Entropy, which have been preferred, as explained below. Therefore, this metric was not selected for our applications.

## 3.5 Spatial Information and Spatial Entropy

In previous work [1], among the existing information-theory based metrics, Spatial Information (SI) was found to be the most promising one in the context of perception in challenging environmental conditions. To compute SI, an edge detector such as a Sobel filter is first used on the input image. SI is then defined as the first standard deviation of the resulting distribution of intensities in the Sobel image, i.e. the intensities of edges in the original image. Since it is evaluating the amount of structure in an image, it can be applied in the same way to heterogeneous sensors such as a visual camera and an infrared camera. However, in this section we show the limitations of SI, mainly due to the Gaussian distribution assumption. This justifies the introduction of Spatial Entropy (SE). Furthermore, we show that combining SI and SE can contribute to discriminating more situations.

### 3.5.1 Contribution to Quality

SI and SE measure the amount of structure in an image. As such, they are particularly relevant to feature-based methods. Setting a minimum threshold of SI and SE can allow to identify when an image is unlikely to be useful for applications using feature-based methods. On the other hand, SI and SE have little relevance to area-based methods. Challenging conditions such as dust and smoke are shown to reduce the values of SI and SE when they obscure the background environment.

### 3.5.2 Limitations of SI

The definition of SI relies on the assumption that the distribution of intensities in the Sobel-filtered image can be modelled as a Gaussian, with an average close to zero. In that case, the distribution can be characterised by its standard deviation. In most edge-filtered-images, this assumption is found to be reasonable. Since dust or smoke clouds tend to obscure features in the background and contain very little structure, SI was shown to be a useful tool to monitor the appearance of such environmental conditions [1], at least in cases where dust or smoke was shown to dim or obscure most background features, i.e. when the Gaussian assumption was acceptable.

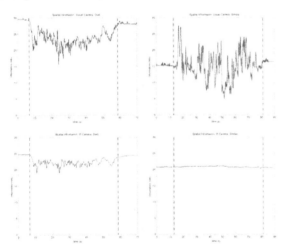

**Figure 9: Evolution of SI for *Dust* (left) and *Smoke* (right), Visual (top row) and IR Camera (bottom)**

However, in some situations, e.g. in the presence of foreground objects, the known challenging conditions can actually highlight the edges of these foreground objects while still obscuring background features. An example is shown in the *Smoke* data set where the smoke obscures much of the background but mostly stays behind the tree that is in the foreground on the right side of the image (see Fig. 10). In this situation the edges of the tree are highlighted as they contrast more with the smoke behind it then with the original background. These high intensity edges have a strong impact on SI (see the high peaks in Fig. 9, right column), making it increase significantly, despite the reduction of structure everywhere else in the image. This same phenomena is also observed for short moments in the *Dust*

data set (most notably at the spike at $t = 24s$). Fig. 10 shows that in these situations the Gaussian assumption is clearly not valid, which means the first standard deviation (and therefore SI) does not characterise the distribution, i.e. the actual amount of structure in the image.

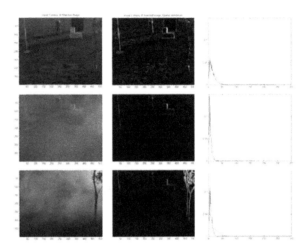

**Figure 10: Representative images (left column) for *Smoke* with Sobel-filtered image (middle column). Right column: corresponding distribution of edge intensities (in blue) and Gaussian approximation of this distribution (in red). Clear Conditions at $t = 1s$; Smoke covering most of image at $t = 50.7s$; Thick smoke cloud at $t = 33.9s$ .**

### 3.5.3 Introduction of SE

To overcome this issue, we introduce a new metric that we call *Spatial Entropy* (SE). SE models the intensity distribution of an edge-filtered image using entropy. The entropy of an edge-filtered-image measures the variety of edge intensity values without giving "weight" to the magnitude of the intensity values, as it happens with SI. An edge image that contains a large variety of intensity values has a greater "information[2] content" than one that has the same spatial distribution of edges all at the same intensity, which usually means the image is more useful for an application, especially feature-based methods.

SE can be used to help discriminate the challenging conditions that SI failed to identify. In situations where most features are behind the obscurant, SI and SE both decrease and jointly confirm that features are being dimmed or lost (e.g. see the *Dust* dataset). However, SI and SE disagreeing usually means the Gaussian approximation of SI is not appropriate. For example if SI is increasing but SE is decreasing, then some features in the environment are being obscured while others are becoming more intense (as in Fig. 10).

### 3.5.4 Experimental Results

Examples of the evolution of Spatial Entropy for both *Dust* and *Smoke* data sets are shown in Fig. 11. The value of SE consistently decreases when dust appears and spreads for visual and infrared images and for smoke in visual images. Once dust and smoke have cleared, SE returns to a

---

[2]information being undestood as *Shannon information* [3] here

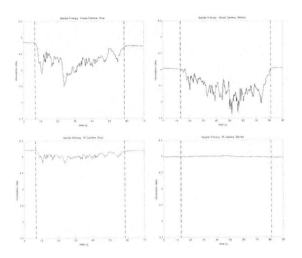

Figure 11: Evolution of SE for *Dust* (left) and *Smoke* (right), Visual (top row) and IR Camera (bottom)

nominal value corresponding to clear conditions. For clear and unchanging conditions, such as seen in the first 8 seconds of both data sets, the value of SE is stable.

### 3.5.5  Discussion

Very low values for Spatial Entropy usually indicate that there is very little information in the image. However, a black and white image of edges (e.g. a checker board) may contain a great deal of useful information for perception but because it uses only two values for intensity, its entropy will be very low. In natural environments, such a situation is extremely unlikely, making SE relevant on its own. However, it should be noted that in this case the value of SI will be high. Therefore, both SI and SE can be used in conjunction to differentiate such situations.

When conditions are clear, both SI and SE are stable. When smoke is covering most of the image, including the tree in the foreground (e.g. at $t = 50.7s$ in Fig. 11), this corresponds to a clear drop in both SI and SE. However, when a thick cloud of smoke is covering much of the background but passes behind the tree in the foreground ($t = 33.9s$), SI increases rapidly while SE decreases. Table 1 summarises the conditions that can be discriminated by monitoring the relationship between SI and SE metrics.

## 4.  METRICS INTERPRETATION

### 4.1  Metrics Evaluation

We consider three main ways to use these metrics to evaluate image quality, in particular in the presence of challenging conditions. The first is to check a single metric value, the second is to monitor its evolution and the third is to compare the relative evolution of multiple metrics.

As discussed for each metric above, due to the generality of metrics and the diversity of environments UGVs operate in, it is rarely possible to discriminate poor quality images from any single metric value, except in extreme cases. Only when the value for the metric is approaching maximum or minimum values, for example if the contrast drops below a critical level, can it definitively indicate that the sensor data is unlikely to be useful for further perception.

The evolution of an individual metric can be used to monitor changes in the environment. Since unmodelled changes in environments will effect perception applications, unexpected changes in a metric may indicate that challenging conditions are occurring. For example, a sudden reduction in SI occurs when features are obscured or lost. Similarly, most metrics were unstable under challenging conditions compared to normal conditions. However, due to the motion of the UGV, the metric will evolve according to the change in the area of the environment which is currently perceived. Consequently, a method to compensate for this influence of motion on the metrics is needed. This is demonstrated in Section 4.2.

The combination of metrics that have some relationship can lead to further discrimination. In this study, the main groups of metrics that should be combined were identified as: Brightness-Contrast-ShI, evaluating changes in intensity, and SI-SE, evaluating changes in structure in the image.

### 4.2  Compensation for Motion

To allow for the use of the selected quality metrics when the UGV is moving, a simple method is used to compensate for the motion of the vehicle. The technique approximates this motion between successive frame acquisitions by an affine transformation, which is calculated using sensing data that must be fully independent from the cameras. In this work we used a cm-accuracy dGPS/INS system which is available on the platform. Once this transformation has been applied, the images can be cropped so that consecutive images approximately register.

Taking into account the field of view and frame rate of the sensors, as well as the operating speeds of our UGV, it was found that five consecutive images guarantee sufficient overlap in images. The evolution of metrics on these overlapping sub-images can then be evaluated for actual changes in quality (e.g. due to challenging conditions) without significant influence from the motion of the vehicle (see Fig. 12).

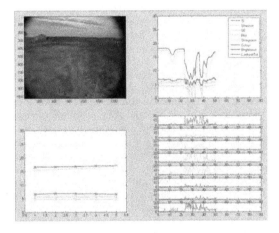

Figure 12: Evolution of multiple metrics for a moving UGV, in a data set with variable presence of airborne dust. Top left: current frame and evaluated ROI in red. Top right: direct evolution of metrics in the ROI. Bottom left: variation of metrics for the last five overlapping regions. Bottom right: variation of the metrics after compensation for motion.

Table 1: The relationship in the evolution of SI and SE can be used to discriminate situations. Normal text: what happens in the image. *Emphasised text*: meaning in case of challenging conditions. ∕ and ∖ stand for "increases" and "decreases", respectively.

| | SI ∕ | SI ∖ |
|---|---|---|
| SE ∕ | Amount of structure is increasing<br><br>*Less Dust/Smoke in front of most objects* | General amount of structure is increasing but some strong edges are getting weaker<br>*Less Dust/Smoke in background. There are objects in front of the cloud* |
| SE ∖ | General amount of structure is decreasing but some edges are getting stronger<br>*More Dust/Smoke in background. There are objects in front of the cloud* | Amount of structure is decreasing<br><br>*More Dust/Smoke in front of most objects* |

## 5. CONCLUSION

This paper has presented image quality metrics and how they relate to evaluating the quality of image data for robotic perception systems. The analysed metrics included in particular Brightness, Contrast, Blur, Sharpness and Spatial Information. While all metrics are affected differently by challenging conditions, the metrics Local Contrast, Blur and SI were found to be the most promising in our context. However, more work is required to properly study the effects of challenging conditions on Blur and Local Contrast in the current form cannot be performed on a real-time system.

Spatial Entropy (SE) was introduced as a novel metric evaluating structure in an image that is more robust in determining challenging conditions than Spatial Information (SI). Additionally, SI and SE were shown to provide even better discrimination of situations when interpreted together.

We have discussed how the metrics may be interpreted specifically to discriminate challenging conditions for perception including thresholding individual values, monitoring the evolution of the metrics and comparing the relationship of metrics.

Besides checking the quality of the data provided by a single sensor, one of the future objective of this work is to be able to check the consistency between heterogeneous sensors such as a visual camera and an infrared camera. Therefore, metrics that transform aspects of the images into characteristics that are comparable between the two types of sensors should be preferred. Indeed, the notion of intensity in a visual image (i.e. luminosity) cannot be directly compared with the intensity in an infrared camera image (representing a temperature). SI and SE are clear candidates for such multimodal comparisons.

Future work will involve studying how to take appropriate decisions in the perception system, based on the interpretation of the metrics. For example, image data considered of insufficient quality may simply be removed to avoid jeopardising the interpretation that will be made by the perception. Another option is to select online the more appropriate type of camera to be used at any time.

## 6. ACKNOWLEDGEMENTS

This work was supported in part by the Centre for Intelligent Mobile Systems (CIMS), funded by BAE Systems as part of an ongoing partnership with the University of Sydney, and the ARC Centre of Excellence programme, funded by the Australian Research Council (ARC) and the New South Wales State Government.

## 7. REFERENCES

[1] C. Brunner, T. Peynot, and J. Underwood. Towards discrimination of challenging conditions for ugvs with visual and infrared sensors. In *Australasian Conference on Robotics and Automation (ACRA)*, 2009.

[2] Y.F. Choong, F. Rakebrandt, R.V. North, and J.E. Morgan. Acutance, an objective measure of retinal nerve fibre image clarity. *British Journal of Ophthalmology*, 87(3):322–326, 2003.

[3] D. Mackay. *Information Theory, Inference & Learning Algorithms.* Cambridge University Press, 2007.

[4] P. Marziliano, F. Dufaux, S. Winkler, and T. Ebrahimi. Perceptual blur and ringing metrics: application to jpeg2000. *Signal Processing: Image Communication*, 19(2):163–172, 2004.

[5] E. Peli. Contrast in complex images. *Journal of the Optical Society of America A*, 7:2032–2040, 1990.

[6] T. Peynot, S. Scheding, and S. Terho. The Marulan Data Sets: Multi-Sensor Perception in Natural Environment with Challenging Conditions. *to appear in International Journal of Robotics Research*, 2010.

[7] S. Susstrunk and S. Winkler. Color image quality on the internet. In *IS&T/SPIE Electronic Imaging: Internet Imaging V*, 2004.

[8] J. P. Underwood, A. Hill, T. Peynot, and S. J. Scheding. Error modeling and calibration of exteroceptive sensors for accurate mapping applications. *Journal of Field Robotics, Special Issue: Three-Dimensional Mapping, Part 3*, 27(1):2–20, January/February 2010.

[9] T. Vlachos. Detection of blocking artifacts in compressed video. *Electronics Letters*, 36(13):1106–1108, 2000.

[10] Z. Wang, A. C. Bovik, and B .L. Evan. Blind measurement of blocking artifacts in images. In *IEEE International Conference on Image Processing*, 2000.

[11] Z. Wang and A.C. Bovik. *Modern Image Quality Assessment.* Morgan & Claypool, 2006.

[12] S. Winkler. *Digital Video Quality: Vision Models and Metrics.* John Wiley & Sons Ltd, New Dehli, 2005.

# Proposals for New UGV, UMV, UAV, and HRI Standards for Rescue Robots

Robin R. Murphy
Computer Science and Engineering
Texas A&M University
College Station, TX
murphy@cse.tamu.edu

## ABSTRACT

This paper summarizes the recommended additions to standards being developed by the ASTM E54.08 Homeland Security committee from the NSF-JST-NIST Workshop on Rescue Robotics held at Texas A&M, March 8-11, 2010, concurrently with the NIST Response Robot Evaluation Exercise #6. The 50 workshop participants represented sixteen universities in the USA, Japan, and China. Over a dozen land, marine, and aerial vehicles were tested at Disaster City® . The workshop produced two recommendations for standards for unmanned ground vehicles, four for small unmanned aerial systems, and two for unmanned marine vehicles, as well as proposed four topics for human-robot interaction evaluation. The eight recommendations were presented at the ASTM meeting on March 12, 2010, although test methods have not been developed or proposed for each new topic. The participants also identified four new classes of standards: tethers, damage to the environment, victim management, and multi-robot coordination and collaboration.

## Categories and Subject Descriptors

K.4 [**Computer Milieux**]: Computers and Society—*public policy issues*; J.2 [**Computer Applications**]: physical sciences and engineering—*engineering*

## General Terms

Theory

## Keywords

rescue robots, metrics, UGV, UAV, UMV, human-robot interaction

## 1. INTRODUCTION

The rescue robotics community is contributing to standards under the ASTM E54.08 technical committee on oper-

Permission to make digital or hard copies of all or part of this work for personal or classroom use is granted without fee provided that copies are not made or distributed for profit or commercial advantage and that copies bear this notice and the full citation on the first page. To copy otherwise, to republish, to post on servers or to redistribute to lists, requires prior specific permission and/or a fee.
PerMIS'10, September 28-30, 2010, Baltimore, MD, USA.
Copyright © 2010 ACM 978-1-4503-0290-6-9/28/10 ...$10.00.

ational equipment for homeland security. As part of a workshop sponsored by the National Science Foundation (NSF), the Japan Science and Technology Agency (JST), and the National Institute for Standards and Technology (NIST) and endorsed by the IEEE technical committee on Safety, Security, and Rescue Robots, 50 researchers considered standards and metrics for robots not covered by the current standards or ASTM working groups. The Rescue Robotics Workshop was held March 8-11, 2010, concurrently with NIST Response Robot Evaluation Exercise #6 held at Texas A&M's Disaster City® . The workshop was hosted by the Center for Robot-Assisted Search and Rescue (CRASAR), sponsored by the National Science Foundation (NSF), the Japan Science and Technology Agency (JST), and the National Institute for Standards and Technology (NIST) and endorsed by the IEEE technical committee on Safety, Security, and Rescue Robots. A total of 50 researchers participated, with 35 attendees from nine Japanese institutions (Chiba Institute of Technology, Kinki University, Kobe City College of Technology, Kyoto University, Nagaoka University of Technology, National Institute of Advanced Industrial Science and Technology, National Research Institute for Earth Science and Disaster Prevention, Tohoku University, and Tokyo Institute of Technology), fourteen attendees from six American universities (Denver University, Ohio State, Texas A&M, University of Pennsylvania, Vanderbilt, Virginia Tech), and one attendee from China (Shenyang Institute of Automation).

This paper presents eight recommendations for new areas and topics for standards encompassing current novel technologies that are not covered and four new classes of standards that anticipate emerging technologies. These areas were presented at the ASTM meeting on March 12, 2010. These recommendations have been also reported as part of a general outbrief of the workshop which appears in [10]; this paper focuses strictly on the standards and provides more justification of the standards.

## 2. UNMANNED GROUND VEHICLES

Small UGVs have been targeted for searching the interior of rubble, in situ medical assessment and intervention, adaptive shoring, acting as a mobile beacon or repeater, and serving as a surrogate for a team member in search and rescue operations.[8] The participants proposed a new standard topic for UGVs that would evaluate robots that are currently not covered (those that can enter extremely small diameter voids) and one new challenge or scenario for ground rescue robots (operation from a vertical access point).

a.

b.

Figure 1: Motivation for standards for operating in small diameter voids: a. Active Scope Camera being inserted into an irregular, naturally occurring void and b.Coring tool creating a regular small diameter void in concrete (photo courtesy of TEEX).

## 2.1 Small Diameter Voids

The motivation for standards for extremely small diameter voids stemmed from the lack of access to the small spaces that currently only a search camera can enter, but cannot penetrate beyond a few feet into the void due to the higher tortorosity of the space. The participants recommended creating metrics based on two types of small void spaces: *irregular, naturally occurring* voids and *regular from a concrete coring tool* used for breaching such as seen in Fig. 1. The widest diameter of the voids would be on the order of 7.62cm (3 inch) to reflect the diameter of common coring tools. Metrics for small diameter voids would permit evaluation of newer snake-like robots, including the Active Scope Camera successfully used at the 2007 Berkman Plaza II collapse [15], and robots such as the TerminatorBot which were designed explicitly to enter through cored holes [17].

## 2.2 Vertical Mobility

The motivation for vertical mobility and perception stan-

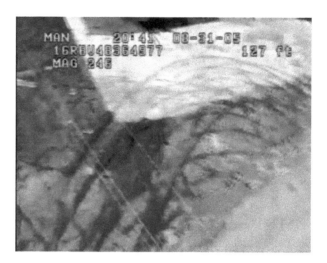

Figure 2: An example of powerlines (lower left, diagonal) as a danger in exterior structural inspection.

dards stems from experiences with responders having to enter the rubble from the top of the rubble. As described in [8], three robot deployments (the World Trade Center [4], the Midas Nevada Gold [5] and Crandall Canyon Utah mine [5] disasters) required robots to be inserted from above and rappel down to the points of interest. Vertical mobility is particularly challenging as it includes being able to maintain the view object of interest while rappelling down. [5] describes problems with a skid-steered ground robot being unable to pan to see critical areas of interest. The participants recommended creating a rappelling rock wall for evaluating a UGV's ability to navigate vertically and search while suspended by a belay line.

## 3. SMALL UNMANNED AERIAL SYSTEMS

The participants proposed four new standard topics for small UAVs that would evaluate: *operating close to structures*, how they *respond to the failures and in external disturbances, performance and non-line of sight operations*, and *take off and landing performance*.

## 3.1 Operating Close to Structures

The motivation for measuring performance in terms of aperture mobility arises from the use of UAVs for exterior structural inspection. Structural inspection is typically close to buildings, power lines, trees, and other difficult to model obstacles. For example, Fig. 2 shows the view from a small fixed wing UAV being used at Hurricane Katrina right before it crashed into powerlines.[14] The powerlines are barely visible. Standards would likely address sensor performance (can the UAV "see" the clutter?) but would go beyond existing visual acuity tests of whether the human can see an object to also consider whether the robot can autonomously detect obstacles and if can withstanding bumping into an object.

## 3.2 Response to Failures and External Disturbances

The motivation for considering failure modes and external disturbances stems from what happens when something goes wrong (e.g., loss of comms, GPS). While there appears to be no statistics on communications losses in small UAVs, this is a distinct possibility. Some systems have an automatic return to home function, others appear to have no contingency function. Likewise, the dependency on GPS for various systems is unclear and the consequences of lost signal could be significant.

### 3.3 Non Line-of-Sight Operation

Although the participants in the workshop were not sure of the exact measures, there was a strong feeling that standards needed to address non line-of-sight (NLOS) operation, both for reconnaissance and mapping (over large areas) and exterior structural inspection (UAV goes behind a building). NLOS operational challenges are closely related to how the UAV responds to failures or external disturbances. It also presumes a higher degree of autonomy, which introduces another challenge for creating standards. Metrics for non line-of-sight operations are also important because in the United States, the Federal Aviation Administration (FAA) does not appear to favor the approval of small UAVs operating out of the line of sight. The creation of meaningful metrics might encourage the FAA to permit such use.

### 3.4 Take-Off and Landing

Measuring take-off/landing difficulty is also important as those regimes may occupy more than 50% of the flight time [13, 14, 6] and maybe the hardest for a human operator to be able to recover from autonomy failures. Small UAVs often expect the pilot to actively handle take-off and landing, with a spectrum of assistance by the robot. Some systems may be easier to pilot and more robust than others, so having metrics is important. It is not clear what test methods would capture this and indeed it may actually be multiple standards for performance and human cognitive load or attention.

### 4. UNMANNED MARINE VEHICLES

Unmanned marine vehicles cover water-based robots (surface, underwater, submersible, etc.) and are a new area for standards. UMVs have been used for post-disaster inspection of littoral structures such as bridges and sea walls and were attempted for use in finding cars and victims after the I-35W bridge collapse in Minneapolis, Minnesota [3, 1]. The test methods used at the Evaluation assumed video camera sensing, which is heavily dependent on the clarity of the water. The participants recommended considering two new topics, *turbidity* and *station-keeping*, and also encouraged consideration of sonars.

### 4.1 Turbidity

Metrics for turbidity would test the performance of underwater sensors in more realistic conditions than clear water. Turbidity is a major limiting factor in manual divers being able to rapidly find and recover drowned victims and to establish the condition of bridges and seawalls. High turbidity was witnessed in the aftermath of Hurricane Wilma [12, 7] and Hurricane Ike.[16, 11] Turbidity sensors exist, the bigger challenge is to create a test method that can inexpensively create turbid conditions.

### 4.2 Station-keeping

Metrics for station-keeping would rate how well the system could respond to environmental effects such as waves, currents, and wind. The real goal is for an object to stay visible and in the same orientation as the user viewed it, rather than disappear and reappear as the vehicle moves about. Since many UMVs have cameras and sonars on pan-tilt mounts, measuring the position and orientation of the vehicle is not sufficient. Instead, measuring how the object moves in the image appears to be the most promising test method and the same measurement scheme would apply to video and sonar.

### 5. HUMAN-ROBOT INTERACTION

The workshop participants found that human robot interaction standards were missing from the current test methods. As noted in [8], poor human-robot interaction has been a major barrier in rescue robots since the first use of robots at the World Trade Center disaster in 2001. Human-robot interaction includes interfaces such as the operator control unit, how well those interfaces support human cognitive limitations in developing situation awareness through computer meditation, and general human performance. Human-robot interaction goes beyond visual acuity and focuses more on understanding. Four types of metrics were recommended: *perception, impact on human, robustness,* and *interface evaluation*.

### 5.1 Perception

The motivation for human robot interaction standards on *perception* is because the mission is perceptually directed, especially manipulation tasks. A perceptually challenging task may be successfully conducted initially with a poor human robot interaction scheme but will eventually lead to failure. Two typical measures of perceptual performance are *situation awareness tests* (ex. SAGAT) and the ability to *correctly estimate outcomes* (e.g., understanding of what to expect).

### 5.2 Impact on Human Operator

The motivation for considering the *impact on the human operator* is that high task loads cannot be sustained. Two methods for measuring the impact on the human include *measuring the cognitive load* (ex. NASA TLX) and *non-interruption testing* (ex. physiological measurements).

### 5.3 Robustness

*Robustness metrics* are motivated by the need for efficiency, maintenance of the appropriate task loading, and ensuring adaptability. Two metrics of robustness are the *error rate* (ex. number of repeats, have to backup, mistakes, slips) and the *choice of modes of operation and camera viewpoint*.

### 5.4 Interfaces

*User interfaces* are a major component of human-robot interaction. The methods for evaluating interfaces are too numerous to list here, but the participants felt strongly that such metrics should become a standard part of the test methods.

### 6. NEW CLASSES OF STANDARDS

In addition to the recommendations above, the workshop participants identified four new classes of areas requiring standards, which are presented below in no particular order:

*Damage to the environment by the robot.* This problem arose as a result of concerns over the possible damage by robots to ancient manuscripts buried in the rubble of the State Archives Building collapse in Cologne, Germany [2]. The building was successfully evacuated before it collapsed due to a cave-in of a subway tunnel, but extremely valuable documents remained in the rubble. However, to navigate and find the location of the oldest manuscripts meant that the robot might have to travel over other documents. This raised the possibility that the effector, in this case tracks, might harm the documents more than continued exposure to the elements.

*Victim management.* While rescue robots have not found to date a live survivor, eventually they will. Therefore, researchers must consider the next step: how robots will interact with the victims? There is both *physical interaction*, where the robot serves as an extension for a medical expert, and *social interaction*, where the robot acts as the conduit between the victim and the outside world. Physical interaction might be evaluated using standards for medical robots such as surgical robots, but measuring social interaction is less clear.

*Multi-robot coordination and collaboration.* Multi-robot coordination and collaboration is a popular topic in research with promising results. It is timely to consider standards that would accelerate adoption of such advances. Multi-robot coordination takes two forms: homogeneous and heterogeneous teams. Homogeneous teams appear to be of the most immediate interest. For UGVs, groups of similar robots would enter rubble through different voids to search and map out the interior. Groups of UAVs could map out large areas, facilitating reconnaissance and mapping functions.

*Tethers.* The motivation for evaluating tethers stems from the practice of using tethers for power or communications and because of vertical mobility [9]. UGVs used in disasters typically have been tethered or had a fiber optic cable.[8] A class of underwater vehicles, remotely operated vehicles or ROV, is distinguished by its use of a tether. Advances in UMV automated tether assistance and in localizing tether position are becoming commercially available. Active tethers have been discussed for ground vehicles. The combination of need and advances in technology suggest the timing is right to consider tether standards. The participants recommended a three dimensional tether maze to test these tether advances.

## 7. OTHER OBSERVATIONS

The participants felt that current research and standards are too focused on components, not informatics, that is: how well information gathered could be transmitted to other stakeholders? The participants saw evidence that while navigational autonomy as possible, mission autonomy (e.g., perceiving victims, understanding structures, etc.) is unlikely due to the extreme conditions and may actually be undesirable from a larger organizational perspective. Instead, mission autonomy is likely to be shared between the robot and a responder. Likewise, the attendees were intrigued by what they termed "learnability." For example the NIST test methods permitted the use of expert drivers but there was

no indication of how long it took the operator to acquire that expertise. Feedback from the response community suggests that training is a major barrier to adoption. A system that cannot be easily learned would be unlikely to be adopted.

## 8. CONCLUSIONS AND CURRENT WORK

In general, the proposed topics for standards addressed *novel technologies*, such as the active scope camera, *challenging applications* of existing technology, for example vertical descents and station-keeping, or *systems-level issues*, especially human-robot interaction and resilience. Currently, standards for station-keeping and turbidity are in progress.

## 9. ACKNOWLEDGMENTS

Participation of researchers from the USA and general organization of the workshop was supported in part by the National Science Foundation under Grant OISE-1029089 and by the National Institute for Standards and Technology through coordination with Elena Messina and Adam Jacoff. Any opinions, findings, conclusions or recommendations expressed in this paper are those of the author and do not necessarily reflect the views of the National Science Foundation. The author would like to especially thank Dr. Paul Oh and and Dr. Anne Emig for their help in expediting the grant, Clint Arnett for his assistance with Disaster City® , Kimberly Mallett for administrative support of the workshop, and the anonymous reviewers for their helpful suggestions.

## 10. REFERENCES

[1] L. Goldwert. Minneapolis honors bridge collapse victims, cbs news, 2007.

[2] T. Linder, V. Tretyakov, S. Blumenthal, P. Molitor, D. Holz, R. Murphy, S. Tadokoro, and H. Surmann. Rescue robots at the collapse of the municipal archive of cologne city: a field report. In *IEEE International Workshop on Safety, Security, and Rescue Robotics*, to appear 2010.

[3] E. Merriam. Mdsu-2 arrives in minneapolis prepared to help, navy.mil the source for navy news, 2007.

[4] R. Murphy. Trial by fire. *IEEE Robotics and Automation Magazine*, 11(3):50–61, 2004.

[5] R. Murphy, J. Kravitz, S. Stover, and R. Shoureshi. Mobile robots in mine rescue and recovery. *IEEE Robotics and Automation Magazine*, 16(2):91–103, 2009.

[6] R. Murphy, K. Pratt, and J. Burke. Crew roles and operational protocols for rotary-wing micro-uavs in close urban environments. In *ACM SIGCHI/SIGART Human-Robot Interaction*, pages 73–80, 2008.

[7] R. Murphy, E. Steimle, E. Griffin, C. Cullins, M. Hall, and K. Pratt. Cooperative use of unmanned sea surface and micro aerial vehicle at hurricane wilma. *Journal of Field Robotics*, 25(3):164–180, 2008.

[8] R. Murphy, S. Tadokoro, D. Nardi, A. Jacoff, P. Fiorini, and A. Erkmen. Rescue robotics (chapter). In B. Sciliano and O. Khatib, editors, *Handbook of Robotics*, pages 1151–1174. Springer-Verlag, 2008.

[9] R. R. Murphy. Navigational and mission usability in rescue robots. *Journal of the Robotics Society of Japan, special issue on Rescue Robotics- Present and Future of Rescue Support System in Disaster*, 28(2):142–146, 2010.

[10] R. R. Murphy. Findings from nsf-jst-nist workshop on rescue robotics. In *IEEE International Workshop on Safety, Security, and Rescue Robotics (SSRR 2010)*. IEEE, to appear 2010.

[11] R. R. Murphy, E. Steimle, M. Lindemuth, D. Trejo, M. Hall, D. Slocum, S. Hurlebas, and Z. Medina-Cetina. Robot-assisted bridge inspection after hurricane ike. In *IEEE Workshop on Safety Security Rescue Robotics*, pages 1–5, Denver CO, 2009. IEEE.

[12] R. R. Murphy, E. Steimle, M. Lindemuth, D. Trejo, M. Hall, D. Slocum, S. Hurlebas, and Z. Medina-Cetina. Robot-assisted bridge inspection. *Journal of Intelligent and Robotics Systems (invited)*, (special issue on Safety Security Rescue Robots), to appear.

[13] K. Pratt, R. Murphy, J. Burke, J. Craighead, C. Griffin, and S. Stover. Use of tethered small unmanned aerial system at berkman plaza ii collapse. In *IEEE International Workshop on Safety, Security, and Rescue Robotics*, pages 134–139, 2008.

[14] K. Pratt, R. Murphy, S. Stover, and C. Griffin. Conops and autonomy rcommendations for vtol suass based on hurricane katrina operations. *Journal of Field Robotics*, 26(8):636–650, 2009.

[15] S.Tadokoro, R. Murphy, S. Stover, W. Brack, M. Konyo, T. Nishimura, and O. Tanimoto. Application of active scope camera to forensic investigation of construction accident. In *IEEE International Workshop on Advanced Robotics and Its Social Impacts (ARSO2009)*, pages 47–50, 2009.

[16] E. Steimle, R. Murphy, M. Hall, and M. Lindemuth. Unmmaned marine vehicle use at hurricanes wilma and ike. In *MTS/IEEE OCEANS 2009*, pages 1–6, 2009. Unknown.

[17] R. M. Voyles and A. C. Larson. Terminatorbot: a novel robot with dual-use mechanism for locomotion and manipulation. *Mechatronics, IEEE/ASME Transactions on*, 10(1):17–25, 2005.

# Metric Selection for Evaluating Human Supervisory Control of Unmanned Vehicles

Birsen Donmez
University of Toronto
Dept. of Mech. and Ind. Engineering
Toronto, ON, Canada
1 (416) 978 7399

donmez@mie.utoronto.ca

M. L. Cummings
MIT
Dept. of Aero-Astro
Cambridge, MA, USA
1 (617) 252 1512

missyc@mit.edu

## ABSTRACT

Broad metric classes were proposed in the literature in order to facilitate metric selection for evaluating human-autonomous vehicle interaction. However, there still lacks a systematic method for selecting an efficient set of metrics from the many metrics available. We previously identified a list of evaluation criteria that can help determine the quality of a metric, and generated a list of potential metric costs and benefits. Depending on research objectives and limitations, these costs and benefits can have different weights of importance. Through an experiment with subject matter experts, we investigated which metric characteristics human factors practitioners consider to be important in evaluating human supervisory control of unmanned vehicles. We also tested two different multi-criteria decision making methods to help practitioners assign subjective weights to the cost/benefit criteria. The majority of participants rated the evaluation criteria used in both tools as very useful. However, the majority of participants' metric selections before using the methods were the same as the suggestions provided by the methods. Since determining weights of metric importance is an inherently subjective process, even with objective computational tools, the real value of using such a tool may be reminding human factors practitioners of the important experimental criteria and relationships between these criteria that should be considered when designing an experiment.

## Categories and Subject Descriptors

C.4 [**Performance of Systems**]: Measurement Techniques
H.1.2 [**User/Machine Systems**]: Human Factors
H.5.2 [**User Interfaces**]: Evaluation/methodology

## General Terms

Measurement, Performance, Experimentation, Human Factors, Standardization, Theory.

## Keywords

Metrics, Metric Quality, Human Supervisory Control, AHP, Analytic Hierarchy Process, Experiments.

## 1. INTRODUCTION

Human-automation teams are common in many domains, such as command and control operations, human-robot interaction, process control, and medicine. With high levels of automation, these teams operate under a supervisory control paradigm. Supervisory control occurs when one or more human operators intermittently program and receive information from a computer that then closes an autonomous control loop through actuators and sensors [1].

A popular metric used to evaluate human-automation performance in supervisory control is mission effectiveness [2, 3]. Mission effectiveness focuses on performance as it relates to the final output produced by the human-automation team. However, this metric fails to provide insights into the process that leads to the final mission-related output. Measuring multiple human-computer system aspects, such as workload and usability can be valuable in diagnosing performance successes and failures, and in identifying effective training and design interventions. However, choosing an efficient set of metrics for a given experiment still remains a challenge. Many researchers select their metrics based on past experience. Another approach to metric selection is to collect as many measures as possible to supposedly gain a comprehensive understanding of the human-automation performance. These methods can lead to insufficient metrics, expensive experimentation and analysis, and the possibility of inflated type I errors. There appears to be a lack of a principled approach to evaluate and select an efficient set of metrics among the large number of available metrics.

Different frameworks of metric classes are found in the literature in terms of human-autonomous vehicle interaction [4-7]. These frameworks categorize existing metrics into high-level metric classes that assess different aspects of the human-automation performance and are generalizable across missions. Pina et al. [5] defined five generalizable metric classes for supervisory control of unmanned vehicles: mission effectiveness, automation behavior efficiency, human behavior efficiency, human behavior precursors, and collaborative metrics. These metric classes can help experimenters select metrics that result in a comprehensive understanding of the human-autonomous vehicle performance, covering issues ranging from automation capabilities to human cognitive abilities. For holistic system assessment, a rule of thumb is to select at least one metric from each metric class. However, there is still a lack of a systematic methodology to select a collection of metrics across these classes. Each metric set has advantages, limitations, and costs, thus the added value of different sets for a given context needs to be assessed to select an efficient set that maximizes value and minimizes cost.

Donmez et al. [8] proposed a list of metric evaluation criteria for human supervisory control of unmanned vehicles: experimental constraints, comprehensive understanding, construct validity, statistical efficiency, and measurement technique efficiency. The following section briefly presents these categories. Detailed discussions and supervisory control metric examples can be found in [8-10].

# 2. METRIC EVALUATION CRITERIA
## 2.1 Experimental Constraints
Time and monetary cost associated with measuring and analyzing a specific metric constitute the main practical considerations for metric selection. Availability of temporal and monetary resources depends on the individual project and such factors are typically limiting in all projects. The stage of system development and the testing environment are additional constraints that can guide metric selection. For example, responses to rare events are more applicable for research conducted in simulated environments, whereas observational measures can provide better value in field testing.

## 2.2 Comprehensive Understanding
It is important to maximize the understanding gained from a research study. Given that it is often not possible to collect all required metrics, each metric should be evaluated based on how much it explains the phenomenon of interest or its coverage. For example, continuous measures of workload over time (e.g., pupil dilation) can provide a more comprehensive dynamic understanding of one aspect of a system compared to static, aggregate workload measures collected at the end of an experiment (e.g., subjective responses).

The most important aspect of a study is finding an answer to the primary research question. The proximity of a metric to answering the primary research question defines the importance of that metric. For example, a workload measure may not tell much without a metric to assess mission effectiveness, which is what the system designers are generally most interested in understanding. Another characteristic of a metric that is important to consider is the amount of additional understanding gained using a specific metric when a set of metrics are collected. For example, a workload measure can provide additional insights into the human-automation performance.

In addition to providing additional understanding, another desired metric quality is its causal relations with other metrics. A better understanding can be gained if a metric can help explain other metrics' outcomes. For example, the underlying reasons for an operator's behavior and the final outcome of an event can be better understood if the initial conditions and operator's state when the event occurs are also measured. When used as covariates in statistical analysis, the initial conditions of the environment and the operator can help explain the variability in other metrics of interest. Thus, in addition to human behavior, experimenters are encouraged to measure human behavior precursors [5] in order to

assess the operator state and environmental conditions, which may influence human behavior.

## 2.3 Construct Validity
Construct validity refers to how well the associated measure captures the metric or construct of interest. For example, subjective measures of situational awareness ask participants to rate the amount of situational awareness they had on a given scenario or task. These measures are proposed to help in understanding participants' situational awareness [11, 12]. However, self-ratings assess meta-comprehension rather than comprehension of the situation: it is unclear whether operators are aware of their lack of situational awareness.

Good construct validity requires a measure to have high sensitivity to changes in the targeted construct. That is, the measure should reflect the change as the construct moves from low to high levels [13]. For example, primary task performance generally starts to break down when the workload reaches higher levels [13, 14], thus primary task performance measures are not sensitive to changes in the workload at lower workload levels.

A measure with high construct validity should also be able to discriminate between similar constructs. An example measure that fails to discriminate two related metrics is galvanic skin response, which has been proposed and used to measure workload and stress levels (e.g., [15]). However, even if workload and stress are related, they still are two separate metrics. Therefore, galvanic skin response alone cannot suggest a change in workload.

Good construct validity also requires the selected measure to have high inter- and intra-subject reliability. Inter-subject reliability requires the measure to assess the same construct for every participant, whereas intra-subject reliability requires the measure to assess the same construct if the measure were repeatedly collected from the same participant under identical conditions. For example, self-ratings are widely utilized for mental workload assessment [16, 17]. However, different individuals may have different interpretations of workload, leading to decreased inter-subject reliability. Some participants may not be able to separate mental workload from physical workload [18], and some participants may report their peak workload, whereas others may report their average workload. Participants may also have recall problems if the subjective ratings are collected at the end of a test period, raising concerns on the intra-subject reliability of subjective measures.

## 2.4 Statistical Efficiency
There are three metric qualities that should be considered to ensure statistical efficiency: total number of measures collected, frequency of observations, and effect size.

Analyzing multiple measures inflates type I error. That is, as more dependent variables are analyzed, finding a significant effect when there is none becomes more likely. The inflation of type I error due to multiple dependent variables can be handled with multivariate analysis techniques, such as Multivariate Analysis of Variance (MANOVA) [19]. However, it should be noted that multivariate analyses are harder to conduct, as researchers are more prone to include irrelevant variables in multivariate analyses, possibly hiding the few significant differences among many insignificant ones. The best way to avoid failure to identify significant differences is to design an effective experiment with the most parsimonious metric/measure set that specifically addresses the research question.

Another metric characteristic that needs to be considered is the frequency of observations required for statistical analysis. Supervisory control applications require humans to be monitors of automated systems, with intermittent interaction, thus human monitoring efficiency is an important metric to measure. The problem with assessing monitoring efficiency is that, in most domains, errors or critical signals are rare, and operators can have an entire career without encountering them. For that reason, in order to have a realistic experiment, such rare events cannot be included in a study with sufficient frequency. Therefore, if a metric requires response to rare events, observed events with a low frequency of occurrence cannot be statistically analyzed unless data is obtained from a very large number of participants, such as in medical studies on rare diseases.

The number of participants that can be recruited for a study is especially limited when participants are domain experts such as pilots. The power to identify a significant difference, when there is one, depends on the differences in the means of factor levels and the standard errors of these means, which constitute the effect size. One way to compensate for limited number of participants in a study is to use more sensitive measures that will provide a large separation between different conditions, that is, a high effect size.

## 2.5 Measurement Technique Efficiency

The data collection technique associated with a specific metric should not be intrusive to the participants or to the nature of the task. For example, eye trackers can be used for capturing operators' visual attention (e.g., [20, 21]). However, head-mounted eye trackers can be uncomfortable for the participants, and hence influence their responses. Wearing an eye-tracker can also lead to an unrealistic situation that is not representative of the task performed in the real world.

The measuring technique itself can also interfere with the realism of the study. For example, off-line query methods are used to measure operators' situational awareness [22], by briefly halting the experiment at randomly selected intervals, blanking the displays, and administering a battery of queries to the operators. The collection of the measure requires the interruption of the task in a way that is unrepresentative of real operating conditions. The interruption may also interfere with other metrics such as operator's performance and workload, as well as other temporal-based metrics.

## 3. MULTI CRITERIA DECISION MAKING METHODS FOR METRIC SELECTION

Donmez et al. [8] translated the above criteria into potential cost-benefit parameters, which can be ultimately used to define cost and benefit functions of a metric set for a given experiment, eqn. (1). The breakdown between cost and benefit parameters are not clear cut, given that some criteria can be considered as a benefit or a cost (e.g., non-intrusiveness vs. intrusiveness to participants). The breakdown in [8] was based on the ability to assign a monetary cost to an item.

$Benefit\ of\ metric\ I = \sum_{i=1}^{NB} WB_i \times MB_{Ii}$    where

$WB_i$: weight of importance for benefit criterion i
$MB_{Ii}$: how well metric I meets benefit criterion i
$NB$: total number of benefit criteria

(1)

$Cost\ of\ metric\ I = \sum_{j=1}^{NC} WC_j \times MC_{Ij}$    where

$WC_j$: weight of importance for cost criterion j
$MC_{Ij}$: how much metric I costs for cost criterion j
$NC$: total number of cost criteria

Depending on research objectives and limitations, the entries in the cost and benefit functions can have different weights of importance (i.e., $WB_i$ and $WC_j$). Two promising techniques identified to help researchers assign subjective weights are the pair-wise comparison approach of the analytic hierarchy process (AHP) [23], and the ranking approach of the probability and ranking input matrix (PRIM) method [24]. Direct assignment of weights is not adopted as an alternative since humans have difficulty with absolute judgment and are better at making relative judgments [25]. Since the probability aspect of PRIM is not applicable to this effort, the method will be referred to as ranking input matrix (RIM) from this point on.

AHP is widely used both in academic research and in the industry. It begins with the user building a decision hierarchy which includes the goals (e.g., identify metric benefits), decision alternatives (e.g., NASA TLX, pupil dilation), and criteria (e.g., non-intrusiveness, construct validity). There are no systematic guidelines for creating the hierarchy or identifying the decision alternatives and criteria. The hierarchies depend on user knowledge and experience.

At each level of a hierarchy, AHP utilizes pair-wise comparisons to express the relative importance of one criterion over another. The relative importance is judged on a five point Likert scale with the end values of equally important and extremely more important. The values obtained from pair-wise comparisons are then used to create a weight matrix. The eigenvectors of this weight matrix correspond to the criteria weights of interest. There are disadvantages associated with AHP identified in the literature suggesting flaws in the methods of combining individual weights into composite weights [26, 27].

Another characteristic of AHP, potentially a user acceptance issue, is the consistency checks that are imposed on the user. AHP forces the user to perform all possible pairwise comparisons even if some of these comparisons are redundant. For example, if the user is comparing A, B, and C, then a comparison between A and B and a comparison between B and C would indicate how A and C would compare. Even if a comparison of A and C is redundant, AHP forces the user to perform it until a consistency criterion is met (consistency ratio ≤ 0.1 as suggested by [28]), with the claim that consistency checks help the user think about his ratings in detail. The consistency ratio criterion of 0.1 is an arbitrary cutoff but is the convention. The consistency ratio takes into account not only the directionality of the responses but also the magnitude. For example, when comparing A, B, and C, if the user indicates that both A and B are moderately more important than C, then he has to indicate that A and B are equally important. Rating A to be even slightly more important than B (or vice versa) would lead to a consistency ratio of 0.19 and would be considered incorrect by

AHP. Thus, AHP does not always allow for finer grain comparisons.

The ranking input matrix (RIM) is similar to more traditional engineering decision matrices such as the ones used in quality function deployment [29]. The RIM method allows people to categorically select weights through a direct perception-interaction interface (Figure 1) [24]. Each item is represented by a puck that can slide (through clicking and dragging) onto a ranking matrix. The ranking matrix consists of 10 slots consisting of five main categories of importance: high, medium-high, medium, low-medium, and low. Each of these main categories has two bins to allow the person to indicate slight variations in the importance of items. The pucks can also be placed side by side indicating equal importance. A numeric weight value is assigned to these bins on a scale of 0.05 to 0.95 with 0.10 intervals. AHP creates hierarchies and only the entries in one level of a hierarchy are directly compared by the user. In contrast, RIM allows the users to see the weights in each category side by side, and manipulate them if necessary. In general, AHP is not as transparent and thus may be harder for the decision makers to understand.

In addition to requiring subjective weights of importance, the cost and benefit functions (1) also require values representing how well each metric meets the evaluation criteria (i.e., $MB_{li}$ and $MC_{lj}$). In some cases, the value of a metric can be represented with an objective number (e.g., time required to collect a metric), however for many criteria finding an objective value is impossible (e.g., construct validity of a metric). To determine the subjective $MB_{li}$ and $MC_{lj}$ weights, AHP and RIM can also be used.

Both AHP and RIM are intended to help decision makers select a choice out of many. However, when trying to answer a research question, the researchers will most likely need more than one metric. When selecting multiple metrics, the benefits and costs for multiple metrics will need to be combined. Moreover, the dependencies between the selected metrics will also need to be incorporated into the combined benefit-cost. For example, the total number of metrics selected would have an influence on the type I error of each individual metric.

The linear combination of benefit-cost values facilitates both the combination of multiple metric costs and benefits, as well as the incorporation of metric dependencies by allowing additional terms to be added or subtracted from the overall value. Therefore, we used the difference of benefit and cost values to rank the metrics. This approach may not be optimal, however, the best method, if one exists, is currently unknown and is an area for future research. However, given that selection of multiple metrics is more realistic than selecting a single metric, it is important to facilitate the incorporation of metric dependencies when combining benefit and cost values. It is also important to assess if people can account for metric dependencies (e.g., statistical implications of collecting multiple metrics) when they evaluate metrics against a set of criteria. The latter issue was investigated as part of a larger experiment conducted to evaluate AHP and RIM methods for metric selection.

# 4. METRIC SELECTION EXPERIMENT

An experiment was conducted to a) investigate the perceived usefulness of the metric evaluation criteria, b) identify which criteria human factors experimenters consider to be important, and

c) evaluate AHP and RIM for supporting metric selection. Thirty-one human factors practitioners were presented with the description of a hypothetical unmanned vehicle supervisory control experiment, which was adapted from an actual experiment conducted by [30]. The participants were then asked to select either one or multiple workload metrics for this hypothetical experiment from a list of potential workload metrics provided to them. After making an initial selection, the participants used both AHP and RIM (order counterbalanced) to evaluate the list of workload metrics. After AHP and RIM solutions were displayed, the participants were given the choice to change their initial metric selection. They could keep their initial selection, pick AHP or RIM solutions, or come up with an entirely different selection. At the end of the experiment, the participants filled out a questionnaire, evaluating AHP and RIM on a multitude of characteristics.

Because this experiment was our initial attempt to evaluate AHP and RIM, we focused on only workload metrics. Moreover, the participants were not allowed to select a workload metric that was not on the list provided to them. Keeping the experiment bounded provided us with a shorter experiment and more control on the experimental conditions, hence a better ability to draw conclusions. Although, a general assumption of this study is that the researchers using RIM and/or AHP are familiar with the set of available metrics through other sources (e.g., [8, 31]).

## 4.1 Participants

A total of 31 participants completed the study. Participants had experience with human subject experimentation and metrics. Experience with human subject experimentation ranged from one month to forty years. Participants were recruited from both academia and industry, and consisted of 9 females and 21 males, ages ranging from 19 to 64 years (average: 36.6, stdev: 13.6). Eleven of the participants currently held an academic position. The highest degrees held included high school (n=1), college (n=12, 5 in academia and 7 in industry), Master's (n=12, 4 in academia and 8 in industry), and Ph.D. (n=6, 2 in academia and 4 in industry). The experiment took 1 to 1.5 hours to complete.

## 4.2 Apparatus

The experiments were conducted in a mobile experimental test-bed mounted in a 2006 Dodge Sprinter. Two 21-inch wall mounted displays were used in the experiment. By integrating an experimental test bed into a vehicle, the experiment was able to travel to the participants. Access restrictions into government facilities, particularly with foreign graduate students, often make it difficult to take such experiments directly into the work place. Thus, the use of the vehicle allowed a high number of human factors practitioners to be recruited for participation.

## 4.3 Experimental Design

The experiment was a 2x2 mixed factorial design with two independent variables: number of metrics to select (a single metric, a subset of all metrics) and weight assignment method (AHP, RIM). Number of metrics to select was a between-subjects variable, with 15 participants selecting a single metric out of all the candidate metrics, and another 16 selecting a subset of all the metrics (one, two, or all). Weight assignment technique was a within-subjects variable with each participant making a decision using both AHP and RIM. In order to control for learning effects, the order of presentation was counterbalanced.

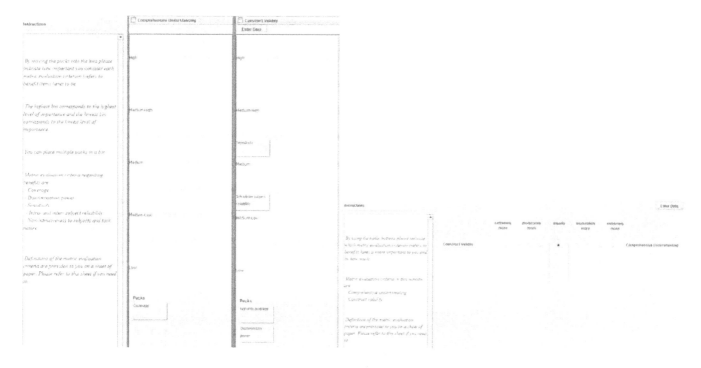

**Figure 1. Experimental interfaces: Ranking Input Matrix (RIM) (left), Analytic Hierarchy Process (AHP) (right).**

## 4.4 Experimental Tasks

The experimental instructions started with the description of the hypothetical experiment and the list of potential workload metrics to choose from: embedded secondary task performance, NASA TLX, and pupil dilation based on eye tracking data. The hypothetical experiment assessed the effects of different auditory alerts on human supervision of multiple unmanned aerial vehicles. When participants finished reading this part of the instructions, they were asked to select either one or a subset of workload metrics depending on the experimental condition they were assigned (i.e., number of metrics to select).

After the initial metric selection, participants read a detailed description of the metric evaluation criteria. A subset of the criteria identified in [8] was selected to be included in this experiment. The selection was based on the relevance to the metrics used in the hypothetical experiment. The cost estimates were provided where applicable. There were no explicit monetary or time constraints imposed on the experiment. To have more experimental control, we did not ask the participants to define a hierarchy structure for AHP but provided the structure below.

*Benefits:*
- Coverage
- Construct validity: a) discrimination power, b) sensitivity, c) inter/intra subject reliability, d) non-intrusiveness
- Type I error (for multiple metric selection)

*Costs:*
- Data gathering: a) time for data collection, b) monetary cost for data collection, c) measurement error likelihood
- Data analysis: a) time for analysis, b) expertise for analysis

The instructions included a detailed description of AHP and RIM, including how the benefit-cost values were calculated. After

reading about the first method (AHP or RIM) the participants used an interface for that method. With this interface, the participants assigned subjective weights of importance to the metric evaluation criteria, and also determined how well potential workload metrics met each criterion. In the RIM condition, the participants used the click and drag interfaces (Figure 1) to rank the evaluation criteria based on importance, as well as to rank the metrics with respect to how well they met the criteria. In the AHP condition, participants conducted pair-wise comparisons to indicate the relative importance of evaluation criteria, and within each criterion they performed pair-wise comparisons to identify how well the metrics satisfied the criteria (Figure 1). Instructions were also provided on the interfaces as reminders on what to do for each window. Since the complete set of written instructions was available throughout the experiment, the participants could also refer back to them if they needed clarification.

In AHP, if participants could not meet the consistency threshold of 0.1 suggested by [28], then they were presented with a pop-up window indicating their inconsistency. The participants were asked to retry and change their responses to achieve the suggested consistency threshold. However, participants were given the ability to skip this step if they felt they had tried "many" times but could not reach the threshold value. The ability to skip was deemed important since we observed in pilot testing that participants would get frustrated to the point that they wanted to quit the experiment. The details on consistency checks were included in the written instructions and were also demonstrated to the participants before they started the AHP trial.

After completing the session with the first interface, the participants read the instructions for the next method (AHP or RIM) and completed their second test session using the next interface.

The experimental tasks for the multiple metric selection condition were slightly different than the single metric selection condition. As previously mentioned, the participants in this condition were told that they could select more than one metric. These participants were also presented with an extra evaluation criterion: type I error. This criterion is not relevant for single metric selection, however, it can be a negative benefit when selecting multiple metrics since analyzing more metrics increases the overall type I error. Participants compared this criterion to the other criteria in terms of importance. In order to assess if participants were aware of how much type I error would change with different number of metrics, they were also asked to compare the number of workload metrics collected (1 to 3) with respect to type I error.

At the end of the experiment, participants were provided with the suggested list of workload metrics ranked based on AHP or RIM solutions. In the multiple metric selection condition, this list could consist of groupings of metrics. For example, the best solution could be NASA TLX and secondary task performance. The participants were then asked to evaluate the solutions provided by AHP and RIM and the initial selection they indicated before using the interfaces. This evaluation helped us assess if the two methodologies result in different selections and if so, which methodology produces results regarded to be better by the participants. Post-test surveys were administered to assess participant opinions about the evaluation criteria and the two methods.

## 5. EXPERIMENTAL RESULTS

Mixed linear models were built for continuous data, whereas non-parametric statistics were utilized to analyze categorical data where appropriate ($\alpha$=.05).

### 5.1 Selected Metrics

For single metric selection, AHP and RIM in general resulted in the same solutions (87%), which also matched most of the participants' initial choices (AHP: 73%, RIM: 87%). Thus, regardless of the method used, participants directed each tool so that the results generally matched their expectations. Participants' self reported experience with the three workload metrics was assessed on a Likert scale (1: no experience, 5: expert). Participants in general had more experience with secondary task (mean=2.3) and NASA TLX (mean=2.3) measures as compared to pupil dilation (mean=1.8). There were approximately an equal number of participants (n=8) who identified secondary task and/or NASA TLX as the metric they have the most experience with. Regardless of this previous experience, 10 out of 15 participants still chose secondary task as their initial metric selection rather than NASA TLX, suggesting that previous experience did not solely determine metric selected.

For multiple metric selection, the majority (n=9) of the participants selected secondary task and NASA TLX as their preferred metrics, which was followed by NASA TLX (n=3) as the second most preferred metric. Interestingly, contrary to our expectation, many of the participants did not choose to collect as many metrics as they could. This finding may be due to the experimental instructions that highlighted resource limitations. Similar to the single metric selection condition, there was no strong evidence to suggest that the participants changed their selections based on the advice from one or the other method.

### 5.2 Type I Error

In this experiment, we focused on type I error as a way of assessing if researchers think about the more hidden ramifications of collecting multiple metrics aside from monetary or time costs.

In the multiple metric selection condition, as part of RIM and AHP, participants were asked to rate how having one, two, and three metrics would affect overall resulting type I error. Six participants out of the 16 total incorrectly indicated that either the overall type I error would not be impacted (n=1) or the type I error would increase as the number of metrics decrease (n=5). Three of these six participants repeated their mistake twice, once with RIM and once with AHP. There were no particular common characteristics for the participants who repeated their mistake. It is unclear if the incorrect responses regarding type I error were due to slips or mistakes. That is, they could be either due to a failure to follow the interface instructions or a lack of knowledge. Regardless of the cause, a fallacy of both methods is that the outputs from AHP and RIM are only as good as the information provided to them.

### 5.3 Subjective Ratings

The evaluation criteria received an average usefulness rating of 4.4 (1-lowest, 5-highest). There was one response with a rating of 3, 18 responses of 4, and 12 responses of 5.

Table 1. Subjective ratings on method usefulness, understanding (* significant at $\alpha$=.05)

|  |  | 1 Low | 2 | 3 Avg. | 4 | 5 High | $\chi^2$(p-value) (4-5 vs. 1-3) |
|---|---|---|---|---|---|---|---|
| Usefulness | AHP | 0 | 6 | 7 | 10 | 8 | .81 (.47) |
|  | RIM | 0 | 3 | 5 | 17 | 6 | 7.26 (.01)* |
| Worth the time | AHP | 1 | 6 | 6 | 15 | 3 | .81 (.47) |
|  | RIM | 0 | 2 | 6 | 20 | 3 | 7.25 (.01)* |
| Understand Method | AHP | 2 | 1 | 7 | 10 | 11 | 3.9 (.07) |
|  | RIM | 0 | 1 | 8 | 8 | 14 | 5.45 (.03)* |

Participants were also asked a list of 1-5 Likert scale questions to assess their understanding and perceived usefulness for the two methods. Table 1 presents statistical results comparing participant ratings with respect to being less than or equal to average vs. being above average ($\chi^2$). Overall, participants' ratings for RIM indicated greater than average perceived usefulness, understandability, and worthiness of their time. For AHP, these responses were not significant, except a marginally significant result assigned to understandability.

### 5.4 Time for Metric Selection

Significant differences were observed on how long it took the participants to select their metric(s). AHP took on average 435 sec longer than RIM (95% CI: 307, 562), a 73% increase. Regardless of the method used, the second trial took on average 214 sec shorter than the first trial (95% CI: 127, 301), a 23% decrease. This finding was expected since both conditions used the same scenario.

## 5.5 AHP Consistency Conformance

Consistency was only an issue when evaluating three or more elements through pairwise comparisons. On average, participants were prompted to retry on 48% of such instances (stdev=20%). On average, the maximum number of times they had to retry in a single instance was 4.8 (stdev=3.2, min=1, max=14).

When the participants were prompted to retry at least once, they skipped without achieving the suggested consistency threshold on average 38% of the time (stdev=39%). Out of the 31 total participants, 11 retried until they achieved consistency (0% skip), whereas 5 chose to skip 100% of the time either after some retrials or none. The rest skipped occasionally with skip rates ranging from 8% to 86%. The skipping consistency values were on average 0.22 (stdev=0.13, max=0.65). The participants who skipped 100% of the time had an average age of 49, whereas the participants who tried until they reached consistency were younger (average age: 29). Experience with workload metrics were similar across the two groups ($t(14)=0.27$, $p=.8$).

## 5.6 Open-ended Comments on Metric Selection Methods

The majority of the positive AHP comments were in regards to the pairwise comparisons (n=12 or 40% of participants). Thirteen percent of the participants indicated that AHP made them think longer and in more detail (n=4). Twenty three percent liked consistency checks (n=7), whereas 16% (n=5) identified them to be frustrating. Thus, the views on consistency checks were split. Thirty percent thought that AHP was too complicated (n=11), and 16% identified it as being time consuming (n=5).

The positive aspects of RIM cited commonly were ease of use (n=10 or 32% of participants), ease of visualizing responses (n=9 or 29% of participants), speed (n=8 or 26% of participants), and being simple (n=5 or 16% of participants). The total number of negative responses for RIM (n=11) was fewer than the total number of negative responses for AHP (n=32). A few participants indicated that they did not think critically at times (n=3 or 10% of participants). The 10-point rating scale was deemed hard by a few participants (n=3 or 10% of participants).

## 6. DISCUSSION

This paper presents an approach for helping experimenters select an efficient set of metrics for evaluating unmanned vehicle supervisory control. The metric evaluation criteria and the relevant cost-benefit parameters presented are guidelines only. It should be noted that there is not a single set of metrics that are the most efficient across all applications. Research-specific aspects such as available resources and the questions of interest will ultimately determine the relative metric quality.

Two different methods to develop principled subjective weights were identified and evaluated through an experiment with human factors practitioners: AHP and RIM. Overall, the participants rated RIM to be more useful, easier to understand, and worth their time. AHP took a significantly longer time, and some participants considered it to be time consuming. In order to keep the experiments short, participants were asked to evaluate only three workload metrics. In reality, researchers not only have to choose from a large number of metrics but they also ideally have to choose from a large number of constructs (e.g., performance, workload, etc.). Because AHP requires pairwise comparisons

between all potential metrics, each additional potential metric would drastically increase the time required to perform AHP. Thus, the appropriateness of AHP selecting from a large set of potential metrics is questionable.

Another AHP problem revealed from the experiment is user frustration and/or lack of conformance to consistency checks. All participants ran into consistency issues where they could not meet the consistency threshold suggested by the AHP inventor [28]. Some participants skipped achieving consistency 100% of the time, whereas some retried until they achieved the threshold. The participants who tried to achieve the threshold indicated that at times they forgot about what they were evaluating, and instead focused on tweaking their responses to obtain a value less than 0.1. In addition, some participants indicated that pairwise comparisons made them lose the big picture. These issues are potential concerns with any method that utilizes pairwise comparisons for assessing subjective responses (e.g., NASA TLX).

When it came to the metrics selected, the majority of participants' initial metric selections matched the solutions proposed by AHP and/or RIM. Thus, no substantial benefits were observed for either of the methods. Even if these methods use mathematical formulas to obtain cost benefit functions, they are inherently subjective as users provide most of the information that goes in the cost benefit functions. Therefore, if the user inputs incorrect information, either by a slip or a mistake, the methods may provide flawed results. For example, participants were asked to indicate the effects of additional metrics on the overall type I error. Responses from 37% erroneously suggested that type I error decreases with additional metrics analyzed. Combined with the weight of importance for type I error, this erroneous information was included in AHP and RIM calculations. But because type I error was only one criterion among many and its weight of importance was not very high, the final solutions of AHP and RIM were not drastically influenced by the incorrect inputs.

While using AHP and RIM, participants referred back to the criteria several times as observed by the experimenter. Approaches like AHP and RIM have the potential to help researchers select metrics by considering many attributes that they may not consider otherwise. Thus, it is essential to provide better information to researchers in terms of how they could view the costs and benefits of a specific metric, before providing them with a mathematical tool that predicts what the best set of metrics would be.

Although this experiment revealed several interesting results, it only focused on selecting from a few workload metrics. Time to complete AHP was reasonable, but RIM was much faster to use. Thus, for evaluating a larger set of metrics and more metrics of different types, RIM appears to be more appropriate. However, the acceptance and effectiveness of RIM for evaluating a larger set of metrics is currently unclear and should be investigated in the future. Moreover, the underlying methodology for RIM should be modified in order to support metric selection when evaluating metrics from multiple classes. For example, a penalty can be introduced to avoid selecting metrics from the same class rather than selecting metrics from different classes. Determining such modifications in the RIM methodology is another point for future research.

# 7. ACKNOWLEDGMENTS

This research was funded by the US Army Aberdeen Test Center (ATC). Special thanks are extended to Meghan Dow, Grace Taylor, and Barden Cleeland, who helped with the experiment. Thanks to Brooke Abounader (ATC) and Luca F. Bertucelli (MIT) for their insightful comments.

# 8. REFERENCES

[1] Sheridan, T. B. 1992. *Telerobotics, Automation, and Human Supervisory Control*. The MIT Press, Cambridge, MA.

[2] Scholtz, J., Young, J., Drury, J. L. and Yanco, H. A. 2004. Evaluation of human-robot interaction awareness in search and rescue. In *Proceedings of the IEEE International Conference on Robotics and Automation (ICRA)*, New Orleans.

[3] Cooke, N. J., Salas, E., Kiekel, P. A. and Bell, B. 2004. Advances in measuring team cognition. In E. Salas and S. M. Fiore (Eds.), *Team Cognition: Understanding the Factors that Drive Process and Performance*. American Psychological Association, Washington, D. C., 83-106.

[4] Olsen, R. O. and Goodrich, M. A. 2003. Metrics for evaluating human-robot interactions. In *Proceedings of NIST Performance Metrics for Intelligent Systems Workshop*.

[5] Pina, P. E., Cummings, M. L., Crandall, J. W. and Della Penna, M. 2008. Identifying generalizable metric classes to evaluate human-robot teams. In *Proceedings of Metrics for Human-Robot Interaction Workshop at the 3rd Annual Conference on Human-Robot Interaction*, Amsterdam, The Netherlands.

[6] Crandall, J. W. and Cummings, M. L. 2007. Identifying predictive metrics for supervisory control of multiple robots. *IEEE Transactions on Robotics - Special Issue on Human-Robot Interaction*, 23, 5, 942-951.

[7] Steinfeld, A., Fong, T., Kaber, D., Lewis, M., Scholtz, J., Schultz, A. and Goodrich, M. A. 2006. Common metrics for human-robot interaction. In *Proceedings of the 1st Annual IEEE/ACM Conference on Human Robot Interaction (Salt Lake City, Utah)*. ACM Press, New York, NY.

[8] Donmez, B., Pina, P. E. and Cummings, M. L. 2009. Evaluation criteria for human-automation performance metrics. In R. Madhavan, E. Tunstel and E. Messina (Eds.), *Performance Evaluation and Benchmarking of Intelligent Systems*. Springer, 21-40.

[9] Donmez, B. and Cummings, M. L. 2009. *Metric selection for human supervisory control*. HAL2009-05, Humans and Automation Laboratory, Cambridge, MA.

[10] Donmez, B., Pina, P. E. and Cummings, M. L. 2008. Evaluation criteria for human-automation performance metrics. In *Proceedings of the Performance Metrics for Intelligent Systems Workshop*, Gaithersburg, MD.

[11] Taylor, R. M. 1989. Situational awareness rating technique (SART): the development of a tool for aircrew systems design. In *Proceedings of the NATO Advisory Group for Aerospace Research and Development (AGARD) Situational Awareness in Aerospace Operations Symposium (AGARD-CP-478)*, 17.

[12] Vidulich, M. A. and Hughes, E. R. 1991. Testing a subjective metric of situation awareness. In *Proceedings of the Human Factors Society 35th Annual Meeting*. The Human Factors and Ergonomics Society, Santa Monica, CA, 1307-1311.

[13] Eggemeier, F. T., Shingledecker, C. A. and Crabtree, M. S. 1985. Workload measurement in system design and evaluation. In *Proceedings of the Human Factors Society 29th Annual Meeting*, Baltimore, MD, 215-219.

[14] Eggemeier, F. T., Crabtree, M. S. and LaPoint, P. A. 1983. The effect of delayed report on subjective ratings of mental workload. In *Proceedings of the Human Factors Society 27th Annual Meeting*, Norfolk, VA, 139-143.

[15] Levin, S., France, D. J., Hemphill, R., Jones, I., Chen, K. Y., Ricard, D., Makowski, R. and Aronsky, D. 2006. Tracking workload in the emergency department. *Human Factors*, 48, 3, 526-539.

[16] Wierwille, W. W. and Casali, J. G. 1983. A validated rating scale for global mental workload measurement applications. In *Proceedings of the Human Factors Society 27th Annual Meeting*, Santa Monica, CA, 129-133.

[17] Hart, S. G. and Staveland, L. E. 1988. Development of NASA-TLX (Task Load Index): results of empirical and theoretical research. In P. Hancock and N. Meshkati (Eds.), *Human Mental Workload*. North Holland B. V., Amsterdam, The Netherlands.

[18] O'Donnell, R. D. and Eggemeier, F. T. 1986. Workload assessment methodology. In K. R. Boff, L. Kaufmann and J. P. Thomas (Eds.), *Handbook of perception and human performance: vol. II. Cognitive processes and performance*. Wiley Interscience, New York, 42-41 - 42-49.

[19] Johnson, R. A. and Wichern, D. W. 2002. *Applied multivariate statistical analysis*. Pearson Education, NJ.

[20] Janzen, M. E. and Vicente, K. J. 1998. Attention allocation within the abstraction hierarchy. *International Journal of Human-Computer Studies*, 48, 521-545.

[21] Donmez, B., Boyle, L. and Lee, J. D. 2007. Safety implications of providing real-time feedback to distracted drivers. *Accident Analysis & Prevention*, 39, 3, 581-590.

[22] Endsley, M. R., Bolte, B. and Jones, D. G. 2003. *Designing for Situation Awareness: An Approach to User-centered Design*. CRC Press, Taylor & Francis Group, Boca Raton, FL.

[23] Saaty, T. L. 2006. *Fundamentals of Decision Making and Priority Theory with the Analytic Hierarchy Process*. RWS Publications, Pittsburgh, PA.

[24] Graham, H. D., Coppin, G. and Cummings, M. L. 2007. The PR matrix: extracting expert knowledge for aiding in C2 sense and decision making. In *Proceedings of the 12th International Command and Control Research and Technology Symposium*, Newport, RI.

[25] Sanders, M. S. and McCormick, E. J. 1993. *Human Factors in Engineering and Design*. McGraw-Hill, New York.

[26] Schenkerman, S. 1997. Inducement of nonexistent order by the anlaytic hierarchy process. *Decision Sciences*, 28, 2, 475-482.

[27] Holder, R. D. 1990. Some comments on the analytic hierarchy process. *The Journal of Operational Research Society*, 41, 11, 1073-1076.

[28] Saaty, T. L. 1980. *The Analytic Hierarchy Process*. McGraw-Hill, New York.

[29] Akao, Y. 1990. *Quality Function Deployment: Integrating Customer Requirements into Product Design*. Productivity Press, Cambridge, MA.

[30] Donmez, B., Cummings, M. L. and Graham, H. D. 2009. Auditory decision aiding in supervisory control of multiple unmanned aerial vehicles. *Human Factors*, 51, 5, 718-729.

[31] Gawron, V. J. 2008. *Human Performance, Workload, and Situational Awareness Measures Handbook*. CRC Press, Boca Raton, FL.

# Performance Measures Framework for Unmanned Systems (PerMFUS): Models for Contextual Metrics

Hui-Min Huang, Elena Messina, Adam Jacoff
National Institute of Standards & Technology
100 Bureau Drive MS 8230

Gaithersburg, MD 20899
+1.301.975.-3427

hui-min.huang@nist.gov

Robert Wade
US Army AMRDEC
Software Engineering Directorate
Redstone Arsenal, AL
Robert.L.Wade@us.army.mil

Michael McNair
Science Applications International Corp.
8303 N. Mopac Expressway
Austin, Texas 78759
MICHAEL.K.MCNAIR@saic.com

## ABSTRACT

In the development of the Performance Measures Framework for Unmanned Systems (PerMFUS), we have established a multiple-axis performance metrics model for the unmanned systems (UMS). This model characterizes the UMS performance requirements by the missions that are to be carried out, the environments in which the missions are to be performed, and the characteristics of the UMS itself. In other words, we focus on the concept of *contextual* metrics and emphasize that performance evaluation and performance specification is based on context.

## Categories and Subject Descriptors

J.2 [physical sciences and engineering] unmanned systems performance

## General Terms

Measurement, Performance, Design, Human Factors, Standardization, Verification

## Keywords

ALFUS, autonomy, collaboration, communication, contextual autonomy, contextual metrics, energy, environment, goal, human-system interaction, HSI, measure, metrics, mission, mobility, perception, power, robot, performance, sensing, task, terminology, test, unmanned system, UMS

## 1. INTRODUCTION

The Performance Measures Framework for Unmanned Systems (PerMFUS) concept has been described in earlier documents [1][2]. It aims at providing a general framework that establishes sets of metrics, describes an approach, and provides a set of guidelines to facilitate UMS performance measurement. PerMFUS describes how one can organize and analyze the requirements, establish the metrics sets by both instantiating from the established generic metrics and generating additional program-specific metrics, and devise methods to test and evaluate the UMS. The following features of PerMFUS are described in the earlier publications:

1. A three-axis model (see Figure 1). The concept stems from the Autonomy Levels for Unmanned Systems (ALFUS) Framework [3]. Autonomy can be considered an aspect of the UMS performance.
2. A set of performance areas to be focused on in PerMFUS, namely, mobility/navigation, sensing/perception, energy/power, communication, human-system interaction, end-effector, collaboration/coordination, and payload.
3. A systematic approach on how the UMS's hardware and software characteristics contribute to the UMS performance.
4. An initial set of generic environmental characteristics and an initial set of generic metrics.

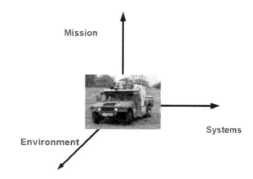

**Figure 1: PerMFUS Main Aspects**

We continued developing the fundamental features regarding the performance measures of UMSs. In this report, we focus on the concept of contextual metrics. In other words, we maintain that metrics must be associated with certain UMS contexts. For example, speed is a UMS metric, which can be used under different environmental contexts:

- Autonomous speed, teleoperation speed
- Flat/paved surface speed, wet surface speed, speed for climbing a 15-degree hill

We start with describing a set of generic metrics and impose it with various types of contexts.

## 2. GENERIC VERSUS SPECIFIC METRICS

A metric is defined as:

An identified characteristic used to measure a particular attribute of a subject, such as how a defined goal fits a user's needs and whether the system generates required results; a metric can be subjective or objective [4].

We examine the concept of a set of core generic metrics that can be instantiated and applied to different types of task or mission goals. They should also be applicable to most, if not all of the performance areas that PerMFUS describes. The set of metrics includes:

1.  Completeness or effectiveness: Is the mission or task goal achieved or to what extent is it accomplished?

2.  Accuracy: How close is the mission or task result to the desired or commanded goal state from the perspectives of time, space, and logic; is the result within the desired or commanded tolerance?

3.  Efficiency: How much time and/or resources are consumed during the execution of the mission or task?

4.  Reliability: What percentage of multiple mission/task executions results in accomplishment of the goals?

5.  Safety, integrity, and security: Does the system perform mission/task without the subject being damaged, disrupted, or anyway modified or disclosed un-intentionally?

6.  Autonomy: Is the system able to accomplish mission or task goal with minimal human intervention?

These metrics need to be associated with the applicable context to be meaningful. Without the proper context, the UMS's performance data can be either ambiguous or subjected to different interpretations. For example:

- The metric "accuracy" can be applied to mobility and to a temperature sensor, which must be clarified.
- An UMS's specified communication range might be achievable in a line-of-sight situation but not achievable in a non-line-of-sight situation. Therefore, the context of application environment must be stated.

The following sections describe how this common set of generic metrics may apply, at a high level of abstraction, to many types of performance concerns. These generic metrics should be able to be superimposed onto the specific performance metrics for each of the performance areas. They include:

- Navigation/mobility (for unmanned ground vehicles, UGV):
  - Traversing: speed, acceleration, turning radius, brake distance
  - Towing: load size, method
  - Obstacle negotiation: types, severity
  - Stealthiness: signatures of sounds, exhausts, smoke/dusts

- Sensing/perception:
  - Object detection, recognition, location
  - Situation awareness
  - Mapping
- Communication:
  - Range, signal strength
  - Line-of-sight (LOS) versus non light-of-sight (NLOS)
- Energy/power
  - Rates, peak power,
  - Sustained load
  - Endurance
  - Restoration time
- Human-System Interaction (HSI)
  - Controllability
  - Resolutions, update rates of displays
  - Pertaining to Human Supervisor/Operator/Partner
    - Situational Awareness
    - Workload
    - Neglect Tolerance
- End-effector
  - Dexterity, load capacity of manipulator
- Collaboration
  - Information sharing
  - Synchronization

## 3. MISSION/TASK GOAL-DRIVEN METRICS

Metrics can cover a wide spectrum of issues. However, the focus of the current version of PerMFUS would be on goal accomplishment, as one of the three axes of the PerMFUS model indicates, also highlighted in [2]. An UMS performs missions or tasks. Metrics are required to measure whether and how the mission/task goals are accomplished. The performance of the UMS depends on how the goal is stated. For a navigation or mobility task, the goal can be stated as:

- Go to (x, y)
- Go to (x, y) at time T
- Go to (x, y) after time T
- Go to (x, y) as soon as possible
- Go to (x, y) within (xx, yy) tolerances
- Go to (x, y) by taking the safest route
- Go to (x, y) by taking the shortest route
- Go to (x, y) stealthily
- Go to the nearest covered area

Whether the task goals are completed is measured with different metrics. A quick review finds that the generic metrics can be applied to all these goals.

# 4. INSTANTIATION TO PERFORMANCE AREAS

Note that the payload performance area is omitted because it can cover too many types of issues.

Performance metrics are required for the various performance areas that PerMFUS identified. Table 1 explores how the generic metrics can be applied.

**Table 1: Generic Metrics for Performance Areas**

| | Mobility | Sensing/ Perception | Comms | Energy/ Power | End-Effector | HSI | Collaboration |
|---|---|---|---|---|---|---|---|
| **Completeness Or Effectiveness** | Y/N or %: reached location; covered area | Y/N or %: detected objects; covered area | Y/N or %: transmitted message; covered area | Y/N or %: delivered capacity or peak load; | Y/N or %: reached location; placed objects | Y/N or %: displayed info; enabled control | Y/N or %: on common tasks; |
| **Accuracy** | spatial; temporal; | from detection through recognition; mapped covered area | from syntactic through semantic | delivered rated/peak/ sustained energy/ power | location; geometric; temporal; load; | info accuracy; control accuracy (vs. resolution, over/under shoots) | on common tasks; |
| **Efficiency** | shorter routes; less obstacles; savings in time, energy, wear and tear, other resources | savings in time, energy, wear and tear, other resources | savings in time, energy, wear and tear, other resources | savings in energy use, wear and tear | savings in time, energy, wear and tear, other resources | amount of displays and devices required; savings in time, energy, wear and tear, other resources | savings in time, energy, wear and tear, other resources |
| **Reliability** | % of trials when goal completed | % of trials when goal completed | % of trials when goal completed | % of trials when goal completed | % of trials when goal completed | % of trials when goal completed | % of trials when goal completed |
| **Safety/ Integrity/ Security/** | goal accomplished without damage or being detected | goal accomplished without damage or being detected | info integrity | acquired sufficient energy for tasks | goal accomplished without system or object damage or being detected | goal accomplished without human or system damage or being detected | goal accomplished without damage or being detected |
| **Autonomy** | goal accomplished with % HSI | sensed or perceived with % HSI | communicated with % HSI | energy/ power delivered with % HSI | goal accomplished with % HSI | task executed requires % human intervention | goal accomplished with % HSI |

# 5. AUTONOMY CONTEXT—MOBILITY PERFORMANCE AREA

Humans have been dealing with various aspects of vehicle performance issues. As such, PerMFUS is set to focus on the unique aspect of the vehicle performance, the "unmannedness." In other words, PerMFUS focuses on a system's performance in the context of autonomy. Meanwhile, it can leverage existing test and evaluation technology that is developed for manned vehicles which do not involve autonomy. For example, there are methods to test and evaluate a vehicle's speed. PerMFUS should focus on only a robot's speed when it is driven without human drivers onboard.

Table 2 should apply to the navigation/mobility performance area.

**Table 2: Autonomy Context for Mobility Performance Areas**

| | | Navigation/Mobility Metrics | | | | | | | | | |
|---|---|---|---|---|---|---|---|---|---|---|---|
| | | Traversal | | | | Tow | | Obstacle Negotiation | | Stealthiness | |
| | | sustained speed | acceleration | braking distance | steering radium | load type | tow method | positive obstacle | negative obstacle | noise level | concealment |
| Autonomy Levels | Remote Control | | | | | | | | | | |
| | Teleoperation | | | | | | | | | | |
| | Human-Directed | | | | | | | | | | |
| | Human-Robot Shared | | | | | | | | | | |
| | Robot-Directed | | | | | | | | | | |
| | Fully Autonomous | | | | | | | | | | |

Similar tables can be drawn for other performance areas.

# 6. ENVIRONMENTAL CONTEXT— MOBILITY PERFORMANCE AREA

The environmental characteristics affect UMSs' performance. Therefore, they should be a part the context of the performance metrics. Table 3 correlates the mobility metrics to the environmental concerns.

As further exploration, in the environmental classification of positive obstacles for ground UMSs, the following, Table 4 can apply. It illustrates how obstacles can be classified in terms of features such as dimensionality, orientation, complexity, and geometry.

**Table 3: Environmental Contexts**

| | | navigation/mobility metrics | | | | | | | | | |
|---|---|---|---|---|---|---|---|---|---|---|---|
| | | traversal | | | | tow | | obstacle negotiation | | stealthiness | |
| environmental context | | sustained speed | acc* | brk dst* | str* rad* | load type | tow method | postv* obs | neg obs | qut* | concl* |
| aerial | wind | | | | | | | | | | |
| | lightness | | | | | | | | | | |
| | rain | | | | | | | | | | |
| ground | terrain | | | | | | | | | | |
| | wind | | | | | | | | | | |
| | lightness | | | | | | | | | | |
| | rain | | | | | | | | | | |
| maritime | sea state | | | | | | | | | | |
| | lightness | | | | | | | | | | |
| | turbidity | | | | | | | | | | |

Key: acc: acceleration; brk: concl: concealment; brake; dst: distance; neg: negative; postv: positive; qut: quietness; rad: radius; str: steering

**Table 4: Ground Mobility Positive Obstacle Architecture**

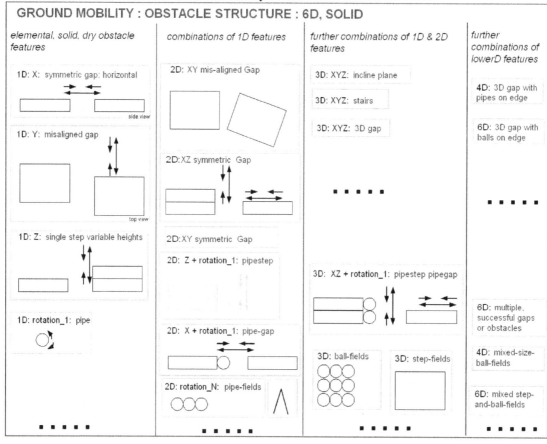

# 7. TOWARD FULL CONTEXT

Besides autonomy and environment, the full context of UMS performance must involve even richer factor descriptions that include missions, tasks, and levels of abstraction. A metric can have different meanings when applied to different levels of abstraction. A laser range sensor can be used to measure a distance at a low level, the same data be used for object recognition at a higher level of abstraction. The issues include:

- Navigation and mobility: A UMS can be commanded in terms of a single explicit position (in some coordinate frame) or sent to an area of concern. Semantic language may be used to describe an area, such as "the other side of this building."
- Sensing and perception: This can range from the pixel level coming out of a sensor up to one through six degrees of freedom; More sophistication can range from detection of entities through object classification; recognition of specific instances of objects ("it's a truck" versus "it's a vehicle") [5].
- Communications: The amount of information transmitted can range from a single data point to composite information. The ability to intelligently plan a communications strategy (e.g., collaborate with other UMSs to form an ad hoc network, save

transmissions until out of the tunnel) contributes to the level of autonomy.

- Energy/Power: Management of resource consumption can range from simply reporting current levels to the ability to plan resupplying its own energy or for a team of UMSs.
- End Effector: The manipulation abilities can range from grasping an object to being able to sense and having enough degrees of freedom to allow dexterous assembly of a composite component or handling of delicate, pliable objects.
- Human-Systems Interaction: The level of discourse can range from communicating based on reporting raw data, or from a limited, fixed vocabulary through semantic information. Further up the scale is an UMS's ability to answer questions or formulate specific requests from a human at higher levels of abstraction.
- Collaboration: This can range from simple coordination of mobility to coordinated mission planning and execution among a team of UMSs.

# 8. CROSS-EFFECTS OF PERFORMANCE AREAS AND UMS SUBSYSTEMS

The ways in which various subsystems might have cross-effects on the areas of performance is an area of study. For example, the mobility subsystem can enhance or impede the coverage areas of sensing and perception as well as the communication. The reverse is true in that the sensing coverage area can affect the mobility and navigation. Further, the degrees of the cross-effects might vary among the various autonomy levels or autonomy modes, making these complex issues.

Table 5 is devised for describing these effects:

**Table 5: Subsystem Cross-effects on Performance Areas**

| | | Subsystem Effects On Performance Areas | | | | | | | |
|---|---|---|---|---|---|---|---|---|---|
| | | Performance Areas | | | | | | | |
| | | Mobility and Navigation | Communications | Sensing and Perception | Energy/ Power | HSI | End Effector | Collaboration | Payload |
| UMS subsystem | Mobility and Navigation | | traversing for coverage | situation awareness coverage | | | reach, stability | facilitate | facilitate |
| | Communications | traverse areas | | n/a | endu. | res., usa. | cmd and cntrl | cmd and cntrl | cmd and cntrl |
| | Sensing and Perception | situation awareness coverage; area reach ability | n/a | | endu. | res., usa. | cmd and cntrl | cmd and cntrl | cmd and cntrl |
| | Energy/ Power | traverse areas; vehicle cntrl | comms avail. | sensing/ percp avail. | | avail. | avail. | avail. | avail. |
| | HSI | cntrllability (C2) for RC and teleop cmding for autonomous | n/a | cmd and cntrl | endu. | | cmd and cntrl | cmd and cntrl | cmd and cntrl |
| | End Effector | n/a | n/a | enhance/ impede sensors | endu. | n/a | | cmd and cntrl | cmd and cntrl |
| | Payload | n/a | n/a | enhance/ impede sensors | endu. | n/a | enhance/ impede reach | cmd and cntrl | |

**Key:**

| | | |
|---|---|---|
| n/a: not applicable | cmd: command | percp: perception |
| res: resolution | cntrl: control | avail: availability |
| endu: endurance | subsys: subsystem | |
| | usa: usability | |

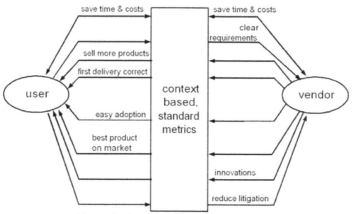

**Figure 2: Benefits of Contextual Metrics**

## 9. MULTIPLE ADAPTIVE LIFECYCLES

Besides the testing and evaluation purposes, contextual metrics provide additional benefits to the communication between the users of the UMS and the vendors. These benefits can be illustrated with Figure 2. When the UMS is clearly specified with context and evaluated, the vendors will get clear and unambiguous requirements, they will have a better chance of deliver the UMS right on the first production (thus reducing the costs), the users will have a better chance of acquiring the best-suited UMS on the market as the performance specification is clear to the requirements, and the vendors will have clear technological objectives to provide innovative solutions on their UMS products.

For the relatively new industry of UMS, technologies are evolving and advancing quickly. Some parts of the market lifecycles might exhibit unique features. As users are exploring wider application of the robots, the requirements might evolve as opposed to being established and essentially fixed for the later acceptance testing purposes. In this situation, the following multiple adaptive lifecycles occur:

- The users will be able to evolve and explore advanced requirements to help their operations due to their continuing familiarity with the UMS tools.
- The vendors will be able to devise innovative UMS technology to address the complex requirements.
- The testing and evaluation developers will be able to evolve and enhance the test methods, including the metrics, measures, apparatuses, and procedures, to better address the requirements.
- The users will become more proficient in operating the UMS tools, thus enhancing their mission capabilities.

These lifecycles all iterate with and leverage against each other while advance along their own trajectories.

## 10. SUMMARY

We described the concept of contextual metrics. Metrics must be associated with proper context to be meaningful. There are many types and layers of contexts that can be associated with metrics. This paper provides a subset. Further development is planned.

## 11. ACKNOWLEDGMENTS

The authors wish to acknowledge the valuable contributions of the ALFUS working group members and of the participants in the SAE AS-4 Unmanned Systems Committee.

## 12. REFERENCES

[1] Huang, H., et al., "Performance Measures Framework for Unmanned Systems (PerMFUS)," PerMIS'08 Workshop, Gaithersburg, Maryland, October 2009.

[2] Huang, H., "Ontological Perspectives for Autonomy Performance" PerMIS'08 Workshop, Gaithersburg, Maryland, October 2008.

[3] *Autonomy Levels for Unmanned Systems (ALFUS) Framework, Volume II: Framework Models Version 1.0,* NIST Special Publication 1011-II-1.0, Huang, H. et al., Ed., National Institute of Standards and Technology, Gaithersburg, MD, December 2007.

[4] *Autonomy Levels for Unmanned Systems (ALFUS) Framework, Volume I: Terminology, Version 2.0,* Huang, H. Ed., NIST Special Publication NIST Special Publication 1011-I-2.0, National Institute of Standards and Technology, Gaithersburg, MD, October 2008.

[5] Albus, J.S., et al., 4D/RCS: A Reference Model Architecture For Unmanned Vehicle Systems Version 2.0, http://www.isd.mel.nist.gov/documents/albus/4DRCS_ver2.pdf

# Towards Standardization of Metrics for Evaluation of Artificial Visual Attention

M. Zaheer Aziz
GET LAB, Universität Paderborn,
33098 Paderborn,
Germany
aziz@upb.de

Bärbel Mertsching
GET LAB, Universität Paderborn,
33098 Paderborn,
Germany
mertsching@upb.de

## ABSTRACT

Standardized methods and metrics for evaluating progress of research is important in every field of science. Computational modeling of visual attention is an important area of research that aims towards machine vision according to the role model of nature. Standards for quantitative evaluation of research achievements in this field are still missing. This paper proposes some measurement methods and metrics that can be used as conventions for evaluation of artificial attention models. The proposed methodology also takes into account the needs of assessing attention under different visual behaviors and considers performance against increasing levels of visual complexity. The measurement methods for the quantities used in the evaluation metrics are designed to make autonomous machine-based evaluation feasible. Creating traces of performance by different attention models using the proposed metrics can provide an objective analysis of the state of the art in this field.

## Keywords

Artificial visual attention, computational model evaluation, performance measures.

## 1. INTRODUCTION

Metrics and measurement methods for quantitative evaluation of developments in an area of knowledge are extremely important for scientific progress in that field. Claims of improved solutions for research problems can only be verified when impartial benchmarks are available and techniques are defined to measure the performance on standardized scales. Visual attention enjoys a key position in natural vision that contributes in selection of relevant and important objects for living beings possessing developed vision systems. This selection process not only confines computationally heavy processes to the attended objects but also helps in robust learning and recognition through vision [22]. Achieving such capability in artificial vision systems can lead to a significant advancement in machine autonomy and intelligence.

Many models of artificial visual attention have been developed during the last couple of decades with the objective to select relevant and important scene portions as done by human vision but a standardized methodology for evaluating output of computational models does not exist so far. This paper addresses the said problem by analyzing the requirements for reaching standardization in visual attention evaluation and proposes some formal procedures and metrics for quantitative assessment of artificial attention. A proposal is also made to regulate the process of data extraction from attention fixations and arranging these quantities into structures in order to facilitate objective comparison of artificial attention with the benchmark data obtained from human attention.

Visual attention has a complex and multi facet nature hence attention models can be evaluated under many contexts. The first step is to define the visual behavior under which attention is to be performed and evaluated. For example, evaluation of an attentive visual search needs different criteria as compared to those for visual attention under free viewing. Secondly, under each behavior there can be multiple aspects that could be evaluated. In some applications a system may be required to select some (or all) of the salient locations in an arbitrary order and unrestricted number of attention fixations. On the other hand the number of allowed fixations and their sequence may be of critical importance in some applications, such as autonomous car driving. The proposal in this paper suggests to explicitly consider the context of visual behaviors in the evaluation schemes. It is also important to measure the capability of computational models to handle different levels of visual complexity. The natural vision remains largely consistent on increasing noise in visibility. Artificial attention models can be graded based upon the complexity level they can handle. The method proposed in this paper investigates this aspect also.

In the existing literature on visual attention modeling some methods can be found that evaluate results of artificial attention for individual cases. A brief survey of these techniques is given in section 2. The survey clearly indicates that there is a need of formalizing the methodology for representation of benchmark data from human visual attention and results of computational models. Also, design of conventions for comparing model output with human output are required. Furthermore, standardized metrics for performance measurement are also missing in this area of science. Section 3 provides a critical analysis of the available techniques and section 4 presents the proposed recommendations and techniques for quantitative evaluation of attention models. In order to demonstrate the utility of the proposed methodology, a sample evaluation is provided in section 5 using an example attention model.

## 2. A SURVEY OF EXISTING METHODS

The model of artificial visual attention proposed in [12] detects bottom-up saliency. Salient locations marked by human subjects in some images are taken as benchmark targets. Experiments for quantitative evaluation are reported for one target per image. The metric used for measuring the model's output is the number of fixations before attending a target with respect to increasing amount of artificial noise introduced in the input. Acceptability of correctness of fixations is decided by human observers.

The scheme given in [21] makes a comparison of ROI clusters. The two compared sets of ROIs are clustered using a distance measure derived from a k-means pre-evaluation. Any two ROIs closer than a certain distance are considered as coincident. The value of similarity metric, representing coincident ROIs in the two sets, is obtained through a string-processing procedure. Each ROI from the ground truth is labeled with a separate letter and these letters are concatenated in the order of appearance of the ROIs to form a ground-truth-string. A similar string is created for the output of the attention model. All the coincident ROIs are labeled with the same alphabetic character. The cost of transforming the model-string into the ground-truth-string is taken as the similarity measure.

The work in [13] proposes to compare the sequence of ROIs identified by an attentional algorithm to those foveated by human observers using two methods of temporal analysis, namely, head-based and time-based. Head-based analysis is used to evaluate sequences in still images where the head remains at a fixed location in space but can rotate to look at a ROI. The scanpath generated from the analysis of head movements is compared with the scanpath followed by the given model using the string editing technique proposed in [21]. In the time-based analysis human fixations and ROIs from the model are compared over frames collected every 100 ms. To allow comparison between ROIs from the model and human fixations in both approaches, human fixations are identified via velocity based analysis of eye movements over the same input given to the attentional model.

The method discussed in [6] extends the technique of [21] by arguing that the said method has a limitation of defining two regions of interest with equal importance as one ROI has to be always preferred over another in order to set up the ground truth and its labeling order. The proposed hybrid approach claims to be able to handle situations of order uncertainties in ROIs. They assign numbers to the ROIs according to the relative order and store the strings in a matrix. These operations are repeated and average of the iterations is obtained in a resultant matrix. Such matrices are created for ground-truth and the test case. Magnitude of the normalized cross-correlation of the two matrices gives the measure of similarity between the sets of ROIs.

The evaluation scheme presented in [7] proposes that a system should be able to attend the same locations in a scene, whether or not the scene has been translated, rotated, reflected or scaled. They quantify the performance of an attention system through two measures. The first looks for gross error rate (GER), that records the percentage of fixations in the test image that are not within a threshold radius of any fixation in the transformed image, once the geometric transformation is compensated for. The second measure is a form of the Hausdorf distance metric that measures positional noise. Robustness against noise is also evaluated in [10] using gross error rate and mean drift. The GER is computed in the same way as [7] whereas they define mean drift as the mean of distances between corresponding fixations on original image and its noisy version. The assessment scheme in [2] has used percentage of erroneous fixations with respect to the total number of target elements as a measure of performance and percentage of erroneous fixations against quantity of distortion, produced by different compression rates, as a measure of robustness.

For the evaluation scheme used in [19] benchmark data was collected by recording scanpaths of human subjects on given scenes under free-viewing behavior. The normalized saliency values produced by the computational model were extracted at fixation locations along a subject's scan path and the mean of these values, named as normalized scan path salience (NSS), was taken as a measure of the correspondence between the salience map and the scan path. NSS values greater than zero suggest a greater correspondence, a zero indicates no correspondence, and negative values indicate an anti-correspondence between human scanpath and model-predicted salient points. Human eye fixations recorded by an eye-tracker are converted into a saliency map in [18] and a correlation coefficient is computed between the human maps and the output of artificial model. The model of [14] has used linear correlation coefficient to compare saliency maps. The method proposed in [11] names its metric as score-$s$. This score is higher if the fixated locations along a scanpath have higher saliency as compared to rest of the input.

The evaluation criteria proposed in [1] gets the salient objects marked by human subjects and then counts the number of fixations taken by the model to cover all of them. They compare the model's performance on the basis of false fixations before focusing on the first required object, before covering 50%, 75%, and 100% of the target locations. A method to evaluate saliency maps by comparing them to a benchmark map is proposed in [3]. A bi-directional comparison is done on the salient areas of the source map with the corresponding areas of the target map. The model in [15] measures the selectivity performance of top-down attention by counting the number of FOA hits and misses on traffic-relevant items like signal-boards and cars in video streams. The evaluation is feedback oriented as human viewers have to decide if the model has fixated on a correct location or not. A fixation is counted as a hit if at least half of the target object is within the FOA.

The evaluation method for top-down attention in [9] measures performance of the search system using two metrics, namely, the average number of fixations per search and the average search time in seconds. Less number of fixations before reaching the target is considered as indication of success. Shorter search time of course comes as a byproduct. The search model in [8] also uses the criteria of hit number to reach the target for evaluation of top-down search performance. They also use a metric of detection rate in which they observe that whether the target was fixated within the first 10 FOAs. The model presented in [16] performs evaluation of the top-down attention by measuring the reaction time versus the number of items in a display. They also use number of attentional shifts before detection of target as a metric.

## 3. CRITICAL ANALYSIS

The best benchmark for measuring performance of computational attention models is the data of human response. Fixations of attention, in terms of locations as well as sequence, largely depend upon the task given to the vision system. The classical psycho-physical experiments reported in [23] clearly support this concept. Therefore it is important to have a clear classification of the benchmark as well as the evaluated data according to the known attentional behaviors, such as search and free-viewing. The first step towards this direction is to acquire behavior dependent response from human subjects on a selected set of visual input. It is also recommendable to arrange the input data in context of complexity based upon some defined criteria such as number of attention candidates, magnitude of noise, and applied transformations. There are two usual ways to obtain human response to saliency. In the first method subjects are asked to mark the salient regions by hand and assign them numbers according to the order of saliency. The other method is to show the test visual input to the subjects on a display device and record the fixations using an eye-tracking equipment. The later method has the advantage of spontaneousness and accuracy.

There are some evaluation criteria of attention models on which the existing literature commonly agrees. Ability of a model to fixate on the human attention scanpath, preferably in the same sequence, is counted in good performance of a given computational model. While capability to cover all salient locations in a scene is a measure of efficiency; fixations falling on non-salient locations are counted as errors that should cause decline in the performance measure. Robustness against noise and transformations in visual input is also among the measures applied by contemporary literature to evaluate performance quality of artificial attention. The basic concept though remains to compare the results of attention obtained on input having varying levels of complexity with the benchmark results. In order to automate the evaluation process with minimum involvement of human intervention, methodologies are needed that allow machine-based comparison of model results with the available human benchmark.

On the other hand, the evaluation measures used so far are not generalizable because of unavailability of standardized benchmark data, unclear definition of evaluation conditions, and lack of standards for representation of attention data. Conventions are needed for representation of the fixation data before results of attention from humans and computational models could be quantitatively compared with each other under standardized metrics. An unbiased performance comparison necessarily needs a standardized shape and size for representing human as well as machine-computed focus of attention (FOA). Also, a formal definition is needed for a successful match between corresponding foci of attention from the different sources under comparison.

## 4. PROPOSED METHODOLOGY

Previous efforts by the authors on methods and metrics for evaluation of attention models [4, 5] resulted in a taxonomy of existing techniques for this purpose and development of some competence tests and validation tests. The work up to that level required intensive involvement of human judgement in extracting measurements from attention data. This could lead to bias based upon personal differences. Here the evaluation metrics are refined and proposals are made to standardize the measurement extraction process.

Keeping in view the requirement analysis in section 3 the evaluation process for computational attention models needs standardization at three steps. Firstly, the data representation of human attention and the results of computational models have to be made consistent with each other. Secondly, the measurement methods to extract comparable values from the attention data have to be devised. Thirdly, performance metrics need to be designed that cover most of the known aspects for performance evaluation of visual attention. The proposed methodology is an effort to address all of these issues. Figure 1 provides a visualization of the conceptual infrastructure of the proposed methodology. The top part of figure 1 represents the proposal of organizing the attention data (benchmark as well as test data) according to different visual behaviors of attention (e.g. free-viewing and search etc.). For each visual behavior the data can also be categorized into defined levels of scene complexity. Attention response from different human subjects has to be combined into a single unified set using the standards for data representation. The middle part of figure 1 reflects the part of the proposal related to extraction of comparable quantities from results of computational models and from unified human benchmark using a regulated measurement methodology. The bottom portion of figure 1 represents the role of standardized metrics based upon the said measurement process leading to objective performance evaluation of attention models. Following subsections explain the proposals at each of these steps.

### 4.1 FOA data representation

As a convention for the shape representation of focus of attention we recommend to use a circle due to its similarity with the circular shape of the human retina as well as the fovea area. The size of this circle may also be standardized according to the proportion of the parafovea area, that contains the highest density of photoreceptors, to the size of retina as reported in human anatomy. Since the horizontal diameter of the parafovea is 2.5 mm as compared to the 42 mm diameter of the retina [17][20] we propose to use a circle having a diameter of $\frac{1}{16.8}w$ to represent the FOA in an input image of width $w$. Therefore, radius of the attention fixation circle $r^\Lambda$ may be standardized to $0.03w$.

### 4.2 Data categorization

The input for attention evaluation may be categorized according to the complexity criteria $\gamma$, for example number

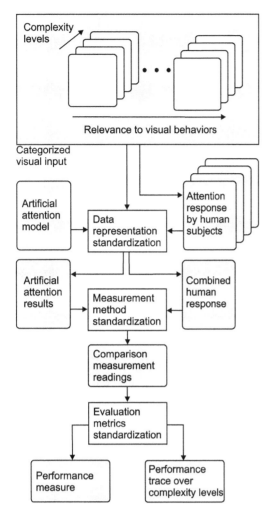

Figure 1: **Visualization of conceptual infrastructure of the proposed methodology for evaluation of artificial visual attention models.**

spectively. These set should have the following format:

$$F_h^H(\beta, I_l^\gamma) = \{L_1(L_x, L_y, L_z), \dots, L_{f_h}(L_x, L_y, L_z)\}$$
$$1 \leq h \leq n_H \quad (1)$$

$$F^H(\beta, I_l^\gamma) = F_\hbar^H(\beta, I_l^\gamma) \bigcup F_h^H(\beta, I_l^\gamma) \,\forall h \,(h \neq \hbar) \quad (2)$$

$$F^M(\beta, I_l^\gamma) = \{L_1(L_x, L_y, L_z), \dots, L_{f_m}(L_x, L_y, L_z)\} \,(3)$$

Where $L_h(L_x, L_y, L_z)$ symbolizes the locations of attention fixations with their Cartesian coordinates. The component $L_z$ may be ignored when dealing with attention in 2D scenes. In equation 2 a set $F_h^H$ possessing the largest $f_h$ is taken as reference $F_\hbar^H$ before creating the combined human response data. This reference is needed to avoid chaining of neighboring FOA locations due to tolerating a distance of $r^\Lambda$ while applying the union operation, i.e., two locations $L_p \in F_\hbar^H$ and $L_q \in F_h^H$ are considered as same when $\overline{L_p L_q} < r^\Lambda$.

For sequence sensitive analysis the data sets will have the provision to store the sequence number $O$ with every fixation. Hence the three datasets will have the following structure:

$$F_h^{H_o}(\beta, I_l^\gamma) = \{(L_1(L_x, L_y, L_z), O_1), \dots,$$
$$(L_{f_h}(L_x, L_y, L_z), O_{f_h})\} \, 1 \leq h \leq n_H \quad (4)$$

$$F^{H_o}(\beta, I_l^\gamma) = F_\hbar^{H_o}(\beta, I_l^\gamma) \bigcup F_h^{H_o}(\beta, I_l^\gamma) \,\forall h \,(h \neq \hbar) \quad (5)$$

$$F^{M_o}(\beta, I_l^\gamma) = \{(L_1(L_x, L_y, L_z), O_1), \dots,$$
$$(L_{f_m}(L_x, L_y, L_z), O_{f_m})\} \quad (6)$$

It is very likely to obtain varying sequence numbers in order of attention fixations by different subjects in $F_h^{H_o}$. Since the sequence followed by one human observer cannot be preferred over another hence a feasible solution is to keep the sequence numbers of all human subjects in record. The evaluation method presented in [6] has also argued in favor of this concept. For this purpose the union operation in equation 5 considers two elements $(L_p, O_p) \in F_\hbar^{H_o}$ and $(L_q, O_q) \in F_h^{H_o}$ as same when $\overline{L_p L_q} < r^\Lambda$ and $O_p = O_q$. It is therefore possible to have multiple entries of the same location with different sequence numbers in $F^{H_o}$. A fixation by a computational model on one of these locations will be considered valid in terms of sequence number if it matches with any of the stored numbers.

## 4.3 Comparison Measurements

The first measurable quantity in the benchmark data is the number of salient locations $N_s$ in a given input $I$ that can be extracted using cardinality of $F^H(\beta, I_l^\gamma)$, hence

$$N_s = |F^H(\beta, I_l^\gamma)| \quad (7)$$

In order to evaluate the artificial models their output may be recorded at two points. First is at completion of $N_s$ attempts and second at the point when the model picks all of the salient locations in the input, denoted by $N_a$. For some cases it may be possible to get $N_a = N_s$ but usually $N_a > N_s$ for complex scenes with the current state-of-the-art of attention models. Sometimes it is possible that a model cannot cover the $N_s$ salient locations at all hence an upper limit $N_t$ has to be imposed on the allowed attempts according to the needs of the application, for which attention is

of attention candidates, noise, or transformations. Each complexity may be available with different levels $l$ such as increasing number of salient objects, growing intensity of noise, or magnitude of transformation. The attention system, human or artificial, may perform fixations on the input while working under different visual behaviors $\beta$. Three types of data sets are involved for each visual input for the evaluation process. The first is the output of human attention obtained from $n_H$ human subjects. These results sets need to be stored individually. Secondly, a structure is needed to record the combination of these sets into a single set, $H$, representing the human response. The third type of dataset, $M$, is required to store the results of artificial attention models. Structure of these datasets may differ when performing evaluation under different aspects. For evaluation of fixation locations we propose to use three sets $F_h^H(\beta, I_l^\gamma)$, $F^H(\beta, I_l^\gamma)$, and $F^M(\beta, I_l^\gamma)$ for individual subjects, combined human response, and model response rebeing evaluated, in order to complete the evaluation within finite number of attempts. Hence, when a model could not detect all the salient locations within $N_t$ attempts then the attention model is stopped at $N_t$ and $N_a = N_t$ is recorded. Having the set of fixations $F_{N_s}^M(\beta, I_l^\gamma)$ by a computational model in the first $N_s$ attempts, the set of matching fixations with the human benchmark within $N_s$ attempts will be obtained by

$$C_{N_s}^M(\beta, I_l^\gamma) = F_{N_s}^M(\beta, I_l^\gamma) \bigcap F^H(\beta, I_l^\gamma) \qquad (8)$$

The intersection operator works with the condition that two elements $L_p \in F_{N_s}^M$ and $L_q \in F^H$ are considered as same when $\overline{L_p L_q} < r^\Lambda$. The set of fixations in $N_a$ attempts by a model will be collected into $F_{N_a}^M(\beta, I_l^\gamma)$ and the set of valid fixations will be extracted using an intersection operation similar to that introduced in equation 8 as follows:

$$C_{N_a}^M(\beta, I_l^\gamma) = F_{N_a}^M(\beta, I_l^\gamma) \bigcap F^H(\beta, I_l^\gamma) \qquad (9)$$

For location based evaluation we define two measurements $N_d$ and $N_f$ that count the number of correctly detected salient locations in $N_s$ attempts and the number of salient locations found in $N_a$ attempts respectively. These quantities can be measured as

$$N_d = |C_{N_s}^M| \qquad (10)$$

$$N_f = |C_{N_a}^M| \qquad (11)$$

For a sequence sensitive assessment of attention the sets of corresponding fixations between human benchmark and model output for $N_s$ and $N_a$ attempts will be collected as

$$C_{N_s}^{M_o}(\beta, I_l^\gamma) = \{ F_q^{H_o} \in F^{H_o} \mid \overline{L(F_q^{H_o}) L(F_j^{M_o})} < r^\Lambda$$
$$\text{and } \Delta(O_q, O_j) = \Delta_{min}, 1 \le j \le N_s \} (12)$$

$$C_{N_a}^{M_o}(\beta, I_l^\gamma) = \{ F_q^{H_o} \in F^{H_o} \mid \overline{L(F_q^{H_o}) L(F_j^{M_o})} < r^\Lambda$$
$$\text{and } \Delta(O_q, O_j) = \Delta_{min}, 1 \le j \le N_a \} (13)$$

where $\Delta(.,.)$ computes the absolute difference between the given numbers and

$$\Delta_{min} = min \left( \Delta(O_q, O_j) \forall j \text{ s. t. } \overline{L(F_q^{H_o}) L(F_j^{M_o})} < r^\Lambda \right)$$

## 4.4 Performance Metrics

Output of computational attention models may be evaluated in terms of three metrics, namely, detection efficiency $\varepsilon^d$, detection capability $\sigma^d$, and sequence proximity $\Psi^o$. $\varepsilon^d$ measures the ability of a system to fixate on all salient locations in minimum number ($N_s$) of attempts. Having $N_s$ salient locations in a given input $\varepsilon^d$ is computed as

$$\varepsilon^d = \frac{N_d}{N_s} \qquad (14)$$

Obviously $0 \le \varepsilon^d \le 1$. The metric $\sigma^d$ allows the system to run for $N_t$ attempts in order to provide an opportunity to fixate on all $N_s$ salient locations in the given scene. The number of salient objects found by a system are counted as $N_f$ and the number of attempts used are counted as $N_a$. As the system is not allowed to go beyond $N_t$ even if it could not mark some of the salient locations, it is obvious that $N_f \le N_s \le N_a \le N_t$. Using readings for these values, the detection capability $\sigma^d$ is defined as

$$\sigma^d = \frac{N_f (N_t - (N_a - N_s))}{N_s N_t} \qquad (15)$$

The first factor $(N_f / N_s)$ quantifies the capability of finding salient objects; a system able to find all salient objects of a given scene scores a 1 in this factor. The second factor $((N_t - (N_a - N_s)) / N_t)$ imposes a penalty on extra (error) fixations taken by the model to cover the $N_s$ salient objects. A system capable of fixating on all $N_s$ locations within $N_a = N_s$ will score a 1 in this factor.

For sequence sensitive evaluation the metrics $\Psi_{N_s}^o$ and $\Psi_{N_a}^o$ are used to assess the proximity of order followed by a model with the order of fixations in human benchmark in $N_s$ and $N_a$ attempts respectively. As mentioned earlier, the sequence number of different human observers may also differ from each other. Therefore the sets of corresponding fixations $C_{N_s}^{M_o}(\beta, I_l^\gamma)$ and $C_{N_a}^{M_o}(\beta, I_l^\gamma)$, defined in the processes mentioned in equations 12 and 13, collect the fixations from human data $F^{H_o}$ overlapping with the model fixations that have the nearest (or same) sequence number. Using members of these two sets $\Psi_{N_s}^o$ and $\Psi_{N_a}^o$ are computed as follows:

$$\Psi_{N_s}^o = 1 - \frac{\sum_{j=1}^{N_s} \Delta \left( O_j(F^{M_o}), O_\alpha(C_{N_s}^{M_o}) \right)}{(max(O(C_{N_s}^{M_o})) - min(O(C_{N_s}^{M_o}))) N_s} \qquad (16)$$

$$\Psi_{N_a}^o = 1 - \frac{\sum_{j=1}^{N_a} \Delta \left( O_j(F^{M_o}), O_\alpha(C_{N_a}^{M_o}) \right)}{(max(O(C_{N_a}^{M_o})) - min(O(C_{N_a}^{M_o}))) N_s} \qquad (17)$$

where $O_\alpha(C_{N_s}^{M_o})$ is the order number of the element from $C_{N_s}^{M_o}$ such that

$$\overline{L_j(F^{M_o}) L_\alpha(C_{N_s}^{M_o})} < r^\Lambda$$

Similarly $O_\alpha(C_{N_a}^{M_o})$ refers to the element that overlaps with $L_j(F^{M_o})$, i.e. it fulfills the condition

$$\overline{L_j(F^{M_o}) L_\alpha(C_{N_a}^{M_o})} < r^\Lambda$$

## 5. EVALUATION CASE STUDY

As a sample implementation of the evaluation methodology proposed in this paper we demonstrate the process of human data collection, extraction of combined human benchmark, record of basic comparison measurements, and outcome of evaluation metrics using a simple lab scene example. In order to show a trace of performance using the proposed metrics on varying levels of complexity in visual input our attention model, presented in [3], was executed on a collection of images containing various scene complexities to record the outcome.

Figure 2(a) shows one of the sample input image on which human subjects were asked to mark salient spots with numbers such that the location with highest saliency is given a 1 and increasing numbers represent decreasing saliency. Figures 2(b) to (f) present five selected samples from the results of marking on this image according to the proposed standards of FOA representation. Centers of these attention marks are stored in $F_h^H$, $1 \le h \le 5$ for this example, and the sequence numbers are stored in $F_h^{H_o}$. The circles in figure 3 provide a visualization of the combined human dataset $F^H$

and the multiple sequence numbers associated per fixation from $F^{H_o}$, which are written around each circle.

Figure 4 shows output of fixations by the attention model ([3]). First $N_s$ fixations by the model are shown with their sequence numbers in figure 4(a). It may be noted in figure 3 that $N_s = 5$. Fixations by the model until $N_a$ attempts, in which it could detect all $N_s$ salient locations, are shown in figure 4(b).

In order to demonstrate extraction of comparable quantities from attention data, the sample output shown in figures 3 and 4 was used to populate table 1. The table presents the values of comparison measurement readings ($N_s$, $N_t$, $N_a$, $N_d$, and $N_f$) and results of performance measures ($\varepsilon^d$, $\sigma^d$, $\Psi^o_{N_s}$, $\Psi^o_{N_a}$). In this case study we have taken $N_t = 2N_s$. This value for $N_t$ may be considered as a convention for evaluation of moderately time-critical systems. On the other hand, $N_t$ may be adjusted according to requirements of the involved application. The values presented in table 1 were computed using equations 14 to 17.

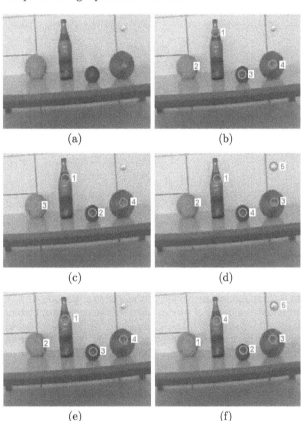

(a)

(b)

(c)

(d)

(e)

(f)

Figure 2: (a) A sample input used for demonstrating an example implementation of the proposed evaluation methodology. (b) to (f) Response from five human subjects representing the sets $F^H_h$ and $F^{H_o}_h$ with $1 \leq h \leq 5$. Smaller sequence numbers refer to higher saliency according to subject's perspective.

A trace of a model's performance can be recorded using the proposed metrics in order to evaluate response of the model against increasing levels of complexity in the visual input.

Figure 3: Combined result of human response representing $F^H$ and $F^{H_o}$ extracted from human response shown in figure 2.

Table 1: Values of the comparison measurement readings and performance measures according to the metrics proposed in this paper using an example implementation with the human benchmark data shown in figures 3 and output of a computational model ([3]) shown in figure 4.

| Measurement/Metric | Value |
|---|---|
| $N_s$ | 5 |
| $N_t$ | 10 |
| $N_a$ | 10 |
| $N_d$ | 4 |
| $N_f$ | 5 |
| $\varepsilon^d$ | 0.80 |
| $\sigma^d$ | 0.50 |
| $\Psi^o_{N_s}$ | 0.90 |
| $\Psi^o_{N_a}$ | 0.82 |

The fixation data of the model of [3] was collected on a set of images containing varying number of salient objects according to human marking on those images. Increasing number of attention candidates can be considered as rising complexity for bottom-up visual attention. Figure 5 shows the graphical representation of the model's performance in terms of $\varepsilon^d$, $\sigma^d$, $\Psi^o_{N_s}$, $\Psi^o_{N_a}$. Mean of these values were taken for all images belonging to a particular complexity level. Such curves drawn together for different attention models can provide a quantitative glimpse of the advancement in the state-of-the-art made by improvements in artificial attention models.

## 6. CONCLUSION

This paper has presented an effort towards standardization of metrics for evaluation of results from computational attention models in comparison to human benchmark. One of the measures for model performance is the ability to cover all salient locations in a given scene. With this, fixations by a model on non-salient locations (in perspective of human vision) should cause a decline in the performance measure. Further, proximity of the sequence of fixations by a computational model with those of humans may also be a criteria

(a)

(b)

**Figure 4: Visualization of the fixations performed by the attention model of [3] on the visual input introduced in figure 2(a) according to the proposed convention of FOA representation. (a) Fixations by the model in $N_s$ attempts. (b) Fixations in $N_a$ attempts until the model could pick all $N_s$ salient locations.**

to evaluate a model. The proposed metrics are designed to cover all these aspects. The detection efficiency $\varepsilon^d$ measures the detection rate of a model in minimum allowable attempts. The detection capability $\sigma^d$ measures the ability to cover all possible salient locations. Error fixations can occur during these attempts hence $\sigma^d$ delivers a decline on these errors. Sequence proximity with the benchmark is evaluated by $\Psi^o_{N_s}$ and $\Psi^o_{N_a}$ that return measure of resemblance of the order of fixations followed by a model with the human attention sequence in $N_s$ and $N_a$ attempts respectively.

The main difference between salient locations of top-down attention and those of bottom-up attention is that the top-down popouts emerge based upon similarity with the search target while for the bottom-up attention this process is data driven. In terms of format of data representation there is no difference between them. Therefore the proposed evaluation methodology is applicable for evaluation of attention under visual search behavior as well. Simply, reference to the behavior $\beta$ in the data representation mentioned in equations 1 to 6 will have to be indicated according to the active visual task.

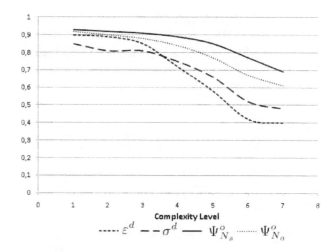

**Figure 5: A sample trace of different performance measures according to the metrics proposed in this paper. The model of [3] is taken as a case study using input with increasing complexity levels in terms of candidate count for bottom-up attention.**

The method proposed for extracting measurement readings from attention data is feasible for automated machine-based computation. The suggestions made for standardization of FOA representation and the metrics designed to provide performance measure in normalized values between 0 and 1 contribute to make objective comparison between different attention models. Availability of such conventions can play a key role in gauging advancements in realistic developments in a research field.

## 7. ACKNOWLEDGMENT

We gratefully acknowledge the funding of this work by the German Research Foundation (DFG) under the grant Me 1289/12-1(AVRAM).

## 8. REFERENCES

[1] T. Avraham and M. Lindenbaum. Esaliency (extended saliency): Meaningful attention using stochastic image modeling. *IEEE Transactions on Pattern Analysis and Machine Intelligence*, 32(4):693–708, 2010.

[2] M. Z. Aziz and B. Mertsching. An attentional approach for perceptual grouping of spatially distributed patterns. In *DAGM 2007, LNCS 4713*, pages 345–354, Heidelberg - Germany, 2007. Springer.

[3] M. Z. Aziz and B. Mertsching. Fast and robust generation of feature maps for region-based visual attention. *Transactions on Image Processing*, 17:633–644, 2008.

[4] M. Z. Aziz and B. Mertsching. Towards standardized metrics and methods for evaluation of visual attention models. In *WAPCV 2008*, pages 180–193, Santorini - Greece, 2008.

[5] M. Z. Aziz and B. Mertsching. Towards Standardization of Evaluation Metrics and Methods

for Visual Attention Models. *Attention in Cognitive Systems, LNAI*, 5395/2009:227 – 241, March 2009.

[6] M. Clauss, P. Bayerl, and H. Neumann. A statistical measure for evaluating regions-of-interest based attention algorithms. In *DAGM 2004, LNCS 3175*, pages 383–390. Springer, 2004.

[7] B. A. Draper and A. Lionelle. Evaluation of selective attention under similarity transforms. In *WAPCV 03*, 2003.

[8] S. Frintrop, G. Backer, and E. Rome. Goal-directed search with a top-down modulated computational attention system. In *DAGM 2005, LNCS 3663*, pages 117–124. Springer, 2005.

[9] N. Hawes and J. Wyatt. Towards context-sensitive visual attention. In *Second International Cognitive Vision Workshop (ICVW06)*, 2006.

[10] M. Heinen and P. Engel. Evaluation of visual attention models under 2d similarity transformations. In *Proceedings of the 2009 ACM symposium on Applied Computing*, pages 1156–1160. ACM, 2009.

[11] H. Hügli, T. Jost, and N. Ouerhani. Model performance for visual attention in real 3D color scenes. In *IWINAC 2005*, pages 469–478. LNCS 3562, Springer, 2005.

[12] L. Itti, U. Koch, and E. Niebur. A model of saliency-based visual attention for rapid scene analysis. *Transactions on Pattern Analysis and Machine Intelligence*, 20:1254–1259, 1998.

[13] G. Marmitt and A. T. Duchowski. Modeling visual attention in vr:measuring the accuracy of predicted scanpaths. In *EUROGRAPHICS 2002*, 2002.

[14] O. L. Meur, P. L. Callet, D. Barba, and D. Thoreau. A coherent computational approach to model bottom-up visual attention. *Transactions on Pattern Analysis and Machine Intelligence*, 28:802–817, 2006.

[15] T. Michalke, A. Gepperth, M. Schneider, J. Fritsch, and C. Goerick. Towards a human-like vision system for resource-constrained intelligent cars. In *ICVS 2007*, pages 264–275. Bielefeld University eCollections, Germany, 2004.

[16] V. Navalpakkam and L. Itti. Modeling the influence of task on attention. *Vision Research*, pages 205–231, 2005.

[17] G. Osterberg. Topography of the layer of rods and cones in the. human retina. *Acta Ophthalmologica*, 6:11–102, 1935.

[18] N. Ouerhani, R. von Wartburg, H. Hügli, and R. Müri. Empirical validation of the saliency-based model of visual attention. *Electronic Letters on Computer Vision and Image Analysis*, 3(1):13–24, 2004.

[19] R. J. Peters, A. Iyer, L. Itti, and C. Koch. Components of bottom-up gaze allocation in natural images. *Vision Research*, 45:2397–2416, 2005.

[20] S. Polyak. *The Retina*. University of Chicago Press, Chicago, USA, 1941.

[21] C. M. Privitera and L. W. Stark. Algorithms for defining visual regions-of-interest: Comparison with eye fixations. *Transactions on Pattern Analysis and Machine Intelligence*, 9:970–982, 2000.

[22] M. Riesenhuber. Object recognition in cortex: Neural mechanisms, and possible roles for attention. In *Neurobiology of attention*, pages 279–287. Elsevier, 2005.

[23] A. L. Yarbus. *Eye Movements and Vision*. Plenum Press, New York, 1967.

# Performance evaluation procedure for vision based object feature extraction algorithms

### Minku Kang
Dept. of Computer Engineering,
Sejong University
98 Gunja-dong Gwangjin-gu
Seoul, 143-747, Korea
+82-2-3408-3243

mkkang@sju.ac.kr

### Wonkook Choo
Dept. of Computer Engineering,
Sejong University
98 Gunja-dong Gwangjin-gu
Seoul, 143-747, Korea
+82-2-3408-3243

wkchoo@sju.ac.kr

### Seungbin Moon
Dept. of Computer Engineering,
Sejong University
98 Gunja-dong Gwangjin-gu
Seoul, 143-747, Korea
+82-2-3408-3243

sbmoon@sejong.ac.kr

## ABSTRACT
In this paper, we introduce the performance evaluation procedure for vision based object feature extraction algorithms. Vision based object feature extraction algorithms are widely employed in object recognition and localization for robots. Our purpose is to establish evaluation procedure and performance measures for these algorithms. The object database, called OFEX(Obejct Feature EXtraction), has been constructed to test the proposed procedures. We also examine experimental results for one of the feature extraction algorithms.

## Categories and Subject Descriptors
H.3.4 [**Systems and Software**]: Performance evaluation – *object recognition*

## General Terms
Algorithms, Measurement, Performance, Standardization.

## Keywords
Object Recognition, Performance evaluation, Illumination, Cluttering, Occlusion, Scale, Features extraction

## 1. INTRODUCTION
In image processing, the meaningful information, called features, may be extracted from the raw image. The features indicate transformed data where unnecessary data has been removed. Transforming the image data into the set of features is called feature extraction.

SIFT(Scale Invariant feature transform)[1] is one of the best known feature extraction algorithms and it is commercially available. SURF(Speeded-Up Robust Features)[2] is also another feature extraction algorithm.

Vision based object feature extraction algorithms are widely used for object recognition[3, 4] and localization[5-8]. Furthermore, it

is extended to the face recognition[9, 10].

The purpose of this paper is to present performance evaluation procedure for the vision based feature extraction algorithms. We designed a database which consists of object images with various conditions. The evaluation procedure and performance measures are also developed in this paper. The initial works has been reported in the earlier studies[11, 12]. The procedure has been adopted as a Korea Intelligent Robot Standard, KOROS, in 2009.

This paper is structured as follows. In Sec. 2, the database, called OFEX(Object Feature EXtraction), is described. The proposed evaluation procedure and performance measures are described in Sec. 3. Experimental results, employing one of the feature extraction algorithms, are shown in Sec. 4. The conclusion is given in the last section.

## 2. OFEX(Object Feature EXtraction) DB
It is difficult to compare the performance of vision based feature extraction algorithms, if we test them in different conditions. Thus, we decided to introduce an object database, which consists of images with various conditions, in testing the performance.

Most of the existing databases[13, 14] for objects contain images that do not reflect the environmental variations such as scale, pose and illumination. However, the robotic application usually has to take these variations into consideration, as the camera attached on the mobile robots experience these variations frequently.

Therefore, we designed and built a database for object images, called OFEX, employing variations in scale, pose, occlusion, and illumination. There are three basic object images, called training set, and 15 images with variations for each basic image, called test set. We also have 50 false positive images for each basic image to test the false positive rate. Table 1 shows the categories of OFEX, where three categories of training set, test set, and false positive set are shown. Training set is used to register object images, and test set is employed to obtain the recognition rates under various conditions. False positive set is used to test false acceptance rate (FAR) when objects in training and test set are similar but different.

**Table 1. Categories of OFEX database**

| Categories | Number of images |
|---|---|
| Training set | 3 |
| Test set | 45 |
| False positive set | 150 |

Fig. 1 shows the objects used in the database – a fire extinguisher, a desktop PC, and a file drawer. These are chosen since we can encounter them frequently in general indoor environments.

**Figure 1. Three basic objects in OFEX DB**

As shown in Fig. 2, center of an object and camera lens forms a straight line, and it is set as x-axis. z-axis is an upward vertical line from the center of an object, and y-axis is determined by right hand rule.

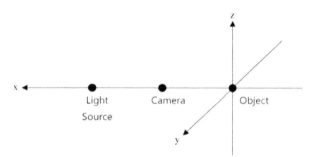

**Figure 2. Object coordinate system**

Table 2 shows database image acquisition conditions in various environmental elements, such as distance, illumination, pose, occlusion, and clutter.

**Table 2. Database image acquisition conditions**

| Environmental elements | | conditions | |
|---|---|---|---|
| | | Training set | Test set |
| Distance | | 1m | 0.5, 1.5m |
| Illumination | | 200lx | 60, 100, 400lx |
| Pose | Roll(x-axis) | 0° | ±20° |
| | Pitch(y-axis) | 0° | ±45° |
| | Yaw(z-axis) | 0° | ±45° |
| Occlusion | | None | 1/4, 2/4, 3/4 |
| Clutter | | No background | Complicated background |

In order to take images in different scales, the object is placed $P_0$ position in Fig. 3. We obtained three images while camera was moved from $P_1$ to $P_3$, where the image at $P_2$ was used as training set.

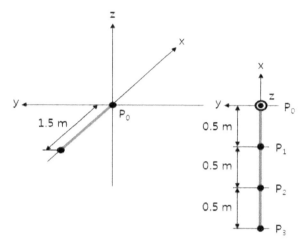

**Figure 3. Image acquisition in different scales**

Images with various poses are taken as shown in Fig. 4. Yaw variance can be easily encountered when a robot moves toward an object in different directions. Pitch variance is also expected when the object is placed in different height. Roll variance is usually not much expected unless the object is placed in slant angle.

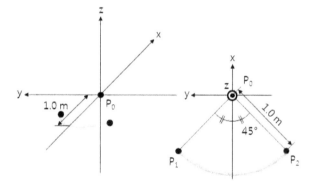

(a)

38

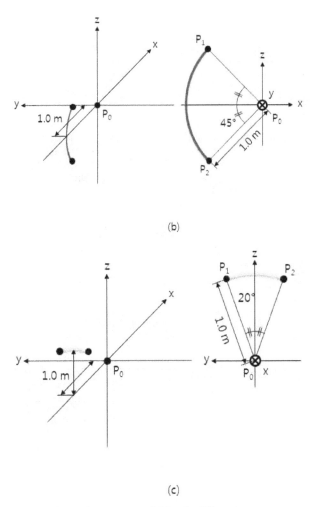

Figure 4. Image acquisition in different poses

(a) Yaw variation (b) Pitch variation (c) Roll variation

We use three filters to build occlusion variation test images, as shown in Fig. 5.

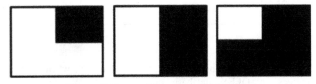

Figure 5. Image filters in occlusion test

We also included cluttered images where basic objects are surrounded by other objects. Finally, we built false positive set images, which are gathered from the internet web sites. For example, we searched fire extinguisher images and gathered similar images with training one. Each object has 50 false positive images. Fig. 6 shows some of the sample images from OFEX database.

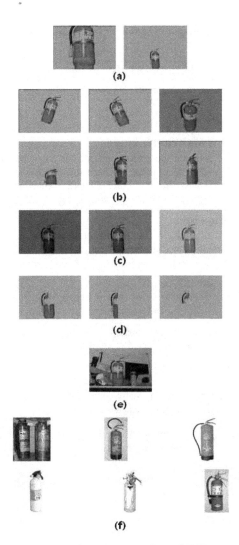

Figure 6. Sample images from OFEX

(a) scale variance (b) pose variance (c) illumination variance
(d) occlusion (e) cluttering (f) false positives

Images in test set are named as "*a_b_c_d_e_f*" style and their meanings are shown Table 3. Similar naming convention is applied to false positive set as in Table 4.

Table 3. Naming convention for test set in OFEX

| | contents |
|---|---|
| a | ID of object: A1, A2, A3 |
| b | Distance between object and camera: 0.5, 1.0, 1.5 |
| c | Pose of camera: R±20, P±45, Y±45 <br> - type : R, P, Y <br> - rotation direction : +(clockwise), -(counter clockwise) <br> - rotation angle : 20(for R), 45(for P and Y) |
| d | Illumination: 60, 100, 200, 400 |
| e | Occlusion scope: 0, 0.25, 0.5, 0.75 |
| f | Clutter condition: 1 or 0 |

**Table 4. Naming convention for false positive set in OFEX**

|   | contents |
|---|---|
| a | ID of object: B1, B2, B3 |
| b | Image numbers: 001, 002, 003, …, 050 |

## 3. Performance measures

In order to compare the performance of the vision based object feature extraction algorithms, we need to develop the objective performance measures. The following performance measures are used to evaluate algorithms in this paper.

### Recognition time

It is one of the most important performance measures since the real-time performance is needed in many applications. It is evaluated as in Eq. (1).

$$\text{Recognition Time(ms)} = \text{(feature extraction time for test image} \quad (1) \\ + \text{ matching time between test and training images)}$$

If the number of features increases, the recognition time generally is expected to increase.

### Feature matching rate

Since the goal of feature extraction algorithm is to find the robust features and match them, feature matching rate is an essential measure for evaluation. It is calculated as in Eq. (2).

$$\text{FMR(\%)} = \frac{\text{number of matched features}}{\text{number of training image features}} \quad (2)$$

The number of matched features is evaluated by matched features between test and training images. This number is used to decide the correct matching if it is larger than the predetermined value, called threshold.

### Recognition rate

The recognition rate is defined as the ratio of the number of correct test images to the number of total test images, as in Eq. (3).

$$\text{RR(\%)} = \frac{\text{number of correct test images}}{\text{number of total test images}} \quad (3)$$

### False acceptance rate

False acceptance means that unregistered object is recognized as the training image. False acceptance rate is evaluated as in Eq. (4).

$$\text{FAR(\%)} = \frac{\text{number of false accepted images}}{\text{number of total test images}} \quad (4)$$

If the recognition rate is high while false acceptance rate remains low, then the algorithm may be considered better than others. Recognition rate and false acceptance rate generally shows trade-off relationship. In another words, if we maintain the lower false acceptance rate, recognition rate tends to be lower. The recognition time is also important if your application requires real-time performance.

## 4. Experiment

In this section, we selected a commercially available object feature extraction algorithm in order to show how the performance measures introduced in this paper could be utilized. We set the threshold, which decides the minimum percentage of features to be accepted as matching, as 5%.

We employed OFEX database in the experiment. In the first experiment, we evaluated the performance measures for each object image set, as shown in Table 5. We noticed that the recognition time depends on the number of features. While fire extinguisher has lowest number of features, desktop PC and file drawer have more number of features.

One of the reasons that the recognition rate is lower for file drawer seems that it has surfaces which reflect the light. The false acceptance rate for fire extinguisher is rather high compared to the other two objects. Possible answer to this is that its main features, such as a grip and a nozzle, are concentrated in one side.

**Table 5. Experimental results for individual object sets**

| Performance Measures | Object image sets (Number of accepted images / Number of test images) | | |
|---|---|---|---|
|  | Fire extinguisher | Desktop PC | File drawer |
| Average number of features | 174 | 291 | 323 |
| Recognition Time(ms) | 28.19 | 36.95 | 36.87 |
| Feature Matching Rate | 35% | 31% | 28% |
| Recognition Rate | 100% (15/15) | 80% (12/15) | 67% (10/15) |
| False Acceptance Rate | 20% (10/50) | 0% (0/50) | 10% (5/50) |

Table 6 shows the performance of the algorithm when all test images in OFEX database are employed. We found the recognition time, feature matching rate, recognition rate, and false acceptance rate. False acceptance rate of 10% might be considered rather high. If we increase the threshold value, FAR could decrease, but the recognition rate will generally be decreased also.

**Table 6. Experimental results for overall object sets**

| Performance measure | Values |
| --- | --- |
| Recognition Time | 34.00ms |
| Feature Matching Rate | 31 % |
| Recognition Rate | 82% |
| False Acceptance Rate | 10% |

Experimental results for subsets with different conditions are shown in Table 7. As expected, clutter image has the highest number of features, while pose variation and occlusion images have lower numbers. Recognition rates are near or above 90% for all cases, except 67% for pose variation case. We may conclude that this feature extraction algorithm is weak for pose variation.

**Table 7. Experimental results for subsets with different conditions**

| Condition | Recognition Time(ms) | Feature Matching Rate(%) | Recognition Rate(%) |
| --- | --- | --- | --- |
| Distance | 69.73 | 20 | 89 |
| Illumination | 44.51 | 55 | 100 |
| Pose | 33.38 | 20 | 67 |
| Occlusion | 34.59 | 35 | 89 |
| Clutter | 113.26 | 37 | 100 |

## 5. Conclusion

We introduced the performance evaluation procedure for vision based object feature extraction algorithms employing OFEX database. It is a useful tool to compare any feature extraction algorithms. The experiment showed that the measures could be used to analyze the performance of the given algorithm.

The drawback of employing a database in evaluating the performance is the possibility of being optimized only to the specific database. However, we feel that this drawback could be overcome by adding more images in the future.

## 6. ACKNOWLEDGMENTS

This work was supported by National Strategic R&D Program for Industrial Technology from Ministry of Knowledge Economy, Korea.

## 7. REFERENCES

[1] Lowe, D. 2004. Distinctive Image Features from Scale-Invariant Keypoints, *International Journal of Computer Vision*, 60, 2, pp. 91-110.

[2] Bay, H., Ess, A., Tuytelaars, T. and Van Gool, L. 2008. Surf: Speeded up robust features, *In Proceedings of Computer Vision and Image Understanding*, vol. 110 no. 3, 346-359.

[3] Lowe, D. 1999. Object recognition from local scale-invariant features, *In Proceedings of International Conference on Computer Vision*, vol. 2, 1150.

[4] Bay, H., Fase, B. and Van Gool, L. 2006. Interactive museum guide: Fast and robust recognition of museum objects, *In Proceedings of First international workshop on mobile vision*.

[5] Tamimi, H., Andreasson, H., Treptow, A., Duckett, T. and Zell, A. 2005. Localization of mobile robots with omnidirectional vision using particle filter and iterative SIFT, *In Proceedings of 2nd European Conf. on Mobile Robots – ECMR'05*, (Ancona, Italy 7-10, 2005), 758-765.

[6] Murillo, A.C., Guerrero, J.J. and Sagüés, C. 2007. SURF Features for Efficient Robot Localization with Omnidirectional Images, *In Proceedings of 2007 IEEE Int'l Conf. Robotics and Automation*, 3901–3907.

[7] Se, S., Lowe, D., and Little. J. 2001. Vision-based mobile robot localization and mapping using scale-invariant features. *In Proceedings of the International Conference on Robotics & Automation* (Seoul, Korea 21-26, May, 2001), 2051-2058.

[8] Cummins, M. and Newman, P. 2008. FAB-MAP: Probabilistic Localization and Mapping in the Space of Appearance, *International Journal of Robotics Research*, Vol. 27, No. 6, 647-665.

[9] Bicego, M., Lagorio, A., Grosso, E. and Tistarelli, M. 2006. On the Use of SIFT Features for Face Authentication, *In Proceedings of Computer Vision and Pattern Recognition Workshop* - 2006, 35–35.

[10] An, S., Ma, X., Song R. and Li, Y. 2009. Face detection and recognition with SURF for human-robot interaction, *In Proceedings of International Conference on Automation and Logistics 2009*(Shenyang, China 5-7, August), 1946-1951.

[11] Kang, M., Moon, S., Back, S. and Ryuh, Y. 2009. Performance evaluation of object feature extraction algorithm for localization of robots, *In Proceedings of Korea Automatic Control Conference*(Pusan, Korea 2-4), 832-835.

[12] Kang, M. and Moon, S. 2009. Database-based performance evaluation of SIFT algorithm, *In Proceedings of annual fall Conf. Institute of Electronics Engineers of Korea* (Seoul, Korea 28, November).

[13] Griffin, G., Holub, A. D. and Perona, P. 2006. *The Caltech-256 Object Category Dataset*. Technical Report. California Institute of Technology

[14] Russell, B.C., Torralba, A., Murphy K.P. and Freeman, W.T. 2008. LabelMe: A Database and Web-Based Tool for Image Annotation. *International Journal of Computer Vision* (May. 2008), 157-173.

# Benchmarks, Performance Evaluation and Contests for 3D Shape Retrieval

Afzal Godil[1], Zhouhui Lian[1], Helin Dutagaci[1], Rui Fang[2], Vanamali T.P. [1], Chun Pan Cheung[1]

[1]National Institute of Standards and Technology, USA

[2]School of Computer Science and Engineering, Michigan State University, USA

godil@nist.gov

## ABSTRACT

Benchmarking of 3D Shape retrieval allows developers and researchers to compare the strengths of different algorithms on a standard dataset. Here we describe the procedures involved in developing a benchmark and issues involved. We then discuss some of the current 3D shape retrieval benchmarks efforts of our group and others. We also review the different performance evaluation measures that are developed and used by researchers in the community. After that we give an overview of the 3D shape retrieval contest (SHREC) tracks run under the EuroGraphics Workshop on 3D Object Retrieval and give details of tracks that we organized for SHREC 2010. Finally we demonstrate some of the results based on the different SHREC contest tracks and the NIST shape benchmark.

## Categories and Subject Descriptors

D.2.8 Metrics: Performance measures

## General Terms

3D Shape retrieval, benchmarks, performance evaluation, contests

## Keywords

3D Shape retrieval, benchmarks, performance evaluation measures, contests

## 1. INTRODUCTION

3D objects are widespread and present in many diverse fields such as computer graphics, computer vision, computer aided design, cultural heritage, medical imaging, structural biology, and other fields. Large numbers of 3D models are created every day using 3D modeling programs and 3D scanners and many are stored in publicly available databases. These 3D databases require methods for storage, indexing, searching, clustering, and retrieval to be used effectively. Hence, content based 3D shape retrieval has become an active area of research in the 3D community. Benchmarking allows researchers to evaluate the quality of results of different 3D shape retrieval approaches. Under a benchmark, different shape matching algorithms are compared and evaluated in term of efficiency, accuracy, robustness and consistence. Results are then obtained and conclusions of the performance are drawn towards the shape matching algorithms.

In section 2, the related work of previous benchmarks is briefly reviewed; in section 3, we discuss benchmarks and the construction of the benchmark; in section 4, we present the evaluation measures used; the NIST shape benchmark is discussed and analyzed in section 5; section 6 describes the SHREC contests and their results; and finally conclusions are drawn in section 7.

## 2. RELATED WORK

*Contest*   The SHape REtrieval Contest (SHREC) [4] is organized every year since 2006 by Network of Excellence AIM@SHAPE under the EuroGraphics Workshop on 3D Object Retrieval to evaluate the effectiveness of 3D shape retrieval algorithms. In 2006, one track was organized to retrieve 3D mesh models on the Princeton Shape Benchmark [1]. In the SHREC 2007, several tracks were organized which focused on specialized problems: the watertight models track, the partial matching track, the CAD models track, the protein models track, the 3D face models track. In the SHREC 2008, following tracks are organized: stability of watertight models, the track on the classification of watertight models and the generic models track, 3D face models. In the SHREC 2009, there were four tracks organized, and we organized two tracks, one based on Generic shape retrieval and the other based on partial shape matching. For the SHREC 2010, there were 11 tracks organized initially, two of them were cancelled because of not enough participants and we organized three Shape Retrieval tracks: Generic 3D Warehouse; Non-Rigid Shapes; and Range Scans.

*Benchmark*   One of the main 3D Shape Retrieval benchmarks is the Princeton Shape Benchmark [1], which is a publicly available database of 3D polygonal models with a set of software tools that are widely used by researchers to report their shape matching results and compare them to the results of other algorithms. The Purdue engineering shape benchmark [2] is a public 3D shape database for evaluating shape retrieval algorithms mainly in the mechanical engineering domain. The McGill 3D shape benchmark [3] provides a 3D shape repository which includes models with articulating parts. Other current shape benchmarks were introduced and analyzed in [10]. We also have developed two Generic shape benchmarks [6], [7] and a Range scan benchmark [8] which we hope will provide valuable contributions to the 3D shape retrieval and evaluation community.

## 3. BENCHMARKS

In this section, the benchmark design principles and how to build the ground truth for benchmarks are discussed, respectively.

### 3.1 Benchmark Design Principles

A number of issues need to be addressed in order to create a 3D Shape benchmark dataset. The dataset must be available free of charge and without copyright issues, so the dataset can be located on a website and can be used freely by everyone for publications. The issue is getting a large collection of 3D models that maybe freely used, which includes those in the public domain, and also ones that are freely licensed, like under the GNU Free Doc. license, or some of the Creative Commons licenses, which offers the Authors/Artists alternatives to the full copyright. There are two main steps to benchmark a shape database, the first of which is to get enough 3D shape models. All the 3D models in the new shape benchmark were acquired by the web crawler. The other step is to classify the 3D shape models into a ground truth database; we discuss it below in detail. 3D models down-loaded from websites are in arbitrary position, scale and orientation, and some of them have many types of mesh errors. Shapes should be invariant to rotation, translation and scaling, which require the process of pose normalization before many shape descriptors can be applied to extract shape features.

## 3.2 Building a Ground Truth for Benchmark

The purpose of benchmarking is to establish a known and validated ground truth to compare different shape matching algorithms and evaluate new methods by standard tools in a standard way. Building a ground truth database is an important step of establishing a benchmark. A good ground truth database should meet several criteria [12], like, having a reasonable number of models, being stable in order to evaluate different methods with relatively high confidence, and having certain generalization ability to evaluate new methods. To get a ground truth dataset, in text retrieval research, TREC [5] uses pooling assessment [12]. In image retrieval research, as there is no automatic way to determine the relevance of an image in the database for a given query image [18], the IAPR benchmark [11] was established by manually classifying images into categories. In image processing research, the Berkeley segmentation dataset and benchmark [14] assumes that the human segmented images provide valid ground truth boundaries, and all images are segmented and evaluated by a group of people. As there is no standard measure of difference or similarity between two shapes, in our shape benchmark [6], two researchers were assigned as assessor to manually classify objects into ground truth categories. When there are disagreements on which category some objects should belong, another researcher was assigned as the third assessors to make the final decision. This classification work is purely according to shape similarity, that is, geometric similarity and topology similarity. Each model was input to a 3D viewer, and the assessor rendered it in several viewpoints to make a final judgment towards shape similarity.

## 4. EVALUATION MEASURES

The procedure of 3D shape retrieval evaluation is straightforward. In response to a given set of users' queries, an algorithm searches the benchmark database and returns an ordered list of responses called the ranked list(s), the evaluation of the algorithm then is transformed to the evaluation of the quality of the ranked list(s). Next, we will discuss the evaluation method that we have used.

Different evaluation metrics measure different aspects of shape retrieval behavior. In order to make a thorough evaluation of a 3D shape retrieval algorithm with high confidence, we employ a number of common evaluation measures used in the information retrieval community [12].

## 4.1 Precision- Recall

Precision- Recall Graph [12] is the most common metric to evaluate information retrieval system. Precision is the ratio of retrieved objects that are relevant to all retrieved objects in the ranked list. Recall is the ratio of relevant objects retrieved in the ranked list to all relevant objects.

Let A be the set of all relevant objects, and B be the set of all retrieved objects then,

$$precision = \frac{A \cap B}{B} \quad \text{and} \quad recall = \frac{A \cap B}{A} \quad (1)$$

Basically, Recall evaluates how well a retrieval algorithm finds what we want and precision evaluates how well it weeds out what we don't want. There is a tradeoff between Recall and Precision, one can increase Recall by retrieving more, but this can decrease Precision.

## 4.2 R-precision

The precision score when R relevant objects are retrieved (where R is the number of relevant objects)

## 4.3 Average precision (AP)

The measure [13] is a single-value that evaluates the performance over all relevant objects. It is not an average of the precision at standard recall levels, rather, it is the average of precision scores at each relevant object retrieved for example, consider a query that has five relevant objects which are retrieved at ranks 1,2,4,7,10. The actual precision obtained when each relevant object is retrieved is 1, 1, 0.75, 0.57, 0.50, respectively; the mean of them is 0.76.

## 4.4 Mean Average precision (MAP)

Find the average precision for each query and compute the mean of average precision [13] over all queries; it gives an overall evaluation of a retrieval algorithm.

## 4.5 E-Measures

The idea is to combine precision and recall into a single number to evaluation the whole system performance [12]. First we introduce the F-measure, which is the weighted harmonic mean of precision and recall. F-measure is defined as

$$F_\alpha = \frac{(1+\alpha) \times precision \times recall}{\alpha \times precision + recall} \quad , \text{ where } \alpha \text{ is the weight.} \quad (2)$$

Let $\alpha$ be 1, the weight of precision and recall is same, and we have

$$F = 2 \times \frac{precision \times recall}{precisionl + recal} \quad (3)$$

Then, go over all points on the precision-recall curve of each model and compute the F-measure, we get the overall evaluation of F for an algorithm.

The E-Measure is defined as E = 1- F,

$$E = 1 - \frac{2}{\dfrac{1}{P} + \dfrac{1}{R}} \qquad (4)$$

Note that the maximum value is 1.0, and higher values indicate better results. The fact is that a user of a search engine is more interested in the first page of query results than in later pages. So, here we consider only the first 32 retrieved objects for every query and calculate the E-Measure over those results.

## 4.6  Discount Cumulative Gain (DCG)

Based on the idea that the greater the ranked position of a relevant object the less valuable it is for the user, because the less likely it is that the user will examine the object due to time, effort, and cumulated information from objects already seen.

In this evaluation, the relevance level of each object is used as a gained value measures for its ranked position $m$, the result and the gain is summed progressively from position 1 to n. Thus the ranked object lists (of some determined length) are turned to gained value lists by replacing object IDs with their relevance values. The binary relevance values 0, 1 are used (1 denoting relevant, 0 irrelevant) in our benchmark evaluation.  Replace the object ID with the relevance values, we have for example:

G'=< 1, 1, 1, 0, 0, 1, 1,0,1,0 . . . . >

The cumulated gain at ranked position $i$ is computed by summing from position 1 to $i$ when $i$ ranges from 1 to the length of the ranking list. Formally, let us denote position i in the gain vector G by G[i]. The cumulated gain vector CG is defined recursively as the vector CG where:

$$G[i] = \begin{cases} G[1] & \text{if } i = 1 \\ CG[i] = CG[i-1] + G[i] & \text{otherwise} \end{cases} \qquad (5)$$

The comparison of matching algorithms is then equal to compare the cumulated gain, the greater the rank, the smaller share of the object value is added to the cumulated gain. A discounting function is needed which progressively reduces the object weight as its rank increases but not too steeply:

$$DCG[i] = \begin{cases} G[1] & \text{if } i = 1 \\ DCG[i-1] + G[i] / \log_2 i & \text{otherwise} \end{cases} \qquad (6)$$

The actual CG and DCG vectors by a particular matching algorithm may also be compared to the theoretically best possible. And this is called normalized CG, normalized DCG. The latter vectors are constructed as follows. Let there be 5 relevant objects, and 5 irrelevant objects in each class, then, at the relevance levels 0 and 1. Then the ideal  Gain vector is  obtain by filling the first vector positions with 1, and  the remaining positions by the values 0. Then compute CG and DCG as well as the average CG and DCG vectors and curves as above. Note that the curves will turn horizontal when no more relevant objects (of any level) can be found. The vertical distance between an actual DCG/CG curve and the theoretically best possible curve shows the effort wasted on  less-than-perfect objects due to a particular matching algorithm.

## 4.7  Nearest Neighbor (NN), First-tier (Tier1) and Second-tier (Tier2)

These evaluation measures [1] share the similar idea, that is, to check the ratio of models in the query's class that also appear within the top K matches, where K can be 1, the size of the query's class, or the double size of the query's class. Specifically, for a class with |C| members, K= 1 for Nearest Neighbor, K = |C| − 1 for the first tier, and K = 2 *(|C| − 1) for the second tier. In the NIST shape Benchmark database [6], C is always 20. The final score is an average over all the objects in database.

## 4.8  Computational Cost

For a number of vision based applications, such as Autonomous Robots, the speed of identification by different algorithms is very important. Computational cost is then related to the time it takes to extract the 3D shape descriptor for an object and perform one query search on the database, and the storage size (byte) of the shape descriptor.

## 5.  THE NIST SHAPE BENCHMARK

In this section, we discuss the generic shape benchmark [6] constructed by our group. It contains 800 complete 3D models, which are categorized into 40 classes. The classes are defined with respect to their semantic categories. In each class there are 20 models. The NIST Shape Benchmark provides a new perspective in evaluating shape retrieval algorithms. It has several virtues: high reliability (in terms of error rate) to evaluate 3D shape retrieval algorithms, sufficient number of good quality models as the basis of the shape benchmark, equal size of classes to minimize the bias of evaluation.

## 5.1  Results

We present results of the ten algorithms that we tested on the generic benchmark. Table 1 compares different performance measures described in the previous section for different algorithms. Figure 1 Shows the overall Precision-recall curve for different algorithms on the new benchmark. In order to examine how different shape descriptors work on the database, we implement several kinds of algorithms to compare on the new benchmark. Moreover, comparison experiments are conducted on both the entire benchmark and a specific class of the benchmark. Several retrieval algorithms are evaluated from several aspects on this new benchmark by various measurements, and the reliability of the new shape benchmark.

Table 1: Retrieval performance of different algorithms on the NIST Shape Benchmark.

|  | NN | Tier1 | Tier2 | E-Measure | DCG | MAP |
|---|---|---|---|---|---|---|
| LFD | 84.50% | 42.58% | 54.03% | 35.05% | 75.40% | 49.79% |
| Hybrid | 81.13% | 45.46% | 57.72% | 36.65% | 76.09% | 48.54% |
| EDT | 77.50% | 39.78% | 52.09% | 33.03% | 72.37% | 42.20% |
| DepthBuffer | 75.88% | 37.37% | 47.96% | 31.15% | 70.08% | 38.46% |
| SIL | 71.00% | 35.54% | 47.98% | 30.06% | 68.57% | 37.16% |
| MRSPRH | 70.00% | 35.15% | 45.99% | 29.98% | 68.77% | 36.38% |
| RSH | 69.13% | 32.83% | 44.11% | 28.18% | 66.43% | 37.16% |
| AAD | 65.00% | 30.61% | 41.69% | 26.67% | 64.58% | 31.59% |
| PS | 50.00% | 21.79% | 29.40% | 20.51% | 56.73% | 22.38% |
| D2 | 49.38% | 22.33% | 32.08% | 20.56% | 56.58% | 22.53% |

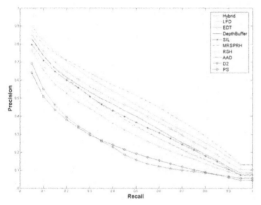

Figure 1: The overall Precision-recall curve for different algorithms on the NIST Shape Benchmark.

## 5.2 Reliability of a Benchmark

The reliability of a new proposed benchmark by testing the effect of class set size on retrieval error is an important issue. Voorhees and Buckley [17] proposed a method to estimate the reliability of retrieval experiments by computing the probability of making wrong decisions between two retrieval systems over two retrieval experiments. They also showed how the topic set sizes affect the reliability of retrieval experiments. We also conducted experiments to test the reliability of retrieval of the new generic 3D shape benchmark [6].

## 6. SHAPE RETRIEVAL CONTEST

In 2010 we organized three tracks in the 3D Shape Retrieval contest. The three tracks were the Generic 3D Warehouse Track [7], the Range scans Track [8], and the Non-rigid shapes Track [9]. These tracks were organized under the SHREC'10-3D Shape Retrieval Contest 2010 (www.aimatshape.net/event/SHREC), and in the context of the EuroGraphics 2010 Workshop On 3D Object Retrieval, 2010. SHREC'10 was the fifth edition of the contest. In the following subsections we will summarize the tracks that we organized.

## 6.1 Generic 3D Warehouse Contest

The aim of this track was to evaluate the performance of various 3D shape retrieval algorithms on a large Generic benchmark based on the Google 3D Warehouse. Three groups participated in the track and they submitted 7 set of results based on different methods and parameters. We also ran two standard algorithms on the dataset. The performance evaluation of this track is based on six different metrics described earlier. All the 3D models in the Generic 3D Warehouse track were acquired by a web crawler from the Google 3D Warehouse [19] which is an online collection of 3D models. The database consists of 3168 3D objects categorized into 43 categories. The number of objects in each category varies between 11 and 177. Figure 2 shows example of each category.

Figure 2: One example image from each class of the Generic 3D Warehouse Benchmark is shown.

### 6.1.1 Results

In this section, we present the performance evaluation results of the Generic 3D Warehouse track. Table 2 shows the retrieval statistics yielded by the methods of the participants and five previous methods. Figure 3 gives the precision-recall curves of all the methods. Observing these figures, we can state that Lian's VLGD+MMR method yielded highest results in terms of all the measures but Nearest Neighbor. While, in terms of Nearest Neighbor, Ohbuchi's MR-BF-DSIFT-E method performed best.

Table 2: The retrieval statistics for all the methods and runs.

| PARTICIPANT | METHOD | NN | FT | ST | E | DCG |
|---|---|---|---|---|---|---|
| Ohbuchi | BF-DSIFT-E | 0.884 | 0.531 | 0.668 | 0.360 | 0.841 |
|  | MR-BF-DSIFT-E | 0.897 | 0.606 | 0.733 | 0.389 | 0.869 |
| Dutagaci | View-based PCA - 18 view | 0.825 | 0.433 | 0.557 | 0.314 | 0.789 |
| Lian | GSMD | 0.875 | 0.491 | 0.624 | 0.344 | 0.824 |
|  | CM-BOF | 0.862 | 0.534 | 0.662 | 0.358 | 0.836 |
|  | VLGD | 0.889 | 0.565 | 0.696 | 0.377 | 0.855 |
|  | VLGD+MMR | 0.889 | 0.647 | 0.791 | 0.390 | 0.880 |
| **AUTHOR** | **PREVIOUS METHODS** | **NN** | **FT** | **ST** | **E** | **DCG** |
| Vranic | DSR472 with L1 | 0.871 | 0.498 | 0.639 | 0.356 | 0.831 |
|  | DBD438 with L1 | 0.809 | 0.407 | 0.532 | 0.306 | 0.770 |
|  | SIL300 with L1 | 0.807 | 0.412 | 0.548 | 0.300 | 0.780 |
|  | RSH136 with L1 | 0.783 | 0.385 | 0.508 | 0.275 | 0.758 |
| Chen | LFD | 0.864 | 0.48 | 0.613 | 0.336 | 0.816 |

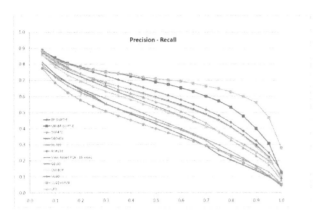

Figure 3: Precision-recall curves of the best runs of each participant.

## 6.2 Range Scan Retrieval Contest

In this contest, the aim was at comparing algorithms that match a range scan to complete 3D models in a target database. The queries are range scans of real objects, and the objective is to retrieve complete 3D models that are of the same class. The query set is composed of 120 range images, which are acquired by capturing 3 range scans of 40 real objects from arbitrary view directions, as shown in Figure 4. The target database is the generic shape benchmark constructed by our group [6]. It contains 800 complete 3D models, which are categorized into 40 classes

Figure 4: Examples from the query set.

### 6.2.1 Results

Two participants of the SHREC'10 track Range Scan Retrieval submitted five sets of rank lists each. The results for the ten submissions are summarized in the precision-recall curves in Figure 5. Figure 6 shows the models retrieved by one of the methods in response to a range scan of a toy bike.

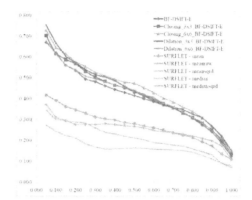

Figure 5: Precision-recall curves.

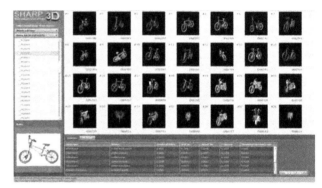

Figure 6: A sample shot from the web-based interface. The query is the range scan of a toy bike.

## 6.3 Non-rigid 3D Shape Retrieval Contest

The aim of this Contest was to evaluate and compare the effectiveness of different methods run on a non-rigid 3D shape benchmark consisting of 200 watertight triangular meshes. Three groups participated. The database used in this track consists of 200 watertight 3D triangular meshes, which are selected from the McGill Articulated [3] Shape Benchmark database.

### 6.3.1 Results

We present the results of the three groups that submitted six results. Figure 7 displays the Precision-recall curves to show retrieval performance of all six methods evaluated on the whole database. We also show the results using a web interface which displays the retrieved models for all objects and methods, to analyze the results as shown in Figure 8.

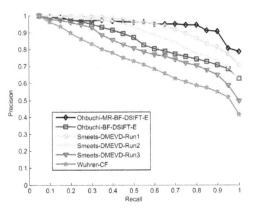

Figure 7: Precision-recall curves of all runs evaluated for the whole database.

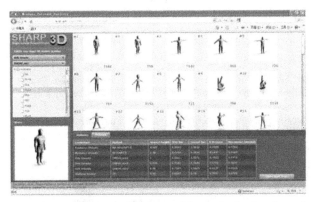

Figure 8. Retrieval example of one of the method using the web interface of the SHREC non-rigid track.

## 7. CONCLUSION

In this paper, we discussed some of the current 3D shape retrieval benchmarking efforts by our group and others and described the various steps involved in developing a benchmark. Then we reviewed the performance evaluation measures that are developed and used by researchers in the 3D shape retrieval community. We also gave an overview of the 3D shape retrieval contests (SHREC) run under the EuroGraphics Workshop on 3D Object Retrieval. Finally, we showed some of the results based on the NIST Shape benchmark and the different shape retrieval contest tracks we organized for SHREC 2010.

## 8. ACKNOWLEDGMENTS

This work has been supported by the SIMA and the IDUS program.

## 9. REFERENCES

[1] Shilane, P., Min, P., Kazhdan, M., Funkhouser, T. 2004. The Princeton shape benchmark *Proceedings of the Shape Modeling International*, 167–178.

[2] Iyer, N., Jayanti, S., Lou, K., Kalyanaraman, Y., Ramani, K. 2006. Developing an engineering shape benchmark for cad models. *Computer-Aided Design 38(9)*, 939–953.

[3] Zhang, J., Siddiqi, K., Macrini, D., Shokouf, A., Dickinson, S. 2005. Retrieving articulated 3-d models using medial surfaces and their graph spectra. *International Workshop On Energy Minimization*

[4] [SHREC, SHREC06, SHREC07, SHREC08,SHREC09] http://www.aimatshape.net/event/SHREC

[5] http://trec.nist.gov/

[6] Fang, R., Godil, A., Li, X., Wagan, A. 2008. A new shape benchmark for 3D object retrieval. *Proceedings of the 4th International Symposium on Visual Computing*, 5358 Lecture Notes in Computer Science, 381–392, Las Vegas, Nev, USA.

[7] Vanamali, T.P., Godil, A., Dutagaci, H., Furuya, T., Lian, Z., Ohbuchi, R. 2010. SHREC'10 Track: Generic 3D Warehouse. *Proceedings of the Eurographics/ACM SIGGRAPH Symposium on 3D Object Retrieval..*

[8] Dutagaci, H., A. Godil, A., Cheung, C.P., Furuya, T., Hillenbrand, U., Ohbuchi, R., 2010SHREC'10 Track: Range Scan Retrieval *Proceedings of the Eurographics/ACM SIGGRAPH Symposium on 3D Object Retrieval.*

[9] Lian, Z., Godil, A., Fabry, T., Furuya, T., Hermans, J., Ohbuchi, R., Shu, C., Smeets, D., Suetens, P., Vandermeulen, D., Wuhrer, S., 2010. SHREC'10 Track: Non-rigid 3D Shape Retrieval in *Proceedings of the Eurographics/ACM SIGGRAPH Symposium on 3D Object Retrieval.*

[10] Tangelder, J.W., Veltkamp, R.C., A survey of content based 3D shape retrieval methods 2008. *Multimedia Tools and Applications*,39, no. 3, 441–471.

[11] http://eureka.vu.edu.au/~grubinger/IAPR/TC12 Benchmark.html

[12] Jones, S., Van Rijsbergen, C.J. 1976. Information retrieval test collections. *Journal of Documentation* 32, 59–75.

[13] Leung, C. 2000. Benchmarking for content-based visual information search. LAURINI, R. (ed.) *Visual LNCS* 1929,442–456. Springer, Heidelberg.

[14] http://www.eecs.berkeley.edu/Research/Projects/CS/vision/grouping/segbench/

[15] Salton, G., McGill, M.J. 1983. Introduction to Modern Information Retrieval. McGraw Hill Book Co., New York

[16] Jarvelin, K., Kekalainen, J. IR evaluation methods for retrieving highly relevant documents. 2000. *Proceedings of the 23rd annual international ACM SIGIR conference on Research and development in information retrieval.* 41–48.

[17] Voorhees, E.M., Buckley, C. 2002. The effect of topic set size on retrieval experiment error. *Proceedings of the 25th annual international ACM SIGIR conference on Research and development in information retrieval.* 316–323.

[18] Leung, C. 2000. *Benchmarking for content-based visual information search.* LAURINI, R. Visual 2000, LNCS 1929, 442–456. Springer, Heidelberg.

[19] http://sketchup.google.com/3dwarehouse/

# Industrial Robots in Warehousing and Distribution Operations

Don Faulkner and Sean Murphy

FANUC Robotics America, Inc.

3900 W. Hamlin Road

Rochester Hills, Michigan 48309

(248) 377-7542 and 609-737-1445

don.faulkner@fanucrobotics.com and sean.murphy@fanucrobotics.com

**ABSTRACT**: Due to the proliferation of the number of SKU's in the warehousing and distribution markets and the need for efficient "direct-to-store" palletizing, the integration of new robotic applications in these market niches is becoming a necessity. This paper will explore the advancements in robotics and applying robotic technologies based on the new demands faced by these markets.

## Categories and Subject Descriptors:

I.2.9 Robotics: Commercial robots and applications

**Keywords:** Robots, Robotic, Palletizing, Mixed Item Palletizing (MIP), Mixed Case Palletizing (MCP), Mixed Load Palletizing (MLP), Random Order Palletizing (ROP), Layer Palletizing, Simulation, SKU, Direct-To-Store, Built-to-Order

## 1.  INTRODUCTION

The warehousing and distribution industry is facing new challenges due to the increasing number of SKU's coupled with the need to provide more "direct-to-store" pallets. This need is causing disruption in an industry where product handling, depalletizing, and palletizing are typically done manually. Having a large number of SKU's and having to supply "direct-to-store" pallets requires an increase in labor, an increase in the quality of the labor, and is a physically demanding job. These new requirements also cause the distributor increased costs due to product damage and fines/penalties in shipping inaccuracies. To combat this, applying robots to key functions in the warehouse and distribution centers is needed… and the time is here and now!

FANUC Robotics has successfully implemented robotic depalletizing and palletizing systems since 1982. Traditionally, these palletizing/depalletizing robots have been used in the food and consumer goods manufacturing arena for *homogenous* palletizing applications, such as building a pallet at the end of a production line with only one type of product on the pallet.    But the warehousing & distribution arena often involves built-to-order custom pallets mixed with multiple SKU's, potentially of widely varying sizes and exterior packaging materials.   One major challenge to

automating this process with a robot is mimicking the high-level decision process that human operators make with each placement of an item on the load, as they carefully fit each one to achieve the highest shipping density combined with pallet load stability and minimal product damage. Another significant challenge is emulating the broad range of adjustability inherent in a pair of human hands. In the past 10 years, great strides in development of intelligent robots, software and tooling have been made to enable robots to meet the needs of the warehousing and distribution market  for building these *mixed* unit load pallets  FANUC Robotics has focused our developments for the warehousing arena on the Receiving/Replenishment and Order Fulfillment/Shipping areas. These are prime target areas where robots can provide a considerable benefit.

In the Receiving/Replenishment areas of a warehouse, robotic layer handling is employed to breakdown homogeneous pallets and either build mixed layer pallets (to go to shipping and be sent directly to stores) or to place a layer of product to a singulator to transport individual items to storage (for subsequent delivery to a palletizing operation in Order Replenishment / Shipping). In the Order Replenishment /Shipping areas, the robots palletize "direct-to-store" pallets, usually involving Mixed Item Palletizing (MIP). Building a "direct-to-store" pallet normally consists of multiple SKU's on a pallet, and potentially, orders for multiple stores on the same pallet. Note that Mixed Item Palletizing (MIP) is a generic naming convention. This type of application is often times referred to as Mixed Case Palletizing (MCP), Mixed Load Palletizing (MLP), and Random Order Palletizing (ROP). Beware that there may be subtle differences, so you will need to investigate the user requirements and the available application solutions on the market to ensure you have what you need.

Layer handling is a straightforward process and a relatively simple application for an industrial robot. It involves a robot equipped with layer handling tooling to accommodate the various products to be handled. Simplified robot programming enables the robot to either build mixed layer pallets or place a layer to a singulator. The mixed item palletizing operation to create "direct-to-store" pallets is considerably more complex, but is the largest robotic opportunity for overcoming the problems facing the industry... to eliminate the notoriously bad ergonomic issues of manual palletizing, reduce product damage, and improve order accuracy.

## 2. WHAT IS A GOOD PALLET?

Before we discuss robotic mixed item palletizing and the associated state-of-the-art technology, we need to define a "good" pallet. In our investigation of warehousing requirements, a good "direct-to-store" pallet has the following attributes:

- Uses the Full Available Height
  - o Maximizes the allowable height for end-user store requirements and shipping.
- Very Dense
  - o Maximizes the Pallet Footprint
  - o Minimizes Air Gap
- Has the Correct Sequence
  - o Reverse Stop/Drop sequencing may be required
    - Involves Mixing Multiple Orders on a Single Pallet
    - Palletizes orders on a "first on - last off" basis
    - Designed to reduce the amount of work that the delivery person has to do.
    - Challenges most algorithms, making it more difficult to hit high density targets.

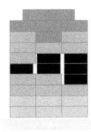

  - o If no pre-defined sequence... Maximizes Density
- Is Conveyable!
  - o Stable enough to survive the Conveyance System (normally to a stretch-wrapper) after the build operation.

These attributes must be weighted and prioritized according to:

1) the industry targeted (beverage, grocery, consumer products, etc),
2) the product being handled (cases, shrink-wrapped bundles, etc...), and
3) the transport system after the pallet build operation... oftentimes, direct fork truck handling.

Specific characteristics of the industry, product, and transport system will determine the correct combination and order of the build attributes in order for a successful system. One of the largest factors is conveyability.

## 3. WHAT MAKES A PALLET CONVEYABLE?

Simply put, a pallet of product must have the ability to withstand the forces applied to it when it moves. This movement may be via a transport system (i.e., conveyor) to a stretch-wrapper or via a fork truck either to a stretch-wrapper or directly to a truck. In building a pallet, a mixed item palletizing (MIP) algorithm must take into account forces due to acceleration and deceleration of the pallet. The three basic pallet building principals are

- Product Mass
- Center of Gravity
- Supported Base

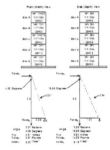

MIP algorithms must analyze the pallet build and take these principles into consideration. The algorithm must be flexible enough to modify the build pattern to maximize the pallet build attributes desired. The MIP algorithm considers the stability of the resultant stack prior to placing each and every item. If stability of the pallet is deemed lower than the configured minimum, no other items are stacked on the pallet and a request is sent for a new pallet.

Many integrators are creative in their approaches to optimize the entire system and allow for higher pallet builds... but caution must be taken to ensure that pallets built for optimal height and density do not sacrifice the overall stability and make the load impossible to transport. In addition, end user requirements must be considered. For example, when a built-to-order pallet arrives at a store and the stretchwrap is cut away: will the built pallet collapse and items fall to the floor? This could be a showstopper, but potentially could be avoided if stability is taken into account while the pallet is being built.

# 4. MIXED ITEM PALLETIZING OPERATIONAL MODES

Automating the Mixed Item Palletizing (MIP) operation is the "holy grail" of warehousing and distribution centers; this is the area that has the largest labor costs, greatest potential for product damage and where order inaccuracies from manual labor are most prevalent. This is where distributors will get the biggest bang for the buck by automating with robots!

MIP automation demands an understanding of two fundamental operational modes that can be implemented. The two operational modes are:

- Preplanned
- Real-Time

In a preplanned mode, customer order data is analyzed well before the order is processed. The various SKU items in the order (perhaps multiple orders) are then picked, sequenced and delivered to the robot based on the results of the preplanning algorithm that defines optimal pallet build solutions. MIP workcell(s) then palletize the variety of SKU items in the customer order(s). Note that an MIP workcell is an island of automation usually consisting of a robot with its end-of-arm-tooling to handle the product, safety fencing surrounding the robot area, infeed conveyors (bringing in product), and outfeed conveyors (sending out mixed item pallet builds).

There are many algorithms on the market that can preplan for manual operations. For robotic building, the list of available algorithms is shorter since the preplanned build must consider the robot's capabilities in terms of reach, robot tooling, and ability to place the product on the pallet when considering limitations of neighboring products and peripheral obstructions. All of these aspects must be considered by a preplanning algorithm to have a successful operation.

The Real-Time mode is where the MIP workcell(s) must determine the best location on a pallet for a variety of SKU items at the moment they are delivered to the robot. While doing this operation in Real-Time, the algorithm must also consider the robot's capabilities in terms of reach, robot tooling, and ability to place the product on the pallet when considering limitations of neighboring products and peripheral obstructions This Real-Time mode is often referred to as a Random Order mode.

# 5. WHAT COMPRISES A MIXED ITEM PALLETIZING WORKCELL?

As mentioned earlier, the robotic workcell is an island of automation with an infeed conveyor (for product coming into the workcell) and an outfeed conveyor (for built mixed case pallets). There are three critical components of the workcell that must be carefully selected:

- Robots
- End-Of-Arm Tooling (EOAT)
- Software

The robots handle the products to the build pallet. The robots can be "stand-alone" robots or they can be mounted on robot transport units (RTU) and move between build pallets to allow for multiple build positions.

The EOAT's handle products of different sizes, shapes and textures. The EOAT's must be extremely reliable and able to pick a wide variety of SKU's. They must also impose minimal restrictions on MIP algorithm(s)... tooling restrictions will limit pallet build options and compromise the quality of the finished load.

The software is the brain of the operation: it determines the best pallet build scenario and directs the robot, with its EOAT, to place each product to the proper location on the pallet. The software must be able to build dense and stable pallets. In the real world, the software must also be intelligent to handle events that go wrong. For example, in a preplanned mode when product arrives at the robot out of sequence, the software must be able to handle the "Broken Play" by determining what has gone wrong and how best to continue placing product on the pallet. FANUC Robotics' Mixed Case Palletizing (MCP) Software Suite has the capability to switch automatically between a Preplanned mode and a Real-Time mode. Without this capability, manual labor must intervene to complete the build, leaving the door open for product damage and order inaccuracies.

# 6. MIXED ITEM PALLETIZING SOFTWARE

FANUC Robotics offers a Mixed Case Palletizing (MCP) Software Suite that provides for a Preplanned mode (whether it is a FANUC Preplanned algorithm or a 3rd-party algorithm) and for a Real-Time Mode. There are many features of the software suite that are needed for any MIP application:

- Ability to handle multiple Preplanning algorithms: choose the best algorithm for your application. Beverage, grocery, and general merchandise are three different industries where the pallet build attributes are different and may require a different preplanning algorithm to provide for the best MIP pallet build. Note that if your SKU content (aka, size variation) is small, a preplanning algorithm may not be needed.

- Ability to control the functions of the robot and its tooling: the tooling needs to be flexible to accommodate the wide variety of products; therefore, the software must be able to control the many functions of the tooling that may be needed to do this. This may include control of servo-motion tooling that optimizes the size of the tooling for the appropriate size of the item to be handled, thus reducing pallet build time and increasing handling reliability (squeeze to a size and force).
- Ability to interface to the robot's surroundings.
- Ability to monitor (Monitor Function) and report (Reporting Function) what is being built and what has been built in order to track and verify order accuracy

These are the run-time aspects of the software, but there are other operational aspects needed to predict if a pallet can be built optimally for an order: ... Virtual Pallet Build and Robot Simulation.

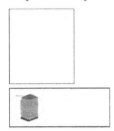

Virtual pallet processing determines the viability of the pallet build *before* product is sent to the MIP workcell and provides historical information *after* a pallet has been built, such as:

- Order Distributions
- Density Distributions
- Height Distributions
- Number of pallets
- Palletizing results at various pallet heights
- Results for actual customer orders
- Analysis for any day

Virtual robotic palletizing with FANUC Robotics' ROBOGUIDE® simulation software determines if a pallet can be built. The simulation automatically generates the product sizes graphically and presents them to a virtual robotic workcell where the robot (with the appropriate EOAT) handles the product in the virtual world. The virtual simulation enables the robot to verify the sequences: from the product pick up, to the approach points, to the place points, to the away points, and finally back to the perch point ready for the next product. In doing all of this, the ROBOGUIDE® virtual simulation analyzes the robot's reach and motion to ensure that the pallet can be physically built.

## 7. MIXED ITEM PALLETIZING SOFTWARE VERSATILITY

In using a Preplanned operational mode, the product must arrive at the robotic workcell in the sequence needed to optimally build a pallet. In the real world... the best laid plans go astray... the products get out of sequence! The question arises: what do you do?

Most operations are forced to go to a manual mode and stack the products by hand. This can be done by having a smart MIP software package that is virtually stacking the pallet and can print out a pictorial (with product item list) of what has been palletized and what remains to be palletized. FANUC Robotics has this feature built into its MCP Software Suite (it also indicates what was stacked automatically and what needs to be stacked manually). Additionally, our MCP Software Suite also incorporates a special feature called the "Broken Play" option. FANUC Robotics' Real-Time algorithm is how to handle the "Broken Play", by automatically taking control and palletizing whatever is presented to the robot to the best available position on the pallet! This "Broken Play" option is unique to FANUC Robotics' MCP Software Suite and will help increase uptime, reduce product damage and order inaccuracies since the human element is not introduced.

Schematically, the FANUC Robotics' MCP Software Suite operates as shown in the following flowchart:

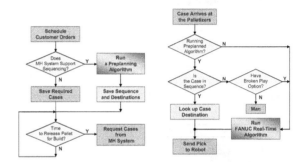

How does the patented MCP Real-Time algorithm work?

- Evaluates a series of prioritized RULES to select and place each case
- Each RULE covers a special condition (full layer, full region, adjacent height, stability, supported area, interlocking, combined similar product, combined space, etc.).
- Remembers previous rule if appropriate (full layer will remember chosen pattern)
- Provides configurable process parameters (which rules to use, pallet size, ...)
- Last rule is BEST SCORE
  - Evaluates each case available against every potential position on the pallet
  - Uses 20 different evaluations: Supported area, stability, size, adjacent height, etc.
  - Each evaluation is weighted or factored differently
  - Factors stability and supported area
  - Highest Score WINS!

# 8. HOW TO CHOOSE WHAT MIXED ITEM PALLETIZING SOFTWARE AND OPERATIONAL MODE IS RIGHT FOR YOU?

Understanding your product mix and typical customer orders is important in determining the best solution for your operation. Pallet Optimization software suppliers and Mixed Item Palletizing suppliers can evaluate your product master list (SKU#, size, weight, etc...) and order data (orders for a peak and average day... consisting of order number, SKU #, quantity per SKU, etc...). These customer-specific attributes will allow these companies to determine their best algorithm to use and validate what operational mode you need. If product mix is low (physical size), the Real-Time algorithm may be your best choice, since its price and complexity are low. If your product mix is high (large physical size variations), the Preplanned algorithm with "Broken Play" may be the answer, but the associated costs and system complexity increase.

The Comparison Matrix below will give you a guide in the choices on the market. The matrix also illustrates key pallet build requirements you may have versus cost and complexity.

| Mixed Case Palletizing Comparison Matrix | | | | | |
|---|---|---|---|---|---|
| Item | Parameter | Real-Time Algorithm | | Preplanned Algorithm | |
| | | Standalone | Buffers | Standalone | Broken Play |
| Features | Delivery Method | Random | Random | Sequenced | Sequenced or Random |
| | Pick Locations | Single | Multiple | Single | Single or Multiple |
| | Delivery Issues[1] | Auto Recovery | Auto Recovery | Manual Recovery | Auto Recovery |
| Pallet | Height[2] | High | Higher | Highest | Highest |
| | Density[2] | Dense | More Dense | Most Dense | Most Dense |
| | Stability[2] | Stable | More Stable | Most Stable | Most Stable |
| System | Price | Low Cost $$ | Moderate Cost $$$ | Expensive $$$$$ | Expensive $$$$$ |
| | Complexity | Easiest to integrate | Moderate Integration | Most Difficult | Most Difficult |

1. Delivery Issues include: Damaged, Missing or out of Sequence cases
2. Pallet quality is a function of the operating mode and product characteristics

FANUC Robotics' MCP Suite is SCALEABLE to meet various production requirements and budgets

# 9. SUMMARY

Warehousing and distribution centers are facing ever increasing customer demands for higher product mix, higher variety of products for each order, multiple store orders on the same pallet, aisle rules, and an unforgiving demand for accurate orders. To face this challenge, automating the warehouse and the use of robotic applications at key points in the warehouse are a necessity... now more than ever!

You are not alone... all warehousing and distribution centers are facing the same battles. The first companies to automate will be able to overcome the ever increasing costs associated with high labor content, an inconsistent labor pool, product damage, order inaccuracies, theft/security, and increased employee injuries.

In the past, there were very few choices for automation and greater limitations regarding which warehouse operations could be automated. The advancement in intelligent robotics has broken the barrier, making it affordable now. The choices, once limited, are now wide and far-reaching. At FANUC Robotics, we have developed software and hardware tools to enable customers and system integrators to tackle this formidable task. The MCP Software suite, available through FANUC Robotics, can allow you to choose the best robot, the best algorithm to meet your needs (either FANUC Robotics' algorithm or a 3rd-party algorithm), and the best End Of Arm Tooling to allow you to build mixed item pallets reliably.

Field-proven Mixed Item Palletizing solutions are now available:

- Real time: smaller investment, good performance
- Preplanned: larger investment, better performance
- Preplanned + Real time = optimal solution --- Only available through FANUC Robotics

The warehouse/logistics market presents a significant new opportunity to software and hardware suppliers, so the costs and complexity will decrease over the next few years making affordability more enticing. The United States has started adding robots to warehousing and distribution centers only within the last 10 years (but concentrating implementation in only the last 3-5 years)... Mixed Item Palletizing is the "Holy Grail". However, US industry is beginning to implement mixed item palletizing at an increasing rate!

# 10. REFERENCES

[1] D. DeMotte, M. Poma, and A. Monique. United States Patent: AUTOMATED PALLETIZING CASES HAVING MIXED SIZES AND SHAPES, US Patent # US 7,266,422 B1, 2007.

# Planning in Logistics: A survey

Pushkar Kolhe
Georgia Institute of Technology
pushkar@cc.gatech.edu

Henrik Christensen
Georgia Institute of Technology
hic@cc.gatech.edu

## ABSTRACT

Planning is an essential part of any logistics system. The paper tries to generalize the view of a logistics planner by framing it as a knapsack problem. We show how the various variants of the knapsack problem compare for different types of industries. We also introduce the pallet stacking problem and survey some of the recent advances made towards this problem.

## Keywords

Planning, Logistics, Bin Packing Problem, Warehouse Management

## 1. INTRODUCTION

Logistics integrates all the operations in an industry. It is a planning system that is supposed to model, analyze and optimize the entire supply chain. Naturally improving the logistics is a key step in industrial automation. Despite significant progress in improving efficiency in pick and place robots, there exists many important problems and much room for improvement. At present many solutions are designed for a particular manufacturer or have many assumptions. The article attempts to bridge the gap between current research and real world problems in logistics. We provide a general overview of the problem and give an introduction to some of the most basic techniques used to solve these problems.

Consider the special cases of a shipping industry or a automated storage and retrieval system where the goal is to improve throughput of the system under some constraints. This can be formulated as a constraint problem, specifically the knapsack problem (KP). We show that logistics operations can be studied theoretically and their performance can be guaranteed by a theoretical upper bound. It is possible the most optimal performance that the system can achieve. If an industry successfully models its logistics as a KP constraint problem, then it is possible to determine the worst case performance of their planner when it is compared to

an optimal planner. New research tools from combinatorics can be used for improving a logistics planner.

We also consider the pallet stacking problem and show some of the recent advancement made in this field. We then list some open problems in logistics from our view point that can be improved solely by providing a good theoretical context to logistics.

## 2. HISTORICAL OVERVIEW

Most recent work in warehouse management systems has focused on satisfying needs of a particular industry. However there has been less work in improving logistics planners. On the other hand the pallet stacking problem, which is closely related to the bin packing problem, has made great advances in the field of combinatorics. It is a well known fact that mixed palletizing is NP-hard, but there are many polynomial and pseudo-polynomial planners which can give an approximate solution which can have a lower bound on its optimality. [31] gives a good overview of the mixed palletizing problem and proves that it is indeed a variant of the KP problem. There is also some work in optimizing robot motion to improve performance of mixed palletizing systems. For example, [28] shows how robot movements can be minimized while packing a pallet. There has also been significant development of software tools to solve this problem. [18] provides an overview of the combinatorial knapsack problem with a few examples for solving the palletizing problem.

The paper is divided into three parts. Section 3 shows how an entire warehouse management process can be formulated mathematically as a knapsack problem. We show how various variants of the knapsack problem can represent logistics for different types of industries. Section 4 introduces some of the most common knapsack problem solving techniques. Section 5 is dedicated to the pallet stacking problem where we show some of the most common techniques used for solving such kind of problems. We refer to a comprehensive list of references as we introduce new concepts.

## 3. LOGISTICS

Logistics is a key part of a warehouse management system. A logistics problem can be framed as a decision problem can be represented numerically as profit, loss or weight, cost value. This has two main advantages: 1. The entire warehouse management system can be framed mathematically and 2. Different approaches can be compared with respect to some benchmarks. Many other industrial problems can be formulated as knapsack problems: cargo loading, cutting stock, project selection and budget control.

Consider the simple example of managing logistics for a shipping industry. Packages are usually shipped through cargo trucks or planes. Every package has a certain weight but the cargo vehicle has a fixed capacity. The cost of sending a package usually does not depend on the weight, since dispatchers get paid on a contract. The dispatchers, therefore, try to maximize their profit by packing efficiently and shipping the maximum weight in a fixed volume. Such a problem can be framed as a optimization problem.

## 3.1 The Knapsack Problem

We can formulate the above logistics problem as a knapsack problem (KP). Consider a knapsack with item set $N$, consisting on $n$ items, where the $j_{th}$ item has profit $p_j$ and weight $w_j$, and the capacity is $c$. Then, the objective function can be formulated as:

$$\max \sum_{j=1}^{n} p_j x_j \qquad (1)$$

subject to

$$\max \sum_{j=1}^{n} w_j x_j \leq c \qquad (2)$$

$$x_j \in \{0, 1\}, \; j = 1, \ldots, n. \qquad (3)$$

In equation (2), $x_j$ can only take integral values and it denotes whether the $j_{th}$ item is included in the knapsack or not. Finding the optimum solution vector $x^*$ having an optimum profit $z^*$ is non-trivial and known to be NP-hard.

However the logistics involved in shipping industries is not as simple as stated above. There can be several additional constraints. For example, a few packages might have to be delivered urgently and so packages also have a priority associated with them. Some packages have to be delivered within a particular time window and some package has exceptionally low weight, but high volume. Because of constraints like these, the definition of profit in equation (1) can change. This leads to many variations in the above problem.

In the above example, if optimal number of packages are transported by shipping the maximum possible weight in a given volume then $p_j = w_j$ in equation (1). This is called the **subset sum problem**. Solutions of the subset problems can be used for designing better lower bounds for scheduling problems [12].

Frequently, a large number of the boxes that are shipped have the same size and weight. To reduce the size of the knapsack problem, $x_j$ can be used to represent a class of boxes rather than a single box. If there are $b_j$ boxes of a class $j$, then equation (3) becomes:

$$0 \leq x_j \leq b_j, j = 1, \ldots, n. \qquad (4)$$

This problem is then called the **bounded knapsack problem**. If $b_j$ is large or unknown, then it is called the **unbounded knapsack problem**.

If you take into account the shipping example again and consider that the boxes have weight as well as volume and both have a maximum bound, then equation (2) should change. After generalizing the problem to include additional constraints we get a **d-dimensional knapsack problem**. We can rewrite equation (2) as:

$$\max \sum_{j=1}^{n} w_{ij} x_j \leq c_i, \; i = 1, \ldots, n. \qquad (5)$$

The knapsack problem given by equations (2), (4) and (5) constitute the most generic of the mixed palletizing problems. In theoretical computer science, this problem is also referred to as the **3D bin packing problem**. If the mixed palletizer has to generate rainbow pallets, then equation (1) will be modified to reflect choice of at least two types of boxes together. This will yield the **quadratic knapsack problem** as:

$$\max \sum_{i,j=1}^{n} p_{ij} x_i x_j \qquad (6)$$

## 3.2 More variants of KP

Consider the generic example of mixed palletizing we formulated in equations (2), (4) and (5). These equations can be further extended as variations of KP to represent entire logistics operations. For example, a shipping industry usually has several cargo vehicles making daily trips between popular locations. In that case the dispatcher has to decide if a particular package goes on a particular trip or the next one. If there are $n$ items on the list of transportation requests and $m$ trips available on a route, we use $nm$ binary variables $x_{ij}$ for representing if a particular item goes on the $m^{th}$ trip.

The mathematical programming formulation of such a problem is called as the **multiple knapsack problem** and is given by:

$$\max \sum_{i=1}^{m} \sum_{j=1}^{n} p_j x_{ij} \qquad (7)$$

subject to

$$\sum_{j=1}^{n} w_j x_{ij} \leq c_i, \; i = 1, \ldots, m, \qquad (8)$$

$$\sum_{i=1}^{m} x_{ij} \leq 1, \; j = 1, \ldots, n, \qquad (9)$$

$$x_{ij} \in \{0, 1\}, \; i, \; j = 1, \ldots, n. \qquad (10)$$

Consider an example of an automated storage retrieval system. In such a system if the items were evenly distributed throughout the warehouse, they could be retrieved efficiently. Each pallet can store only one variant of each type of item, so that the overall utility value is maximized without exceeding the capacity constraint. This problem can be expressed as the following multiple-choice knapsack problem. Using the decision variable $x_{ij}$ to denote whether variant $j$ was chosen from the set $N_i$, the following model appears:

$$\max \sum_{i=1}^{m} \sum_{j \in N_i} p_{ij} x_{ij} \qquad (11)$$

subject to

$$\sum_{i=1}^{m} \sum_{j \in N_i} w_{ij} x_{ij} \leq c, \qquad (12)$$

$$\sum_{j \in N_i} = 1, \ i = 1, \ldots, m, \qquad (13)$$

$$x_{ij} \in \{0,1\}, \ i = 1, \ldots, m, \ j \in N_i. \qquad (14)$$

Evaluating the efficiency of a warehouse system is an important factor in logistics. There are at least two ways in which we can measure the efficiency of a logistics scheme. Firstly, we can look at the output of the supply chain. For a shipping industry these may be factors like number of packages shipped, packages arriving late, wrongly delivered packages. These factors describe the quantity and quality of the items coming through the supply chain. Secondly, we can look at the planning algorithm and determine the efficiency of the logistics planner. Comparing the planner means comparing the algorithm that solves the effective knapsack problem which the logistics operation represents. Many such techniques are described in [18] and [25].

### 3.3 Comparing Algorithms

Algorithms that solve the knapsack problem are not similar. Algorithms that find the most optimum solution often do so by doing a exhaustive search. They are computationally very inefficient when compared to approximate algorithms which are computationally far more efficient. However, approximate algorithms have the drawback that they can only find a near optimum solution. It is also important to note the complexity for each algorithm. Simple algorithms which are easy to implement are desired. However, performance can be improved by adding appropriate complexity, for example, storing items in a tree instead of a list improves running time.

Algorithms that solve NP-hard problems can be divided into two parts: **exact algorithms** and **approximate algorithms**. Exact algorithms find the most optimal solution of a given problem whereas approximate algorithms find an approximate solution. Usually, approximate algorithms are faster because they only find a near optimal solution. Because of this, running time becomes an important criteria in comparing exact algorithms while approximate algorithms can be compared by finding out how close they come to the most optimal solution.

It is not always possible to do an exhaustive search over a problem space. Algorithms are usually run over several data sets and their performance is determined analytically. One of the most common way to check is to compare running time of the algorithm after the data set is doubled. The time required to find the solution should not increase exponentially for polynomial or pseudo polynomial algorithms.

The most common way to measure the performance of an algorithm is to perform the worst-case analysis. It is denoted by the big-Oh notation as described in [5]. The most efficient algorithms have a polynomial running time bounded by $O(n)$, $O(n \log n)$, $O(n^k)$. Pseudo-polynomial algorithms have running time bounded by $O(nc)$ which is better than $O(2^n)$ or $O(3^n)$ for non-polynomial algorithms [18].

### 3.4 Designing the KP problem

It is not obvious how a logistics problem can be formulated

as a KP problem. Answering this question involves further research into studying and understanding industry specific parameters. The problem is to design the profit, that is (1), and weight constraints, that is (2), for a logistics problem.

Profit depends on several factors. In a shipping industry it will depend on the throughput, that is number of shipments per hour, the correctness of the delivery and the total number of cargo vehicles used. The relationship between profit and all these factors is non-linear, in the sense that they depend on each other or improving throughput comes through compromising the number of vehicles used. Similar problems arise when designing the relationship between maximum capacity and actual industrial constraints.

However, the simplest way to formulate the problem is to simply formulate profit or capacity as a linear combination of all the parameters that influence profit and capacity. The weights used will decided by the industry depending upon their specific needs and requirements. Similarly a system of equations can be formulated for a warehouse. The main idea is to formulate the logistics in such a way that it can tell us back what are the specific operations that can be compromised upon and still performing near the optimum.

## 4. LOGISTICS PLANNERS

As we have seen in Section 3.2 a logistics system can be expressed as a Knapsack problem. This gives us many insights into logistics. There are lower bounds available from theoretical computer science, which give a theoretical indication that the running time of an exact algorithm for (KP) can not beat a certain threshold under reasonable assumptions on the model of computation. Many (KP) instances can be solved within reasonable time by exact solution methods. This fact is due to algorithms like primal-dual dynamic programming recursions, the concept of solving a core, and the separation of cover inequalities to tighten the formulation [18].

### 4.1 Basic Algorithms

The greedy algorithm is perhaps the most basic algorithm that can be used to solve the KP problem. We also explain the basic idea behind exact algorithms like branch and bound, dynamic programming and approximate algorithms like polynomial time approximate schemes (PTAS) and fully PTAS.

#### 4.1.1 The Greedy Algorithm

This is by far the most popular algorithm currently used to solve the bin packing problem. For every item, an efficiency factor is calculated as,

$$e_j := \frac{p_j}{w_j}. \qquad (15)$$

We want the first bin to have the maximum profit to weight ratio. All items are arranged in a descending order based on its efficiency factor. Items are selected to be in the knapsack in this order until equation (2) is not violated.

The Greedy solution is arbitrarily bad as compared to the optimal solution, but it can yield at least a 0.5 of the optimal solution [18].

#### 4.1.2 Branch and Bound

The general idea of the branch and bound technique is to intelligently enumerate the entire solution space and pick the best solution. It basically consists for two fundamental principles: *branching* and *bounding*. In the branching part, the solution space is divided and the optimum solution is found locally. In the bounding part, the algorithm derives upper and lower bounds of the solution space. The upper bound is found trivially in $O(n)$ by relaxing the KP integral constraint given in equation (3). Thus, $0 \leq x_j \leq 1$. The upper bound is used to prune parts of solution space whose optimum value is less than this value. The lower bound is the most optimum solution if no other local solution space has a greater lower bound.

To make the search process more efficient, the entire solution space can be divided so that it forms a tree structure. This way the search for the most optimum value can be done with a recursive depth-first or breadth-first search.

### 4.1.3 Dynamic Programming

Instead of optimizing the knapsack problem over all items, dynamic programming only optimizes the knapsack for a small subset of items. Then it adds an item iteratively to the problem and the solution. (KP) has the property of an optimal substructure, that is, if $x^*$ is an optimum solution of a knapsack with capacity $c$, then $x^* - j$ is an optimum solution of a knapsack with capacity $c - w_j$. KP has the property of an *optimal substructure* as described in [5].

A simple dynamic programming approach to solve this problem would involve using the *Bellman recursion*. Consider $l$ items which are a subset of the original $j$ items. We formally solve the KP problem for $l$ items and a knapsack capacity of $d \leq c$. The optimal solution at this point is given by $z_{j-1}(d)$. For a new item $j$, if $d \geq w_j$ and $z_{j-1}(d - w_j) > z_{j-1}(d)$, then it is added into the knapsack.

### 4.1.4 Polynomial Time Approximation Schemes (PTAS)

Algorithms that solve the knapsack problem either compromise on running time to get an optimal solution or run in pseudo-polynomial time to get an approximate solution. PTAS algorithms are also more formally known as the $\varepsilon$-*approximation scheme*. $\varepsilon$ will determine how close the solution is to the optimal solution. Running time will increase if a solution near the optimal is desired.

These algorithms have the basic idea of guessing a certain set of items included in the optimal solution by going through all the possible candidate sets and then filling the remaining capacity in a greedy way [18]. In a simple scheme, the Greedy algorithm can be extended so that a subset of item are compared before inserting them in the bin. Item with maximum efficiency factor given by equation (15) within the subset is selected. The size of the subset determines the running time of this algorithm. The classical PTAS in [27] requires $O(n^{\frac{1}{\varepsilon}})$ time. The CKPP algorithm given in [4] had an improved runtime over the one in [4]. They explored the monotonicity of the arranged items for the Greedy algorithm to create subsets. This reduced their search space and time. The running time for their algorithm is $O(n^{\frac{1}{\varepsilon}-2})$ for $\varepsilon < \frac{1}{3}$.

### 4.1.5 Fully Polynomial Time Approximation Schemes (FPTAS)

Dynamic programming techniques discussed in 4.1.3 can be modified so that they can run in polynomial time. The earliest FPTAS technique for KP was given in [15]. Later [21] and [16] introduced new partition techniques for partitioning the profit space which improved the FPTAS algorithm further. Some of the most recent work in improving

on these algorithms was done by [17, 16].

The basic idea behind the FPTAS technique is to scale the profits values or the weight values and then apply a dynamic programming technique. The optimal solution value of the scaled instance will always be at least as large as the scaled profits of the items of the original optimal solution [18]. Usually, the upper bound on the most optimal solution is found out using a Greedy method and the scaling factor is determined whose value determines the approximation of the solution. Most of the earlier solutions were impractical because they compromised memory to get better running time. However, some of the new techniques given in [17, 16] have a running time of approximately $O(n \log n \log \frac{1}{\varepsilon})$ and space complexity of $O(n + \frac{1}{\varepsilon^2})$.

## 4.2 All capacities problem

In several planning problem, the exact capacity is not known in advance, but it may be changed based on the proposed solutions. For example, carrying huge amounts of loads also increases transportation cost. There is obviously a non-linear relationship between actual profit and profit as defined by the KP problem. A natural way to overcome this problem is to calculate optimal solutions for each capacities including $c_{max} > c$ to find the most optimal solution. As we have stated earlier KP has the property of an optimal substructure [5]. The dynamic programming techniques exploit this property to solve the KP problem along with the all capacities problem.

## 5. 3D BIN PACKING PROBLEM

Packaging or storing is an integral part of many warehouse systems. Hence, many logistics planners are designed to optimize packing and storing of goods or items. As we have seen in Section 3.1, this problem can be represented as a variant of the knapsack problem. It is a well studied problem in literature. It is closely related to other three dimensional container loading problems: *Knapsack loading*, where the problem is to find a subset of items that will fit into a single bin; *Container Loading*, where the problem is to find a feasible arrangement of items in which the height of the bin filled is minimum and *Bin Packing*, where the items are packed into finite sized bins and the problem is to find the solution with the minimum number of bins.

To formulate orthogonal packaging or cutting constraints for packaging into the bin packing problem it has to be expressed as an integer programming problem, that is, condition (3) should hold. Many methods add constraints to this problem to get a structured pallet. Usually a pallet layer can be formulated as an integer programming problem and a feasible packing can be found. This is referred to as the cutting problem. There are two widely studied cutting problems: *guillotine* and *non-guillotine* cutting problems. Guillotine patterns refer to pattern that are cuttable. Most bin packing algorithms will have a two step process: one which selects the most profitable items to go in a bin followed by a feasibility check to see if these items can fit the bin.

Integer Programming formulations for packaging have been studied by [1, 13, 3]. Algorithms that solve the 2DKP using a branch and bound algorithm and then run a feasibility check which checks for overlaps for every new assignment are described in [9, 10, 8]. An enumeration technique for checking feasibility of an assignment is shown in [24]. Recent work in using advanced graphical technique to feasibility check an assignment called sequence triple is introduced in [7]. [6] is some earlier work that discusses some exact algorithms and heuristic techniques to solve the packaging problem.

## 5.1 Heuristics for the packing problem

The problem we consider in this section is that of selecting a subset of items and assigning coordinates $(x_j, y_j, z_j)$ to each item, such that no item goes outside the bin, no two items overlap and the total volume of the items does not exceed the maximum capacity. We assume that the origin of the coordinate system is in the left-bottom-back corner of the bin. We have the obvious constraints

$$0 \le x_i \le W - w_i,$$
$$0 \le y_i \le H - h_i,$$
$$0 \le z_i \le D - d_i.$$

To ensure that no two packed boxes $i$, $j$ overlap we will add more constraints

$$x_i + w_i \le x_j,$$
$$y_i + h_i \le y_j,$$
$$z_i + d_i \le z_j,$$
$$x_j + w_j \le x_i,$$
$$y_j + h_j \le y_i,$$
$$z_j + d_j \le z_i.$$

These ensure that the boxes $i$ and $j$ are packed and that they must be located on the left, right, up, down, above or below each other. In the packaging sense, these constraints are enough. Many methods that solve the bin packing problem [7, 22] use the above constraints. However, in practice there are many other issues that concern the stability of a bin or pallet. These can be added as additional constraints to the above integer programming problem. The stability of a pallet is more when it has a lower center of mass, the distribution of pressure and weight is even and there are interlocking boxes. Interlocking can be guaranteed by maximizing the surface area of a box that will touch other boxes. Many of these factors are application specific but the problem of assigning constraints to maximize stability of a pallet remains an open problem.

Heuristic techniques use statistics to determine the most optimal packaging. As the size of the problem increases, exact algorithms' runtime complexity increases exponentially. Here, heuristic solutions are very popular. [7, 29] use a heuristic simulated annealing procedure to pack boxes together. [22, 14] presents a good overview of heuristic techniques to solve the bin packing problem.

## 5.2 On-Line bin packing problem

Consider a bin packing example, where boxes are coming down a conveyor and a pick and place robot is arranging the boxes onto a pallet. In this scenario the data of the items and their number is unknown. As soon as the item is seen by the sensor the on-line planner has to decide whether to pack the item or discard it. In literature on-line algorithms are analyzed for their worst case when their solutions is compared with the optimal solution given by an exact algorithm with complete input data. This analysis is called the *competitive analysis* and it is widely studied and surveyed in [2,

11].

[18] provides a brief overview of this problem and some solutions. A programming compiler usually can optimize the program by modeling breaks in the program. This way it can avoid processor cache misses and improve efficiency of the processor. Similarly a KP algorithm can also create a stochastic model of the distribution of profit and weights of items. This can give rise to a simple on-line greedy algorithm. From the a-priori knowledge of the distribution one can determine a threshold for efficiency given by equation (15). The planner will pack all items that have efficiency more than this threshold. If the knowledge about distribution of profits and weights is known a lower bound can be determined on the performance on this algorithm as shown in [23].

### 5.2.1 Time Dependent On-Line bin packing problem

In this model the time dependence is explicitly taken into account. For example on a shipping yard, transportation requests are made randomly and they have to be accepted or rejected without delay. If they are accepted they consume a resource and gain some price, but if they are rejected then their is no resource lost but price is lost due to cost in storage space, customer goodwill etc.. [18]. These problems are formally known as *dynamic and stochastic knapsack problems* and they were extensively studied in [20, 26, 19].

In stochastic models discussed in the literature the requests arrive by a stochastic process, usually a Poisson process. The entire setup can be modeled as a Markov decision process. The time dependence does not allow us to compare performance of these algorithms with the classical knapsack problem. However, the achieved results contain general characterizations of optimal policy and optimal threshold policy for greedy algorithms. Some recursive algorithms in the context of freight transportation and scheduling in batch processes are discussed in [19]. A similar problem in the context of airline yield management problem is discussed in [30]. They also extend their work to include a stochastic version of the multidimensional knapsack problem (d-KP).

Recent work in designing algorithms for solving the palletizing problem on-line uses statistical methods. The idea behind these methods is very intuitive. In greedy methods items need to be arranged in the descending order of their efficiency and then they are added in the bin in order. In the on-line variation, statistical methods are used to predict the rank of an item around the last $n$ items based on previous observations. If the efficiency of an item is below the threshold efficiency it is discarded, otherwise it is added to the bin.

## 6. OPEN PROBLEMS

Many algorithms and techniques to solve logistics and mixed palletizing are industry specific. On of the advantages of providing a theoretical context is to generalize this problem and use a theoretical framework to improve logistics. However there are many open questions. As we discussed in section 3.4 every industry is different and converting their entire logistics into constraints that can be fed to a combinatorics problem is an open question. In the context of mixed palletizing the most important question remains of improving stability. There are very few solutions that also accommodate stability into their problem formulation.

## 7. CONCLUSIONS

We showed how the logistics planner can be formulated as the knapsack problem. We can use this to determine theoretical performance measure over a logistics system. We also introduced a 3D bin packing algorithm and provided a comprehensive reference to some of the latest work in combinatorics for solving it.

We have tried to generalize the common planning problem in industries so that they can be studied theoretically. Our future work will involve understanding and surveying various industries and grounding their logistics planner in combinatorics. We also think that if the gap between industrial logistics and theoretical computer science research were closed, we can widely improve the scope of industrial automation.

## 8. ACKNOWLEDGEMENT

The work has been sponsored by the United States Department of Commerce/National Institute of Standards and Technology (NIST) under the grant - Logistics Design and Benchmarking Manufacturing System. Their support is gratefully acknowledged.

## 9. REFERENCES

[1] J. Beasley. Algorithms for unconstrained two-dimensional guillotine cutting. *Journal of the Operational Research Society*, pages 297–306, 1985.

[2] A. Borodin and R. El-Yaniv. *Online computation and competitive analysis.* Cambridge University Press Cambridge, 1998.

[3] M. Boschetti, A. Mingozzi, and E. Hadjiconstantinou. New upper bounds for the two-dimensional orthogonal non-guillotine cutting stock problem. *IMA Journal of Management Mathematics*, 13(2):95, 2002.

[4] A. Caprara, H. Kellerer, U. Pferschy, and D. Pisinger. Approximation algorithms for knapsack problems with cardinality constraints. *European Journal of Operational Research*, 123(2):333–345, 2000.

[5] T. Cormen. *Introduction to algorithms.* The MIT press, 2001.

[6] K. Dowsland and W. Dowsland. Packing problems. *European Journal of Operational Research*, 56(1):2–14, 1992.

[7] J. Egeblad and D. Pisinger. Heuristic approaches for the two-and three-dimensional knapsack packing problem. *Computers & Operations Research*, 36(4):1026–1049, 2009.

[8] S. Fekete and J. Schepers. A new exact algorithm for general orthogonal d-dimensional knapsack problems. In *AlgorithmsâĂŤESA '97*, pages 144–156. Springer, 1997.

[9] S. Fekete and J. Schepers. On more-dimensional packing III: Exact algorithms. *Discrete Applied Mathematics*, 1997.

[10] S. Fekete, J. Schepers, and J. van der Veen. An exact algorithm for higher-dimensional orthogonal packing. *Arxiv preprint cs/0604045*, 2006.

[11] A. Fiat and G. Woeginger. *Online algorithms: The state of the art.* Springer Berlin, 1998.

[12] C. Guéret and C. Prins. A new lower bound for the open-shop problem. *Annals of Operations Research*, 92:165–183, 1999.

[13] E. Hadjiconstantinou and N. Christofides. An exact algorithm for general, orthogonal, two-dimensional knapsack problems. *European Journal of Operational Research*, 83(1):39–56, 1995.

[14] E. Hopper and B. Turton. An empirical investigation of meta-heuristic and heuristic algorithms for a 2D packing problem. *European Journal of Operational Research*, 128(1):34–57, 2001.

[15] O. Ibarra and C. Kim. Fast approximation algorithms for the knapsack and sum of subset problems. *Journal of the ACM (JACM)*, 22(4):463–468, 1975.

[16] H. Kellerer and U. Pferschy. A new fully polynomial approximation scheme for the knapsack problem. *Approximation Algorithms for Combinatiorial Optimization*, pages 123–134, 1998.

[17] H. Kellerer and U. Pferschy. Improved dynamic programming in connection with an FPTAS for the knapsack problem. *Journal of Combinatorial Optimization*, 8(1):5–11, 2004.

[18] H. Kellerer, U. Pferschy, and D. Pisinger. *Knapsack problems.* Springer Verlag, 2004.

[19] A. Kleywegt and J. Papastavrou. The dynamic and stochastic knapsack problem. *Operations Research*, 46(1):17–35, 1998.

[20] A. Kleywegt and J. Papastavrou. The dynamic and stochastic knapsack problem with random sized items. *Operations Research*, pages 26–41, 2001.

[21] E. Lawler. Fast approximation algorithms for knapsack problems. In *18th Annual Symposium on Foundations of Computer Science, 1977.*, pages 206–213, 1977.

[22] A. Lodi, S. Martello, and D. Vigo. Heuristic and metaheuristic approaches for a class of two-dimensional bin packing problems. *INFORMS Journal on Computing*, 11(4):345–357, 1999.

[23] A. Marchetti-Spaccamela and C. Vercellis. Stochastic on-line knapsack problems. *Mathematical Programming*, 68(1):73–104, 1995.

[24] S. Martello, M. Monaci, and D. Vigo. An exact approach to the strip-packing problem. *INFORMS Journal on Computing*, 15(3):310, 2003.

[25] S. Martello and P. Toth. *Knapsack problems: algorithms and computer implementations.* 1990.

[26] J. Papastavrou, S. Rajagopalan, and A. Kleywegt. The dynamic and stochastic knapsack problem with deadlines. *Management Science*, 42(12):1706–1718, 1996.

[27] S. Sahni. Approximate algorithms for the 0/1 knapsack problem. *Journal of the ACM (JACM)*, 22(1):115–124, 1975.

[28] S. Taboun and S. Bhole. A simulator for an automated warehousing system. *Computers & Industrial Engineering*, 24(2):281–290, 1993.

[29] R. Tsai, E. Malstrom, and W. Kuo. A three dimensional dynamic palletizing heuristic. *Progress in Material Handling and Logistics*, 2:181–201.

[30] R. Van Slyke and Y. Young. Finite horizon stochastic knapsacks with applications to yield management. *Operations Research*, 48(1):155–172, 2000.

[31] H. Yaman and A. Sen. Manufacturer's mixed pallet design problem. *European Journal of Operational Research*, 186(2):826–840, 2008.

# Metrics for Mixed Pallet Stacking

Stephen Balakirsky
National Institute of Standards
and Technology
100 Bureau Drive
Gaithersburg, MD USA
stephen@nist.gov

Thomas Kramer
National Institute of Standards
and Technology
100 Bureau Drive
Gaithersburg, MD USA
thomas.kramer@nist.gov

Frederick Proctor
National Institute of Standards
and Technology
100 Bureau Drive
Gaithersburg, MD USA
frederick.proctor@nist.gov

## ABSTRACT

Stacking boxes of various sizes and contents on pallets (i.e. making mixed pallets) is a primary method of preparing goods for shipment from a warehouse to a store or other distant site. Many billions of dollars are spent each year in preparing, shipping, and unloading mixed pallets. Designing the load on a pallet well can save money and effort in all three phases. But what is a good design? In this paper we discuss quantitative metrics for mixed pallets. We have built a graphical simulator called PalletViewer, also described here, that displays pallets being built and calculates metrics.

## Categories and Subject Descriptors

I.2.1 [**Computing Methodologies**]: Atrificial IntelligenceApplications and Expert Systems; D.2.8 [**Software**]: Software EngineeringMetrics

## General Terms

Algorithms, Performance

## Keywords

Palletizing, Simulation, Metrics, Mixed, Pallet

## 1. INTRODUCTION

Stacking objects (boxes or containers) onto pallets is the most widely used method of bulk shipping, accounting for over 60% of the volume of goods shipped worldwide. A significant portion of the pallets are loaded with boxes (or other containers) of different sizes containing different goods. These are called mixed pallets. Shipping mixed pallets is a primary method of preparing goods for shipment from a warehouse to a store or other distant site. Many billions of dollars are spent each year in preparing, shipping, and unloading mixed pallets. For whole sale items it is estimated that more than 50 % of the consumer price is related to post-manufacturing costs such as shipping and handling.

In the literature, the mixed palletizing domain for which we are developing metrics is often called "the distributor's pallet packing problem". It is one of a set of closely-related packing (or unpacking/cutting) problems, all of which are known to be hard to solve as pure geometry problems. A

This paper is authored by employees of the United States Government and is in the public domain. *PERMIS' 10 September 28-30, 2010, Baltimore, MD USA. ACM 978-1-4503-0290-6-9/28/10*

.

solution is finding an optimally efficient packing. More details are given in Section 2. The most closely related of these is "the manufacturer's pallet packing problem" in which all the boxes are the same size and contain the same items. That is much less difficult (but still very difficult). We are not focusing on that problem or any of the other variants. We are interested in helping with the real-world mixed palletizing problem, which goes far beyond geometry.

Designing the load on a pallet well can save money and effort in all three phases. But what is a good design? In the Manufacturing Engineering Laboratory of the National Institute of Standards and Technology, we are developing a set of quantitative metrics for mixed pallets. We have gone through two rounds of developing metrics. The metrics from the second round are discussed in Section 3.

We are not developing methods for designing stacks of boxes ourselves, and this paper touches on design methods only briefly. We are interested in methods of calculating and presenting metrics. The primary tool we have for that is called palletViewer, which simulates execution of a plan to make a stack of boxes on a pallet in a 3D view and calculates and displays metrics. PalletViewer is discussed in Section 4. The PalletViewer tool was utilized as the primary evaluation tool for the Virtual Manufacturing Automation Competition which is discussed in section 5. Finally, conclusions are provided in section 6.

## 2. RELATED WORK

A great deal of work has been done on the purely geometric aspect of palletizing: packing a container of fixed size and shape with the largest possible volume of objects. In mathematical literature, there are both 2-D and 3-D versions of the problem, and the nature of objects to be packed varies from version to version. The problem is often cast as a cutting problem rather than a packing problem – for example, how can a set of moldings be best cut from a cylindrical log. It is well-known that all versions of the geometric packing/cutting problem are, in general, hard to solve. The problem is provably a member of a class of problems called NP-hard (non-deterministic polynomial-time hard). The best algorithms for finding optimal solutions to these problems take computer time that increases exponentially with the number of objects to be packed. For a typical palletizing problem with, say, 50 boxes, the estimated time taken on a supercomputer may be expected to be larger than the lifetime of the universe. Currently, few (if any) researchers believe that an algorithm that can produce an optimal solution in a reasonable amount of time will be found in the near future.

Adding other requirements as discussed in Section 3 (such as a low center of gravity) adds further complexity to the problem and has not been addressed in mathematical research. There is general agreement that automatic pallet building systems must use heuristic approaches. With heuristic systems, however, there is no guarantee of being anywhere near optimal. One can only hope that the heuristic methods will produce good results for at least the types of problems for which the heuristics were designed.

The United States Air Force, which ships pallets in airplanes, conducted research on pallet planning in the last decade of the twentieth century and the first decade of the twenty-first [2] [3]. The first of those has a good literature review and bibliography. It also contains C language source code for a pallet planner and substantial documentation of the method implemented by the code. Extensive testing on problem sets generated in-house and elsewhere was conducted.

Bischoff and Ratcliff [5] discussed loading multiple mixed pallets and presented an algorithm for planning for multiple pallets. A flowchart of the algorithm was included. The algorithm was tested on 9600 problems.

Bischoff and Ratcliff [4], almost uniquely among journal papers, presented a number of practical, non-geometric requirements for designing mixed pallet stacks. These included, for example, orientation, load bearing, and stability. They presented a stacking algorithm that has both dense packing and stablility as objectives. They also presented an automatic method for generating problem sets that has been used by other researchers.

Bischoff, Janetz, and Ratcliff [6] discussed mixed pallet planning further.

The collections of boxes in the problem sets of [2], [5], and [4] however, tend to lend themselves to dense packing, whereas real-world collections of boxes may not. Problem sets at the other extreme, where the density of the densest possible packing is near zero might also be devised. Consider, for example, packing very thin boxes in a cubical container where the length of the boxes is almost as large as the diagonal of the floor of the container. Such boxes may be put in the container on the diagonal. If we make the length of the box long enough that the edges of the box touch the sides of the container and we make make the width of the box equal to the length of a side of the container, exactly one such box can be loaded. Since the thickness may be made arbitrarily small, the volume of the box may be made arbitrarily small. For this problem set, the densest possible packing is as close to zero as we choose to make it. As a more realistic example, consider packing the same container with cubical boxes whose side length is slightly more than half the side length of the container. Again, exactly one such box may be loaded. In this case the largest possible density is a little over one eighth ($0.5 \times 0.5 \times 0.5$).

A few commercial pallet planning systems are available [1]. Some of these generate multiple solutions and allow the user to pick one.

---

[1] Certain commercial software tools and hardware are identified in this paper in order to explain our research. Such identification does not imply recommendation or endorsement by the authors, nor does it imply that the software tools and hardware identified are necessarily the best available for the purpose.

Neither the papers on pallet packing mentioned above nor the commercial systems say much about the metrics themselves, other than packing density. Brief mention is made in [2] of intersection, overlap, overhang, and center of gravity (as described in Section 3).

Along with Pushkar Kohle and Henrik Christensen of The Georgia Institute of Technology, we presented a paper [1] describing the metrics used in the previous version of Pallet Viewer and the Pallet Viewer software. We also described the pallet stacking competition held in May 2010 at the Virtual Manufacturing Automation Competition (VMAC) that was part of the IEEE International Conference on Robotics and Automation (ICRA).

## 3. METRICS

Roughly speaking, a metric for palletizing is a quantitative measure of some aspect of any of the following:

- one box that is part of a stack on a pallet
- the entire collection of boxes in a stack on a pallet
- a set of stacked pallets
- the process of building stack(s) of boxes on pallet(s).

### 3.1 Input Data

To evaluate metrics, data is needed. Currently, we are using three types of data files as input for calculating metrics. Parsers are available for each type of file.

- Order file
  - describes the pallets available to use.
  - describes types of package and gives the barcodes of the boxes of each type (thereby giving the number of each type).
  - is an XML data file corresponding to an XML schema.
  - is available before planning.

- Packlist file
  - describes the design of the stack and the plan for building it.
  - can represent multiple pallets.
  - is an XML data file corresponding to an XML schema.
  - is available after planning.

- As-built file
  - describes the as-built stack on the pallet.
  - has a home-brewed format (is not an XML file).
  - implicitly references an order file.
  - is available after the simulation has executed the plan.

The order file and packlist file can represent only four orientations for a box (top up with sides parallel to the sides of the pallet). The as-built file can represent a full 6 degrees of freedom. The limitation on orientations simplifies calculating metrics for planned stacks immensely as compared with what would be necessary if more degrees of freedom were allowed. If there were a full 6 degrees of freedom in plans, a solid modeler would be needed to calculate metrics, and the definitions of some metrics would need to be extended.

The XML schemas mentioned above may be downloaded from [10] and are described in the document "Interface Specification for Mixed Palletizing Competition" which was prepared for the VMAC competition and may be downloaded from the same site.

Data for box positions is given in terms of the coordinate system of the pallet. That (right-handed) coordinate system is assumed to have its origin at a corner of the (rectangular) pallet at the top of the pallet. The X axis lies on one edge of the top, and the Y axis lies on another edge so that the top of the pallet is in the first quadrant of the XY plane. The Z axis is the cross product of the X and Y axes. In normal use, the top of the pallet is horizontal so that the Z axis is vertical. Some of the metrics refer to this coordinate system. In pallet data, "length" is assumed to be along the X axis and "width" along the Y axis.

In the packlist file, each box may be identified by the number giving the order in which to box is put on the stack. This number is used with the metrics to make it clear which box is under consideration.

This section discusses details of specific metrics, but before getting specific, more general discussions of weight support and box robustness are given to set the stage.

## 3.2  Weight Support Mode

There are at least two different common modes for the way in which boxes are supported by other boxes. What constitutes a good stack is very different between the two.

In one mode, which we might call the *cardboard* mode, when anything (such as another box) is put on top of a box, it is the material from which the box is made that bears the weight. The *cardboard* mode occurs with boxes containing breakable items such as glassware and tomatoes. These boxes may be made of more sturdy material such as wood or thick plastic or may have additional internal supports such as columns at the corners.

In the other, *contents* mode, it is the contents of the box that provide most of the support for any weight placed on top of the box. The *contents* mode occurs with boxes containing relatively robust items such as cans of soda or reams of paper. In the *contents* mode, the material from which the box is made may have very little resistance to compression. The contents have it, instead.

The goodness or badness of metrics such as how much boxes overlap varies widely between the two modes. In *cardboard* mode, overlap is usually a bad thing because the edges of the boxes (the load-bearing part) are not lined up vertically. One web site [9] says overlap (also called interlocking) "can destroy up to 50 % of the compression strength". In *contents* mode, overlap is generally good, since it tends to hold the stack together. The edges of the boxes are not load bearing in *contents* mode. All shippers expect pallets to be wrapped with plastic and possibly also with straps or nets. The wrapping and strapping hold the stack together and fasten it to the pallet, so the benefits of overlap are usually not large. If the pallet is moved from a loading area to a wrapping area, however, it is useful to have a cohesive stack.

The work we have done so far has used pallets of boxes of supermarket items. These are mostly *contents* mode boxes, so overlap has been looked upon favorably.

## 3.3  Box Robustness

Boxes of different items have different maximum loads and maximum pressures. No box on a pallet should have its maximum load or pressure exceeded. The XML schema for boxes we have been using includes an optional Robustness element, which has as sub-elements: MaxPressureOnTop, SourcePalletLayers, and RelativeRobustness. Currently, our metrics use only MaxPressureOnTop (which is the maximum *allowed* pressure on top). We could calculate the maximum load number as the maximum allowed pressure times the area of the top of the box, but that number would probably not be correct. Also with that number, the maximum allowed pressure would always be exceeded if the maximum allowed load were exceeded, so the "maximum pressure exceeded" error would be triggered, making a maximum load error redundant.

SourcePalletLayers, the number of layers on a pallet of identical boxes on which a product is received, is an empirical measure of robustness. If the manufacturer piled boxes N layers deep for shipment, and they arrived intact, it should be "ok" for the builder of a mixed pallet to do likewise.

RelativeRobustness is an enumeration of VeryWeak, Weak, Normal, Strong, and VeryStrong. This is in order of increasing robustness, but no quantitative meaning has been assigned.

## 3.4  Specific Metrics

### 3.4.1  Connections Below

Connections below is a measure of package overlap. A larger number indicates more overlap. For a single box **B**, if the box rests on the pallet, connections below is 1. Otherwise, connections below is the number of boxes below **B** whose tops are in contact with the bottom of **B**.

For a stack of boxes on a pallet, the pallet average connections below is the average of the connections below over all the boxes.

The way the computation is being done, the first layer of a stack always has a pallet average connections below value of 1, and the more layers there are, the larger the pallet average connections below tends to get.

An alternate method of calculating the pallet average connections below might be to disregard boxes directly on the pallet. This would eliminate the effect described in the preceding paragraph and might be more useful.

### 3.4.2  Overlap

Overlap is a measure of the percent of a box that rests on a support surface. The number ranges between 0 and 1 with 1 being the optimal value. For a single box **B**, the overlap fraction is the fraction of the bottom of **B** that is in contact with the top of the pallet or with the top of some box below it. If **B** has a small overlap fraction, **B** is likely either to be intersecting the pallet or a box below **B** (possible in a plan, impossible in a real stack) or to produce an unstable stack. In the intersection condition, the bottom of **B** is inside the pallet or box below, not in contact with the top of the pallet or the top of the box below. We have been treating a low overlap fraction for a single box as a plan error.

For a pallet, the pallet average overlap fraction is the average of the overlap fraction over all the boxes. This could also be computed by dividing (1) the total area of the bottoms of boxes in contact with the tops of other boxes or the top of the pallet by (2) the total area of the bottoms of boxes. That would usually be a slightly different number since each box would, in effect, be weighted by the area of the bottom of the box. If there were two boxes **B1** and **B2**, the bottom of **B1** was a square millimeter, the bottom area of **B2** was a square meter, **B1** had an overlap fraction of 0, and **B2** had an overlap fraction of 1, our calculation would give an average of 0.5 while the alternate calculation would give something over 0.999.

### 3.4.3 Overhang

Overhang is a measure of a box or the stack extending outside the pallet.

For a single box **B**, the overhang of each side beyond the four sides of the pallet may be calculated. If there is no overhang, the value is given as 0.

For a pallet, the overhang beyond a side of the pallet is the maximum of the overhangs of all the boxes beyond that side.

Many shippers, including the US Postal Service [11] and UPS [12], require that there be no overhang. The Great Little Box web site [9] says overhang is bad: "With as little as 1/2 inch [12.7 mm] hanging-over, as much as 30 % of their strength is lost!". Overhang will also be undesirable if pallets must be loaded with little clearance between them, a common situation for trucks, airplanes, and large shipping containers. In some situations, however, overhang may be acceptable or desirable.

In order to provide space for netting, the U.S. Air Force [2] requires 5 cm (2 in) of clearance between each side of the stack and a vertical plane through the nearest edge of the pallet. This could be calculated as negative overhang, but we are currently not doing that calculation. It would be simple to do it.

### 3.4.4 Maximum Pressure on Top

The concept of maximum pressure on top applies to a single box. Exceeding the maximum allowed pressure over a small area might result in a hole being punched in the top of the box. Exceeding the maximum allowed pressure over a larger area might result in the box collapsing.

To determine whether the maximum allowed pressure on top of a box **B** is being exceeded, we calculate the pressure on **B** exerted by each box **T** that rests on top of **B**.

To find the pressure exerted by **T**, let $F_t$ be the total downward force exerted by **T** and $A_t$ be the total area of the bottom of **T** in contact with other boxes.

$A_t$ may be found using the data in the order and the plan giving the positions and sizes of the boxes.

$F_t$ is the weight of **T** plus the force exerted on **T** by boxes on top of it. For boxes on the top of the stack, $F_t$ is just the weight of the box. If we assume that the downward force of each box is uniformly distributed over the bottom of the box, the pressure exerted by **T** on **B** is $F_t/A_t$. We can calculate the force and pressure exerted by each box on the boxes below it by starting at the top and working downwards. The pressure is found as just described, and the downward force is the pressure times the area of contact.

The assumption that $F_t$ is uniformly distributed over the part of the bottom of box **T** that is supported by other boxes is a naive assumption. The actual distribution of force will depend on several factors such as the elasticity and deformability of the boxes and their contents as well as on the way in which they are stacked. Only a finite element analysis requiring detailed data that is not available could hope to provide a good picture of the actual distribution of force.

The metric for a single box is the maximum pressure in kilograms per square meter exerted on the top of **B** by any other box. If the maximum allowed pressure on **B** has been exceeded, that is reported as an error.

The metric for a stack of boxes is the total number of boxes for which the maximum allowed pressure is exceeded.

If all the boxes in a stack have the same maximum allowed pressure on top, the method of calculating maximum pressure we are using will never return a false report that the maximum allowed pressure has been exceeded since the situation can only be worse if force is not distributed uniformly. However, the method may fail to find a situation in which maximum allowed pressure has been exceeded.

It would be a good idea to check the pressure on the bottom of each box, but no figure for maximum allowed pressure on the bottom is available.

### 3.4.5 Box Intersections

The format for a design for a stack of boxes allows boxes to be placed anywhere, so it is possible to make a design in which boxes intersect. Such a design is impossible to make, of course, so the design is in error. Calculating whether boxes in a design intersect is easy to do with the current limitation on the orientation of boxes.

For a single box **B**, the metric is the number of other boxes that intersect **B**. It is helpful if the id numbers of the other boxes are given.

For a stack, the metric is the total number of intersection errors. The intersection of two boxes is a single error, not one error for each of the two intersecting boxes.

### 3.4.6 Center of Gravity

The center of gravity (COG) is a useful measure for determining pallet stability. In almost all real situations, a low COG for a stack of boxes is better than a higher one. The lower the COG, the less likely the stack is to fall over if the pallet is tilted. In addition, it may be important that the XY location of the COG be near the XY center of the pallet, so that a fork lift, truck, or airplane carrying the pallet is not unbalanced. The Air Force is reported to prefer that the COG not be more than 10.16 cm (4 in) from the center of the pallet for a pallet 274.32 cm by 223.52 cm (108 in by 88 in) [2].

The COG of a single box is assumed to be at the center of the box (halfway between each of the three pairs of parallel sides). This may or may not be a good assumption. The input data format does not have a place to put the location of the COG of a box.

The XYZ location of the COG is easy to calculate from the input data. The metrics currently used for the COG are its height above the pallet in meters and its relative offsets from the pallet center in the X and Y directions. The relative offset in the X direction is the difference between the X coordinate of the COG and the X coordinate of the pallet center divided by half the length of the pallet. With that definition: if the value is 0, the COG is at the center of the pallet in X; if the value is 1, the COG is at the +X edge of the pallet; and if the value is -1, the COG is at the

-X edge of the pallet. The relative offset in the Y direction is defined similarly but using the width. The relative offsets provide a measure that is intuitive and independent of the size of the pallet. The XY location of the COG may be easily calculated from the relative offsets as long as the length and width of the pallet are known.

### 3.4.7 Loading Order Errors

Loading order errors provide one measure of the "build-ability" of a pallet. As mentioned earlier, the packlist files we are using for input provide both the design for a stack and a plan for building the stack. Among other things, the packlist specifies the order in which boxes are to be added to the stack. It is almost always necessary in the real world to place all the boxes on which a given box **B** rests before putting **B** on the stack. The metric we are using for a single box is the number of boxes below **B** that are not in place when **B** is put on the stack. The metric for a stack is the sum of those numbers over all boxes. It is helpful if the id numbers of the missing boxes are given.

### 3.4.8 Number of Boxes on Stack

The number of boxes on the stack is useful for keeping track of progress while the stack is being built and, when the stack is completed, for comparison with the number of boxes in the order.

### 3.4.9 Total Weight

Shipping charges are often based on weight, and many shippers have a maximum allowed weight for a pallet, so this is an essential metric. Also, the total weight is needed to ensure the load capacity of the pallet is not exceeded. The total weight of the stack (excluding the pallet) is calculated as the sum of the weights of the boxes on the stack.

### 3.4.10 Stack Height

The stack height is the height above the top of the pallet of the highest point on the stack. This is used for finding the pallet storage volume (and hence the volume density).

Almost all shippers have a maximum allowed height that includes the pallet. Another height metric should be added that includes the height of the pallet. The pallet height, however, is not included in the input data we are currently using.

### 3.4.11 Volume of Boxes

The volume of boxes is the sum of the volumes of the boxes on the stack. Its primary use is in finding the volume density of the stack.

### 3.4.12 Pallet Storage Volume

This is the maximum volume of boxes a stack with the current stack height could have (in the absence of overhang). This is calculated as the area of the top of the pallet times the height of the stack. Its primary use is also in finding the volume density of the stack.

### 3.4.13 Volume Density

The volume density of a stack is a significant measure of the quality of a stack. It is computed as the volume of boxes divided by the pallet storage volume. Its value is never greater than 1 (unless there is overhang).

### 3.4.14 Total Errors

One more metric is provided for the stack. That is the total number of errors. This is the sum of the total overlap errors, the total intersection errors, the total loading order errors, and the total maximum pressure errors.

## 3.5 Combining Metrics

Depending on the nature of the goods, boxes, shipping methods, warehouse procedures, and unloading procedures, combining the quantitative metrics to produce an overall measure of goodness must be done in different ways with different weights or thresholds applied.

We have not yet found a method of generating a single score for a shipping situation with a specific set of characteristics. Such a method is desirable since it would save a great deal of time on the part of shippers. Commercial palletizing software generates alternatives from which a user must choose according to his or her preferences.

## 3.6 Additional Metrics

Several additional metrics may be useful, as follows. For several of these, it will be necessary to revise the input file format.

### 3.6.1 Connections and Overlap on Top

The metrics listed above for connections and overlap are currently calculated only for the bottoms of boxes. It may be useful to calculate them for the tops as well.

### 3.6.2 Other Measures of Connectedness

The point of finding connections and overlaps is to get a measure of how well the stack holds together. It may be useful to calculate a more direct measure of holding together, such as the number of connected sub-areas on the top side of a layer (fewer being better). Intuitively, a sub-area is formed by a number of boxes in a layer being linked together by boxes in the layer above.

### 3.6.3 Families of Boxes

To unload a pallet efficiently, it should be possible to unload all boxes that have the same destination at once without having to move boxes that have a different destination. To support this idea, the order schema has a place to put an identifier for the family of a box. A metric could be calculated giving the number of families that can be unloaded from a pallet without moving other boxes.

### 3.6.4 Error Metrics

It would be useful to have metrics for more kinds of plan and execution errors. These include:

- the number of boxes that should be on the pallet that are not there.

- the number of boxes on the pallet that should not be there.

- the number of non-fatal syntax errors in the packlist file.

## 3.7 Other Considerations of Metrics

### 3.7.1 Multiple Pallets

We have not yet tackled metrics for multiple pallets. For example, if more than one pallet is required, is it going to be better to have roughly equal loads on all pallets than to load all but the last pallet full and put the remaining boxes (which may be few in number) on the last pallet?

### 3.7.2 Box Orientation

The representation of a plan we are currently using allows placing a box in only four orientations – bottom down with sides parallel to the sides of the pallet. It would be practical to allow a wider range of orientations. As long as the sides of the boxes on the stack are parallel to the sides of the pallet, the difficulty of calculating metrics will not change much. Without the parallel sides limitation, calculating metrics would probably require using a solid modeler.

### 3.7.3 Location Tolerances

It is practical to treat differences of a millimeter or so in height as unimportant in building stacks of boxes of the size typically stacked on pallets. However, it is not clear how to model a stack with non-zero but negligible height differences or how to calculate metrics in this case.

### 3.7.4 Box Spacing

A metric for spacing between the sides of boxes should be devised. Some automatic planning systems leave spaces between the sides of boxes and have the edges of every layer line up with the edges of the pallet. Other planning systems leave as little space as possible between the sides of boxes. Some boxes may be safely manipulated by suction grippers holding on to the top of the box. For other boxes, side and/or bottom gripping is necessary. In the latter case, it may be necessary to leave spaces between boxes for the gripper.

### 3.7.5 Design Vs. Plan

Currently, the packlist we are using specifies both the design for the stack and the plan for building the stack. The plan includes waypoints for each box as it is loaded onto the stack. There are many ways in which a given design may be built, and some are more efficient than others. In addition, some designs are easier to build than others. Metrics might be developed both for the buildability of designed stacks and for the efficiency of plans for building a stack with a given design.

For evaluating plans that include specific paths (as they do in the current plan format), one metric might be the number of times boxes being loaded collide with the partially built stack. To calculate that, a solid modeler may be necessary.

## 4. PALLET VIEWER

## 4.1 Functionality

Pallet Viewer was originally built at the Georgia Institute of Technology. We have made major revisions twice at NIST. The first NIST revision was described in [1]. The latest NIST revision is described here.

The Pallet Viewer utility displays in a 3D color view a pallet and the as-planned stack of boxes on it. Figure 1 shows a typical Pallet Viewer image. The Pallet Viewer executable is called with at least two arguments: the name of an order file and the name of a plan file. A third, optional,

argument may also be given: the name of an as-built file. If the third argument is given, the Pallet Viewer shows the as-built stack in a color wire frame view off to the side of the as-planned stack.

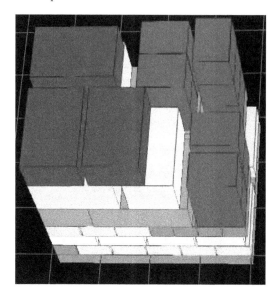

**Figure 1: Pallet Viewer Image**

Pallet Viewer calculates and displays 23 metrics for the as-planned stack, as shown in Figure 2. These are as described in Section 3. In addition to what is shown in Figure 2, the following additional information will be printed for the current package.

- If the overlap fraction is less than 0.4, "Error!" is printed after the value of the "Overlap fraction".

- If there are intersection errors, the package numbers of the packages that intersect the current package are shown on the "Intersection errors" line immediately after the number of errors. All packages are checked for intersections, not only those shown in the picture.

- If there are loading order errors, the package numbers of the packages that should be under the current package but are not on the stack are shown on the "Loading order errors" line immediately after the number of errors.

- If the maximum allowed pressure on top is exceeded, "Error!" is printed after the value of the "Maximum pressure on top". The value shown for maximum pressure on top is for the complete stack.

The stack of boxes shown in Pallet Viewer may be built or unbuilt by using keyboard keys. The metrics are calculated for all partial stacks when Pallet Viewer starts. Each time a box is added or removed, the metrics for the current package and current partial stack are displayed. The metrics and the stack are shown in different graphics windows. The current view may be saved in a ppm (portable pixmap image) graphics file. The ppm file combines the two windows into a single image.

The Pallet Viewer is a C++ program using OpenGL graphics. Manipulating the view is done entirely with the mouse,

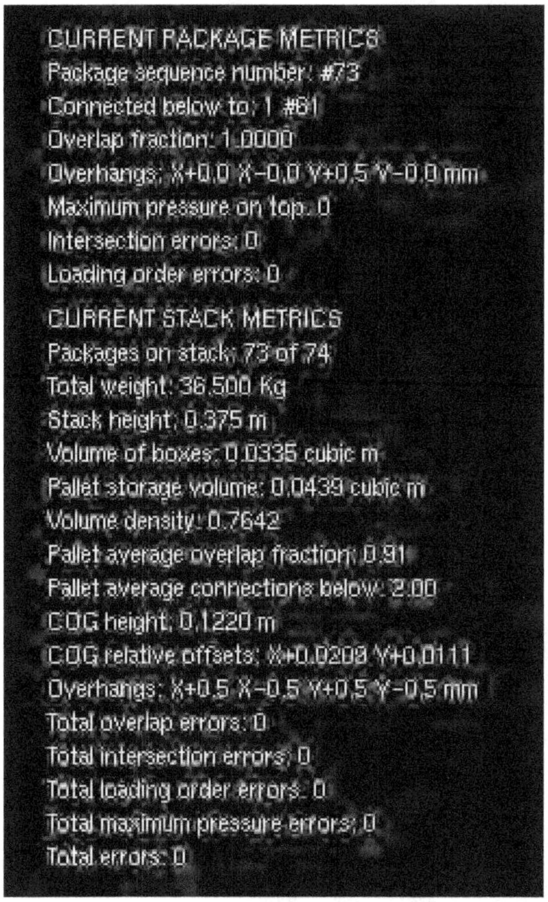

CURRENT PACKAGE METRICS
Package sequence number: #73
Connected below to: 1 #61
Overlap fraction: 1.0000
Overhangs: X+0.0 X−0.0 Y+0.5 Y−0.0 mm
Maximum pressure on top: 0
Intersection errors: 0
Loading order errors: 0

CURRENT STACK METRICS
Packages on stack: 73 of 74
Total weight: 36.500 Kg
Stack height: 0.375 m
Volume of boxes: 0.0335 cubic m
Pallet storage volume: 0.0439 cubic m
Volume density: 0.7642
Pallet average overlap fraction: 0.91
Pallet average connections below: 2.00
COG height: 0.1220 m
COG relative offsets: X+0.0208 Y+0.0111
Overhangs: X+0.5 X−0.5 Y+0.5 Y−0.5 mm
Total overlap errors: 0
Total intersection errors: 0
Total loading order errors: 0
Total maximum pressure errors: 0
Total errors: 0

**Figure 2: Pallet Viewer Metrics**

except that the h key returns the view to its default position. The stack may be rotated and translated. The view may be zoomed in and out.

The Pallet Viewer program is useful for analyzing the process of creating a pallet. Since metrics are calculated for placement of every box on the stack, the software can assess whether the stack will remain stable when it is being constructed. Another important aspect of palletizing is the order in which boxes are put on the stack. By observing the Pallet Viewer display an expert user can to determine if the planner is making motion planning hard or impossible.

## 4.2 Limitations

The Pallet Viewer application is used to evaluate the quality of a pallet plan based on the geometry of the objects and their placement. Its metrics apply to the geometry and loading forces of a planned pallet and may be used to answer the question, "will this be a good pallet when built?" These metrics don't answer the questions, "how well does this pallet lend itself to being built?" or "when the pallet was actually built, how good was it?" It is a static evaluation that does not evaluate dynamic effects such as objects sliding, tipping or being crushed.

An intermediate step toward dynamic simulation is to use Pallet Viewer to apply static quality metrics after each object has been stacked, so that problems with the interme-

diate condition of a pallet can be detected. However, since Pallet Viewer does only static analysis, problems such as objects sliding will not be detected.

Dynamic simulation is utilized to supplement Pallet Viewer's static evaluation. There are two aspects of dynamic evaluation: qualitative visualization by an expert, and comparisons of the as-built pallet and the planned pallet to examine object slipping, tipping, crushing or misplacement.

A shortcoming of dynamic evaluation is that the source of problems can't be easily isolated to the pallet building process or the pallet plan itself. For example, if an object slips or tips, it could be due to an improper stacking order as chosen by the robot controller, or it could be due to the plan itself, and no stacking order would fix the problem.

As discussed in Section 2, we use the Unified System for Automation and Robot Simulation (USARSim) [8] to evaluate the pallet build process and resulting built pallet. USARSim runs in real time. As a consequence, the evaluation takes as long as the pallet build process, typically on the order of tens of minutes. This makes it unsuitable as a way to compare many different object stacking plans to quickly select the best plan for execution.

## 5. COMPETITIONS

The first real trial of the metrics being developed for this effort occurred during the 2010 Virtual Manufacturing Automation Competition (VMAC) [7] that was part of the IEEE International Conference on Robotics and Automation (ICRA) robot challenge. During this event, three different palletizing approaches were evaluated through the use of our metrics. These approaches included a university created neural network learning-based approach, a university created deterministic planning approach, and a commercial product that is commonly used by industry.

**Figure 3: View of the USARSim physics-based simulation of a mixed-pallet under construction.**

At the VMAC event, teams were presented with the XML order file and were required to generate a compliant XML packlist file. This file was then passed through the Pallet Viewer software and the values of the metrics were computed. While this provided a measure of the final pallet's quality, it did not evaluate the buildability of the pallet. Therefore, teams were next tasked with running their packlist file on a simulated palletizing cell. This cell was implemented in the Unified System for Automation and Robot Simulation (USARSim) and is shown in Figure 3. USARSim performs a physics simulation that includes friction and gravity, so that problems such as sliding and tipping (which Pallet Viewer will not find) are evident. USARSim runs in real time, however, so it is not able to evaluate plans quickly. USARSim provided an "as-built" file at the end of the pallets construction that could be utilized by the Pallet Viewer software for evaluation of the correctness of the build.

**Figure 4:** 1/3 **scale palletizing cell used during the ICRA Competition**

The final step of the competition was to allow successful teams to try and build their pallets on a 1/3 scale palletizing cell shown in Figure 4 This competition is an ongoing event and will be held during the 2011 ICRA conference. Sample palletizing code may be found through the VMAC website and new teams are encouraged to participate.

## 6. CONCLUSIONS

We have adopted a model of palletizing, used it to define metrics, and held a palletizing competition. A Pallet Viewer utility has been built that calculates the metrics, displays them, and displays a naive simulation of executing a palletizing plan. The USARSim system has been used to simulate execution of a palletizing plan more realistically and produce an as-built description of a stack of boxes on a pallet. We have collaborated with industrial partners to ensure that our work is practical.

The palletizing model we are using is limited in the following ways:

- It supports placing a box in only four orientations.

- It mixes the design of a finished pallet with the plan for producing the design.

- It does not provide for using any buffer space where boxes might be stored temporarily during palletizing.

- No allowance for multiple robots loading a pallet or multiple pallets being loaded.

- No allowance for expressing a constraint on the minimum space between boxes.

We need to improve our palletizing model so that it addresses these limitations. We plan to do that and to continue

developing metrics. We are aware of a few additional metrics that might be calculated. We need to consult with more commercial firms to determine what metrics are important in what environments.

We need to develop methods for combining individual metrics in order to produce a single score for the design of a stack on a pallet. Different methods will be needed for different shipping environments.

There is a commercial need for a pallet planner that:

- Uses many of the metrics described in Section 3.

- Includes user preferences for weighting the metrics.

- Includes user preferences while generating designs.

- Can handle multiple pallets.

## 7. REFERENCES

[1] S. Balakirsky, F. Proctor, T. Kramer, P. Kolhe, and H. Christensen. Using simulation to assess the effectiveness of pallet stacking methods. In *Proceedings of the 2nd International Conference on Simulation, Modeling, and Programming for Autonomous Robots (SIMPAR 2010)*, 2010.

[2] E. Baltacioglu. The distributor's three-dimensional pallet-packing problem: A human intelligence-based heuristic approach. Master's thesis, Air Force Institute of Technology, 2001.

[3] E. Baltacioglu, J.T. Moore, and R.R. Hill Jr. The distributor's three-dimensional pallet-packing problem: a human intelligence-based heuristic approach. *International Journal of Operational Research*, 1(3):249–266, 2006.

[4] E. E. Bischoff and M. S. W. Ratcliff. Issues in the development of approaches to container loading. *Omega, International Journal of Management Science*, 23(4):377–390, 1995.

[5] E. E. Bischoff and M. S. W. Ratcliff. Loading multiple pallets. *Journal of the Operational Research Society*, 46:1322–1336, 1995.

[6] E. E. et al Bischoff. Loading pallets with non-identical items. *European Journal of Operational Research*, 84:681–692, 1995.

[7] VMAC Executive Committee. Virtual manufacturing automation competition homepage. http://www.vma-competition.com, June 2010.

[8] USARSim Community. Usarsim wiki homepage. http://usarsim.sourceforge.net/wiki/index.php/Main_Page, June 2010.

[9] Great Little Box Company. Palletization. http://www.greatlittlebox.com/packaging/storing, June 2010.

[10] NIST. Scm repositories - moast. http://moast.cvs.sourceforge.net/viewvc/moast/devel/src/manufact/sampleData, August 2010.

[11] US Postal Service. Special standards - pallets, pallet boxes, and trays on pallets. http://pe.usps.com/text/QSG300/Q705b.htm, June 2010.

[12] UPS. Ups: Preparing your freight shipment. http://www.ups.com/content/us/en/resources/ship/packaging/prepare/freight.html, June 2010.

# Mixed Pallet Stacking: An Overview and Summary of the 2010 PerMIS Special Session

Stephen Balakirsky
National Institute of Standards
and Technology
100 Bureau Drive
Gaithersburg, MD USA
stephen@nist.gov

Henrik I. Christensen
RIM@GT,CoC
Georgia Institute of
Technology
Atlanta, GA USA
hic@cc.gatech.edu

Thomas Kramer
National Institute of Standards
and Technology
100 Bureau Drive
Gaithersburg, MD USA
thomas.kramer@nist.gov

Pushkar Kolhe
RIM@GT,CoC
Georgia Institute of
Technology
Atlanta, GA USA
pushkar@cc.gatech.edu

Frederick Proctor
National Institute of Standards
and Technology
100 Bureau Drive
Gaithersburg, MD USA
frederick.proctor@nist.gov

## ABSTRACT

Stacking boxes of various sizes and contents on pallets (i.e. making mixed pallets) is a primary method of preparing goods for shipment from a warehouse to a store or other distant site. A special session of the 2010 PerMIS workshop was held to examine mixed palletizing issues. Papers were presented by end-users, vendors, researchers, and evaluators of palletizing solutions. This paper presents a summary of this session and discusses issues ranging from how to construct pallet build plans to metrics for evaluating these plans to competitions that feature novel palletizing approaches.

## Categories and Subject Descriptors

I.2.1 [**Computing Methodologies**]: Artificial Intelligence Applications and Expert Systems; D.2.8 [**Software**]: Software EngineeringMetrics

## General Terms

Algorithms, Performance

## Keywords

Palletizing, Simulation, Metrics, Mixed Pallet, Order Picking

## 1. INTRODUCTION

The warehousing and distribution industry is an important part of the supply chain that transports goods from the factory to the end user. A typical scenario is receiving pallets containing a single type of Stock Keeping Unit (SKU), depalletizing the product, and then creating new mixed SKU pallets for transport to customers. About 140,000 containers per week are imported into the US. About 30 % of these

containers are immediately repacked onto mixed pallets for distribution to stores. In the grocery industry alone, more than 80 million SKUs (half of which are for beverages) are distributed to stores each week. Much of this work is performed as a physically demanding manual task which has the largest labor costs, greatest potential for product damage, and most prevalent occurrence of order inaccuracies [5] of an activity in the distribution process. Increasing numbers of SKUs coupled with the manual nature of the task is causing a disruption in this industry due to increased costs from product damage and fines/penalties for shipping inaccuracies [5].

There is thus no doubt that a major challenge for supply chain management and logistics is optimization of mixed palletizing systems. At the PERMIS session, it was estimated by C&S Wholesale Grocers that the manufacturing costs only represent 30 % of the consumer costs for grocery items. The remaining costs are related to distribution, handling, and sales. Optimization of the process has the potential to reduce consumer prices significantly. Applying robotics to this problem has the potential to greatly reduce both product damage and order inaccuracies, thus further reducing consumer prices.

There are multiple providers of logistic systems and complete solutions for distribution centers. This includes methods for depalletizing, warehouse management, order management, palletizing algorithms, gripper design, robot automation, mixed palletizing, and infrastructure support such as conveyors or Automated Guided Vehicles (AGV) systems. This paper concentrates on the palletizing robotic work-cell which may be seen as an automation center that has an in-feed conveyor for product coming into the cell, a robotic arm with end-of-arm tooling and planning software, and an out-feed conveyor for carrying the mixed case pallets from the robot cell to a distribution center. While several companies already provide solutions for this problem, there is no consistent world view on what makes a good pallet, nor standards for the information models required to complete this task.

The 2010 Performance Metrics for Intelligent Systems workshop featured a special session on mixed palletizing that addressed these deficiencies. This session brought together representatives from the end-user community, robot vendors, and researchers to share and compare ideas on the current state and future challenges of automation for mixed palletizing. Several papers and talks were presented, and a panel discussion was held. The papers included an end-user perspective of the palletizing problem [12], a description of the state-of-the-art and continuing challenges for robotic palletizing systems [5], a survey of current planning systems for mixed palletizing [8], and a discussion of emerging information standards and benchmarks for palletizing metrics and evaluation tools [1]. In this paper we summarize this session by presenting an overview of the generic needs of a palletizing solution and some present palletizing systems, planning systems for palletizing, and evaluation benchmarks.

Section 2 of this paper presents an overview of current pallet planning algorithms. A summary of the discussion on the information model is next presented in Section 3, followed by a summary of the metrics discussion in Section 4. Information on a competition that is striving to advance the state-of-the-art in palletizing is presented in Section 5, and conclusions are presented in Section 6.

## 2. PALLET PLANNING TECHNIQUES

Planning for the creation of mixed pallets is not a single problem, but a class of related planning problems that vary depending on a particular industry's packaging types, warehousing systems, delivery methods, order profiles, and customer expectations. Not all packages are of the same type (e.g. cardboard boxes, shrink wrap items, wooden boxes, etc.), and therefore the planner may need to treat some SKUs differently than others.

For example, there are at least two different common modes for the way in which boxes are supported by other boxes. In one mode, the structure of the box bears the weight of any item placed on top of the box. This mode occurs with boxes containing breakable items such as glassware and tomatoes. These boxes may be made of more sturdy material such as wood or thick plastic or may have additional internal supports such as columns at the corners. For other boxes, it is the contents of the box that provides most of the support for any weight placed on top of the box. This mode occurs with boxes containing relatively robust items such as cans of soda or reams of paper. In this mode, the material from which the box is made may have very little resistance to compression. The contents have it, instead. The planning system must be able to vary its strategy depending on the support structure of the boxes.

When building a stack of boxes where the box must bear the weight, overlap (a box resting on multiple boxes beneath it) is usually a bad thing because the edges of the boxes (the load-bearing part) are not lined up vertically. One web site [4] states that overlap (also called interlocking) "can destroy up to 50 % of the compression strength". However, when the contents of the box are load-bearing, overlap is generally good, since it tends to hold the stack together.

The shipping container type (pallet vs. roller cages) and the delivery method also impact the packing design. For example, some customers may require family grouping, reverse stop sequencing, or bay mapping for their containers. A family group is a construct that is established to cluster items that are often sold together or items with specific storage or handling requirements. These items should be co-located on the final pallet in order to minimize the work load during the unloading process. Reverse stop sequencing groups multiple orders on one pallet that are sorted by the sequence of locations that the delivery truck will visit along its route. At each stop, another set of packages is removed for delivery. Bay mapping considers truck configurations when optimizing a set of pallets for transport. It will include the construction of various height pallets to be able to fit in odd sized areas of the truck (e.g. bays over a wheel are often smaller than other bays).

Some customers may also include order profile constraints that are used to simplify the auditing process on the receiving side. For example, a beverage order may be constrained to have an individual layer of ten 12-packs of soda cans even though ten 12-packs and a 6-pack fit onto the layer. Finally, various customers have specific constraints that are driven by their expectations on how pallets should be packed. For example, they may specify that detergents or pet food may not be put on the same pallet as regular food.

Other constraints on the planning system deal with the amount of *a priori* data available to the planner. In offline planning systems, the planner is able to not only specify the final resting location of each box, but is also able to plan the order in which the boxes are placed on the in-feed conveyor. In online planning systems, the planner does not have *a priori* knowledge of the box ordering and must compute a location for each box as it is received. Some industries require a hybrid planning approach to add robustness to their system. A hybrid planning system generates a plan using an offline planning algorithm, but can switch over to an online approach if the preplanned sequence is violated.

The planner has to be able to consider all of these constraints and deliver pallets that are both high density and stable. The remainder of this paper will deal with offline planning systems for boxes whose contents provide support and will include creation of pallets with single or multiple SKUs.

Mixed palletizing is a multi-objective multi-constraint optimization problem. In the literature, the mixed palletizing domain for which we are developing metrics is often called "the distributor's pallet packing problem". It is one of a set of closely-related packing (or unpacking/cutting) problems, all of which are known to be hard to solve as pure geometry problems. In fact, the pallet stacking problem is related to the bin packing problem which is a standard NP-hard (non-deterministic polynomial-time hard) problem in computational complexity theory [7].

In this problem, objects of different volumes must be packed into a finite number of bins of limited capacity in a way that minimizes the number of bins used. By restricting the number of bins to one (our one pallet), and characterizing each item by both a volume and a value, we have a problem known as the knapsack problem. Our palletizing problem is then a special case of the knapsack problem where each box is represented by a volume/weight and a potential profit (the value) for including that box on the pallet. Consider a knapsack with item set $N$, consisting of $n$ items, where the $j_{th}$ item has profit $p_j$ and weight $w_j$, and the capacity is $c$. Then, the objective function can be formulated as:

$$\max \sum_{j=1}^{n} p_j x_j \, , \qquad (1)$$

subject to

$$\max \sum_{j=1}^{n} w_j x_j \le c \, , \qquad (2)$$

$$x_j \in \{0,1\}, \ j = 1, \ldots, n. \qquad (3)$$

In equation (2) $x_j$ can only take integral values and it denotes whether the $j_{th}$ item is included in the knapsack or not. Finding the optimum solution vector $x^*$ having an optimum profit $z^*$ is non-trivial and known to be NP-hard [7]. There are 2 main aspects of the palletizing problem that need to be defined: the constraints and the model.

## 2.1 Planning Constraints

### 2.1.1 Stability Constraints

The stability constraints of a mixed palletizing problem can be specified by studying the shear and stress properties and doing a finite element analysis (FEM) on the pallet. Stress and strain failure are caused by the load or pressure on each SKU. The planner has to take these into account for scheduling the order in which boxes should be packed.

These constraints are formally expressed as compressive or shear stress and yield equations. Compressive stress causes the package to reduce its height due to pressure and buckle. The strength of the pallet is determined by the elastic properties of the boxes it contains. This property allows us to constrain the maximum allowable pressure on each box by (4). The stress strain curve is a standard tool used in FEM analysis which gives (5). It puts a limit on the assumed yield strength of a package.

$$\rho = \frac{F}{A} \propto \frac{\pi^2 E}{h^2} \, . \qquad (4)$$

$$\partial \rho \le k \frac{dh}{h} \, . \qquad (5)$$

Here $E$ is the Young's modulus and $h$ is the height of the package, a constant of elasticity specific to the packaging material being used. $F$, $A$ are the total force and the total surface area of the package. From (4) we can determine that shear stress can be reduced by creating interlocking patterns which would increase the area under contact for each package. A trivial approach to model this would be to maximize,

$$P \propto \frac{n A_0}{A}, \qquad (6)$$

where $n$ is the total number of boxes touching the current box and $A_0$ is the total area encompassed by all the boxes. We normalize it by $A$, which is the total surface area of the box.

### 2.1.2 Packaging Constraints

Finding a feasible packing for a pallet is referred to as the cutting problem. There are two widely studied cutting problems: guillotine and non-guillotine cutting problems. Guillotine patterns refer to patterns that are cuttable. The problem we consider in this section is that of selecting a subset of items and assigning coordinates $(x_j, y_j, z_j)$ to each item, such that no item goes outside the bin, no two items

intersect and the total volume of the items does not exceed the maximum capacity. We have the following constraints,

$$0 \le x_i \le W - w_i,$$
$$0 \le y_i \le H - h_i,$$
$$0 \le z_i \le D - d_i.$$

To ensure that no two packed boxes $i$, $j$ intersect we add more constraints,

$$x_i + w_i \le x_j,$$
$$y_i + h_i \le y_j,$$
$$z_i + d_i \le z_j,$$
$$x_j + w_j \le x_i,$$
$$y_j + h_j \le y_i,$$
$$z_j + d_j \le z_i.$$

Many methods that solve the bin packing problem use the above constraints.

### 2.1.3 Empirical Constraints

Empirical constraints constitute the generic statistics that are known to be related to stability such as the center of mass and density of the pallet.

## 2.2 Planning Models

### 2.2.1 Variations of the Packing Problem

Variations of the packing problem include knapsack loading, container loading, and bin packing. In knapsack loading, the problem is to find a subset of items that will fit into a single bin. In container loading, the problem is to find a feasible arrangement of items in which the height of the filled bin is minimum, and in bin packing, the items are packed into finite sized bins and the problem is to find the solution with the minimum number of bins. Usually one of these problem determines a cost function for the knapsack problem.

Any logistics or a mixed palletizing system can be modeled by a Knapsack problem variant [8]. If the planning problem involves many constraints then we can frame it as a *d-dimensional knapsack problem*. Planning for rainbow palletizing (a pallet where different layers of the pallet are created out of different products) can be performed by modifying the problem as a *quadratic knapsack problem*. Other interesting variants of the problem can be used to model complex warehousing systems for shipping industries. The *multiple knapsack problem* and the *multiple-choice knapsack problem* can be used to model package priority, packages arriving late or even wrongly delivered packages. If the rate or the number of packages coming into a warehouse is not fixed, a variant called *stochastic knapsack problem* can be used for modeling on-line bin packing problem. All these different models can give us insight into the measure of efficiency a logistics scheme is capable of. There are lower bounds available from theoretical computer science, which give a theoretical indication that the running time of an exact algorithm for the knapsack problem can not beat a certain threshold under reasonable assumptions on the model of computation. Many knapsack instances can be solved within reasonable time by exact solution methods.

### 2.2.2 Planning Algorithms and Benchmarks

Algorithms that solve NP-hard problems can be divided into two parts: *exact algorithms* and *approximate algorithms*. Exact algorithms find the most optimal solution of a given problem whereas approximate algorithms find an approximate solution.

There are many standard algorithmic approaches that can be used to solve this problem. Greedy, branch and bound, dynamic programming and polynomial time approximation schemes are used to solve palletizing problems modeled as the knapsack problem. Each of these different class of algorithms scale the profit or weight space to achieve a near optimal solution. For problems with stochastic input, heuristics are used which are learned from statistical distribution techniques to model the profit and weight space.

### 2.2.3 Algorithmic Benchmarks

Algorithms that solve the knapsack problem are not similar. Algorithms that find the most optimum solution often do so by doing an exhaustive search. They are computationally very inefficient when compared to approximate algorithms which are computationally far more efficient. However, approximate algorithms have the drawback that they can only find a near optimum solution. It is not always possible to do an exhaustive search over a problem space.

Algorithms are usually tested over several data sets and their performance is determined analytically. One of the most common way to check is to compare running time of the algorithm after the data set is doubled. The time required to find the solution should not increase exponentially for polynomial or pseudo polynomial algorithms. The most common way to measure the performance of an algorithm is to perform the worst-case analysis.

## 2.3 An Exact Approach

Consider the robot packable bin packing problem. The problem is strongly NP-hard. However we discuss here an exact branch and bound algorithm for solving the bin packing problem. The three dimensional bin packing problem consists of orthogonally packing all the boxes in the minimum number of bins.

A greedy approach to solve this problem would assume that the packages are sorted according to decreasing efficiencies

$$\frac{p_1}{w_1} \geq \frac{p_2}{w_2} \geq \cdots \geq \frac{p_n}{w_n} \ . \tag{7}$$

An obvious disadvantage of this approach is that only the first bin would be efficiently filled. The exact algorithm due to [10, 9] is based on a two level decomposition principle: the main branching algorithm and the single bin filling algorithm. The main branching algorithm assigns boxes to each bin, while a separate branch and bound algorithm tests whether the box can be placed in the bin by determining its location and cost. The main branching algorithm is an approximation algorithm and limits the number of executions of the single bin filling algorithm. The approximation algorithm can be defined by many complementary heuristics.

Consider our objective function is to maximize the number of boxes to fit in a bin. Let $Z$ be the solution value and let $M = \{1, 2, \ldots, m\}$ be the current set of bins to which the boxes are assigned.

### 2.3.1 The main branching algorithm

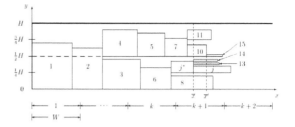

Figure 1: The shelf approach used for packing boxes in shelves [10]. A free box is assigned to the same shelf or a new shelf is created.

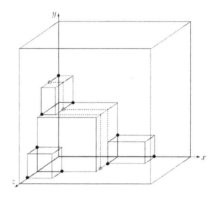

Figure 2: The 3D corners approach is used to find all possible feasible positions for a box [9]. The black dots indicate all starting positions available for a free box.

The exploration of the main branching algorithm follows a depth-first strategy. At each decision node the free box is assigned to all open bins. It is also assigned to a new bin if $|M| < Z-1$. Then the two heuristics on the single bin filling algorithm are used to find feasible packaging combinations. A node is not explored further if the lower bound is more than one or no feasible solution is found with the single bin filling algorithm. A box is assigned to the bin with the maximum upper bound.

### 2.3.2 The single bin filling algorithm

Here we consider two bin packing heuristics which have a complementary behavior. A poor performance on one of them corresponds to a good performance on the other.

In Figure 1, boxes are sorted according to their heights. All the boxes which lie within $\{\frac{h}{2^i}, \frac{h}{2^{i+1}}\}$ are put in group $i$. For every group $i$, boxes are sorted in slices of their width and length. If a new free box cannot be assigned to a particular shelf, it is put on the next shelf which starts from the highest box in the current shelf.

In Figure 2, is the 3D corners algorithm which decides feasible location after every assignment based on geometry. The packaging constraint equations in Section 2.1.2 correspond to this particular heuristic.

If a box cannot be assigned using one of the above heuristics it is rejected.

## 3. INFORMATION MODEL

An information model provides a sharable, stable, and organized structure of information for representing domain specific data. For the case of mixed palletizing, there are three categories of data that need to be represented. These include *a priori* data about possible articles and constraints, plan data that specifies how a pallet is to be constructed, and as-built data that provides a description of the pallet as it was actually constructed. In our case, all of these information models are provided as XML schemas [6]. The *a priori* and plan models are based on extensions of KUKA Systems[1] information models. The as-built model is a newly created construct.

### 3.1 A priori information model

The *a priori* information model contains all of the data necessary for the planner to construct and optimize its plans. It contains information on pallet constraints, individual articles, and the bill of lading. Pallet constraints include information such as the pallet dimensions, allowed overhang, and maximum capacity. Article information includes quantities such as the article dimensions, weight, robustness, and family group. Finally, the bill of lading contains order information such as the desired quantities for each article.

### 3.2 Plan information model

The plan information model contains all of the information necessary to construct the pallet. This includes article information and plan-build information. The article information contains the same data as in the *a priori* information model described above with the addition of the pallet build order. The build order enumerates the order in which an upstream sequencing or sorting system should deliver the articles to the assigned mixed palletizing robot or manual palletizing station that is building the actual pallet.

The plan-build information contains the final resting location (or target point) of each article along with article approach information. This approach information contains a set of via points which describes the approach movement of the robot to arrive at its final drop location without colliding with articles that have already been placed on the target pallet. In the optimal case, the target point can be reached by all four sides. However, depending on the cell layout, the gripper technology utilized, and the loading container, the allowed approach direction may be limited.

### 3.3 As-built information model

The as-built information model contains information on the pallet as it was actually constructed by the robotic platform (either simulated or in reality). The file contains the actual 6-degree-of-freedom location of article after completion of the build as well as information on the actual article size. The reason that size information is necessary is that packages are deformable. Their shape may change as pressure is applied to them from packages placed on top, or due to damage from the manipulation task. In addition, the actual packages used in the pallet build may differ from the expected models. If it is possible to obtain the as-built information during the build process, an additional use of the information would be for the planner to adjust article drop point locations during the build process to account for the package deformations and irregularities. The build process would also be able to be interrupted in case the virtual model and actual model differ by too great of an extent. At the current time, the packages used in simulation are not deformable, and are of uniform size and shape. Therefore, the information model contains an identifier for each package. The identifier may be used to obtain more information about the package from the order file. However, this is an area that we hope to expand upon in our future work.

## 4. PALLET METRICS

Due to the fact that planning for a mixed pallet is NP-hard, we know that computed plans will be suboptimal. We further know that packing strategy depends on the type of packages being stacked and pallet utilization depends on shipping constraints. However, given a packing plan, we would still like to answer the question of *how good is the plan?* In order to answer this question, metrics must be devised. Neither papers on pallet packing found in the literature nor the commercial systems say much about the metrics themselves, other than packing density. Brief mention is made in [2] of intersection, overlap, overhang, and center of gravity. In an attempt to better answer this question, the authors have developed a series of metrics that may be decomposed into the categories of Article Specific Metrics, Pallet-Wide Metrics, and Error Metrics.

### 4.1 Article Specific Metrics

Article specific metrics are those metrics which apply to a single article or package. They include measures that contribute to the stability (e.g. connections below and overlap) and integrity (e.g. overhang and maximum pressure) of individual packages.

The connections below measures the number of packages on which this package rests. This measure is designed to indicate the degree of interlocking that occurs on the pallet, where more interlocking may imply improved pallet stability. It should however be noted that for some pallets, interlocking may significantly reduce the load capacity of individual articles. The overlap of a package represents the fraction of the bottom of the article that rests on other packages. Small values would mean poorly supported articles which could result in pallet instability.

The overhang indicates the amount of the article that extends over the pallet edge. Large overhang could make the article vulnerable to to damage, and may make loading the pallet into a truck, plane, or container difficult or impossible. The maximum pressure indicates the maximum static pressure that will be exerted on this package. Note that dynamic loads, for example when a package is dropped on top of this article, may cause the article to experience larger pressures.

### 4.2 Pallet-Wide Metrics

Pallet-wide metrics are those metrics which apply to the pallet when taken as a whole. They include measures that relate to the raw construction data for the pallet such as the number of articles on the pallet and overall pallet statistics such as the pallet's total weight, maximal height, and vol-

---

[1]Certain commercial software tools and hardware are identified in this paper in order to explain our research. Such identification does not imply recommendation or endorsement by the authors, nor does it imply that the software tools and hardware identified are necessarily the best available for the purpose.

| Metric | Pallet (a) | Pallet (b) |
|---|---|---|
| Average Overlap | 0.95 | 0.53 |
| Average Connections | 2.00 | 1.00 |
| Intersection Error | 1 | 9 |
| Stack Height | 0.125 m | 0.209 m |
| Volume Density | 0.6054 | 0.4410 |
| Center of Gravity (height) | 0.04 m | 0.08 m |

Table 1: **A few metrics generated by palletViewer on the pallets from Figure 3**

ume. In addition, efficiency and handling characteristics are represented with these metrics.

Efficiency measures strive to measure how efficient the pallet construction is. They include storage volume and volume density. The storage volume represents the warehouse space that is required to store the pallet based on the calculation of the pallet base area times its height. Volume density is a ratio that compares the sum of the individual article volumes to the storage volume. It may be used to indicate how much "empty space" is required to be stored.

Handling measures indicate how easy it will be for the final pallet to be maneuvered during shipping and the complexity of unloading the pallet. It includes such measures as the pallet's center of gravity and the number of product families that are contained on the pallet. A product family is a set of articles that will be unloaded at a single location at the pallet's destination. In the case of product families, a particular product family's distribution on the pallet is also considered. For example, a pallet that contains three layers of articles with layer one and three belonging to the same family would be said to contain three different families. The reason for this is that the pallet would need to make three stops to unload (stop one for the family in layer three, stop two for the family in layer two, and then back to stop one for layer one).

### 4.3 Error Metrics

The error metrics deal with problems in the packing plan. These problems include plan errors, stocking errors, and syntax errors. Plan errors occur when some planning constraint has been violated. These include constraints on article placement (e.g. two articles intersect) as well as constraints on article integrity such as the maximum pressure that may be exerted on an article and pallet integrity such as the overall pallet weight, height, and overhang.

Stocking errors occur when the content of the pallet does not match the order. This can include missing or extra articles. Finally, syntax errors occur when the plan file does not properly conform to the predefined XML schema for the plan.

### 4.4 Metric Tools

The above metrics define a set of raw values that can be computed from a combination of the raw order data, plan constraints, and final packing plan. In order to dictate that one packing plan is superior to another, these raw values must be combined and weighted into a single value. This weighting may be application and industry specific. In order to experiment with various weightings and examine the

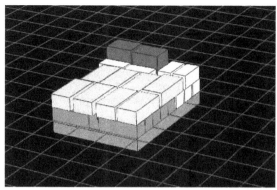

(a) Pallet generated with an offline algorithm.

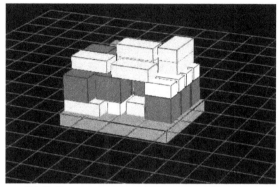

(b) Pallet generated with an online algorithm.

Figure 3: **Pallets generated by two different planning algorithms on the same order as displayed in palletViewer.**

specific values of individual metrics, a tool has been created which computes these metrics. This tool is called the *Pallet Viewer* and is a C++ program that uses OpenGL graphics [11].

The application simulates the exact execution of the final packing plan by placing one article at a time on the pallet. Metrics are computed for each article as it is added, and pallet-wide metrics are also displayed. A sample of the pallet display may be seen in Figure 3 and a sample of the computed metrics are shown in Table 1. The user is able to rotate, translate, and zoom this image as well as adding or subtracting articles from the pallet.

## 5. ICRA VIRTUAL MANUFACTURING COMPETITION

The first real trial of the metrics being developed for this effort occurred during the 2010 Virtual Manufacturing Automation Competition (VMAC) [3] that was part of the IEEE International Conference on Robotics and Automation (ICRA) robot challenge. During this event, three different palletizing approaches were evaluated through the use of our metrics. These approaches included a university-created neural network learning-based approach, a university-created deterministic planning approach, and a commercial product that is commonly used by industry.

At the VMAC event, teams were presented with the XML

**Figure 4: View of the USARSim physics-based simulation of a mixed-pallet under construction.**

order file and were required to generate a compliant XML packlist file. This file was then passed through the Pallet Viewer software and the values of the metrics were computed. While this provided a measure of the final pallet's quality, it did not evaluate the ability to build the pallet. Therefore, teams were next tasked with running their packlist file on a simulated palletizing cell. This cell was implemented in the Unified System for Automation and Robot Simulation (USARSim) and is shown in Figure 4. USARSim performs a physics simulation that includes friction and gravity, so that problems such as sliding and tipping (which Pallet Viewer will not find) are evident. USARSim runs in real time, however, so it is not able to evaluate plans quickly. USARSim provided an "as-built" file at the end of the pallet's construction that could be utilized by the Pallet Viewer software for evaluation of the correctness of the build.

**Figure 5: 1/3 scale palletizing cell used during the ICRA Competition**

The final step of the competition was to allow successful teams to try and build their pallets on a 1/3 scale palletizing cell shown in Figure 5. This competition is an ongoing event and will be held during the 2011 ICRA conference. Sample palletizing code may be found through the VMAC website and new teams are encouraged to participate.

## 6. CONCLUSIONS

Due to the lack of widely accepted metrics, it is currently very difficult to judge the quality of a mixed pallet solution. In addition, most of the current mixed palletizing solutions are catered to a particular industry. There is a desire to obtain more flexible solutions and techniques to compare these solutions. For this, we have proposed generic problem modeling and benchmarking techniques. By comparing the mixed palletizing technique to the knapsack problem we have tried to theoretically reason benchmarks.

In our future work, we endeavor to grow as a community dedicated to the study and analysis of automation in logistics.

## 7. REFERENCES

[1] S. Balakirsky, T. Kramer, and F. Proctor. Metrics for mixed pallet stacking. In *Proceedings of the Performance Metrics for Intelligent Systems (PerMIS) Workshop*, 2010.

[2] E. Baltacioglu. The distributer's three-dimensional pallet-packing problem: A human intelligence-based heuristic approach. Master's thesis, Air Force Institute of Technology, 2001.

[3] VMAC Executive Committee. Virtual manufacturing automation competition homepage. http://www.vma-competition.com, June 2010.

[4] Great Little Box Company. Palletization. http://www.greatlittlebox.com/packaging/storing, June 2010.

[5] D. Faulkner and S. Murphy. Industrial robots in warehousing and distribution operations. In *Proceedings of the Performance Metrics for Intelligent Systems (PerMIS) Workshop*, 2010.

[6] Kuka SysTec GmbH. Xml schema for article. http://moast.cvs.sourceforge.net/viewvc/moast/devel/src/manufact/sampleData/Schema, June 2010.

[7] H. Kellerer, U. Pferschy, and D. Pisinger. *Knapsack problems*. Springer Verlag, 2004.

[8] P. Kolhe and H. Christensen. Planning in logistics: A survey. In *Proceedings of the Performance Metrics for Intelligent Systems (PerMIS) Workshop*, 2010.

[9] S. Martello, D. Pisinger, and D. Vigo. The three-dimensional bin packing problem. *Operations Research*, pages 256–267, 2000.

[10] S. Martello and D. Vigo. Exact solution of the two-dimensional finite bin packing problem. *Management science*, 44(3):388–399, 1998.

[11] NIST. Pallet viewer user's manual. http://sourceforge.net/apps/mediawiki/moast/index.php?title=Pallet_Viewer_User%27s_Manual, November 2010.

[12] L. Sweet. Mixed palletizing in transformed supply chains: Operational requirements and technical challenges. Presentation at the Performance Metrics for Intelligent Systems (PerMIS) Workshop, 2010.

# Modeling and Simulation Analysis Types for Sustainable Manufacturing

Deogratias Kibira, Guodong Shao and Y. Tina Lee
Manufacturing Systems Integration Division
National Institute of Standards and Technology
100 Bureau Drive, Gaithersburg, MD 20899, Mail Stop 8261
301-975 2192, 301-975 3625 and 301-975 3550

deogratias.kibira@nist.gov, guodong.shao@nist.gov and yung-tsun.lee@nist.gov

## ABSTRACT

Sustainable manufacturing could be promoted by the effective use of Modeling and Simulation (M&S) applications. These applications can evaluate manufacturing operations in light of increasing legislation and awareness for environmental protection. They can help determine the operational policy and strategy, and evaluate day-to-day manufacturing decisions to comply with regulations and to improve a company's image. However, in order to accomplish these objectives, existing and future simulation applications need to be enhanced to include sustainability constructs. This paper describes a classification of M&S application areas along functionality and data requirements axes that are necessary to achieve sustainable manufacturing objectives. The classification can in turn be used to perform requirements analyses for those applications and develop data repositories necessary to build and execute the simulation models.

## Categories and Subject Descriptors

I.6.1 [Simulation and Modeling]: Simulation Theory – *model classification, systems theory.*

## General Terms

Management, Measurement, Documentation, Performance, Design, Human Factors, Standardization, Theory.

## Keywords

Sustainable manufacturing, metrics, sustainability data, simulation analysis requirements

## 1. INTRODUCTION

Manufacturing systems use raw materials and auxiliaries such as water and air, and transform them into finished products. The transformation process requires inputs of energy. Solid and liquid wastes and gaseous pollution are often produced as byproducts of the manufacturing process. Figure 1 shows the basic inputs and outputs of a manufacturing system. Therefore, production systems and production activities can have both positive and negative impacts on the natural environment, natural resources, economy, and the surrounding communities. The negative effect may imply

This paper is authored by employees of the United States Government and is in the public domain.
PerMIS'10, September 28-30, 2010, Baltimore, MD, USA.
ACM 978-1-4503-0290-6-9/28/10.

that soil is contaminated, and natural resources, water sources, energy sources, and pristine land mass depleted at such a rate that manufacturing activities cannot be sustained in the long-term without exceeding the natural limits. With this new awareness to minimize the impact of economic activities on the environment and natural resources, the term "sustainable manufacturing" has been coined.

The Sustainable Manufacturing Hub (Sustainable Manufacturing Hub 2009) defines sustainable manufacturing as *"creating a product in a way that considers the entire product's life cycle and its full impact surrounding the use and reuse of raw materials and auxiliary materials, impact on the environment and impact on the surrounding community. The goal is to be able to manufacture in a way which is so sustainable that it is able to continue into the future."* This definition implies the importance of analyzing a product's entire life from raw material acquisition to its disposal and, if possible, recovery and reuse of its components or materials into new products.

This paper gives an overview of the types of simulation models that can be developed for sustainable manufacturing. It contrasts traditional simulation model objectives and sustainable objectives, and highlights the types and role of data in these models.

**Figure 1. Basic inputs and outputs of a manufacturing system**

What is simulation? Simulation can be defined as *"the process of designing and creating a computerized model of a real or proposed system for the purpose of conducting numerical experiments to give us a better understanding of the behavior of that system for a given set of conditions"* (Kelton et al. 2004). Modeling and simulation (M&S) methods have a high potential to contribute to sustainable manufacturing. Therefore, it is necessary to capture and formalize descriptions of the product design, manufacturing, use and disposal processes, and their interactions. Because of the complexity of the problems, M&S will play a large part in understanding (Rachuri et al. 2009). As such, M&S applications can play an important role in decision making either before or during each stage of a product's or production system's life cycle. Such stages include site selection, product design, production system design, machine and process selection, material selection, product useful life, product replacement, and product disassembly and reuse/recycle. A simulation model can be developed for targeted stage in a product's life or one model could be constructed to simulate the entire product lifecycle. An example of this is the Arena model developed to investigate lifecycle cost reduction in domestic appliances for manufacturers under the Waste Electrical and Electronic Equipment (WEEE) regulation for product sale, product use, repair, and disposal (Xie et al. 2006).

By describing what to simulate, the classification of objectives would support to perform requirements analyses of M&S tools for enhancement and development of new applications for sustainable manufacturing. The rest of the paper is organized as follows: the next section reviews literature related to simulation of sustainable manufacturing and classification strategy. Section 3 describes the classification issues along the dimension of functional requirements for the simulation model. Section 4 presents a description of the data requirements for executing the simulation models. Section 5 describes an example of a simulation model that can be developed to include sustainability concepts in the functions, and its data requirements. Section 6 concludes the paper.

## 2. RELATED WORK AND SIMULATION CONTEXTS

### 2.1 Assessing Sustainable Manufacturing

A region or country can be assessed whether or not it is on a trajectory to sustainable development by measures such as genuine savings, ecological measures, ecological footprints, environmental space, socio-political measures, and quality of life indicators (Moffatt et al. 2001). In a standardized Life Cycle Assessment (LCA) the goals are first defined to eliminate the case where some indicators can be seem as conflicting. Lifecycle simulation has also been proposed to evaluate the effectiveness of different lifecycle phases, i.e., remanufacture, reuse, recycle, maintenance, and final dumping (Takata et al. 2003). By this method the given parameters, indicators, performance metrics, and indexes are defined, tracked and evaluated against set benchmark values.

### 2.2 Modeling and Simulation Issues

M&S tools have been used for sustainable manufacturing for specific cases. For example; collecting and recycling policies of used products under the Extended Producer Responsibility (EPR) system (Kamazawa and Kobayashi 2003); evaluating process design for optimizing material and water consumption (Turon et al. 2005); selecting processes to be outsourced, new suppliers, and new manufacturing styles by using life cycle simulation by original equipment manufacturers (Komoto et al. 2003); evaluating alternative operating processes regarding CO2 emission, energy use, resource use, and waste in a smelter plant (Khoo et al. 2001); determining manufacturing for environmental waste and indirect costs associated with disposal and containment (Russell et al. 1998); and reducing and streamlining material, energy used, and cost of energy (Sakai et al. 2003). Environmental and ergonomic issues have been analyzed using simulation (Heilala et al. 2008) and an integrated framework for

analyzing both economic and ecological objectives in manufacturing has been developed (Herrmann et al. 2007).

The review shows that simulation of manufacturing systems for sustainability is scanty and scattered. There is also a lack of concerted effort to structure requirements for modeling, simulation and analysis of sustainable manufacturing.

### 2.3 Decisions at Different Abstraction Levels

Different decisions are made at different levels of hierarchy. The interaction between the decision making systems can complicate the process of achieving economic, social, and environmental objectives. Each level may require a different simulation study type due to different data and analysis objectives. For example, the evaluation of impact of a new plant on overall business performance is a long term strategic decision as compared to determining a daily production schedule, which is a short term operational decision.

#### Industrial Policy

M&S is important for decision making at the industrial level for long term or strategic planning because of the increasing complexity of systems, processes, and data. At a macro level, sustainable manufacturing policy can be determined by the use of system dynamics modeling. System dynamics facilitates decision support for policy making by helping to determine long term effects of industrial activities on natural resources, energy, and the environment. It can also evaluate the impact on the economic viability of the industry. To benefit from these models, the analyst needs to first determine the indicators of manufacturing sustainability. Measures such as genuine financial benefits, ecological measures such as pollution, ecological footprints, and environmental space need to first, be defined. The inputs to this model would be factors such as population, investment, interest rates, imports, regulatory policies, incentive, and taxes.

#### Factory and workstation level

M&S for sustainable manufacturing at workstation and machine level can be done in different ways, depending on the objective. Workstation simulation can model setup options to improve waste handling and disposal or to determine human-machine interaction to reduce energy use and toxic waste. Virtual reality can also be used to determine the ergonomic and kinematics movement of resources during operation. In can also analyze issues such as worker safety, and posture noise level and measures.

#### Process

M&S of machining operations, called virtual numerical control, is used to validate numerical control (NC) program, to ensure that the program would produce the part and to prevent possible machine crashes and damage. Thus, a module can be attached to the virtual machine model to track the energy consumed, quantity of coolant used, wastes generated, quality, surface finish, and gaseous pollution for an operation.

M&S can guide to select a particular model of NC machine tool for a job given the stock and required product. Different machine tools could have different specific energy consumption for machining given engineering materials. As M&S determines whether a given NC program can produce the part it can also determine sustainability indicators. With this approach, production scheduling will not only produce a schedule which can best utilize resources and meet customer requirements but also minimize the environmental impact of a given work order.

## 2.4 Classification Strategy

The classification identifies the nature of the simulation, i.e., the major issues and elements within sustainable manufacturing that are to be modeled. These issues form a basis for identifying the functionalities required within the simulation applications. The need for M&S is often due to, for example, the introduction of a new manufacturing plant in a community, evaluation of effect of compliance with a newly introduced environmental regulation, or modification of existing manufacturing process for a particular purpose. We identify two dimensions along which to perform the requirements analysis and classification. The first is the stage in the product lifecycle. The other dimension is the data categories.

## 3. REQUIREMENTS ANALYSIS – FUNCTIONAL

This section describes the functional requirements of a simulation model for traditional and sustainable situations. These two situations or views form the structure of the work to be described in this section.

## 3.1 Product Lifecycle

The stages in a production lifecycle start with product design and end with disassemble, reuse, and recycle. At each stage, different simulation models need to be constructed. It is the requirements and goals of the simulation model at each stage that will form the basis for problem classification. The Figure 2 shows the hierarchical display of the stages.

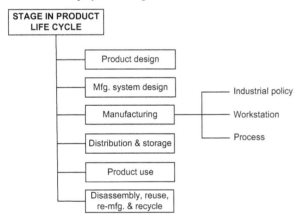

**Figure 2. Framework for classification of sustainable manufacturing M&S problem types**

## 3.2 Functional Categories

### 3.2.1 Product Design

Product design defines the determination and specification of components of a product so that they all function as the requirements specify. The design phase is important because it is estimated that 70 to 80 percent of the product cost is determined by decisions made during the design stage (Savari et al. 2008). It is beneficial to introduce Lifecycle Engineering early in the design stage and assess both ecological and economic impacts of a product design. There are many areas in the design process where

M&S can play a major role. They include performance analysis, process planning and manufacturing requirements, and economic and safety objectives.

**Performance**

*Traditional* – Eliminate the need to build physical prototypes as a means of determining behavioral characteristics and manufacturability before a product is eventually built. As such, product simulation is carried out to understand the problem that the design intends to solve, and a synthesis phase in which the solutions are generated. The different solutions are evaluated using M&S. Novel approaches such as Applied Signposting Model (Wynn et al. 2006) used to simulate the effect of design on various options for manufacturing in a concurrent engineering environment.

*Sustainable* – Test alternative designs, materials, and component parts with a view to analyzing energy consumption during production and use, product durability, and pollution. It can also be useful in issues such as investigation of product function when using alternative operating conditions.

**Process planning and manufacturing requirements**

*Traditional* – Virtual reality simulation of assembly processes where, through the concept of virtual manufacturing, the parts manufacturing and assembly of a product can all be done in a 3-D simulated environment. M&S is also useful to evaluate different process plans for product flow time, facilities utilization, alternative work flows, resource utilization, waiting times, and load balancing.

*Sustainable* – Model the process according to clean manufacturing processes, equipment, and the use of alternative materials.

**Economic**

*Traditional* – Assessment of costs involved in materials purchase, parts production, labor, and equipment.

*Sustainable* – Analysis of costs of sustainable inputs and toxicity of materials, cost of non-compliance, material reuse, tradeoff between sustainable process costs, and maintenance and disposal costs under the extended user responsibility.

**Safety**

*Traditional* – Evaluation of worker capacity and physical burden and strain to carry out the task for efficiency of operation, allowance for resting, and production rate while minimizing or eliminating injury to person. Reduction of claims and expense from worker related health problems and/or loss of body part.

*Sustainable* – Place greater emphasis on safety, including exposure to hazards, injury prevention mechanisms, and elimination of potential harm from infection. Emphasize long-term health by elimination of carcinogens, task diversification, and employee morale.

### 3.2.2 Manufacturing System Design

Manufacturing system design involves equipment specification, determination of labor requirements, and layout. This process normally follows product design so that the required facilities, equipment, machinery, staffing, and control systems can be put in place to manufacture the product. In case of jobbing shops, a production system may already be in place and equipped with general purpose machine tools with given capabilities. New product designs or orders are accepted on the basis of equipment capability and capacity. However, it is also possible that a new product design would need modifications on existing equipment and facility layout. But with concurrent engineering the design of the product and manufacturing system design would take place simultaneously.

Regardless of the situation, M&S can be used to select a manufacturing process and in turn determine the requirements. Effective design of a manufacturing system using M&S contributes to efficiency and sustainability of its operations.

**Manufacturing process selection**

*Traditional* – Evaluate and select manufacturing processes that are cost effective and efficient in operation, matching machine capacity, labor skills, and operator comfort.

*Sustainable* – Evaluate and select process for minimal environmental impact such as evaluation and selection between casting and sintering in the making of some classes of products.

**Manufacturing facilities selection**

*Traditional* – Investigate equipment capability and identify problem areas, quantify or optimize system performance under different loading conditions and investigate queue sizes, resource utilizations, existence and identification of bottlenecks, and staffing levels. Determine effect of facilities on throughput.

*Sustainable* – Consider additional sustainability issues to equipment such as pollution, greenhouse gas emissions, maintenance requirements, equipment life while carrying out the selection process.

**Manufacturing facilities layout**

*Traditional* – Evaluate effect of different layout configurations on system performance, floor space requirements and materials handling costs, buffer storage needs and throughput, effect of materials handling, storage areas, scheduling, and determination of work routing.

*Sustainable* – Evaluate effect of layout on factors such as energy usage, machine idle times, operational and maintenance accessibility, and housekeeping.

**Materials handling**

*Traditional* – Determine material handling capacity, materials holding storage, sufficient space for movement, level of automation, visualize proposed system, integration of materials handling with other manufacturing systems and testing of alternative handling policies.

*Sustainable* – Minimize energy costs in handling, reduction of handling, deployment of reusable containers and containers, and the use of sustainable materials handling methods.

### 3.2.3 Manufacturing

One of the largest application areas for M&S is that of manufacturing systems, with the first use dating back to at least the early 1960's (Law and McComas 1997). Hence, manufacturing is perhaps the largest application stage in product realization because of the large potential for performance improvement and the need to avoid costly mistakes. Current M&S applications enable analysts to model and validate manufacturing processes, work flow, schedules; introduce new products and processes; determine material, labor, equipment, tooling,

inventory, material handling, and maintenance requirements; and plan for equipment breakdowns and repairs. However, the current commercial off-the-shelf simulation tools most often do not address sustainability.

**Planning and control**

*Traditional* – Reduce costs, minimize production lead times, evaluate schedules, and improve product quality. Others are to identify bottlenecks, determine inventory policies, throughput, and capacity (equipment and personnel) utilization. Also, evaluate effect of inventory policy, location, size, deliveries, and inventory tracking mechanisms on system performance.

*Sustainable* – Determine material, energy, and waste flows in manufacturing and consideration of issues such as energy or water used per unit of final product.

**Quality improvement**

*Traditional* – Determining the number of inspection stations, their placement and impact on throughput and outgoing quality. It can also be used in investigating the effect of process parameters on defect formation in the product.

*Sustainability* – Investigate the shift to sustainable manufacturing processes and products and the effect that the shift can have on product quality.

**Maintenance management**

*Traditional* – Determine optimal preventive maintenance policy, sizing of repair crew and tools for dealing with breakdowns, improving system life, improving production and quality, and safety. M&S can support decision making to determine operating policy, performance management, dynamic maintenance system, maintenance cost control, and system downtime.

*Sustainable* – Investigate use of more environmentally friendly parts, lubricants, and procedures. Schedule maintenance to collect used parts in bins of same material composition for easy recycling or rework. M&S can be applied to evaluate and decide maintenance procedures and policy for longer product service and optimal policy for product (especially equipment) replacement.

### 3.2.4 Distribution and Storage

Virtually all products from the manufacturer pass through a distribution system that involves storage and handling until it reaches the final consumer. Control of the distribution system is concerned with measuring the cost, service level, and flexibility or a tradeoff while considering different strategies and structural conditions. By selecting a criteria or measure of performance, an analyst can determine an operating policy or strategy.

**Distribution and warehousing strategy**

*Traditional* – Meeting delivery requirements, minimization of costs, and customer satisfaction. For a new supply chain that means location of distribution points and fleet capacity, and determination of optimal inventory levels.

*Sustainable* – Minimization of costs while considering environmentally friendly transportation and storage alternatives.

### 3.2.5 Product use

M&S of a completed unit of product use could include different ranges of operating conditions such as loading and environments, to ensure that it would perform as designed. This helps to increase product confidence in manufacturers and users by using virtual testing to cover a range of product usage situations.

**Product maintenance**

*Traditional* – Evaluate component and product reliability, availability and maintenance. Such an analysis can be used to determine maintenance crew and policy and what the benefits are of reduction of breakdowns.

*Sustainable* –Develop more conscientious maintenance programs for support equipment. This includes heating, ventilation, and air conditioning systems in work areas so as to reduce outputs of pollutants, energy use, and maintenance costs.

### 3.2.6 Disassembly, Reuse, Remanufacturing, and Recycle

In recent years, interest has increased in recovering and reusing materials from products after the end of their lives. Products are now designed for easy recovery of materials for reuse. The term "end of life product" has been changed to "end of use product." The main reasons include increasing cost of materials, rising cost of disposing used products, toxic substances being dumped into the environment, and government legislation.

*Traditional* – Evaluate product design for least cost, shortest time, etc. for disassembly and optimal communication of disassembly information and optimal sequence of disassembly processes.

*Sustainable* – Determine: i) recycling and reuse policy for local, state or federal government, ii) technologies for recycling, iii) the cost of recycling, iv) the end of life recycling value in a product, v) material and recovery reclamation strategy, and vi) whether to reuse, remanufacture or recycle an end of use product.

## 4. REQUIREMENTS ANALYSIS – DATA

M&S for sustainable manufacturing requires data for quantitative information to execute the models and obtain results to aid decision making. This section overviews this data.

## 4.1 Role of Data

The simulation models for each stage of product life cycle and abstraction level would typically require different types of data. Simulation execution data is input for a particular model or run. Stored data or reference data should be available for access by any simulation model and can be stored in plain text format or in remote databases. It could also be stored in relational databases. Figure 3 shows the relationship between data input, the simulation model, and output. This data can be categorized in the domains: environmental, social, and economic.

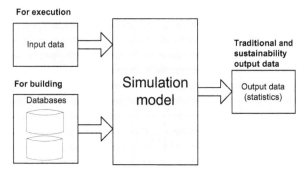

**Figure 3. Process flow for sustainable manufacturing modeling and simulation**

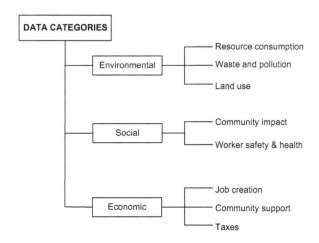

**Figure 4. Classification of M&S data requirements for sustainable manufacturing**

## 4.2 Data Categories

### 4.2.1 Environmental

The categories of data relevant to environmental impact are resource consumption, waste and pollution, and land use.

**Resource consumption**

This refers to natural resources available and those required in making the product. Such resources include raw materials, energy, air quality, and water. Different manufacturing systems consume different resources. The excessive use of local natural resources can affect both plant and animal life in the community.

**Waste and pollution**

Quantity and type of waste and emission produced throughout a product's life cycle. This category includes all solid, liquid and gaseous byproducts with a description of their content and lethal potential. Pollution includes also that produced by energy producers and transporters. Noise is also a form of pollution.

**Land**

This refers to the land available and land use per unit of product and for disposal of waste.

### 4.2.2 Social

This is the data input to evaluate the social impact of the investment on the population. The type of modeling relevant for this category is the continuous high-level simulation for policy setting. It is perhaps one of the most difficult to quantify and evaluate. The key elements in the social domain are:

- General population and health status
- Potential manufacturing workforce
- Skilled people
- Housing
- Community amenities
- Other manufacturers as social institutions

- Supporting infrastructure and institutions
- Social laws and regulations

### 4.2.3 Economic

Economic data is relevant for all levels of abstraction from the decision to set up a manufacturing plant to the payment of manufacturing bills. The income largely comes from sales and other benefits or services. The cost for each stage in product life cycle, i.e., material, labor, equipment (plant), energy, water, transportation, fines, and taxes is set against price tag and sales. Other economic data categories include:

- Financial markets
- Financial regulations
- Financial institutions
- Shareholders
- Individual wealth in the community
- Disposable income
- Manufacturing wages
- Manufacturers as financial entities
- Manufacturing throughput
- Manufacturing profits
- Other manufacturing investments

## 5. EXAMPLE OF SIMULATION MODEL

## 5.1 Machining Manufacturing Modeling

Machining falls into the categorization of manufacturing where the concern is production planning and control, quality, and maintenance. The objectives include: minimize waste, energy use and meet production requirements.

Machining uses energy, cutting fluids and lubricants that have to eventually be disposed of as waste. The chips formed during the process are often mixed with these fluids, and have to be cleaned before recycle. Cutting tools, made of hard materials, have a large life cycle environmental impact. Overall, machining is a "dirty" process with a negative impact on the environment. Therefore, modeling and simulation of the process using virtual numerical control for manufacturing sustainable products could aid decision making to reduce the environmental impact.

After a virtual model of the machine is constructed, the next step is to input the models of the part blank and the cutting tools to produce the virtual product. The part stock size and geometry plays an important role for deciding how much waste will be generated, energy consumed, and production time. The numerical control (NC) program is the basic input to the virtual machine, required, and is validated using the model. An optimized NC program may mean shorter production time thereby reducing energy consumption, tool usage, coolant and lubricant, and total emission. Different NC programs provide different scenarios for calculation of the environmental impact. Other controlled variables such as speed of cut and depth of cut influence cutting conditions and substantiality output. In addition, different NC programs for the same design part can be used to evaluate the difference in environmental impact. This analysis has functional and data requirements.

## 5.2 Functional Requirements

Modeling NC would need functionality to represent and visualize the machine tool, and input the workpiece, cutting tool, and NC program in addition to sustainability constructs. These are the machine tool builder, machine tool controller, machining process, energy use, coolant, and lubricant. The outputs are models of product, solid waste, liquid, waste, gaseous waste and other sustainability reports. It should also be able to model relationships between different sustainability indicators so that they can be evaluated with a common unit. There should also be functionality to vary different controllable inputs in the model. Other requirements are connections to databases and any optimization function and display of sustainability reports.

## 5.3 Data Requirements

**Validation data**

This process requires data. Some of this data is substituted into the simulation model by that particular run. Such data includes the NC program, work piecework model, and cutting tool data. The other is stored reference data.

**Reference data**

This is any data other than what can be provided by the model for the determination of the environmental impact. It includes machine specification data, lifecycle assessment (LCA) data, cutting speed data, feed rate, specific energy tables, tool tables, spindle power specification, and other real world data.

Real world data is collected from machine systems on the shop floor. The data could be collected directly from devices or come from a database or other information system. For example, the output that includes sustainable data from a real machine may be extracted by the following systems:

- **MTConnect**

This is a data exchange standard that allows for disparate entities in a manufacturing system along with their associated devices to share data in a common format. This middleware standard can facilitate direct extraction of data from Computer Numerical Controlled (CNC) machines during operation to other systems for further processing using the eXtensible Markup Language (XML) standard (Vijayaraghavan et al. 2008).

- **The Object Linking and Embedding for Process Control (OPC)**

OPC is a technique for monitoring manufacturing systems and their status (OPC Foundation 2010). The OPC standards specify the communication of industrial process data, alarms and events, historical data and batch process data between sensors, instruments, controllers, software systems, and notification devices.

## 6. CONCLUSIONS AND FUTURE WORK

This paper has presented an overview of the class of sustainable manufacturing simulation problem types and data. Different levels within each category and objectives of modeling have been discussed for both traditional and sustainability approaches. It has been found that M&S applications for sustainable manufacturing are relatively few and are often geared to the solution of a given problem using existing simulation models in their current form or a combination of approaches. Enhancement of M&S for sustainable manufacturing will require new metrics and standards and standards interfaces to be developed. It will also need a depository of data to execute simulation models and compare output against the best in class performance. To support sustainability, modeling tools will need to provide additional functional capabilities as well as validated methods and models that will help the analyst develop technically correct simulations. This paper has described the requirements. This description can then be used to perform requirements analysis for the applications that could form the basis for enhancement of or development of the required simulations systems and the model structures.

What remains to be done includes the description of characteristics of each type of simulation model and objectives, and searches into the sources of data. It would also link the data to the simulation model type.

# 7. ACKNOWLEDGMENTS

Work described in this report was sponsored by the Sustainable and Lifecycle Information-based Manufacturing (SLIM) program at the National Institute of Standards and Technology (NIST), Gaithersburg, Maryland. The SLIM program applies information technologies and standards-based approaches to manufactured product lifecycle problems. The work described was funded by the United States Government and is not subject to copyright.

# 8. DISCLAIMER

Any software products identified in context in this paper does not imply a recommendation or endorsement of the software products by the authors or NIST, nor does it imply that such software products are necessarily the best available for the purpose.

# 9. REFERENCES

[1] Heilala, J., S. Vatanen, H. Tonteri, J. Montonen, S. Lind, B. Johansson, and J. Stahre. 2008. Simulation-based Sustainable Manufacturing Systems. In *Proceedings of the 2008 Winter Simulation Conference* (Orlando, Florida, December 07-10, 2008). Institute of Electrical and Electronics Engineers, Piscataway, New Jersey: 1922–1930. DOI= http://www.informs-sim.org/wsc08papers/237.pdf

[2] Herrmann, C., L. Bergmann, S. Thiede, and A. Zein. 2007. Framework for Integrated Analysis of Production Systems. In *Proceedings of the 14th CIRP Conference on Lifecycle Engineering* (Waseda University, Tokyo, Japan, June 11-13, 2007). 195–200. DOI= http://www.springerlink.com/content/w83jj11vn2675j54/fulltext.pdf.

[3] Kamawaza, T. and H. Kobayashi. 2003. Feasibility Study of Sustainable Manufacturing System. In *Proceedings of the EcoDesign2003: Third International Symposium on Environmentally Conscious Design and Inverse Manufacturing* (Tokyo, Japan, December 11-13, 2003). 517–520.DOI= http://ieeexplore.ieee.org/stamp/stamp.jsp?arnumber=0132 2727

[4] Kelton, W., R. D. Sadowski, and D. T. Sturrock. 2004. *Simulation with ARENA*. 3rd ed. The McGraw-Hill Companies, Inc.

[5] Khoo, H. H., T. A. Spedding, L. Tobin, and D. Taplin. 2001. Integrated Simulation and Modeling Approach to Decision Making and Environmental Protection. *Environment, Development and Sustainability* 3, (June. 2001), 93–108. DOI=

http://www.springerlink.com/content/k8n268234r74l823/full text.pdf

[6] Komoto, H., T. Tomiyama, S. Silvester, and H. Brezet. 2006. Life Cycle Simulation of Products in a Competitive Market. In *Proceedings of the 13th CIRP International Conference on Life Cycle Engineering* (Leuven, Belgium, March 31 – June 2, 2006) 233–237. DOI= http://www.mech.kuleuven.be/lce2006/147.pdf

[7] Law, A. M. and M.G. McComas. 1997. Simulation of Manufacturing Systems. In *Proceedings of the 1997 Winter Simulation Conference* (Atlanta, Georgia, December 07-10, 1997). Institute of Electrical and Electronics Engineers, Piscataway, New Jersey: 86–89.

[8] Moffat, I., and N. Hanley. 2001. Modeling Sustainable Development: Systems Dynamics and Input-output Approaches. *Environmental Modeling & Software* 16, 6 (September 2001):545–557.

[9] OPC Foundation. 2010. *OPC Resource Page.* DOI= http://www.opcfoundation.org

[10] Rachuri, S., R.D. Sriram, and P. Sarkar. 2009. Metrics, Standards and Industry Best Practices and Sustainable Manufacturing Systems. In *Proceedings of the annual fifth IEEE International Conference on Automation Science and Engineering Conference, CASE 2009* (Bangalore, India, 2009), Institute of Electrical and Electronic Engineers, Piscataway, New Jersey: 472–477. DOI = http://www.nist.gov/customcf/get_pdf.cfm?pub_id=903008

[11] Russell, D.K, P. A. Farrington, S. L.Messimer, and J.J. Swain. 1998. Incorporating Environmental Issues in a Filament Winding Composite Manufacturing System Simulation. In *Proceedings of the 1998 Winter Simulation Conference* (Washington DC, December 13-26, 1998). Institute of Electrical and Electronics Engineers, Piscataway, New Jersey: 1023–1027. DOI = http://ieeexplore.ieee.org/stamp/stamp.jsp?tp=&arnumber=7 45837&userType=inst

[12] Sakai, N., G. Tanaka, and Y. Shimomura. 2003. Product Life Cycle Design Based on Product Life Control. In *Proceedings of the EcoDesign2003: Third International Symposium on Environmentally Conscious Design and Inverse Manufacturing*, (Tokyo, Japan, December 8-11, 2003), 102–108. DOI = http://ieeexplore.ieee.org/stamp/stamp.jsp?arnumber=013226 45

[13] Savari, M., L. Newnes, A. R. Mileham, and Y.G. Goh. 2008. Estimating Cost at the Conceptual Design Stage to Optimize Design in terms of Performance and Cost. In *Proceedings of the 15th ISPE International Conference on Concurrent Engineering (CE2008)*, Book Series: Advanced Concurrent Engineering. 123–130.DOI = http://www.springerlink.com/content/g27h3x74632r1628/full text.pdf

[14] Sustainable Manufacturing Hub: The National Council for Advanced Manufacturing, *What is Sustainable Manufacturing?*, DOI = http://nacfam01.stage.web.sba.com/Default.aspx.

[15] Takata S., T. Ogawa, Y. Umeda, and T. Inamura. 2003. Framework for Systematic Evaluation of Life Cycle Strategy by means of Life Cycle Simulation. In *Proceedings of the EcoDesign2003: Third International Symposium on Environmentally Conscious Design and Inverse Manufacturing.* (Tokyo, Japan, December 8-11, 2003), 198–205, DOI= http://ieeexplore.ieee.org/stamp/stamp.jsp?arnumber=013226 61

[16] Turon, X., J. Labidi, and J. Paris. 2005. Simulation and Optimization of a High Grade Coated Paper Mill. *Journal of Cleaner Production* 13, 15 (December 2005):1424–1433,

[17] Vijayaraghavan, A., W. Sobel, W., A. Fox., D. Dornfeld, and P. Warndorf. 2008. Improving Machine Tool Interoperability Using Standardized Interface Protocols : MTConnect™. In *Proceedings of the 2008 International Symposium on Flexible Automation* (Atlanta, Georgia, June 23-26, 2008). DOI= http://www.escholarship.org/uc/item/4zs976kx?display=all

[18] Wynn, D.C., C.M. Eckert, and P.J. Clarkson. 2006. Applied Signposting: A Modeling Framework to Support Design Process Improvement. In *Proceedings of the IDETC/CIE ASME 2006 International Design Engineering Technical Conferences & Computers and Information in Engineering Conference,* (Philadelphia, Pennsylvania, September 10-13, 2006). DOI = http://www-edc.eng.cam.ac.uk/p3/06-dtm06-wynn.pdf

[19] Xie, X. and M. Simon. 2006. Simulation for Product Life Cycle Management. *Journal of Manufacturing Technology Management* 17,4:486–495.

# Metrics for the Cost of Proprietary Information Exchange Languages in Intelligent Systems

John Horst
NIST
100 Bureau Drive / MS 8230
Gaithersburg, MD 20899
1.301.975.3430

john.horst@nist.gov

Nathan Hartman
Purdue University
401 Grant Street
West Lafayette, IN 47907-2021
1.765.496.6104

nhartman@purdue.edu

George Wong
The Boeing Company
5301 Bolsa Ave. / MS H012-B438
Huntington Beach, CA 92647
1.714.372.1917

george.s.wong@boeing.com

## ABSTRACT

The increasing number of intelligent software components is accompanied by an increasing number of proprietary information exchange languages between components. One of the challenges for the smart technology worker is to achieve intelligent system component interoperability, at the lowest cost possible, without sacrificing the freedom to choose from the entire spectrum of current and future software product offerings. This is best achieved when correct, complete, and unambiguous information exchange standards are implemented in vendor products worldwide. If this is the common sense solution to information incompatibility costs and risks, why is standards-based interoperability so rarely seen? One reason is that a required investment in standards must precede the savings gotten from true interoperability. Corporate management is commonly reluctant to commit to this investment, partly because there appears to be no published set of interoperability cost metrics which technology workers can employ to make an evidence-based business case. This research seeks to remedy this situation by defining realistic, comprehensive, and sector-independent cost-risk metrics.

## Categories and Subject Descriptors

D.2.8 [**Information Systems**]: Metrics – *process metrics, complexity metrics.*

D.2.12 [**Software**]: Interoperability – *interface definition languages.*

K.1 [**Computing Milieu**]: The Computer Industry –*standards.*

## General Terms

Measurement, Performance, Economics, Standardization, Languages.

## Keywords

Interoperability, information, information exchange languages, intelligent systems, intelligent system components, return on investment, standards, information exchange standards, standard languages, interoperability costs, metrics, interoperability metrics, interoperability cost metrics, interoperability risk metrics, proprietary exchange languages.

## 1. INTRODUCTION

Intelligent system performance is not maximized by smart system design and manufacture alone, but also by a smart technology infrastructure and a smart system lifecycle, and to achieve the latter includes the interchangeability of system components from multiple vendors, *i.e.*, system manufacturers and end users are able to swap in and out any component of the system from any component vendor worldwide with minimal cost or risk.

### 1.1 Illusory Interoperability

Component interchangeability is related but not identical to the plain meaning of interoperability: "the ability of two or more systems or components to exchange information and to use the information that has been exchanged." [9]

A common path taken to achieve interoperability (by this definition) is to build systems consisting of components made from a single vendor. Such systems are generally interoperable[1], but not typically interchangeable with components from other vendors[2]. Single vendor mandated interoperability limits freedom of component choice, incurs risk of vendor viability and corporate mergers, and commonly pushes information translation costs down to suppliers and vendors, who pass the cost right back to the end user in the form of higher component prices. Little is saved and much is risked. [12] It is an illusory interoperability. [6]

Furthermore, single vendor mandates generally do not deliver the interoperability as planned due a variety of factors, including vendor volatility, corporate mergers, and acquisitions. Enter language translation. With translation, systems consisting of components made from multiple vendors now become "interoperable," as well as interchangeable, albeit at a cost, since translation incurs labor costs, information quality losses, license fees, and training costs. To make matter worse, the number of translators required for interoperability increases multiplicatively with respect to the number of component vendors at each interface in the system[3]. This too is illusory interoperability.

---

[1] The infamous Airbus A380 interoperability failure is a notable exception: different versions of same vendor's software were not interoperable, leading to billions of dollars of losses. 4

[2] Reference to specific commercial vendors and their products does not imply endorsement by the authors or their affiliate organizations.

[3] If there are $M$ interfaces in the system and $n_m$ component vendors on both sides of the $m^{th}$ interface ($m \in \{1, 2, \dots, M\}$), then the system requires roughly $\sum_{m=1}^{M} n_m(n_m - 1)$ translators.

## 1.2 Interoperability and Communication

Some have defined interoperability as "the ability of systems, units, or forces 1) to provide services to and accept services from other systems, units, or forces and 2) to use the services so exchanged to enable them to operate effectively together." Part 1 of this definition is called "technical interoperability" and part 2 is called "operational interoperability." [2]

The distinction between technical and operational interoperability is an analog to the distinction between properly encoding and decoding a message, since 1) interoperability is a measure of the degree that a sender correctly encodes a message and the receiver correctly decodes that message and 2) the ways we measure the correct operations of sender and receiver are not the same.

Here's how we measure whether a message is **encoded** correctly. Since correct syntax and semantics are both measurable[4], correct encoding can be measured directly, without observing system behavior. Of course, a precisely defined language must exist to define correct encoding.

Here's how we measure whether a message is **decoded** correctly. There is no other way of knowing whether the message was correctly decoded except by observing the "operation" of the message receiver. Of course, the receiver must decode according to the language known and used by the sender, perhaps through a translator, though that adds unnecessary cost.

"Technical interoperability" is then "the ability to correctly and completely encode and deliver a message" and "operational interoperability" is "the ability to perform the correct action inherent in the message." This principle is encapsulated in the statement, "information is as information does." [10]

## 1.3 Standard Languages

With these ubiquitous costs and risks inherent in so-called "interoperable" systems, it is therefore preferable to redefine interoperability.

> Interoperability is the state of a system wherein the cost of attaining and maintaining correct encoding and decoding of the information exchanged between component pairs is minimized, and minimum cost is attained only when each component pair conforms to a correctly defined standard language, correctly and widely implemented.

Simply put, interoperability is optimized when a single apt language, and none other, is encoded and decoded at each component interface in real systems worldwide. [6] "Correctly defined" standard languages are

- Correct, complete, unambiguous, and timely
- Developed within a standards-generating organization ensuring IP protection, low implementation cost, and open participation

"Correctly implemented" means

- Conformance and interoperability tested
- Certified via conformance tests
- Widely implemented
- Purchased by end users only if certified

Standard languages for component-to-component information with standards-certified implementations maximize interoperability since interoperability success is directly linked to successful component-to-component communication, and successful communication is dependent on well-defined languages and correct encoding/decoding. Widely implemented and correctly defined standards eliminate all the costs associated with sub-optimal interoperability.

When standards do not exist, we do not have the freedom of interchangeability, or else we must pay extra for it. For example, anyone in a household with multiple cell phones knows well that when he/she misplaces or damages the power charger to his/her phone, the power chargers for other phones in the home typically do not work with his/her phone. Either he/she has to spend time searching for his/her charger, pay for a new one, or go for a time without access to his/her cell phone – all achieving "interoperability" at a cost. If there were a cell phone power charger standard, well defined and implemented worldwide, each charger in the home would work with all other phones – and this is not as elusive a goal as it may at first appear.

## 1.4 Measuring Interoperability

Using our definition of interoperability, measuring interoperability must be directly related to the ability of one system component[5] to encode and the other system to decode in the context of a language. The language must be well-defined and well-implemented by both the encoding and decoding components. Syntactical rules and a dictionary are all that are required to measure **encoding** success. Measuring component behavior is all that is required to measure **decoding** success.

To the degree that the language definition and its encoding and decoding fail, interoperability fails. So, standard language definition and its encoding and decoding are directly proportional to this quality we are calling interoperability.

It appears that measuring interoperability directly is hard, [3] because it is hard to define (and apply) a metric for syntactical and semantic communication. Happily, measuring **the cost** of less than perfect interoperability (by our definition above) is quite a bit easier than measuring interoperability itself [3] and more importantly, it has greater pragmatic usefulness at helping achieve better interoperability in real organizations.

## 1.5 Return on Investment

Knowing the cost of interoperability failures and risks in an organization is not the only cost needed. Also needed is the cost of generating, implementing, and supporting standard interface languages. The difference between these two costs has been called the "Interoperability ROI (return on investment)." The cost of developing standards is addressed in earlier work. [5][6]

## 2. Defining and Measuring Interoperability Costs and Risks

Defining, implementing, and maintaining standard languages between all software systems will generate huge savings of cost and quality. However, measuring that cost savings is difficult for these reasons:

---

[4] However, measuring semantics can be much more difficult than measuring syntax. Shannon identified but ignored semantics in defining his communication theory. [11]

[5] A "system component" can be anything from a temperature sensor to a nation state.

- Businesses do not have a solid understanding of the nature of "interoperability costs"
- Savings due to benefits of mandated standard languages are considered to be a corporate secret
- Costs due to interoperability lapses are an embarrassment, so companies are reluctant to measure these costs

We suggest a new way to address this problem:

- Define interoperability costs metrics
- Describe a process for efficiently and cheaply applying those metrics to get accurate cost numbers to corporate planners

# 3. The Process for Applying Interoperability Metrics

## 3.1 Define Organizational Scope

Determine the precise scope of the organizational entity targeted for application of interoperability cost metrics. The entity might be an enterprise, a factory, a division, a work cell, or a manufacturing sector, where a sector might include any or all of the following: enterprise resource planning, product lifecycle management, product design, process planning, machining, assembly, quality control, measurement analysis. End user organizations must include operations of all tier suppliers and product vendors within the scope. Tier suppliers must include operation of all product vendors within the scope. Product vendors need only determine the scope in their own organization.

## 3.2 Define Activity/Component Diagram

End user organizations should develop an activity diagram for each organizational entity. Each activity in the activity diagram must be performed by one or more standalone system components corresponding to real products in the market (otherwise there is necessarily no interoperability problem at that interface). Depending on the organizational entity, there may be duplicate activities in the entity, for example, transfer of information is known to be common between design activities in one part of an entity and design activities in another part of the entity, e.g., CAD-to-CAD, requiring CAD-to-CAD translation/validation.

If the organizational entity is a tier supplier, or if tier suppliers are part of the end-user organizational entity, develop detailed activity diagrams for all tier supplier operations supporting the scope of the organizational entity.

Vendor software/systems entities should identify all activities for which there are software/system products in the (vendor) organizational entity under active support

## 3.3 Identify All Interface Languages

### 3.3.1 End users and tier suppliers

Identify all languages, either proprietary or standard, actually in use in the organizational entity at each of the interfaces between activities where information is known to be transferred. In manufacturing, common activities include enterprise resource planning, product lifecycle management, product design, process planning, product machining, product assembly, quality control, and results analysis

### 3.3.2 Vendor software/system organizations

For each supported product, identify all languages supported, either proprietary or standard, via the maintenance of translators, either internally or via 3rd party

## 3.4 Prioritize interoperability cost measurements

Assign high priority to interoperability costs suspected to be higher than other costs and whose cost information can be more easily/cheaply gathered. Generally CAD-to-CAD translations and validations are more costly than translating CAD for downstream applications. These is no need to gather cost data for all cost categories, since the requirement is to persuade management of the magnitude of the problem, without spending a lot of time and money gathering the cost data.

## 3.5 Measure actual interoperability costs

If there are multiple languages at any of the interfaces identified in the activity diagram, translation is required. To keep the expense of measuring interoperability costs low, some measurements may need to be estimated. For those values estimated, if will be necessary to seek and find realistic estimation error values. All costs related to translation and validation can be considered direct interoperability costs.

Costs such as translation and validation must occur when there are multiple languages at a single interface, since an organization must move its information. We consider translation and validation unnecessary costs in an organization, because neither translation nor validation is needed where there exists a single widely-used information standard that is correct and complete. Therefore, translation and validation are considered "interoperability costs" and not considered merely "the cost of doing business." Validation is done after translation and attempts to ensure that the translation was done correctly. If validation is not performed, then clearly only translation costs apply. Here is the list of (direct) costs:

- Information translation/validation of both format and meaning
  - Translation/validation task labor: the cost of each translated/validated file (or cost per average data rate) and the time it takes may be computed from file sizes (or average data rate)
  - Translation/validation software license fees
  - Reduced engineering software usage skill due to multiple platforms
  - Non-optimal software usage with downtimes due to multiple vendor support
  - Translation/validation software product development [vendor cost]
  - Translation/validation software execution labor, which might be gotten from bytes of data translated/validated
  - Unnecessary system maintenance and software training
  - Unnecessary software development
  - If translation/validation is necessary but not performed because it is too costly,
    - loss of expert knowledge in those files
    - reprogramming costs
    - new software purchase costs
  - Proprietary license fees for "direct CAD interface" to downstream activities, such as manufacturing process planning or supplier bidding
  - Information access fees, e.g., Product Manufacturing Information (PMI) with CAD
  - Manual or automatic editing of information due to lost information quality (erroneous syntax or meaning)

- o Quality check and repair healing software licenses
- o Increase support (staff and equipment)
- o Manpower (time) for translation and support of the additional systems
- o The cost of storage of actual amount of translated information
- Storing and maintaining information in more than one proprietary version (keeping the information up-to-date)

## 3.6 Indirect costs

Certain costs of interoperability, unlike translation for example, are not directly related to interoperability, but can be quite substantial. [1][12] These costs are real, but are the indirect consequence of translation/validation errors:

- Information quality degradation due to translation/validation errors, either from omission or commission, leading to decreased product quality; must check cost to all downstream activities affected by the information quality degradation
  - o Diminished customer product/service confidence
  - o Lost contracts
  - o Contract penalties
  - o Reduced perception of quality
  - o In-warranty service/replacement
  - o Functional failures in product traceable to translation/validation errors (versus traceable to design or manufacturing errors) leading to the following costs
    - Property damage, injury, and legal fees
    - Reduced product/service image causing revenue losses
    - Product recall
    - If there is vendor-software incompatibility due to a merger or acquisition, end user must pay either to
      - choose and implement new single vendor enterprise-wide or
      - pay for all interoperability costs, such as translation, validation, fees, training, etc. (listed above)
- Increased product development times
- Reduced perception of quality
- Uselessness of long term stored proprietary information
- Profit/market loss due to lack of freedom to choose best-in-class
- Restraints on corporate or technical agility
- Reduced product and process innovation

## 3.7 Identify and estimate cost risks

The following risks are potential costs, each of which must be traceable to interoperability failures:

- Vendor corporate failure (scandal, mismanagement, poor economy)
- Lost contracts
- Contract penalties
- Increased product price due to interoperability costs
- Competitive disadvantage leading to
  - o Reduced profits
  - o Loss of market share due to
    - Customer dissatisfaction with high cost
    - Competitors' lower product cost

- o Indecision due to interoperability issues and complexities
- o Lost opportunities
- o Inability to capitalize on revolutionary technological breakthroughs by other vendors

## 3.8 Single language mandate costs

If there is a single vendor language mandate anywhere in the organizational scope under test, the same cost areas mentioned in the last two sections will also be suffered by companies down the supply chain, which may not be in the organizational scope. One cost commonly unique to a single language mandate environment is higher fees due to reduced competition, which should also be measured.

## 4. Conclusion

We have made the argument that to define and implement interoperability cost metrics against the ideal, *i.e.*, complete, correct, and unambiguous interface language, widely and correctly implemented by components worldwide, should help greatly to mitigate information exchange incompatibility (interoperability) problems, since interoperability is directly and inextricably related to correct and complete communication between a sender and receiver, so the proliferation of multiple, redundant (usually proprietary) languages (consisting of both format and meaning) is the heart of the problem.

Managers and intelligent systems workers commonly have the problem of convincing corporate executives and funding sources, of the magnitude and seriousness of the interoperability problem, and ultimately that support of language standards is of fundamental importance, since such standards are the only optimal way to eliminate the many costs that have been identified in this research.

The following work needs to be done which, along with the cost metrics already defined, will help workers easily and accurately determine the cost of interoperability in their enterprise.

- Describe where and how to do cost data collection (i.e., "sensor" placement) to (preferably) automatically collect cost data
- Give guidance on cost and risk uncertainty estimation
- Conduct pilots on the application of the metrics, the process, and cost collection
- Revise and augment cost and risk details based on results from pilots
- Publicize these interoperability cost measurement tools in appropriate venues

## 5. REFERENCES

[1] Bartholomew, D., PLM: Boeing's Dream, Airbus' Nightmare. In *Baseline* (February 5, 2007)

[2] Kasunic, M., Andrew, T., Ensure Interoperability. In *DoD Software Tech News* (June 2010) Vol 13, No. 2

[3] Kasunic, M., Measuring Systems Interoperability: Challenges and Opportunities. Software Engineering Institute, Carnegie Mellon University, (2001)

[4] DoD Directive Number 4630.05. (May 5, 2004)

[5] Hartman, N. Using metrics to justify interoperability projects and measure effectiveness. In *Proceedings of the*

*Collaboration and Interoperability Congress.* (May 2009). http://www.3dcic.com.

[6] Horst, J., Hartman, N., and Wong, G. Defining quantitative and simple metrics for developing a return-on- investment (ROI) for interoperability efforts. In *Proceedings of the Collaboration and Interoperability Congress.* (May 2010). http://www.3dcic.com.

[7] Horst, J. Update on Quality and Metrology. In *Proceedings of the Collaboration and Interoperability Congress.* (May 2010). http://www.3dcic.com.

[8] Horst, J. Reduce Costs and Increase Quality with Information Exchange Standards for Manufacturing Quality. In *CMM Quarterly Special DMSC Edition*, (2009)

http://www.cmmquarterly.com/ezine/current-issure/special-edition

[9] Institute of Electrical and Electronics Engineers. *Standard computer dictionary: a compilation of IEEE standard computer glossaries*, (New York, 1990)

[10] McKay, D. M., Information, Mechanism, and Meaning. *The MIT Press.* (1969)

[11] Shannon, C.E. A Mathematical Theory of Communication. In *Bell System Technical Journal.* 27 (July, October, 1948) 379-423, 623-656

[12] Tyrka, K. Interoperability: Tying Industry in Knots. In *Global Design News.* (February, 2000), 58 – 62.

# Component Models in Robotics Software

Azamat Shakhimardanov, Nico Hochgeschwender, Gerhard K. Kraetzschmar

Bonn-Rhine-Sieg University of Applied Sciences
Department of Computer Science
Grantham-Allee 20, 53757 Sankt Augustin, Germany

## ABSTRACT

In recent years increased research activity in robotics has led to advancements in both hardware and software technologies. More complex hardware required increasingly sophisticated software infrastructures to operate it, and led to the development of several different robotics software frameworks. The driving forces behind the development of such frameworks is to cope with the heterogeneous and distributed nature of robotics software applications and to exploit more advanced software technologies in the robotics domain. So far, though, there has been not much effort to foster cooperation among these frameworks, neither on conceptual nor on implementation levels. Our research aims to analyse existing robotics software frameworks in order to identify possible levels of interoperability among them. The problem is tackled by determining a set of software concepts, in our case centering around component-based software development, which are used to determine a set of common architectural elements in an analysis of existing robotics software frameworks. The result is that these common elements can be used as interoperability points among software frameworks. Exploiting such interoperability gives developers new architectural design choices and fosters reuse of functionality already developed, albeit in another framework. It is also highly relevant for the development of new robotics software frameworks, as it opens smoother migration paths for developers to switch from one framework to another.

## 1. INTRODUCTION

The development of complex robotic applications is a very difficult, time-consuming, and error-prone exercise. The need to cope with vastly heterogeneous, networked hardware, to manage the complexities arising from developing and running distributed software applications, and to integrate highly diverse computational approaches for solving particular functional problems of the application are the major contributing factors to task complexity. Furthermore, the integration of legacy code such as device drivers or functional modules implementing algorithms for e.g. localization, mapping, navigation, or path planning), and the need to meet quality-of-service requirements, such as real-time constraints, are factors increasing the overall complexity. In principle, such problems are well-known also in domains like telecommunications, avionics, and automation. In these somewhat more mature domains these problems are often tamed by relying on widely accepted architectural principles, control models, robust software technologies, and well-defined implementation standards. In robotics, the situation is quite different, as none of the previous—architecture principles, control models, software technologies, and implementation standards—is widely accepted or even exists. There is no existing break-through service robot application, for example, which could serve as a reference model for future developments. Scientific debate is fierce on all of the above levels, and it is not clear whether and how fast community consensus can be reached in the foreseeable future.

To cope with such challenges during the development and deployment of complex robotic applications, the robotics community introduced various and diverse tools and software frameworks. During the last two decades almost every second year a new robotic software framework has been introduced. Ranging from frameworks with a particular emphasis on real-time issues, such as Orocos [1], to more general-purpose frameworks, like Player/Stage [2], Orca [3], GenoM [4], SmartSoft [5], Miro [6], YARP [7], ROS [8], and OpenRTM [9].[1] Taking the multidisciplinary nature of robotics into account, this diversity of software frameworks is not surprising. On one hand, this diversity leads to improvements which are beneficial for the whole robotics domain. On the other hand, however, it also hinders progress. Whenever a new robot is developed, developers are faced with the question which software framework to choose, which is, due to a missing sound methodology to assess robotics software frameworks, a difficult decision-making process in itself. As none of the existing frameworks seems to offer the best, or at least an adequate, solution to all problems to be solved during development, developers very often either stick with their known, but technological constrained frameworks and try to extend it, or start from-scratch developments of completely new frameworks. In both cases, they tend to reinvent the wheel and to waste effort [11]. Usually, they also underachieve their initial goals, end up haunted by hard-to-maintain and hard-to-extend workarounds induced by underlying outdated technology, or have to live with incomplete, immature, and non-robust new developments.

---

[1] Refer to Scheutz and Kramer [10] for an exhaustive survey.

Recently, the robotics community started to adapt the component-oriented programming paradigm [12] (e.g. Open-RTM [9], Orca [13]) in order to increase re-use of existing functional components and to decrease the effort for from-the-scratch developments. A component encapsulates a functionality (e.g. a SLAM algorithm) and restricts the access to that functionality via explicitly defined interfaces [14]. In addition, interfaces are used to define the services on which a component depends in order to provide its functionality. The core idea behind component-oriented programming is to use components as building blocks and to implement an application by composing them from components.[2] Albeit component-oriented robot software frameworks foster re-use of functional components, developers of robot applications are still facing a core problem: After having chosen a particular framework, they are locked into it and cannot make use of functionality developed in another framework. As an example, lock-in makes it impossible or at least very difficult to re-use a localization component developed in Orca in an OpenRTM application. So far, component-level interoperability between robotic software frameworks is not well supported.

This paper analyses four component-oriented robotic software frameworks, namely Orocos, ROS, GenoM, and Open-RTM, from a model-level interoperability perspective. The evaluation is based on a step-wise approach introduced in [11]. Interoperability is first considered on a system-level, then refined in detail on the component-level, through analysing a set of software concepts relevant for component-oriented programming. Section 2 formalizes a set of relevant modeling primitives and relationships among them. Section 3 uses these primitives to assess component and system models used in the selected frameworks. Section 4 concludes and discusses implications of this work and future research to achieve interoperability between frameworks both on modeling and implementation levels.

## 2. COMPONENT MODEL CONCEPTS

Assessing, evaluating, and comparing complex systems is a very delicate and difficult issue. This is particularly true for robot software frameworks, for which we lack sets of commonly agreed-upon evaluation criteria and well-established procedures for their assessment. Most evaluation criteria considered are abstract notions, for which no quantitative metrics are known and which can at best be assessed in a qualitative manner by expert judgment. The weighting and integration of different evaluation criteria is influenced by the domain or the targeted application, and general statements like "system A is better than system B" are highly problematic. The best we can do in such a situation is to look at systems at different levels of abstraction and granularity, and analyse and compare concepts as concretely as possible on each of them. Documenting the analysis and separating this analysis from the interpretation of their results and the conclusions to be drawn from them, should help to re-use the analysis part of the exercise, even if another target domain warrants drawing different conclusions.

This work identifies two levels of abstraction for analysis and evaluation: *systems* and *system constituents*. This reflects a highly relevant distinction of perspectives when talking about reuse in the context of robot software frameworks: Vendors supplying hardware devices for integration in robot systems would like to enable and simplify the use of their products by supplying software that is easy to integrate into an application, however this application may look like. Likewise, robotics researcher focusing on particular functional problems like object recognition, object manipulation, or SLAM, like to supply software modules that can be easily integrated into a larger software system when building a robot application. Both groups are mainly, if not exclusively, concerned with developing software that will, hopefully, become constituents of larger systems. In contrary, developers of complete robot applications are faced with the problem to design and implement an appropriate system architecture (both functional and on the software level), devise adequate control models, and implement both by applying suitable software technologies and relevant standards. In order to minimize own development effort, such system integrators prefer to re-use as many pre-existing functionality as possible, providing that they are available in a form which allows them to use them system constituents. Component-based programming seems to be very attractive from both perspectives, as the concept of a component captures the nature of a system constituent very well.

Software systems can be analysed in terms of two views:

- A **structural view**, focusing on which components constitute a system, which types these components may be, which components are connected to each other, and which types these connections may be.

- A **functional view**, focusing on which functional interfaces the components provide or require, and how the interactions between components are defined.

Below, we describe a set of components and systems concepts which relate primarily to the structural view and will serve as criteria to analyse different software system models.

**System:** A system can be defined as the composition of a set of interacting and interdependent entities [16]. Note, that an entity refers to both components *and* the connections between them, which represent interactions and inter-dependencies among the components.

**Component:** Components are the system constituents providing functionality. There are almost as many definitions of the notion of a component as there are papers about component-based design and development. From a software life-cycle point of view, a component can be a modeling block/class represented in UML in the design phase, a function in the form of C source code during implementation phase, and a running process in the deployment phase. In the context of robotics software frameworks, a component often represents an encapsulation of robot functionality (e.g. access to a hardware device, a simulation tool, a functional library) which helps to introduce structure. Other possible responsibilities include achieving code-level or framework-level interoperability and reusability, and being composed with other software by third parties [12, 17, 18]. In our work, a component is represented as a block (black box) which defines the boundaries of particular functionality the robot provides. A component can consist of many fine-grained primitives such as classes, functions, etc.

---

[2]See Brugali et al. [15] for an introduction into component-oriented programming for robotics.

**Port:** Components need to interact with other components in their environment. The primitives making this interaction possible include ports, interfaces, data types, and connections. The latter three will be discussed below. A port is the software equivalent to the concept of a connector in hardware, and are a component's communication end-points for its connections to other components. Ports play an important role in component-based design. While in object-oriented programming a class usually provides a single public interface, which can actually be used by any entity that obtains an object reference to an instance of the class, the use of ports allows developers to provide several functionally different interfaces and to constrain their use to well-defined entities that will be connected to a port (see Connections below).

Ports can be typed. The port type may impose constraints on which type of connection may be associated with it. For example, the connection may be required to use particular communication protocols or synchronization mechanisms. Two types of ports are frequently needed in robotics:

- **Data Flow Port:** A data flow port is used in situations where there is single supplier providing data in regular intervals to one or more consumers. An example is a component which encapsulates a laser scanner device and sends laser scans every 20 msec to anyone connected to it via such a data flow port. Syntactically, the port has a name (e.g. *scan2D, position2D*) and an interface for reading and writing data. Via this interface, the port can only communicate information with *data semantics* to and from other components' ports; the interaction is supposed to not directly influence control flow on both the sender and the receiver side, and mechanisms for synchronization or advanced handling of communication errors are not foreseen.

- **Service Port:** Although important for robotics, data flow ports are not sufficient to build sophisticated robot control architectures. For instance, modifying a component's configuration or coordinating its activity via a data flow port would be difficult, require extra effort, and lead to suboptimal designs. Therefore, a component model should feature a port type with *control flow semantics*. Syntactically, the port has a name and an interface made up of a collection of methods or functions, referred to as services.

In addition to the difference in information semantics, data flow ports and service ports are usually associated with different interaction patterns. While service ports usually imply synchronous interaction between components with clearly assignable client and server roles, data flow ports usually imply asynchronous interaction between components with clearly identifiable publisher and subscriber roles.

**Interface:** An interface is a set of operations made available to the outside by a software entity. An interface is usually defined by a set of method signatures.

**Data Type:** The classification of data which is communicated between components of the system is done through data types. Both the arguments and return values for the functions/methods specified in the interfaces used in component ports need to be agreed upon in order to ensure correct representation and interpretation of the communicated data, especially if the two connected components eventually reside on different computers running different operating systems, and are implemented in different programming languages. Automatic translation or conversion of data types across languages and systems can be difficult or even impossible if incompatible data types are used. Interoperability can be fostered by providing a standardized library of domain-specific data types, which should be designed to minimize or avoid such incompatibilities.

**Connection:** Connections provide the actual wiring between ports of different components. That is, while a port is a component-level mechanism to make a particular component interface available to the outside, connections perform the linking between ports. With this role, connections are the concept suitable to encapsulate any details about communication protocols and synchronization. This is in line with the definition in [19], where connections *mediate interactions among components. That is, they establish the rules that govern component interaction and specify any auxiliary mechanisms required.* From an implementation perspective, connections may be realized as simple as memory access or a UNIX pipe, or as sophisticated as TAO, ICE, ZeroMQ middleware runtimes and their respective interaction patterns. For instance, publisher/subscriber, client/server, peer–to–peer are most common interaction patterns. From a modeling perspective, a connection is a directed link connecting two ports.

These essential concepts are used as common denominator to analyse the component models defined in common robot software frameworks. The analysis aims to identify commonalities and differences, and to eventually estimate the effort required to make these frameworks interoperable both on modeling and implementation levels.

## 3. ANALYSIS AND EVALUATION

The assessment approach adopts several features from the benchmarking and software architecture evaluation methods. By combining them we cover the evaluation process from both practical and theoretical perspectives. Figure 1 provides a simple view of the evaluation method. This procedure can be considered as a top-down approach, moving from general to more specific system aspects. We identified four stages for this procedure. The output of each stage serves as an input to the proceeding one, thus narrowing the problem to several specific operational situations. Please refer to [11] for further details. With respect to interoperability among frameworks, the second stage consists of identifying a set of refinements directly influencing this quality attribute. These were explained in section 2. Below we detail assessment results for the second step and draw conclusions for steps three and four which will focus on implementation level (compile and runtime) interoperability.

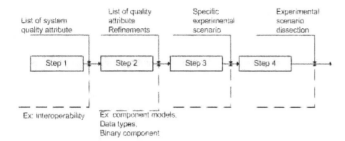

**Figure 1: Different steps of the analysis and assessment.**

## 3.1 OpenRTM

OpenRTM (version 1.0) is component-oriented software developed by AIST in Japan. It is an open-source implementation of OMG Robot Technology Component specification [20]. OpenRTM relies on omniORB CORBA implementation for its communication infrastructure.

- **Component:** OpenRTM defines the component in terms of two parts. A functional part of the component, called `core logic`, contains functional algorithms and is structurally represented by a class as in OOP. A non-functional part of the component, called `wrapper` or `component skin`, provides means to expose functionality of the `core logic` by attaching platform resources to it.

- **Port:** OpenRTM components can interact with other components through ports. OpenRTM components include *ports* as stand-alone construct. OpenRTM allows to define a polarity (`required, provided`) for ports. There are two types of ports. A `data port`, as its name suggests, is semantically equivalent to the data-flow port primitive defined in Section 2. Data ports are unidirectional and used to transfer data using a publisher/subscriber protocol. Components that have only data ports for interaction are referred to as `data flow components` in OpenRTM. The second type of port defined in OpenRTM is the `service port`. It relies on CORBA's interface description language (IDL) for the specification and implementation and allows components to interact with RPC semantics.

- **Data Types:** OpenRTM relies on primitive types as defined by the CORBA IDL. There is no library of robotics-specific data types (e.g. `forceVector`, `positionVector2D` etc).

- **Connection:** On the model level, OpenRTM uses the concept of `connector` to realize inter-component interactions. `Connectors` are specified through their `connector profiles` which contain a connector name, an id, the ports it is connecting, and additional attributes. These connector profiles are implicitly deduced from the connections between components and the ports used for these connections.

## 3.2 GenoM

GenoM (ver 2.0) has been developed at LAAS CNRS robotics group. It relies on a shared memory approach for communication among modules. One of the distinct features of GenoM is that it was the first to apply a model-driven code generation process in robotics software [4]. GenoM module's structure, behavior, and resources are defined in generic way by the GenoM module description language. The GenoM tool parses this module description to generate compilable code [22, 23, 24].

- **Component:** In GenoM, a component is referred to as `module`. Like in OpenRTM, GenoM components can also be decoupled into functional and non-functional parts. A component developer is required to implement only the functional part of the module, which is represented by a set of so-called `codels`. Codels are defined as non-preemptable, atomic code units, usually in the form of C functions. The non-functional part of the module is auto-generated by the GenoM code generator tool.

- **Port:** The concept of data flow port does not exist in its given interpretation in GenoM modules. In order to exchange data, GenoM modules use *posters*, which are sections of shared memory. There are two kinds of posters. `Functional posters` contain data shared between modules (e.g. sensor data). Something semantically equivalent to service ports are `control posters`. `Control posters` contain information on the state of the module, running services and activities, client IDs, thread periods, etc. But a component cannot write/send to `control posters` of another component. Therefore control posters do not provide the same functionality as service ports in Section 2.

- **Data Types:** GenoM does not provide a robotics-specific library of data types, but supports the communication of both simple and complex data types as they are defined in the C programming language.

- **Connection:** Connections do not exist as a separate entity. The developer needs to specify in a model description file for each model which shared memory section it needs to have access to. On the `request/reply` interface level, connections are set up through a Tcl[3] interpreter, which plays the role of an application server to all running modules. Developers write Tcl scripts in which they define the module connections. This is very similar to the Player approach, where the role of the Tcl interpreter is taken by the Player device server.

## 3.3 ROS

The open-source Robot Operating System (ROS, version 'boxturtle') developed by WillowGarage aims to provide a software development environment for robotics. The underlying analogy of this robot software framework is that of an operating system, including package management, inter-process communication, and software development tools.

- **Component:** The main computational entity in ROS is called a `node`. A `node` is a process which provides some specific functionality. Thus, a node can be considered as the ROS equivalent of a component as exemplified in Section 2.

---

[3]Tcl = Tool Command Language

- **Port:** ROS features the concepts of `topics` and `messages`, which effectively implement an equivalent to a data flow port with publish/subscribe interaction pattern. A `topic` can be considered as a named communication channel which is used to send and receive `messages` between `nodes` in an anonymous manner. This kind of interaction helps to decouple `nodes` and achieve more fault-tolerant systems. Synchronous interaction between `nodes` in ROS is achieved through the concept of `services`. In contrast to the traditional understanding of service ports, `services` are not groupable through service ports in ROS. However, as `nodes` and `messages`, `services` are encapsulated through a hierarchical naming structure (called `names`), leading to decreased naming conflicts and a more structured development of complex applications.

- **Data Types:** ROS provides a messages description language to specify data structures (called `messages`). `Messages` are composed of arbitrarily nested primitive data types (as integers, float, etc.). These `messages` are used as a mean for communication between `nodes` through `topics` and `services`. In addition, ready-to-use robot-specific data types as geometry and pose `messages` are available.

- **Connection:** The concept of a connection does not exist in ROS. Location-transparency between `nodes` is achieved through the concept of a `master node`. The `master node` provides naming and registration facilities for all nodes. However, the parametrization of the communication link between `nodes` (e.g. the size of the queue) is performed in the `nodes` itself.

### 3.4 Orocos

Orocos (ver 1.8) is developed at robotics group of Katholieke Universiteit Leuven. It focuses on developing a general purpose modular software framework for robot and machine control. The framework provides basically a set of libraries, among which the Real Time Toolkit (RTT) library delivers infrastructure and functionality to build component based systems [26].

- **Component:** The RTT explicitly defines a component primitive. Conceptually, the RTT component is similar to OpenRTM components. A component's functional core is decoupled from the part responsible for platform resources. The component implements five different types of interaction endpoints. They differ according to the information semantics (data, event, property end-points) and synchronization mechanisms (command, method end-points). In practice, it does not seem to be so easy to clearly determine the right type of port, and the developers are recently re-thinking their approach in this regard.

- **Port:** Orocos components use data flow ports as thread-safe data transport mechanism for (un)buffered communication of data among components. Data port-based exchange is asynchronous/non-blocking. In Orocos `methods` behave similar to service ports as defined in Section 2.

- **Data Types:** Orocos provides a set of predefined standard data types for robotics. Developers can also create custom data types.

- **Connection:** Orocos provides an explicit connection concept between components.

The results of our analysis can be summarized in Table 1:

|  | Comp. | Data Flow Port | Service Port | Data Types | Conn. |
|---|---|---|---|---|---|
| OpenRTM | ✓ | ✓ | ✓ | ✓ | ✓ |
| Genom | ✓ | — | — | ✓ | — |
| ROS | ✓ | ✓ | — | ✓ | — |
| Orocos | ✓ | ✓ | ✓ | ✓ | ✓ |

**Table 1: Overview on component modeling primitives in different robot software systems.**

## 4. CONCLUSIONS

This paper provided a review of some well-established component-based software frameworks in the robotics domain. The review focused on the analysis and comparison of these frameworks from a component model perspective. The assessment was performed with respect to major structural entities often defined and required in component-based software development. The goal of the assessment was to identify possible interoperability points for robot software on the model level.

The results of the assessment in Table 1 show that there is not only a zoo of robot software frameworks, but also a zoo of different component models. However, most of these component models adopt quite similar concepts for components and component-related concepts, e.g. data flow ports and service ports. Most component models lack an `explicit` concept of connections. Connections seem to be a promising alley to follow in order to explore interoperability concerns. A library of well-defined, standardized data types for the robotics domain, designed with expressiveness, performance, and robustness, but also communication and interoperability issues in mind, seems more than overdue. Also, developing a common ontology of concepts for the robotics domain appears to hold the potential for identifying many similarities between differently names concepts and ideas, for streamlining much of the development work invested by the community, and for greatly simplifying the currently complex world of a robot software developer.

Although all the analysed component software has common features and attributes, there is no systematic approach to reuse software (models and code) across the systems. Observing current trends in robotics software development, it is realistic to expect that the number of new software packages will grow in the future. This situation is similar to the operating systems domain some time ago, when there were a handful of systems which then grew in number. Most of those systems eventually provided some means for interoperability among each other. A similar approach should be taken in the robot software domain, since there is an abundance of robot software systems and component models with largely the same functionalities out there. At the same time, there is no way to persuade people to use *The Grand Unifying Solution*, and the best approach to make progress is to achieve interoperability between existing systems on different levels, i.e. on model level, code level, etc.

This research concerned two initial phases of an assessment process in [11]. The next phases of the assessment will focus on practical implications of component software for interoperability purposes.

## 5. ACKNOWLEDGMENTS

The research leading to these results has received funding from the European Community's Seventh Framework Program (FP7/2007-2013) under grant agreement no. FP7-ICT-231940-BRICS (Best Practice in Robotics). We also thank doctoral students Michael Reckhaus and Jan Paulus from the Bonn-Rhine-Sieg University of Applied Sciences for their detailed comments and insights on this work.

## 6. REFERENCES

[1] P. Soetens, *A Software Framework for Real-Time and Distributed Robot and Machine Control*. PhD thesis, Department of Mechanical Engineering, Katholieke Universiteit Leuven, Belgium, May 2006.

[2] B. Gerkey, R. Vaughan, and A. Howard, "The Player/Stage project: Tools for multi-robot and distributed sensor systems," in *In Proc. of the International Conference on Advanced Robotics*, 2003.

[3] A. Brooks, T. Kaupp, and A. Makarenko, "Orca: Components for robotics," in *IEEE/RSJ International Conference on Intelligent Robots and Systems, Workshop on Robotic Standardization*, 2006.

[4] S. Fleury, M. Herrb, and R. Chatila, "GenoM: A tool for the specification and the implementation of operating modules in a distributed robot architecture," in *In Proceedings of the IEEE/RSJ International Conference on Intelligent Robots and Systems (IROS)*, pp. 842–848, September 1997.

[5] C. Schlegel, "Communication patterns as key towards component interoperability," in *In Davide Brugali, editor, Software Engineering for Experimental Robotics*, vol. 30, Springer, STAR series, 2007.

[6] H. Utz, S. Sablatnoeg, S. Enderle, and G. Kraetzschmar, "MIRO - middleware for mobile robot applications," in *IEEE Transactions on Robotics and Automation*, vol. 18, IEEE Press, August 2002.

[7] P. Fitzpatrick, G. Metta, and L. Natale, "Towards long-lived robot genes," *Robotics and Autonomous Systems*, vol. 56, pp. 29–45, 2008.

[8] M. Quigley, K. Conley, B. Gerkey, J. Faust, T. Foote, J. Leibs, R. Wheeler, and A. Y. Ng, "Ros: an open-source robot operating system," in *ICRA Workshop on Open Source Software*, 2009.

[9] N. Ando, T. Suehiro, K. Kitagaki, T. Kotoku, and W.-K. Yoon, "Rt-component object model in rt-middleware- distributed component middleware for rt (robot technology)," in *IEEE International Symposium on Computational Intelligence in Robotics and Automation*, June 2005.

[10] K. James and S. Matthias, "Robotic development environments for autonomous mobile robots: A survey," *Autonomous Robots*, vol. 22, no. 2, pp. 101–132, 2007.

[11] A. Shakhimardanov and E. Prassler, "Comparative evaluation of robotic software integration systems: A case study," in *Intelligent Robots and Systems, 2007.*

[12] C. Szyperski, *Component Software: Beyond Object-Oriented Programming*. Addison-Wesley Professional, 2 ed., 2002.

[13] A. Brooks, T. Kaupp, A. Makarenko, S. Williams, and A. Orebaeck, "Towards component-based robotics," in *In Proc. of the IEEE/RSJ Int. Conf. on Intelligent Robots and Systems IROS*, 2005.

[14] E. D. Richard N. Taylor, Nenad Medvidovic, *Software Architecture: Foundations, Theory, and Practice*. Addison-Wesley Professional, February 2009.

[15] D. Brugali and P. Scandurra, "Component-based robotic engineering (part i) [tutorial]," *Robotics Automation Magazine, IEEE*, vol. 16, pp. 84 –96, december 2009.

[16] R. S. Henry George Liddell, "Λ greek-english lexicon." [online] http://www.perseus.tufts.edu/hopper/.

[17] A. J. A. Wang and K. Qian, *Component-Oriented Programming*. Wiley-Interscience, 1 ed., 2005.

[18] I. Crnkovic and M. Larsson, eds., *Building Reliable Component-Based Software Systems*. Artech House Publishers, 1 ed., July 2002.

[19] N. R. Mehta, N. Medvidovic, and S. Phadke, "Towards a taxonomy of software connectors," in *ICSE '00: Proceedings of the 22nd international conference on Software engineering*, pp. 178–187, ACM, 2000.

[20] Y. Tsuchiya, M. Mizukawa, T. Suehiro, N. Ando, H. Nakamoto, and A. Ikezoe, "Development of light-weight rt-component (lwrtc) on embedded processor-application to crawler control subsystem in the physical agent system," in *SICE-ICASE International Joint Conference*, pp. 2618–2622, 2006.

[21] R. Alami, R. Chatila, S. Fleury, M. Ghallab, and F. Ingrand, "An architecture for autonomy," *International Journal of Robotics Research*, vol. 17, April 1998.

[22] B. Lussier, R. Chatila, F. Ingrand, M. Killijian, and D. Powell, "On fault tolerance and robustness in autonomous systems," in *3rd IARP - IEEE/RAS - EURON Joint Workshop on Technical Challenges for Dependable Robots in Human Environments, (Manchester, UK)*, 7-9 September 2004.

[23] R. Alami, R. Chatila, F. Ingrand, and F. Py, "Dependability issues in a robot control architecture," in *2nd IARP/IEEE-RAS Joint Workshop on Technical Challenge for Dependable Robots in Human Environments*, LAAS-CNRS, October 7- 8 2002.

[24] P. Soetens, *The OROCOS Component Builder's Manual*, 1.8 ed., 2007.

# Benchmarking Production System, Process Energy, and Facility Energy Performance Using a Systems Approach

Jorge Arinez and Stephan Biller
General Motors
30500 Mound Road
Warren, Michigan
Jorge.Arinez@gm.com

Kevin Lyons, Swee Leong, Goudong
Shao, B.E. Lee, and John Michaloski
National Institute of Standards and Technology
100 Bureau Drive
Gaithersburg, Maryland
Kevin.Lyons@nist.gov

## ABSTRACT

Evaluating overall energy performance of a manufacturing system requires accurate information on how, when, and where energy is being used. Collecting and tracking energy data is necessary for determining performance benchmarks and reducing energy consumption. Optimizing energy efficiency in manufacturing systems is difficult to achieve since energy management is typically performed separately from the production monitoring and control systems. Further, low-level equipment energy data collection is costly to do, and, if done, is often not well-linked to production data.

The smarter integration of production system, process energy, and facility energy data is a significant opportunity to improve manufacturing sustainability. This paper will examine the issues related to the linking of these three types of data as well as develop a methodology for jointly modeling and evaluating production, process energy, and facility energy performance. A case study of a sand casting production line will be discussed to better understand the integration issues, validate the methodology, test performance benchmarks, and investigate sustainable manufacturing opportunities.

## Categories and Subject Descriptors

J.1 [**Computer Applications**]: [manufacturing]

## General Terms

Management, Measurement, Performance, Standardization

## Keywords

Sustainability, Discrete Event Simulation, production, energy, methodology, analysis, key performance indicators (KPI)

## 1. INTRODUCTION

The goal for manufacturing to be cleaner, more efficient, and environmentally benign is part of the dynamics contributing to a closer examination of manufacturing sustainability. Further, costs related to carbon emissions seen in the form of a potential "Cap and Trade" or a "Carbon Tax" scheme are considered by some to be inevitable. To stay competitive, companies must assess and improve their energy use within production in order to reduce their carbon footprint. Organizing, quantifying, and reporting of cumulative energy consumption and greenhouse gas emissions of manufacturing processes can be found in International Organization for Standardization (ISO) standards 14064-1, -2, and -3 [9, 10, 11] and ISO 14065-2006 [12], but thus far, there has been limited analysis of more automated, synergistic approaches to combined production and energy management.

More intelligent integration of process and energy data offers a significant opportunity to reduce manufacturing energy consumption [1, 2]. Energy management is challenging for manufacturing due to the difficulty that arises from the diversity of energy use – there are thousands of processes each having unique energy consumption characteristics as well as different production requirements based on the product, product quality, environmental compliance, and other business factors [16]. Today, most production energy management is done by separate plant information systems and is frequently not well-linked to production data. Though possible, it is quite costly, especially in older facilities, to perform extensive energy data collection at the equipment level. Consequently, low-level energy consumption within production is also not well understood. Clearly, without insight into the fundamental energy consumption behavior of equipment, it becomes challenging for plant and manufacturing engineers to make effective decisions. Further, facility energy such as heating, ventilation, and air-conditioning (HVAC) and lighting, which is viewed from an indirect perspective, is also loosely correlated to production needs. The smarter integration of production system, process energy, and facility energy management is a significant opportunity to improve manufacturing sustainability. If a smarter, more holistic, view of the manufacturing system were in place, simple actions such as the timely shut off an air handler when a production line is down could lead to energy reductions.

General Motors (GM) and the National Institute of Stan-

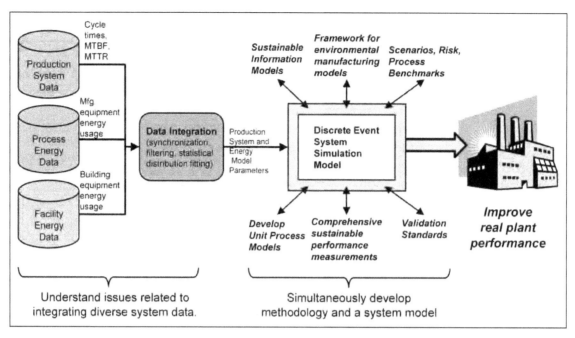

Figure 1: Integration of Production System, Process Energy, and Facility Energy Data for Sustainable Manufacturing

dards and Technology (NIST) are partners in an effort to investigate the feasibility of smarter integration of production, process energy, and facility energy data from the plant floor to improve sustainability. The goal of this effort is to understand the key technical and implementation issues in combining such data. The strategy adopted in this work focuses on developing a methodology to extract process and energy data from the plant, and then formalize this approach to allow future reuse at other production facilities. The formalism to measure and benchmark sustainability performance is considered a critical aspect as currently this production/process energy/facility energy integration is not done in a systematic fashion.

Fundamental to a smarter understanding of a process is the ability to measure it. Currently, prescribed energy reduction methods in industry are often related to lean manufacturing concepts and include energy treasure hunts, value stream mapping, Six Sigma, and Kaizen events [6]. Most of these methods rely on empirical observation and basic analysis. However, informative, accurate and timely shop-floor production data should be considered vital to understanding a process. Only with accurate data from the shop-floor can analysis and benchmarking be suitably done to eliminate waste and inefficiencies.

The research into energy efficiency of manufacturing processes covers the spectrum of industrial processes [7]. The majority of the research is on energy-intensive processes, where the energy gains would be most pronounced. Most of the research conducts a static analysis of a manufacturing process and then compares and contrasts various processing options and areas for potential improvement. Generally, energy efficiency research does not include consideration for automating the data collection and analysis in order to perform continuous monitoring of factory floor energy consumption.

Solding considered design issues related to energy and power utilization inside an iron foundry [15]. Heilala proposed an integrated factory simulation tool for the design phase to help maximize production efficiency and balance environmental constraints and present methods for calculating energy efficiency, carbon dioxide ($CO_2$) emissions and other environmental impacts [8]. This research considers energy consumption, but only estimates energy consumption based on equipment power ratings. Kuhl shows sustainability modeling and simulation of logistics and transportation systems, but does not incorporate real-time data collection [14]. Research into industrial process and energy analysis using Discrete Event Simulation (DES) has been shown to be possible, but illustrates the difficulty in incorporating real energy data into the DES process analysis.

Though many companies cannot afford sophisticated factory data collection, the low cost of networks and computers is continually lowering the financial threshold of acquiring plant information systems that can perform real-time data collection and archiving of the operational behavior of their HVAC, PLCs, automation, and other auxiliary equipment. Increasingly, companies collect process and energy data from the various control and supervisory systems on the plant floor and store the data in several different databases. Although process and energy data collection is routinely done, there are often many (and unconnected) data collection subsystems involved. Given such systems and databases, this work seeks to build an integrated production system and process energy and facility energy DES benchmarking model.

This paper will study the issues related to integration of production system and process energy and facility energy data as well as to develop a methodology for modeling and evaluating performance. Section 2 will discuss the concepts involved in the systems approach to the integration of energy and process for sustainable production. Section 3 will present a walk-through of the methodology as applied to production and process energy integration for a sand casting production line at General Motors. The methodology will include goals, objectives and assumptions; functional requirements; data collection; and modeling and analysis. Finally, section 4 will present a discussion on the results and future directions.

## 2. PRODUCTION SYSTEM, PROCESS ENERGY, AND FACILITY ENERGY INTEGRATION

Figure 1 highlights the concepts involved in the systems approach to integration of energy and production system data for sustainable manufacturing. Production system event, process energy, and facility energy data are all required to be collected from the factory floor and stored into archival databases. At this point, it is assumed that facility energy and production system data is not synchronized and stored in different databases. Process energy on the other hand such as the electricity used to power a computer numerical control (CNC) milling machine could be linked with event data. However, this data is frequently not readily available nor integrated unless a specific effort has been made to acquire the data from the machine controller or via power monitoring sensors. Data integration would thus involve a number of steps: data collection, cleaning and filtering, state and event correlation, and finally data fitting to statistical distributions. Given the production and energy (for both process and facility) data and statistical characterization, the factory is modeled in DES so that potential scenarios can be run to project different operational outcomes. The development of the DES model is a large undertaking but can be handled in phases to incorporate increasingly detailed parameterization, at first, starting with the basic key performance indicators (KPI) such as, cycle time, throughput, and bottlenecks, and then adding energy KPI: cost and energy consumption and $CO_2$ emissions.

For the determination of productivity, the use of DES is considered critical to developing a production and energy benchmarking methodology. In manufacturing, DES simulates a real or virtual model of production based on statistical characterization of a manufacturing process, such as cycle time, idle time, and failure rates. Once developed, the DES model can then be used to predict outcome given different parameterization scenarios. DES can also be used in the design of new facilities using historical production data to ensure modeling accuracy.

Assuming a robust model, DES is aptly suited as a way to understand energy consumption as it relates to process and facility control, as a DES model can run benchmark data to uncover optimizations, savings and drawbacks, as well as mitigate risks, and help avoid potential crisis points. For example, benchmarks could be used to understand the implications of energy usage during production stoppages, to understand the effect of changing production schedules, or to see what can be done to lower the risk associated with rising energy costs or energy shortages. Development of the DES model provides an apt framework in which to develop an integrated process and energy strategy. However, a one-time DES model is a necessary but not sufficient goal for this effort. Part of the mission is to generalize any modeling

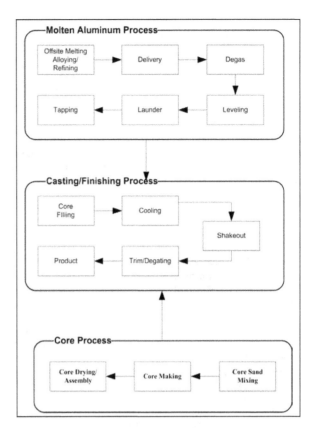

**Figure 2: Casting Process**

and analysis work to become part of standard sustainable technology. A goal of the work is to leverage the integrated production and process and energy modeling and develop a methodology that will allow such work in the future to be done in a systematic and formal manner. Understanding the issues related to integrating the diverse process and facility energy with production system data is a core part of the effort. The effort will contribute to the ongoing evolution in improving and standardizing sustainable manufacturing constituent technologies, including integrated frameworks based on composable components, information models, and performance metrics.

Figure 1 shows related technologies that assist and simplify sustainable manufacturing efforts, including unit processes, sustainable information models, sustainable frameworks, and performance metrics. Unit processes are defined as the individual steps required to produce finished goods by transforming raw material and adding value to the workpiece as it becomes a finished product [5]. Unit processes within manufacturing can involve one or more mechanical, thermal, electrical, or chemical processes. Improving the quality of the final product depends on improvements to the unit processes themselves. Sustainable information models use formal representations to model the full range of the product lifecycle and sustainable manufacturing, including reuse, recycle (disassembly), and remanufacturing. A framework for environmental manufacturing models allows composing sustainable manufacturing systems based on sustainable manufacturing components [13].

Given the goals of this work, numerous GM plants and

Figure 3: Energy and Process Model Methodology Steps

processes were investigated as a suitable candidate for a specific production and process energy and facility energy sustainable manufacturing study, in the end an aluminum casting production line was selected as it combined several key factors: significant energy consumption, extensive production system process and facility energy data collection, and the opportunity to benchmark the effectiveness of new technologies.

Casting has seen over 5000 years of technological advances. Figure 2 shows a high-level overview of the casting process at GM that is dedicated to making aluminum engine blocks. The molten aluminum process is responsible for melting the aluminum, refining the melt, and adjusting the molten chemistry. Once molten, the aluminum is degassed, leveled, and laundered to remove deleterious gases before being tapped to flow into cores. Cores are made of sand which is poured into molding machines to create the contours of the casting, pressed and heated to bind the sand. Since the sand casting process is an expendable mold metal casting process, the core process builds a new sand core for each casting. Overall, core parts are molded from sand and binding elements, assembled into the engine block core, and then dried before casting. The casting and finishing process is where the molten aluminum flows into the sand cast core, after which, the casting is cooled and then casting sand is removed from around the now solidified aluminum engine block by shakeout, trim, and degating operations.

## 3. METHODOLOGY

The goal of this GM/NIST effort is to develop a methodology that combines low-level production data and energy data in order to derive sustainable manufacturing benchmarks and cost projections. Ideally, the methodology should be generic and applicable to any process and facility.

A large number of modeling factors are critical in effectively developing a production and energy methodology for a manufacturing system. Manufacturing systems involve a number of interrelated elements, including equipment strategy, number of product options, material handling systems, system size, process flow configuration, processing time of the operations, system and workstation capacity, and space utilization. The model must be combined with other constraints such as unpredictable machine breakdowns, varying operational requirements, schedule variation, and different production demands.

Figure 3 shows the general foundation of the methodology that will be refined in the course of developing the production system and process energy and facility energy model. The application of these general methodology steps, as applied to the GM sand casting process, will be discussed in the following sections.

### 3.1 Problem Statement and Objectives

First, a problem statement with goals, objectives, assumptions, and simplifications must be developed. The problem is to model the relationship between process energy and facility energy within a production environment. The objectives are to better understand these relationship to improve energy efficiency, process efficiency, part quality, yield rate, and other established production objectives. The assumptions that facility energy and process data is available will be assumed, but the data may be poorly correlated or the energy data may not be of sufficient granularity to establish meaningful measures. Some simplifying assumptions will be made if the energy data does not satisfy the analysis needs, such that a future data collection plan will be developed that would enable the proper data collection to allow the energy and process control to be properly modeled. Another simplification is that high-level process KPIs will be sufficient for understanding process flow, and can be derived directly from the existing plant-floor information systems in place. The existence of data is high-fidelity will be assumed.

### 3.2 Functional Requirements

In this step, a list is made of the functional requirements that need to be satisfied for the model to be accurate. This step is also used to determine the appropriate scope and level of detail of the effort. For the functional requirements, the goal is to understand the key performance and sustainability indicators for the production and process energy consumption. Some of the related tasks involved in developing the detailed requirements include the following.

- Define the high-level methodology for efficient DES modeling of energy and process production.

- Develop reusable unit process model templates for casting and other production systems.

- Enumerate scenarios for the production and process energy study.

- Describe the tasks to correlate facility energy management with process energy and production system data.

- Structure the data collection and integration of energy data and process data.

- Identify potential energy optimizations and related decision tradeoffs.

### 3.3 Conceptual Design

Next, a conceptual design is required that provides a system model of the manufacturing system. The system model gives a high level description of the inputs and outputs for the parts, equipment, and general process flow, including energy requirements. At this point, only a rough estimate of the timing and interconnections of all the elements is required. The basic information required by the conceptual design analysis includes:

1. process flow,

2. production statistics,

3. resources – equipment list,

4. and energy resources

Resource energy consumption can be modeled quite effectively using a state model, which maps machine energy usage to particular states [4]. Equipment such as fans, machinery, or lighting all can be modeled by finite state machines. Figure 4 shows the basic state model for machinery resources in our project, where the equipment has states for off, busy, idle, down, starved, and blocked states. Such a model is particularly useful because it is equally applicable to equipment whether they be for production or for the facility. The only difference is that for facility equipment, the starved or blocked states would never arise.

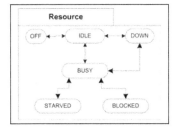

**Figure 4: Production Equipment State Model**

The Off state indicates that the process equipment is not in use (unpowered). The Busy state indicates the equipment is working to produce product. The Starved state indicates that there are missing input materials so the equipment is paused. If the storage facility for the process output is full, the process is in the Blocked state and the equipment is paused. When equipment has a breakdown or fault, the process stops and the equipment is in the Down state.

Some equipment need not have such a complex state model and instead may only exhibit the Off or Busy or Down states. For example, a light has on/off states, but can also be down (i.e., broken). Understanding the necessary state model for each piece of equipment is important so that correct data can be properly collected. For example, knowing the amount of total energy that is consumed during the entire day may not be sufficient. Rather, knowing the average amount of energy consumption within each state is more important in developing a robust model.

Detailed information contained in the system model of the production line should include:

- number of resources – including state model,

- number and size of buffers,

- type of parts,

- estimated energy required to make parts,

- general high level overview of material in parts,

- transport between resources, conveyor speeds,

- and overview part routes between resources.

## 3.4 Data Collection

Data collection involves the activities required for obtaining accurate and meaningful representations of all the relevant input parameters for the system model. Specific data interfaces and acquisition logic is required to collect both static and dynamic data. Static data defines constant values, such as buffer sizes, and can be fed into the conceptual design. Dynamic data refers to process and energy state that can change over time.

In our study, production system and process energy data are routinely archived to databases. Normal data handling operations, such as filtering of the raw data into event data as well as cleansing of the data, are required, as in any modeling work. Production data can be described by raw, cumulative eventŬbased, or statistical distribution parameters.

Raw data obtained via regular polling contains a timestamp, the current state and any other knowledge deemed important. If the energy data is uncorrelated to process data, the most useful form of energy data would be as archived raw data with timestamp and energy intensity values, (e.g., kW). Table 1 shows an example for raw data entry the production system.

**Table 1: Raw process data**

| Line | Object | State | Timestamp |
|------|--------|-------|-----------|
| PSC | Machine1 | Idle | 02/22/2010 06:19:00 |
| PSC | Machine1 | Busy | 02/22/2010 06:20:00 |
| PSC | Machine1 | Busy | 02/22/2010 06:21:00 |

Raw polled data can become voluminous without some filtering or aggregation into cumulative data. The casting plant data collection filtered raw data into event data containing events and time duration within the event. Table 2 shows an example of event–based data that describes production.

**Table 2: Filtered Event Process Data**

| Line | Object | Event | Start Time | End Time |
|------|--------|-------|------------|----------|
| PSC | Machine1 | Idle | 02/22/2010 06:19:00 | 02/22/2010 06:19:06 |
| PSC | Machine1 | Busy | 02/22/2010 06:19:08 | 02/22/2010 06:22:44 |
| PSC | Machine1 | Blocked | 02/22/2010 06:22:46 | 02/22/2010 06:23:04 |

Assuming the data has been collected, database queries can then retrieve the relevant process and energy data to characterize the factory operation. Production can then be succinctly characterized by fitting event data to a statistical distribution. Throughput, utilization, and cycle time are some KPIs that often statistically characterize manufacturing performance.

Table 3 shows a statistical characterizations of cycle time and down time that is required for DES to model production. The data must be in the form of production system data, such as cycle time per part, not as cumulative time equipment spends in each state, that is, total time spent in the busy versus idle state during the course of a shift. This is due to the need to understand the relationships of cycle time to part yield as well as to incorporate equipment failure and its influence on the overall system model.

| Line | Object | Average Cycle Time | MTBF | MTTR | |
|---|---|---|---|---|---|
| PSC | Machine1 | 67.7 | 38.0 | 42.0 | |
| PSC | Machine2 | 70.0 | 27.7 | 15.2 | |
| PSC | Machine3 | 72.2 | 23.5 | 36.5 | |

Table 3: Statistical Process Data

On the other hand, process energy data is based on integrated measurements over time to determine power consumption, but may include peaks, spikes, and other cost-sensitive parameters. For this analysis, the key energy parameter is not only power consumed, but now, instead of time-based readings, the energy needs to be correlated to the underlying process state, for example, the amount of energy being consumed while processing, versus the amount of energy being consumed when the equipment is down. However, synchronizing the energy data to the process within the plant is difficult as energy collection is integrated over time, and energy collection is uncorrelated to process performance. This means that energy data needs to be transformed from timed into state-based power consumption. If the energy data is of fine enough granularity, the transformation can be programmatically determined by correlating the power consumed during a process state and integrating over time. Should the energy data be coarse readings, such as daily or shift summaries, numerical algorithms will be required to perform statistical and selective modeling techniques that can roughly estimate the power consumed for the process states.

In general, the following is a representative but not exhaustive list of data that should be collected:

- resource and production data and statistics,

- process cycle times,

- process setup times,

- resource mean time between failure (MTBF),

- resource mean time to repair (MTTR),

- process scrap percentage (if any),

- resource/process energy consumption,

- and resource conveyor speeds.

## 3.5 Simulation Modeling

Building the DES model links the system model with the data collection activity. It assumes that statistical fitting of the data collected yields acceptable results. The DES model will then assist in the manufacturing decision-making process. The major consideration during this phase is the level of detail to model. To attain more insightful energy related decisions, a finer granularity of modeling is necessary. If possible, the energy consumed by each piece of equipment should be incorporated into the DES model. If the data collection phase is able to determine state-based equipment energy consumption, then it can be easily calculated during DES analysis scenarios.

## 3.6 Validation

A validated model is both accurate and able to meet the high-level functional requirements of the problem statement. The purpose of validation is to guarantee that the behavior of the model is representative for the system modeled. Numerous validation tests can be done, but the comparison with the real casting production system as a means of establishing whether the system model is accurate will be used. Of course, further mathematical analysis can be used to augment and confirm the accuracy of the initial validation. If the DES system outputs do not compare well with the actual system outputs, then further analysis for missing items in the system model, or closer attention to the data collected to verify its accuracy will need to be done. This process is repeated until the model is satisfactory either through empirical observation or by statistical analysis [3].

## 3.7 Analysis/Results

When the model has been validated and is ready for use then various scenarios can be created to evaluate production system, process energy, and facility energy performance. DES can then benchmark the overall manufacturing system to evaluate concepts, identify problem areas, and quantify or optimize system performance.

First, DES can benchmark process performance. Often, improving process performance will correspond to energy savings, but not always. If the production line is often down, and the production equipment use less power while idling, then less energy will be used. So, some production improvements such as better yield may end up using more energy, but are a positive. Clearly, reducing scrap corresponds to energy savings. This implies that production really needs to study the energy cost per part yield to truly understand the performance benchmarking of energy consumption. Potential process scenario criteria include:

- throughput and bottleneck identification,

- utilization of resources, labor, and machines,

- staffing requirements, capacity, and work shifts,

- storage needs, and queuing at work locations,

- routing of materials,

- and maintenance and down time.

Typical industrial energy consumption analysis relies heavily on empirical observation. This has proven useful but most of the easily sustainable savings have been realized. Using integrated production system and process energy data, new potential savings will have to be identified based on automated and more scientific scenarios and assessment. First, with an automated approach the data is more reliable than with empirically observed phenomenon, but may be harder to understand. Second, real data will help detect subtle problems that are not readily apparent. For example, process and energy variability can be monitored with real data, and significant variability may imply underlying production problems.

The foreseen scenario analysis includes:

- Correlate total energy consumption to parts produced per shift to develop a production energy yield.

- Determine average and peak loads for given energy yield. Assess variability.

- Compare energy yield against an equipment energy baseline determined from rated power to compute equipment energy sizing factor.

- Compare daily variability of process energy consumption. Determine root cause in cases of high variability.

- Compare energy consumption pre/post preventive maintenance. This scenario can assess operation when equipment and processes are expected to run efficiently.

- Compare energy consumption between high and low scrap rate.

- Compare yield to energy to outdoor temperature.

- Adjust electrical cost to determine change in per unit cost.

- Change fault times to determine change in electrical consumption.

- Assess amount of equipment energy consumed versus rated power of equipment. Excessive powered equipment should be replaced with smaller equipment tailored to the specific needs of manufacturing cells.

- Maximize electricity purchasing power, evaluate opportunities to reduce energy costs through load shifting of electricity use to off-peak times, assuming energy deregulation is applicable.

- Determine if real-time power shedding to reduce the load and limit the peak load cost is required, compare to production efficiency, where high production efficiency correlated to minimal or no corresponding downtime, blocked or starved subprocesses, assuming the capability for power metering to predict the electrical demand.

## 4. DISCUSSION

In this paper, a methodology for analyzing the smarter integration of production system, process energy, and facility energy data was outlined. In this section some preliminary results and related modeling issues from our analysis of the selected GM casting production system and process energy integration will be presented. Note that this initial work does not yet include the facility energy data, however, the specific details and issues with the integration of this data is ongoing at the time this paper was written and will be left for a future report.

Some initial observations are in order. This particular GM sand casting production is a large process, with hundreds of electrical equipment being controlled – robots, conveyors, elevators, sand core making machines, saws, etc. The extent of the casting production size necessitated narrowing the initial analysis scope to one of the finishing lines. The analysis was also limited to data already being collected by the plant's production system.

DES modeling to integrate production system and process energy data requires that traditional production KPIs be combined with process energy KPIs. Raw and event process production data was available and easily adapted into process KPI parameters. The casting production facility has a target castings yield per hour that it must achieve. This target served as the baseline process performance benchmark. Access to baseline energy equipment data for rated and peak energy loads was also available for most of the plant equipment. Logically, the production system data and the process energy data were not an exact match within production line, with production data being grouped a little differently than that of the energy data. For this analysis, the modeling was restructured to satisfy the structure of the energy information.

Using a commercial DES software package, a model was developed to correlate the production activity with the process energy consumption. This was not straightforward as the DES package did not inherently support manufacturing sustainability concepts, but correlation of the data by separating the integration into production and process energy submodels was possible. The Finishing process was condensed into three steps to better match the energy data: Spiral Cooling, Blast Robot, and Degating. Cycle times were determined by summing constituent process data substep cycle times. In simulation, the casting is moved from process to process. The operations (Spiral Cooling, Blast Robot, and Degating) have equipment resources that were simulated with the Sieze–Delay process model [17]. Once the simulated delay is completed, the casting is moved forward in the simulation lines. Input and output queues are associated with each operation, but queue states (blocked/starved), conveyor times, buffering, were not addressed in this initial analysis.

A state-based model to calculate energy consumption was used, where the resource utilization is used to determine the amount of energy consumed. For the initial benchmarking analysis, the rated equipment electrical demand loads as estimates for determining the "Busy" and "Idle" power consumption was used. Energy consumed was calculated using the native DES performance statistics for resource utilization, which provides values in the range from zero to one, and the total time of the simulation. The total resource energy consumed in the "Busy" state is determined by multiplying the resource utilization by the simulation time and by the average power used in this state. "Idle" is calculated similarly but uses 1 minus the utilization. Down time was not factored into the current stated based energy calculation. As an example, we can determine the total energy consumed for the blast robot during the simulation by the following equation:

$$
\begin{aligned}
E_{BR}^{Total} = & ((SU(BRR, Busy) == 1) \\
& \times E_{BR^{Busy}} \\
& + 1.0 - (SU(BRR, Busy) \\
& \times E_{BR^{Idle}}) \times T_s
\end{aligned}
$$

where

$BR = Blast\ Robot\ Process\ Module$
$BRR = Blast\ Robot\ Resource$
$E_x = Energy\ for\ Resource\ at\ State\ x$
$SU(resource, state) = utilization : u \in [0,1]$
$T_s = Total\ Simulation\ Time$

The total energy is the sum of each process energy consumption and the total energy cost is based on industry estimate of 5 cents per kWh price.

In summary, this paper has presented an approach to develop system models which can be used to evaluate the overall energy performance of any given manufacturing system. The total energy consumed in a manufacturing plant is comprised of process and facility energy components. Process energy is directly related to the operation of production lines that must meet specified targets. Facility energy consumption though not directly linked to production system performance nevertheless can be indirectly attributed and correlated with the requirements of the manufacturing system. The distinction between these two types of energy data though seemingly obvious is not trivial. Facility energy data typically resides in plant energy management systems that monitor and control the operation of equipment such as HVAC and other building related automation. Process energy on the other hand is not so readily available and often requires additional programming and interfacing effort with machine controllers to extract it and subsequently store it in some plant-floor system database. Many times, such process energy data is viewed in isolation from both the production system and certainly from that of the facility energy management system. The separation of these two types of energy data clearly represents an integration challenge, however, if successfully done, the association and correlation of this data can tremendously enhance the capability of a plant to make better energy related decisions. Therefore, any attempt to obtain meaningful understanding of a plant's total energy consumption thus requires a modeling approach that encompasses the interactions of the production system with that of the energy consumption characteristics of its equipment whether they be process or facility related.

In addition, process and facility energy analysis requires systematic study of strategic points within production lines. Production facilities can be very complex that makes integrated energy assessments quite difficult. Using a systematic methodology with appropriate benchmarks and evaluation criteria can make this a more manageable activity. However, energy results and the relationships to production are not always intuitive. For example, a paradox of lean manufacturing principles applied to energy consumption is that process improvements may in fact lead to increased energy consumption, but will improve part energy yield. Given an environment where energy efficiency improvements and technologies are not as easy to come by, production system, process energy, and facility energy data integration and benchmark measures are even more important to determine the expected return-on-investment of any energy-related improvements.

## Disclaimer

Commercial equipment and software, many of which are either registered or trademarked, are identified in order to adequately specify certain procedures. In no case does such identification imply recommendation or endorsement by the National Institute of Standards and Technology or General Motors, nor does it imply that the materials or equipment identified are necessarily the best available for the purpose.

## 5. REFERENCES

[1] J. Arinez and S. Biller. Innovations in energy measurement and control for manufacturing systems. In *NIST National Workshop on Challenges to Innovation in Advanced Manufacturing: Industry Drivers and R&D Needs*, Gaithersburg, MD, 2009.

[2] J. Arinez and S. Biller. Integration requirements for manufacturing–based energy management systems. In *2010 IEEE PES Conference on Innovative Smart Grid Technologies*, Gaithersburg, MD, 2010.

[3] J. Banks, J. Carson, B. L. Nelson, and D. Nicol. *Discrete-Event System Simulation (4th Edition)*. Prentice Hall, 4 edition, December 2004.

[4] N. Bengtsson, J. Michaloski, F. Proctor, G. Shao, and S. Venkatesh. Discrete event simulation of factory floor operations based on MtConnect data. In *2010 ASME International Conference on Manufacturing Science and Engineering*, Erie, PA, 2010.

[5] N. R. Council. *Unit Manufacturing Processes: Issues and Opportunities in Research*. National Academy Press, 1995.

[6] EPA. Lean energy toolkit. Technical Report EPA-100-K-07-003, Environmental Protection Agency, Washington, DC, 2007.

[7] T. Gutowski, J. Dahmus, and A. Thiriez. Electrical energy requirements for manufacturing processes. In *13th CIRP International Conference on Life Cycle Engineering*, Leuven, 2006.

[8] J. Heilala, S. Vatanen, H. Tonteri, J. Montonen, S. Lind, B. Johansson, and J. Stahre. Simulation-based sustainable manufacturing system design. In *Winter Simulation Conference (WSC) '08: Proceedings of the 40th Conference on Winter Simulation*, pages 1922 – 1930, 2008.

[9] ISO. *ISO 14064-1:2006 Greenhouse gases - Part 1: Specification with guidance at the organization level for quantification and reporting of greenhouse gas emissions and removals*. International Organization for Standardization, Geneva, Switzerland, 2006.

[10] ISO. *ISO 14064-2:2006 Greenhouse gases - Part 2: Specification with guidance at the project level for quantification, monitoring and reporting of greenhouse gas emission reductions or removal enhancements*. International Organization for Standardization, Geneva, Switzerland, 2006.

[11] ISO. *ISO 14064-3:2006 Greenhouse gases - Part 3: Specification with guidance for the validation and verification of greenhouse gas assertions*. International Organization for Standardization, Geneva, Switzerland, 2006.

[12] ISO. *ISO 14065:2007 Greenhouse gases – Requirements for greenhouse gas validation and verification bodies for use in accreditation or other forms of recognition*. International Organization for Standardization, Geneva, Switzerland, 2007.

[13] D. Kibira, S. Jain, and C. McLean. A system dynamics framework for sustainable manufacturing. In *27th International Conference of the System Dynamics Society*, Albuquerque, NM, USA, 2009.

[14] M. E. Kuhl and X. Zhou. Sustainability toolkit for simulation-based logistics decisions. In *Winter Simulation Conference (WSC) '09: Proceedings of the*

*41st Conference on Winter Simulation*, pages 1466 –
1473, 2009.

[15] P. Solding and P. Thollander. Increased energy
efficiency in a swedish iron foundry through use of
discrete event simulation. In *Winter Simulation
Conference (WSC) '06: Proceedings of the 38th
Conference on Winter Simulation*, pages 1971 – 1976,
2006.

[16] U.S. Congress, Office of Technology Assessment.
*Industrial Energy Efficiency, OTA-E-560*. U.S.
Government Printing Office, Washington, DC, 1993.

[17] R. S. W. Kelton and N. Swets. *Simulation with Arena*.
McGraw-Hill, Inc., New York, NY, USA, 2009.

# Complexity Measures for Distributed Assembly Tasks

M. Ani Hsieh
Scalable Autonomous Systems Lab
Drexel University
Philadelphia, PA 19104
mhsieh1@drexel.edu

Joshua Rogoff
Mechanical Engineering & Mechanics Dept.
Drexel University
Philadelphia, PA 19104
joshua.rogoff@drexel.edu

## ABSTRACT

We present complexity measures for distributed assembly tasks for a team of homogeneous robots with applications in intelligent construction and manufacturing. The objective is to define an appropriate metric to inform online partitioning of assembly tasks to maximize assembly parallelization. In this work, we consider the assembly of two-dimensional polygonal structures composed of homogeneous building blocks. We demonstrate our metric with different two dimensional assemblies and discuss briefly preliminary hardware results.

## Categories and Subject Descriptors

I.2.11 [**Distributed Artificial Intelligence**]: Multiagent systems

## 1. INTRODUCTION

In this work, we describe a complexity measure for distributed assembly tasks where a team of homogeneous robots are tasked to assemble complex structures with applications in intelligent construction and manufacturing. The objective is to develop an appropriate complexity measure that can be used to inform the partitioning of the assembly task to maximize assembly parallelization. We consider the assembly of two-dimensional structures composed of homogeneous building blocks where assembly is achieved by first partitioning the structure into subcomponents. These subcomponents can then be assembled by individual robots that have the ability to identify, carry, and assemble the components as well as navigate within the workspace. To this end, our goal is to develop measures that will take into account the geometry of the desired structure and its impact on the traversability of the workspace as the structure is being assembled.

Existing works in the area of robotic assembly have mostly focused on the design of local assembly rules that can meet high-level task specifications. Klavins *et al.* achieved distributed self-assembly by pre-programming component parts with a set of probabilistic attachment and detachment rules

[1, 6, 5]. Assembly is achieved by actively mixing the components using an external shaking or stirring mechanism. As parts collide with one another, the individual components bind and detach following the pre-programmed probabilistic rule set. In [9, 10, 8], distributed assembly by a team of mobile robots was achieved by pre-specifying the local attachment rules for the parts to be assembled. In these works, robots rely on the information stored on the assembly components. The interconnection rule set is then carefully designed to ensure completeness and correctness of the final structure. Matthey *et al.* considered the autonomous assembly of distinct products from a collection of heterogeneous parts by a team of mobile robots in [4]. Here, the mobile robots wander the workspace and assembly is achieved when two robots with matching subassemblies encounter one another. While these control policies provide theoretical guarantees on the overall yield of the system, the approach requires the enumeration of all possible interconnections between the various subcomponents.

More recently, Yun *et al.* proposed a distributed mass-based partitioning of the assembly task to enable parallel construction of a desired structure by a team of mobile robots [2, 11]. Here, an iterative Voronoi decomposition of the workspace was employed to partition the space into a set of convex cells. The partitioning strategy was designed such that each Voronoi cell contains roughly the same amount of subcomponent mass. At each iteration, the individual robot positions were used to obtain the Voronoi tessellation of the workspace. The mass contained within each cell was then computed and robot positions were modified to minimize the mass differential between the cells. While this approach provides an approximately equal allocation of parts to be assembled, it does not take into account the additional path planning costs that may arise due to the increasing complexity of the workspace as the various subcomponents of the structure are put together by the team. Furthermore, as the geometric complexity of the target structure and the number of robots increase, the accuracy of the approximations decreases which results in an unbalanced allocation of workload among the team. This is because the objective function employed in this approach is non-convex and thus the optimization strategy can potentially be stuck in a local minimum that is far off from the global minimum.

In this work, we take inspiration from the approach proposed in [2, 11] and define complexity measures that takes into account the geometry and mass of the target structure as well as the number of connected components, narrow passages, and holes, *i.e.* empty space, within the desired structure. Similar to [7] and [3], this work focuses on the development of a metric that can be used for comparison and/or to inform the synthesis of distributed assembly strategies such as the one proposed in [2].

## 2. COMPLEXITY MEASURES

In general, given a two-dimensional structure, we have an intuitive understanding of the complexity of the structure to be assembled. Figure 1 shows three example structures, each partitioned into four roughly equal mass substructures. If we employ the assembly strategy described in [11], a construction robot would be assigned to each cell while a part delivery robot would be tasked to deliver building materials to each of the assembly robots. Each construction robot would be tasked to remain within its convex work cell and assemble the individual parts as they are delivered. From a motion planning perspective, one would expect that the structures shown in Figures 1(b) and 1(c) would result in increased inter-agent collision and obstacle avoidance maneuvers as the structures are assembled compared to the one in Figure 1(a). As such, to enable efficient parallelization in assembly, an ideal partitioning of the target structure must take into account these navigation costs that result from the decreased in open space as the structure is assembled by the mobile robot team.

The target structures shown in Figures 1 include examples of geometric features that make the design of distributed assembly strategies challenging. For the structure shown in Figure 1(a), one strategy is to task the robots to assemble the subcomponents within each cell starting from the center of the target structure. While the structure is non-convex, this simple strategy ensures both completeness and correctness of the distributed assembly task. Applying the same assembly strategy to the structure shown in Figure 1(b) may provide similar results. The presence of the narrow entrance at the bottom, however, may require the robots to execute more complex navigation maneuvers as they negotiate the workspace around the narrow entrance as the structure is assembled. This is particularly true for the structure shown in Figure 1(c). Further, in this third case, the presence of the enclosed empty areas within the structure will require more complex coordination strategies to ensure robots do not trap themselves within these regions as they complete their tasks.

While what constitutes a complex target structure can be somewhat subjective and may depend on the type of hardware, i.e., the types of sensors, robots, and building materials used, our goal is to define a metric that can provide an estimate to enable comparisons and inform the design of distributed strategies. As such, we formalize these properties in the following section before presenting our metric to describe the complexity of the assembly task.

### 2.1 Definitions

In this section, we briefly describe the set of structure properties that will be used to assess the complexity of the desired structure. We limit our discussion to two dimensional polygonal structures in convex workspaces.

We consider the distributed assembly of a given target structure $S$ by a team of $N$ homogeneous robots. We assume that the workspace, $\mathcal{W}$, is a convex polygonal space and is obstacle free before the assembly of $S$. Let $\mathbf{q}$ denote a point in $\mathcal{W}$ and $\phi_t(\mathbf{q})$ the target mass density function for $S$ similar

to [2, 11]. We note that $\phi_t(\mathbf{q}) > 0$ for all $\mathbf{q} \subset S \subset \mathcal{W}$. Let $S_i$ denote the $i$ connected component in $S$ such that $S = \cup_{i=1}^{M} S_i$. In addition, we denote the $j$ massless connected component enclosed in $S_i$ as $O_{ij}$, i.e. $\phi_t(\mathbf{q}) = 0$ for $\mathbf{q} \in O_{ij}$, and define $O_i = \cup_{j=1}^{m_i} O_{ij}$ with $\mathcal{O} = \cup_{i=1}^{M} O_i$. Next, let $E$ and $H$ denote the number of entrances into and hallways in $S$. We will consider any opening into the structure as an entrance.

For the example structures shown in Figures 1(a) - 1(c), $S$ is represented by the shaded areas. For Figure 1(a), $M = 1$ since there is only one connected component in $S$. Further, $\mathcal{O}$ is the null set and $E = H = 0$. Figure 1(b) shows a target structure with two connected components $S_1$ and $S_2$ corresponding to the interior rectangle and the exterior fence. In this example, $M = 2$ with $\mathcal{O} = 0$ and $E = H = 1$. Similarly, Figure 1(c) is an example with $M = 1$ and $O_i = \cup_{j=1}^{2} O_{ij}$ with each $O_{ij}$ given by the interior empty squares with $E = H = 1$.

Finally, let $\partial S$ and $\partial \mathcal{O}$ denote the boundaries of the structure and of the set of massless connected components respectively. We denote the length of these boundaries by $L(\cdot)$. The area of each of these sets will be given by $A(\cdot)$ and let $w_i$, $v_i$, and $l_i$ represent the width of the $i$ entrance, the width of the $i$ hallway, and the length of the $i$ hallway. Since the desired metric must be independent of the size of individual robots, we define $R$ as the radius of the smallest circle that circumscribes the robot.

### 2.2 Measures of Complexity

Given a target structure $S$, we define the complexity of the distributed assembly task for $S$ as:

$$C = k_1 \left( \frac{L(\partial S)}{\sqrt{A(S)}} \right)^M + k_2 \left( \min\{0, \frac{L(\partial \mathcal{O})}{\sqrt{A(\mathcal{O})}}\} \right)^{\sum_{i=1}^{M} m_i} + $$

$$k_3 \left( \min\{0, \sum_{i=1}^{E} \frac{2R}{w_i}\} \right)^E + k_4 \left( \min\{0, \sum_{i=1}^{H} \frac{l_i}{v_i}\} \right)^H \quad (1)$$

where $k_1, k_2, k_3, k_4$ are weighting positive constants.

The first term in (1) captures the geometric complexity of the target structure $S$. In general, given $S$, the larger the discrepancy between the perimeter of the structure and the normalized area, i.e., $\sqrt{A(\cdot)}$, implies more protrusions and indentations associated with the structure. In addition, as $M$ increases, the more complex the workspace becomes as $S$ is being assembled since every $S_i$ introduces an obstacle into the environment.

Similarly, the second term in (1) describes the complexity introduced by massless regions enclosed in $S_i$ for all $i = 1, \ldots, M$. Holes within a structure pose significant challenges in the synthesis of provably correct distributed algorithms unless an assembly prioritization scheme can be imposed for certain portions of $S$. The third and fourth terms in (1) describe the complexity induced by the presence of narrow entry points into and hallways within $S$. Such features can introduce significant traffic congestion for part delivery robots as well as assembly robots. As the width of the entrances and hallways shrinks, the complexity increases since localization and navigation errors can detrimentally affect the performance of the entire system.

We note that while the complexity of the distributed assembly task $C$ is given by (1), it is possible to consider

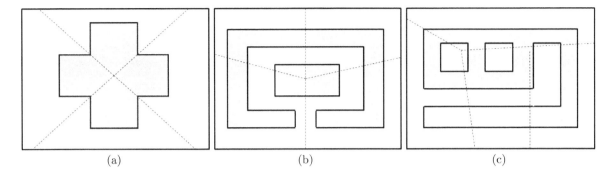

Figure 1: Three toy examples of assembly structures of (a) low, (b) medium, and (c) high complexity. The dotted lines denote cell boundaries where each cell roughly contains equal mass.

the individual terms as distinct measures for a given structure/task. These measures can be used to adjust the target mass density function $\phi_t(\mathbf{q})$ to affect the partitioning of the assembly task or be used to determine the order in which components must be assembled.

## 3. EXAMPLES

We present six example structures and their resulting complexities using the metric defined by (1). The target structures are shown in Figure 2. The target mass density function for each structure was set to unity for every point in $\mathcal{S}$, i.e. $\phi_t(\mathbf{q}) = 1$ for all $\mathbf{q} \in \mathcal{S}$. The structures were then partitioned into six equal mass components using the Voronoi-based decomposition strategy described in [2]. The Voronoi-based partitions are shown in Figure 2 and the distribution of mass in the Voronoi cells for each structure and the standard deviation as a percentage of total mass of $\mathcal{S}$ are summarized in Table 2. We note that while the resulting Voronoi cells contain roughly the same mass, the resulting partitioning may require complex navigation strategies or may be unrealizable unless robots become trapped within the structure, i.e. Figures 2(e) and 2(f).

The complexity measures described in Section 2 for the structures shown in Figure 2 are provided in Table 1. These values where obtained by assuming $R = 1$ and $k_1 = k_2 = k_3 = k_4 = 1$. Based on our chosen metric (given by (1)), the most challenging structure is the one shown in Figure 2(f). The complexity of the structure arise from the set of holes $\mathcal{O}$ within the target structure. One surprising result is the relatively low complexity value of the structure shown in Figure 2(d). This is partly because the proposed complexity metric does not take into account the size of the robot team that will be used to assemble the desired structure.

## 4. CONCLUSION

In this work, we define a set of complexity measures for distributed assembly tasks based on the geometry of the desired structure. The proposed complexity measures were then combined to define a complexity metric which can be used to inform the synthesis of partitioning strategies of the target structure to maximize parallelization of the assembly task. This work has open many avenues for further investigation. In particular, we are interested in investigating the use of topological invariants such as Euler characteristics to

| $\mathcal{S}$ | % of Total Mass in Each Cell | | | | | | Std Dev |
|---|---|---|---|---|---|---|---|
| | 1 | 2 | 3 | 4 | 5 | 6 | (%) |
| (a) | 18.4 | 15.7 | 14.9 | 16.8 | 17.9 | 16.2 | 1.3 |
| (b) | 12.8 | 17.1 | 18.1 | 16.9 | 19.2 | 16.0 | 2.2 |
| (c) | 14.8 | 15.8 | 19.0 | 16.3 | 17.8 | 16.4 | 1.5 |
| (d) | 16.1 | 17.7 | 13.4 | 17.4 | 17.7 | 17.7 | 1.7 |
| (e) | 14.1 | 16.4 | 19.0 | 16.7 | 16.5 | 17.3 | 1.6 |
| (f) | 14.7 | 16.1 | 15.9 | 16.6 | 18.9 | 17.8 | 1.5 |

Table 2: Mass distribution across the Voronoi partitions for the structures shown in Figure 2.

further refine our complexity measure. Such an approach will enable us to extend our measures to describe three dimensional structures as well as structures whose boundaries are given by smooth curves and surfaces.

A second direction for future work is the development of complexity aware task partitioning algorithms that can allocate the assembly task to minimize navigational costs. Rather than partition the assembly task solely based on the density of assembly parts, we have shown that it may make more sense to partition the task based on the traversability of the resulting workspace as the structure is being assembled. Finally, we are currently developing a set of hardware experiments based on the mini-mobile manipulator platform ($M^3$ robot shown in Figure 3) to enable hardware experimentation of our proposed strategies.

## 5. REFERENCES

[1] E. Klavins, S. Burden, and N. Napp. Optimal rules for programmed stochastic self-assembly. In *Proc. Robotics: Science and Systems II*, pages 9–16, Atlanta, GA, 2007.

[2] S. kook Yun, M. Schwager, and D. Rus. Coordinating construction of truss structures using distributed equal-mass partitioning. In *Proc. of the 14th International Symposium on Robotics Research*, Lucerne, Switzerland, Aug-Sept 2009.

[3] K. Lee, M. Moses, and G. S. Chirikjian. Robotic self-replication in structured environments: Physical demonstrations and complexity measures. *The International Journal of Robotics Research (IJRR)*, 27(3-4):387 – 401, March/April 2008.

[4] L. Matthey, S. Berman, , and V. Kumar. Stochastic strategies for a swarm robotic assembly system. In

| $\mathcal{S}$ | $M$ | $\dfrac{L(\partial\mathcal{S})}{\sqrt{A(\mathcal{S})}}$ | $\sum_{i=1}^{M} m_i$ | $\dfrac{L(\partial\mathcal{O})}{\sqrt{A(\mathcal{O})}}$ | $E$ | $\sum \dfrac{w_i}{2R}$ | $H$ | $\sum \dfrac{l_i}{v_i}$ | $C$ |
|---|---|---|---|---|---|---|---|---|---|
| (a) | 1 | 4.0 | 0 | NA | 0 | NA | 0 | NA | 4.0 |
| (b) | 1 | 10.2 | 1 | NA | 2 | 1.00 | 4 | 20.2 | 11.2 |
| (c) | 1 | 6.9 | 2 | 4.3 | 1 | 0.14 | 1 | 0.5 | 25.1 |
| (d) | 1 | 10.0 | 3 | NA | 1 | 1.00 | 2 | 14.5 | 11.0 |
| (e) | 2 | 15.9 | 4 | NA | 2 | 1.00 | 1 | 70.5 | 253.3 |
| (f) | 1 | 9.2 | 6 | 10.2 | 0 | NA | 0 | NA | 1.1e6 |

Table 1: **Complexity measures for the structures shown in Figure 2 with** $R = 5$.

*2009 IEEE International Conference on Robotics and Automation (ICRA'09)*, Kobe, Japan, May 2009.

[5] N. Napp, S. Burden, and E. Klavins. Setpoint regulation for stochastically interacting robots. In *Robotics: Science and Systems V*. MIT Press, 2009.

[6] N. Napp, D. Thorsley, and E. Klavins. Hidden markov models for non-well-mixed reaction networks. In *Proc. of the American Control Conference*, St. Louis, MO, June 2009.

[7] A. C. Sanderson. Part entropy method for robotic assembly design. In *Proc. of Int. Conf. on Robotics & Automation (ICRA'84)*, pages 600–608, March 1984.

[8] J. Werfel, Y. Bar-Yam, and R. Nagpal. Building patterned structures with robot swarms. In *Proc. of the 19th Int. Joint Conf. on Artificial Intelligence (IJCAI'05)*, pages 1495–1502, Pasadena, CA USA, July 2009.

[9] J. Werfel, Y. Bar-Yam, D. Rus, and R. Nagpal. Distributed construction by mobile robots with enhanced building blocks. In *Proc. of the Int. Conf. on Robotics & Automation (ICRA'06)*, pages 2787 – 2794, Orlando, FL USA, May 2006.

[10] J. Werfel, D. Ingber, and R. Nagpal. Collective construction of environmentally-adaptive structures. In *Proc. of the IEEE/RSJ Int. Conf. on Intelligent Robots and Systems (IROS'07)*, pages 2345 – 2352, San Diego, CA USA, Oct 2007.

[11] S. K. Yun and D. Rus. Adaptation to robot failures and shape change in decentralized construction. In *Proc. of the Int. Conf. on Robotics & Automation (ICRA'10)*, pages 2451 – 2458, Anchorage, AK USA, May 2010.

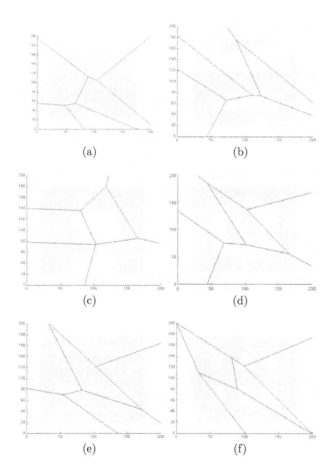

(a)    (b)

(c)    (d)

(e)    (f)

Figure 2: **Four target structures decomposed into 6 equal mass partitions. The shaded region corresponds to the structure and the solid lines represent the borders of each Voronoi cell.**

Figure 3: **The mini mobile manipulator (M³) robot assembled from the iRobot Create and Lynxmotion platform assembling a 2-D structure out of interlocking blocks.**

# Advanced Sensing Towards Improved Forklift Safety

Roger Bostelman, Will Shackleford
National Institute of Standards and Technology
100 Bureau Drive, Stop 8230
Gaithersburg, MD 20899
(301) 975-3426

roger.bostelman@nist.gov

## Abstract
The National Institute of Standards and Technology's Intelligent Systems Division has been researching advanced three-dimensional (3D) imaging sensors and their use in manufacturing towards improving forklift safety. Experiments are presented in this paper and that show how the sensors can augment a forklift operator's perception of obstacles nearby. Interoperability of the obstacle/pedestrian detection information from these sensors to the facility or other forklifts for broader alerts is also possible.

## Categories and Subject Descriptors
B.7.0 [Advanced]; C.2.1 [Sensor Networks]

## General Terms
Algorithms, Measurement, Performance, Design, Experimentation, Human Factors, Verification.

## Keywords
3D imagers, forklift, ANSI B56.5, driver alert

## 1 Introduction
There are over 1 million forklifts in operation in the United States with an estimated 2 million operators (6 million including part time operators) [1] and nearly 2 000 automated guided vehicles (AGVs) in use in the US. Forklifts are a necessary piece of material handling equipment for many industries. If used properly, they can reduce employee injuries. Unfortunately, they can also pose some safety risks to drivers, pedestrians, and other equipment and goods.

The National Institute of Standards and Technology's (NIST) Intelligent Systems Division (ISD) held a Special Session at the 2009 Performance Metrics for Intelligent Systems (PerMIS) Conference to address the safety of forklifts. A White Paper [2] summarized presentations and discussions from the Special Session on "Performance Measurements Towards Improved Forklift Safety." In this paper,

This paper is authored by employees of the United States Government and is in the public domain. PerMIS'10, September 28-30, 2010, Baltimore, MD, USA.
ACM 978-1-4503-0290-6-9/28/10

forklift safety statistics were listed along with recommendations for improving forklift safety. For the readers convenience, several of the statistics are listed here:

o OSHA estimates that there are 110 000 accidents each year.

o $135 000 000 immediate costs are incurred due to forklift accidents

o Approximately every 3 days, someone in the US is killed in a forklift related accident

o Almost 80 % of forklift accidents involve a pedestrian

o One in six of all workplace fatalities in this country are forklift related

o According to OSHA, approximately 70 % of all accidents reported could have been avoided with proper safety procedures

A definition for interoperability [3] is "the ability of systems to provide services to and accept services from other systems, units or forces and to use the services exchanged to enable them to operate effectively together." Interoperability of forklifts with facilities was also discussed in the Special Session and in the White Paper, including:

o automatic barrier guards which can be installed to prevent fork trucks from falling off a vacant receiving dock that can detect approaching forklifts and trucks,

o radio frequency (RF)-tags placed in safety vests worn by warehouse workers that can communicate with RF receivers on forklifts alerting drivers to the presence of any workers within the detection radius of the receiver,

o presence detection sensors of a vehicle being within the detection distance or zone and can indicate potential collisions at intersections and can communicate with other forklifts.

The White Paper also listed two recommendations suggested by NIST to add sensors and cameras to new forklifts and also to retrofit them to the nearly 1 million forklifts in use today. Sensor systems added to forklifts can potentially detect nearby obstacles and pedestrians and provide alerts to drivers and/or, through communication with the facility, to pedestrians or other forklift drivers nearby. Moreover, non-contact sensing devices are discussed in the ANSI/ITSDF B56.5 Safety Standard for Driverless, Automatic Guided Industrial Vehicles and Automated Functions of Manned Industrial Vehicles Standard draft (currently under ballot) [4] stating that "a sensing device or combination of devices shall be supplied to prevent contact of the vehicle structure and installed equipment with people or objects appearing in the path of the vehicle in the main direction of travel." Also, "if used as a primary sensing device, … (the sensor) shall cause a safety stop of the vehicle prior to contact…" In the case of manned forklifts, the operator is responsible for prevention of accidents. However, the operator's view is sometimes blocked by, for example, the forklift and/or its payload. ISD has performed non-contact 3D imager experiments to recommend language to add to the ANSI B56.5 standard to support sensor and AGV manufacturers. [5]

ISD has, therefore, continued to research advanced sensors applied to forklifts through experiments using forklifts outfitted with 3D imagers and operator alerts (e.g., lights). This paper will discuss these experiments and discuss next steps to collect data in real manufacturing environments. The paper begins with discussion of the advanced 3D imagers used. Following are sections on the experimental configuration, software developed, and experimental results. Last are conclusions and references.

## 2 Advanced 3D Imaging Sensors

The imaging sensors used in the forklift experiments were 3D LIDAR (light detection and ranging)[1], time-of-flight measurement sensors, [6] each having a 64 x 48 pixel array and photonic mixing device technology to provide data that can be used to identify an object in its field of view (FOV). The sensors measure 122 mm long x 75 mm wide x 95 mm high. The array projects 3072 points of reference onto an object, capturing the entire FOV in three dimensions. The sensors provide their own active lighting with background lighting suppression for use in various lighting conditions. Each pixel within the array is able to compute the phase difference on-board the sensor chip allowing the

sensor to pre-process the signal. Variations in color cause challenges with traditional photoelectric sensors. White objects reflect more than dark objects. The sensor manufacturer's specification states that this issue is minimized and creates a more consistent measurement throughout the color spectrum. Without direct comparison and evaluation of this sensor with a different manufacturer's sensor, this claim could not be verified.

The sensor used is stated as having a 40° x 30° field of view (FOV) allowing approximately 11 mm x 11 mm pixel size with 840 mm x 580 mm FOV at 1 m from the sensor. Distance resolution for white objects at 1 m distance is ± 3 mm versus ± 5 mm for gray objects. Unambiguous object detection ranges are stated to be 6.5 m in the single frequency mode and 48 m in the dual frequency mode. Figure 1 shows images from the sensor brochure of a pallet of boxes and the corresponding sensor data surface map. Range and intensity are available at each pixel and output is via Ethernet to a computer.

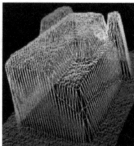

Figure 1 – Images from the sensor brochure showing (left) a pallet of boxes and (right) the corresponding 3D imager sensor data surface map.

Navigation support and collision avoidance on automated guided vehicles (AGVs), among other applications, are suggested as possible applications of these sensors. Based on the product specifications, the sensor appears appropriate for mounting on forklifts to measure objects and pedestrians when they are near the vehicle. Through wireless Ethernet, the object detection information could perhaps be interoperable with facility systems to provide off-board vehicle alerts.

## 3 Experiments with 3D Imagers on Forklifts
### a Sensors Configuration

Experiments were performed using the 3D imaging sensors mounted on forklifts. The sensors were retrofitted to two different commercial forklifts to test the retrofit feasibility, test obstacle detection capability and to provide appropriate operator alerts.

---

[1] Commercial systems equipment and materials are identified in order to adequately specify certain procedures. In no case does such identification imply recommendation or endorsement by the National Institute of Standards and Technology, nor does it imply that these materials or equipment identified are necessarily the best available for the purpose.

Forklift #1 was smaller than Forklift #2. Forklift #1 was retrofit with five sensors and Forklift #2 was later retrofitted with six sensors. Available space between the Forklift #1 front wheels and below the fork frame allowed for a single sensor to be mounted for detection of the front floor. Forklift #2 did not have this space and instead was retrofitted with six sensors where two sensors, one above each front wheel, detected the front floor. Sensors were mounted to detect the: rear parallel-to-the-floor; rear floor; front parallel-to-the-floor (fork-side); front floor ahead of the front wheels; and the ceiling. Figure 2 shows a concept for ideal forklift sensing and photos of the two forklifts with sensors mounted for use in the experiments. In the concept drawing, 3D imagers are shown on the forks frame and on an extendible boom, among others shown. These tilting-concept (to provide a larger FOV from one sensor) 3D imagers were not tested and instead replaced with fixed mounted 3D sensors and a camera. Figure 2 (b) and (c) show Forklift #1 and Forklift #2, respectively, with red arrows that indicate each of the sensor locations and the directions they sensed.

The ceiling and front parallel-to-the-floor sensors are mounted to the fork frame and move up and down with the forklift tines. Fork height for the moving 3D imaging sensors, with respect to the forklift, was measured using a one-dimensional (1D) laser measurement sensor mounted to the moving fork frame. This sensor indicates the fork height above the floor to correct for the position of the two moving sensors.

(b)

(c)

Figure 2 – (a) Concept for ideal sensing for forklifts; (b) Forklift #1 and (c) Forklift #2 used in experiments showing sensor mount locations and sense directions (red arrows).

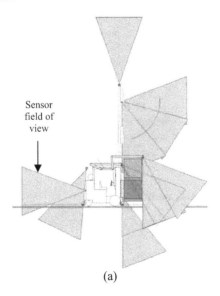

Sensor field of view

(a)

Commercial-off-the-shelf forklift camera systems also mount rigidly to the fork frame or forklift frame and provide extended views (e.g., forward and rear) to the driver. A payload, however, can block at least the front camera. For ISD's experiments, a camera, instead of a 3D imager depicted in Figure 2 (a), was mounted to a manual sliding boom to place the camera in front of payloads to see around them. Figure 2 (b) shows Forklift #1 with a camera mounted on an extendable boom wrapped in safety tape, with a monitor in the cab to allow the operator to see in front of the payload. This concept was tested with a payload blocking the driver's FOV. The driver was able to use the camera and monitor, along with viewing side to side of the load, to drive from one room, through doors, through a machine shop, through another set of doors and through a metal storeroom to a loading dock without any safety personnel support. This concept was tested with good results and is a minor extension to commercial forklift camera systems. As opposed to 2D cameras displayed to the operator, 3D imagers could process the data, instead of the driver, and simply send an alert to the driver and others through interoperability of forklifts with facilities if/when there is a safety issue.

## *b  Data Processing Software*

The sensor positions and orientations are calibrated by starting with values taken with a tape measure and level and then fine-tuning using the display of overlapping data on simple recognizable targets. This step is needed since some sensors FOV overlap one another. Some of the sensors are mounted on the fork's frame and the positions of those sensors need to be updated in real-time based on the height of the forks. This height is measured with the 1D laser range sensor on the fork frame.

The software processes the 3D LIDAR sensor data so that if a sufficient number of data points are within that volume, the volume is assumed to be obstructed and an operator alert could be provided. Otherwise the entire volume is considered clear with no alert provided. Similarly, signaling negative obstacles when the floor is not detected (e.g., at the loading dock edge) is important and accomplished with the software. The threshold for each volume is determined after data are collected for both known clear and known obstructed data sets.

For each 3D LIDAR sensor a process is run dedicated to reading and time-stamping each frame of data from that sensor. The data are converted from a vendor specific XML-RPC (eXtensible Markup Language-Remote Procedure Call) network protocol to NML (Neutral Message Language) [7], configured to use shared memory. The data structures used within NML have been used with 3D LIDAR sensors from several other vendors and therefore tools written to work with this interface can be easily configured to work with other sensors.

A separate process reads all of the NML buffers and combines the data from all sensors. Each sensor provides both a range image and an intensity image. Data points can be excluded if the intensity is too high or too low since both conditions may indicate the range value is likely to be invalid. Also, data points may be excluded if the range value differs too much from all their neighboring pixels in the image. Data points not filtered are converted from range to a 3D Cartesian point relative to the center-front-bottom

part of the vehicle using a calibrated position and orientation for each sensor.

Each 3D Cartesian data point is then checked to see if it is within a 3D rectangular volume associated with each of the warning lights that will be shown to the operator (see Figure 3).

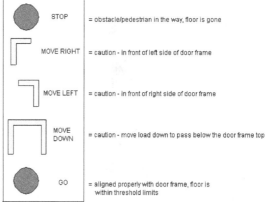

Figure 3 – Forklift operator alerts provided on an onboard vehicle laptop

Another alert panel (shown in Figure 4 (b)) was built and installed as opposed to the Figure 3 laptop-based alerts tested. This panel is potentially simpler for the driver to interpret quickly because the lights indicated the general area an obstacle was detected so that the operator could immediately check that area for issues. In Figure 4 (a), an obstacle is behind the forklift. Figure 4 (b) shows the operator alert panel with the rear light lit indicating that an obstacle is directly behind the vehicle. The obstacle was detected by the rear parallel-to-the-floor sensor and interpreted by software to indicate that an obstacle was in the sensor FOV. The simpler light panel was remote from the computer and connected through a USB interface eliminating the need to include a laptop onboard the forklift. A series of lights also appear adequate to provide the information shown in the Figure 3 operator alerts although this was not tested.

Wired Ethernet was used onboard the vehicle to interconnect all sensor data with the onboard laptop computer. However, wireless Ethernet or other cable-less data intercommunication could interoperability between forklifts and facilities, such as:

- Onboard forklift sensors sending alerts to nearby persons using facility alerts (e.g., lights, audibles).
- Off-board forklift sensors sending alerts to forklift drivers.
- Forklift to forklift communication.

(a)

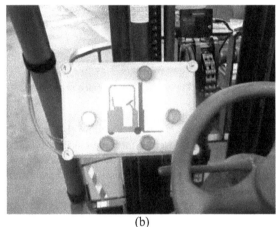

(b)

Figure 4 (a) – An obstacle is directly behind the forklift and (b) is indicated on the operator alert light panel used in forklift safety experiments.

## 4 Experimental Results

Figure 5 shows a snapshot of results of the merged data from sensors used in the experiment. The results show that the sensors clearly detect the ceiling above the forks, obstacles behind the forklift, and the missing floor in front of the forklift (obstacles are shown in red). The forward facing sensor mounted parallel to the floor was blocked by the carried load as indicated by the blue box. When not blocked, this sensor detected obstacles similar to the rear sensor. A height threshold for the floor can be selected in software as indicated by the red and green dots. The slope in front of the forklift indicates either that the floor is sloped or drops-offs. Either case is not safe for the forklift. The detected missing/sloped floor and the obstacles can be processed using software to send alerts to the operator and/or others.

Just as important is to detect if a truck is not completely backed to the loading dock. In this case, the forklift must detect that there is a gap that cannot

be crossed between the dock and truck and stop prior to the gap. The 3D sensors clearly detected the gap as shown by the sloped green dots on the lower right of Figure 5.

Figure 5 - Snapshot of results of the merged data from sensors used in the Forklift #1 experiment.

Important to note is that while the sensors detected the gap, their front, low mounting locations and angles between or just above the front wheels may not provide enough stopping time when the gap or missing floor is detected depending upon vehicle speed. There may be a better mounting location for these sensors if vehicle speed is allowed to remain high or sensors mounted low may be combined with forced slow speeds in these situations. The rear sensor can detect sloped or gapped floors in either case since it is mounted on top of the vehicle roll-cage and therefore, measures far enough from the vehicle for an appropriate operator alert at higher speed.

Both forklift operator alert panels functioned properly and as expected. Several videos were captured [8] of the Figure 3 panel to prove that when a load was carried and for example, could not fit through a doorway, appropriate indicator lights would alert the operator to move the load left, right, or down to fit through the opening. Similarly, stop and go (path is clear) indicators worked well when the path was blocked or not, respectively. Similarly, the Figure 4 panel control software indicated appropriate lights when obstacles were detected.

Another experiment using Forklift #2 provided similar results to the previous experiment using Forklift #1 with sensors being mounted above each of the front wheels. However, in this experiment the sensors also detected the fork frame when the forks were lowered to the ground since these two sensors were mounted above each front wheel. Software, therefore, was developed to mask the pixel lines viewing the forks and only view the pixels that were in front of the wheel and behind the forks to detect missing floor or obstacles. There was also a concern as to whether these two sensors would return useful data due to too much light returned from the fork frame. In past experience with 3D LIDAR sensors, for example in [9 and 10], we found that the sensor light-emitting diodes can 'wash-out' the data when they are too close to an object. However, these two sensors provided useful returned data without wash-outs. This may be due to the steep angle of the sensor with respect to the forklift frame or from manufacturing differences of different sensors.

## 5   Conclusions

Forklifts are useful and widely-used material handling tools. However, their safe use is being researched due to the high number of accidents that occur. The ANSI/ITSDF B56.5 standard states that the operator of a manned forklift is responsible for prevention of accidents. Augmenting forklifts with safety devices may be useful to support accident prevention.

Several types of interoperable (forklift with people and/or facility) safety systems have been or are being applied to forklifts. NIST ISD has been researching advanced 3D imaging sensors mounted on forklifts. Ideally, 3D sensors could surround forklifts and provide drivers and those nearby with alert information when obstacles and pedestrians are detected with these sensors.

In experiments performed at NIST, 3D imagers were mounted on two different sized forklifts and obstacle detection data were collected from sensors that viewed the front, rear, and overhead forklift areas. Data processing software was developed to interpret the sensor data as obstacles, including negative (missing or steeply sloped floor) obstacles, or clear space and to send driver alerts. Initial experimental results show that the 3D imagers used can provide enough information to detect obstacles with promising results. Various operator alerts were also tested providing simple obstacle detection (light on) or no detection (light off) alerts as well as showing the operator which way to move the load to clear a passageway. Early results showed that processed 3D image sensor data can augment a forklift driver's perception of his/her surroundings and can provide knowledge of obstacles to the driver through alerts.

Planned next steps for this research are to retrofit the sensors to a forklift in a real manufacturing facility, collect data and determine whether 3D imagers can play a useful role in forklift safety.

## 6   Acknowledgements

The authors would like to thank the NIST Machine Shops and the NIST Construction shop for letting us borrow their forklift and truck, respectively, for the secondary experiments.

## 7   References

[1] Chugh, Kevin, 2009. "A PC Based Virtual Reality Simulation for Forklift Safety Training," SBIR Phase II, http://www.cdc.gov/od/science/phresearch/

[2] Bostelman, Roger, 2009. "White paper, Towards Improved Forklift Safety," PerMIS 09 Proceedings.

[3] Wikipedia, 2010. "Interoperability" definition under telecommunications: http://en.wikipedia.org/wiki/Interoperability#Public_safety

[4] ANSI/ITSDF B56.5 -2010 "Safety Standard for Driverless, Automatic Guided Industrial Vehicles and Automated Functions of Manned Industrial Vehicles."

[5] Bostelman, Roger, 2009; Shackleford, Will, "Performance Measurements Towards Improved Manufacturing Vehicle Safety," NIST Intelligent Systems Division, PerMIS 09 Proceedings.

[6] Ifm Efector, 2009, "3D Image Sensing Using Smart Pixel Technology," http://www.ifm-electronic.com/obj/ifm_o3d200_brochure_gb.pdf

[7] XML-RPC definition, http://en.wikipedia.org/wiki/XML-RPC, October 27, 2010.

[8] Roger Bostelman, Will Shackleford, 2008. "Manufacturing Vehicles - Towards Improved Forklift Safety (avi files)" http://www.nist.gov/mel/isd/ms/manufacturing-vehicles.cfm.

[9] Roger Bostelman, Will Shackleford, 2008. "Test Report on Highly Reflective Objects Near the SR3000 Sensor, NIST Internal Report to Consortium CRADA Partners, February 27.

[10] Roger Bostelman, Will Shackleford, 2008. "Test Report of Performance Measurements of a 3D Imager and Color Camera Viewing Forklift Tines," NIST Internal Report to Consortium CRADA Partners, September 24.

# A Multi-Vehicle Testbed for Underwater Motion Coordination

Nitin Sydney
Department of Aerospace
Engineering
University of Maryland,
College Park, MD 20742
nsydney@umd.edu

Seth Napora
Department of Aerospace
Engineering
University of Maryland,
College Park, MD 20742
snapora@umd.edu

Derek A. Paley
Department of Aerospace
Engineering
University of Maryland,
College Park, MD 20742
dpaley@umd.edu

## ABSTRACT

The Synthetic Collective Unmanned Underwater Laboratory (SCUUL) testbed is a multi-vehicle testbed that is used to evaluate the performance of underwater motion coordination algorithms in a dynamic environment. The SCUUL testbed consists of six propellor-driven vehicles, a 367,000 gallon tank, and an underwater motion capture system. The tank is the Neutral Buoyancy Research Facility (NBRF) located at the University of Maryland and operated by the Collective Dynamics and Control Laboratory (CDCL) and the Space Systems Laboratory. The motion capture is a state-of-the-art system developed by Qualisys in Gothenburg, Sweden. Initial results have shown the capabilities of the separate components of SCUUL and its ability to test and evaluate a multitude of motion coordination algorithms in a laboratory environment.

## Keywords

Underwater vehicles, cooperative control, motion coordination

## 1. INTRODUCTION

Testing of cooperative motion algorithms can be difficult in a real world underwater environment. Issues such as limited communication, environmental setbacks, deployment costs and many other problems can be detrimental to vehicle testing and the implementation of algorithms. Verifying the performance of the algorithms can be challenging, if not impossible, in such an environment. There is a need for a testbed in which motion coordination algorithms for underwater vehicles can be tested without the challenges listed above.

The Synthetic Collective Unmanned Underwater Laboratory at the University of Maryland provides a controlled environment where algorithms for underwater motion coordination can be tested and verified while avoiding many of the problems encountered in real world environments. SCUUL is a multi-vehicle testbed consisting of six propeller-driven unmanned underwater vehicles (UUVs) operated at the University of Maryland's Neutral Buoyancy Research Facility (NBRF). The NBRF is a 367,000 gallon tank filled with clear, filtered water that is equipped with a state-of-the-art underwater motion capture system. The motion capture system is used for two purposes: to stream data in real time to the UUVs for feedback control and to verify cooperative motion algorithms.

The objective of SCUUL is to apply dynamical systems theory to implement and verify nonlinear motion coordination algorithms for underwater vehicles. The focus of this paper is to show the utility of the SCUUL testbed for UUV navigation, sampling, performance and control. Examples of such algorithms are shown in [4],[1],[3],and [2].

Section 2 will describe the testbed and it's capabilities in detail. Section 3 will describe the preliminary results and ongoing work of the project.

## 2. THE SCUUL TESTBED

This section describes the SCUUL testbed, which consists of six propeller driven submarines, the NBRF and an underwater motion capture system.

### 2.1 The UUVs

The SCUUL testbed includes six propellor-driven UUVs as shown in Figure 1. The submarines are 1:60 scale models of the USS Albacore. They are RC kits purchased from Mike's Sub Works LLC that can be operated using a standard RC radio transmitter.

The outer hull consists of a nose cone, tail cone, a mast, and a two-part main section. Attached to the tail cone are four control surfaces: two rudders and two elevators. The interior of the submarines contains two pressure vessels. The first pressure vessel houses the battery which powers the submarine during operation. The second pressure vessel, called the main pressure vessel (MPV), contains all the electronics. This includes two servos, a DC motor, a Viper speed controller, an automatic depth controller, a HITEC Laser4 radio control system, and a voltage regulator to manage power fluctuations. Both the MPV and battery compartments are sealed by two endcaps with O-rings. The interior of the submarines is shown in Figure 2.

The depth of the submarines is regulated by an automatic depth controller, which controls the elevators. The desired depth is adjustable using a potentiometer. The yaw motion

**Figure 1: The SCUUL testbed.**

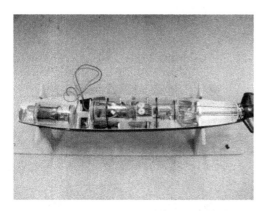

**Figure 2: The interior view showing the battery compartment and the main pressure vessel.**

**Figure 3: The custom circuit board containing a PIC microcontroller, a single-axis gyroscope, and four digital potentiometers.**

planar coordination algorithms. For the algorithms SCUUL is currently testing, the AU needs to know the desired heading rate. The desired heading rate is sent to the AU via the underwater motion capture system (described in Section 2.3). The desired heading rate is calculated using nonlinear control laws developed for a reduced order model [4]. The AU uses the desired heading rate, $\dot{\theta}_d$, and the current heading rate, $\dot{\theta}$, given by the gyroscope to close the loop on the rudder dynamics with a proportional gontroller controller, given below

$$u = -K(\dot{\theta}_d - \dot{\theta})$$

where $K > 0$ is the proportional gain. Figure 4 shows the AU attached to the bottom of a SCUUL UUV.

**Figure 4: The autopilot unit attached to the bottom of a SCUUL submarine.**

## 2.2 NBRF

The NBRF is a 367,000 gallon tank containing clear, filtered water kept at a nominal temperature of 90° F. The tank is 50 ft across and 25 ft deep making it the largest neutral buoyancy facility at any university worldwide. The CDCL uses NBRF as a dive tank to conduct all tests of the SCUUL UUV fleet. The NBRF is shown in Figure 1.

Research is currently being conducted on methods to generate water currents in the tank. One such example of this is a 3600 gallon-per-hour waterfall pump that can be used in NBRF with the submarines. This pump can generate significant flows that allow for a laboratory-scale test of control algorithms in a dynamic environment. The waterfall pump used by the CDCL is shown in Figure 5.

## 2.3 Underwater Motion Capture System

The NBRF is equipped with a state-of-the-art underwater motion capture system. This system consists of twelve underwater cameras designed and manufactured by Qualysis, based in Gothenburg, Sweden. The camera placements in the tank are shown in Figure 6 below.

There are eight cameras at anupper level and four on a lower level. The cameras are angled to maximize the cov-

of the UUV is controlled either by human in teleoperation using an RC transmitter, or autonomously by an autopilot, which is described below.

Attached to the bottom of each submarine is an autopilot unit (AU) that provides onboard feedback control to the submarines to close the loop on the second order dynamics of the rudder. In the AU there are two main assemblies. The first assembly consists of the components needed for wireless communication. This includes a HITEC Laser4 radio control system to respond to commands from the top side and a modified radio transmitter to communicate from the AU to the submarines radio receiver. The second assembly consists of a single-axis gyroscope mounted vertically a PIC micro controller. The gyroscope is attached to the PIC using an SPI connection and provides the submarines turning rate up to ±300°/sec. The PIC relays the turning commands to the submarine by the means of four digital potentiometers, which are meant to take the place of the physical potentiometers in the original transmitter.

Due to a limited amount of space in the AU pressure vessel, some of the components were printed onto a custom circuit board. This reduces the amount of wiring in the AU and hence increases the available space. The components on the circuit board include the PIC microcontroller, the one-axis gyroscope and the four digital potentiometer. The printed circuit board is shown below.

The depth controller enables the SCUUL testbed to test

Figure 5: Waterfall pump used to generate underwater currents.

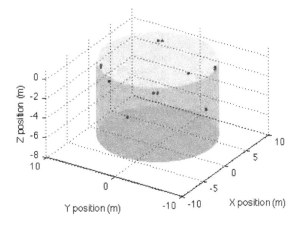

Figure 6: Locations of the motion capture cameras
.

erage of the system. The upper and lower cameras are two and fifteen feet in depth, respectively, from the surface.

The upper-level cameras are mounted in pairs while the lower cameras are mounted individually as seen in Figure 6. One of the upper level mounts is shown below in Figure 7. The cameras are all connected to a single operating computer via four ethernet switches. Data streams to the computer from each camera at a nominal rate of 20 Hz, but can be adjusted to capture at up to 100 Hz.

The motion capture cameras have two modes of operation. The first mode is video capture. In this mode the cameras behave like an ordinary video camera, with the footage being stored on the operating computer. The second mode is marker tracking. In this mode, the cameras track reflective markers specially made for the purpose of underwater tracking. The data given is the 3D position of every marker, as well as a residual for the error in the estimate. Depending on the calibration, this error is usually between 0.5-1.0 cm. When there are three or more markers on a single object, the markers can be formed into a rigid body. The data given for rigid-body tracking is the 3D position of the center of mass of the object, the associated 3-2-1 Euler angles for the rotation, and the rotation matrix. This mode also has the capability of streaming data in real-time.

Using the motion capture system in real-time mode allows information to be sent to the AU and used by the inner-loop controller to perform closed-loop feedback control for each of the vehicles in the fleet. This architecture can be utilized

Figure 7: Upper level mount of two Qualisys motion capture cameras.

to test a multitude of coordination algorithms, such as those developed in [1], [3], and a multitude of other algorithms.

The UUVs in the SCUUL fleet each have six markers at varying positions on the outer hull. This ensures that the software will not confuse the submarines and that occluded markers will not have a significant effect on the tracking capabilities of the system. The markers are 30 mm in diameter so that the Qualisys cameras can see them from across the tank. Figure 8 shows one of the SCUUL UUVs with markers attached to it.

Figure 8: A SCUUL UUV equipped with reflective markers.

The real-time data is sent to the AU using a PCTx interface. The motion capture system streams data to a control computer, which is connected to the PCTx interface. The PCTx interface interprets the data and sends it to a transmitter, which then transfers the data to the AU. Since the transmitter uses standard RF communication there is a limited line of sight through water in which the signal will successfully transmit, however, the conditions at the NBRF allow penetration of the signal to at least the depth of the lower level cameras.

A schematic of the SCUUL architecture is shown in Figure 9. The Qualisys data is sent from the control computer to the PCTx box, which transmits the desired turning rate to the AU of each submarine. The AU calculates the control signal needed to control the loop on the second-order dynamics and transmits it to the submarine it is attached to.

## 3. PRELIMINARY RESULTS AND ONGO-ING WORK

This section describes the progress made in the SCUUL testbed so far and describes our current efforts to improve

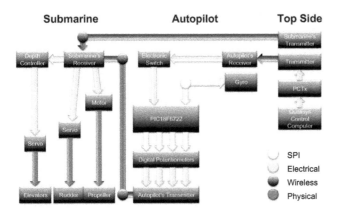

Figure 9: Schematic of topside interface and the submarine/autopilot architecture.

the system.

## 3.1 Results

The performance of the proportional controller for the rudder dynamics has been evaluated. Figure 10 shows the performance of the controller to an impulse starting at approximately 0.25 seconds. The error settles to a nominal value of zero within only one second, which is an acceptable settling time for the purposes of the control laws currently being verified by SCUUL. The settling time, and peak response, can be adjusted according to the need of the algorithm that is under testing.

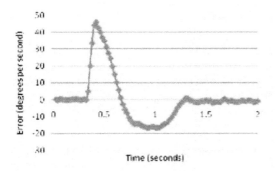

Figure 10: Impulse response of the one-axis gyroscope in the UUVs

An operational version of the autopilot unit was attached to one of the SCUUL UUVs and placed in the tank to determine its performance capabilities. The submarine was preprogrammed to travel in a downward spiral at a given angular rate. This test was also used to evaluate the quality of data produced by the Qualisys motion capture system. Figure 11 shows a visual representation of the 6DOF tracking data using a visualization developed in Matlab.

While the vehicle did perform a downward spiral, the center of the spiral tended to drift. This may have been due to the increased drag on the vehicle from the addition of the AU, which caused the vehicle to drift while turning.

Once the performance of the AU was determined, the ability of the motion capture system to identify and track mul-

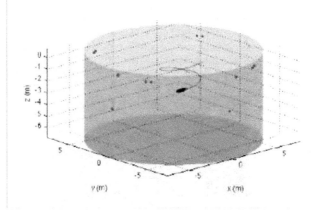

Figure 11: Motion capture tracking of one submarine under autopilot control is followed.

tiple bodies was assessed. Two subs under RC control were placed in the tank to determine the performance. Figure 12 shows the 6DOF tracking data for the collected data set.

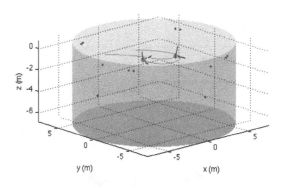

Figure 12: Motion capture tracking of two UUVs.

Even in the case where there are multiple objects in the water, the Qualisys system is able to track the submarines with sub-centimeter accuracy. The only condition placed on the UUV is that its marker configuration be unique from any other objects in the tank.

## 3.2 Ongoing Work

It was determined during the testing of the AU that attaching a pressure vessel to the bottom the UUVs greatly increases the drag on the vehicle, thereby reducing the speed. This introduces effects in the vehicle dynamics, such as roll/yaw coupling and turning drift. Since most of the control algorithms currently being tested in SCUUL use a self-propelled particle model for the underlying dynamics this may cause the heading-rate control law to produce undesired results.

Current work is focusing on moving the autopilot electronics to the main pressure vessel. The new architecture, shown in Figure 13, will place an ArduPilot controller, made by DIY Drones, and the gyroscope in the MPV of the submarine. Control commands from the Qualisys system will be sent directly to the UUVs onboard receiver, eliminating the need for a transmitter on the vehicle. These components can be powered from the battery already inside the UUV. With this new architecture, there is no need for a separate AU, it is instead integrated into the MPV. The ArduPilot and the gyroscope are shown below.

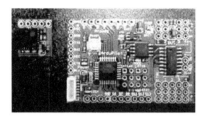

**Figure 13: The new gyroscope (left) and ArduPilot (right).**

In addition, it was determined that the fleet would be more versatile if the automatic depth controller was upgraded to a custom version designed by CDCL. The new architecture includes a pressure sensor which is attached directly to the ArduPilot. The ArduPilot can use the pressure reading in a proportional controller to adjust the depth of the vehicle. The desired depth can be hard-coded or it can be sent via the PCTx interface. This architecture is also shown in Figure 14.

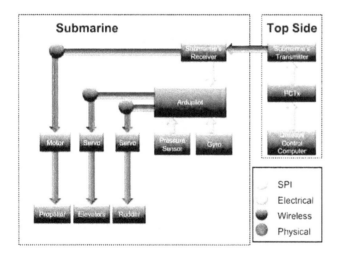

**Figure 14: Future interface between the UUVs and top side operations.**

This improved architecture increases the accuracy of the model used for the cooperative control laws that are currently being implemented in SCUUL and will therefore lead to enhances capabilities for test and evaluation of motion coordination algorithms for underwater vehicles.

## 4. CONCLUSIONS

This paper describes the University of Maryland SCUUL testbed. The testbed consists of six, propellor-driven UUVs, a 367,000 gallon dive tank, and a state-of-the-art underwater motion capture system. The current architecture has an autopilot unit attached to the bottom of each submarine

through which closed-loop control of the vehicle can be performed. The motion capture system outputs data in real time. The data is processed to generate a desired heading rate to be sent to the submarines.

So far, the performance of the autopilot unit has been examined in and out of the water. An ArduPilot will be placed in the main pressure vessel of each submarine and will receive commands directly from the submarines receiver. Tests have also been conducted to examine the ability of the motion capture system to handle multiple rigid bodies. Preliminary results show that the system can handle at least two rigid bodies provided the placement reflective markers is unique to each UUV.

Efforts are currently underway to examine the ability to inject controlled flow fields into the NBRF. This would allow the simulation of real underwater flows in a controllable environment. With this architecture, the SCUUL testbed provides an environment where collective control laws for UUVs can be tested and evaluated in a safe and predictable environment.

## 5. ACKNOWLEDGMENTS

The authors would like to acknowledge the University of Maryland Space Systems Laboratory for supporting our underwater testing and maintaining the NBRF. We would also like to thank Levi DeVries, Colin Parker, Steve Sherman, Patrick Mohl, and Patrick Nolan for their continued support in submarine trials. We want to acknowledge the efforts of all past and present CDCL members for building and maintaining the UUV fleet. This work is supported by Army contract W9124Q09P0230 as part of the Unmanned Autonomous Systems Test program.

## 6. REFERENCES

[1] G. Hoffman, S. Waslander, and C. Tomlin. Mutual information methods with particle filters for mobile sensor network control. In *Proceedings of the 45th IEEE Conference on Decision and Control*, pages 1019–1024, 2006.

[2] E. W. Justh and P. S. Krishnaprasad. Equilibria and steering laws for planar formations. *Syst Control Lett*, 52(1):25–38, 2004.

[3] C. Peterson and D. A. Paley. Multi-vehicle coordination of autonomous vehicles in an unknown flowfield. In *Proc. AIAA Conf. Guidance, Navigation, and Control (electronic)*, number AIAA-2010-7585,, August 2010.

[4] R. Sepulchre, D. Paley, and N. E. Leonard. Stabilization of planar collective motion: All-to-all communication. *IEEE Trans. Automatic Control*, 52(5):811–824, 2007.

# Measurement of Autonomous Operation

W. Hamel
NAVAIR, Integrated Battlespace Simulation and Test (IBST)
48150 Shaw Road, Bldg 2109, N213
Patuxent River, MD 20670-1907

## ABSTRACT

While robotic systems and the field of Artificial Intelligence (AI) have been funded through the Department Of Defense (DoD) and Industry for decades, it was not until recent years that the combination of these two technologies has made truly significant advances in the area of Autonomous Operation (AO) systems. Through the efforts of the Defense Advanced Research Project Agency (DARPA) challenges in 2004-2007 timeframe, the academic and industrial communities came together to overcome some significant hurdles for the development of AO ground vehicles in both the rural and desert environments (DARPA Grand Challenge 2004-2005) and the urban environment (DARPA Urban Challenge 2007). Although no AO vehicle succeeded in the 2004 event, the following year four systems completed the 132 mile course within the 10 hour time limit. The winner of the 2005 event (The Stanley from Stanford University) designed an autonomous (learning system) vehicle that fused five Lidars, Radar, and an Electro Optic sensor in addition to the waypoint GPS (provided by DARPA) and an internal Inertial Measurement Unit (IMU) system to produce the situational awareness required to meet the challenge. The team took approximately one year "training" the perception and planning sections of the software to compensate for various types of terrain and maneuvering. It was through extensive planning, meticulous design, and thorough testing that the final goal was achieved and it will take a much greater level of effort for DoD to realize a similar capability in the air environment.

In the Air domain, DoD will not have the luxury of releasing autonomous vehicles (without significant constraints) within an operationally relevant environment (like the National Air Space (NAS)) until a very high level of confidence is achieved in their ability to perform the mission while providing a level of safety commensurate with manned operation. For DoD to succeed, it is imperative that we provide the Unmanned Air System (UAS) development community the tools required to assess all of the engineering components necessary for transition of AO vehicles into the NAS and operational environments. These tools should include a model of the required environments (emulated with access to standardized hardware/software in the loop), standard set of operational test procedures (with desired metrics), and a framework through which individual components can be assessed. It is ironic that the success of AO unmanned systems will require a structured collaborative learning process within the human domain for our goals to be realized.

## Categories and Subject Descriptors

I.2.9 [**Artificial Intelligence**]: Robotics – *autonomous vehicles*

## General Terms

Measurement, Performance, Verification

## Keywords

*unmanned aerial system, autonomous operations, C4ISR, Automated Decision Aid (ADA), autonomous control*

## 1. INTRODUCTION

Before venturing too far into a discussion of the unmanned communities ability to develop and field autonomous air vehicles capable of safely interacting with manned air vehicles in both the National Air Space (NAS) and an operational environment (including modern warfare), it is important to understand the current state of manned aviation. The manned aviation community (in conjunction with the Research and Development (R&D) community) have been in the process of developing and fielding Automated Decision Aids (ADAs) for over a decade (like Multi-Sensor Integration (MSI), Combat Identification (CID), Threat Evaluation and Weapons Assignment (TEWA), Automated Target/Threat Recognition (ATR), Distributed Sensor Coordination (DSC), and Distributed Weapons Coordination (DWC)). The primary focus of these tools are to either reduce the operator workload (thus allowing an operator to focus on more important aspects of their area of responsibility) and/or to improve Situational Awareness (SA) within an Area of Interest (AOI). While many of these capabilities have been developed and tested successfully in lab environments (Technology Readiness Level 5 (TRL 5)) they have yet to transition from the R&D community to the operational community, especially for the C4ISR platforms. The reasons for the slow rate of transition are far more complicated than can be addressed within the scope of this paper; however, many of these types of automated decision aids will become the basis for the development of autonomous combat vehicles of the future.

The challenge for developing a set of ADAs for a specific platform is directly related to the quantity of disparate sensors it utilizes to generate SA and the volumetric area of surveillance/collection. Platforms like the E-2C/D Hawkeye, P-8 Poseidon, and EP-3 ARIES II represent significant challenges due to their large volumetric search areas and their rich set of sensors. In addition to the development challenge, ADAs represent a significant Test and Evaluation (T&E) challenge due to the large volumes of coherent data required to insure that processes like data fusion are being performed correctly prior to passing the fused data to ADAs (in a two step process). The role of the ADAs is to transform the fused sensor data into actionable information that can be presented to an operator for subsequent processing (typically within the human brain).

In this construct both the association/correlation of sensor data (input) and the formation of actionable information must be assessed by the T&E community to verify that the right actionable information is being produced from the raw data.

MSI (DATA) ➡ ADAs (Actionable Information) ➡

While the manned community is wrestling with the transition to ADAs, the UAS autonomy community has to grapple with the additional challenge of developing Autonomy Engines (AE) that will "eventually" replace the human factor (for achieving high levels of Autonomy).

MSI (DATA) ➡ ADAs (Actionable Information) ➡ AE (Reasoning)

From a T&E perspective this creates the additional challenge of determining not only if the sensor data was combined correctly, or the proper actionable information was produced, but did the machine take the appropriate action based on the inputs provided (assuming they are all correct). An equally important test case is the evaluation of what action the machine will take if some (or even all) of the inputs are either corrupted or not available in the absence of human intervention. For example what decisions will be made based on loss of communications (either due to equipment failure or intentional/unintentional electromagnetic interference) but with a fully functional onboard sensor suite (in the NAS versus a warfare environment). Or even more stressing, how will the same system react to a partially capable onboard sensor suite in the same scenario? While these scenarios are very simplistic compared to the myriad decisions that will be required of unmanned combat vehicles in a warfare environment, they highlight the level and complexity of T&E that will be required to insure that autonomous UAS can be trusted in either the NAS or an operational environment.

## 2. BUILDING TRUST

One of the initial challenges for the UAS community is to obtain a level of access to the NAS that is on par with the manned aviation (at least for segments of the NAS that are critical to performing their mission). A key focus area to support this objective is the development of Sense and Avoid (SAA) technologies or procedures that can be utilized to marshal specific UAS within the NAS. Currently there are two general approaches that are being pursued to address this topic:

- Ground Based Sense and Avoid (GBSAA)
- Airborne Sense and Avoid (ABSAA)

GBSAA (as its name implies) capitalizes on the extensive infrastructure investment that is in place throughout the United States to both monitor and control an UAS within the NAS in a manner similar to that of manned aviation platforms. This approach is dependent upon a man to machine tether for controlling the actions of a specific UAS if it deviates from a flight path or requires in flight re-routing. For this construct, the UAS may have the potential for AO (in case of communication failure) or may be simply a Remotely Piloted Vehicle (RPV). While this approach has broad extensibility across a wide range of UAS platforms, its dependency on terrestrial and airborne

communication segments may limit its utility to specific areas of interest within the NAS.

ABSAA can be utilized in conjunction with GBSAA to provide an extra layer of security, typically at the cost of additional sensors/sources of data and more complex software processing. ABSAA has the potential for fully autonomous operation within both the NAS and in an operational environment if the sensors/sources of data have sufficient ability to provide the situational awareness (actionable information) required for an AE to determine a proper course of action for a specific set of circumstances.

While the details associated with these programs are important, the focus of this paper is to concentrate on both the test methodology/strategy and the tools required to objectively measure or assess the progress made towards achieving the final objective of NAS integration (and future endeavors of AO). The Test Resource Management Center (TRMC) in conjunction with the joint services has recently embarked on a program to develop a capability for evaluating the performance of UAS within the NAS. Over the course of the next four years, the Joint UAS Mission Environment (JUAS ME) program will develop an environment and tools that will become the basis for the Developmental Test and Evaluation (DT&E) of the NAS integration objectives across the three services (USA, USAF, USN). JUAS ME was designed to leverage the developmental engineering work being performed under the GBSAA and ABSAA programs in addition to UAS Program of Record (POR) efforts like the Live Virtual Constructive Distributed Engineering (LVCDE) program for the USN Broad Area Maritime Surveillance (BAMS) platform. "Trust but Verify" was a favorite quote of President Ronald Reagan when discussing the nuclear treaties between the US and the Soviet Union. The same premise should be applied for the beginning stages of AO (NAS integration), through a structured and collaborative process with the Federal Aviation Administration (FAA), the DoD should be capable of developing technologies and establishing a process/framework through which those technologies are vetted for facilitating UAS integration into the NAS.

## 3. AUTONOMOUS OPERATIONS TEST METHODOLOGIES

Over the past several decades, systems have become more complex (and capable), especially in the area of software. This rapid expansion of software (refer to Figure 1) represents a formidable testing challenge and has required that the T&E community rethink the way we have been doing business.

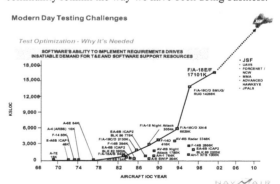

Figure 1. Software Growth

In order to overcome this challenge, the T&E community has evolved and will continue to evolve as we move into the age of unmanned autonomous systems (Figure 2). Whether the transition to AO vehicles and the need to assess AEs will result in the requirement for evolutionary or revolutionary changes in T&E capability is still to be determined.

Figure 2. T&E Capabilities Evolution [1]

The evolution of T&E capabilities has provided the system developer the option of testing design concepts at much higher levels of realism and fidelity than was previously available and at much earlier stages of system development. Not only can the developer test individual hardware/software components, they can assess how individual components would react within a complex system and/or a Family/System of Systems (FoS & SoS respectively). What makes this possible is the decades of investment that have resulted in a distributed T&E environment that can simulate all aspects of the modern battlefield at a level of fidelity and realism that can be tuned in accordance with the needs of the user (Figure 3).

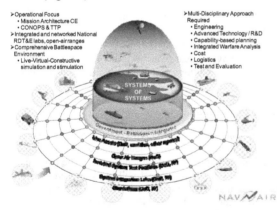

Figure 3. Battlespace Integration [1]

Figure 4 depicts a representation of the Live Virtual Constructive (LVC) domains that are currently in place for testing both manned and unmanned air systems. It is important that Figure 4 be viewed in the context of Figure 3 or as a subset of the larger construct. The Open Air Range (OAR) represents the "Live" aspect of the three domains. The Traditional Modeling Simulation and Analysis (MS&A) represents the "Constructive" domain. The Installed System Test Facility (ISTF) (which has the flexibility of including (and often does) a myriad of joint government, industry and academia labs in addition to stimulation of live assets) represents the "Virtual" domain.

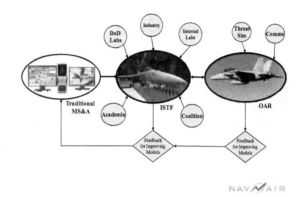

Figure 4. Live Virtual Constructive Domains

Two important points to glean from Figure 4 are:

- It is imperative that the results of testing/analysis from the individual domains are fed forward to provide the basis/foundation upon which the next domain (of higher level of fidelity) can build upon.
- The need for feedback and a comparison of results (including a reconciliation of differences) is required to insure that future assessments provide a baseline that can be trusted to generate the most accurate results possible.

Each of the domains depicted in Figure 4 will be discussed separately in the context of the measurement of AO developmental engineering and DT&E.

## 3.1 Constructive

Figure 5 depicts the Traditional MS&A Pyramid that explains the rolls and uses of the four categories of models associated with the constructive domain. This is the traditional starting point for most system developments and although the models developed within this domain can be quite complex it is essentially the lowest level of fidelity (with potentially the lowest cost). The DoD R&D and acquisition communities utilize this domain for everything from high level trades to estimating performance of individual engineering components (and the software tools or models for performing analysis are quite diverse). In the area of AO many of the AEs of the future have started or will start here (as did data fusion and ADAs for manned systems in the previous decades).

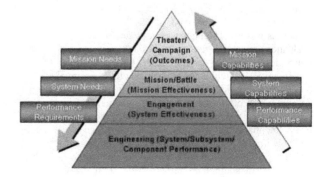

Figure 5. Traditional MS&A Pyramid

119

At a recent Science of Autonomy Workshop held at the Naval Research Lab (NRL) and sponsored by the Office of Naval Research (ONR), approximately 40 presentations were provided on basic research associated with the development of algorithms to support AO. The research that was presented at the workshop focused on behavioral models, control algorithms, reasoning, ADAs, swarming or collaborative behavior technologies, and architectures to support autonomy. As expected, the overwhelming majority of this work was in the constructive domain (or earlier).

## 3.2 Virtual

The virtual domain represents a hybrid of both the constructive and live domains in that it can contain elements of both for any given scenario. It is best understood as a distributed collection of high fidelity laboratories and facilities whose main objective is to provide a ground based environment that is representative of a batlespace (Figure 6). At its core, this digital battlespace has a Virtual Warfare Engine (VWE) that coordinates/synchronizes all of the activities necessary to support the acquisition of specific information related to a user derived scenario based;

- Virtual R&D Experiment
- System/Unit Under Test
- FoS/SoS Test.
- CONOPs Development
- Tactics Techniques Procedure Development
- Mission Rehearsal

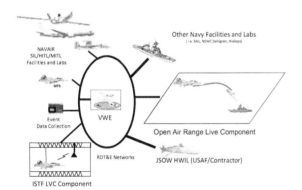

Figure 6. Surface Warfare Virtual Scenario

While the DoD acquisition communities utilize this domain for performing mission level testing of both new systems or improvements to existing systems (typically prior to or in parallel with testing in the live domain), the R&D communities use of this domain is mixed. The higher level of fidelity (over constructive evaluation) within the domain comes at a cost which is typically much less than the live domain but possibly more than constructive. It is within this domain that the majority of the work on NAS Integration (Section 2) is being performed and the domain which offers the best promise for maturing technologies for the future of AOs. The main reason that this domain offers so much potential is that while the TRL for constructive evaluation is typically limited to the 3-4 range (by definition) demonstrations of technologies in a high fidelity virtual environment could achieve TRL 5-6. In addition as the feedback from the live domain continues to increase the fidelity of the virtual domain it is more commonly being used to augment live flight testing at the

technology readiness 7-9 levels (typically for identification of issues that are hard to replicate in the live domain) .

## 3.3 Live

In the context of a discussion on the development of AO UAS, the live domain refers to the utilization of actual air vehicles in the open air environment. While the live domain is (and will/should continue to be) the last and most important step in verifying the performance of DoD weapon system performance, it is the most costly component of a T&E plan/strategy. The major advantage of the live domain is the operational environment in which a system is tested. While the virtual domain can replicate a large number of the operational components of the environment, there is no substitute for the real thing. It is often the unpredictable nature of the live domain that makes it so valuable. While engineers can work in both the constructive and virtual domains and achieve positive results, many failure mechanisms do not become evident until a system is in flight and being utilized in a manner commensurate with real flight operations. This does not diminish the need for the other domains, but solidifies the need for all.

Live testing of AO capable UAS (including the ABSAA component of NAS Integration) will be required for deployment/fielding. For ABSAA developmental test and engineering, it is hard to envision a live test event that includes two aircraft converging on each other to determine if the SUT meets its performance requirements. It is for this reason that significant high fidelity work should be performed in the other domains to provide a high level of confidence before entering the live phase of testing.

## 4. OPERATIONAL ENVIRONMENT

The operational environment for AO capable UAS are highly complex and are not limited to just the in flight segment of its operation. The operational environment as a minimum would include the following;

- Control Segment (Control Station)
- Communication Segment
- Environmental factors that could affect operation
- Mission Environment (whether it be the NAS or exposure to battlefield conditions with all of the related high level interactions)
- Unmanned Aircraft Segment (including AE)
- Payload Segment

Other elements could include provisions for deck operations of USN carrier based systems, launch and landing (including marshalling activities), aerial refueling, etc.. The two aspects of the operational environment that will be addressed are the NAS (which will be crucial to GBSAA/ABSAA development and a focus area for the JUAS ME program) and the Warfare Environment (which is a logical step for AO UAS development that support DoD missions). Both of these environments will be described in relation to the virtual domain.

## 4.1 National Airspace (NAS)

The NAS environment is a major component of the overarching Airspace Integration effort to specifically examine the integration of the Unmanned Aircraft System (UAS) into the NAS. The major elements of the NAS required to support the development of GBSAA and ABSAA technologies and procedures are;

- Air Traffic Control (ATC)
- Commercial Aviation
- General Aviation
- Military Aviation (both Manned and Unmanned)
- Data Extraction and Analysis Tools

A realistic representation of the NAS must recreate the civil airspace structure (traffic patterns/routes, elevation profiles, separations), civil air traffic (traffic densities, and time dependencies), and civil air traffic control. An accurate air traffic generator should be developed using historical recorded air traffic data to enable both static and dynamic flight representations and facilitate the V&V process. NAS data must be translated into ATC useable data files for input to the ATC in a manner identical to normal operations. The NAS should incorporate dynamic routes for enabling flights to be flown by human-in-the-loop pseudo-pilots responding to ATC controller instruction. [2]

To create a valid virtual environment for T&E, the NAS representation should consist of models, including air traffic generators, and integrated operator in the loop Air Traffic Control capabilities to accurately conduct procedures and operations in conjunction with UAS operators and other aircraft in the T&E mission. By integrating with OAR (live) controllers and systems, this capability can provide end to end T&E event conduct or rehearsal from launch to recovery. Additionally, to support Sense and Avoid test events an NAS representation must provide for a high fidelity General Aviation "intruder" pilot/aircraft. [2]

## 4.2 Warfare Environment

Within the virtual domain, the stimulation of installed systems in a realistic warfare environment provides a deterministic approach for assessing the baseline performance of existing and future weapon systems. This process provides an important step in the evaluation of complex platform and/or SoS/FoS constructs within an environment that is controlled and understood. An accurate T&E warfare environment can be best described by the phrase "test like we fight". To support this goal for the development of AO capable UAS this would require doctrine based UAS specific scenarios that accurately portray;

- Major and limited contingencies
- Homeland defense
- Mission, Engagement, and Engineering level fidelity

The warfare environment should include all aspects of the battlespace that could affect the evaluation of the AO capable mission under consideration, including;

- Mission Scenarios (i.e. Strike, Close Air Support (CAS), Intelligence Surveillance Reconnaissance (ISR), Stand off/in Jamming, etc.)
- Blue entities (air, ground and surface, space, communications, etc.)
- Red entities (Integrated Air Defense System (IADS), Threats (air, ground/surface), communications, etc.)
- Other entities (civil traffic (air/surface), ally entities, buildings, etc.)
- Weather effects
- Data Extraction and Analysis Tools

Warfare environments have been developed for the manned aviation community for decades and should be highly leveraged to support AO capable UAS developmental efforts.

## 5. RISK BASED TEST APPROACH

The previous sections of this paper were focused on guiding the reader to conclude that the T&E community is well suited (both infrastructure and expertise) to become an active partner in the engineering development (at all stages) of AO capable UAS. This section focuses on an approach or process that could be utilized for both the evaluation and maturation of AO technologies. Figures 7 and 8 depict the T&E and V&V Findings/Challenges that were briefed to the Defense Science and Technology Advisory Group (DSTAG) by the R&D Communities of the joint services.

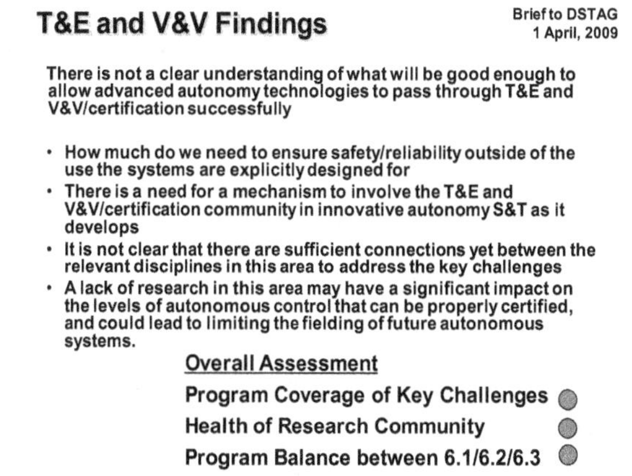

### T&E and V&V Findings

Brief to DSTAG
1 April, 2009

There is not a clear understanding of what will be good enough to allow advanced autonomy technologies to pass through T&E and V&V/certification successfully

- How much do we need to ensure safety/reliability outside of the use the systems are explicitly designed for
- There is a need for a mechanism to involve the T&E and V&V/certification community in innovative autonomy S&T as it develops
- It is not clear that there are sufficient connections yet between the relevant disciplines in this area to address the key challenges
- A lack of research in this area may have a significant impact on the levels of autonomous control that can be properly certified, and could lead to limiting the fielding of future autonomous systems.

**Overall Assessment**

Program Coverage of Key Challenges ⬤
Health of Research Community ⬤
Program Balance between 6.1/6.2/6.3 ◐

Figure 7 Brief to Defense S&T Advisory Group [3]

### T&E and V&V Challenges

Brief to DSTAG
1 April 2009

- T&E and V&V approaches that support
  - Exponential growth projected in Software Lines of Code
    - Prohibitively expensive to exhaustively test
  - New algorithms (e.g., non-deterministic)
- Timely and efficient certification (and re-certification) of intelligent and autonomous control systems
- Analytical tools that work with realistic assumptions
- Approaches to bound uncertainty caused by learning/adaptation or other complex non-linearities that may make behavior difficult to predict
- Proving not just safety, but also level of competence at mission tasks

Autonomy may replace decision-making that requires years of training for humans. This will challenge test and certification techniques

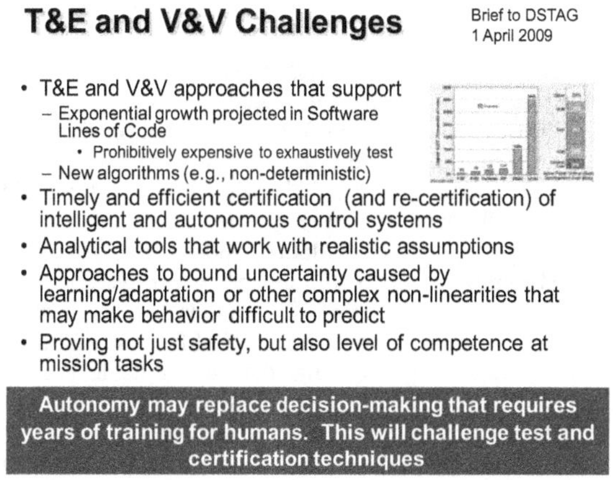

Figure 8 Brief to Defense S&T Advisory Group [3]

Careful examination of the findings and challenges reveal several key points;

- That the R&D and T&E communities need to coordinate their activities in the very early stages of the developmental cycle of AO capable UAS
- Both the R&D and T&E communities see the growth and sophistication of software in modern aviation systems (Figure

1) as a formidable challenge that will require a new approach to T&E/V&V

- New analytical tools will be required to facilitate the T&E of AO capable UAS

The Battlespace Modeling Verification and Validation (BMV&V) Branch of the NAVAIR Integrated Battlespace Simulation and Test Department (IBST), has been refining a process for Risk Based Verification, Validation, and Accreditation (VV&A) of models and simulation for the past several years. A risk based approach to VV&A "provides a strategic method for tailoring VV&A efforts based on the criticality of the decision being supported by the M&S and the availability of resources (schedule, personnel, and funds)."[4] The topic is the subject of several papers and will only be synopsized here, while the exploration/investigation into the extensibility of the approach beyond the current VV&A process (T&E of complex weapon systems like AO capable UAS) will be the subject of future papers. Figure 9 provides a flowchart of the actions required as part of the risk based VV&A process.

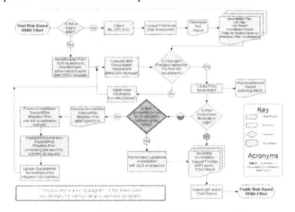

Figure 9 Risk Based VV&A Process [4]

The process itself starts by working with the user to define the "intended use" and "role of the M&S" in the decision making process. The model/simulation that will be used for the decision process must be analyzed to determine the likelihood that it will generate an incorrect result. This process involves significant insight into the working level of the model/simulation and requires access to the Subject Matter Experts (SMEs) that created the model/simulation and SMEs for the system/systems that the model/simulation will represent. The end result of this analysis is a Summary of Limitations and Errors (SALE) (part of a detailed risk report that describes the limitations of the model/simulation within the context of its intended use) that will be utilized in the accreditation phase (with the user) to reduce the level of risk. Once the intent and role are defined, the maximum acceptable risk level the user is willing to accept must be determined. The maximum risk level is based on the likelihood (described above) and the consequence if the model/simulation results are wrong (resulting in a wrong decision).[5] The accreditation process trades off the investment required of reducing the likelihood of M&S error and the consequence associated with a poor decision. The trade off could range from zero investment (user willing to accept risks) to potentially large investments (if the likelihood that the limitations or errors within the M&S are unacceptable).

In the context of testing AO capable UAS, the current approach could be tailored to determine the limitations/errors for a UAS

(versus M&S) within a specific mission set (intended use) and basing the consequence on a number of variables (safety, security, attrition, cost, etc.). The user could manage the overall risk by limiting the utilization of classes of UAS to mission sets that represent an acceptable risk level for the variable of interest. Approaching it in this manner would have the effect of buying time to invest in the reduction of risk at a point in time when the expansion of the mission sets is required. The user could define a program that starts with a limited operational capability that would diminish over time.

## 6. SUMMARY

Figure 9 illustrates the projection for the development and fielding of UAS at various Autonomy Control Levels (ACL) (circa 2009, although the original data (in black) seems to be circa 2005-2006 based on when UCAR and J-UCAS were canceled at DARPA). The blue and red lines are new estimates based on current uncertainty related to ACL of the UCLASS LOC (follow on of J-UCAS => N-UCAS => UCAS-D) platform. How much time is actually available for the RDT&E communities to determine a way forward for the best approach on testing high level of AO is difficult to say, however, there is no time like the present to start the dialogue.

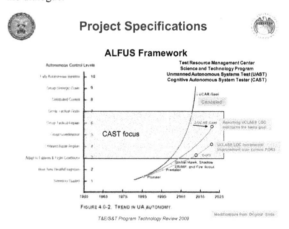

Figure 9 UAS Autonomy Trends [6]

The LVC domains were briefly described and it was suggested that the best method for economically meeting the goal of supporting the engineering development and test of AO capable UAS lies in the virtual domain. This domain offers significantly higher levels of test fidelity than the constructive domain at a cost that is significantly less than that of the live domain. In addition, the introduction of UAS into the NAS (through the efforts of GBSAA/ABSAA) is the first step to AO within a program of record UAS and the acquisition and T&E communities are already engaged in a path forward. Through the efforts of TRMC, the JUAS ME program (for testing NAS Integration) will become the basis for T&E of research and engineering efforts to develop higher levels of AO capable UAS.

Finally, the RDT&E community has recognized the need for new approaches to the T&E/V&V of future software intensive systems. While the NAVAIR IBST Department has successfully utilized a risk based approach for V&V, determining whether an approach of this nature is extensible to an AO capable UAS will require some additional investigation.

# 7. REFERENCES

[1] NAVAIR, "Integrated Battlespace Simulation and Test Department (Internal Brief)," Patuxent River, MD, August 2010

[2] NAVAIR, "JUAS ME Program Management Plan (DRAFT), "Patuxent River, MD, September 2010

[3] ONR, ARL, AMRDEC, DARPA, AFRL, ARO, "Science of Autonomy Technology Focus Team Brief," Arlington, VA, April 2009

[4] J. Elele, PhD, J. Smith, "Risk-based verification, validation, and accreditation process (Internal Manuscript)," Patuxent River, MD, March 2010

[5] J. Elele, PhD, "How To Assess and Prioritize The Risks Associated with Verification, Validation and Accreditation Of Models And Simulations Internal Briefing," Patuxent River, MD, July 2009

[6] TRMC, "Unmanned Autonomous Systems Test (UAST), Cognitive Autonomous System Tester (CAST) (Brief)," Arlington, VA, 2009

# DCF® – A JAUS and TENA Compliant Agent-based Framework for UAS Performance Evaluation

Nicholas Lenzi
(301) 294-4769
nlenzi@i-a-i.com

Benjamin Bachrach, PhD.
(301) 294-5237
bach@i-a-i.com

Vikram Manikonda, PhD
(301) 294-5245
vikram@i-a-i.com

Intelligent Automation Inc., 15400 Calhoun Dr., Suite 400 Rockville MD, 20855

## ABSTRACT

Real-world applications for UAS teams continue to grow, and the scale and complexity of the teams is continually increasing. To reduce life cycle costs and improve T&E, there is increasing need for a generalized framework that can support the design and development of T&E approaches for multi-UAS teams and validate the feasibility of the concepts, architectures and algorithms. This challenge is most significant in the cognitive/social domains, where the development of test approaches and methodologies are difficult because of the emergent nature of behaviors in response to dynamic changes in the battlespace. Current DOD T&E capabilities and methodologies are insufficient to address these needs. Today much of the initial validation effort is done using simulations, which unfortunately very rarely capture the complexity of this problem. Current simulations rarely capture the complexity of real world effects related to net-centric communications, vehicle dynamics, distributed sensors, the physical environment (terrain), external disturbances, etc. Furthermore, very often high fidelity simulations do not scale as the number of UAS increases. On the other extreme, directly implementing hardware platforms without high resolution simulations to help refine the design induces significant risk. For large unmanned system teams, shortcomings in design decisions related to the control architecture, information flow, sensor fusion, assumptions on communication bandwidths, and robustness of the algorithms may only become apparent when deployment on several hardware platforms has been completed, resulting in a significant loss of time and resources. In response to this need, under a recently completed effort with TRMC, IAI has developed the Distributed Control Framework (DCF), an Integrated Agent-based T&E Framework for Simulated, Mixed-Model (Virtual and Live/hardware in the loop) and Live Testing of Teams of Unmanned Autonomous Systems. In recent efforts, DCF has been made JAUS compliant, and integration with TENA has been achieved. In this paper we discuss the development of this framework, details of JAUS compliance implementation and

initial results of its deployment at ARDEC in Picatinny Arsenal on use cases involving teams of FireAnt Robots performing cooperative surveillance tasks.

## Keywords
Unmanned Systems Teams, T&E of Unmanned systems, Unmanned and Autonomous System Testing, JAUS compliance.

## 1. INTRODUCTION
The successful deployment of unmanned platforms in the battlefield has led to an increased demand for greater numbers of unmanned and autonomous systems (UAS). Coupled to this increase in demand is the expectation of greater levels of autonomy for these systems [1]. As the rate at which new and more complex systems are developed accelerates, there is a compelling need for the development of flexible T&E frameworks that can address the challenges associated with testing increasingly complex systems over shorter testing cycles [2]. This challenge is most significant in the cognitive/social domains, where the development of test approaches and methodologies are difficult because of the emergent nature of behaviors in response to dynamic changes in the battlespace [3].

Under a recently completed effort with the Test Resource Management Center (TRMC), Unmanned and Autonomous System Testing (UAST) program, IAI has developed an Integrated Agent-based T&E Framework for Simulated, Mixed-Model (Virtual and Live/hardware in the loop) and Live Test and Evaluation (SMML-T&E) of Teams of Unmanned Autonomous Systems. At the core of this T&E architecture is IAI's Distributed Control Framework (DCF) (see [4][5][6]). As part of this effort, an enhanced JAUS [7] and TENA [8] compliant version of DCF was developed and tested. A user interface with integrated T&E environment development, simulation and C2 capabilities was implemented. DCF was also evaluated at the Armament Research Development and Engineering Center (ARDEC) in Picatinny Arsenal in a relevant test environment.

In this paper, we discuss the details of DCF and present initial results from a technology development conducted at ARDEC. The paper is organized as follows. In Section 2 we introduce DCF. In Section 3 we present the features of the Vignette Editor. Our implementation of JAUS and TENA compliance are discussed in Section 4. In Section 5 we discuss the details of the technology

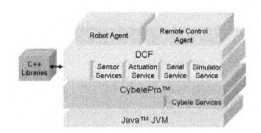

**Figure 1: Layered architecture of the Distributed Control Framework (DCF)**

demonstration conducted in collaboration with ARDEC personnel at Picatinny Arsenal.

## 2. DISTRIBUTED CONTROL FRAMEWORK

Written entirely in the Java programming language, DCF (see [4][5]) is a small and lightweight framework that may be deployed on any computing architecture that supports the Java Virtual Machine (JVM). A key element of DCF is the ability to deploy on real hardware the same UAS control and coordination code that is verified through simulation. In fact, DCF makes no distinction between real and simulated UAS. This powerful feature is possible because of the modeling of UAS teams as "software agents". Software agents are autonomous and event driven, they do not share their encapsulated data, and they interact exclusively via messaging. The key features of DCF include:

- Agent-based Modeling – DCF simplifies the implementation of distributed algorithms, supports mixing of virtual robot agents with real robot agents and enables data sharing via peer-to-peer messaging
- Controls-centric Design – DCF adopts a control-centric architecture with a Sensor Layer, State Estimators, Motion Planners and an Actuation Layer
- Modular Architecture – In DCF algorithms are implemented as plug-ins and include hardware device abstraction, self-contained sensor/actuator drivers, with components loaded at run-time via XML configuration files
- Robust Simulation Capabilities – DCF provides hardware-in-the-loop support, discrete-time and real-time simulations, built-in equation solvers, distribution across multiple computing resources with repeatable results, cross layer (network –level) modeling and human in the loop support.

DCF is built on top of the CybelePro™ agent-based framework developed at Intelligent Automation, Inc. (see [10][11]). Figure 1 shows a high-level representation of the DCF and its relationship to CybelePro™. CybelePro™ is built on top of the Java 2 platform and provides the runtime environment for control and execution of agents. The architecture consists of a kernel and several service implementations. The architecture kernel provides application interface methods for agent programmers to write classes representing activities using the Activity Centric Programming (ACP) paradigm. The agent-infrastructure adopts a service-layered architecture promoting plug-n-play capability of agent services. The services and their interfaces are defined in such a way that performance can be fine-tuned by loading

different service implementations as appropriate to the OS/platform/network and/or the agent application domain, without having to re-write the agent code. The agent services include error handling, concurrency management, event handling, thread-management, internal event services, communication, timer, data sharing, GUI services, sender side filtering, dynamic data distribution migration, and load balance services. Events currently supported include message, timer, and agent internal events. CybelePro provides support for different concurrency models between activities of an agent, and data-sharing among activities for high efficiency. Location independent communication between agents is supported via publish-subscribe based messaging, with support for synchronous, asynchronous, broadcast messaging, multicast, and point-to-point messaging. Both continuous and discrete clock capabilities (for event driven large-scale distributed simulations) are supported by CybelePro.

DCF adds support for robot team coordination and management, a pluggable architecture for sensing and estimation, support for heterogeneous robot platforms, robust simulation capabilities with hardware in the loop, and an extensible planner and plan execution engine. DCF also provides rich fast simulation capabilities for verifying the complete distributed control system prior to deployment on physical hardware. To support fast-time simulation, DCF uses the discrete clock feature of CybelePro™. To utilize these simulation capabilities, the user must provide appropriate kinematics and/or sensor models for the agents to be simulated. A simulation service manages the execution of these models at discrete time steps and also handles routing information to the various DCF activities. Simulations are limited only by the availability of computing resources. Multiple computing resources may be chained together when simulating large numbers of agents or when the control algorithms are particularly numerically intensive. As mentioned previously, DCF also supports mixed-mode operation in which simulated and physical agents interact seamlessly with one another. To support mixed-mode or pure execution on hardware, DCF uses a real-time clock.

As seen in Figure 1, The DCF architecture features two distinct agents: a *Robot Agent* and a *Remote Control Agent*. The Robot Agent embodies a real or simulated robot that is part of a multi-agent system, while the Remote Control Agent (RCA) provides the command and control GUI enabling a human operator to interact with the robot team. Block diagrams of the Robot Agent and Remote Control Agent architectures appear in Figure 2 and Figure 3 respectively.

### 2.1 Robot Agent

The Robot Agent represents either a simulated or a real physical robot; since the DCF does not distinguish between real and simulated agents, users are able to simulate complex missions with real hardware in the loop. The Robot Agent uses four classes of *Activities* (Activities are lightweight software components that perform work on behalf of the Agent) to perform its work: *State Estimators*, *Robot Coordinators*, *Robot Planners*, and *Custom Tasks*. Multiple instances of each Activity class are supported and instances within the same class may run either concurrently or sequentially. The arrows shown in Figure 2 depict the flow of information through the Robot Agent.

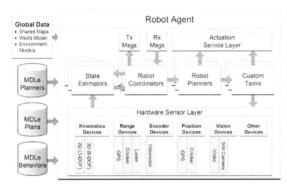

**Figure 2: Architectural block diagram of the DCF Robot Agent**

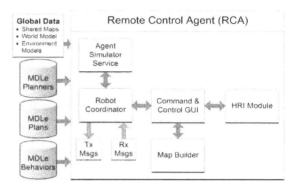

**Figure 3: Architectural diagram of the DCF Remote Control Agent**

State Estimators receive and process raw sensor data from onboard hardware and from other connected agents via the Robot Coordinators. The State Estimators maintain and update models of the team and world state that are shared with other agents and supplied to the Robot Planners. Robot Planners process the team state data and invoke high-level behaviors using rules defined in the currently executing plan. Finally, Custom Tasks perform application-specific tasks and may be executed periodically or in a background process.

System developers can augment the DCF functionality by implementing new algorithms for execution by the Robot Agent Activities. A new algorithm is added to the DCF by writing a Java class that implements one of the Activity *models*. For example, we have developed an indoor navigation system that uses an extended Kalman filter to fuse robot odometry and range measurements from a network of Cricket® sensors. The software navigation module implements the *Estimation Model*, which is executed by a State Estimator Activity whenever new odometry or range data is available. Activity models are loaded by the Robot Agent at runtime according to an XML configuration file that specifies the desired models, and if applicable, the physical hardware sensors to be used. This model-based architecture enables libraries of algorithms to be developed and shared with other DCF users.

Notice that hardware devices are classified according to the functionalities they provide (see Figure 2). For example, a GPS receiver can function either as a position device or as a range device. In Java terminology, a robot *device* is an interface – a contract specifying the methods that must be provided by an implementing class. This device interface architecture enables a loose coupling between the control/estimation algorithms and the underlying hardware; alternative hardware sensors supporting the required device(s) may be interchanged freely (for example, GPS may be substituted for the Cricket sensors in our navigation system since GPS is a *Range Device*).

## 2.2 Remote Control Agent

The counterpart of the Robot Agent is the Remote Control Agent (RCA), which provides the human operator command and control

GUI. A block diagram of the RCA is shown in Figure 3. Core components of the RCA include the GUI and the HRI (Human Robot Interface) modules. Using the GUI, an operator can quickly assess the team's shared situational awareness and perform robot tasking using simple drag and drop operations. The human-robot interface was designed specifically for ease of use on a tablet PC, where the agent tasking operations are performed with a stylus. Next section includes a detailed discussion of the user interface.

The DCF also provides various hardware support services for interfacing with sensors and actuators. So far, a number of important features and capabilities have been implemented, including the ability to interface with a rich variety of platforms (ARIA Amigobot and Pioneer, DARPA developed LAGR platform, Robotic Research Corporation's FireAnt platform and iRobot Create) and sensors (cameras, LADAR, sonar, among others).

## 3. Vignette Editor

DCF also provides a user interface called the *Vignette Editor* (shown in Figure 4). The functions of the Vignette Editor are various; from visualizing the state of the UAS team, creating T&E scenarios, monitoring the UAS team performance and generating automated T&E reports. Most importantly, the Vignette Editor provides the user the ability to issue real-time commands to the team and to upload a new distributed control algorithm (mission) on-the-fly.

The Vignette Editor is written in Eclipse. Eclipse is a Java open-source plug-in architecture most notably known for its Java Integrated Development Environment (IDE). Implemented as a series of cascading plug-ins providing a variety of functionality including OSGi the plug-in loading and management platform, SWT the Java Native Interface (JNI) to the native widgets of the operating system, and JFace the user interface level event management API. Additionally, it provides support for developing new plug-ins and deploying applications within itself. A description of the main components of the Vignette Editor follows:

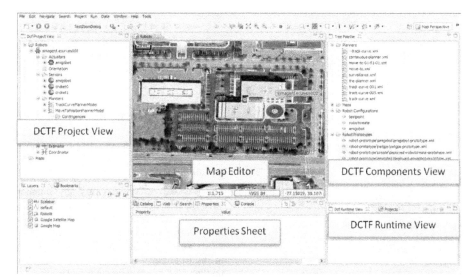

**Figure 4: DCF Vignette Editor**

*DCF Project View:*

The DCF Project View (see Figure 5) provides a tree view of all of the robots, and their corresponding software components, of the running scenario. From this view, robots can be added and configured and missions can be built and assigned. Each robot element displays the set of *Actuators*, *Sensors*, *State Estimators*, *Coordinators*, and *Planners* based on the DCF Robot Agent Architecture (see Figure 2). Each element within the tree can be selected, and the corresponding parameters such as serial port or desired position can be manipulated via the Properties Sheet View provided by Eclipse.

**Figure 5: DCF Project View**

*DCF Runtime View:*

The DCF Runtime View (see Figure 6) provides a view of all of the *Robot Agents* in the DCF Community. Robots appear as children of the root node of the tree. From this view, the contents of the sensor map and the active plan are displayed. Each element within the tree can be selected, and the corresponding parameters such as serial port or desired position can be view via the Properties Sheet View provided by Eclipse. The runtime view can be extended to support new device types, as programmers create them. Via the context menu and the local toolbar, users can assign, pause, and resume plans, display a live video feed, and remote control the robot.

**Figure 6: DCF Runtime View**

*DCF Components View:*

The DCF Components View (see Figure 7) provides a view of all components that can be configured within a scenario. This includes the *Robot Prototypes* which are the basis of each robot added to a scenario, the *Behaviors* and *Behavior Interrupts*, and the map of the environment. The user simply has to drag the selected component onto the map to make the necessary change.

*Mission Building Editors:*

The Serial Mission Editor allows mission builders to chain *Discrete Behaviors*, and execute them at runtime sequentially. Using this editor, users can manually select waypoints on a map for behaviors that require them. Once the user assembles the mission as they see fit, the mission is saved to an XML file and assigned to the robot.

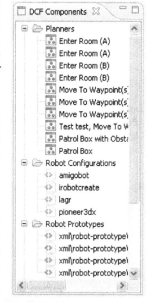

**Figure 7: DCF Components view**

The Serial Mission Editor allows the user to string discrete behaviors into a serial sequence. These behaviors are then executed by the robot sequentially (see Figure 8 and Figure 9). The State Machine Mission Editor allows mission builders to use

**Figure 8: Serial Mission Editor. Mission Sequence List defining the order of the Behaviors.**

127

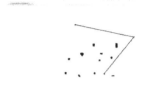

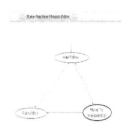

**Figure 9: Serial Mission Editor. Serial Mission Editor with Selected Waypoints**

**Figure 10: State Machine Editor.**

*Behaviors* from the DCF Component View, and visually configure them in a finite state machine (see Figure 10). Once the user assembles the mission as they see fit, the mission is saved to an XML file and assigned to the robot. Missions assembled using these editors also fit the DCF description of *Behaviors,* so they can then be used in the Serial or State Machine Missions Editors as components *Behaviors.*

### *Map Editor:*

The Map Editor is an Eclipse Editor implemented within the UDig application to provide a way to display a series of map layers such as political maps and road locations. UDig is a popular open source Eclipse-based GIS application, which was used as the foundation of the DCF Vignette Editor. It provides a two dimensional canvas to display layers on a map. In the Vignette Editor, it is a fundamental tool for displaying the location of the robots on two dimensional canvas. The Map Editor supports editing the DCF scenario graphically. User's can drag robots to adjust their positions and orientations. Robots can be added by dropping a *Robot Prototype* XML document onto the map.

### *Web Map Tile Server Visualization:*

A series of UDig renderers, using any standard web map tile server for the back end, were created to visualize street maps, aerial photographs, and terrain maps. These components download the images from web servers, cache them locally, and display them accordingly based on the geo location of the Map Editor (see Figure 11).

**Figure 11: DCF Map View with Open Street Maps**

### *Digital Terrain Elevation Data (DTED) Visualization:*

DTED is a file format, used by the military to encode elevation data over a large scale. Leverage an existing technology, a DTED based UDig renderer was built. The DTED rendered displayed a topographic map build from DTED level 0, 1, or 2, from a

**Figure 12: Screenshot Google Map with DTED Topographic Overlay**

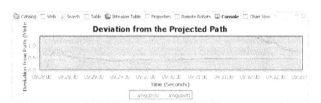

**Figure 13: Real-time Metric Display**

local directory on the file system (see Figure 12).

### *Streaming Video:*

The Vignette Editor supports any number of incoming video streams, as long as their sources are known. Users can right-click a robot in the Runtime View, and select "Show Video Stream" to bring up the video window for a particular robot. Launching the video window is also quite simple. Users can right-click a robot in the Runtime View, and select "Show Video Stream" to bring up the video window for a particular robot.

### *Metrics Evaluation Integration:*

Visualization capabilities for real-time metrics have been incorporated to the Vignette Editor. Users may visualize metrics via configurable plots during runtime using the JFreeChart library. Simply by selecting a robot, a separate eclipse view is launched displaying the value of the given metric. Numerous types of plots are supported via JFreeChart so different types are trivial to implement. An example of a time sequence chart showing the navigation error of a robot is shown in Figure 13.

## 4. JAUS / TENA Compliance

### 4.1 JAUS Compliance

The Joint Architecture for Unmanned Systems (JAUS) is a messaging standard that has been mandated by the DoD to facilitate interoperability between unmanned systems. In addition to the messaging standard, JAUS also defines a series of hierarchically organized software naming scheme to reduce confusion. These object names are Subsystem, Node, Component, and Instance.

A Subsystem is generally viewed as a complete hardware and software solution such as a UGV Platform or an Operator Control Unit (OCU). A Node is generally viewed as a process running on a dedicated CPU. Components are logically organized software components that generally perform some specific sensing or driver level task within the Node.

There are three levels of JAUS compliance, Level 1, Level 2, and Level 3. Level 1 compliance indicates that all communication between JAUS Subsystems is done via JAUS messages. Level 2 compliance indicates that all communication between JAUS Nodes is done via JAUS messages. Level 3 compliance indicates that all communication between JAUS Components is done via JAUS messages.

A DCF-style JAUS Controller was implemented that sends JAUS messages to specific JAUS Components on the platform. As part of transitioning DCF to ARDEC at Picatinny Arsenal, the JAUS Controller was designed to directly interface with the Primitive Driver, Reflexive Driver, Local Waypoint Driver, and Global Waypoint Driver to support driving the platform. Additionally, periodic updates of important sensor data were required. Global Pose Sensor and Local Pose Sensor were implemented to support the creation of higher-level DCF Behaviors that allowed more complex task such as perimeter surveillance.

Other data that was implemented included the image data from the Visual Sensor and platform operation data from the Primitive Driver. Additionally, FireAnt-specific experimental custom messages were implemented to support control of the Pan/Tilt/Zoom Camera, Querying the Encoders, and Querying the LIDAR. In this model, DCF is JAUS Compliant Level 1 since it sends and receives messages at the Subsystem Level.

## 4.2 TENA Compliance

Test and Training Enabling Architecture (TENA) is a middleware to support interaction between remote software components. The specific applications that use TENA are T&E applications where users want to integrate with data collected from remote test ranges. TENA classes are implemented in their own programming language, which is similar in syntax to C++, and compiled remotely by the TENA community at the TENA Software Development Architecture website (www).

The DCF-TENA integration approach was to support relaying DCF Robot Agent data across the TENA infrastructure, and support waypoint tasking from remote TENA applications. A series of TENA classes were developed and compiled, which are available via the tena-sda website, which integrates with DCF. TENA application programmers can task DCF robots to an (X, Y) location using the TENA method moveToLocation. Additionally, they can query the position of the robots as well. Future development will be done by integrating with an existing TENA repository, and log DCF data to it.

## 5. Evaluation of DCF at ARDEC in Picatinny Arsenal

ARDEC personnel at Picatinny Arsenal have developed the Firestorm system, a fully integrated and scalable decision support tool suite for the mounted/dismounted Warfighter/Commander. Firestorm is an open, extensible and scalable family of tools that support network centric warfare and can be configured for user experimentation in either virtual or field environment. ARDEC is also developing the concept of a joint manned-unmanned system team (JMUST), for which target handoff and sharing of situational awareness (SA) data between humans and UAS working together have been demonstrated. This is a groundbreaking program in terms of implementation of advanced concepts for human-UAS teaming in combat operations. Some examples of unmanned systems currently being integrated at ARDEC include military robots such as the FireAnt, PackBot, Talons, and Scouts (See Figure 14). However, as new unmanned platforms (manufactured by different vendors with different levels of JAUS compliance, if at all) are being integrated into Firestorm, new challenges are emerging. There is a critical need for a framework to coordinate the behavior of these platforms and to test the performance of teams of unmanned systems.

Based on our interactions with ARDEC personnel, use cases for "perimeter surveillance" scenarios and implemented in two stages:

a) Single UGV Perimeter surveillance: In order for an unmanned system to conduct autonomous perimeter surveillance, the operator would provide a region (such as a building, for example) around which the unmanned system should conduct surveillance. The unmanned platform would have to generate a surveillance path plan around the region of interest as a sequence of way-points. At each way point the unmanned system would conduct a surveillance activity, such as searching for candidate targets using a camera (the target could be predefined or a moving object). If such a target is identified, a message would be sent to the OCU, together with an image of the target.

b) Multiple UGV Perimeter surveillance: As in the previous discussion, the operator would provide a region around which the team of unmanned systems should conduct surveillance. The unmanned platforms would collaboratively generate a surveillance path plan around the region of interest as a sequence of way-points for each of the unmanned platforms. At each way point the unmanned systems would conduct a surveillance activity,

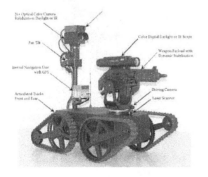

**Figure 14: Some of ARDEC UGV platforms: a) FireAnt, b) Talon and c) Packbot**

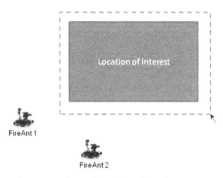

**Figure 15: Selection of Region of Interest**

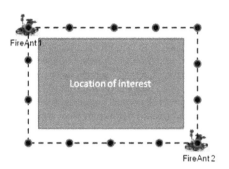

**Figure 17: Deployment of UGV team**

as in the single platform case. Higher and more interesting behaviors can be achieved by multi-UAS system. For example, if a given target is identified by UAS-1 (say UGV 1), it could be confirmed or handed over to UAS-2. UAS-2 could be commanded to follow the target while UAS-1 continues the surveillance, etc. This decision could be taken with or without operator intervention.

The main stages of the perimeter surveillance mission implemented in collaboration with ARDEC personnel were the following:

a) **Selection of Region of Interest:** The operator uses the mouse to indicate on the Vignette Editor the region over which the UGVs are to perform surveillance (see Figure 15). This region can be any non-intersecting polygon. Once the region is selected, the planner defines a sequence of way points which the UGVs are to traverse during the surveillance.

b) **Deployment of UGV team:** The UGV Robot Agents negotiate over equally-spaced starting position of each platform. Once a starting point for each platform is assigned, both platforms navigate to their respective starting positions (see Figure 17).

c) **Surveillance:** Both robots start a clockwise rotation pattern traversing each of the way points in the perimeter of the Region of

Interest. At each waypoint the platforms stop and conduct a target detection search where they pan their cameras towards the outside of the Region of Interest (see Figure 16).

d) **Target Detection:** If a target is detected during any point of the surveillance mission, a pop-up menu is displayed on the Vignette Editor prompting the operator to take an action such as "Continue surveillance", "Remote Control", "Follow Target", etc. If no action is taken by the operator within a timeout period, the surveillance mission continues.

e) **End of Mission:** At the completion of the mission the operator has the choice of manually tele-operating each of the platforms or giving them all a command to go back to their starting positions.

The use cases listed above were implemented over a number of visits to Picatinny Arsenal. On June 2010, a coordinated perimeter surveillance mission using two FireAnt UGVs was successfully demonstrated. Figure 19 and Figure 18 shows the two platforms while performing the mission.

## 6. Conclusions

Real-world applications for UAS teams in military scenarios continue to grow, and the scale and complexity of the teams is rapidly increasing. To reduce life cycle costs and improve T&E, there is an increasing need for a generalized framework that can support the design and development of T&E approaches for multi-

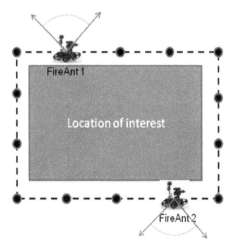

**Figure 16: Surveillance**

**Figure 18: FireAnt 1 and FireAnt 2 during coordinated perimeter surveillance mission**

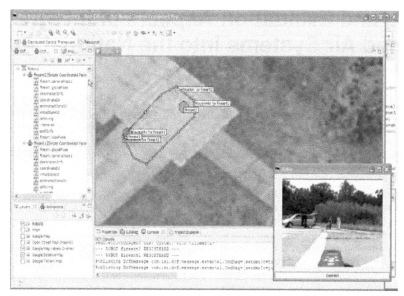

**Figure 19: IAI's Vignette Editor operating as OCU to control a coordinate perimeter surveillance mission at Picatinny Arsenal. The light blue disks correspond to the UGVs (Fireant 1 and Fireant 2); the perimeter under surveillance is shown as a sequence of waypoints which the UGVs are to follow. The bottom right corner shows a live video of Fireant 2 taken in real time.**

UAS teams and validate the feasibility of the concepts, architectures and algorithms. To address this need, IAI has developed a JAUS and TENA compliant Integrated Agent-based T&E Framework for Teams of Unmanned Autonomous Systems developed. IAI has also developed the Vignette Editor which fulfills a variety of functions from visualizing the state of the UAS team, creating T&E scenarios and monitoring the UAS team performance. IAI has already integrated a variety of drivers into DCF which allow the framework to interface with a rich family of platforms, sensors and by providing the tools to develop missions. This enhanced system has already reached a TRL 5, and thanks to the support of TRMC, it is currently in the process of being transitioned to ARDEC personnel at Picatinny Arsenal.

## Acknowledgment

The work reported in this paper has been made possible by funding from Test Resource Management Center (TRMC), Unmanned and Autonomous System Testing (UAST) under contracts No. W9124Q-07-C-0685 and W9124Q-09-P-0272. We would also like to acknowledge the Intelligent Systems Laboratory at the Intelligent Systems Branch, Network Lethality & Int. Systems Div. at Picatinny Arsenal, NJ for their support in this effort.

## 7. REFERENCES

[1] "FY2009 – 2034 Unmanned Systems Integrated Roadmap,".

[2] "Unmanned and Autonomous Systems Testing Roadmap," March 3, 2009.

[3] James J. Streilein, "Test and Evaluation of Highly Complex Systems," *ITEA Journal*, vol. 30, pp. 3-6, 2009.

[4] Zachary Kulis, Vikram Manikonda, Babak Azimi-Sadjadi, and Priya Ranjan, "The Distributed Control Framework: A Software Infrastructure for," in *American Control Conference*, Seattle, WA, 2008. See Also DCF: http://products.i-a-i.com/view.asp?pid=5

[5] V. Manikonda, P. Ranjan, Z. Kulis and B. Azimi-Sadjadi. "An Agent-based Distributed Control Framework for Design, Simulation and Deployment of Unmanned Vehicle Teams". In Proc. of Simulation Interoperability Workshops, Providence, RI 2008.

[6] V. Manikonda, Z. Kulis and Nick Lenzi. "A Motion Description Language and its Applications to Test, Evaluation and Control of Unmanned Autonomous System Teams". 2008 Annual ITEA Technology Review, Colorado Springs 2008 (Presentation only).

[7] JAUS: [Online] http://www.openjaus.com

[8] TENA: [Online] www.tena-sda.org

[9] The Test and Training Enabling Architecture. Architecture Reference Document

[10] "Cybele: An Agent Infrastructure for Modeling, Simulation, and Decision Support", V. Manikonda, G. Satapathy and R. Levy AgentLink, Issue 15, September 2004

[11] CybellePro: [Online] www.cybelepro.com

# Testing and Evaluation Aspects of Integration of Unmanned Air Systems into the National Air Space

Mauricio Castillo-Effen
General Electric Global Research
1 Research Circle
Niskayuna, NY 12309, USA
Castillo-Effen@GE.com

Nikita Visnevski
General Electric Global Research
1 Research Circle
Niskayuna, NY 12309, USA
Nikita.Visnevski@GE.com

## ABSTRACT

Current developments show that the integration of Unmanned Aerial Systems (UAS) into the National Airspace System (NAS) is a process that will inevitably happen. Arguably, it may be viewed as one of the key milestones in the history of aviation. Whereas the majority of research and development efforts are being invested on developing the core technologies and regulations to enable such a leap, there are currently a number of gaps that need to be addressed to transition those new technologies to daily operations with no detriment to performance of the NAS and chiefly, to safety of the NAS. One of those gaps relates to the efficient Testing and Evaluation (T&E) methodologies and procedures that need to be applied to guarantee smooth integration of UAS with varying levels of autonomy. Another main gap relates to the performance metrics that need to be considered to support these new T&E processes. This paper elaborates on those two aspects and it shows examples of how to streamline T&E to accelerate UAS integration.

## Keywords

Unmanned Aerial Systems, NAS Integration, Modeling and Simulation, Test and Evaluation, Verification and Validation

## 1. INTRODUCTION

Considering all modalities of unmanned vehicles, namely: aerial, ground, surface, underwater, and space, it is the aerial modality which seems to be advancing the technology readiness levels (TRL) at the fastest pace. Part of this rapid development stems from the strong need of military and civilian entities for utilizing unmanned aerial systems (UAS) in a large variety of applications. The numerous environmental, economic, and safety benefits have been demonstrated and documented exhaustively [3]. The large number of UAS being developed, manufactured and acquired by several entities and governments all over the world create a new composition mix in the total number of aerial vehicles with potential access to airspace. Most aviation experts predict

the inevitable advent of the time when manned aircraft will share the airspace with their unmanned counterparts [12]. The exact time frame when this will happen is at this point unknown. What are the challenges associated with the integration of UAS into civil airspace? This question has driven a lot of research and it has captured significant attention in the aviation community. Since we appear to be witnessing the beginnings of a rising technology, we see a lot of work aiming at creating structure in this complex problem, and at defining commonly accepted terminology [2]. In addition to the conceptual and technological gaps, the thought of unmanned aircraft flying alongside manned airspace users or even above populated areas causes a great deal of uneasiness, specially for institutions responsible for the safety of the air transportation system.

Gaps may be identified and technologies addressing those gaps may be developed. However, there remains the question of how to guarantee that technology indeed addresses those gaps fully, or that it does not cause unforseen interactions. Is it possible to guarantee that all gaps have been identified? The current report on "Technology Horizons" issued by the U.S Air Force points to the numerous advantages originating from the utilization of autonomous systems. However, it cautiously highlights the need for methods to establish "certifiable trust in autonomy" [8]. A formal methods-based approach to the Verification and Validation (V&V) of autonomous systems inhabiting environments with high levels of stochasticity may be intractable [11]. We propose Test and Evaluation (T&E) as one of the essential tools to guarantee a reasonable "level of trust" in an autonomous system.

The lack of data has been also frequently mentioned as a major gap preventing safety authorities to progress on the path of UAS integration. T&E may be seen as a major generator of data. Moreover, advanced and principled T&E methodology may not only provide data in quantity and quality, but if may also guarantee a level of efficiency in the utilization of resources needed for obtaining valuable data. Although there is a long tradition in the successful practice of T&E applied to technical systems of diverse nature, it has been shown that T&E needs to evolve considerably to cope with the complexity implied by Unmanned and Autonomous System T&E (UAST). The challenges of UAST have been documented and expounded in several sources [14],[6]. Hence, one of the main objectives of this paper is to introduce an important methodological tool whose utilization may increase the efficiency of T&E procedures considerably, specially when dealing with autonomous systems.

Section 2 introduces the problem of integration of UAS into the NAS in general terms. It also defines terminology which is accepted and used in the aviation community to communicate and understand the UAS integration issues. Section 3 delves into more details of T&E concepts, as they apply to the general UAS integration problem. This section also contrasts traditional T&E methodology and procedures against new methods proposed in the Unmanned and Autonomous System T&E (UAST) community, targeting aspects specific to unmanned systems, such as autonomy. Section 4 explores the application of the concepts presented in the previous section at a high analytical level. Finally, section 5, points to important conclusions and future perspective of this work.

## 2. UAS AIRSPACE INTEGRATION BACKGROUND

### 2.1 Related Work

Numerous studies have attempted to identify the key challenges of UAS airspace integration. For example, the Department of Defense's (DoD) Joint UAS Center of Excellence (JUAS COE) has identified 35 issues, which have been categorized into five groups [15]: 1) sense-and-avoid, 2) airworthiness, 3) operating standards and procedures, 4) equipage, and 5) pilot qualifications. Many of the challenges are specific to each type of UAS. One contribution of the JUAS COE work is a UAS categorization schema, based on maximum gross takeoff weight, normal operating altitude, and speed, which is used frequently in the UAS integration community.

MITRE has also worked on the key airspace integration challenges for UAS. For instance in [4], Lacher et al. classify those challenges into four groups: 1) technical, 2) operational, 3) policy, and 4) economic. In Lacher's work, major emphasis is placed on three technical challenges: 1) the lack of an onboard capability equivalent to "see-and-avoid," 2) vulnerabilities of UAS command and control link, and 3) possible need for UAS-specific procedures for air traffic management (ATM) integration.

There seems to be consensus in assigning the highest priority to the sense-and-avoid (SAA) problem. In accordance to that, the FAA organized a series of workshops with the main objective of acquiring technical insight into this matter, which could be utilized for guiding policy and regulatory developments. The main conclusions from these workshops were condensed in a publicly available document [10]. Another important contribution of the SAA workshop is a set of specific definitions, functions, and concepts, which may be used as a basis for defining SAA requirements. Also in this report, the TLS is put forward as the most desirable means for quantification of safety of a SAA system.

### 2.2 UAS Integration and NextGen

The Air Transportation System in the US is undergoing a major, highly needed transformation, which is described partially in a document called the Concept of Operations (ConOps) of the Next Generation Air Transportation System (NextGen) [1]. NextGen envisions a National Airspace

System (NAS) populated by heterogeneous aircraft types, with highly variable levels of equipage in terms of automation, considering even UAS. The authors of this paper argue that SAA is a subfunction of a more general trajectory deconfliction capability [5], which may possess another higher layer, directly related to trajectory-based operations (TBO), lying at the core of NextGen. SAA seems to be essential for the integration of UAS into the current NAS. However, another strategic deconfliction layer is needed that will enable UAS to autonomously synchronize and negotiate its trajectory with Air Traffic Control (ATC). This layer, which may be referred to as the *Trajectory Management layer* will guarantee smooth integration of UAS into NextGen.

### 2.3 Basic Concepts

Some basic concepts are provided, to establish a clear framework for the UAS integration problem, considering the deconfliction aspects.

**Conflict.** An event triggered when any of the constraints that a 4D trajectory is subject to is NOT met. The most well-known conflict type is the event triggered by a *loss of separation*. However, any possibility of invading restricted airspace, proximity to ground, proximity to no-fly zones subject, weather, etc., may be viewed as conflicts.

**4D-Trajectory.** A path defined in space and time.

**Loss of separation, PAZ, CAZ.** Loss of separation is a violation of the Protected Airspace Zone (PAZ) around an aircraft. In civil aviation, the PAZ is defined by legal separation requirements, which vary according to airspace category and to other factors. For instance, the PAZ could be defined by a cylinder with a radius of 5NM and an altitude of 2000ft. A conflict with a higher degree of urgency of attention is generated when there is a violation of the Collision Avoidance Zone (CAZ), e.g.: 0.15NM radius, 600ft altitude.

**Deconfliction.** A comprehensive deconfliction solution for UAS integration may be partitioned into three main components:

- Trajectory Management Layer. according to the NextGen ConOps document [1]: "Trajectory Management (TM) is the adjustment of individual aircraft within a flow to provide efficient trajectories, manage complexity, and ensure that conflicts can be safely resolved." The generation of conflict-free trajectories will require global knowledge about potential conflicts, which is accessible to ground systems. However, trajectory generation also requires performance data, which may be only available to airspace users. Hence, it is foreseeable that strategic deconfliction will be a collaborative effort manifest though some form of *trajectory negotiation*. Furthermore, a basic prerequisite for trajectory negotiation is a common view of the aircraft trajectory, airspace structure, restrictions, etc. This is only going to be achievable through another process essential to trajectory management, known as *trajectory synchronization*.

- Separation Management. "Separation management tactically resolves conflicts among aircraft and ensures avoidance of weather, airspace, terrain, or other hazards." Weather, terrain, restricted airspace and other hazards may be treated as *generic conflicts*. Separation management is usually handled by ATC. However, there are several instances when ATC delegates separation responsibility to the airspace user. In those cases we talk about *self separation*. In UAS in whose operation there is a large amount of human involvement, the UAS operators are in charge of self separation. However, it is envisioned that in the future, UAS will autonomously perform self separation.

- Collision avoidance. An urgent "last ditch" effort to avoid the occurrence of a collision. It should only be activated when other deconfliction measures have failed

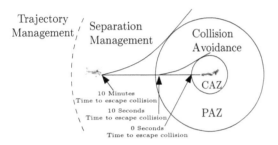

**Figure 1: Comprehensive UAS Deconfliction**

## 3.  T&E IN UAS AIRSPACE INTEGRATION

As described in previous sections, an efficient T&E process is essential for the introduction of new technologies posing significant challenges to safety. T&E is particularly challenging when dealing with complex autonomous systems. It has been shown that traditional component-focused requirement-traceability T&E has severe limitations when dealing with complex systems. An example that is often cited to support this notion is the Predator MQ-1 UAS, which failed operational T&E but proved extremely useful on the battlefield [14]. The case of the Predator proves that metrics for complex systems need to be tied to measures of effectiveness (MoE) and not necessarily to measures of performance (MoP). Frameworks such as the Mission and Means framework (M&M) can help in establishing a hierarchical relationship between mission effectiveness, tasks, capabilities and system components [9]. By using this framework it is also possible to trace back mission success or failure to specific tasks, to capabilities, and to components.

To guarantee that tests are truly relevant and efficient, a formal approach to test planning is necessary. Statistical techniques such as Design of Experiment (DoE) have been already proposed as viable tools [7]. The authors adhere to that notion and to the view of T&E of UAS airspace integration as a DoE problem. The main objective is to obtain a minimal set of experiments which yields the maximum information with respect to the hypothesis that need to be tested. To maximize the efficiency of physical tests in terms

of time and resources, test planning is crucial. The only way to avoid the curse of dimensionality in designing experiments with a large number of independent variables is by including as much knowledge of the process as possible. This is where modeling and simulation (M&S) is most valuable. M&S can be seen as the main vehicle for incorporating knowledge about the system into the test planning process.

What we propose is a test generation system based on modeling and simulation tools along with search techniques. A test or experiment $E$ corresponds to a specific selection of independent variables $X_i$, where each independent variable represents a factor affecting the outcome of a mission, whose success is measured via a single or aggregate metric $\mathcal{M}$. The simulation of the system that needs to be tested assists in exploring the search space of experiments $E$. The final objective is to find through simulation experiments combinations of independent variables $X_i$ that produce abnormal behavior, thus making the system fail the mission (measured via the metric $\mathcal{M}$). These are the tests that if executed on the real system provide the richest set of data. The information gathered from the data may be then fed back to the testing planner, which uses the data to increase the fidelity of the models in certain aspects that are relevant to the chosen metrics. Hence, we not only have a recursive procedure within the test planner, but also the test planner interacts with the T&E aspect by generating test plans which help refine the search for weaknesses. The recursive search process within the planner is depicted in Figure 2.

The blocks labeled with number (1) represent elements that may provided by a third-party simulation tool vendor. The elements of the autonomous testing planner are shown with the label (2). For the T&E of deconfliction capability, we developed a high fidelity model of the UAS of its environment, and of the interactions between both. As it may be observed in Figure 3, central to the UAS model is a Flight Management System (FMS). We support the concept that if UAS will share the airspace with their manned brethren, they will need to possess similar capabilities, specially for trajectory management, which is provided by the FMS. This aspect is commonly neglected in current UAS airspace integration work, although it has been demonstrated that an FMS may prove essential for the insertion of UAS into civilian airspace [13].

With a fast-time executable simulation of the model presented in Figure 3, it is possible to explore the search space of experiments, looking for weaknesses or combinations of independent input parameters that cause failures, as determined by a specific metric to be chosen.

## 4.  CASE STUDIES

Two scenarios of high relevance to UAS airspace integration efforts were selected for the application of the proposed test generation methodology. These scenarios were originally designed for demonstrating some technological solutions for UAS integration. However, since simulations need to be developed for these demonstrations, they can also be used for test generation purposes. In both scenarios, appropriate quantitative outcomes were identified, which could serve as metrics in the search for meaningful T&E experiments. Furthermore, input variables were also determined to allow for

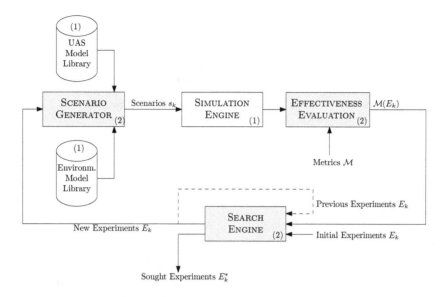

Figure 2: Automated Test Planning System

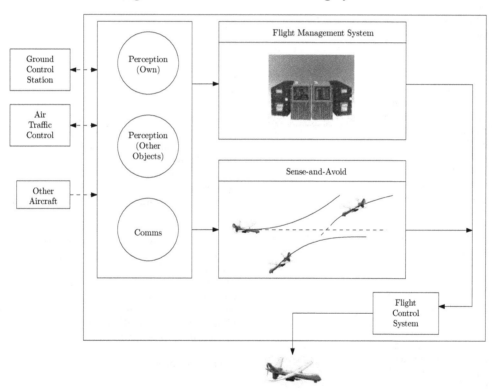

Figure 3: UAS Autonomous Deconfliction Model

a rich search space universe. In other words, the test generation methodology we propose helps testers to find situation when things could go wrong.

## 4.1 Logistics

UAS manufacturers and users are often faced with the logistics problem of getting UAVs delivered to the operations site from the manufacturing facility. Same problem arises when UAV units in need of service or maintenance are re-

quired to be transported to a maintenance or testing facility that is geographically separated from the UAS's operational base. Ideally, manufacturers, users, and testers should be able to fly UAVs from/to operational bases. Currently, due to safety restrictions on UAS operations, this is extremely inefficient and complicated to do.

We acknowledge the fact that one of the serious obstacles to UAS in the NAS operations is the absence of integrated and certified UAS sense-and-avoid capabilities. This capability is essential for UAVs in Class B/C/D/G and the lower portion of Class E airspaces, where they need to interact with general aviation and other types of possibly unequipped aircraft. However, in Class A airspace, ATC is assumed to be fully in charge of air traffic separation. The original goal of this demonstration scenario was to illustrate that the absolute reliance on a sense-and-avoid capability, which is tactical in nature, can be minimized or possibly completely eliminated for UAV operations in Class A airspace by shifting focus to trajectory-based management, which acts in the strategic time horizon.

The scenario involves a flight of a Predator B from Fort Huachuca, AZ army base (KFHU) to Griffiss maintenance facility (KRME) in Rome, NY. It illustrates both the difficulties associated with the lack of sense-and-avoid capabilities, and the benefits to Class A airspace UAS operations provided by trajectory synchronization and negotiation.

Event sequence:

1. The operating agency creates and files a flight plan for the UAV that is not very different from the typical commercial flight plan with the exception that it states UAS operation.

2. The filed flight plan has to be approved and results in the set of Temporary Flight Restrictions (TFR) established around the departure and arrival points of the UAV route and distributed through NOTAMS as outlined in FAA AIM 5-1-3.

3. UAV takes off under the ground based "sense-and-avoid" support. A chase plane is assigned to this flight, to ensure collision avoidance with potential non-TFR-compliant traffic.

4. UAV climbs to FL180. During the climb, the Class A airspace portion of the trajectory is negotiated by the UAV and ATC taking into account other traffic in the vicinity of the requested UAV trajectory. Once in Class A, the chase plane is released and is free to return to the starting airport.

5. From this point on, UAV trajectory does not differ from the typical commercial airplane trajectory. Trajectory synchronization guarantees that Air Traffic Control has complete situational awareness of the UAS' 4D-trajectory and intent.

6. As the UAV approaches the end of its Class A airspace trajectory segment, a ground-based "sense-and-avoid" system is engaged. Descent is initiated and the landing at the destination airport is completed.

In this scenario, the control variables could be various flight conditions (winds aloft, etc.) and the traffic density along the travel route of the UAV. The key objective is the ability for the UAV to meet the specified navigation performance and be able to communicate and follow accurate four dimensional trajectory.

## 4.2  Border Patrol

This scenario exemplifies the needs of UAS integration into the NAS for their intended applications. These needs are more complex than those described in the previous scenario. Specifically, unlike the case in the logistics scenario where a UAV flight resembles the point-to-point flights of a typical commercial or GA aircraft, typical UAS operations involve trajectories that can be different from those flown by commercial airplanes. An example of such operational needs is the DHS use of Predator B aircraft in US/Mexico border patrol missions. Similar operations are contemplated along the US/Canada borders. Also, forest fire detection and law enforcement UAS applications would have similar operational needs and UAV trajectory structures.

As in previous scenario, lack of comprehensive sense-and-avoid capability places restrictions on operations of UAS in Class B/C/D/G and the lower portion of Class E airspaces. However, advanced 4D-trajectory synchronization and negotiation mechanisms can be enabling factors of UAS operations in Class A airspace despite the lack of comprehensive sense-and-avoid strategies.

The scenario evolves around DHS Predator B operation at the New Mexico/Arizona/California Mexican border. The Predator flies loitering patterns between FL180 and FL500 that are repeatedly re-negotiated with ATC services. The loitering pattern crosses multiple commonly used IFR routes with air traffic travelling to/from Mexico as well as the South- and Central American countries. Trajectory synchronization is engaged to give ATC accurate positions of the UAV. Trajectory is negotiated by the UAV based on its strategic and tactical mission needs as well as performance limitations and threat priorities. Under normal circumstances, commercial air traffic remains largely unaffected by the presence of the UAV. UAV has to adapt its loitering patterns to accommodate commercial traffic and be unobtrusive.

Situation reverses if a high security threat is detected. Commercial traffic routes will be re-negotiated by ATC to give way to the high priority UAV trajectory. Similar situation occurs in the case of UAV malfunction when an immediate emergency landing is required. This is especially relevant in the reduced crew case of the manned aircraft with the single pilot. Such an aircraft essentially becomes a UAV in case when a pilot becomes physically incapacitated.

Event sequence:

1. The demo starts with Predator B already in class A airspace initiating negotiation with ATC of its proposed loitering pattern. Traffic in the airspace is low and UAV loitering pattern is approved.

2. User is given an option to increase the commercial air traffic density in the vicinity of the UAV operations. Eventually, a conflict between the UAV and the commercial traffic arises. It requires ATC to modify UAV trajectory. UAV re-negotiates trajectory and adjusts to ATC requests.

3. The user of the demonstrator is given an option to change UAV mission priorities. For instance, an area

of the border becomes a suspect and requires close investigation. This results in a need for the UAV to re-negotiate its trajectory with ATC. The negotiation process is initiated and conflicts with commercial traffic are resolved, yielding a new loitering pattern for the UAV.

4. User is given an option to trigger"high security threat" event that will require UAV to re-negotiate high priority trajectory with ATC. The new UAV trajectory is established and commercial traffic trajectories are also re-negotiated to accommodate high security threat UAV request.

In this scenario, the control variables are commercial traffic density, ATC and ground control communication latency, and threats injected into the scenario. The goal of the UAV is to detect as many threats as possible, so threat detection capability as well as threat handling capacity are test and evaluation objective functions.

## 5. CONCLUSIONS

The advantages of the use of a T&E-approach to the advancement of safety critical technologies has been presented along with a general framework for test generation. T&E may be seen as an essential tool for risk reduction and for generation of relevant data. On the other hand, M&S complements the T&E process by providing understanding about the system and about its possible interactions with the environment. Due to the complexity of current systems, it would be challenging to identify all issues without the help of computer simulation tools. Although the methodology introduced is general and it may apply to manned, unmanned, and autonomous systems, its actual application to the problem of UAS airspace integration has been developed in higher detail in this work.

The model of UAS presented in this paper contains a complete deconfliction solution, including a trajectory management aspect realized by an FMS, as expected in future UAS systems participating in the NextGen air transportation system. The scenarios presented in the last section are being studied with the help of the test generation tool. Actual results will be included in future publications reporting this work.

## 6. ACKNOWLEDGMENTS

The authors would like to thank the Test Resource Management Center (TRMC) Test and Evaluation/Science and Technology (T&E/S&T) Program for their support. This work is funded by the T&E/S&T Program through the White Sands Missile Range, NM, contract W9124Q-08-C-0562.

## 7. REFERENCES

[1] Concept of Operations for the Next Generation Air Transportation System, Version 2.0. Technical report, Joint Planning and Development Office, June 13th 2007.

[2] Sense and Avoid (SAA) for Unmanned Aircraft Systems (UAS). Technical report, FAA Sponsored "Sense and Avoid" Workshop, October 9 2009.

[3] Unmanned Aircraft System Integration into the United States National Airspace System: An Assessment of the Impact on Job Creation in the U.S. Aerospace Industry. Technical report, Association for Unmanned Vehicle Systems International, 2010.

[4] Andrew Lacher, Andrew Zeltin, Chris Jella, Charlotte Laqui, and Kelly Markin. Analysis of Key Airpsace Integration Challenges and Alternatives for Unmanned Aircraft Systems. Technical report, MITRE, July 2010.

[5] M. Castillo-Effen and N. Visnevski. Analysis of autonomous deconfliction in Unmanned Aircraft Systems for Testing and Evaluation. In *Aerospace Conference, 2009 IEEE*, pages 1 –12, mar. 2009.

[6] M. Castillo-Effen, N. A. Visnevski, and R. Subbu. Modeling and Simulation for Unmanned and Autonomous System Test and Evaluation. In *Performance Metrics of Intelligent Systems PerMIS'09*, Gaithersburg, MD, September 2009. NIST.

[7] M. L. Cohen, J. E. Rolph, , and D. L. Steffey, editors. *Statistics, Testing, and Defense Acquisition: New Approaches and Methodological Improvements*. National Academy Press, 1998.

[8] W. J. Dahm. Report on Technology Horizons – A Vision for Air Force Science & Technology During 2010-2030. Technical report, United States Air Force Chief Scientist (AF/ST), May 15 2010.

[9] P. A. Djang and F. Lopez. Unmanned and Autonomous Systems Mission Based Test and Evaluation. In *Performance Metrics of Intelligent Systems PerMIS'09*, Gaithersburg, MD, September 2009. NIST.

[10] FAA Sponsored "Sense and Avoid" Workshop. Sense and Avoid (SAA) for Unmanned Aircraft Systems (UAS). Technical report, Federal Aviation Administration, October 2009.

[11] M. Hinchey, J. Rash, and C. Rouff. Verification and validation of autonomous systems. In *Software Engineering Workshop, 2001. Proceedings. 26th Annual NASA Goddard*, pages 136 –144, 2001.

[12] T. Hoffman. Eye in the Sky – Assuring the Safe Operation of Unmanned Aircraft Systems. *FAA Safety Briefing*, pages 20–23, May/June 2010.

[13] John Croft. Unmanned Flight Tests to Advance Airline Reduced-Crew Concepts. *Flightglobal / Aircraft, http://www.flightglobal.com/articles/2009/12/28/336641/unmanned-flight-tests-to-advance-airline-reduced-crew.html*, December 2009.

[14] F. Macias. The Test and Evaluation of Unmanned and Autonomous Systems. *ITEA Journal*, 29(4):388–395, December 2008.

[15] Michael Johson, Michael Mixon, Dennis Steed, and Frank Villanueva. DoD's Joint UAS Center of Excellence Tackles Airspace Integration Issues. *Unmanned Systems*, 28:21–24, August 2010.

# Evaluating Intelligent Systems with Performance Uncertainty in Large Test Spaces

Miles S. Thompson
Georgia Tech Research Institute
7220 Richardson Rd.
Smyrna, GA 30080
+1 (404) 407- 7837
miles.thompson@gtri.gatech.edu

## ABSTRACT
This paper proposes a new methodology, the Spatial Variance Bounding Methodology, for designing tests/experiments for intelligent systems based on a meta-model method for characterizing a discontinuous, stochastic system. The intent of these designs is to provide a framework for evaluating the performance of these intelligent systems across large test spaces that may take months or years to complete via traditional test/experiment design methods.

## General Terms
Performance, Design, Experimentation

## Keywords
performance, uncertainty, complex, stochastic, Kriging, testers nonlinear, autonomous, intelligent, test matrix

## 1. INTRODUCTION
Traditional test methods for physical systems rely on their performance being continuous with best and worst performances occurring at the extremes of the test space. When testing a manned vehicle such as a truck, testers determine operational requirement limits on the system and test the vehicle at these limits. The assumption is that if the system performs well at the limits of its operational realm, it will perform well at all points between the limits.

On the other hand, software systems are deterministic and very likely to have a discontinuous performance across a test space. Intelligent robotic systems and other systems that are highly software based physical systems become discontinuous and stochastic in their performance. This means that if the intelligent system performs well at all the operational limits, there is no confidence that it will perform well at all points between the limits. It is these points of uncertainty in an intelligent system's behavior that are more commonly referred to as emergent behavior. More often than not, emergent behavior is undesirable

not only because of the risk of lower performance, but also because of the inability to predict or understand an intelligent system's behavior at these points. Additionally, an intelligent system of significant complexity running the same test multiple times will produce a mean performance with some variability because of the testers' inability to reproduce the exact same stimuli or because of inherent noise added by the system itself. Together with emergent behavior, these two concerns represent the majority of performance uncertainty in an intelligent system and need to be accounted for with an appropriate test or experiment methodology.

Before researching the methodology, it was wise to concentrate on certain goals. The methodology must be:

- applicable to intelligent systems, both purely software and mobile
- applicable to systems with discontinuous and/or stochastic performance
- able to provide general system performance information for evaluation purposes (e.g. probability of success, confidence in probability)

In addition to these goals, it was clear that this methodology should target systems that are not already sufficiently testable with other methods. Of particular interest were systems with large test spaces. Intelligent systems are considered to have large test spaces when sufficiently testing them with traditional methods would takes months or years.

[Note: the terms test and experiment are used interchangeably in this document not because they are the same, but rather because the proposed methodology could be used for either.]

## 2. METHODOLOGY DESIGN
### 2.1 Organizing the Test Matrix
Traditional test matrices are designed by using the test parameters as axes. This methodology uses the same set up by defining a specific test with a parameter value chosen from each of the parameters. Since intelligent systems will typically have many influencing parameters, the high number of axes produces a P dimensional hypercube where P is the number of parameters.

Assuming the metrics have already been established for the system under test for this task, the metrics can then be incorporated into the test matrix. The P dimensional hypercube in replicated M times, once for each of the M number of metrics.

This will ensure that performance is being evaluated independently for each metric.

## 2.2 Utilizing Meta-Model Methods

There are many methods that estimate a system's performance through observation of outputs to a variety of inputs. Meta-model techniques such as Response Surface Methods (RSM) and Kriging are extremely useful when dealing with black box systems with complex behaviors and/or unknown parameters. RSMs use a quadratic or cubic interpolation between data points to determine an approximation of a system. Typically, RSMs are most useful for systems with continuous outputs because the model cannot account for deterministic outputs that lead to output discontinuities. Because RSMs are not ideal for discontinuous systems, they would not be appropriate for this methodology.

Kriging was originally developed as a group of geostatistical techniques to interpolate the value of a stochastic field at an unobserved location from observations of its value at nearby locations. Its main use was to determine the most likely locations of valuable minerals based on the results of a few varied locations. The variability in the concentration of ore at these locations compared to their distance from each other gave rise to a probability function that could be maximized to locate the highest likelihood of finding a precious metal.

While geology is an unlikely surrogate for system testing, there are a surprising number of connections. First, ore placement is random in the ground. Just because ore is at one location does not guarantee that it will be in any surrounding locations. Likewise, just because an intelligent system performs well at one location in the test space does not mean it will perform well in the immediate surrounding tests. Second, the probability function that geologists maximize to find ore could be correlated instead to risk of mission failure or even safety violations for intelligent systems. In fact, a separate probability function can be developed for each metric for the intelligent system under test allowing evaluators to easily discern system performance risks to a requirement. Finally, geostatistical Kriging typically involves only three parameters (latitude, longitude, and depth) but is actually scalable up to hundreds of different parameters.

A particular form of Kriging called Blind Kriging assumes an unknown mean output and builds an expected mean output meta-model of a system iteratively as more combinations of inputs are run. While knowing a mean performance for each metric across the entire test space is extremely useful, using the spatial variance to bound the expected performance has been so far overlooked. The spatial variance function is calculated during the Kriging methods and is typically displayed in a graph known as a variogram (Figure 1).

This variogram shows the maximum variance in a metric as a function of distance between any two tests. If a scalar distance could be calculated between tests, the variogram would be used to create an upper and lower expected bound of performance for all tests that have not be run. Assuming that the stochastic performance distribution at each test was a normal distribution, the bounds on performance would then be compared to a required level of performance and an expected probability of success could be determined (Figure 2).

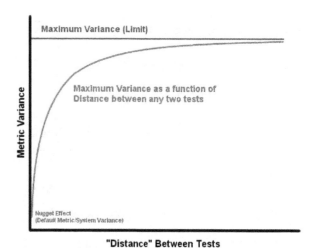

**Figure 1: A sample metric variogram.**

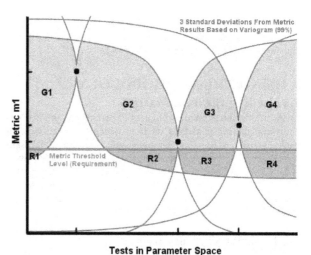

**Figure 2: Example of three tests providing bounds on remaining test.**

## 2.3 Similarity between Tests

The major issue with using Kriging methods for testing is determining a scalar distance between tests. Parameters, if even continuous, are often in different units that don't reflect their importance. One parameter could be linear distance from start to end in meters while another parameter could be average ambient temperature in Kelvin. Calculated a distance between two tests with these parameters would result in a vector of differences for parameter. Of course, a vector would only work for those parameters where a difference could be determined. Categorical parameters such as type of precipitation or terrain would make calculated a difference very difficult. However, a normalized similarity between tests based on the differences in parameters would provide a scalar distance that would allow each test to be related to every other test in the test space.

To calculate a test's similarity to another, one needs to know the values of each parameter in each test (the location of each in the matrix), the weight of the system's sensitivity to each parameter, and an estimated relation between values of each categorical parameter. The normalized similarity S between two tests is then

$$S = 1 - \frac{\sum_{n=1}^{P} \Delta R_n \cdot W_n}{\sum_{n=1}^{P} W_n}$$

where $\Delta R_n$ is the normalized relation between the parameter n for each test and $W_n$ is the weight of each parameter on expected performance. A similarity S equal to one means the tests are identical and a similarity S equal to zero means the tests do not share common ground and the results of one should not be used to create an expected performance of the other. The scalar distance between tests D = 1 – S which means

$$D = \frac{\sum_{n=1}^{P} \Delta R_n \cdot W_n}{\sum_{n=1}^{P} W_n}$$

This scalar distance can be used to build the variogram and allow this methodology and Kriging to be applied.

# 3. USING THE METHODOLOGY
## 3.1 Seeding the Test Matrix
Given a defined test matrix from a set of parameters, the first step is to seed the initial sample set from which to work. Seeding methods such as Random Sampling and Non-orthogonal Latin Hypercube Sampling and excellent choices, but either will work as long as the sample set is spread to cover the test matrix. The number of tests in the sample set is largely dictated by the sampling method and the amount of time it takes to set up and run a test.

## 3.2 Iterative Operations
With the test matrix setup and the sample set of tests selected, the method is ready to enter its iterations. The following steps are repeated until an ending condition is met.

A) Run the selected tests and enter the results into each metric's replicated test matrix.

B) Calculate the variogram for each metric based on all results available.

C) Calculate the expected performance and bounds for each metric.

D) Update the variables such as parameter weighting based on correlation of sensitivity.

E) Select the next sample set of tests.

In step E, sample sets can be chosen by one of three methods. The first is to do another random sample. The second is to select a set of tests where the expected bounds on performance are greatest. This method gives the most amount of knowledge by running tests with the most amount of uncertainty. The final

method is to choose tests with an expected performance closest to the threshold requirement for a metric. This method is useful when much of the expected performance is too close to be definitively above or below a threshold.

## 3.3 Ending the Iterations
Like much of the methodology thus far, testers have a choice on ending the iterations. Many times time and money are constraints on testing so the iterations simply have to end when resources are diminished. When using this ending requirement, it is highly advised to select sample sets based on the greatest expected bounds so that it will maximize knowledge.

When time and money are less of a constraint, the best ending condition is when the confidence level in the model reaches some pre-determined point. It is important to note that not only should the confidence level reach this point, but that the metric variograms should be more or less constant the last three iterations.

# 4.0 CONCLUSION AND FUTURE WORK
The methodology presented here is a variation on an existing form of Kriging that provides additional insight into the variation of performance throughout the test space. The methodology, tentatively called the Spatial Variance Bounding Methodology, gives testers a method for testing intelligent systems with stochastic and discontinuous performance characteristics in large test spaces. In order to use this methodology, testers will need set of operational parameters, operational values for theses parameters, and a set of metrics that can be linked to performance requirements.

For intelligent systems without stochastic performance (e.g. pure software systems), this methodology may prove to be too cumbersome and tedious as it is currently written. However, the methodology is designed to work with deterministic (i.e. zero nugget variance) and discontinuous systems and should provide an excellent starting point.

Though no experiments have been run with this methodology at time of publishing, the first trials will be in Q4 2010 on a heterogeneous system of autonomous systems and results will be published.

# 5.0 REFERENCES
[1] Joseph, V. Roshan and Hung, Ying, "Blind Kriging: A New Method for Developing Metamodels", ASME Journal of Mechanical Design, March 2008 (Vol 130).

[2] Thompson, Miles S., "Testing the Intelligence of Unmanned Autonomous Systems", ITEA Journal 2008; 29: pg 380-387

# The Multi-Relationship Evaluation Design Framework: Creating Evaluation Blueprints to Assess Advanced and Intelligent Technologies

Brian A. Weiss
National Institute of Standards and Technology
100 Bureau Drive, MS 8230
Gaithersburg, Maryland 20899
1-301-975-4373

brian.weiss@nist.gov

Linda C. Schmidt
University of Maryland
0162 Glenn L. Martin Hall, Building 088
College Park, Maryland 20742
1-301-405-0417

lschmidt@umd.edu

## ABSTRACT

Technological evolutions are constantly occurring across advanced and intelligent systems across a range of fields including those within the military, law enforcement, automobile, and manufacturing industries. Testing the performance of these technologies is critical to (1) update the system designers of areas for improvement, (2) solicit end-user feedback during formative tests so that modifications can be made in future revisions, and (3) validate the extent of a technology's capabilities so that both sponsors, purchasers and end-users know exactly what they are receiving. Evaluation events can be minimally designed to include a few basic tests of key technology capabilities or they can evolve into extensive test events that emphasize multiple components and capabilities along with the complete system, itself. Tests of advanced and intelligent systems typically assume the latter and can occur frequently based upon system complexity. Numerous evaluation design frameworks have been produced to create test designs to appropriately assess the performance of intelligent systems. While most of these frameworks allow broad evaluation plans to be created, each framework has been focused to address specific project and/or technological needs and therefore has bounded applicability. This paper presents and expands upon the current development of the Multi-Relationship Evaluation Design (MRED) framework. Development of MRED is motivated by the desire to automatically create an evaluation framework capable of producing detailed evaluation blueprints while receiving uncertain input information. The authors will build upon their previous work in developing MRED through an initial discussion of key evaluation design elements. Additionally, the authors will elaborate upon their previously-defined relationships among evaluation personnel to define evaluation structural components pertaining to the evaluation scenarios, test environment, and data collection methods. These terms and their relationships will be demonstrated in an example evaluation design of an emerging technology.

## Categories and Subject Descriptors

B.8.0 [**Performance of Systems**]: m*easurement techniques, modeling techniques, performance attributes.*

## General Terms

Measurement, Performance, Design, Experimentation, Verification.

## Keywords

MRED, SCORE, performance evaluation, model, framework

## 1. INTRODUCTION

Advanced technologies and intelligent systems are emerging across a range of domains including those within the military, law enforcement, automobile, manufacturing and oil industries. An example of a technology are the remotely operated underwater vehicles (ROVs) currently being used to support the Gulf of Mexico oil spill [5]. One commonality of these systems is the human robot interface (HRI) or human computer interaction (HCI) component [11] [12]. Evaluating the performance of these intelligent systems is of paramount importance to (1) inform the technology designers of shortcomings, (2) solicit end-user feedback, and (3) validate the technology's final capabilities. The former occurs in formative evaluations so that modifications can be made in upcoming design iterations; the latter occurs in summative evaluations so that buyers and technology users know exactly what they are getting. These HRI and HCI technologies still feature human-in-the-loop operation. The user's involvement with the technology can range from having full control over all system functions to simply monitoring the system's behavior and can include dynamically varying the levels of control between these two limits.

Both formative and summative evaluations can be minimally structured to include several basic tests of key system capabilities or they can take the form of comprehensive test events that focus on multiple sub-system components and capabilities [8]. Evaluation events of advanced and intelligent systems usually focus on these multiple levels. These tests can justifiably occur more frequently based upon their inherent system complexity.

Extensive evaluations of emerging and intelligent technologies have occurred in numerous domains. Examples include the evaluations of autonomous ground vehicles along with several constituent components (i.e., intelligent control architectures, automated positioning and mapping technologies, obstacle and pedestrian tracking systems) [1] [2] [13]. Likewise, considerable resources have been exerted to test the advanced technologies of Urban Search and Rescue (US&R) and bomb disposal robotic systems. To date, a widespread range of tests have been designed, fabricated, implemented, and iterated to test US&R and bomb disposal robots across a collection of operational situations [6] [7]. The tests designed to evaluate these technologies range from specific test methods aimed at assessing individual system capabilities to scenarios targeted at testing the entire system.

Assessing the performance of advanced and intelligent systems has motivated research into creating methods and frameworks to design evaluation plans. Many of the frameworks developed have been sufficient to evaluate given technologies and accomplish program-specific objectives. To date, no individual framework has been recognized as being suitable to attain both quantitative and qualitative performance across a range of virtual and physical systems including those with both human-controlled and autonomous functions.

The National Institute of Standards and Technology (NIST) has created the System, Component, and Operationally-Relevant Evaluation (SCORE) framework to evaluate emerging and intelligent systems at various levels [8]. SCORE has been effectively applied to fifteen evaluations across several technologies [9] [10] [17] [19]. SCORE enabled tests have yielded extensive quantitative and qualitative data that has proven valuable to the technology developers, evaluation designers, potential end-users, and funding sponsors.

Weiss, a co-developer of SCORE, has drawn upon that success to introduce a new evaluation framework that will automatically generate evaluation blueprints (test plans). This new evaluation plan design tool is known as the Multi-Relationship Evaluation Design (MRED) framework. MRED's ultimate objective is to take inputs from three specific groups, each complete with their own uncertainties, and output an evaluation blueprint that specifies all characteristics of the tests [18]. MRED's evaluation blueprint is defined as a detailed technology evaluation plan that states the levels and values of the test variables and how they will be combined to set up and implement the test. The blueprint also specifies the class(es) of metrics to be collected which would either include quantitative and/or qualitative data.

This paper will present the following: the author's initial development of the MRED framework. The discussion will include those elements leveraged from SCORE and further expansion of the MRED framework. MRED will be validated by applying it to an evaluation design to test an emerging technology. Finally, strategies to further develop and augment MRED will be stated.

## 2. OTHER FRAMEWORKS

Development of MRED is motivated by the desire to create an evaluation framework capable of producing detailed evaluation blueprints while factoring in numerous uncertainties. There are currently many test development systems that are used to evaluate complex advanced and intelligent systems. For instance, an evaluation framework was produced to test mobile robots for planetary exploration across relevant terrains [15]. However, evaluations did not consider HRI factors. Likewise, Calisi et al. [3] have devised an evaluation framework to specifically assess intelligent algorithms. Its success has been well-documented in capturing technical performance in the virtual world, yet it has not been employed to capture feedback from human users or evaluate physical systems.

The SCORE framework was created to evaluate technologies at the component level, capability level, and system level across numerous environments from highly-controlled laboratory settings to real use-case domains [16]. To date, SCORE has been successful in allowing evaluation designers to recognize the most practical blueprints for evaluating a range of intelligent technologies. MRED not only leverages some of the successes of the SCORE framework in its own design, but it also introduces several innovative features. They include (1) MRED's ability to identify relationships and interdependencies among many evaluation elements and (2) an ability to address the uncertainties from the various evaluation inputs including how they impact the blueprints.

Due to SCORE's success in identifying evaluation designs for testing speech-to-speech translation technologies, advanced soldier-worn sensor systems, along with mapping and navigation algorithms, MRED will adapt the SCORE framework's prescribed evaluation goal types [9] [10] [14] [17] [19]. These will be discussed in subsequent sections as the MRED framework is presented.

## 3. MRED MODEL

The Multi-Relationship Evaluation Design (MRED) model is introduced by presenting the significant design inputs and the features of the output "evaluation blueprint." These inputs and outputs are shown in Figure 1.

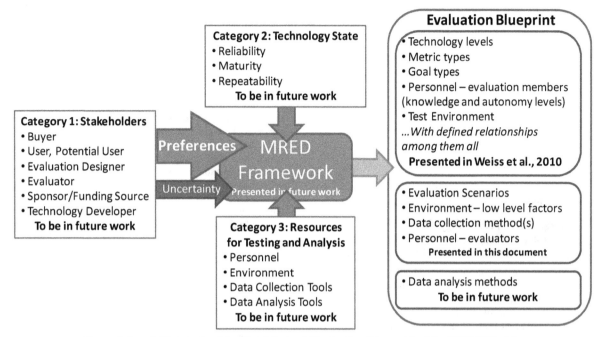

**Figure 1. Input (Categories 1 to 3) and Output (Evaluation Elements) of the MRED Model**

Development of the MRED model began with identifying elements of the evaluation blueprint [18]. The unique parts of this paper are the expansion and elaboration of three evaluation blueprint elements. They are *Explicit Environmental Factors, Data Collection Methods, Evaluation Scenarios*, and *Personnel - evaluators* (shown in Figure 1). Additionally, previously-identified parts of the evaluation blueprint will be presented section 3.3 as shown in Figure 1 [18].

## 3.1 Example MRED Application

These MRED pieces will be applied to a technology that is currently being tested by NIST personnel as each of the critical input categories and output blueprint criteria are discussed. The selected project is the assessment and evaluation of multiple pedestrian tracking algorithms whose test design and implementation is conducted jointly by NIST and members of the Army Research Laboratory's (ARL) Collaborative Technology Alliance (CTA) [2]. Specifically, the CTA/NIST testing is focused on evaluating algorithms produced from numerous companies and organizations which use Laser Detection and Ranging (LADAR) and video sensor data taken from a moving test vehicle. This vehicle travels through the test environment and the vehicle-mounted sensors collect and feed data to the on-board detection and tracking algorithms.

From 2007 to the present day, the CTA/NIST team has jointly planned and implemented several evaluations. To expand the evaluation capabilities of the MRED, the ARL work will be discussed using the terms of the initial MRED framework design.

## 3.2 Input Categories

The MRED framework identifies three critical input groups that provide data into the planner. Each group will be briefly described in the following subsections. These categories will be further elaborated upon including their relationships and sources of uncertainty in future efforts.

### 3.2.1 Category 1 – Stakeholders

Test stakeholders are classified into six categories or parties interested in a technology's evaluation. Stakeholders could have an impact over the design of a technology evaluation. Members of these categories have their own motivation in the test plan and interests in the results of a technology's performance. Their individual motivations will reflect personal uncertainties based upon their changing preferences. An example of uncertainty within stakeholder preferences could be the sponsor's expectation of what system capabilities are crucial for testing. Based upon uncertain and/or changing information, directives from their superiors, etc, the sponsor's preference of what capabilities should be tested could be moving a target. The six personnel categories are summarized in Table 1.

**Table 1. Personnel with a Stake in a Technology Evaluation**

| STAKEHOLDER GROUPS | WHO THEY ARE... |
|---|---|
| *Buyers* | Stakeholder purchasing the technology |
| *Users, Potential Users* | Stakeholder that will be, or are already using the technology |
| *Evaluation Designers* | Stakeholder creating the test plans by determining MRED inputs |
| *Evaluators* | Stakeholder implementing the evaluation test plans |
| *Sponsors/Funding Sources* | Stakeholder paying for the technology development and/or evaluation |
| *Technology Developers* | Stakeholder designing and building the technology |

There may be some overlap among the stakeholders which occurs on a technology-by-technology basis. Figure 2 presents the potential relationships among the stakeholders.

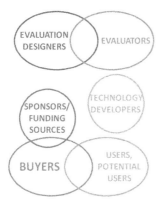

**Figure 2. Stakeholder Relationships**

### 3.2.2  Category 2 – Technology State Factors

This class or category comprises the factors that influence the technology's state at the time of its test. These factors include:

- *Reliability* – This term defines the technology's ability to be evaluated under certain conditions and/or use specific functionalities. Reliability is important because it determines if the technology is robust enough to undergo specific tests and/or if its current level of reliability limits the tests it can perform.
- *Maturity* – This term describes the technology's state or quality of being fully developed. This factor is critical because it states the degree to which the technology is equipped with all of its intended functionalities. Only a subset of expected features may be operational at the time of testing.
- *Repeatability* – This term refers to the technology's ability to yield the same or comparable results as determined from previous test(s). Repeatability is a significant factor that notes the degree to which the technology has undergone previous testing. The output test data may be used to iterate upon the design along with provide baseline data for future testing.

Understanding each of these factors will provide knowledge as to to the high-level intent of the test. The evaluation will either output formative data (intended to inform on a technology's design while it's still in development and not fully mature) or summative data (intended to validate the final design of a technology) [14].

### 3.2.3  Category 3 – Resources for Testing and Analysis

This last input group is composed of various types of material, personnel and technology to be included in the evaluation exercise. Resource availability (or lack thereof) and resource limitations can have a tremendous influence on the final evaluation design.

- *Personnel* –those individuals that will use the technology during the test(s), those that will indirectly interact with the technology during the test(s), those that will collect data during the test(s), and those that will analyze the data following the test(s).
- *Test Environment* –the physical test venue, supporting infrastructure, artifacts and props that will support the test.

- *Data Collection Tools* –the tools, equipment, and technology that will collect quantitative and/or qualitative data during the test(s).
- *Data Analysis Tools* –the tools, equipment and technology capable of producing the necessary metrics from the collected evaluation data.

## 3.3  Previously-defined Blueprint Outputs

Previously-defined key terms in MRED's evaluation blueprint are presented here prior to introducing the new blueprint concepts. These existing terms include technology levels and metric types, which are also combined to form goal types. Additionally, evaluation personnel and environments are discussed. These previously-defined outputs were applied to the ARL CTA test case in earlier work [18]. An example will be briefly presented in the following subsections to better enable understanding of how the newly-defined outputs are applied.

### 3.3.1  Technology Levels

A system (often called a "technology") is made up of constituent components and they can be evaluated at multiple levels. There are several terms related to technology levels as follows:

- *System* – Group of cooperative or interdependent *Components* forming an integrated whole intended to accomplish a specific goal.
- *Component* – Essential part or feature of a *System* that contributes to the *System's* ability to accomplish a goal(s).
- *Sub-Component* – Element, part or feature of a *Component*.
- *Capability* – A specific ability of a technology where a System is made up of one or more *Capabilities*. A *Capability* is provided by either a single *Component* or multiple *Components* working together.

### 3.3.2  Metric Types

Evaluations are capable of capturing two distinct types of metrics. In defining the two metric types, it is essential to define metrics and measures in the context of the MRED model.

- *Measures* – A performance indicator that can be observed, examined, detected and/or perceived either manually or automatically.
- *Metrics* – The analysis of one or more output measures elements, e.g. measures that correspond to the degree to which a set of attribute elements affects its quality.

Specifically, the two metric types are:

- *Technical Performance* – Metrics related to quantitative factors (such as accuracy, precision, time, distance, etc). These metrics may be needed by the program *Sponsor* to get a status of the technology's current performance, update the *Technology Developers* on their design, etc.
- *Utility Assessments* – Metrics related to the qualitative factors that judge the condition or status of being useful and usable to the target user population. Like *Technical Performance*, these metrics may be of value to any of the stakeholders.

### 3.3.3  Goal Types

Goal types, extracted from the SCORE framework, are combinations of technology levels and desired metrics [9] [16]. There are five goal types employed in the MRED framework (shown in Table 2).

**Table 2. Goal Types Employed by the MRED Framework**

| TECHNOLOGY LEVEL | METRIC TYPE | DESCRIPTION |
|---|---|---|
| *Component Level Testing* | *Technical Performance* | Evaluation type breaks down a system into components in order to separate the subsystems that are essential for system functionality and can be designed or altered independently of other components. |
| *Capability Level Testing* | *Technical Performance* | Evaluation type requires the identification and isolation of specific capabilities from overall system behavior to the measure the individual capabilities' contribution to technical performance. |
| *System Level Testing* | *Technical Performance* | Evaluation type targets a full system assessment where environmental variables can be isolated and manipulated to capture their impact on system performance. |
| *Capability Level Testing* | *Utility Assessments* | Evaluation type assesses the end-users' utility of a specific capability where the complete system's behavior is composed of multiple capabilities. In this instance, the SCORE framework defines utility as the value the application provides to the end-user. |
| *System Level Testing* | *Utility Assessments* | Evaluation type focuses on the end-users' utility of the entire system. |

Each of these goal types requires different blueprint components and characteristics within an evaluation. Specific goal and metric types make it possible to design evaluations to collection the necessary quantitative and/or qualitative data

Due to the current level of technology maturity, the ARL CTA is currently isolating the pedestrian detection and tracking algorithms to yield technical performance metrics. Based upon this knowledge, NIST's involvement in the program has focused on conducting exercises in the *Goal Type* of *Capability Level Testing – Technical Performance*. Further discussion of *Metrics* can be found in [2] [18].

### 3.3.4 Personnel – Evaluation Members

Various individuals and groups are required to perform an effective evaluation. They are classified into two categories: primary (direct interaction) technology users and secondary (indirect interaction or evaluation support). The primary technology users are defined as *Tech User*. These individuals directly interact with the technology during the evaluation. They receive any training necessary to use the technology and are responsible for engaging/disengaging the technology's usage during the test event. There are multiple classes of *Tech Users* that have been extensively defined in previous efforts [18]. *Tech Users* are usually the predominant source of qualitative data when the evaluation goal(s) include capture of utility assessments.

- *Tech User: End-User* – Individuals that are the intended users for the technology. Depending upon the level and extent of the evaluation, all, some, or none of the *Tech Users* will be from the *End-User* class.
- *Tech User: Trained User* – Individuals selected to be *Tech Users*, yet are not *End-Users*.
- *Tech User: Tech Developer* – Members of the research and development organization that developed the technology under evaluation.

The secondary personnel feature those that indirectly interact with the technology during the evaluation and fall into three categories:

- *Team Member* – Individuals that work with *Tech Users* during the evaluation as they would to realistically support the use-case scenario in which the technology is immersed. Team *Members* may or may not be in a position to indirectly or directly interact with the technology during the evaluation, but they are often in a position to observe a *Tech User's* interactions with the system.

- *Participant* – Individuals that indirectly interact with the technology during an evaluation. Typically, *Participants* are given specific tasks to either interact with the *Tech Users* and/or with the environment, but not with the technology.
- *Evaluator* – Personnel on the evaluation team present within the *Test Environment* that task the *Participants* and/or captures data, but do not interact with the technology. Depending upon the test, the *Evaluator* may interact with the *Tech User* to capture data.

As discussed in previous efforts [18] each of these *Personnel Groups* (excluding evaluators) has varying *Knowledge Levels* about the technology (*Technical Knowledge*) and the testing and/or use-case environment (*Operational Knowledge*). Additionally, *Autonomy Levels* are identified for these personnel groups where each has varying decision-making authority regarding the technology they were using (*DM Autonomy – Technical*) and their interactions with other personnel and the environment (*DM Autonomy – Environmental*).

Presently, the ARL CTA test effort calls for a *Tech User: Trained User* to operate the technology during the test runs. It should be noted that since the capability being tested will ultimately be incorporated into a larger system, it is premature to recognize the intended user group. Prior tests have not featured any *Team Members*, yet include numerous *Participants*. These *Participants* play the role of "walkers" where they are assigned to walk specific paths during the test. *Knowledge* and *Decision-making Autonomy* levels for these *Evaluation Members* can be found in [18].

### 3.3.5 Test Environments

The setting in which the evaluation occurs can have a significant effect on the data since the environment can influence the behavior of the personnel and can limit which levels of a technology can be tested. MRED defines three distinct environments that are:

- *Lab* – Controlled environment where test variables and parameters can be isolated and manipulated to determine how they impact system performance and/or the *Tech Users'* perception of the technology's utility.
- *Simulated* – Environment outside of the *Lab* that is less controlled and limits the evaluation team's ability to control influencing variables and parameters since it tests the technology in a more realistic venue.

- *Actual* – Domain of operations that the system is designed to be used. The evaluation team is limited in the data they can collect since they cannot control environmental variables.

Significant relationships exist between Technology Levels, Metric Types, Tech Users and *Test Environments* which were highlighted in previous efforts [18]. Likewise, extensive relationships have been noted between *Personnel, Knowledge Levels*, and *Autonomy Levels* have been documented in this same effort.

The ARL CTA testing is currently being conducted in *Simulated* environments that include some Military Operations in Urban Terrain (MOUT) characteristics. This type of venue enabled the evaluation team to control many key parameters and variables within the *Test Environment*. It also allowed them collect extensive ground truth necessary for calculating several of the quantitative metrics.

## 3.4 Latest Key Blueprint Outputs

This work defines and further illustrates several new output elements from MRED. Specifically, they are *Evaluation Scenarios, Explicit Environmental Factors*, and *Data Collection Methods*. Although introduced in previous work, *Evaluators* (Personnel) will be discussed again in the context of their responsibilities and interactions with the three latest output categories. Relationships that link these blueprint components will be also be explored.

### 3.4.1 Evaluation Scenarios

The *Evaluation Scenarios* govern exactly what the technology will encounter and the challenges it will have to meet within the identified *Test Environments*. Three unique types of *Evaluation Scenarios* are identified below where each is unique in the relationships they have with *Tech User: Knowledge Levels, Tech User: Decision-Making Autonomy*, and *Environment – High Level Venues*. The three *Evaluation Scenario* types are:

- *Technology-based* – Evaluation scenarios in this category feature specific instructions to the user in how they should use the technology within the testing environment.
- *Task/Activity-based* – Evaluation scenarios in this category state the user complete a specific task within the environment where they may use the technology as they see fit.
- *Environment-based* – Evaluation scenarios in this category enable the user to perform the relevant activities within the environment based upon an advanced Operational Knowledge.

Typically, *Technology-based Evaluation Scenarios* occur in the *Lab* or *Simulated* environments where the evaluation team can determine the exact test parameters and control the various test variables. Likewise, *Task/Activity-based Evaluation Scenarios* can occur across any of the three (*Lab, Simulated, Actual*) environments where the evaluation team still has specific measures of control of both the test parameters and variables. The

*Environment-based Evaluation Scenarios* can only occur in the *Simulated* and *Actual* environments where the evaluation team has no control over test parameters and variables. The specific relationships among the *Evaluation Scenarios* and the *Tech User's Knowledge Levels* and *Decision-making Autonomy* are shown in Table 3. Refer to [18] for a detailed presentation of *Knowledge and Decision-Making Autonomy Levels*.

The *Evaluation Scenarios* designed for the ARL CTA testing can be classified as *Technology-based* (see Table 4). Specifically, the *Tech User* is restricted in how they can interact with the technology. They are only allowed to engage the technology at the beginning of a run and disengage it at the run's conclusion. It is clear that the *Evaluation Scenarios* are neither *Task/Activity-based* nor *Environment-based* since the *Tech User* has no freedom to interact with the environment or has to complete a specific mission with the technology during the testing.

Since the *Evaluation Scenarios* are *Technology-based, meaning* the *Tech User* is fully-constrained as to when they can use the system, the *Tech User* then has a *DM Autonomy-Technical* value of "None." Likewise, since *Evaluators* drove the test vehicle around the site, the *Tech User* has a *DM Autonomy-Environmental* of "None." The *Tech User* has no other responsibilities and more specifically, is a *Trained User*, with some working knowledge of the technology thereby specifying the *Technical Knowledge Level* of "Medium." Multiple tracking algorithms from different organizations were evaluated simultaneously. So, it was not practical or proper to have a *Tech Developer* engage the technologies. Since the *Tech User* had no control over their activities within environment nor was it a place they had prior experience, their *Operational Knowledge* can be defined as "Low."

### 3.4.2 Explicit Environmental Factors

The *Explicit Environmental Factors* are significant characteristics within the environment that impact the technology and therefore, influence the outcome of the evaluation. These factors pertain to the overall physical space which is composed of *Participants* (constituent actors), structures along with any integrated props and artifacts. These factors are broken down into two characteristics, *Feature Density* and *Feature Complexity*. Together, these two elements determine the *Overall Complexity* of the environment.

- *Feature Density* – Refers to the number of features within the *Test Environment* given the size of the test area. The greater the *Feature Density*, the more challenging it is for a technology to effectively and efficiently interact with, identify objects/events/activities, operate within, etc. The *Test Environment*. *Feature Density* of a testing environment can be characterized as "Low," "Medium," and "High" referring to the level within the testing environment.

**Table 3. Relationship Among the Evaluation Scenarios, Test Environments, Knowledge and Decision-making Autonomy**

| EVALUATION SCENARIOS | TEST ENVIRONMENT(S) | TECH USER'S KNOWLEDGE LEVEL | | TECH USER'S DECISION-MAKING AUTONOMY | |
|---|---|---|---|---|---|
| | | *TECHNICAL* | *OPERATIONAL* | *TECHNICAL* | *ENVIRONMENTAL* |
| Technology-based | Lab, Simulated | MED - HIGH | LOW - MED - HIGH | NONE - LOW | NONE - LOW |
| Task/Activity-based | Lab, Simulated, Actual | LOW - MED - HIGH | LOW - MED - HIGH | LOW - MED - HIGH | LOW - MED - HIGH |
| Environment-based | Simulated, Actual | MED - HIGH | MED - HIGH | MED - HIGH | MED - HIGH |

- *Feature Complexity* – Refers to the intricacy of various features within the environment. For example, a baseball (sphere) has a lower *Feature Complexity* as compared to a car. Similar to *Feature Density*, the greater the *Feature Complexity*, the more difficult it is for the technology to accurately and appropriate operate and be beneficial to the *Tech User(s)*. As with *Feature Density*, *Feature Complexity* can also be characterized as "Low," "Medium," and "High" referring to the level within the testing environment.
- *Overall Complexity* – This factor refers to the global combination of *Feature Density* and *Feature Complexity* within the testing environment. *Overall Complexity* can range from "Low," "Low/Medium," "Medium," "Medium/High," and "High" since it integrates both density and complexity.

**Table 4. ARL CTA Test Evaluation Scenario, Environment, and Tech User Parameters**

| EVALUATION SCENARIOS | TEST ENV. | KNOWLEDGE | | DM AUTONOMY | |
|---|---|---|---|---|---|
| | | TECH. | OP. | TECH. | ENV. |
| Technology-based | Simulated | MED | LOW | NONE | NONE |

Figure 3 presents the relationship between the *Test Environment* and the *Low Level Environmental Factors*. Note that "Low" and "High" *Overall Complexities* are achieved by single combinations of "Low" "Low" and "High" "High" *Feature Densities* and *Feature Complexities*, respectively. "Low/Medium" and "Medium/High" *Overall Complexity* can be obtained by two combinations of *Feature Density* and *Feature Complexity*. "Medium" *Overall Complexity* is achieved by three unique combinations. Since the *Lab* environment is heavily controlled by the *Evaluators* and it's usually desired to obtain specific *Technical Performance* data during the technology's early stages of development, it's unlikely that the *Overall Complexity* will exceed the "Medium" level. Note that it is possible to obtain *Utility Assessment* data in the *Lab*, but this *Test Environment* limits the type and range of qualitative data that can be captured since the *Lab* is not indicative of the *Actual* Environment. The *Simulated* and *Actual* environments are capable of producing the full range of *Overall Complexities* where the significant difference between the two is that the *Evaluators* have some measure of control over the parameters and variables present within the *Simulated* environment whereas the *Evaluators* have no control over test parameters and variables within the *Actual* environment.

It is also critical to note that the *Feature Density* and *Feature Complexity* ranges from "Low" to "Medium" to "High" correspond to global values across a specific *Test Environment*. For instance, the global *Feature Density* of an environment may be classified as "Medium" yet one local spot in the environment could have a large cluster of features indicating a "High" local *Feature Density*. Likewise, another spot within this same *Test Environment* could be sparsely populated so its local *Feature Density* could be classified as "Low." Altogether, the global *Feature Density* of the entire *Test Environment* is still "Medium."

Matching the appropriate *Explicit Environmental Factors* of the ARL CTA testing effort based upon previous test events is not trivial. Since NIST personnel have limited prior algorithm testing, it's difficult to state how the *Feature Density*, *Feature Complexity*, and *Overall Complexity* compare in the current test venue from prior testing environments. Also, since this technology will be integrated onto a greater system for its intended usage, it's difficult to state what the *Actual* environment will be, especially since the greater system(s) are somewhat unknown at this point. This highlights another challenge in accurately defining this blueprint category. Should *Explicit Environmental Factors* be referenced from the same test types with the technology at comparable states or do values of *Explicit Environmental Factors* range across all test types? In the case of the ARL CTA testing effort, the former would mean that "Low" *Feature Complexity* in the *Lab* is much lower and vary different to "Low" *Feature Complexity* in a *Simulated Environment*. The latter would mean that "Low" *Feature Complexity* in the *Lab* is comparable to "Low" *Feature Complexity* in a *Simulated Environment*.

The MOUT *Simulated Test Environment's Explicit Environmental Factors* that the ARL CTA/NIST team most recently evaluated the technology could be classified as having an *Overall Complexity* of "Medium" where *Feature Density* and *Feature Complexity* were both globally "Medium." This determination is based upon the overall consideration of the number of pedestrians within their environment, their motion paths, the number and type of fixed obstacles, number of lanes and other ambient features and/or obstacles. However, looking at specific artifacts and personnel activities within the environment, a case could be made that local *Feature Density* ranged from "Low" to "Medium" since multiple personnel were close proximity to one another in some spots while other personnel stood by themselves in other spots. Comparably, it can be stated that local *Feature Complexity* also ranges from "Low" to "Medium" considering that there were various environmental features present including several rectangular buildings and about a dozen *Participants*.

Further exploration needs to be completed on the exact method(s) to determine global and local complexities and densities both in general and specific to the CTA/NIST example. Additional time will be spent with the CTA/NIST test designers to obtain a greater understanding of their specific wants regarding the features and obstacles specifically placed in the environment.

The authors envision refining these blueprint specifications and solidifying the issue raised regarding if levels of *Explicit Environmental Factors* range within each *Test Environment* or across all *Test Environments*. Additionally, the authors will determine if the MRED framework will identify specific *Feature Density* and *Feature Complexity* levels, leading to unique *Overall Complexities* or if the framework will simply specify the *Overall Complexity* allowing the designer some freedom to specify *Feature Densities* and *Complexities* based upon the relationships identified in Figure 3.

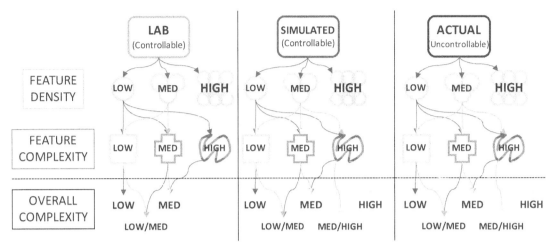

**Figure 3. Relationship between the Test Environment and its Low Level Environmental Factors**

### 3.4.3 Data Collection Methods

Technology-specific and/or customized *Data Collection Methods* are used to capture experimental and ground truth data depending upon the technology being evaluated and the environment it's being tested. *Data Collection Methods* are classified as being an observation device placed at a specific location in the environment to collect experimental test and/or ground truth data. No matter the type of tools are being used, *Data Collection Methods* include several factors that influence the techniques being employed. These two factors include *Mode* and *Collector Location* and are discussed further.

- *Mode* – This factor refers to the nature of the *Data Collection* Method that will be employed. Specifically, there are two different types of *Modes* that can collect data.
  1) *Automated Modes* involves collecting data with a calibrated technology that is independent of the system undergoing testing. An example of this would be using a radar gun to determine the speed of a vehicle.
  2) *Manual Modes* features an *Evaluator* actively managing a calibrate technology or collecting data by hand. Either way, *Manual Modes* are impacted by the *Evaluator* and are subject to human error. An example of *Manual Modes* would be a human starting and stopping a stop-watch to determine the time it takes a vehicle to go from point A to point B. Note that an evaluation can include *Data Collection Methods* of both *Automated* and *Manual Modes*.

- *Collector Location* – This factor refers to where the *Data Collection Methods* are located relative to the technology under test. The different perspectives include (i.e. physical locations from which observations are taken) include:
  1) From that of the technology (subject of the testing) – For those data collection tools used from this perspective during the evaluation, it's important that they are as discreet as possible so they do not interfere with the technology's functions.
  2) From that of a *Tech-User* – Depending upon the exact nature of the test and the type of data being collected (quantitative vs. qualitative metrics) it may be imperative for the *Data Collection Methods* to be as unobtrusive as possible so as not to influence the *Tech User* as they are using the technology.

3) From that of a *Team Member* – Although the same types of data can be collected from this perspective as compared to that of the *Tech-User,* the captured data is distinct. The *Team Member(s)* have the ability to provide feedback about not only their perceptions of the technology's effectiveness, but also their perception of how it's impacting the *Tech-User* in their ability to complete their task, mission objective, etc.

4) From that of a *Participant* – Data collected from this perspective is also distinct from that collected by the *Tech Users and Team Members*. The evaluation team gets insight from individuals who usually have the least familiarity with the technology. It should also be noted that *Participants* rarely support *Data Collection Methods* used during the evaluation since this can be perceived by the *Tech-Users* and *Team Members* as part of the evaluation scenario and not something that is purely for the evaluation.

5) From the environment – Data collected from this perspective usually includes sensors automatically collecting data and/or evaluation team members manually collecting data from various points within the test environment.

Table 5 shows several example *Data Collection Methods* from both *Automated* and *Manual Modes* across the five *Collector Locations.*

The CTA/NIST team deployed numerous *Automated Data Collection Methods* from the *Collector Location* from within the test environment. Specifically, an Ultra-Wideband (UWB) tracking system is deployed to capture position ground truth data of the test vehicle, key environmental features and pedestrians (*Participants*) within the testing environment [4]. Data is used to capture quantitative *Technical Performance* data of the sensors and algorithms in order to generate the necessary evaluation metrics. A filter, devised by evaluation personnel, is incorporated into the raw UWB tracking data to minimize the impact of any potential data collection errors resulting from artifacts within the environment or from the UWB technology, itself. Additionally, numerous cameras are setup throughout the environment to automatically capture additional position data of test vehicle, key environmental features and *Participants*.

The experimental data is composed of each algorithm reporting detection information such as positions and velocities of the humans at the end of each CTA algorithm cycle. Some of the underlying assumptions for the outputs of the algorithms included:

- Only obstacles seen and classified as human were reported.
- Unique identification numbers were assigned to individual algorithm detections within a run.

- Algorithms demonstrated tracking of an individual by maintaining the same ID in successive frames.

Since the fixed test area was instrumented to capture ground-truth data, all detections were excluded if they occurred outside the test area. The correspondence algorithm found the correspondence between the detections and the ground-truth based on location and time stamp. Detections were compared with all the ground-truth objects on the course to attain the desired metrics [2].

**Table 5. Example Data Collection Methods from various Collection Perspectives and Modes**

| COLLECTION PERSPECTIVE | DATA COLLECTION METHODS: Examples | |
| --- | --- | --- |
| | MEANS - AUTOMATED | MEANS - MANUAL |
| From the Technology | Sensor and/or tool collecting technical information during the evaluation | Evaluator capturing data with sensors, tools |
| | Output of log files following the evaluation | Evaluator making notes of behavior |
| From the *Tech User* | Sensors (e.g. helmet camera) attached to the *Tech User* that collect data during testing | Surveys prior to and/or following the evaluation(s) |
| | | Interviews prior to and/or following the evaluation |
| | | Verbal and/or physical feedback provided by the *Tech User* during the evaluation (e.g. thumbs-up or thumbs-down at key way points) |
| From the *Team Member* | Sensors (e.g. microphone) attached to the *Team Member* that collect data during testing | Surveys prior to and/or following the evaluation(s) |
| | | Interviews prior to and/or following the evaluation |
| | | Verbal and/or physical feedback provided by the *Tech User* during the evaluation (e.g. thumbs-up or thumbs-down at key way points) |
| From the *Participant* | NONE (usually) | Surveys prior to and/or following the evaluation(s) |
| | | Interviews prior to and/or following the evaluation |
| From the Environment | Sensors (e.g. radar gun, thermal camera, motion detector) setup throughout the environment that collect data during testing | Evaluation personnel stationed in various parts of the environment taking notes and/or manually using a sensor and/or tool to collect data |

### 3.4.4 Personnel – Evaluators

There are three classes of evaluation personnel that are necessary to ensure that the evaluation proceeds accordingly to plan and that the necessary data is captured to evaluate a technology's performance. They fall into the three classes below:

- *Evaluators: Data Collectors* – These *Evaluators* are responsible for either setting up/implementing automated collection methods and/or performing manual collection methods. This class of *Evaluators* is also responsible for collecting experimental data directly from the technology at the conclusion of each test scenario (as necessary).
- *Evaluators: Test Executors* – These *Evaluators* are responsible for initiating the test including instructing *Participants* on when to engage in their specified activities within the environment.
- *Evaluators: Safety Officers* – These *Evaluators* are solely responsible for ensuring the safety of all personnel within the *Test Environment* along with protecting the technology and the environment, itself.

Depending upon the nature of the technology being evaluated and the range of *Data Collection Methods* employed, it's possible that some *Data Collectors* may also be *Test Executors* and vice versa. Although safety is everyone's responsibility on a test site, including *Data Collectors* and *Test Executors*, *Safety Officers* have no other role other than ensuring a safe test. The exact responsibilities and number of each of these personnel is heavily dependent upon the size and scope of the evaluation.

The ARL CTA/NIST testing featured both *Data Collectors* and *Test Executors* facilitating the test exercises. Specifically, the

*Data Collectors* included personnel responsible for deploying and calibrating the UWB tracking system and cameras prior to the test event. These same personnel were also responsible for managing the UWB tracking system and cameras during test to ensure it was operating within normal limits. Numerous *Test Executors* also played a significant role in the evaluation. This personnel class included one individual who signaled the start and conclusion and another individual that signaled the *Participants* to walk in their prescribed paths. Additionally, another *Test Executor* was employed to signal when the vehicle should begin its motion and when the sensors and algorithms under test should be engaged. This test exercise featured numerous *Safety Officers* stationed throughout the environment. Additionally, several *Safety Officers* were positioned at key locations along the test environment's perimeter to prevent non-evaluation personnel or vehicles from entering.

## 4. CONCLUSION

The MRED model's new blueprint elements have shown they can be applied to a current technology through test plan matching with the ARL CTA test plans. This has already highlighted some areas to address in this continuing work. The next steps for the MRED model are to identify the remaining evaluation blueprint pieces and continue to validate its design against a technology whose own tests were inspired by other successful methods, such as the SCORE framework. Once the entire blueprint has been specified, the three input categories will be addressed in detail. Since each input is nondeterministic in nature (based upon human preference, an unknown technology state, or uncertain resource availability), uncertainty will be factored. The inner workings of the framework will then be outlined and devised, first assuming certain inputs, and then uncertain data.

With MRED leveraging some of the success of a previous evaluation framework, MRED presents expanded capabilities in the detailed evaluation blueprints it prescribes along with the defined relationships among them. It is envisioned that MRED will be an invaluable tool in devising comprehensive technology test plans of emerging and advanced intelligent systems allowing evaluation designers to be more effective and efficient in producing and implementing the appropriate tests.

# 5. ACKNOWLEDGMENTS

The authors would like to thank Harry Scott, the NIST project leader for the ARL CTA testing effort, for his continued support throughout this work. Further, the lead author would like to thank Craig Schlenoff of NIST for his support and encouragement in this effort.

# 6. REFERENCES

[1] Albus, J.S., Barbera, A.J., Scott, H.A., Balakirsky, S.B., 2006, "Collaborative Tactical Behaviors for Autonomous Ground and Air Vehicles," *Proc. of the Unmanned Ground Vehicle Technology VII – SPIE Conference*, **5804**, pp. 244-254.

[2] Bodt, B., Camden, R., Scott, H., Jacoff, A.S., Hong, T., Chang, T., Norcross, R., Downs, T., Virts, A., 2009, "Performance Measurements for Evaluating Static and Dynamic Multiple Human Detection and Tracking Systems in Unstructured Environments," *Proc. of the 2009 Performance Metrics for Intelligent Systems (PerMIS) Workshop.*

[3] Calisi, D., Iocchi, L., and Nardi, D., 2008, "A Unified Benchmark Framework for Autonomous Mobile Robots and Vehicles Motion Algorithms (MoVeMA benchmarks)," In *Workshop on Experimental Methodology and Benchmarking in Robotics* Research (RSS 2008).

[4] Fontana, R., Richley, E. and Barney, J., 2003, "Commercialization of an Ultra Wideband Precision Asset Location System," In *2003 IEEE Conference on Ultra Wideband Systems and Technologies.*

[5] Galvin, C., 2010, "Gulf Oil Spill: Responding with Robots," *Robotics Trends.* DOI = http://www.roboticstrends.com/service_robotics/article/gulf_oil_spill_responding_with_robots

[6] Jacoff, A.S., and Messina, E., 2007, "Urban Search and Rescue Robot Performance Standards: Progress Updated," *Proc. of the Unmanned Systems Technology IX – SPIE Conference*, G.R. Gerhart et al., eds., **6561**, pp. 65611L..

[7] Messina, E., 2009, "Robots to the Rescue," *Crisis Response Journal*, **5**(3), pp. 42-43.

[8] Schlenoff, C.I., Steves, M.P., Weiss, B.A., Shneier, M.O., and Virts, A.M., 2007, "Applying SCORE to Field-Based Performance Evaluations of Soldier-Worn Sensor Technologies," *Journal of Field Robotics – Special Issue on Quantitative Performance Evaluation of Robotic and Intelligent Systems*, **24**, pp. 671-698.

[9] Schlenoff, C.I., Weiss, B.A., Steves, M.P., Sanders, G., Proctor, F., and Virts, A.M., 2009, "Evaluating Speech Translation Systems: Applying SCORE to TRANSTAC Technologies," *Proc. of the Performance Metrics for Intelligent Systems (PerMIS) Workshop.*

[10] Schlenoff, C.I., Weiss, B.A., Steves, M.P., Virts, A.M., and Shneier, M.O., 2006, "Overview of the First Advanced Technology Evaluations for ASSIST," *Proc. of the Performance Metrics for Intelligent Systems (PerMIS) Workshop.*

[11] Scholtz, J.C., Antonishek, B., and Young, J.D., 2004, "Evaluation of Human-Robot Interaction in the NIST Reference Search and Rescue Test Arenas," *Proc. of the 2004 Performance Metrics for Intelligent Systems (PerMIS) Workshop.*

[12] Scholtz, J.C., Theofanos, M.F., and Antonishek, B., 2006, "Development of a Test Bed for Evaluating Human-Robot Performance for Explosive Ordnance Disposal Robots," *Proc. Of the 1st Annual Conference on Human-Robot Interaction.*

[13] Scrapper, C.J., Madhavan, R., Balakirsky, S.B., 2008, "Performance Analysis for Stable Mobile Robot Navigation Solutions," *Proc. of the Unmanned Systems Technology X – SPIE Conference*, **6962**(6), pp. 1-12.

[14] Steves, M.P., 2007, "Utility Assessments of Soldier-Worn Sensor Systems for ASSIST," *Proc. of the 2006 Performance Metrics for Intelligent Systems (PerMIS) Workshop.*

[15] Sukhatme, G.S. and Bekey, G.A., 1995, "An Evaluation Methodology for Autonomous Mobile Robots for Planetary Exploration," *Proc. of the First ECPD International Conference on Advanced Robotics and Intelligent Automation*, pp. 558-563.

[16] Weiss, B.A. and Schlenoff, C.S., 2008, "Evolution of the SCORE Framework to Enhance Field-Based Performance Evaluations of Emerging Technologies," *Proc. of the 2008 Performance Metrics for Intelligent Systems (PerMIS) Workshop*, pp. 1-8.

[17] Weiss, B.A., and Schlenoff, C.I., 2009, "The Impact of Scenario Development on the Performance of Speech Translation Systems Prescribed by the SCORE Framework," *Proc. of the Performance Metrics for Intelligent Systems (PerMIS) Workshop.*

[18] Weiss, B.A., Schmidt, L.C., Scott, H.A., and Schlenoff, C.I., 2010, "The Multi-Relationship Evaluation Design Framework: Designing Testing Plans to Comprehensively Assess Advanced and Intelligent Technologies," *Proc. of the ASME 2010 International Design Engineering Technical Conferences (IDETC) – 22nd International Conference on Design Theory and Methodology (DTM).*

[19] Weiss, B.A., Schlenoff, C.I., Sanders, G.A., Steves, M.P., Condon, S., Phillips, J., and Parvaz, D., 2008, "Performance Evaluation of Speech Translation Systems," *Proc. of the 6th edition of the Language Resources and Evaluation Conference.*

[20] Weiss, B.A., Schlenoff, C.I., Shneier, M.O. , and Virts, A.M., 2006, "Technology Evaluations and Performance Metrics for Soldier-Worn Sensors for ASSIST," *Proc. of the 2006 Performance Metrics for Intelligent Systems (PerMIS)Workshop.*

# Implementation and Application of Maximum Likelihood Reliability Estimation from Subsystem and Full System Tests

Coire J. Maranzano
The Johns Hopkins University
Applied Physics Laboratory
11100 Johns Hopkins Rd
Laurel, Maryland, 20723-6099, USA
coire.maranzano@jhuapl.edu

James C. Spall
The Johns Hopkins University
Applied Physics Laboratory
11100 Johns Hopkins Rd
Laurel, Maryland, 20723-6099, USA
james.spall@jhuapl.edu

## ABSTRACT

This paper provides an overview and examples of a novel and practical method for estimating the reliability of a complex system, with confidence regions, based on a combination of full system and subsystem (and/or component or other) tests. It is assumed that the system is composed of multiple processes, where the subsystems may be arranged in series, parallel, combination series/parallel, or other mode. Maximum likelihood estimation (MLE) is used to estimate the overall system reliability based on the fusion of system and subsystem test data. The method is illustrated on two real-world systems: an aircraft-missile system and a highly reliable low-pressure coolant injection system in a commercial nuclear-power reactor. The examples are used to demonstrate the following properties of the method. One, increasing the number of full system tests improves the confidence in the full system reliability estimate. Two, increasing the number of tests of one subsystem stabilizes the subsystem reliability estimate. Three, the likelihood function and optimization constraints can readily be modified to handle systems consisting of repeated components in a mixed series/parallel configuration. Four, the asymptotic normal assumption for computing confidence intervals is not always appropriate, especially for highly reliable systems. Five, performing a mixture of full system and subsystem tests is important when the model that relates the subsystem reliability to the full system reliability is uncertain.

## Categories and Subject Descriptors

G.3 [**Probability and Statistics**]; J.2 [**Physical sciences and engineering**]

## Keywords

Test and Evaluation, Performance Evaluation, Series and Non-Series Systems, Reliability Metric, Maximum Likelihood Estimation

## 1. INTRODUCTION

System, subsystem, component, interface, and other[1] tests are often carried out on complex systems to ensure that an operational reliability requirement is satisfied. Fusing full system and subsystem test data to evaluate the reliability of a complex systems is desirable when full system testing can be very costly, dangerous or requires the destruction of the system itself. Additionally, it is desirable to include full system testing in an overall reliability assessment to help guard against possible mis-modeling of the relationship between the subsystems and full system in calculating overall system reliability. One method of fusing full system and subsystem reliability test data to form a full system estimate of reliability is the method of maximum likelihood [8]. This general maximum likelihood formulation for the fusion of reliability test data applies across all system configurations (series, parallel, etc); only the optimization constraints change, leading to an appropriate maximum likelihood estimate (MLE). The method of maximum likelihood provides a characterization of the estimation uncertainty—statistical uncertainty about the model parameters—through the Fisher Information on the parameters of the system reliability model.

The general maximum likelihood method of reliability estimation combines data from subsystem tests and full system tests via a model that reflects the constraints associated with the operation of the full system. If the reliability of the system must be known within a specified confidence interval or if the test plan is limited by cost, there exists an inherent trade off between performing full system tests or subsystem tests. However, the model is often subject to error, leading to an inaccurate system reliability estimate when subsystem tests alone are performed. Performing full system tests guards against error in the system reliability estimate due to an imperfect model. The general method is extended in [4] to include a robust test planning capability to simultaneously minimize estimation uncertainty and the effect of

---

[1]To avoid the need to repeatedly refer to tests on subsystems, components, processes, and other aspects of the system as the key source of information other than full system tests, we will usually only refer to subsystem tests; subsystem tests in this context should be considered a proxy for all possible test information short of full system tests.

modeling error on the full system reliability estimate for a series system. The capability enables a planner to determine the optimal number of system and subsystem tests to include in an experiment.

This paper provides an overview and examples of a novel and practical method for estimating the reliability of a complex system, with confidence regions, based on a combination of full system and subsystem tests. It is assumed that the system is composed of multiple processes, where the subsystems may be arranged in series, parallel (i.e., redundant), combination series/parallel, or other mode. The general MLE method of [8] is used to estimate the overall system reliability. The MLE approach provides asymptotic or finite-sample confidence bounds through the use of Fisher information or Monte Carlo sampling (bootstrap). The examples below also demonstrate the need for developing a robust test plan that includes a mixture of full system and subsystem tests to reduce the influence of model error on the system reliability estimate and minimize testing costs.

The method is illustrated on three systems. First, a hypothetical system is used to demonstrate the value of combining full system and subsystem test data for reducing the uncertainty in the full system reliability estimate even with model error. Second, the MLE method is used to form estimates of system and subsystem reliability on the series aircraft-missile system described in [6]. The example demonstrates that increasing the number of full system tests improves the confidence in the full system reliability estimate and that increasing the sample size of one of the subsystems stabilizes the subsystem reliability estimate but only slightly improves confidence in the full system reliability estimate. The asymptotic and Monte Carlo (bootstrap) confidence intervals are computed and compared. The system reliability MLE and 90% confidence interval is also compared with the Bayesian posterior distribution on the system reliability computed in [6]. The comparison shows that prior information significantly influences the full system reliability estimate. Also, prior information on the subsystem reliabilities is used to determine a minimum cost test program for achieving a specified mean square error (MSE) given that the system reliability model is in error. Third, the MLE method is used to form estimates of system and subsystem reliability on a highly reliable low-pressure coolant injection system in a commercial nuclear-power reactor described in [5]. The example shows that likelihood function and optimization constraints can readily be modified to handle systems consisting of repeated components in a mixed series/parallel configuration. Through the presentation of the empirical distribution of the bootstrap sample used to determine the confidence interval, the example also shows that the asymptotic normal assumption for computing confidence intervals is not always appropriate, especially for highly reliable systems.

# 2. MLE APPROACH

## 2.1 Background

Consider a system composed of $p$ subsystems. The general estimation formulation involves a parameter vector $\boldsymbol{\theta}$, representing the parameters to be estimated. Let $\rho$ and $\rho_j$ represent the reliabilities (success probabilities) for the full system and for subsystem $j$, respectively, $j = 1, 2, \ldots, p$. The vector $\boldsymbol{\theta} = [\rho_1, \rho_2, \ldots, \rho_p]^T$. Let $\boldsymbol{\Theta}$ represent the feasible region for the elements of $\boldsymbol{\theta}$. To ensure that relevant

logarithms are defined and that the appropriate derivatives exist, it is assumed, at a minimum, that the feasible region $\boldsymbol{\Theta}$ includes the restriction that $0 < \rho_j < 1$ for all $j$. The system reliability $\rho$ is not included in $\boldsymbol{\theta}$ because it is uniquely determined (or bounded) by the subsystem reliabilities $\rho_j$ for $j = 1, 2, \ldots, p$ and possibly other information via relevant constraints. Herein, the relation is restricted such that $\rho$ is uniquely determined by a function $h(\boldsymbol{\theta})$. The mapping, $h$, between $\boldsymbol{\theta}$ and $\rho$ dictates the arrangement of the system, which may be configured in series ($\rho = h(\boldsymbol{\theta}) = \prod_{i=1}^{p} \rho_i$), parallel ($\rho = h(\boldsymbol{\theta}) = 1 - \prod_{i=1}^{p}(1 - \rho_i)$), combination series/parallel, or some other configuration, and it is analogous to a *model* of system reliability in terms of its subsystems. To mirror the lexicon commonly used in the literature, $h$ will be referred to as the model for the system reliability. Thus, an estimate of the system reliability $\hat{\rho}$ is found by evaluating $h(\cdot)$ at the estimate $\hat{\boldsymbol{\theta}}$.

Further consider the test data on the system and its subsystems. Let $Y$ be the number of successes in $n$ independent identically distributed (i.i.d.) tests of the system, and let $X_j$ be the number of successes in $n_j$ i.i.d. tests of the $j^{th}$ subsystem, for $j = 1, \ldots, p$. And, let $\hat{\boldsymbol{\theta}} = \hat{\boldsymbol{\theta}}(\boldsymbol{Z})$ be a function that produces an estimate of $\boldsymbol{\theta}$, where $\boldsymbol{Z}$ is the set of test data on the full system and its subsystems $\{Y, X_1, \ldots, X_p\}$.

## 2.2 MLE Formulation

Consider the following general maximum likelihood estimator of the parameter vector $\boldsymbol{\theta}$,

$$\hat{\boldsymbol{\theta}} = \hat{\boldsymbol{\theta}}(\boldsymbol{Z}) \equiv \arg\max_{\boldsymbol{\theta} \in \boldsymbol{\Theta}} \mathfrak{L}(\boldsymbol{\theta})$$

$$\text{subject to } \rho = h(\boldsymbol{\theta}), \quad (1)$$

where $\mathfrak{L}(\boldsymbol{\theta}) \equiv \log(p(\boldsymbol{Z}|\boldsymbol{\theta}, \rho))$, [8]. Given both system and subsystem test data, $\boldsymbol{Z}$, the estimate of $\rho$ is derived from the MLE for $\boldsymbol{\theta}$ through the model for the system, $h$. The model dictates how the subsystems are arranged in the full system ($\mathfrak{L}(\boldsymbol{\theta})$ is the same regardless of whether, the subsystems are in series or parallel). For a given parameter vector $\boldsymbol{\theta}$, the definition of $\mathfrak{L}(\boldsymbol{\theta})$ does *not* depend on the model for the system. However, the MLE does change as a function of the model for the system. This is a consequence of the system model being used as a constraint in the optimization problem that is solved to produce the MLE. Given that the test data are independent, the probability mass function is:

$$p(\boldsymbol{Z}|\boldsymbol{\theta}, \rho) = \underbrace{\binom{n}{Y} \rho^Y (1 - \rho)^{(n-Y)}}_{\text{system}}$$

$$\times \underbrace{\binom{n_1}{X_1} \rho_1^{X_1} (1 - \rho_1)^{(n_1 - X_1)} \cdots \binom{n_p}{X_p} \rho_p^{X_p} (1 - \rho_p)^{(n_p - X_p)}}_{p \text{ subsystems}},$$

$$(2)$$

leading to the log-likelihood function:

$$\mathfrak{L}(\boldsymbol{\theta}) = Y \log \rho + (n - Y) \log(1 - \rho) +$$

$$\sum_{j=1}^{p} [X_j \log \rho_j + (n_j - X_j) \log(1 - \rho_j)] + \text{constant}, \quad (3)$$

where the constant does not dependent on $\boldsymbol{\theta}$. The MLE is determined by finding a root of the score equation $\partial \mathfrak{L}(\boldsymbol{\theta})/\partial \boldsymbol{\theta} =$

**0.** The solution to $\partial \mathcal{L}(\boldsymbol{\theta})/\partial \theta = \mathbf{0}$ must generally be found by numerical search methods.

## 2.3 Theoretical Properties

Except in trivial cases, the analytic expression for the variance of the general MLE for system reliability is not easily found. However, [8] showed that the Fisher Information, $\boldsymbol{F}(\boldsymbol{\theta})$, is easily obtained for the general maximum likelihood estimator of the parameter vector $\boldsymbol{\theta}$. Further, [9] showed that the general MLE of system and subsystem reliability has a strong (a.s.) convergence property and that the rate of convergence for the system reliability estimate to the true reliability $\rho^*$ is

$$O\left( \sqrt{\frac{\log\log (n + n_s)}{n + n_s}} \right), \qquad (4)$$

where $s$ is the index of the slowest increasing subsystem sample size. Invoking the Cramer-Rao inequality, the inverse of the Fisher information is a lower bound on the variance of the MLE (for an unbiased estimator). Although, proof of asymptotic normality has not yet been formally established for the general MLE described in Section 2.2, standard results in MLE, [3], show that the estimate is asymptotically normal. Therefore, the variance of the general MLE, $\hat{\boldsymbol{\theta}}$, is approximated with the inverse Fisher Information and the variance of the general MLE of the full system reliability, $\hat{\rho}$, is approximated by

$$h'(\boldsymbol{\theta})^T \boldsymbol{F}(\boldsymbol{\theta})^{-1} h'(\boldsymbol{\theta}). \qquad (5)$$

Aside from being used to form approximate confidence regions for the MLE when the sample size is sufficiently large, the Fisher information is helpful in determining when the estimation problem in Section 2.2 is well posed (i.e., when $\rho$ and/or $\boldsymbol{\theta}$ is identifiable) through an evaluation of the conditions ensuring that the information matrix is positive definite (e.g., [2], pp. 104 and 139; [10]; and [1]). Further, the Fisher information matrix is used in determining the optimal combination of subsystem and full system tests for estimating reliability when performing test design [4].

## 2.4 Confidence Bounds

There are two general methods for constructing confidence bounds for the estimate $\hat{\rho}$, a large-sample approach based on an asymptotic normal distribution (and accompanying inverse Fisher information matrix for variance calculation) and a finite-sample approach based on Monte Carlo (bootstrap sampling) methods. The discussion below is a summary of key aspects of both of these general methods.

For the large-sample approach, the asymptotic distribution provides an approximate probability distribution for $\hat{\rho}$ for use in finite-sample (practical) analysis. Herein, the inverse average information matrix for $\boldsymbol{\theta}$ (or information number for $\rho$) is used as the covariance matrix (or variance) appearing in the asymptotic distribution of the appropriately normalized MLE (see Section 2.3).

There are, however, potential problems in the use of the asymptotic approach in practical reliability settings. The problem is especially acute when sample sizes are too small to justify the asymptotic normality and/or when confidence intervals from the asymptotic normality fall outside of the interval $[0, 1]$ as a consequence of the need to approximate the true asymmetric distribution with the symmetric normal

distribution. The latter factor is exacerbated by the fact that practical reliability estimates are often very near unity. Therefore, we provide a summary of a bootstrap (Monte Carlo)-based method below. Bootstrap methods are well-known Monte Carlo procedures for approximating important statistical quantities of interest when analytical methods are infeasible (e.g., Efron and Tibshirani, 1986; Ljung, 1999, pp. 304 and 334; and Aronsson et al., 2006). The bootstrap-based method for constructing confidence intervals for the full system reliability estimate $\hat{\rho}$ relies on the assumption that $\hat{\rho}$ is uniquely determined from $\hat{\boldsymbol{\theta}}$. Ref. [8] presented sufficient conditions for such a function via the implicit function theorem.

The steps below describe a parametric bootstrap approach to constructing confidence intervals for $\hat{\rho}$. Parametric bootstrap methods rely on many Monte Carlo samples from the distribution associated with the likelihood function, where the unknown parameters in the distribution are replaced by their estimated values (in contrast, a standard bootstrap method uses Monte Carlo samples from the raw data, typically from a histogram of the raw data). The bootstrap approach performance is compared with the asymptotic approach in example 2 below (see Section 4).

*Bootstrap Method for Computing Confidence Intervals for $\hat{\rho}$:*

**Step 0:** Treat the MLE $\hat{\boldsymbol{\theta}}$, and associated $\hat{\rho} = h(\hat{\boldsymbol{\theta}})$, as the true value of $\boldsymbol{\theta}$ and $\rho$.

**Step 1:** Generate (by Monte Carlo) a set of bootstrap data of the same collective sample size $\{n, n_1, n_2, ..., n_p\}$ as the real data $\boldsymbol{Z}$ using the assumed probability mass function in (2) and the value of $\boldsymbol{\theta}$ and $\rho$ from Step 0.

**Step 2:** Calculate the MLE of $\boldsymbol{\theta}$, say $\hat{\boldsymbol{\theta}}_{\text{boot}}$, from the bootstrap data $\boldsymbol{Z}$ in Step 1, and then calculate the corresponding full system reliability MLE, $\hat{\rho}_{\text{boot}}$.

**Step 3:** Repeat Steps 1 and 2 a large number of times (perhaps 1000) and rank order the resulting values; one- or two-sided confidence intervals are available by determining the appropriate quantiles from the ranked sample of $\hat{\rho}_{\text{boot}}$ values.

## 2.5 Estimator Uncertainty with Model Error

The system reliability model, $h$, is a function that relates the subsystem reliabilities to the system reliability based on the layout of the subsystems. As $h$ is a mathematical representation of the true relation among reliabilities, it is imperfect. For example, a subsystem may be neglected and not included in the model, or two subsystems assumed to be stochastically independent in the model may have a subtle dependence. An imperfect mathematical model results in a true system reliability that is *not* uniquely determined by the model for the system, $h(\cdot)$. Ref. [4] develops a method for test planning that minimizes MSE of the MLE using a local design for a series system assuming that the system reliability is uniquely determined from the subsystem reliability and the model error $\beta(\boldsymbol{\theta})$; that is,

$$\rho = h(\boldsymbol{\theta}) - \beta(\boldsymbol{\theta}). \qquad (6)$$

where, in general, $-\rho \le \beta(\boldsymbol{\theta}) \le (1 - \rho)$ to ensure $0 \le \rho \le 1$ (the model error subtracted from $h$ as it is desirable to avoid overestimating the system reliability). The expression for the MSE is formed to explicitly include a contribution from the modeling error. The result is summarized next for completeness.

Given the relation in (6), the estimator of system reliability, $\hat{\rho} = h(\hat{\boldsymbol{\theta}})$ no longer satisfies the conditions for a.s. convergence to $\rho^*$ as described in [9], and the optimal test plan depends on $\boldsymbol{\theta}, h,$ and $\beta$. However, a test planner does *not* know $\boldsymbol{\theta}$ or $\beta$ before testing the system (and determining $\beta$ may be intractable). To cope with the optimal test plan's dependence on $\boldsymbol{\theta}$, test planners assume a nominal value of $\boldsymbol{\theta}$ and develop an optimal test plan based on this fixed value. For a fixed value of $\boldsymbol{\theta}$, the function $\beta$ becomes a constant, and only a single value of the model error needs to be determined. Hence, to cope with the optimal test plan's dependence on $\beta$, test planners can also assume a maximum value for the model error, $\tilde{\beta} = \max \beta(\boldsymbol{\theta})$, and develop a test plan based on the fixed maximum value. Using this approach, a test planner can avoid explicitly determining the function $\beta(\boldsymbol{\theta})$ (analogous to a *local design*, see [7], Sect. 17.4) and develop a test plan so that the estimate of system reliability is robust to modeling errors.

The MLE of $\boldsymbol{\theta}$ with a fixed model error, $\tilde{\beta} = \max \beta(\boldsymbol{\theta})$, is assessed by modifying the constraint in (1) such that it is $\rho = h_{\tilde{\beta}}(\boldsymbol{\theta}, \tilde{\beta}) \equiv h(\boldsymbol{\theta}) - \tilde{\beta}$. The addition of the modeling error to the constraint does *not* change the log likelihood function of the general MLE. However, the relationship between $\rho$ and the $\rho_j$ differs, and so, the MLE of $\boldsymbol{\theta}$ differs from what it would be if there were no modeling error. The MSE of the general maximum likelihood estimator is composed of the asymptotic variance of the estimate from (5) and the approximate expected bias of the estimate. The expression for the MSE is,

$$E\left[(h(\boldsymbol{\theta}) - \rho)^2\right] \approx h'(\boldsymbol{\theta})^T \boldsymbol{F}(\boldsymbol{\theta})^{-1} h'(\boldsymbol{\theta}) + E\left[\hat{\rho}_{\tilde{\beta}} - \hat{\rho}\right]^2. \quad (7)$$

The expression for the expectation of the quantity $|\hat{\rho}_{\tilde{\beta}} - \hat{\rho}|$ is,

$$E\left[\hat{\rho}_{\tilde{\beta}} - \hat{\rho}\right] \approx \tilde{\beta} \left. \frac{\partial h_{\tilde{\beta}}}{\partial \boldsymbol{\theta}} \right|_{E[\hat{\boldsymbol{\theta}}]} (\boldsymbol{F}(\boldsymbol{\theta}))^{-1} E\left[\frac{g_{\text{MLE}}(\boldsymbol{\theta}, \tilde{\beta})}{\partial \tilde{\beta}}\right]_{\tilde{\beta}=0} - \tilde{\beta}, \quad (8)$$

where the function $g_{\text{MLE}}(\boldsymbol{\theta}, \tilde{\beta})$ is the value of the score function , where the function $h$ is replaced with $h_{\tilde{\beta}}$. Note that that for implementing a local design, $\boldsymbol{\theta}$ and $E[\hat{\boldsymbol{\theta}}]$ are replaced with a nominal estimate of the parameter vector. Eqn. (8) is an approximation for the bias in the MLE, for a specific test plan $n, n_1, \ldots n_p$, given $h$, a nominal estimate of $\boldsymbol{\theta}$, and the maximum model error, $\tilde{\beta}$. When *only* full system tests are planned, model error does not contribute any bias to the full system reliability MLE. When full system tests are *not* planned, $E\left[\hat{\rho}_{\tilde{\beta}} - \hat{\rho}\right] = \tilde{\beta}$ and $\tilde{\beta}^2$ is the bias squared term of the MSE for the MLE.

# 3. EXAMPLE 1: UNCERTAINTY REDUCTION FROM COMBINING TEST DATA

For an asymptoticly efficient MLE, increasing the estimation sample size reduces the asymptotic uncertainty (increases the statistical information) about the variate being estimated. Herein, an example is designed to demonstrate that the general MLE method described in Section 2.2 and [8], decreases the asymptotic uncertainty about the system

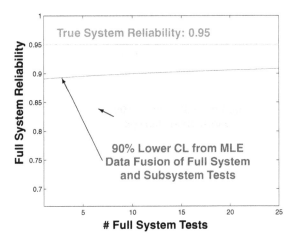

Figure 1: The 90% asymptotic lower confidence limits (CLs) about the true reliability of a hypothetical series system.

reliability estimate when subsystem reliability test data is added to full system reliability test data. A variation on this example demonstrates that the benefit, in terms of decreased full system reliability estimate uncertainty, can still be realized if there is error in the model that relates the subsystem reliabilities to the full system reliability.

Consider a system with four independent subsystems in series. Assume that each subsystem is tested 22 times. Further assume that the true reliability of each subsystem is 0.987. This implies a full system reliability $0.987^4 = 0.95$.

The system reliability and and the asymptotic 90% lower confidence limit about the true system reliability are plotted as a function of the number of full system tests in Figure 1. The lower confidence limit is computed using two different samples of data. First, the lower confidence limit is computed using only full system test data. Second, the lower confidence limit is computed using full system test data and all available subsystem test data (22 tests for each subsystem). As expected, the lower confidence limit computed from full system test data alone is below the lower confidence limit from the combined full system and subsystem data samples. This indicates that the estimation uncertainty about the full system reliability estimate is decreased by adding the available subsystem test data to the full system test data. Also, the difference between the two confidence intervals depicted in Figure 1 is greatest when the number of full system tests is small. Thus, in this example, the greatest potential for decreasing the estimation uncertainty exists when adding the subsystem test data to a few tests of the full system. The example also illustrates that by combining the system and subsystem test data via MLE, test planners require fewer full system tests to meet evaluation objectives in terms of statistical confidence.

As discussed in Section 2.5, the model that relates the subsystem reliabilities to the system reliability may be in error. Because the subsystem test data are combined with full system test data that is not subject to model error, the addition of a deterministic model error to the model does not uniformly increase the uncertainty in the full system reliability estimate as the number of full system tests is increased. To illustrate this property, the 90% lower confidence limit

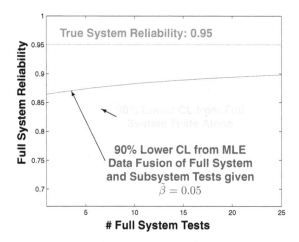

True System Reliability: 0.95

90% Lower CL from Full System Tests Alone

90% Lower CL from MLE Data Fusion of Full System and Subsystem Tests given $\tilde{\beta} = 0.05$

**Figure 2: A 90% lower confidence limits (CLs) about the true reliability of a hypothetical series system given a maximum model error $\tilde{\beta} = 0.05$.**

about the true system reliability is modified. Specifically, the asymptotic variance use in the confidence bound computation is replaced with the MSE, computed via (7) with a maximum model error of $\tilde{\beta} = 0.05$. The resulting bound is plotted in Figure 2, and represents the uncertainty in the full system reliability estimate assuming a maximum model error of $\tilde{\beta} = 0.05$. The resulting bound is not a simple translation of the bound in Figure 1. In addition, the figure shows that, even under assumption of modest model error, there is advantage, in terms of reducing the estimate uncertainty, to fuzing the subsystem and full system reliability test data using the MLE method, especially when there are few full system tests avalible.

## 4. EXAMPLE 2: AIRCRAFT-MISSILE SERIES SYSTEM

The second example consists of three parts. First, the MLE method described in Section 2.2 and [8] is applied to test data from a certain series air-to-air heat seeking missile system described in [6]. Second, the test data from [6] are modified to illustrate the effect on the MLE of increasing system and subsystem sample sizes. Third, the prior information from [6] is used as the basis for designing a hypotheical robust test program for the example system using the method described in Section 2.5 and [4]. Herein, comparisons are drawn between the reliability estimates from the general MLE method and the naive maximum likelihood system and subsystem reliability estimator of the form (# Successes/Total # Tests). To avoid confusion, these estimates of the individual subsystems or full system are referred to as ratio estimates.

### 4.1 Aircraft-Missile System Reliability

For simplicity, the aircraft-missile system example in [6] is restricted to the aircraft and aircraft-to-missile interface, which consists of nine subsystems in series (the subsystems are listed in Table 1). The binomial test data and ratio estimates for the aircraft system and its subsystems are listed in Table 1. The product of the subsystem ratio estimates is 0.954, which is larger than the full system ratio estimate.

The aircraft system and subsystem MLEs are also listed in Table 1. The subsystem MLEs are slightly smaller than the ratio estimates and the aircraft system MLE is larger than the system level ratio estimate. The MLEs represent a compromise between the ratio estimates from subsystem and system test data. The MLEs reflect increased information about the subsystem and system reliability as a result of fuzing the test data; the degree of change in the estimates depends on the statistical information in the data samples used for estimation (represented by the Fisher Information, see Section 2.3).

The two-sided 90% confidence interval on the aircraft system reliability is computed using the large sample approach (the inverse Fisher Information is used as the asymptotic variance) and using the bootstrap method described in Section 2.4. The asymptotic 90% confidence interval on the MLE of system reliability is (0.921, 0,962), and the 90% bootstrap confidence interval from 500 Monte Carlo trials is (0.920, 0.961). In this case, the two confidence intervals are very similar. The MLE of aircraft system reliability and 90% confidence interval are much different from the aircraft system reliability estimate and 90% credible interval derived from the posterior distribution presented in [6]. The posterior mean and 90% credible interval derived from the posterior distribution are 0.927, (0.925, 0.928). The Bayesian aircraft system reliability estimate is significantly less than the MLE and ratio estimate because the Bayesian reliability estimate is heavily influenced by the prior distributions selected for the subsystem and system reliabilities (prior means are listed in Table 4). The total number of prior parameters needed to form the Bayesian estimate is 20. The Bayesian estimate also provides a 90% credible interval on the system reliability estimate that is much smaller than the 90% confidence interval provided by the MLE approach because the additional prior information narrows the distribution about the posterior mean (reduces the estimate uncertainty).

### 4.2 MLE Estimate Sensitivity to Sample Size

The aircraft-mssile system example described above is modified to illustrate the effect of (i) increased full system testing and (ii) increased subsystem testing on the MLEs of system and subsystem reliability.

To demonstrate the MLEs sensitivity to full system testing, the number of full system tests is increased to 1000 and the total number of successful tests is increased such that the system reliability ratio estimate remains 0.932 (the same as in the original example). The resulting MLEs of the aircraft system and its subsystems are in Table 2 (four of nine subsystems shown to save space). The 90% confidence interval on the system estimate is (0.923, 0.947). The aircraft system MLE is much closer to the system reliability ratio estimate, it reflects the additional information from increased full system testing. The system reliability confidence interval width is significantly decreased from the original example (the confidence interval shrinks from 0.041 to 0.024 as the full system sample size increases from 205 to 1000) representing more certainty about the system reliability estimate. The additional information from increased system testing also decreases the MLEs of the subsystem reliabilities. They are smaller than the subsystem ratio estimates and MLE estimates in the original example (see Table 1).

To demonstrate the MLEs sensitivity to subsystem testing, the number of subsystem tests about the acquisition/fire

**Table 1: Subsystem and System Test Data and MLE Reliability Estimates for the Aircraft System**

| Subsystem | # of Tests* | # of Successes* | $\frac{\text{\# Successes}}{\text{\# Tests}}$ | MLE Estimate |
|---|---|---|---|---|
| 1. Flight Structure | 130 | 129 | 0.992 | 0.990 |
| 2. Avionics | 130 | 130 | 1.000 | 1.000 |
| 3. Power | 130 | 129 | 0.992 | 0.990 |
| 4. Flight Control | 130 | 129 | 0.992 | 0.990 |
| 5. Environmental | 130 | 130 | 1.000 | 1.000 |
| 6. Acquisition/Fire Control | 250 | 247 | 0.988 | 0.986 |
| 7. Launching | 130 | 129 | 0.992 | 0.990 |
| 8. Missile Interface | 250 | 249 | 0.996 | 0.995 |
| 9. Human Intervention | 130 | 130 | 1.000 | 1.000 |
| Aircraft System | 205 | 191 | 0.932 | 0.941 |

*Data are from [6].

**Table 2: Modified Subsystem and System Test Data and MLE Reliability Estimates for the Aircraft System Demonstrating the Effect of Increased System Testing**

| Subsystem (4 of 9 Shown) | # of Tests | # of Successes | $\frac{\text{\# Successes}}{\text{\# Tests}}$ | MLE Estimate |
|---|---|---|---|---|
| 1. Flight Structure | 130 | 129 | 0.992 | 0.988 |
| 2. Avionics | 130 | 130 | 1.000 | 1.000 |
| 4. Flight Control | 130 | 129 | 0.992 | 0.988 |
| 6. Acquisition/Fire Control | 250 | 247 | 0.988 | 0.985 |
| Aircraft System | **1000** | **932** | 0.932 | 0.935 |

control subsystem is increased to 1000 and the total number of successful tests is increased such that the subsystem reliability ratio estimate remains 0.988 (the same as in the original example). The resulting MLEs of the aircraft system and its subsystems are in Table 3 (four of nine subsystems shown to save space). The 90% confidence interval on the system estimate is (0.922, 0.962). The aircraft system MLE is slightly larger (but virtually unchanged) from the original example, it reflects the additional information from increased subsystem testing. The increased subsystem testing results in a very stable estimate of the acquisition/fire control subsystem. It is identical to the subsystem ratio estimate and the MLE derived 90% confidence interval about the acquisition/fire control subsystem is (0.982, 0.993) vs. (0.975, 1.004) for the flight structures subsystem. The MLE system reliability confidence interval width is virtually unchanged from the original example (it shrinks from 0.041 to 0.040 as the subsystem sample size increases from 205 to 1000) indicating that increasing the testing about one subsystem does not greatly improve confidence in the system reliability estimate. The subsystem MLEs are slightly increased to reflect the additional information about the acquisition/fire control subsystem (compare Tables 1 and 3).

## 4.3 Optimum Test Planning

In this section, the optimal combination of system and sets of subsystem tests[2], in terms total test plan cost, is determined for the aircraft series system using the methodology described in Section 2.5. Let the presumed reliabilities of the nine subsystems be equal to the prior means (see Table 4). These estimates represent the best knowledge, information,

---

[2]The robust test planning method of [4] is not restricted to optimizing the number of sets of subsystem tests for test sizing. The number of sets of subsystem tests are optimized herein to simplify the the presentation of the approach.

**Table 4: Initial Reliability Estimates for Aircraft Subsystems Derived from Subsystem Prior Distributions in [6]**

| Subsystem | Initial Reliability Estimate |
|---|---|
| 1. Flight Structure | 0.989 |
| 2. Avionics | 0.984 |
| 3. Power | 0.992 |
| 4. Flight Control | 0.989 |
| 5. Environmental | 0.994 |
| 6. Acquisition/Fire Control | 0.992 |
| 7. Launching | 0.996 |
| 8. Missile Interface | 0.996 |
| 9. Human Intervention | 0.971 |
| Aircraft System* | 0.907 |

*Product of subsystem reliabilities

and experience about the system before testing has begun. Among other reasons, model error may arise because some of the subsystems are dependent or because a component is left out of the subsystem definitions or test plan. The methodology described in Section 2.5 and [4] allows a test planner to assume that the system reliability model may be incorrect and supply a maximum model error, $\tilde{\beta}$. The model error contributes a bias to the MSE of the general maximum likelihood estimator based on the number of full system/subsystems tests planned. Loosely, full system tests contribute unbiased information to the general maximum likelihood estimator. Thus, as the number of full system tests increases relative to the number of sets of subsystem tests, the model error contributes less to the bias term of the MSE.

To achieve an MSE of 0.005 or less (root mean squared error 0.07 or less) many different test plans can be devised. Thus, the design of a test plan should also account for the cost of the tests. To illustrate the effect of cost on the test

Table 3: Modified Subsystem and System Test Data and MLE Reliability Estimates for the Aircraft System Demonstrating the Effect of Increased Subsystem Testing

| Subsystem (4 of 9 Shown) | # of Tests | # of Successes | # Successes / # Tests | MLE Estimate |
|---|---|---|---|---|
| 1. Flight Structure | 130 | 129 | 0.992 | 0.989 |
| 2. Avionics | 130 | 130 | 1.000 | 1.000 |
| 4. Flight Control | 130 | 129 | 0.992 | 0.989 |
| 6. Acquisition/Fire Control | **1000** | **988** | 0.988 | 0.988 |
| Aircraft System | 205 | 191 | 0.932 | 0.942 |

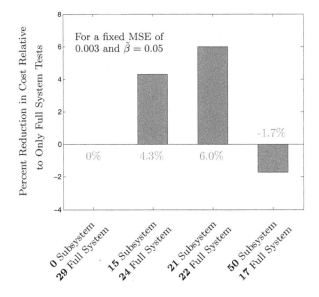

Figure 3: The potential cost reduction from performing a mixture of full system and subsystem tests instead of performing only full system tests; numerical values in the labels are the number of sets of subsystem tests and number of full system tests.

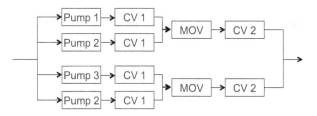

Figure 4: LPCI System Block Diagram from [5]: LCPI, Low Pressure Coolant Injection; MOV, Motor-Operated Valve; CV, Cheek Valve.

plan design, assume that a set of subsystem tests costs a fourth as much as a full system test. The cost benefit, relative to only performing full system tests, is depicted in Figure 3. Four test plans are listed, each having an a MSE of 0.005, given $\tilde{\beta} = 0.050$. The baseline test plan consists of performing only full system tests. The other three test plans consist of a mixture of full system and subsystem tests. The potential cost reduction from performing one of these three test plans instead of performing only full system tests is plotted as a percentage. For $\tilde{\beta} = 0.050$, the minimum cost test plan consists of 21 sets of subsystem tests and 22 full system tests. If several other test plans have the same total cost, then it is optimal to perform the maximum number of full system tests that can be performed while achieving the desired MSE for the least cost.

# 5. EXAMPLE 3: LOW PRESSURE COOLANT INJECTION SYSTEM

A third example is carried out on a highly reliably low pressure coolant injection (LCPI) system in a commercial nuclear-power reactor. The system provides coolant to the reactor vessel during accidents in which the vessel pressure is low. The system consists of six subsystems (listed in Table 5), some of which are repeated in a mixed series/parellel

system configuration (see Figure 4). The system was used by [5] to illustrate Bayesian reliability estimation methods.

The LCPI system reliability estimate from subsystem data alone is 1.0 to sixteen decimal places. With 200 successful tests of the full system the, the system reliability MLE is unchanged. However, the subsystem reliability MLEs increase slightly with information from the 200 successful system level tests.

To illustrate the properties of the MLE method, consider the following modification to the example. Let the test data on check valve (CV) 2 and the test data about the LPCI system be modified so that the reliability estimates from system and subsystem data alone disagree significantly (see Table 6). In this case, the system reliability estimate from subsystem testing alone is 0.999999999547. The LCPI system MLE is 0.999994756507. Again, the MLEs represent a compromise between the ratio estimates from subsystem and system test data; the degree of change in the estimates depends on the statistical information in the data sample used for estimation. In this case, the CV 2 subsystem MLE differs the most from its ratio estimate because it has largest statistical variance of any subsystem estimate and, based on the system configuration (see Figure 4), it has the largest potential of any subsystem to affect the system level reliability estimate.

The confidence interval is computed using 500 Monte Carlo iterations of the the bootstrap method described in Section 2.4. The 90% bootstrap confidence interval on the LCPI system is (0.999982353026, 0.999999083859). Because the system reliability is so close to unity, the interval is not symmetric about the MLE estimate. In fact, the normality of the uncertainty about the estimate is questionable given the proximity of the estimate to 1.0. The empirical cumulative distribution function of the system reliability MLE generated via the bootstrap Monte Carlo procedure is plotted in Figure 5 alongside the best fit normal distribution function. The empirical cumulative distribution function is clearly not normal.

**Table 5: Subsystem and System Test Data and MLE Reliability Estimates for the LCPI System**

| Subsystem | # of Tests | # of Successes | # Successes / # Tests | MLE Estimate |
|---|---|---|---|---|
| 1. Pump 1 | 240 | 236 | 0.98333 | 0.98341 |
| 2. Pump 2 | 240 | 238 | 0.99167 | 0.99168 |
| 3. Pump 3 | 190 | 189 | 0.99474 | 0.99478 |
| 4. Check Valve (CV) 1 | 14232 | 14231 | 0.99993 | 0.99993 |
| 5. Check Valve (CV) 2 | 240 | 240 | 1.00000 | 0.99999 |
| 6. Motor Operated Valve (MOV) | 470 | 469 | 0.99787 | 0.99790 |
| LPCI System | 200 | 200 | 1.00000 | 1.00000 |

**Table 6: Modified Subsystem and System Test Data and MLE Reliability Estimates for the LCPI System**

| Subsystem | # of Tests | # of Successes | # Successes / # Tests | MLE Estimate |
|---|---|---|---|---|
| 1. Pump 1 | 240 | 236 | 0.98333 | 0.98333 |
| 2. Pump 2 | 240 | 238 | 0.99167 | 0.99167 |
| 3. Pump 3 | 190 | 189 | 0.99474 | 0.99474 |
| 4. Check Valve (CV) 1 | 14232 | 14231 | 0.99993 | 0.99993 |
| 5. Check Valve (CV) 2 | **100** | **99** | 0.99000 | 0.90003 |
| 6. Motor Operated Valve (MOV) | 470 | 469 | 0.99787 | 0.97709 |
| LPCI System | **500** | **495** | 0.99000 | 0.99999 |

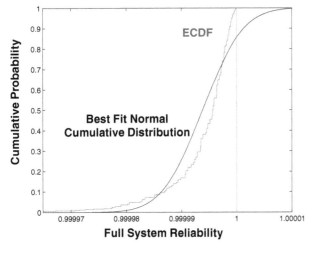

Figure 5: Non-normality of the bootstrap MLE reliability estimates.

## 6. CLOSURE

The main purpose of this paper was to develop three examples of the general MLE method for reliability. The examples illustrated a few of the important properties of the method. Namely, the method appropriately combines data from subsystem and full system reliability tests based on the statistical information in the respective samples. In addition, an extension of the method enables robust test plans to be developed for system reliability estimation involving trade-offs between the MSE (estimation accuracy), the degree of modeling error, and the cost of doing full system and subsystem tests.

## 7. REFERENCES

[1] M. Gevers, A. Bazanella, X. Bombois, and L. Miskovic. Identification and the information matrix: how to get just sufficiently rich? *IEEE Transactions on Automatic Control*, 54(12):2828–2840, 2009.

[2] G. Goodwin and R. Payne. *Dynamic system identification: experiment design and data analysis*. Academic Press, 1977.

[3] B. Hoadley. Asymptotic properties of maximum likelihood estimators for the independent not identically distributed case. *The Annals of mathematical statistics*, 42:1977–1991, 1971.

[4] C. J. Maranzano and J. C. Spall. Robust test design for reliability estimation with modeling error when combining full system and subsystem tests. In *Proceedings of the American Control Conference*, number ThB17.6, pages 3741–3746, Baltimore, MD, June-July 2010.

[5] H. Martz and R. Waller. Bayesian reliability analysis of complex series/parallel systems of binomial subsystems and components. *Technometrics*, 32(4):407–416, 1990.

[6] H. Martz, R. Waller, and E. Fickas. Bayesian reliability analysis of series systems of binomial subsystems and components. *Technometrics*, 30(2):143–154, 1988.

[7] J. C. Spall. *Introduction to Stochastic Search and Optimization: Estimation, Simulation, and Control*. Wiley Interscience, Hoboken, New Jersey, 2003.

[8] J. C. Spall. System reliability estimation and confidence regions from subsystem and full system tests. In *Proceedings of the American Control Conference*, number FrB14.1, pages 5067–5072, St. Louis, MO, June 2009.

[9] J. C. Spall. Convergence analysis for maximum likelihood-based reliability estimation from subsystem and full system tests. In *Proceedings of the 49th IEEE Conference on Decision and Control*, Atlanta, GA, December 2010.

[10] P. Stoica and T. Marzetta. Parameter estimation problems with singular information matrices. *IEEE Transactions on Signal Processing*, 49(1):87–90, 2001.

# "What do you do with a drunken robot?"

## *In Situ Performance Measurements of Intelligent Mobile Robots*

J. P. Gunderson

Gamma Two, Inc.

209 Kalamath St, Unit 13
Denver, CO, USA, 80223
1 303 778 7400

jgunders@gamma-two.com

L. F. Gunderson

Gamma Two, Inc.

209 Kalamath St, Unit 13
Denver, CO, USA, 80223
1 303 778 7400

lgunders@gamma-two.com

## ABSTRACT

This paper explores the characteristics of intelligent systems, focusing on impact of intelligence on performance metrics. The feedback loops required for intelligence cause areas of stable and unstable performance over environmental characteristics. The stable areas result in wide zones of nearly identical performance, surrounded by unstable zones where performance degrades.

We present design criteria for probing the envelope of stability, and present the results of performance metrics for an mobile autonomous robot.

## CATEGORIES AND SUBJECT DESCRIPTORS

D.2.5 [Testing and Debugging]
D.2.8 [Metrics]
I.2.9 [Robotics]

## GENERAL TERMS

Algorithms, Measurement, Performance, Reliability, Experimentation,

## KEYWORDS

Artificial Intelligence, Autonomy, Performance Metrics, Robotics, Test Design, Testing

## 1 INTRODUCTION

Performance metrics are a well accepted methodology for testing both software and hardware. These metrics have the advantage of

not requiring any knowledge of the internal structure or mechanisms of the system being tested, and they allow systems that perform essentially the same functions to be compared directly, with respect to that function. This makes performance metrics an ideal candidate for testing robots.

However, the nature of intelligent systems can make it difficult to design and implement good performance metrics. Unlike a simple deterministic system, such as a sort routine, intelligent systems adapt their behavior to the environment. This typically results in a wide range of environmental conditions under which the performance is nearly identical. Within this environmental envelope, we expect the performance to be near optimal. To compare two intelligent systems it is often the case that the comparison must be between the performance of the system at limits of the envelope, and the performance of the system outside the bounds of the envelope.

We look at the aspects of intelligent robots that place them into this class of systems. We then explore the process of designing tests that will push the intelligent systems to the edges of their envelopes, so that significant measurements can be made of individual systems, and meaningful comparisons can be made between systems.

This paper concludes with an analysis of a robotic system, and the performance metrics resulting from such testing. However, we begin by providing a short discussion of the nature of intelligent systems, and a working definition of intelligence for autonomous intelligent robots.

## 2 DEFINING INTELLIGENCE FOR EMBEDDED SYSTEMS

For this work we will use an extension of the working definition of intelligence derived from the work of Albus and Mystel:

> *Intelligence* is the ability of a system to act appropriately in an uncertain environment, where an *appropriate* action is that which increases the probability of success, and *success* is the achievement of behavioral sub-goals that support the system's ultimate goal[8].

We initially modify this definition as follows:

> "Intelligence is the ability of a system to select actions or behaviors, which, if executed

successfully, increase the probability of achieving sub-goals that support the system's ultimate goal."

This definition focuses on the cognitive task of selecting actions or behaviors – the process of producing a information based solution that would satisfy the system's goals. However, for embedded systems, such as robots, the problem is more complex. For these systems, just selecting a solution is not enough. They must implement that solution in the real world. This means that they are subject to additional cognitive and physical demands that the environment may create.

The first extension of the definition concerns a set of assumptions that may be correct when applied to a disembodied artificial intelligence, but are almost never true for an embedded system:

- There is always enough time to find a solution;

- There are always enough computational resources;

- The system is independent of its environment; and,

- The description of a solution is sufficient.

This involves modifying the definition as follows:

> "Intelligence is the ability of a system to select **and execute** actions or behaviors **in a timely manner**, which, if executed successfully, increase the probability of achieving sub-goals that support the system's ultimate goal **under changing environmental conditions**."

To illustrate this, consider a human taking an IQ test. Then consider that same human taking an IQ test after being sleep deprived. Better yet, consider the sleep deprived human drinking a few beers and taking an IQ test. How about after a fight with a loved one? What is the "correct" IQ measurement? Has the intelligence of the drunk/sleep deprived/angry human changed?

There is a tendency to consider the reasoning ability of humans as independent of emotion, and indeed of the body and its needs. The way in which the emotions interact with cognition is discussed in detail in Damasio's work[1].

The requirement that the system execute actions also expands the basic definition of intelligence. Following Howard Gardner's work on multiple intelligences [4], the definition must include at least two additional dimensions of intelligence, in addition to the *logical-mathematical* intelligence required to create a plan. These are *spatial* intelligence, which is required to perceive the world accurately and *bodily-kinesthetic* intelligence, which is required to move smoothy through the world.

To illustrate this, consider a drink serving robot that has the goal of offering a drink to people in each section of a large room. The metric for the logical-mathematical intelligence of the robot is the speed with which it comes up with a satisficing plan. It will come up with a plan to visit each section of an empty room quickly. If the robot is given a snapshot of people's positions in the room, it will take longer to plan, since it is necessary to determine the spatial aspects of the distribution of the people. Then place the robot in the room with the people. If the people are moving while it is planning, the robot must also utilize kinesthetic intelligence to avoid collisions, and to intercept the moving people. Given the limited computational resources of the robot, there may not be enough time to plan and execute – in short it may fail to achieve its goals.

If it is also moving and avoiding people, using its bodily-kinesthetic intelligence, it may not have enough computational resources to do the planning. In any case, the planning while moving in a crowded room will take significantly longer than the planning for an empty room. Then, to make the problem harder, allow the environment to affect the robot, by requiring the robot to report on all the people it encounters, so that it's ability to plan is compromised or, as is discussed below, allow it to be distracted by other demands. We demonstrate that under the latter condition, the planning and execution process suffers. So what is the "true" intelligence of the robot. The speed with which it plans in an empty room with a full battery and no distractions or the speed with which it plans in in a crowded room with a partial charge and many computational needs?

## 3  CHALLENGES FOR PERFORMANCE METRICS ON ROBOTS

Intelligent robots are complex embodied software/hardware systems that operate by observing the environment, becoming oriented within that environment with respect to the system goals and abilities, deciding an appropriate set of actions or behaviors, and then applying those actions or behaviors and monitoring the results. This loop has been variously described as a "Sense-Act Loop", a "Sense, Plan, Act Loop", or as the "Observe, Orient, Decide, Act (OODA ) Loop".

Inherent in all these descriptions are two common elements – the system is operating in a continuous loop, and there is significant feed-back between the intelligent system and the world in which it operates. This feed-back causes specific problems in designing performance metrics for an intelligent system.

An autonomous robot has feed-back loops running at many different time scales and levels of abstraction. These feed-back loops might range from low level, high frequency loops controlling power in the drive system, to high level, lower frequency loops selecting actions to get from the front door to the kitchen, to higher level, very low frequency loops designed to allow the robot to learn from its mistakes. The overall performance of the robot depends not only on the individual loops working correctly, but these loops must also interact successfully if the robot is to achieve its goals.

These feed-back loops are designed to give the robot the ability to function in a dynamic, uncertain world, and respond appropriately to changes in knowledge, changes to the environment, and changes to the systems goals. If the system is designed correctly, it will achieve its goals across a wide range of environmental states, and in response to a broad range of dynamic changes to its environment.

## 4  EFFECT OF ENVIRONMENT

We can look at the example of the drinks serving robot (presented above) from this perspective. There are four test conditions across two characteristics:

1. An empty room;

2. A room with people standing around;

3. A room with people moving around; and,

4. A room with people moving around and a reporting requirement.

There are two characteristics in the description: the complexity of finding and serving food to the people, and the need to log the locations of people. These two characteristics interact, since the additional computational load will affect the robot's ability to plan paths and perform precise motions, which in turn impact it's ability to actually get to the people, to achieve the goal.

We can look at this graphically as a two dimensional field (See Illustration 1)

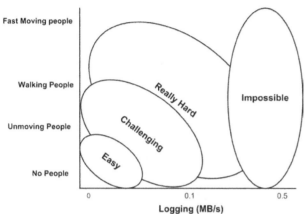

**Illustration 1: The difficulty of achieving the goal "Serve people food" under different environmental conditions.**

The effect of a feedback system is that within some portion of this environment space, the performance will be essentially constant. If the system can achieve the goal, it will do so. So rather than the gradient from easy to really hard, there will be an envelope within which the robot will perform stably, and outside the envelope the robot will have progressive failures and unstable performance. This is shown in Illustration 2.

## 4.1  Designing Performance Tests

The key to using performance metrics to assess the capabilities of a single system or to compare one system to another, is the design of the test conditions. If all the performance tests are drawn from inside the stable zone of the system under test, we learn very little about the capabilities of the system.

One can envision the test setup as a probe into the environment space in which the robot is operating. Ideally, we can design tests that probe the boundary of the envelope, and also probe the unstable area to assess the performance degradation as we move away from the envelope. The response of the robot just outside the envelope can vary in a number of significant ways – it can simply fail outside the envelope, it can degrade smoothly as the distance from the envelope increases, or it could have a very non-linear performance degradation.

## 4.2  Unstable Zone  Environments

If we label the area outside the envelope as unstable environments (e. g., the demands exceed the capacity of the system under test) we can look at comparing performance across systems. By probing this environment space, we can compare the stability zone of two systems, if one system has a stable zone that contains the zone of the other, and extends beyond it, the first system dominates the other. If the envelopes overlap, but each has areas

where the other performs unstably, intelligent choices can be may about which system to use under what circumstances.

Also, if the capabilities of all available systems are marginal – if the expected environments are close to, or outside the envelopes – the performance degradation can be used to inform decisions about which system is more appropriate.

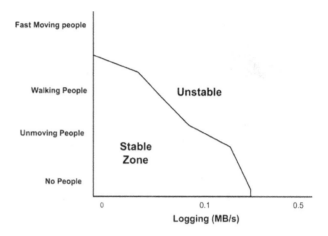

**Illustration 2: The zone in which the robot's performance is stable, versus unstable.**

## 5  EXPERIMENTAL SETUP

In our experiments, we focus on probing the envelope of a single robot. This robot is intended to function in home and office environments and to provide fetch and carry services for the people in the environment. It is the same robot that is used to serve food to people who drop by our lab during our monthly open house.

The robot can also be assigned a security (or guard robot) role. In this role it patrols a specified route (a sequence of locations to observe) and monitors the environment at these locations and along the route between them. Since it monitors the environment, and builds a Mental Model of what it encounters, it can detect both the presence of unauthorized people, and the evidence of intrusion (noticing a door that was open is now closed for example). This requires the ability to monitor and log the state of the world on a symbolic level, which is provided by the Cybernetic Brain.

## 5.1  Robot

The robot is a BSL series autonomous mobile robot manufactured by Gamma Two. It is a roughly cylindrical robot, designed for deployment into home and office environments (see Illustration 3). It is equipped with 12 forward looking ultrasonic ranging sensors, thermal infrared sensor, encoders, and a magnetic compass. The drive system is based on two co-axial drive motors and fore and aft casters. This enables the robot to turn in place as well as execute straight line and curving forward motion.

**Illustration 3: BSL Series robot manufactured by Gamma Two, Inc.**

The control system is a two tiered structure, with a lower tier real-time control system directed by the upper tier Cybernetic Brain. The lower tier (cerebellum) is responsible for sending control signals to the drive system, monitoring the sensors, and reflex actions such as collision avoidance. The Cybernetic Brain is responsible for planning, execution monitoring, fault analysis and correction, and maintaining a multi-resolution representation (mental model) of the world as it changes and is changed by the robots actions.

## 5.2 Cybernetic Brain Architecture

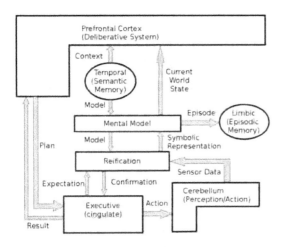

**Illustration 4: The Cybernetic Brain architecture is derived from the structure of vertebrate brains in living systems. Rather than being mathematically principled, it is based on the biological principles that lead to natural intelligence.**

Our approach to an intelligent architecture is biologically principled. Rather than attempting to construct *a priori* a system the embodies intelligence, we rely on the large number of exemplars of intelligent systems presented by living systems. Recent advances in brain imaging have provided significant indicators of the structure of one successful solution to the problem of producing an intelligent system.

From this recent research we have designed and implemented a Cybernetic Brain. This brain displays the capabilities normally associated with intelligent behavior, and conforms to the definition of intelligence outlined above. The design and architecture of this system is presented in *Robots, Reasoning, and Reification*[6].

In order to function in the complex, dynamic, and uncertain world, living systems have evolved complex, multilevel feedback/feed-forward structures in their brain architecture, and rely on significant levels of redundancy supporting multiple representations of information organized for different purposes. It is believed that these redundant, multi-resolutional representations are necessary to support complex intelligence.

We have emulated this complexity in our design not because we like complexity, but because the only working models of intelligent behavior seem to require it.

## 5.3 Goal

The goal of this experiment is to investigate the impact of environmental conditions on the measured performance of the robot. The goal given to the robot is to complete a tour of specified locations. The robot is instructed by voice command to execute a tour. The robot must control its velocity (both linear and angular), and heading during an approximate 10 meter closed path.

## 5.4 Metrics

The performance of the robot on its assigned tasks is measured by the total time from the assignment of the goal to the completion. This metric was chosen for several reasons:

1. It is a 'black box' metric – no knowledge of the internal mechanisms of the robot is required;

2. It is applicable across many types of robots;

3. It integrates both the planning ability and the execution of the actions (this would penalize a robot that produced plans that it was incapable of reliably executing); and,

4. It requires the robot to perform these tasks while monitoring the environment and adapting to failures.

This provides a single metric that captures the ability of the robot to achieve its goals – a hallmark of an intelligent system.

## 5.5 Setup

The tests were run in the lab at Gamma Two, with a six station patrol route. The route (See Figure 5) requires the robot to cross open areas, skirt the edge of obstacles, and avoid potential obstacles such as the stair-rail on leg E.

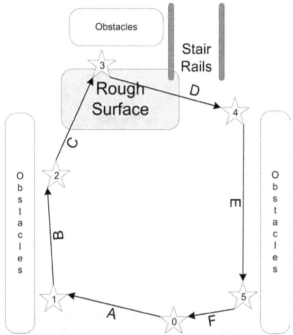

**Illustration 5: The patrol route for the experiment. The total length is approximately 10m.**

## 5.6 Drunken robots

The BSL series robots maintain a multi-resolution representation of the world, and maintain a history of recent actions, tasks, and events. As with living systems, this Episodic Memory requires space, and processing power; and like living systems, the robot has limited resources (bounded rationality is the term used by Newell and Simon[9])

In living systems, this linear, time sequenced Episodic Memory is processed into a more structured representation (Semantic Memory) during sleep. Several studies have demonstrated that there is significant degradation of cognitive function as a result of sleep deprivation[3]. This may be, in part, due to the increasing cognitive load of maintaining the unprocessed Episodic Memory[5]. It has been reported that chronic sleep shortage of as little as 1 to 2 hours per night has effects on cognition, judgment, and motor skills equivalent to alcohol intoxication[10]. Under normal operation, the robot uses downtime to re-process its Episodic Memory. Since it is a service robot, this reprocessing is designed to occur when there are no unsatisfied tasks. By preventing the robot from offloading this memory, (analogous to sleep deprivation, which approximates drunkenness) we force the robot towards the edge of its stability envelope, and into the unstable performance area of Illustration 2.

The effect of this 'drunkenness' is to limit the resources available to the kinesthetic control system. The robot is designed to constantly monitor its environment, and adjust its movement in response to changes in the sensed environment. This enable the robot to re-calculate the direction it needs to travel, and the

distances and speed needed to arrive at a desired location regardless of roughness on the floor, different surfaces, close approaches to obstacles, and dodge moving obstacles. This kinesthetic intelligence is needed to successfully execute the planned actions in an uncertain and dynamic world.

To stress the kinesthetic intelligence, we prevent periodic offloading of the Episodic Memory. This forces the Cybernetic Brain to assign increasing amounts of resources to the tasks of maintaining Episodic Memory. Since the computer is limited in resources, if additional resources are needed for 'maintenance' tasks – then fewer resources are available for the primary tasks (See Illustration 6). In short, the logical-mathematical, linguistic, and kinesthetic intelligence of the robot will be compromised. It will take longer to plan, the processing of voice input and output will be degraded, and the ability of the robot to move smoothly and accurately will be impaired.

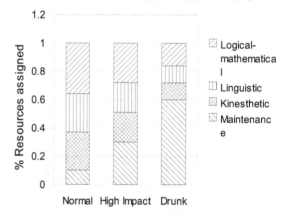

**Illustration 6: Resource allocation under varying environmental conditions.**

We allow the maintenance tasks to require increasing resources, and measure the time to task completion. As fewer and fewer resources are available for kinesthetic computation, the robot has greater and greater difficulty navigating around the space in a timely manner. It takes longer to plan the actual movements (how many degrees to turn, how far and fast to travel). It also impacts the fine motor control needed for stopping at the appropriate location. As the fine motor control degrades we expect to see slower approaches to targets, more and larger mid course corrections during travel, and repeated overshooting and undershooting on final target approaches. All of these will impact the total time until to task completion.

We ran the robot around the patrol route and recorded data for

- Unprocessed Episodic Memory size

- Total Execution Time

The protocol was to:

1. Place the robot in a known location and orientation (room-center facing north – point 0 in Illustration 5);

2. Inform the robot of its location and pose;

3. Task the robot with a single patrol; and,

4. When the robot completed its task, query it for total time and Episodic Memory size.

Since the robot is constantly monitoring it's own performance, and state, it automatically tracks the needed information and can simply be asked to report the values.

This process was repeated until the Episodic Memory size grew to over 100MB, well outside the operating specifications, and by the same token, well outside the envelope. Once we reached 100MB files, we allowed the robot to process its Episodic Memory, and started over with an empty memory.

# 6  RESULTS

The typical patrol required 129 seconds, and we collected a total of 129 data points. During the course of this testing the robot traveled over 1.5 kilometers.

Since we began each run inside the envelope, and ended it well outside, we have data points from both the stable zone, and the unstable area for the robot. The raw data is shown below as a scatter plot of execution time versus Episodic Memory size.

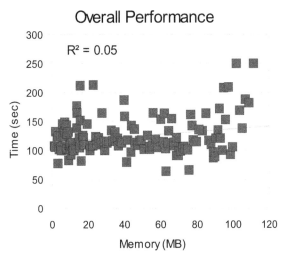

**Illustration 7: Overall Performance of the robot during all tests**

It is clear from these data that there is very little correlation between the execution time and the Episodic Memory size. In effect, the state of the Episodic Memory would appear to have no correlation with performance. However, since our hypothesis is that we would have very low correlation within the stable zone, and much higher correlation in the unstable region. When we partition the data into stable and unstable regions we get the results listed in Table 1.

| Zone | Data Points | Linear Correlation (r2) |
|---|---|---|
| Stable | 80 | 0 |
| Unstable | 49 | 0.26 |
| Overall | 129 | 0.05 |

*Table 1: The relative correlation of the stable zone and the*

*unstable area*

From these data it is clear that we have differential behavior inside and outside the envelope boundary. Which is consistent with our hypothesis. Further more, the performance outside the stability envelope shows a significant linear degradation, from which we can predict the performance.

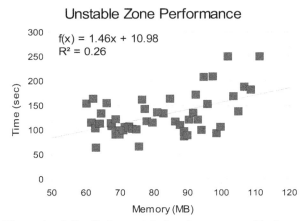

**Illustration 8: Predictive model of performance outside the stable zone.**

# 7  CONCLUSIONS

In this paper, we have discussed the ways in which a definition of intelligence must change when the system being analyzed is embedded. These changes include an extension of the intelligence metric to include, at the least, spatial and bodily-kinesthetic intelligence.

We have also shown that the performance of an embedded artificial intelligence can be degraded by environmental conditions. We have analyzed the expected performance of an intelligent system with complex feedback control systems. After discussing the expectation of both stable and unstable zones controlled by environmental demands, we analyzed the impact of this on performance metrics. We concluded that we would see areas of self-similar near optimal performance, surrounded by an unstable zone of degraded performance.

With this in mind, we concluded that there is little value in running multiple performance metrics within the stable zone, since they would produce similar measurements. However, there is significant advantage to probing the edges of the stability envelope, and probing the unstable areas to assess performance degradation.

We designed and ran tests based on this methodology on a service robot, to assess its performance and showed that it displayed characteristics that matched our predicted behaviors, and found that its measured performance was significantly affected by the environmental characteristics.

This finding has two important corollaries. First that any metric for intelligent systems must include performance over a variety of environmental stresses. These stresses should be related to the types of environmental conditions that the embedded system will be exposed to under normal conditions. Second, and perhaps more important, the result of this testing will indicate the direction that further work should go, in order to make a more robust system.

As a side note, one of the most challenging aspects of collecting data for performance metrics on robots is the sheer time required. Unlike a simulation, where it might be possible to run hundreds or thousands of simulated 'patrols' in a few seconds, the robot must physically traverse the floor, encounter the obstacles, and respond appropriately. And this just takes time. However, good science requires investment.

# 8   REFERENCES:

[1] Damasio, A. 1994. *Descartes' Error: Emotion, Reason, and the Human Brain*. J. P. Putnam's Sons, New York, NY.

[2] Dean, T. and Bonasso, R. P. 1993. The 1992 AAAI Robot Exhibition and Competition. *AI Magazine.* 14, 1 (Spring 1993) 34-48.

[3] Durmer, J. S. and Dinges, D. F. 2005. Neurocognitive Consequences of Sleep Deprivation. *Seminars in Neurology.* 25, 1, 117 - 129.

[4] Gardner, H. 1983. *Frames Of Mind.* Basic Books.

[5] Girardeau,G., Benchenane, K., Wiener, S. I., Buzsáki, G. , and Zugaro, M. B. 2009. Selective suppression of hippocampal ripples impairs spatial memory. *Nature Neuroscience.* 12 (Sep. 2009), 1222-1223. DOI: 10.1038/nn.2384

[6] Gunderson, L. F. and Gunderson, J. P. 2009. *Robots, Reasoning, and Reification.* Springer Press.

[7] Miller, David P. 1993. Intelligent Mobile Robots: Perception of Performance. In *International Conference on Advanced Robotics (ICAR).*

[8] Mystel, A. M. and Albus, J. S. 2002. *Intelligent Systems: Architecture, Design, and Control.* Chapter 1, 3. Wiley-Interscience, New York.

[9] Simon, H.A. 1955. A Behavioral Model of Rational Choice. *Quarterly Journal of Economics.* 69, 1 (Feb. 1955), 99-118.

[10] Williamson A. M, Feyer A. M . 2000. Moderate sleep deprivation produces impairments in cognitive and motor performance equivalent to legally prescribed levels of alcohol intoxication. *Occup Environ Med.* 57, 10 (October 2000), 649–55. doi:10.1136/oem.57.10.649. PMID 10984335. PMC 1739867. http://oem.bmj.com/cgi/pmidlookup?view=long&pmid=10984335.

# Comprehensive Standard Test Suites for the Performance Evaluation of Mobile Robots

Adam Jacoff, Hui-Min Huang, Elena Messina, Ann Virts, Anthony Downs
National Institute of Standards & Technology
100 Bureau Drive MS 8230
Gaithersburg, MD 20899
+1.301.975. 3427
hui-min.huang@nist.gov

## ABSTRACT

Robots must possess certain sets of capabilities to suit critical operations such as emergency responses. In the mobility function, ground robots must be able to handle many types of obstacles and terrain complexities, including traversing and negotiating positive and negative obstacles, various types of floor surfaces or terrains, and confined passageways. Additional mobility requirements include the ability to sustain specified speeds and to tow payloads with different weights. Standard test methods are required to evaluate how well candidate robots meet these requirements. A set of test methods focused on evaluating the mobility function has been collected into a test suite. Likewise, in other functions such as sensing, communication, manipulation, energy/power, Human-System Interaction (HSI), logistics, and safety, corresponding test suites are required. Also needed are test suites for aerial and aquatic robots. Under the sponsorship of DHS, NIST researchers are collaborating with others to establish such a collection of test suites under the standards development organization ASTM International. Apparatuses must be set up to challenge specific robot capabilities in repeatable ways to facilitate direct comparison of different robot models as well as particular configurations of similar robot models.

## Categories and Subject Descriptors

J.2 [physical sciences and engineering] unmanned systems performance

## General Terms

Measurement, Performance, Design, Human Factors, Standardization, Verification

## Keywords

energy, environment, goal, human-system interaction, HSI, measure, metrics, mobility, power, radio communications, robot, performance, sensor, standard, task, terminology, test, test method, test suite

## 1. INTRODUCTION

U.S. emergency responders face extremely dangerous or hazardous environments when responding to natural or man-made disasters. Urban search and rescue (US&R), bomb disposal, and law enforcement are a few of these critical operational areas. Major efforts have been underway to improve the effectiveness of the emergency responses. The Department of Homeland Security (DHS) Federal Emergency Management Agency (FEMA) and the National Institute of Justice (NIJ) co-sponsored an effort to identify and define functional requirements for new and/or improved technologies that meet the needs of both urban search and rescue teams as well as law enforcement agencies. The report [8] stated needs included "Reliable non-human, non-canine search and rescue systems - robust systems that combine enhanced canine/human search and rescue capabilities without existing weaknesses (i.e., robots)."

The National Response Framework [1] states that "Governments at all levels have a responsibility to develop detailed, robust, all-hazards response plans."
It would be extremely helpful for the successfully tested robots to be made available to the emergency responders.

Under the sponsorship of the DHS, NIST has embarked on an effort for the research and development of the performance evaluation methodology of the response robots since 2005. Earlier papers [5,6] described some initial results. This paper provides an update as well as an overall structure of the standard test methods.

## 2. APPROACH

DHS and NIST adopted an iterative, user-oriented approach for developing the robotic performance evaluation standards. See Figure 1. The process starts with collecting operational requirements, which must be provided by the emergency responders. The project objective is, then, to be able to employ robots to accomplish the required tasks.

For example, one requirement is for a robot to sustain its speed when navigating in an obstacle-rich environment. A

[1] National Response Framework, U.S. Department of Homeland Security, January 2008, www.fema.gov/NRF.

test method to characterize how well a candidate is able to do so is developed. This test method would entail sets of apparatus, metrics, and procedure, as indicated in Figure 1.

The draft test methods evolve through several validation steps, where they are applied to candidate robots to see how effective they are. The validation can be conducted through organized robotic exercises or competitions. The matured test methods are submitted for standardization. They are also proliferated for wide application, for the purpose of verifying that the subject testing is reproducible, and for responder proficiency training of the robotic tools. Beyond validating test methods, robot exercises further serve to educate developers about the domain requirements, as well as to allow responders to experiment with deploying robots in realistic scenarios.

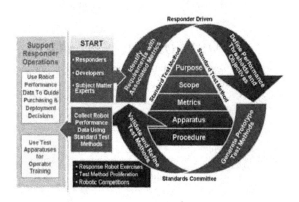

**Figure 1: Test Method Development Cycle[2]**

## 2.1 REQUIREMENTS CAPTURE

The original intent of this standardization effort was to enable the Department of Homeland Security to make well-informed decisions about the application of robots to urban search and rescue missions. A major requirement capture process was conducted in 2005 through a series of workshops attended by FEMA US&R task force members [7]. These requirements have been the foundation for the standards development efforts. Over the years, the focus of the work has expanded to include other civilian response applications, such as bomb disposal. The requirements definition process for the latter has been less formal and has also benefitted from prior studies, in particular funded by the National Institute of Justice. [8]

Over the years, the requirements have been refined and updated as the responders have become increasingly familiar with robotic capabilities. They gain familiarity through the continued participation in the standards development and evaluation process, especially during test exercises. Responders evaluate the test methods and provide constructive feedback throughout the development

process. Their input serves to ensure that the test methods measure real world functionality in meaningful ways.

The objective is for the robots to meet the requirements before they can be adopted by and integrated into the agencies' operating processes.

## 2.2 Test method standardization

The NIST team has joined the ASTM International for developing the standard procedures, test methods, and metrics to fully to address the requirements. This effort is under Committee on Homeland Security (E54), Subcommittee on Operational Equipment (.08), Robotics Task Group (.01). In other words, the designation for this response robot performance evaluation effort is (ASTM E54.08.01).

According to the ASTM classification, the following are the relevant types of standards:
  o terminology
  o practice: a definitive set of instructions for performing one or more specific operations that does not produce a test result
  o test method—a definitive procedure that produces a test result

From these, we establish the following major milestones for the standardization effort. The various test methods evolve at different paces. Currently, three standards have been approved by ASTM [1, 2, 3]. About 20 test methods are in the balloting, validating or prototype status.

1. Prototype: when a test procedure and apparatus is conceived, built, and under evolution.
2. Validating: when a prototype has progressed enough after going through several sets of tests by robots. A Work Item description might have been submitted to ASTM to indicate that the standardization balloting process may be ready in months.
3. Standards:
   a. Standard Practice: the balloted and approved test procedure; meanwhile, the team continues collecting test data to fine tune the metrics, the evaluation form, and the accompanying performance repeatability issue.
   b. Standard Test Method: the goal of the prototype; once the team has gathered sufficient data to prove the performance repeatability, the metrics/evaluation form will be finalized and added into the previously approved standard practice to be re-balloted as a standard test method.

## 3. TEST METHOD

Each of the test methods corresponds to the requirements as specified by U.S. emergency responders and additional constituents. A robot's performance in this test is indicative of its capabilities needed in such operations as emergency responses. ASTM has a standard style guide for

---

[2] Figure based on original by Dr. Bert Coursey, Department of Homeland Security Standards Executive.

the test methods. Parts of the essential information generated by the test method development team are:

- Metrics: We identify the characteristics for measuring the corresponding aspect of the robotic performance that addresses a particular requirement or subset of requirements. For example, the emergency responders may require a robot to be able to drive around, on, or through particular obstacles or challenging terrains. We must identify the characteristics (sizes, severity) of the obstacles to be measured.

  Associated with the metrics is the issue of performance requirements, in other words, what measured values are acceptable. These values can be derived from the requirements.

- Apparatus: To measure the performance, we must design and develop the testing setup such that the metrics can be applied for the performance evaluation. The apparatuses associated with the test methods challenge specific robot capabilities in repeatable ways to facilitate direct comparison of different robot models as well as particular configurations of similar robot models.

  The apparatus can contain either notional or operational objects or setups. With notional objects or setups, we can easily standardize the design characteristics, such as size, weight, surface type, color, etc., of the apparatus. This would facilitate reproducing the apparatus. The opposite approach, using operational objects or objects with operational flavors, might have the benefit of close to reality but might suffer the drawback of difficult to standardize.

- Procedure: A procedure is generated based on the apparatus and how we want to exercise the metrics to measure the performance.

- Test Form: Corresponding to a test method and contains fields for recording the testing results and the associated information, including:
  o Metrics and corresponding measurement scales and ranges;
  o Any additional testing features such as those reflecting performance proficiency;
  o Important notes to be recorded during the test, including particular fault conditions that occurred, the reason the robot developer abstained from participating in this test (if this was the case), any observations by the test administrator that could augment the recorded results in either positive or negative ways, or any comments that the robot's operator requests to be put on the form;
  o Testing administrative information; including: names for the involved personnel,

organizations, and robot; the testing date(s) and time; version number of the form; and the testing conditions on the environment, apparatus, and robotic configuration (tether versus radio communication, for example). If audio/video recording is done during the testing, the file names should be recorded on the form.

- Repeatability analysis: Tests must be conducted with a statistically significant number of repetitions to establish the reliability of the testing method and the associated confidence levels.

- Reproducibility analysis: A test method must be reproduced at multiple locations to verify that similar levels of reliability and confidence can be obtained.

# 4. TEST METHOD ORGANIZATION

The entire set of requirements and the corresponding testing standards are organized into the following categories:

- Terminology
- Robotic Subsystems
  - Mobility
    o Ground Locomotion
    o Aerial Maneuvering
    o Aquatic Maneuvering
  - Energy and Power
  - Sensing
  - Communications
  - Manipulation and Other Payloads
  - Chassis
- Human-System Interaction (HSI)
- Logistics
- Safety/Operating Environment

A collection of test methods is to be developed for each of the subsystems. These test methods are called a test suite for the subsystem. The test methods in a test suite are intended to collectively characterize a robot's performance in a particular functional area.

For example, a set of test methods has been developed for the Mobility subsystem. A robot with a larger size may be better suited for the gap crossing test but may be more constrained in the confined space traversal test. Therefore, the collective test evaluation, as opposed to individual test methods, should give a comprehensive perspective for the robot's mobility capability in the response environments.

Note that a lot of the requirements may involve multiple robotic subsystems. Particularly, the Mobility subsystem is involved in most of the other subsystem requirements. For example, a radio communication requirement is irrelevant unless the robot can navigate to a location of concern. The endurance requirement for the battery is relies on the robot's mobility capability, since the test method entails having the robot drive a prescribed pattern over a designated apparatus terrain repeatedly. The Mobility subsystem is therefore considered the enabling subsystem and a heavy focus has been placed upfront on test methods for this subsystem.

# 5. TEST SUITES AND TERMINOLOGY

## 5.1 Terminology

Terms must be formally defined to facilitate proper communication among all the test method development efforts. Given that this effort covers multiple communities, terms might be used with different meanings. Consistent terminology is crucial.

The applicability of the terms varies, ranging from: test method specific, common to a test suite, and common to all response robots standard test methods. As such, the terms are identified and defined correspondingly throughout the whole test method organization.

## 5.2 Cache Packaging Test Suite

The following standards are being developed to evaluate the cache packaging performance:

Standard Practice for Establishing the Test Configuration and Associated Cache Packaged Weight and Volume of Emergency Response Robots for
o   FEMA Urban Search and Rescue Teams (ASTM E2592-07)
o   Federal/State/Local Bomb Squads (P)[3]

## 5.3 Mobility Test Suite

Suitable ground robots must be able to handle many types of obstacles and terrains. Standard test methods are required to evaluate whether candidate robots meet these requirements. The following test methods are being prototyped and validated:

Standard Test Method for Evaluating the Mobility Capabilities of Emergency Response Robots Using
o   Terrains: Flat/Paved Surfaces (V)[4]
o   Terrains: Continuous Pitch/Roll Ramps (V)
o   Terrains: Crossing Pitch/Roll Ramps (V)
o   Terrains: Symmetric Stepfields (V)
o   Terrains: Sand (P)
o   Terrains: Gravel (P)
o   Terrains: Mud (P)
o   Obstacles: Inclined Planes (V)
o   Obstacles: Gap Crossings: Static, Horizontal, Parallel (V)
o   Obstacles: Gap Crossings: Dynamic, Horizontal, Parallel (P)
o   Obstacles: Pipe Steps (V)

o   Obstacles: Stair/Landings (V)
o   Towing Tasks: Grasped Sleds (V)

See Figure 2, Figure 3, Figure 4 for the apparatuses of three of the mobility test methods.

**Figure 2: Paved Surface Terrain-for Sustained Speed and Towing Test Methods**

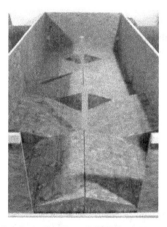

**Figure 3: Crossing Ramps Terrain Test Method**

**Figure 4: Stairs Obstacle Test Method**

## 5.4 Energy/Power Test Suite

The following test methods are being developed to evaluate the energy/power subsystem performance:

Standard Test Method for Evaluating the Energy/Power Capabilities of Emergency Response Robots Using
o   Endurance Tasks: Terrains: Continuous Pitch/Roll Ramps (V)
o   Peak Power Tasks: Obstacles (P)

See Figure 5 for the apparatus of the endurance test method.

---

[3] P - Indicates the development status as being Prototyped

[4] V - Indicates the development status as having completed the Prototyping stage and being Validated.

Figure 5: Endurance Test Method

## 5.5 Radio Communications Test Suite

The following test methods are being developed to evaluate the radio communications subsystem performance:

Standard Test Method for Evaluating the Radio Communication Capabilities of Emergency Response Robots Using

o Control and Perception Tasks: Line-of-Sight Environment (V). See Figure 6.
o Control and Perception Tasks: Non-Line-of-Sight Environment (V)
o Control and Perception Tasks: Structure Penetration Environment (P)
o Control and Perception Tasks: Interference Signal Environment (P)
o Control and Perception Tasks: Urban Canyon Environments (P)

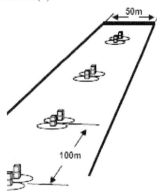

Figure 6: Light-of-Sight Radio Comms Test Method

## 5.6 Sensor Test Suite

The following test methods are being developed to evaluate the sensor subsystem performance:

Standard Test Method for Evaluating the Sensor Capabilities of Emergency Response Robots Using

o Video Acuity Charts and Field of View Measures (ASTM E2566-08) (See Figure 7.)
o Video Directed Search Tasks: Complete (V) (See Figure 8.)
o Video Directed Search Tasks: Rapid (V)
o Audio Rhyming Words and Loudness Measures (at the Operator and Robot) (V)
o Audio Spectrum Tones (at the Operator and Robot) (P)
o Laser Ranging Targets and Spatial Resolution Measures (P)
o Localization and Mapping Tasks: Hallway Labyrinths with Complex Terrain (P)
o Localization and Mapping Tasks: Wall Mazes with Complex Terrain (P)
o Localization and Mapping Tasks: Sparse Feature Environments (P)
o Localization and Mapping Tasks: Tunnel Mazes (P)

Figure 7: Video Acuity Charts and Field of View Measures Test Method

Figure 8: Video Directed Search Tasks: Complete Test Method

## 5.7 Manipulation Test Suite

The following test methods are being developed to evaluate the manipulator subsystem performance:

Standard Test Method for Evaluating the Manipulation Capabilities of Emergency Response Robots Using

- Directed Perception Tasks in Elevated Shelves: Open Access (V)
- Directed Perception Tasks in Elevated Shelves: Reach-Over Access (P)
- Directed Perception Tasks in Elevated Shelves: Reach-Under Access (P)
- Gasping Dexterity Tasks in Elevated Shelves: Open Access (V) (See Figure 9.)
- Gasping Dexterity Tasks in Elevated Shelves: Reach-Over Access (P)
- Gasping Dexterity Tasks in Elevated Shelves: Reach-Under Access (P)
- Door Opening and Traversal Tasks (V)

**Figure 9: Gasping Dexterity Tasks in Elevated Shelves: Open Access Apparatus**

## 5.8 Human-System Interaction (HSI) Test Suite

The following test methods are being developed to evaluate the HSI subsystem performance:

Standard Test Method for Evaluating the Capabilities of Emergency Response Robots Using
- Navigation Tasks: In Unknown Environments with Complex Terrain (V)
- Search Tasks: In Unknown Environments with Complex Terrain (V) (See Figure 10.)
- Search Tasks: Under-Body Voids with Complex Terrain (V)

**Figure 10: HSI Search Test Method Using a Random Maze Apparatus**

## 6. TESTING POLICY

A testing policy has evolved to ensure consistent testing efforts. The main points include:

- All tests are conducted with the robot operator stationed remotely from the robot. The robot must be out of sight of the operator and ideally out of sound of testing apparatus.
- The operator can choose to abstain (withdraw from) the test, which causes the result to be not reported. By doing so, the robot developer acknowledges the omission of the performance data while the test method was available at the test time. The operator typically abstains when the robot configuration is not designed nor equipped to perform the tasks as specified in the test method. The abstention should be granted only before the test. The testing authority should make a consistent policy about the timing.
- Testing is conducted by a test administrator. She/he is to ensure the readiness of the apparatus, the test form, and any required measuring devices.
- The test administrator ensures that the specified or required environmental conditions are met.
- She/he will also explain the test to the robot operator. This includes fault conditions before the test starts.
- She/he will inform the operator when the safety belay (if needed to protect the robot from damage) is available and ensure that the operator has either decided not to use it or assigned a person to handle it properly.
- The administrator is to call the operator to start and end the test and record the performance data and any notable observations during the test.
- Verbal communication between the operator and the administrator regarding the performance of a test repetition is not allowed other than instructions on when to start and notification of faults and any safety related conditions. The operator has the full responsibility to determine whether the robot has reached a test goal.
- Operator is allowed to have as much practice time as practical before entering a test.

## 7. TESTING

### 7.1 Testing Results

Extensive testing has been conducted for the purposes of prototyping and validating the test methods as well as supporting the project sponsor's objectives. Some representative testing results are shown in Figure 11, which shows that two of the nine testing robots successfully traversed 45° stairs and Figure 12 shows the endurance test distances of the participating robots. The endurances traversing distances for the nine participating robots range from 6915 m to 345 m.

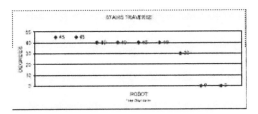

Figure 11: Stair Traversing Tests for Nine Robots

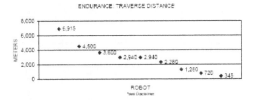

Figure 12: Endurance Test Results for Nine Robots

## 7.2 Operational Testing

The NIST team also developed a collection of test operational scenarios that require combinations of the aforementioned test suite capabilities. The scenarios include suspected package on a bus (for bomb squads), which requires the mobility, manipulation, and sensing capabilities. Other scenarios include aerial post-disaster assessment and search in a rubble pile (Figure 14), which are conducted in a Texas Engineering Extension Service (TEEX) training facility called Disaster City [9].

**Figure 13: Test Scenario of Suspected Packages on Bus**

**Figure 14: Rubble Pile Scenario**

### 7.1 Test Site Proliferation

The project aims at utilizing or implementing various testing resources, not only in the U.S. but also in the world.

Testing has been extensively conducted at the NIST site, the TEEX Disaster City site, Montgomery County training facility in Maryland, the Southwest Research Institute (SwRI) in Texas [10], etc. Plans are being made to implement the testing apparatuses in Asia and Europe. Ultimately, selected test sites will be certified within the United States and internationally and will be responsible for conducting robot testing.

## 8. SUMMARY

The key principles of the program are:

- user-focused requirements capturing process
- easily reproducible standards evaluation processes
- individually developed but collectively presented standard performance evaluation test suites
- teleoperation based testing [4]
- human level sizes and weights for robots and objects

As of September 2010, 3 standards have been approved and published, 4 are being balloted within ASTM, and over a dozen test methods have been validated and are in the process of final review and formatting so that they can be submitted for balloting. About 10 additional test methods are being prototyped as the next wave of the validation. Once approved, the resulting test suites will form a foundation for characterizing the performance of robots functionality. This will facilitate informed purchase decisions for response organizations and foster growth in the market and further innovations in the robots' capabilities.

## 9. ACKNOWLEDGEMENTS

This work was supported by the Department of Homeland Security, Science and Technology Directorate, Office of Standards, the National Institute of Justice, and the NIST Office of Law Enforcement Standards.

## 10. REFERENCES

[1] ASTM Standard E 2521 – 07a, *Standard Terminology for Urban Search and Rescue Robotic Operations,* ASTM International, West Conshohocken, PA.

[2] ASTM Standard E 2592 – 07, *Standard Practice for Evaluating Cache Packaged Weight and Volume of Robots for Urban Search and Rescue,* ASTM International, West Conshohocken, PA.

[3] ASTM Standard E2566, *Standard Test Method for Determining Visual Acuity and Field of View of On-Board Video Systems for Teleoperation of Robots for Urban Search and Rescue Applications*, ASTM International, West Conshohocken, PA.

[4] Autonomy Levels for Unmanned Systems (ALFUS) Framework, Volume II: Framework Models Version 1.0, NIST Special Publication 1011-II-1.0, Huang, H. et al., Ed., National Institute of Standards and Technology, Gaithersburg, MD, December 2007.

[5] Jacoff, A., and Messina, E, "Urban Search and Rescue Robot Performance Standards: Progress Update," SPIE Defense and Security Conference 2007.

[6] Messina, E. and Jacoff, A. S. "Measuring the Performance of Urban Search and Rescue Robots," IEEE Conference on Homeland Security Technologies, 2007.

[7] Messina, E. R., et al., Statement of Requirements for Urban Search and Rescue Robot Performance Standards, NIST Draft Report, May 2005

[8] Urban Search and Rescue Technology Needs Identification of Needs, DHS/FEMA and National Institute of Justice Report, June 2004.

[9] http://www.teex.com/index.cfm

[10] http://www.swri.org/

# Towards a Standardized Test for Intelligent Wheelchairs

Joelle Pineau[*]
Centre for Intelligent Machines
McGill University
Montreal, QC CANADA
jpineau@cs.mcgill.ca

Robert West
Centre for Intelligent Machines
McGill University
Montreal, QC CANADA
robert.west@mail.mcgill.ca

Amin Atrash
Centre for Intelligent Machines
McGill University
Montreal, QC CANADA
aatras@cs.mcgill.ca

Julien Villemure
Centre for Intelligent Machines
McGill University
Montreal, QC CANADA
julien@cs.mcgill.ca

François Routhier
Institut de réadaptation en
déficience physique de
Québec
Québec, QC CANADA
Francois.Routhier@rea.ulaval.ca

## ABSTRACT

Many people who have to rely on electric wheelchairs find it hard or even impossible to fulfill daily navigation tasks with their chairs. The SmartWheeler project aims at developing an intelligent wheelchair that minimizes the physical and cognitive load required in steering it. In this paper we briefly outline the SmartWheeler project and its goals. We then argue that it is important to have a standardized test to evaluate autonomous wheelchairs in terms of performance quality, safety, and usability. No such test exists as yet for intelligent wheelchairs, but there has been an effort in the clinical community to design tests for conventional wheelchair usage. We discuss the existing Wheelchair Skills Test (WST). We then suggest a paradigm that allows us to use this test to benchmark the quality of intelligent wheelchairs, and in particular their interface, in a task context that is relevant to clinical practice in rehabilitation.

## 1. INTRODUCTION

Many people who suffer from chronic mobility impairments, such as spinal cord injuries or multiple sclerosis, use a powered wheelchair to move around their environment. However, factors such as fatigue, degeneration of their condition and sensory impairments often limit their ability to use standard electric wheelchairs. According to a recent survey, 40% of powered wheelchair users surveyed found daily steering and maneuvering tasks to be difficult or impossible [2]; and according to the clinicians who treat them, nearly half of those patients unable to control a powered wheelchair by conventional methods would benefit from an automated navigation system [2].

---

[*]Corresponding author.

Such numbers make it seem likely that intelligent wheelchairs catering to those patients' needs would have a deep societal impact. One might argue that the transition to wheelchairs that cooperate with the user is at least as important as that from manual to electric wheelchairs—possibly even more important since this would mark a paradigmatic rather than merely a technological shift. However, to the best of our knowledge, there is no general method of evaluating the performance of intelligent wheelchairs yet [11]. And in particular, no formal tools exist to evaluate the safety and effectiveness of the interaction between the intelligent wheelchair and its operator.

In this paper we try to make a first step by suggesting a methodology based on work done in the clinical rehabilitation community. In particular, we investigate the use of a specific corpus of tasks, as defined by the Wheelchair Skills Test (WST) [10]. The use of such a well-defined set of tasks has many advantages for the objective evaluation of the intelligent wheelchairs. It ensures the evaluation criteria is relevant to the end-user (since the task domain was originally defined for standard powered wheelchair users), it provides a repeatable evaluation protocol between test subjects, and it admits an objective performance measure.

We first describe the SmartWheeler project and the intelligent wheelchair developed by our research team. The rationale that supports the use of a standardized test and the relevant literature are exposed. The WST is then described, followed by results pertaining to the evaluation of the human-robot interface component of our platform. Finally, future perspectives are presented.

## 2. THE SMARTWHEELER PROJECT

The SmartWheeler project [1, 8] aims at developing—in collaboration with engineers and rehabilitation clinicians—a prototype of a multi-functional intelligent wheelchair to assist individuals with mobility impairments in their daily locomotion, while minimizing physical and cognitive loads.

Figure 1 shows a picture of the SmartWheeler platform (built on top of a commercially available Sunrise Quickie Freestyle which was extended in-house at McGill's Centre for Intelligent Machines).

Most of the software components governing the autonomous navigation are being developed by some of our collaborators [3]. The main contribution of the authors is in the development and validation of the human-robot interface. Figure 2 presents an overview of the software architecture controlling the human-robot interface onboard the robot. The primary mode of interaction is a two-way speech interface. We employ a number of technologies to achieve robust interaction, including natural language processing (automatic speech recognition and grammatical parsing) and high-level dialogue management using Partially Observable Markov Decision Processes. A tactile/visual interface system is also installed, and used primarily for provided visual feedback to the human regarding the state of the dialogue system.

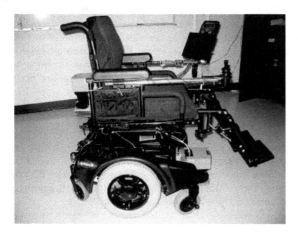

**Figure 1: The SmartWheeler robot platform.**

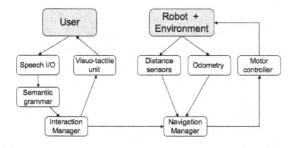

**Figure 2: The SmartWheeler Interaction Architecture.**

Speech provides a natural interface for human operators. Yet it is subject to significant failure rates due to the noise and ambiguity inherent in speech-based communication. Both the choice of tasks and physical environment can further affect the performance of a automated dialogue system. Thus it is imperative that we be able to carefully quantify the performance of the speech-based interface in the context of natural interactions and in a realistic environment.

## 3. REASONS FOR A STANDARDIZED TEST

All engineered research needs to be assessed in terms of the results it produces. Quantifying the efficacy of a robotic device designed to aid people is also a necessary step in the evaluation of its impact. A machine will only be accepted by people if it is of use to them. In this section we list the

major reasons we see for adopting a standardized test for intelligent robotic wheelchairs.

In a recent review of intelligent wheelchair projects Simpson concludes that, "[while] there has been a significant amount of effort devoted to the development of smart wheelchairs, scant attention has been paid to evaluating their performance. [...] Furthermore, no smart wheelchair has been subjected to a rigorous, controlled evaluation that involves extended use in real-world settings." [11]

However, such a "rigorous, controlled evaluation" is essential particularly in the context of health-related projects like SmartWheeler. Performance and safety requirements for wheelchairs are high, since users rely heavily on the device. There must be a rigorous way of proving that these requirements are met before a wheelchair can be deployed. This is especially true for *intelligent* wheelchairs, which will eventually act at least partly in an autonomous manner. As more control is taken from the user and given to the wheelchair, it becomes more important to make guarantees about its performance. Certainly a standard evaluation scheme is also a crucial step if the use of intelligent wheelchairs is to be funded by public health services and insurance companies.

Also, one generally strives to supply a person with the wheelchair that fits them best. This is true for regular wheelchairs, and it applies equally to intelligent wheelchairs. For instance, certain features (e.g. an eye tracker) might be expensive, so one would like to dispense with them if they are not necessary. A standardized test might help figure out the best configuration for a user. Again, this will be essential for funding purposes.

Moreover, as more projects of the kind described above come into being it will be helpful to benchmark the efficacy of the technologies employed. On the one hand this can serve to assess how well the algorithms and hardware being developed within one research project work in a setting that is close to the real world, which can guide researchers towards the problems that have to be addressed next. On the other hand a standardized test facilitates the comparison of similar projects by different research teams, thus highlighting the most promising approaches.

Finally, from a practical point of view, a standardized test can be helpful during the development process because it makes work more target-driven. Keeping the test in mind can help the research team get 'boot-strapped' by providing a useful basis for thinking of possible deployment scenarios. For instance, a first English grammar for the natural language understanding component of a voice recognition system could cover the set of commands that represent the skills required in a standardized test.

## 4. RELEVANT LITERATURE

If a test is to be used for the reasons just listed it should be valid and reliable from a clinical point of view, i.e. it should actually measure what it is intended to measure, and do this in a reproducible way. Designing such a test can be difficult for a computer scientist or engineer lacking the necessary background in clinical rehabilitation. Fortunately the rehabilitation literature offers many possibilities.

Several wheelchair skills tests have been proposed in the literature, and Kilkens *et al.* [4] and Routhier *et al.* [9] fairly recently provided the first systematic overviews. In this section we will briefly summarize their results. Later we will describe the test we chose for evaluating the SmartWheeler project and how we are planning to use it.

Both Kilkens *et al.* [4] and Routhier *et al.* [9] come to the conclusion that no standard test to measure wheelchair skill performance exists as yet, despite a considerable clinical and academic need for such a measure. From a clinical point of view, a standard test should allow for extrapolation of test results to assess subjects' everyday wheelchair performance, in order to guide training and facilitate the selection of a suited wheelchair. From an academic perspective, a standard test would alleviate the current difficulty in comparing study results due to the lack of a common benchmark. As a first step towards standardization, both articles give surveys about existing non-standard wheelchair tests.

Kilkens *et al.* [4] conclude that, while more research is needed to identify the skills to be included in a standard test, out of the 24 tests they reviewed only the Wheelchair Skills Test (henceforth WST) has been "adequately tested on both validity and reliability" [4] (for the results of the evaluation of the WST see [6]). Note that, although Kilkens *et al.* center their discussion on manual chairs, the WST happens to be conceived for powered wheelchairs as well.

The article by Routhier *et al.* [9] is slightly more general in that it considers tests for manual as well as powered wheelchairs and reviews not only controlled environments (as Kilkens *et al.* [4] do) but also distinguishes between three categories of test environments:

1. Real environments (observing subjects' daily wheelchair activities).

2. Controlled environments (e.g. obstacle courses).

3. Virtual environments (using a simulator).

Routhier *et al.* [9] recommend the controlled-environment para-digm. It is interesting to note that they have recently abandoned the design of their own test [10] in favor of the WST, which seems to become the 'gold standard' in the clinic and research communities, being deployed by many institutions across North America. This is due to the aforementioned reason that it is the only test that has been rigorously checked for validity and reliability in statistical terms. If there is to be a standard test for wheelchair skills in the future it seems that it will most likely be the WST.

Another reason that makes the WST particularly appropriate is that, unlike many other tests, it has not been designed for a specific target group (e.g. stroke patients) but for wheelchair users in general (manual and powered). This is important if the intelligent wheelchair shall serve as an aid to more than just a fraction of patients.

# 5. THE WHEELCHAIR SKILLS TEST

The WST, currently in version 4.1 [5], is being developed as part of the Wheelchair Skills Program (WSP) at Dalhousie University in Halifax, Canada, as a "standardized evaluation method that permits a set of representative wheelchair skills to be objectively, simply and inexpensively documented." [5] Extensive information about the test can be found at the WSP website (`www.wheelchairskillsprogram.ca`). The creators envision several situations in which to apply the WST:

1. In the early rehabilitation process it can serve to identify the skills that should be addressed during training.

2. It can serve as an outcome measure to compare a subject's performance before and after rehabilitation.

3. It can be used to test research hypotheses and to assist engineers in the development of new technologies.

Since the WST strives to be as general as possible, it specifies four test categories, one for each combination of wheelchair type (manual vs. powered) and test subject (wheelchair user alone vs. wheelchair user with caregiver). Some of the tasks do not apply to all of the four categories (e.g. 'Picks object from floor' is not applicable if a caregiver is present, since it is assumed that the latter rather than the wheelchair user will do this when the situation arises). For our use of the WST it is crucial to note that it is also explicitly conceived to provide a means of evaluating caregivers. Our goal is not to rate the performance of wheelchair users but that of the intelligent control system. We will do so by considering it a caregiver: Like a caregiver, the software cooperates with the wheelchair user in order to help him/her master everyday situations.

## *Tasks covered*

The powered wheelchair version of the WST (WST-P) test covers 32 skills which are considered representative for general wheelchair performance. The assumption is that a person doing well (performance and safety) on the 32 tasks included in the WST can be considered a skilled wheelchair user because the situations he/she encounters on a daily basis will resemble those tested. In other words, the WST abstracts from a real-world setting to measurable wheelchair skills. It is based on realistic scenarios but is still standardized enough to allow for precise performance measurements. As one would expect, most tasks test navigation skills (e.g. 'Rolls forward 10 m in 30 s', 'Gets over 15-cm pot-hole'), but there are some other actions as well, e.g. those concerning the wheelchair configuration, like 'Controls recline function'. Figure 3 shows an experimenter undergoing some of the skills included in the test. One pass over all tasks takes about 30 minutes [6].

## *Evaluation method*

The test evaluates skill performance and safety. Each skill is graded in terms of these two criteria in a binary manner: a person either passes or fails a task, and he/she does so either in a safe or in an unsafe way. The overall score consists of two numbers, which are simply percentages: one indicates the proportion of tasks that were successfully passed, the other one states how many of the tasks were carried out safely. A task is considered unsafe if injury on the patient's part seems likely or actually occurs during task completion.

The pass/fail grading method makes the evaluation simple and as objective as possible. This is reflected in the high test-retest, intra- and interrater reliabilities achieved by the WST [6][7].

The WST requires the presence of a tester (giving instructions and being in charge of conducting the test) and a spotter (ensuring safe test execution); both roles can, however, be assumed by the same person.

To summarize, the WST takes little time (around 30 minutes) and effort (no special tools required) and is easy to evaluate (just percentage scores). More important, we think that it makes most sense to adopt a test developed by the rehabilitation community and emphasize that the latter seems

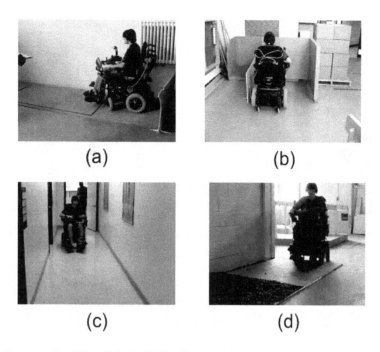

Figure 3: Various stations of the Wheelchair Skills Test, with an intelligent wheelchair. (a) The wheelchair must travel along a sloped platform. (b) The wheelchair must be aligned to the left wall. (c) The wheelchair must move forward through a door. (d) The wheelchair must travel through increased rolling resistance (in this case, gravel).

to converge on the WST as a standard. This is why we have decided to use this test in order to evaluate the SmartWheeler project and propose that it be used by similar projects, too.

## 6. PROPOSAL OF A TEST PARADIGM

As mentioned above, it is desirable to use a test developed by the rehabilitation research community to evaluate the performance of intelligent wheelchairs. The WST (like the other tests reviewed in [4] and [9]) was designed principally to evaluate the joint performance of the disabled person with their wheelchair, rather than evaluating specifically the person, or wheelchair, alone. This is an important aspect, one that is worth considering also in the context of evaluating intelligent wheelchairs.

The expected outcome of applying the WST consists of two numbers indicating the percentage of skills that were accomplished successfully and safely, respectively. These numbers are absolute though, and there is no obvious way of interpreting them. For instance, what does it mean if a disabled person in an intelligent wheelchair (or, to stay within our paradigm, rather the intelligent wheelchair in cooperation with a disabled person) achieved a score of 60%? Is 60% a good or a bad score? In order to attribute more meaning to the result, one should apply the test under different conditions.

A standard way of doing this in clinical practice is to use the WST with a given individual using a variety of wheelchairs. This setup measures the change in the skills exhibited by the person onboard the various wheelchair platforms, and can allow the selection of a wheelchair matched to a person's needs. In the context of intelligent wheelchairs, the WST could be applied to compare the performance and

safety achieved by an individual using both a conventional powered wheelchair and an intelligent wheelchair. The difference between the two outcomes measures how helpful the intelligent software was to the wheelchair user.

The WST has also developed for assessing the efficacy of rehabilitation, by comparing the results of taking the test before and after training or modification to the wheelchair. The WST can thus be applied to evaluate the impact of incorporating different intelligent systems onboard the smart wheelchair (e.g. speech vs. tactile interface, semi-autonomous vs. fully autonomous navigation, etc.) The WST can be further used to evaluate the effectiveness of the training phase, when the human is becoming acquainted with the intelligent wheelchair.

Finally, the WST could be used to faciliate the comparison of results produced by different research teams working on similar projects.

Yet there are limitations to using such a constrained evaluation procedure The set of tasks included in the WST is very constrained, which makes it difficult to test the system for higher-level tasks such as 'Leave the house'. We will touch on this problem in the next section. Another limitation is that the presence of a qualified tester/spotter is required. However, dispensing with such personnel is possible only if an experiment does not involve actual patients. We see our methodology in between these two extremes: We are not arguing that the WST be the *only* evaluation tool used to validate intelligent wheelchairs, but rather that it serves a useful purpose to benchmark systems at a crucial point in their development, namely when the state of the project already warrants experiments with real patients, without being as advanced yet as to necessitate long-term studies in real environments.

# 7. PRELIMINARY EVALUATION

A preliminary evaluation was conducted to evaluate the design and implementation of the communication interface of the intelligent wheelchair. Seven healthy subjects, all of them university students without involvement in the project, were asked to go through the tasks of the WST, using appropriate vocal commands to communicate each task. The physical robot was not involved in this task; the only measures of interest were the performance of the speech recognition and the dialogue management modules through the set of WST skills. These results were reported in earlier publications [1].

A second round of experiments involving eight healthy subjects, all of them clinicians in local rehabilitation centers but without involvement in the project, was performed more recently. These experiments were performed on a different robotic platform developed at École Polytechnique de Montréal [3]; this second platform features substantial differences from the SmartWheeler in terms of hardware and autonomous navigation software, however the user interaction modules are the same. Results analyzing the performance of the communication interface during these experiments are presented in Figure 4. This evaluation involved the full robot capabilities, from the robust communication to autonomous navigation. However the results presented here focus primarily on the speech interface, which is the primary contribution of the authors.

As shown in Figure 4, the robot's current architecture provides a robust architecture for handling communication with the user. Users were able to complete the test using between 114 and 219 commands. The word error rate for some subjects (subjects 4 and 8) was quite high. However the appropriate use of queries allowed the system to reach a performance level comparable to that of other users, as shown by the low incidence of incorrect actions.

Overall, the test subjects were satisfied by the functionality of the robot's interface and appreciated the visual feedback capabilities. While the word error was in some cases quite high, the use of probabilistic techniques allowed the system to maintain a low rate of incorrect actions, thus providing satisfactory performance overall. Some subjects felt they needed more time to get familiar with the platform to exploit it more successfully. Training time for all subjects was on the order of 30 minutes.

Based on these results, the system was judged to be sufficiently usable and robust to move forward with experiments involving the target population (disabled people). Therefore a third round of experiments involving eight subjects with mobility impairments is currently underway.

# 8. FUTURE PERSPECTIVES

The WST has been designed for evaluating skill performance and safety in a controlled environment. As just stated, we think that this paradigm is generally well-suited for the purpose of testing intelligent wheelchairs. Referring to the distinction made in [9] and summarized in section 4, we will briefly comment on the other two test categories as well:

## Real environments

Observing users in their everyday setting in order to assess their performance in a standardized manner is difficult both practically and theoretically. First, from a practical point of

| Subject id | Number of commands | Word error rate | Number of queries | Number of correct actions | Number of incorrect actions |
|---|---|---|---|---|---|
| 1 | 136 | 8.8% | 10 | 121 | 5 (3.7%) |
| 2 | 159 | 13.8% | 18 | 136 | 5 (3.1%) |
| 3 | 165 | 13.5% | 11 | 152 | 2 (1.2%) |
| 4 | 201 | 23.6% | 37 | 155 | 9 (4.5%) |
| 5 | 114 | 6.2% | 13 | 97 | 4 (3.5%) |
| 6 | 219 | 2.3% | 10 | 208 | 1 (0.5%) |
| 7 | 210 | 13.1% | 25 | 175 | 10 (4.8%) |
| 8 | 141 | 19.3% | 26 | 111 | 4 (2.8%) |

**Figure 4: Performance of the Interaction Manager for the Wheelchair Skills Test. The second column shows the number of vocal commands issued by the user throughout the test. The third column reports the raw speech recognition error rate. The fourth column shows the number of clarification queries issued by the robot in cases where the command was misunderstood or ambiguous. The fifth column presents the number of correct actions carried by the robot, as identified by human labeling of video sequences. Finally, the last column reports the number of times the robot selected an incorrect actions; users were instructed to recover from such situations by issuing a *Stop* command, or starting a new command.**

view, it is time-consuming and thus expensive, as a clinician would have to examine the test subject's daily wheelchair performance over a sufficiently long period of time. Second, the high variance in terms of environment properties makes it conceptually hard to compare scores. Coping with this high variance is, however, one of the foremost challenges in the development of an intelligent wheelchair, so evaluating how well the device can deal with it is crucial for assessing the success of the project. Consider, for instance, a user utterance like "I'm hungry." There is no standardized way of benchmarking the wheelchair's reaction in such a situation because the best reaction depends very much on the setting: Downtown the best option might be to ask the user which restaurant he/she wants to go to, whereas at home it might be best to take him/her to the kitchen. A modified test paradigm will be necessary to rate the quality of intelligent control software in such real environments. But to rigorously assess more basic performance quality we need the more restricted and controlled type of scenario we have presented.

## Virtual environments

Virtual tests involving a simulator are probably even cheaper to conduct than controlled-environment tests as proposed in this article. Routhier *et al.* [9], however, state that such tests have demonstrated a "limited applicability to assessment" mainly due to technical weaknesses of the simulators used. However, since big parts of the technology developed for intelligent wheelchairs (e.g. the interaction manager) are software rather than hardware, it might indeed make sense to evaluate these parts in a simulator. As the respective technology advances, this will clearly become more feasible than it is today. But to assess the entire project it will be necessary to evaluate the interplay of both software and hardware. This is why we deem a controlled-environment test like the WST better suited.

## 9. CONCLUSION

In this paper we have suggested a methodology to quantify the performance of intelligent wheelchairs, and have applied this test to the evaluation of the speech interface of an intelligent wheelchair. Rather than designing a test from scratch we are building on work done by specialists in the field of rehabilitation. We have picked the WST, which seems to emerge as a *de facto* standard in the clinical and research communities. It is based on situations occurring in the daily lives of wheelchair users but still abstract enough to allow for precise measurements. The WST has been checked for validity and reliability by the developing team, which is crucial both principally and practically if a passing score is to be used as evidence that a wheelchair is ready to be deployed and funded by public health services and insurance companies. In this sense, a strict evaluation is a critical step towards both establishing and gauging the efficacy of intelligent wheelchairs.

## Acknowledgement

**Active participants in the project:** The project was carried out in close collaboration with researchers at the École Polytechnique de Montréal (Paul Cohen, Sousso Kelouwani, Hai Nguyen, Patrice Boucher) who developed the intelligent wheelchair platform used for the human subject experiments. Researchers at the Universite de Montreal (Robert Forget) and at the Centre de réadaptation Lucie Bruneau (Wormser Honoré) acted as the primary clinical investigators. **Collaborators:** The project also benefitted from contributions by researchers at the Université de Montréal (Louise Demers), and also clinicians and technicians at the Centre de réadaptation Lucie Bruneau (Claude Dufour) and at the Constance-Lethbridge Rehabilitation Centre (Paula Stone, Daniel Rock, Jean-Paul Dussault). **Sponsors:** Financial support was provided through the Canadian Foundation for Innovation, the Natural Sciences and Engineering Council of Canada, and the Fonds québécois de la recherche sur la nature et les technologies. Additional funding was provided by the Fondation du Centre de réadaptation Lucie Bruneau, the Fondation Constance Lethbridge, and Robovic. Materials were donated by Sunrise Medical Canada and LiP-PERT.

## 10. REFERENCES

[1] A. Atrash, R. Kaplow, J. Villemure, R. West, H. Yamani, and J. Pineau. Towards the deployment of an intelligent wheelchair in a standardized rehabilitation environment. *Interaction Studies*, pages 345–356, 2009.

[2] L. Fehr, E. Langbein, and S. B. Skaar. Adequacy of power wheelchair control interfaces for persons with severe disabilities: A clinical survey. *J. of Rehabilitation Research & Development*, 37:353–360, 2000.

[3] W. Honoré, A. Atrash, P. Boucher, R. Kaplow, S. Kalouwani, H. Nguyen, J. Villemure, R. West, F. Routhier, P. Stone, C. Dufour, J.-P. Dussault, D. Rock, P. Cohen, L. Demers, R. Forget, and J. Pineau. Human-oriented design and initial validation of an intelligent powered wheelchair. In *RESNA Annual Conference*, 2010.

[4] O. J. E. Kilkens, M. W. M. Post, A. J. Dallmeijer, H. A. M. Seelen, and L. H. V. van der Woude. Wheelchair skills tests: A systematic review. *Clinical Rehabilitation*, 17:418–430, 2003.

[5] R. L. Kirby. *Wheelchair Skills Program (WSP), Version 4.1. Wheelchair Skills Test (WST) Manual*, 2007. http://www .wheelchairskillsprogram.ca/eng/4.1/WST_Manual_ Version_4.1.pdf (accessed 04/27/2008).

[6] R. L. Kirby, D. J. Dupuis, A. H. MacPhee, A. L. Coolen, C. Smith, K. L. Best, A. M. Newton, A. D. Mountain, D. A. MacLeod, and J. P. Bonaparte. The Wheelchair Skills Test (version 2.4): Measurement properties. *Arch. Phys. Med. Rehabil.*, 85:794–804, 2004.

[7] R. L. Kirby, J. Swuste, D. J. Dupuis, D. A. MacLeod, and R. Monroe. The Wheelchair Skills Test: A pilot study of a new outcome measure. *Arch. Phys. Med. Rehabil.*, 83:10–18, 2002.

[8] J. Pineau and A. Atrash. SmartWheeler: A robotic wheelchair test-bed for investigating new models of human-robot interaction. In *AAAI Spring Symposium on Multidisciplinary Collaboration for Socially Assistive Robotics*, pages 59–64, 2007.

[9] F. Routhier, C. Vincent, J. Desrosiers, and S. Nadeau. Mobility of wheelchair users: A proposed performance assessment framework. *Disability & Rehabilitation*, 25:19–34, 2003.

[10] F. Routhier, C. Vincent, J. Desrosiers, S. Nadeau, and C. Guerette. Development of an obstacle course assessment of wheelchair user performance (OCAWUP). *Technology & Disability*, 16:19–31, 2004.

[11] R. C. Simpson. Smart wheelchairs: A literature review. *J. of Rehabilitation Research & Development*, 42:423–436, 2005.

# Evaluation of Ultra-Wideband Technology for use in 3D Locating Systems

**Adam Kopp**
Fire Fighting Technologies, BFRL, NIST
100 Bureau Dr., Stop 8661
Gaithersburg, MD 20899
301-975-5965
akopp@nist.gov

**Kamel Saidi**
Construction Metrology and Automation, BFRL, NIST
100 Bureau Dr., Stop 8611
Gaithersburg, MD 20899
301-975-6069
kamel.saidi@nist.gov

**Hiam Khoury**
American University of Beirut
P.O. Box 11-0236 / FEA-CEE
Riad El Solh / Beirut 1107 2020, Lebanon
+961-1-340460 ext.3428
hk50@aub.edu.lb

## ABSTRACT

A high-powered (5 Watt peak power) ultra-wideband (UWB) ranging system was evaluated for use as the basis of a 3-Dimensional (3D) locating system by comparing tracking results to a ground truth system. The UWB ranging system is composed of five ranging radios. One radio is connected to a computer and the others communicate to it wirelessly. The distance between any two of the radios is determined using a time-of-flight (TOF) algorithm provided with the system from the manufacturer. Four of the radios were placed at known locations and the fifth radio was placed at an unknown location to be tracked. The distance from each of these four fixed radios to the fifth radio was continuously measured and different tracking algorithms were implemented to calculate the unknown radio's 3D position in real-time. The algorithms tested utilized trilateration, multilateration, error minimization, and low-pass filtering. Position-versus-time data were obtained from each algorithm and compared to position-versus-time data obtained from a 3D ground truth locating system known to have an uncertainty of approximately 5 mm. Both moving and stationary tests were performed for each algorithm. During moving experiments, the tracked radio was moved along a predetermined path by an experimenter holding the radio while walking. During stationary experiments, the tracked radio remained at a single location while 1000 positions were measured by the various algorithms. The tests took place in an indoor laboratory environment which was free of obstruction in order to promote optimum performance of both the UWB and ground truth tracking systems. By analyzing the data from the UWB and ground truth systems, the error of the UWB system's 3D location measurement was expressed as a function of time.

## 1.0 INTRODUCTION

The ability to track first responders in real-time at the scene of emergency incidents is of interest to the first responder community. For this reason, locating systems for first responders are an emerging technology being researched and developed. While locating technologies such as global positioning systems (GPS) are well understood and well developed, they are not applicable to locating systems for first responders because they are not able to function reliably under the harsh conditions experienced by first responders. One of the most significant challenges of developing a locating system for first responders is developing a system that works indoors. This is a significant challenge because modern construction materials such as concrete and metal are very effective at blocking radio frequency (RF) signals at the wavelengths that locating systems traditionally operate (this range consists primarily of several hundred MHz to several GHz). One attempt to rectify this problem is the use of ultra-wideband (UWB) technology. UWB technology operates in the several GHz range and uses a very large (several GHz) bandwidth to make very short (several nanoseconds in duration) pulses of RF energy. While operating in the several GHz range makes UWB systems susceptible to path loss when propagating through materials, the short-duration pulses utilized by UWB systems offer fine spatial resolution, making UWB an ideal technology for time of flight (TOF) based ranging and locating systems. Furthermore, non-line of sight (NLOS) mitigation techniques have been proposed for UWB systems, which show the potential for rectifying ranging errors that occur due to UWB signals attenuating through building materials (Alsindi et al. 2009).

In order to evaluate the potential of UWB technology to be used for 3D locating systems, various localization algorithms utilizing different mathematical and geometric concepts were developed. The algorithms were able to calculate the position of a tracked UWB radio[1] in real-time from the known locations of four stationary radios and the respective distance from each stationary

---

1 Certain commercial equipment, instruments, or materials may be identified in this paper in order to specify the experimental procedure adequately. Such identification is not intended to imply recommendation or endorsement by the National Institute of Standards and Technology, nor is it intended to imply that the materials or equipment identified are necessarily the best available for the purpose.

radio to the tracked radio. These algorithms will be used in future research to study the ability of different UWB ranging systems to act as the basis for a 3D locating system, as well as study the effectiveness of UWB NLOS mitigation techniques when applied to a 3D locating system.

The algorithms were applied to an UWB-based ranging system to evaluate their performance under LOS conditions. The performance of the UWB ranging system used under ideal conditions was well understood and characterized. Therefore, experiments were designed to allow the UWB system to operate under near-ideal conditions. This allowed inaccuracies of the algorithms being tested and inaccuracies of the UWB ranging system being utilized to be distinguished. The algorithms that were tested utilized trilateration averaging, error minimization, and multilateration. The data obtained from these tracking algorithms were compared to a ground truth system in order to characterize their respective errors.

Finally, experimental data obtained from both the UWB and ground truth systems were applied in a 3D virtual application that tracks the position of workers on a construction site (Khoury and Kamat 2009). This was done to visually evaluate the performance of the UWB-based locating system against the ground truth tracking system in order to explore the UWB system's feasibility for construction applications.

## 2.0 SYSTEM IMPLEMENTATION
### 2.1 Hardware
The UWB ranging system used during testing consisted of individual radios that were able to measure the distance between each other. One radio was connected to a computer through a serial connection. On the radio connected to the computer was a field programmable gate array (FPGA), which controlled the radio. A library to control the FPGA was provided by the vendor of the UWB ranging system. This library interfaced with C++, allowing programs written in C++ to be carried out by the UWB ranging system. In this setup, a program written in C++ controlled the FPGA on the radio directly connected to the computer. The radio connected to the computer was able to wirelessly control the remaining UWB radios in order to continuously gather ranging data from all of the radios. These ranging data were used by the various algorithms to calculate the position of the tracked radio.

The radios used UWB pulses to wirelessly communicate with each other and to find the distance between each other. To communicate with each other, the radios sent and received UWB pulses, which they interpreted as digital data. To measure distance, an UWB radio sent out a pulse that was detected by another radio. This radio then sent back a pulse to the radio that sent the initial pulse. The total time for this process was recorded and sent to the computer via the radio connected to the computer. From this time (known as the time of flight (TOF) of the UWB pulse), a distance was calculated using the known speed of light.

### 2.2 Software
All software that was used during testing to control the UWB ranging system was written in C++ using the library provided by the vendor. Data obtained from the algorithms were analyzed by commercially available high-level mathematics software. This software was used to gather statistics and create plots of the data obtained from the algorithms.

## 2.3 Algorithms
### 2.3.1 Trilateration Averaging
The trilateration averaging algorithm treated each stationary radio and its known location as the center of a sphere, and the distance from that radio to the tracked radio as the radius of the sphere. Four equations of spheres were thereby created; one for each stationary radio.

$$(x_i - x_{tracked})^2 + (y_i - y_{tracked})^2 + (z_i - z_{tracked})^2 = r_i^2$$

*Where i=1, 2, 3, 4 for stationary radios 1, 2, 3, 4, and $r_i$ represents the measured range from stationary radio, i, to the tracked radio.*

The algorithm evaluated each combination of three spheres at a time and used the Newton-Raphson method to solve for their point of intersection as described in [2]. This gave four sets of 3D coordinates that described the position of the tracked radio. The four values of $x_{tracked}$, $y_{tracked}$, and $z_{tracked}$ were averaged to estimate the location of the tracked radio. If three spheres were ever described that did not yield a common point of intersection (i.e. any of the measured range values were too short), each of the lengths was increased to a point where a solution did exist.

### 2.3.2 Error Minimization
The error minimization algorithm defined the distance from any of the stationary radios to the tracked radio using the known Cartesian coordinates of that radio and the variables $x_{tracked}$, $y_{tracked}$, and $z_{tracked}$ (representing the unknown coordinates of the tracked radio) in the Pythagorean Theorem.

$$d_i = \sqrt{(x_i - x_{tracked})^2 + (y_i - y_{tracked})^2 + (z_i - z_{tracked})^2}$$

*Where $d_i$ represents the true distance from stationary radio, i, to the tracked radio.*

The error in the measured range from a stationary radio to the tracked radio at any point in time was therefore defined as the measured distance minus the distance solved for by the Pythagorean Theorem. This yielded four error expressions, each of which described the measured distance from a stationary radio to the tracked radio.

$$E_i = d_i - r_i = \sqrt{(x_i - x_{tracked})^2 + (y_i - y_{tracked})^2 + (z_i - z_{tracked})^2} - r_i$$

*Where $E_i$ represents the error in the measured distance from stationary radio, i, to the tracked radio.*

These expressions were squared and then added together to make an overall square of residuals expression.

$$S(x,y,z) = \sum_{i=1}^{4} E_i^2 = \sum_{i=1}^{4} (\sqrt{(x_i - x_{tracked})^2 + (y_i - y_{tracked})^2 + (z_i - z_{tracked})^2} - r_i)^2$$

*Where $x_{tracked}$, $y_{tracked}$, and $z_{tracked}$ are the parameters x, y, and z, respectively, of S.*

When this expression was minimized for the parameters x, y, and z, the calculated values of x, y, and z gave the best estimate of the coordinates of the tracked radio. The tested algorithm used a Davidon-Fletcher-Powell (DFP) minimization as described in [9].

$$\min S(x, y, z)$$

*Where the calculated values of x, y, and z represent the best estimate of the coordinates of the tracked radio.*
(Coope 2000).

### 2.3.3 Multilateration
Multilateration is a popular method of calculating the 3D position of a tracked object. Locating systems that utilize multilateration consist of a tracked transmitter and four or more stationary radios at known locations. The tracked transmitter transmits an RF signal that is received by the stationary receivers. The time

difference of arrival (TDOA) of the RF signal at the separate receivers is measured and converted to a distance using the known speed of light. This distance is used as the difference between the distances from the stationary radios to the tracked radio. By using these differences in distance and the known coordinates of four stationary radios, three separate hyperboloids can be described, and the location of the tracked radio is defined as their point of intersection.

$$(\sqrt{(x_1 - x_{tracked})^2 + (y_1 - y_{tracked})^2 + (z_1 - z_{tracked})^2} - \sqrt{(x_i - x_{tracked})^2 + (y_i - y_{tracked})^2 + (z_i - z_{tracked})^2} = (r_1 - r_i)$$

*Where i=2,3,4 for stationary radios 2,3, and 4.*
(Mathias and Leonardi 2008).

### *2.3.4 Filtering of 3D Tracking Data*
Along with different localization algorithms, an attempt to filter the ranging data from each pair of radios was made in order to improve performance. A low-pass Butterworth filter was applied to the ranging data to reduce the noise in measurements (Jagannathan and Patel 1986). The filtered data was sent through the various localization algorithms and the calculated coordinates were compared to the coordinates calculated from the unfiltered ranging data. Finally, a different filtering method was used, in which low-pass Butterworth filters were applied to the end-value coordinate data. This was attempted because it was seen that the algorithms caused different amounts of noise in the different axes of the calculated coordinates. Furthermore, since this locating system is used to track humans, it is reasonable to assume that the tracked radio will move differently in the z-axis (perpendicular to the earth's surface) than the x and y-axes (parallel to the earth's surface). Therefore different filters were designed to more accurately reflect the behavior of the system along the different axes.

## 3.0 EXPERIMENTAL DESIGN AND SETUP
### 3.1 Determining Uncertainty of UWB-Based Ranging System
The uncertainty of the UWB ranging system was measured as a function of distance. Each pair of radios was set at distances of 1.52 m to 10.67 m in increments of 1.52 m. These distances were measured with a tape measure. At each distance, 10,000 ranges were measured. From these data, the average distance and the standard deviation of the measured distances were calculated in order to determine the uncertainty in distance measurements obtained from the UWB ranging system.

### 3.2 Determining the Uncertainty of UWB-Based 3D Locating system
To measure the uncertainty of the UWB-based 3D locating system, both stationary and moving experiments were performed. During moving experiments, the tracked radio was moved along a predetermined path by an experimenter holding the radio while walking. During stationary experiments, the tracked radio remained at a single location while 1,000 positions were measured by the various algorithms.

In both the stationary and moving experiments, a ground truth 3D tracking system known to have an uncertainty of approximately 5 mm was used to measure the tracked radio's position in real-time. Position data collected from the tested algorithms were compared to data collected from the ground truth system in order to determine error as a function of time, maximum error, average error, and the standard deviation of errors (i.e. the uncertainty of the measured position). For all experiments, the stationary UWB radios were placed on the outside perimeter of the testing area in

an approximately rectangular shape. This orientation was chosen because it represents the most likely setup for a potential first responder locating system, in which stationary radios are placed around the perimeter of a building at the scene of an emergency incident in order to track first responders inside. The ground truth system was setup in such a way that it could accurately measure the 3D position of the tracked radio at all times during experiments. The testing area was an indoor laboratory environment measuring approximately 5.49 m x 13.7 m. The area was arranged to allow for both the UWB and ground truth systems to operate in LOS conditions in order to promote near-ideal behavior of each.

## 3.3 Application of UWB-Based Locating System to a 3D Virtual Application
In recent years, the need for localization and tracking has been increasing in many fields and currently offers the potential for improving manual processes and supporting decision-making tasks in the construction field (Khoury 2009). In order to evaluate the UWB-based locating system's potential applicability to position tracking in indoor construction environments, position data collected from the UWB-based locating system were compared to data collected from the ground truth system in a 3D virtual world. Results are shown in Section 4.3.

## 4.0 RESULTS AND DISCUSSION
### 4.1 Uncertainty of UWB-Based Ranging System
The standard deviations of the measured ranges were taken as a percentage of the total distance. This yielded a relationship between the uncertainty of the UWB-based ranging system and the distance from one radio to another that was best described by the general equation, $\sigma_p = a * x^b + c$, where a, b, and c are experimentally derived values, x is the nominal distance between the radios being evaluated, and $\sigma_p$ is the standard deviation of the measured ranges as a percentage of the distance, x (i.e. $\sigma_p = \sigma/x$, where $\sigma$ is the standard deviation of the measured ranges at distance x). Results from these tests are shown below in table 1 and figure 1. Because of the similarity of results, data from only one pair of radios is shown as an example.

**Table 1: Ranging data between two UWB ranging radios.**

| Nominal distance (m) | Average measured range (m) | σ (standard deviation of measured ranges in m) | σ_p (standard deviation of measured ranges as a percentage of nominal range) |
|---|---|---|---|
| 1.52 | 1.58 | 0.044 | 0.0290 |
| 3.05 | 3.06 | 0.026 | 0.0085 |
| 4.57 | 4.57 | 0.018 | 0.0039 |
| 6.10 | 6.10 | 0.022 | 0.0036 |
| 7.62 | 7.64 | 0.022 | 0.0029 |
| 9.15 | 9.16 | 0.037 | 0.0040 |
| 10.67 | 10.67 | 0.022 | 0.0021 |

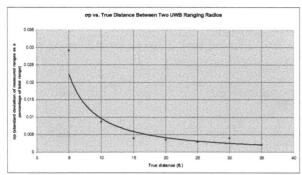

**Figure 1: Standard deviation of ranging data as a percentage of total distance between two UWB ranging radios.**

In these data, it can be seen that the error of the ranging system was greater at close distances. While no explanation for this behavior was provided by the vendor of the system, it is possible that this trend is a product of the circuit used by the system to measure TOF. Such a circuit would measure time in discrete intervals. As the distance between two radios that are ranging each other decreases, so does the TOF between the two radios. As the TOF decreases, it approaches the time step of the time measuring circuit used by the UWB system. The system therefore offers diminishing resolution in comparison to the distance between two radios ranging each other as the distance between those radios decreases. Furthermore, although the time step of the time measuring circuit is assumed to be constant, it actually fluctuates. When the distance between two radios ranging each other is great, the effect of these fluctuations is negated. This is because a large distance between two radios is associated with a long TOF. Likewise, a long TOF allows for the time measuring circuit to take many time steps. As more time steps are taken, the average of the actual time steps is more likely to be closer to the expected time step. This makes the measured TOF, and therefore measured distance, more accurate and decreases the uncertainty in the values reported by the system.

## 4.2 Uncertainty of UWB-Based 3D Locating System

The error of each tracking algorithm was measured as a function of time by comparing the 3D positioning data obtained from the algorithms to the ground truth positioning data. During each test, the average 3D error and the standard deviation of the 3D error was calculated in order to determine the uncertainty of the system. Results are shown below in Figures 2-7 and Tables 2-3. Because of the similarity of results, only visual representations of the paths created by the error minimization algorithm during one moving and one stationary test are shown as examples.

### 4.2.1 Results of Moving Tests

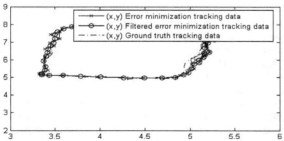

**Figure 2: Overhead view of path created by error minimization algorithm during moving test. Axes are in m.**

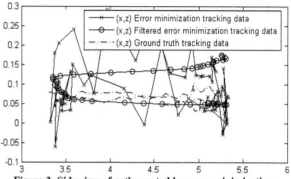

**Figure 3: Side view of path created by error minimization algorithm during moving test. Axes are in m.**

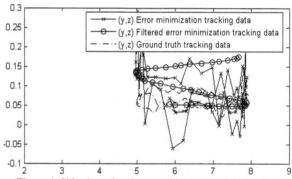

**Figure 4: Side view of path created by error minimization algorithm during moving tests. Axes are in m.**

**Table 2: Maximum error, average error, and standard deviation of errors in locating data obtained during moving tests by various algorithms.**

|  | Max error (m) | Average error (m) | Standard deviation of errors (m) |
|---|---|---|---|
| Trilateration averaging | 0.381 | 0.210 | 0.109 |
| Filtered trilateration averaging | 0.360 | 0.199 | 0.095 |
| Error minimization | 0.238 | 0.083 | 0.038 |
| Filtered error minimization | 0.168 | 0.074 | 0.030 |
| Multilateration | 1.930 | 0.763 | 0.498 |
| Filtered multilateration | 1.677 | 0.730 | 0.480 |

## 4.2.2 Results of Stationary Tests

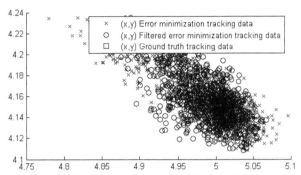

**Figure 5: Overhead view of points calculated by error minimization algorithm during stationary test. Axes are in m.**

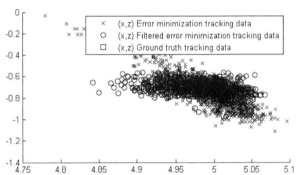

**Figure 6: Side view of points calculated by error minimization algorithm during stationary test. Axes are in m.**

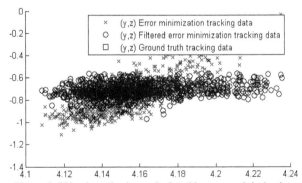

**Figure 7: Side view of points calculated by error minimization algorithm during stationary test. Axes are in m.**

**Table 3: Maximum error, average error, and standard deviation of errors in locating data obtained during stationary testing by various algorithms.**

|  | Max error (m) | Average error (m) | Standard deviation of errors (m) |
|---|---|---|---|
| Trilateration averaging | 0.573 | 0.291 | 0.109 |
| Filtered trilateration averaging | 0.345 | 0.290 | 0.026 |
| Error minimization | 0.701 | 0.191 | 0.135 |
| Filtered error minimization | 0.198 | 0.071 | 0.036 |
| Multilateration | 0.747 | 0.170 | 0.124 |
| Filtered multilateration | 0.198 | 0.062 | 0.031 |

The results of these experiments show that the error minimization algorithm exhibited the most consistent behavior of the algorithms tested. While the uncertainty of the trilateration averaging and multilateration algorithms was greater in moving experiments than in stationary experiments, the uncertainty of the error minimization algorithm decreased slightly during moving experiments. It is believed that this behavior is due to the natural tendencies of the algorithms tested and the non-ideal behavior of the UWB-based ranging radios.

Each of the algorithms tested has its own characteristic response to errors inherent in the input ranging data. For example, multilateration algorithms experience their greatest uncertainty when the tracked radio is in the middle of the stationary radios (such as the setup used for testing). Furthermore, it was observed that in many cases, the greatest uncertainty in the calculated 3D position occurred in the calculated z-coordinate. This is believed to be a property of the algorithms used.

From preliminary testing, it was shown that the UWB-based ranging radios exhibited non-ideal behavior when their front faces were not turned directly towards each other. This occurred whenever the tracked radio was placed too far to the side or too far above any of the stationary radios. This caused the measured range to be greater than the nominal range and increased the uncertainty in the measurement. As explained previously, these errors in the measured distances affected the 3D positions calculated by the various algorithms differently.

One attempt to correct the errors in the calculated 3D positions was to apply a low-pass Butterworth filter to the ranging data before using those data in the various algorithms to calculate 3D position. However, it was found that the effect of this was negligible because of the the slow sampling rate of the UWB system. Because the sampling rate was slow, random noise occurred at approximately the same rate as actual changes in the measured distances. The low-pass filter was therefore unable to effectively distinguish random noise from a true change in measurement and did little to correct the measured distances. To mitigate this problem, similar low-pass Butterworth filters were applied separately to the calculated x, y, and z coordinates. This was effective because of the different time-dependent behavior of the calculated x, y, and z coordinates. These differences in behavior occurred because of the tendencies of the tracking algorithms and because of the semi-predictable motion of humans (humans generally move more sporadically when moving parallel to the earth's surface - along the x-and-y-axes than when moving perpendicular to the earth's surface - along the z-axis).

## 4.3 Results of 3D Virtual Application

The objective of the 3D application was to further evaluate the performance of the UWB-based locating system and demonstrate its suitability for construction applications. This was achieved by collecting data from one of the aforementioned moving experiments where a mobile user or experimenter (i.e. inspector, construction engineer, etc.) was continuously tracked as s/he moved along a predetermined path inside a laboratory. Position data collected from the developed algorithms were compared to data collected from the ground truth system The results were virtually depicted through two different users in one tracking application.

In order to visualize the mobile user's path, a 3D environment with sufficient underlying computer graphics support to allow the manipulation of entities in a 3D scene was needed. In this case, a C++-based computer graphics toolkit was adopted (Khoury 2009). Selected virtual snapshots of tracked users at different locations in the testing laboratory are shown in Figure 8.

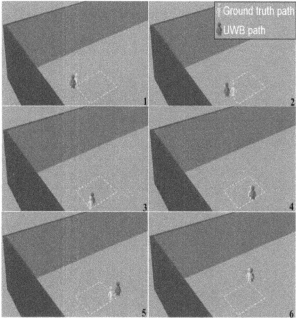

**Figure 8: Virtual representation for comparative indoor tracking of mobile users, using UWB and ground truth locating systems.**

## 5.0 CONCLUSIONS

The results of these experiments both validate the algorithms that were used and suggest that UWB has potential for use in 3D locating systems. The UWB system tested was relatively low-cost and simple, yet still yielded uncertainties in measurements that could potentially be useful to groups such as first responders or construction workers. Much of the uncertainty in calculated 3D positions was likely due to simple design flaws of the UWB ranging system. These flaws likely existed because the system was not intended to be converted to a 3D locating system. Furthermore, many of these design flaws could be corrected with simple solutions. The shortcomings of the UWB ranging system include its slow sampling rate, sequential ranging, and directionality.

From experimental data, it was found that the UWB locating system sampled at approximately 2.6 Hz. This caused several problems; it did not allow for effective low-pass filtering of the measured ranges and it meant that measured distances from stationary radios to the tracked radio were not from the same point in time. The former could be improved only by increasing the sampling rate of the UWB system. This could be accomplished through more efficient circuitry. The latter could be improved by increasing the sampling rate, or by redesigning the system to not obtain ranging data sequentially. The tested system obtained ranging data by sequentially sending pulses from stationary nodes to the tracked node. If, instead, the system was designed in such a way that the tracked radio sent out a single pulse that was detected by each of the stationary radios, the measured ranges would be from the same point in time.

Preliminary testing showed that when two UWB radios did not directly face each other, the measured distance between them was consistently larger than the nominal distance. This implies that the UWB radios were not truly omni-directional, so that when the tracked radio was in certain locations relative to the stationary radios, the uncertainty of the calculated 3D position would increase. This could be resolved by fashioning the radios with omni-directional UWB antennas similar to those discussed in [4].

With the development of better systems that will incorporate more optimized hardware and NLOS mitigation techniques, the future of UWB technology is promising. UWB shows the potential to solve the problem of indoor 3D localization. For the purpose of first responder or construction worker locating systems, future research should include NLOS mitigation techniques so that algorithms such as those examined can be applied to develop 3D locating systems capable of accurately working in an indoor environment.

## 6.0 References

[1] Alsindi et al. (2009), "NLOS Channel Identification and Mitigation in Ultra Wideband ToA-Based Wireless Sensor Networks", Mitsubishi Electric Research Laboratories, Inc., Cambridge, MA.

[2] Chapra, S.C and Canale, R.P. (1988), "Numerical Methods for Engineers", 2nd edition, McGraw-Hill Book Company.

[3] Coope, I.D. (2000), "Reliable Computation of the Points of Intersection of $n$ Spheres in $R^n$", Anziam J., 42 (E), pp.C46-477.

[4] Gentile, C. and Kik, A. (2007), "A Comprehensive Evaluation of Indoor Ranging Using Ultra-Wideband Technology," *EURASIP Journal on Wireless Communications and Networking*, vol. 2007, Article ID 86031, 10 pages, 2007. doi:10.1155/2007/86031

[5] Jagannathan, S., and Patel, R. C. (1986), "Digital Filters for Noise Reduction in Optical Kinetic Experiments", Analytical Chemistry 58(2), 421-427.

[6] Khoury, H. M. (2009). "Context Aware Information Access and Retrieval for Rapid On-Site Decision Making in Construction, Inspection and Maintenance of Constructed Facilities", Ph.D. Dissertation, Department of Civil and Environmental Engineering, University of Michigan, Ann Arbor, MI.

[7] Khoury, H. M., and Kamat V. R. (2009), "Indoor User Localization for Context-Aware Information Retrieval in Construction Projects", Automation in Construction, 18 (4), Elsevier Science, New York, NY, 444-457.

[8] Mathias, A., Leonardi, M., and Galati, G. (2008), "An Efficient Multilateration Algorithm," Digital Communications – Enhanced Surveillance of Aircraft and Vehicles 2008, TIWDC/ESAV 2008. Tyrrhenian International Workshop on.

[9] W.H. Press, B.P. Flannery, S.A. Teukolsky, and W.T. Vetterling (1992), *Numerical Recipes in C: The Art of Scientific Computing*, 2nd edition, Cambridge University Press.

# Detecting Humans under Partial Occlusion using Markov Logic Networks

Raghuraman Gopalan
Dept. of ECE
University of Maryland
College Park, MD 20742 USA
raghuram@umiacs.umd.edu

William Schwartz
Dept. of Computer Science
University of Maryland
College Park, MD 20742 USA
schwartz@cs.umd.edu

## ABSTRACT

Identifying humans under partial occlusion is a challenging problem in unconstrained scene understanding. In contrast to many existing works that model human appearance *in isolation*, we address this problem by studying the semantic context between human face and other body parts using Markov logic networks. By learning a set of probabilistic first-order logic rules that capture interactions between body parts under varying degrees of occlusion, and the relationship they share with the neighboring spatial windows, we obtain a graphical model representation of these instances to facilitate inference. We illustrate the efficacy of our method through experiments on standard human detection datasets, and an internally collected dataset with several occluding humans.

## Categories and Subject Descriptors

I.4.8 [**Computing methodologies**]: Image processing and computer vision—*Scene analysis, Object recognition*

## General Terms

Algorithm

## Keywords

Human detection, Occlusion, Context, Learning

## 1. INTRODUCTION

Detecting humans from still images is an extensively studied problem in computer vision. It is a challenging problem due to the presence of scene-induced variations like pose, lighting, inter- and intra- person occlusions, among others. Occlusions, in particular, pose a significant challenge since there is no analytical model for the nature of variations it could inflict on the person's appearance.

The vast majority of the literature on human detection can be classified into the following two categories: holistic

window-based and part-based. In the first category, features extracted from sliding windows are used holistically to perform classification. Some examples include the work of Dalal and Triggs [1] that used histogram of oriented gradients (HOG) features, and Tuzel et al [14] using covariance matrices. Part-based approaches, on the other hand, view a human as a combination of different sub-parts and model their interaction to perform classification. For instance, Wu and Nevatia [16] used edgelet features in a boosting framework to learn nested cascade detectors for each part. Mikolajczyk et al [5] used probabilistic combination to fuse information across body parts.

However, there are only very few works that explicitly account for the effect of occlusion in detecting humans. For instance, Shet et al [12] used a bilattice based logical reasoning framework to detect occluding humans by considering the responses of different low level parts-based detectors as logical facts. Schwartz et al [11] combined the outputs of detectors corresponding to different human parts, and the face using first order logic to model cases that study interactions between them.

**Contributions:** However, logic (by itself) can not accommodate for the probabilistic nature of the real world, and hence a more formal approach that accommodates the uncertainties of the visual scene is needed. Further, by focusing on different aspects of human in isolation (within a single window), the existing works do not account for the information conveyed by the surrounding scene. Since human vision perceives the real world by associating a set of contextual constraints prevalent in nature [13], we propose

- Modeling contextual information between different human parts, and the relation they share with the surrounding spatial windows.

- Learning the source of context using the framework of Markov logic networks [8], which integrates first-order logic with probabilistic reasoning to perform robust inference.

**Outline of the paper:** We first motivate our approach in Section 2 and discuss the details of the detectors, and the sources of context. In Section 3 we introduce the basics of Markov logic networks, including the construction of the network and performing inference. We also highlight our adaptation of this framework in terms of detecting humans under occlusion. We then validate our method in Section 4 on datasets, with and without occlusion, and provide comparisons with the existing methods. We also analyze the advantage of Markov logic when compared with other ways

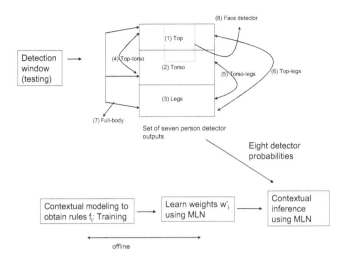

Figure 1: An overview of the proposed approach

of integrating information from detectors. We then discuss the merits and demerits of our approach, and conclude the paper in Section 5.

## 2. AN OVERVIEW OF OUR APPROACH

Our method to detect humans under partial occlusion stems from the notion of parts. We specifically focus on modeling the contextual interactions of these parts in performing inference. Given a set of $N$ detectors corresponding to different body parts, and a set of detection windows $\{d_i\}_{i=1}^M$ in a close spatial neighborhood, we propose the following:

- Learn the relation shared between the $N$ detectors under varying degree of occlusion - **Intra-window context**

- Learn the relation of a window with the surrounding windows under visual uncertainties - **Inter-window context**

- Formulate the contextual information with a set of logic rules, and perform probabilistic inference within the framework of Markov logic networks.

We discuss more details in the following sections.

### 2.1 Design of detectors

We divide the human into the following $N = 8$ parts, full body, top, torso, legs, top-torso, top-legs, torso-legs, and face (trained on a higher resolution than other human parts). An illustration is given in figure 1. We then learn individual detectors for these parts using training data with and without occlusion. The detectors are based on Partial least squares (PLS) [15], and we use the following set of features [10] to learn the appearance variations of these parts: co-occurrence matrices [14] to extract texture features, edge information using HOG [1], and color frequency [10].

Let $\mathbb{X} \in R^m$ denote an m-dimensional space of feature vectors and similarly let $\mathbb{Y} \in R$ be a 1-dimensional space representing the class labels. Let the number of samples (training patches) be n. PLS decomposes the zero-mean

matrix $\mathbf{X}$ ($n \times m$) and zero-mean vector $\mathbf{y}$ ($n \times 1$) into

$$\mathbf{X} = \mathbf{TP}^T + \mathbf{E} \tag{1}$$

$$\mathbf{y} = \mathbf{Uq}^T + \mathbf{f} \tag{2}$$

where $\mathbf{T}$ and $\mathbf{U}$ are ($n \times p$) matrices containing $p$ extracted latent vectors, the ($m \times p$) matrix $\mathbf{P}$ and the ($1 \times p$) vector $\mathbf{q}$ represent the loadings and the ($n \times m$) matrix $\mathbf{E}$ and the ($n \times 1$) vector $\mathbf{f}$ are the residuals. The PLS method, using the nonlinear iterative partial least squares (NIPALS) algorithm [15], constructs a set of weight vectors (or projection vectors) $W = \{w_1, w_2, ..., w_p\}$ such that

$$[cov(t_i, u_i)]^2 = \max_{|\mathbf{w}_i|=1}[cov(\mathbf{Xw}_i, \mathbf{y})]2 \tag{3}$$

where $\mathbf{t}_i$ is the $i^{th}$ column of matrix $\mathbf{T}$, $\mathbf{u}_i$ the $i^{th}$ column of matrix $\mathbf{U}$ and $cov(t_i, u_i)$ is the sample covariance between latent vectors $\mathbf{t}_i$ and $\mathbf{u}_i$. After the extraction of the latent vectors $\mathbf{t}_i$ and $\mathbf{u}_i$, the matrix $\mathbf{X}$ and vector $\mathbf{y}$ are deflated by subtracting their rank-one approximations based on $\mathbf{t}_i$ and $\mathbf{u}_i$. This process is repeated until the desired number of latent vectors had been extracted. The dimensionality reduction is performed by projecting the feature vector $\mathbf{v}_i$, extracted from a $i^{th}$ detection window, onto the weight vectors $W = \{w_1, w_2, .., w_p\}$, obtaining the latent vector $\mathbf{z}_i$ ($1 \times p$) as a result. This vector is then used in classification to obtain the detection probability $p_{w,N}$ of a particular window, $w$ belonging to the $N^{th}$ part.

### 2.2 The sources of context

The set of $p_{d_i,N}$ for all $N$ detectors across windows $d_i, i = 1\ to\ M$ are our primary information using which we learn the contextual information. The choice of $M$ depend on the application of interest, and we chose $M = 10$ windows equally spaced around a center window $d_c$ in an image at which the decision about a human is to be taken. This process will be repeated across all possible locations ($d_c$) in an image, in a sliding window fashion.

This type of context, being built from the intermediate detector probabilities, is generally referred as the *semantic context* [2]. We now learn contextual rules using $p_{d_i,N}$ as follows,

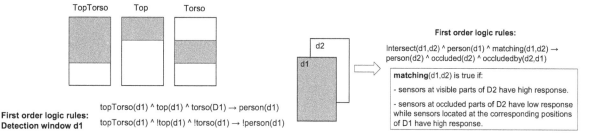

Figure 2: Examples of Contextual modeling. (a) Intra-window context. (b) Inter-window context

- **Intra-window context:** This is done for a single $d_c$ across all $N$. The main focus behind these rules is to see how different parts of humans supplement information under varying degrees of visual uncertainties such as, occlusions, pose among others. The general terminology for these rules can be written as,

$$p_{d_c,1} \circledast p_{d_c,2} \circledast ... \circledast p_{d_c,N} = Out_{d_c} \qquad (4)$$

where $\circledast$ denotes to function operation between the probabilities, which can be either the union $\vee$, intersection $\wedge$, or inversion of probabilities $\neg$. *Out* refers to the decision pertaining to a window $d_c$, which can be any semantic state such as, human present, human absent, human present with occlusion, which part is occluded among others.

- **Inter-window context:** We now analyze how $p_{d_i,[1..N]}$ interact with $p_{d_j,[1...N]}, \forall j = 1$ to $M, j \neq i$. This is motivated by the fact the an object does not occur in isolation, but share some properties with the surrounding scene. Rules to encode this information take the following form. For a center detection window $d_c$,

$$p_{d_c,j_1} \circledast p_{d_i,j_2} \circledast Out_{d_c} \circledast Relation(d_c, d_i) = Out_{d_c}^\star \quad (5)$$

where $Out_{d_c}^\star$ refers to semantic decision like human present or absent, which window is occluding others etc., and *Relation* refers to high level analysis of two detection windows in that, how their holistic probabilities are matching, are they intersecting, among others. An illustration is given in figure 2.

Let us now refer all possible rules (or formulas) in the form of (4,5) as $\mathbb{F} = \{f_i\}_{i=1}^{N_f}$. With these set of rules and training samples belonging to positive (human) and negative (non-human) class illustrating occlusions, we use Markov logic networks [8] to perform inference.

## 3. INFERENCE USING MARKOV LOGIC NETWORKS

Markov logic networks (MLN) is a first-order knowledge base (KB) with a weight $w_i'$ attached to each formula $f_i$. Together with a set of constants representing objects in the domain (in our case, detection windows $d_i$'s), it specifies a ground Markov network containing one feature for each possible grounding of a first-order formula in the KB, with the corresponding weight. Inference in MLNs is performed by Markov Chain Monte Carlo (MCMC) over the minimal subset of the ground network required for answering the query. Weights are efficiently learned from relational databases by

iteratively optimizing a pseudo-likelihood measure. Optionally, additional clauses are learned using inductive logic programming techniques.

A first-order KB can be seen as a set of hard constraints on the set of possible worlds: if a world violates even one formula, it has zero probability. The basic idea in MLNs is to soften these constraints: when a world violates one formula in the KB it is less probable, but not impossible. The fewer formulas a world violates, the more probable it is. Each formula has an associated weight that reflects how strong a constraint it is: the higher the weight, the greater the difference in log probability between a world that satisfies the formula and one that does not, other things being equal.

### 3.1 Constructing the network

With this idea, an undirected network, called a Markov Network, is constructed to predict the outcomes (or events like a presence of human, the type of occlusion) such that,

- Each of its nodes correspond to a ground atom (an event) $e_k$.

- If a subset of ground atoms $e_{\{i\}} = \{e_k\}$ are related to each other by a formula $f_i$, then a clique $C_i$ over these variables is added to the network. $C_i$ is associated with a weight $w_i'$ and a feature $fe_i$ is defined as follows

$$fe_i(e_{\{i\}}) = \begin{cases} 1, & \text{if } f_i(e_{\{i\}}) \text{ is true} \\ 0, & \text{otherwise} \end{cases} \qquad (6)$$

Thus first-order logic formulae in our knowledge base serve as templates to construct the Markov Network. This network models the joint distribution of the set of all ground atoms, E, each of which is a binary variable. It provides a means for performing probabilistic inference.

$$P_E = P(Event = E) = \frac{1}{Z} \exp(\sum_i w_i' fe_i(e_{\{i\}})) \qquad (7)$$

$$P_E = \frac{1}{Z} \exp(\sum_i w_i' f_i) \qquad (8)$$

where $Z$ is the normalizing factor.

### 3.2 Inference

Based on the constructed Markov network, the marginal distribution of any event $E$ given some evidence (observations) can be computed using probabilistic inference. Since the structure of the network may be very complex (e.g. containing undirected cycles), exact inference is often intractable. MCMC sampling is a good choice for approximate

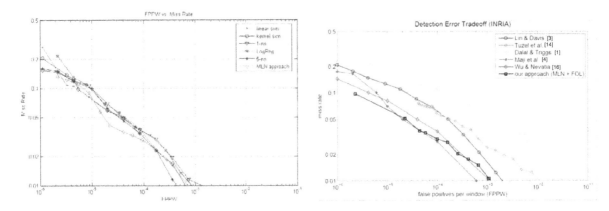

Figure 3: Experimental validation. (a) Comparing different combination strategies on INRIA [1] dataset. (b) Detection performance in INRIA dataset.

reasoning. In MLN, the probability that a ground atom $E_i$ is equal to $e_i$ given its Markov blanket (neighbors) $B_i$ is

$$P(E_i = e_i | Bi = bi) = \frac{\exp(\sum_{fe_j \in f_i} w'_j fe_j(E_i = e_i, B_i = b_i))}{Z_1} \quad (9)$$

where $Z_1 = \sum_{k1 \in \{0,1\}} \exp(\sum_{fe_j \in f_i} w'_j fe_j(E_i = k1, B_i = b_i))$.

where $f_i$ is the set of all cliques that contain $E_i$ and $fe_j$ is computed as in (6). Basic MCMC (Gibbs sampling) is known to have difficulty dealing with deterministic relations, which are unavoidable in our case. It has been observed that using simulated tempering [8] gives better performance than the basic Gibbs sampling. Simulated tempering is a MC method that is closely related to simulated annealing. However, instead of using some fixed cooling schedule, a random walk is also performed in the temperature space whose structure is predetermined and discrete. These moves aim at making the sampling better at jumping out of local minima.

Hence, with the set of contextual rules $\mathbb{F}$ as the input to MLN, we learn the weights $w'_i$ and perform inference over detection windows $d_i$'s using the open source Alchemy system [8].

## 4. EXPERIMENTS

We evaluated our method on datasets containing humans with and without occlusion. For the first task we used the widely followed benchmark of INRIA pedestrian detection images [1], with the main goal of comparing the performance of our method with other standard approaches. Then to study performance under occlusion, we used images from an internally collected dataset.

### 4.1 Training stage

We estimate the parameters of our system using a 10-fold cross-validation procedure on the training dataset provided by INRIA Person Dataset. This dataset has 2416 positive samples of size $64 \times 128$ pixels and images containing no humans, used to obtain negative exemplars. We sample this set to obtain our validation set containing 2000 positive samples and 10000 negative samples. This was used to estimate the detection thresholds of seven human part detectors. For

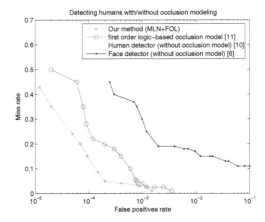

Figure 4: Detecting humans under occlusion on an internally collected dataset

the face detector, high resolution images of $240 \times 320$ pixels from the CMU-MIT dataset [9] were used (since faces generally require higher resolution for detection when compared to humans).

### 4.2 Testing

We first evaluate whether the integration of the 8 detectors using MLN is better than other standard combination method. The INRIA testing dataset was used for this purpose, and the following methods were compared with: linear and kernel SVM [7], logistic regression and k-nearest neighbor. We provide the results in figure 3(a) where we see that MLN offers better performance. We then compared our approach with other standard methods ([1, 16, 3, 14, 4]) for human detection. As noted before, this dataset has very few occluded images. The results are given in figure 3(b), where we see that in regions with stringent requirements on false positives, our method has very low miss rates.

We then used our internally collected dataset with lots of occluding humans to test the proof of concept. We had nearly 70 images containing nearly 300 humans. We compare our method with methods for detecting humans [10] and faces [6] without occlusion handling, and a first-order logic based method to model occlusions [11]. The results are

**Figure 5: Sample detection results on images from an internally collected dataset. Semantic decisions on occluding humans are a part of the output.**

given in figure 4, and some examples of detection in figure 5 which, in addition to providing the location information of humans, gives semantic knowledge of occluding persons. These results exemplify the efficacy of our approach.

## 5. CONCLUDING REMARKS

We proposed a method to model contextual information of humans, and perform inference using Markov logic networks to handle partial occlusions. Through this, we illustrated the importance of context, and the use of probabilistic interpretation of first-order logic to perform robust inference under visual uncertainties. A study of more formal model for occlusion and other sources of context, and incorporating them in this framework is an interesting future work to improve robustness to noise.

## 6. ACKNOWLEDGEMENTS

This work was supported by a MURI Grant N00014-08-1-0638 from the Office of Naval Research.

## 7. REFERENCES

[1] N. Dalal and B. Triggs. Histograms of oriented gradients for human detection. In *IEEE Conference on Computer Vision and Pattern Recognition*, pages 886–893, 2005.

[2] S. Divvala, D. Hoiem, J. Hays, A. Efros, and M. Hebert. An empirical study of context in object detection. *IEEE Conference on Computer Vision and Pattern Recognition*, pages 1271–1278, 2009.

[3] Z. Lin and L. S. Davis. A pose-invariant descriptor for human detection and segmentation. In *European Conference on Computer Vision*, pages 423–436, 2008.

[4] S. Maji, A. Berg, and J. Malik. Classification using intersection kernel support vector machines is efficient. In *IEEE Conference on Computer Vision and Pattern Recognition*, pages 1 –8, 2008.

[5] K. Mikolajczyk, C. Schmid, and A. Zisserman. Human detection based on a probabilistic assembly of robust part detectors. *European Conference on Computer Vision*, pages 69–82, 2004.

[6] H. Moon, R. Chellappa, and A. Rosenfeld. Optimal edge-based shape detection. *IEEE Transactions on Image Processing*, 11(11):1209–1227, 2002.

[7] E. Osuna, R. Freund, and F. Girosi. Training support vector machines: an application to face detection. In *IEEE Conference on Computer Vision and Pattern Recognition*, pages 130–137. Published by the IEEE Computer Society, 1997.

[8] M. Richardson and P. Domingos. Markov logic networks. *Machine Learning*, 62(1):107–136, 2006.

[9] H. Rowley, S. Baluja, and T. Kanade. Neural network-based face detection. In *IEEE Transactions on Pattern Analysis and Machine Intelligence*, volume 20, pages 23–38, 1998.

[10] W. Schwartz, A. Kembhavi, D. Harwood, and L. Davis. Human detection using partial least squares analysis. In *Proceedings of the International Conference on Computer Vision*, pages 24–31, 2009.

[11] W. R. Schwartz, R. Gopalan, R. Chellappa, and L. S. Davis. Robust human detection under occlusion by integrating face and person detectors. In *International Conference on Biometrics*, pages 970–979, 2009.

[12] V. Shet, J. Neumann, V. Ramesh, and L. Davis. Bilattice-based logical reasoning for human detection. In *IEEE Conference on Computer Vision and Pattern Recognition*, pages 1 –8, 2007.

[13] A. Torralba. Contextual priming for object detection. *International Journal of Computer Vision*, 53(2):169–191, 2003.

[14] O. Tuzel, F. Porikli, and P. Meer. Human detection via classification on riemannian manifolds. In *IEEE Conference on Computer Vision and Pattern Recognition*, pages 1 –8, 2007.

[15] H. Wold. Partial least squares. *Encyclopedia of statistical sciences*, 6:581–591, 1985.

[16] B. Wu and R. Nevatia. Detection of multiple, partially occluded humans in a single image by bayesian combination of edgelet part detectors. In *IEEE International Conference on Computer Vision*, pages 90–97, 2005.

# Transitional or Partnership Human and Robot Collaboration for Automotive Assembly

Jane Shi
GM Global R&D Center
30500 Mound Road
Warren, MI 48090-9055
248-807-4212

Jane.Shi@gm.com

Roland Menassa
GM Global R&D Center
30500 Mound Road
Warren, MI 48090-9055
586-986-3890

Roland.Menassa@gm.com

## ABSTRACT

Traditional automotive manufacturing tasks that are automated to date by industrial robots utilize a human robot *exclusion* strategy for normal production. Although new generations of robots are envisioned to *emulate* humans' capabilities to collaborate with people, we propose a near term and a practical strategy for robots to *complement* humans' capabilities instead in order to achieve a shared goal in a shared context of manufacturing task execution. We describe two types, transitional and partnership, of human and robot collaborations in the automotive manufacturing environment. We illustrate both types of human robot collaboration with detailed manufacturing tasks. We explore potential solutions to the human and robot collaboration problem in manufacturing: how to interact optimally and fail-safely for a given task collaboration between a human and a robot.

## Categories and Subject Descriptors

C.3 [**Special-Purpose and Application-Based Systems**]: Process control systems; Real-time and embedded systems.

## General Terms

Human Robot Collaboration, Automotive Assembly

## Keywords

Human Robot Collaboration, Industrial Robots, Automotive Assembly

## 1. Introduction

The recent market shift from high volume single lot size to mid-volume production of smaller customized products is driving a higher level of manual labor and highly automated and flexible systems in one integrated manufacturing system. However, all traditional automotive manufacturing tasks automated so far by industrial robots are utilizing a human robot *exclusion* strategy for normal production. Industrial robots fully automate the

ergonomically stressing tasks using precision fixtures and rigid process flows that are cost-effective in large volume production as illustrated by Figure 1. For this type of robotics automation, humans are prohibited inside the production workcells by extensive perimeter guards and system level PLC electronic interlocking control.

**Figure 1 Traditional Human Robot Exclusion in Automotive Robotic Manufacturing Workcells**

When a human operator presence around the automation workcells becomes necessary for part inspection or loading and unloading as dictated by the manufacturing process design, the human and robot exclusion practice is enforced by utilizing an intermediate mechanical transfer mechanism that would transfer the physical workpiece out of the robot work envelop / workcell so that the human operator can perform a task such as quality inspection as shown by Figure 2.

The idea of a robot as a "co-worker" working side by side with humans as a teammate in unstructured environments remains to be a grand challenge as discussed by Groom et al [3]. It is a far reaching vision for robots to *emulate* humans' capabilities for human robot collaborations. On the other hand, it is possible for robots to *complement* humans' capabilities to achieve a shared goal in a shared context of manufacturing task execution. In this regard, progress has been made through ongoing research to enable humans and robots collaboration successfully in a manufacturing assembly environment in Europe as reported by

Kruger et al [1] and Schraft et al [5], in Japan by Wojtara et al [2] and Tan et al [6].

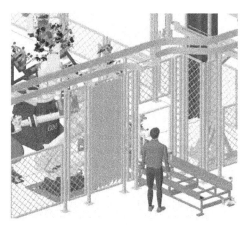

**Figure 2 A Workpiece is Transferred out of Robot Workcell in order for the Human to Perform an Inspection Task**

Major research activities in the area of human robot collaboration (HRC) have been addressing challenges including (1) effective human robot interaction and collaboration interfaces utilizing speech, vision, touch, gesture etc [13], (2) social, mental, and physiological relationship and behavior dynamics in a human and robot team [3,4,8,9], and (3) safe human robot collaboration that includes new robotic hardware, software, and control methods to prevent human robot collision [10, 11, 12]. Many critical issues [1, 14] have to be resolved completely and robustly at a fundamental level before realistic human robot collaborations can become a common practice in the future. To help illustrating these critical technical issues in the human and robot collaboration, we will first define a transitional or partnership human and robot collaboration in automotive manufacturing applications. Section 2 will outline two manufacturing tasks that could potentially benefit from a transitional or partnership human and robot collaboration. Section 3 will illustrate a detailed transitional human robot collaboration and interaction mechanisms as well as new robotic capabilities to achieve direct part transfer between humans and robots. Section 4 will detail the partnership human and robot collaboration to achieve part installation in a human and robot team setting. We examine the action transition between a human and a robot and how to interact optimally and fail safely for a given action transition.

## 2. Complementary Human and Robot Collaboration for Manufacturing Tasks

Complementary human and robot collaboration is the type of collaboration that utilizes the strongest capability of one party to compensate a relative weak capability of another party in the human and robot team. For example, robots do not have any mental models and a sense of self and weak on learning [Groom et al 2007] where humans are strong in this area and are able to be adaptive and predictive to a changing environment. Likewise,

robots could have physical strength that complements human's intelligence.

We present two manufacturing tasks here to define and illustrate complementary human and robot collaboration for automotive manufacturing tasks.

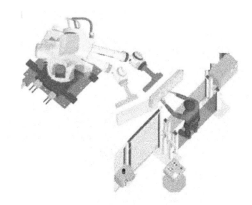

**Figure 3 Human Directly Places a Part to (or Picks up a Part from) the Robot End of Arm Tool**

Figure 3 illustrates the first manufacturing task where both the human and robot collaborate directly on the manufacturing plant floor. The main task in this station is to produce a quality assembled part. The main subtask is automated assembly through welding in this case of two parts assigned to the robot. Another subtask is the random quality inspection of the part which is assigned to the operator. With traditional manufacturing processes design that enforce a human and robot exclusion strategy, a fixture will be placed near the gate of the workcell in order to isolate the operator from the robot during a part pick-up operation. An example is illustrated in Figure 4 where the robot first places the part to the fixture and the human then picks it up from the fixture.

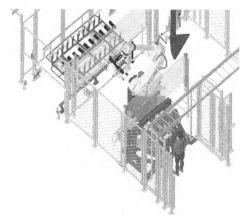

**Figure 4 Traditional Design of a Human Loading a Part to a Fixture and Robot Picking up a Part from the Fixture**

When a direct human and robot collaboration is required for this manufacturing task, the robot is programmed to directly hand off a part to the human. The operator proceeds to pick up the part directly from the robot end of arm tool (EOAT) while the robot servo is active. We define this type of human robot collaboration as _transitional_ collaboration. One of its main characteristics is task transition between human and robot within a relative short period of time. During this short period of time, both the human and robot are expected to synchronize their activities. The shared common goal of the _transitional_ human and robot collaboration is for the task to transition from one party to another party.

The key collaborative communication of information includes the signals of _when_ the transition starts, _when_ the transition ends, and the _status_ of success or failure of such transition collaboration. The robot tasks prior to the transitional collaboration are not relevant to the human and the same holds true for the operator tasks. In the time domain, prior or after the transitional collaboration both robot and human tasks are serially executed. However, the success of the transitional collaboration will impact subsequent subtasks in the serial chain.

Figure 5 is the illustration of a serial subtask execution in the transitional human and robot collaboration. We will discuss the detailed interaction mechanism for this human robot transitional collaboration in section 3.

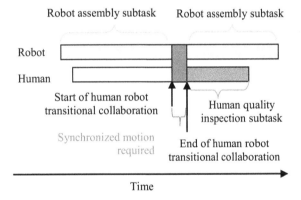

**Figure 5 Human and Robot _Transitional_ Collaboration in Serially Executed Subtasks**

Figure 6 illustrates the second manufacturing task that depicts the principle of complementary human and robot collaboration on the manufacturing plant floor. Again, if this manufacturing process is designed with the traditional human and robot exclusion practice, either a robot or human will have to place the moon roof onto the vehicle body and fasten and secure all bolts, nuts, and wiring harnesses. While a team of operators are able to complete the entire task of installing a moon roof, industrial robots are not yet capable to perform the entire assembly in an efficient and low cost way on the manufacturing plant floor. The main technology gap is mainly due to the lack of dexterous hands to grasp and

manipulate automotive parts for placing, fastening, and securing various bolts, nuts, and wiring harnesses.

When the human and robot team is employed to accomplish this moon roof installation task, the robot is best at moving heavy and bulk objects such as the moon roof and placing it onto a vehicle body and holding it in place while the human performs more dexterous manipulation such as placing and securing bolts, nuts, and wiring harnesses. We define this type of human robot collaboration as _partnership_ human and robot collaboration. One of its main characteristics is robot subtasks and human subtasks are executed in parallel and these subtasks are coordinated in time and space during the entire cycle time of the station. During the full cycle of the station, both human and robot are expected to synchronize their motion, in two ways either by: 1- operator will follow the robot's motion when the robot runs through its programmed motion, or 2- operator drives the robot based on a reactive force compliance method. The shared common goal of the _partnership_ human and robot collaboration is for the entire installation task to be completed successfully.

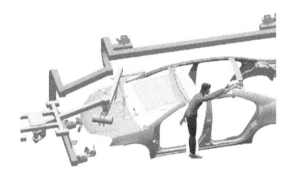

**Figure 6 Robot Transports and Places a Heavy Bulky Moonroof while Human Performs Dexterous Fine Manipulative Assembly**

A successful partnership between a human and robot will rely on a well devised communication scheme of information to include the signals of when the partnership starts, when the partnership ends, and the signals reflecting back from all levels of the interaction. In this case, robot subtasks' status are important for the human partner so that dexterous and fine dexterous manipulation subtasks can be coordinated with the robot.

Figure 7 illustrates a parallel subtask execution during a human and robot partnership. The tasks during the entire installation can be accomplished by this robot and human partnership collaboration. In section 4, we will discuss the detailed interaction mechanisms.

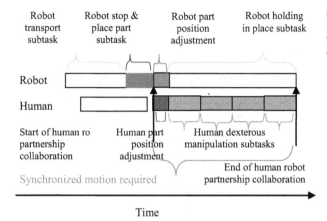

Robot transport subtask | Robot stop & place part subtask | Robot part position adjustment | Robot holding in place subtask

Robot

Human

Start of human ro partnership collaboration | Human part position adjustment | Human dexterous manipulation subtasks

End of human robot partnership collaboration

Synchronized motion required

Time

**Figure 7 Human and Robot Partnership Collaboration in Parallel Executed Subtasks**

## 3. Interaction Mechanisms in Transitional Human and Robot Collaboration

There are several challenges that arise in a transitional human and robot collaboration that need to be solved:

1- Define the mechanisms that allow human and robot to collaborate in order to achieve a shared goal.

2- Identify the dependency of the interaction mechanisms on specific subtasks.

3- Identify the valid fail-safe choices during the interaction.

4- Determine the error conditions and their error recovery choices for that collaboration.

The next section will detail one automotive manufacturing task to highlight these research questions.

A material handling robot used for automatic part pickup and drop off is a popular robotic automation application in the automotive industry. Each robotic material handling application has its own customized robot end of arm tool (EOAT) that is designed to pick up and secure a specific part as shown in Figure 8. Most importantly, the part has to be at a specific location accurately within the robot EOAT. Otherwise the robot will not be able to place the part accurately when it drops the part off at a specified position for the manufacturing process. Figure 8 below illustrates a robotic EOAT and the robotic actions for automatic part pick up and drop off applications. The second action block, "Robot EOAT detects part presence at P(pick)," will allow the robot to move to its next action to close the clamping devices in order to secure the part within its EOAT. If the part is NOT present, the robot will be waiting on its second action until it is timed out. Then a system fault condition will be signaled to the system controller for proper fault recovery action.

In order to directly transfer the part from the human to the robot or from the robot to the human, the transitional human and robot collaboration is executed using different interaction mechanisms. In the first case, human to robot interaction, the third robotic

action in Figure 8, "Robot EOAT closes and secures the part with EOAT", will apply. In the second case, robot to human interaction, the third to the last robotic action in Figure 8, "Robot EOAT opens and drops the part off", will apply.

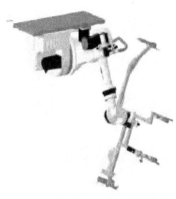

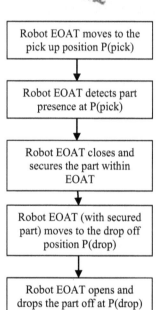

Robot EOAT moves to the pick up position P(pick)

↓

Robot EOAT detects part presence at P(pick)

↓

Robot EOAT closes and secures the part within EOAT

↓

Robot EOAT (with secured part) moves to the drop off position P(drop)

↓

Robot EOAT opens and drops the part off at P(drop)

**Figure 8 Robotic Actions for Automatic Part Pick up and Drop off Applications**

When transferring a part from the human to the robot, the question becomes whether the robot needs to differentiate between the interactive case and the automated pick up case. Other factors to consider in this scenario include the specification of the pickup position P(pick) and whether it is fixed or dynamic based on the human's position as well as dealing with the uncertainty of the human premature release of the part to the robot EOAT. In this case a fail safe way to ensure successful part transfer from the human to the robot needs to be put in place.

Similarly, when transferring the part from the robot to the human, the robot needs to determine unambiguously the exact time to open its EOAT in order to release the part. In this second scenario the question of whether the robot needs to differentiate between the automated drop off case and the human interactive drop off case is examined. Other factors to consider in this scenario include the specification of the drop off position P(drop) and whether it needs to be fixed or dynamic based on the human's position as well as dealing with the uncertainty of the premature release of the part from the robot EOAT and while the human is not ready to pick up the part. In this case a failsafe procedure is necessary to ensure a successful part transfer from the robot to the human.

Figure 9 below illustrates both human and robot actions in the transitional collaboration for the part transfer from the human to the robot. Robot actions are R1 through R6 and human actions are H1 through H6 and they are executed in a collaborative sequence to achieve the goal of the part transfer from human to robot. To ensure a safe and successful part transfer, two human decision actions, HR1 and HR2, are critically important. In addition, the retry loop including action steps H3, R6, H4, R3, and R4, for repositioning and re-securing the part in the robot EOAT is essential when the human decides for a retry.

The outlined transitional human and robot collaboration in Figure 9 relies heavily on the decision skills of a human and adaptations to environmental conditions in (1) deciding when it is the right time to place a part into the robot EOAT, (2) deciding if the part is secure enough in the robot EOAT, (3) deciding to reposition and re-secure the part in the robot EOAT, and (4) deciding that the robot can continue to the next step after the part is secured in the robot EOAT. These critical human skills are highlighted as yellow actions in Figure 9 and they are critical elements of the *system intelligence* in this transitional human robot collaboration. In this case, human and robot relationship is not peer-to-peer. Robot can automatically perform its actions when the condition for the actions is ready, but the human is responsible to ensure the condition is right for the robot to carry out appropriate actions. Therefore, the robot's role in the transitional human and robot collaboration as illustrated by Figure 9 is simple: it does not require the robot to be able to develop the mental model of its spatial environment and contextual task execution sequences [3]. It is easily implementable on today's industrial robots with a new development of an effective interaction mechanism for humans to provide a signal to the robot, and for the robot to receive the signal from the human, to either open its EOAT or move to next drop off position as highlighted by flow arrows between H3 and R6 as well as between H6 and R5. This interaction between the robot and the human is no different than the palm button that an operator has to push to allow the robot to continue its next motion in a manual loading station.

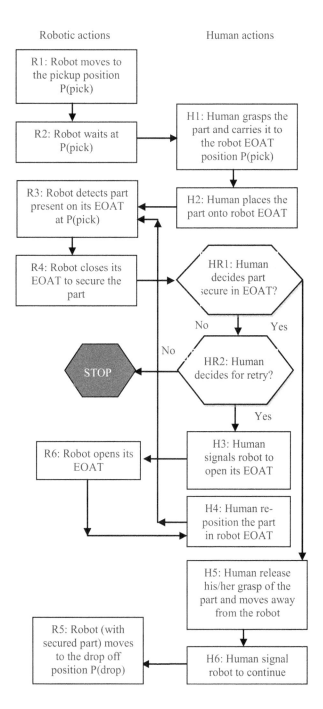

**Figure 9 Robot and Human Actions in the Transitional Collaboration for the Part Transfer from the Human to**

Figure 10 below illustrates both human and robot actions in the transitional collaboration for the part transfer from the robot to the human. R1 through R5 are robot actions and H1 through H6 are human actions. All actions are executed in a collaborative sequence to achieve the goal of the part transfer from the robot to the human. Similarly two human decision actions, H3 and H6, are critically important in ensuring a safe and successful part handover. In this case, human decision skills and adaptations to environmental conditions come into play in (1) deciding when is the right time to reach for the part in the EOAT, (2) deciding when to open the robot EOAT after the human securely grasps the part, and (3) deciding that the robot can continue to the next step after the part is removed from the robot EOAT and the human has safely moved away from the robot.

Two yellow actions in Figure 10 are interactions for the human to provide a signal to the robot, and for the robot to receive the signal from the human, to either open its EOAT or move to the next drop off position. This interaction is similar in the part hand over from the human to the robot case.

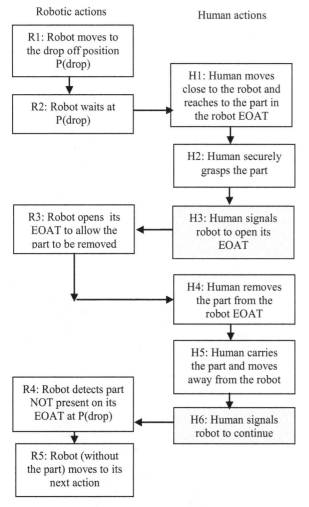

Robotic actions

Human actions

R1: Robot moves to the drop off position P(drop)

R2: Robot waits at P(drop)

H1: Human moves close to the robot and reaches to the part in the robot EOAT

H2: Human securely grasps the part

R3: Robot opens its EOAT to allow the part to be removed

H3: Human signals robot to open its EOAT

H4: Human removes the part from the robot EOAT

H5: Human carries the part and moves away from the robot

R4: Robot detects part NOT present on its EOAT at P(drop)

H6: Human signals robot to continue

R5: Robot (without the part) moves to its next action

**Figure 10 Robot and Human Actions in the Transitional Collaboration for the Part Transfer from the Robot to the Human**

Traditional robots are designed to accomplish their tasks independent of humans in an industrial automation environment. By leveraging the intelligence of humans and the direct role they play in signaling a robot to perform its next intended set of actions,

the above transitional human and robot collaboration is achievable using current today's industrial robot technologies

However, significant new robotic capabilities have to be developed in order for robots to be more intelligent and cooperate with humans at a peer level to accomplish the transitional collaboration more efficiently and robustly.

The first new capability is for robots to detect and utilize the interactive force to secure part placement inside the robot EOAT when the part is being handed over by a human. Two human peers utilize this interactive force naturally to ensure safe part handover from one party to the other. Today's industrial robots lack this capability to "intelligently interpret" the interactive forces so that an automatic decision can be made when to open the EOAT to allow the part to be transferred or when a part is securely being held by the EOAT.

The second new capability is for robots to detect humans' position so that the robot pick up position P(pick) or drop off position P(drop) can dynamically be adjusted to follow a human's position. Again, in a human peer to peer collaboration, it seems natural for humans to move to the other party's location for part transfer collaboration. Today's industrial robots lack this critical capability to "intelligently adapt" to the human's proximity so that robots can automatically decide to continue on their next action when a human moves away from the robot.

With the above two proposed robotic capabilities that are reliable and robust, the human and robot interaction signals, as highlighted by two yellow human actions H3 and H6 in both Figure 9 and 10, can be replaced by robotic intelligence so that a more peer to peer like collaboration between humans and robots would be achievable.

## 4. Interaction Mechanisms in Partnership Human and Robot Collaboration

In this section, we will detail another automotive manufacturing task utilizing partnership human and robot collaboration to discuss similar research questions and critical new robotic capabilities.

In the partnership human and robot collaboration, robot actions and human actions are executed in a parallel fashion and these actions are coordinated in time and space during the entire cycle time of the station. The actions in the partnership are dependent on each other. There is a strong "belief and trust" in the other partner's ability in carrying out his actions reliably and in a coordinated fashion so that one's own actions can be successfully carried out at the same time. The shared common goal of the partnership human and robot collaboration is for the entire installation task to be completed successfully.

Figure 11 below illustrates both human and robot actions in the partnership human and robot collaboration for a moonroof installation on a vehicle.

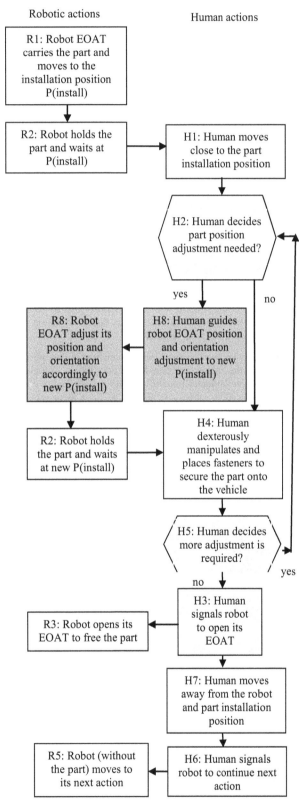

Robotic actions | Human actions

R1: Robot EOAT carries the part and moves to the installation position P(install)

R2: Robot holds the part and waits at P(install)

H1: Human moves close to the part installation position

H2: Human decides part position adjustment needed?

yes | no

R8: Robot EOAT adjust its position and orientation accordingly to new P(install)

H8: Human guides robot EOAT position and orientation adjustment to new P(install)

R2: Robot holds the part and waits at new P(install)

H4: Human dexterously manipulates and places fasteners to secure the part onto the vehicle

H5: Human decides more adjustment is required?

no | yes

R3: Robot opens its EOAT to free the part

H3: Human signals robot to open its EOAT

H7: Human moves away from the robot and part installation position

R5: Robot (without the part) moves to its next action

H6: Human signals robot to continue next action

**Figure 11 Robot and Human Actions in the Partnership Collaboration for a Moon Roof Installation**

R1 through R5 are robot actions and H1 through H7 are human actions. All actions are executed in a collaborative sequence to achieve the goal of the part installation on a vehicle body. Similarly to the transitional collaboration, two human decision actions, H3 and H6, are critically important in ensuring safe and successful operations.

The human and robot partnership collaboration key feature is the new interaction capability as highlighted by the collaborative human action H8, in blue as illustrated in Figure 11, and corresponding robot action R8 , in blue as illustrated in Figure 11 The key function of human action H8 is 1) to estimate the robot EOAT position and orientation adjustment for the next assembly task and 2) to provide this required adjustment to the robot so that robot action R8 will result in a satisfactory part position for a human to accomplish the next assembly task. This human and robot partnership collaboration, H8+R8, requires a strong "belief and trust" in the other partner's ability in carrying out actions reliably and in a coordinated fashion so that one's own actions can be successfully carried out at the same time. For example, a human has to trust the robot's ability to adjust the position of the part while the robot is "trusting" the human to provide the position that is best for a successful assembly, i.e. robot will not be directed by the human to "collide" with the vehicle body. The ultimate result of such interactive human and robot actions, H8+R8, is the adaptive positioning of part held by the robot EOAT for the human to easily manipulate several parts for the successful assembly of the moonroof onto the vehicle.

The challenge in this scenario is to devise an implementation plan for the new human and robot interaction, H8+R8. The final goal of such an interaction is to achieve robotic adaptive positioning of the part to its environment with human's active guidance. We highlight two potential approaches:

First we propose the static approach. The static approach mainly consists of an iterative step of (1) estimate position adjustment by the human, (2) input the required position adjustment to the robot by the human via a robotic interface, and (3) the robot moves to the newly adjusted position. This is very similar to how a robot program is edited by a human operator. While this approach is implementable on current industrial robots, the static approach is tedious, time consuming, and inefficient.

Second we propose a dynamic approach. In this approach the robot can utilize interactive forces applied by the human so that it adjusts its position accordingly. This is the same concept as the robotic force feedback control or compliant motion control. Instead of assembly forces being generated by assembly contact surfaces, the human in this case supplies guidance forces for the robot to adjust its position. Wojtara etc al [2] have experimented with this approach and reported some success by partnering a human with a robot as teammates to jointly position a part on a vehicle body using cooperative control. Park etc al [7] also proposed an algorithm that could be used to implement the dynamic approach. The dynamic approach is more efficient, but the main challenge is to achieve accurate part position with quick dynamic response under the force feedback control.

# 5. Summary

In this paper, we proposed a near term and a practical strategy for robots to *complement* humans' capability to achieve a shared goal in a shared context of manufacturing task execution.

We described two types, transitional and partnership, of human and robot collaborations and illustrated how the human and the robot can interact and collaborate to accomplish an automotive assembly task. We illustrated detailed transitional human robot collaboration and interaction mechanisms as well as new robotic capabilities to achieve direct part transfer between a human and a robot. We discussed the partnership human and robot collaboration to install parts in a team setting. We examined action transitional states between a human and a robot and how to interact optimally and fail safely for a given action transition between a human and a robot.

To enable effective human robot collaboration, two new critical robotic capabilities are identified. The first new capability is for a robot to detect and utilize the interactive force to ensure secure part placement in its EOAT when the part is being transferred. Today's industrial robots lack this capability to "intelligently interpret" the interactive forces to ensure a robust transition. The second new capability is for robots to detect humans' position so that they can dynamically adjust their position based on presence and proximity of a human. Today's industrial robots lack this critical capability to "intelligently adapt" to the human's presence.

# 6. Acknowledgments

We would like to acknowledge the graphic illustration provided by Dr. Gao, Mr. McGraw, Mr. Miller, Mr. Ahlstrom of General Motors.

# 7. References

[1] Kruger, J., Lien, T.K., and Verl, A. 2009. *Cooperation of Humand and Machines in Assembly Lines.* CIRP Annals - Manufacturing Technology Vol. 58, Issue 2, 2009, Pages 628-646

[2] Wojtara, T., Uchihara, M., Murayama, H., Shimod, S., Sakai, S., Fujimoto, H. and Kimura, H. 2009. *Human–robot collaboration in precise positioning of a three-dimensional object* Automatica Volume 45, Issue 2, February 2009, Pages 333-342

[3] Groom, V. and Clifford, N. 2007 *Can robots be teammates? Benchmarks in human-robot teams* Interaction Studies, Vol 8, Number 3, pp. 483-500, John Benjamins Publishing Company

[4] Groom, V. 2008 *What's the Best Role for a Robot?* Proceedings of the International Conference on Informatics in Control, Automation and Robotics (ICINCO) 2008, pp. 323-328

[5] Schraft, RD.,, Meyer, C., Parlitz, C. Helms, E., *PowerMate – A safe and intuitive robot assistant for handling and assembly tasks,* Proceedings of the 2005 IEEE International Conference on Robotics and Automation, 2005, pp. 4074-4079

[6] Tan, JTC., Duan, F., Zhang, Y. , Watanabe, K. , Kato, R., Arai, T. *Human-Robot Collaboration in Cellular Manufacturing: Design and Development*, Proceedings of the 2009 IEEE/RSJ International Conference on Intelligent Robots and Systems, 2009, pp. 29-34

[7] Park, Chan Hun; Kyung, Jin Ho; Park, Dong Il; Park, Kyung Taik; Kim, Doo Hyung; Gweon, Dae Gab, *Direct Teaching Algorithm for a Manipulator in a Constraint Condition using the Teaching Force Shaping Method,* Advanced Robotics, Volume 24, Numbers 8-9, 2010 , pp. 1365-1384(20)

[8] Fong, T. Nourbakhsh, I, Kunz, C., Fluckiger, L., Schreiner, J. *The peer-to-peer human-robot interaction project*, Space, 2005-6750

[9] Prewett, M S.; Saboe, K N.; Johnson, R C.; Coovert, M D.; Elliott, L R. *Workload in Human-Robot Interaction: A Review of Manipulations and Outcomes* Human Factors and Ergonomics Society Annual Meeting Proceedings, Volume 53, Number 18, 2009 , pp. 1393-1397(5)

[10] Martínez-Salvador B., Pérez-Francisco M.. Del Pobil A.P., *Collision Detection between Robot Arms and People,* Journal of Intelligent and Robotic Systems, Volume 38, Number 1, 200309 , pp. 105-119(15)

[11] Kulić, D, Croft, E, 2007, *Pre-collision safety strategies for human-robot interaction,* Autonomous Robots, Vol. 22, N. 2, Feb 2007, pp. 149-164

[12] Michael Zaeh and Wolfgang Roesel, Safety Aspects in a Human-Robot Interaction Scenario: A Human Worker Is Co-operating with an Industrial Robot, Progress in Robotics, Part 2, p53-62, Springer Berlin Heidelberg, 2009

[13] T. Salter, K. Dautenhahn and R. Boekhorst *Learning about natural human–robot interaction styles* Robotics and Autonomous Systems, Volume 54, Issue 2, 28 February 2006, Pages 127-134 Intelligent Autonomous Systems

[14] A. De Santisa, , B. Sicilianoa, A. De Lucab, and A. Bicchic, *An atlas of physical human–robot interaction* Mechanism and Machine Theory, Volume 43, Issue 3, March 2008, Pages 253-270

# Performance Assessment of Face Recognition Using Super-Resolution

Shuowen Hu
U.S. Army Research Laboratory
2800 Powder Mill Rd.
Adelphi, MD 20783
(301)394-2526

shuowen.hu@arl.army.mil

Robert Maschal
U.S. Army Research Laboratory
2800 Powder Mill Rd.
Adelphi, MD 20783
(301)394-0437

robert.maschal@arl.army.mil

S. Susan Young
U.S. Army Research Laboratory
2800 Powder Mill Rd.
Adelphi, MD 20783
(301)394-0230

ssyoung@arl.army.mil

Tsai Hong Hong
NIST

100 Bureau Dr.
Gaithersburg, MD 20899
(301)975-3444

hongt@nist.gov

Jonathon P. Phillips
NIST

100 Bureau Dr.
Gaithersburg, MD 20899
(301)975-5348

jonathon@nist.gov

## ABSTRACT

Recognition rate of face recognition algorithms is dependent on the resolution of the imagery, specifically the number of pixels contained within the face. Using a sequence of frames from low-resolution videos, super-resolution image reconstruction can form a higher resolution image, aiding the face recognition stage for improved performance. In this work, images from a video database of moving faces and people are used to assess the performance improvement of face recognition using super-resolution.

## Categories and Subject Descriptors

D.3.3 [**Image Processing and Computer Vision**]: Enhancement.

## General Terms

Algorithms, Performance

## Keywords

Super-resolution image reconstruction, face recognition, image enhancement, video surveillance

## 1. INTRODUCTION

Performance of face recognition algorithms is dependent on a host of factors including resolution/scale, lighting conditions, facial expression, head orientation, occlusion, and image compression. In general surveillance video applications, the imagery is not only low-resolution (typically 480×760), but the person of interest may be at a far distance with respect to the camera, further compounding the problem of limited number of face pixels. The video database of moving faces and people [1] contains similar

imagery as surveillance videos, and was used in this work. Using a sequence of frames from the low-resolution videos, super-resolution image reconstruction can form a higher resolution image, aiding face recognition systems for improved performance.

Super-resolution image reconstruction algorithms are generally composed of two stages: a registration stage and a reconstruction stage. During the registration stage, the shift of a given frame with respect to a reference frame is computed to subpixel accuracy, which is then utilized by the reconstruction stage to interpolate the low-resolution frames onto a higher-resolution grid. A necessary condition for super-resolution benefit is the presence of differing subpixel shifts between frames within the low-resolution video sequence to provide distinct information from which the super-resolved image can be constructed. In this work, the super-resolution algorithm developed by Young and Driggers [2] is used to assess the performance improvement of face recognition with super-resolved imagery. For improved registration accuracy, the super-resolution algorithm [2] separates the registration stage into a gross shift (i.e. integer pixel shift) estimation substage and a subpixel shift (i.e. decimal pixel shift) estimation substage; both substages are based on the correlation method in the frequency domain to estimate shifts. The reconstruction stage uses the error-energy reduction method with constraints in spatial and frequency domains to generate a super-resolved image with resolution improvement proportional to the square root of the number of frames [2].

Although face recognition performance improves with increased resolution, the improvement is highly nonlinear. Boom et al. [3] examined the effect of image resolution on performance of a face recognition system using face image resolutions of 8×8 to 128×128. Their results indicated that the performance of the face recognition algorithm in terms of equal error rate exhibited large improvement from 8×8 to 32×32, but only slight improvement from 32×32 to 128×128; these results suggests that face recognition performance is highly dependent on resolution for lower resolutions, but ceases to depend on face resolution past some threshold resolution. The results from the Facial

Recognition Vendor Test 2000 [4] confirm the findings of Boom et al. [3]. To assess the impact of resolution on face recognition performance, Blackburn et al. [4] used a high resolution gallery for training and varied the resolution (defined in terms of eye-to-eye distance) of the query set using a standard reduction algorithm. Results show that the tested face recognition systems yielded similar performance for query sets with eye-to-eye distance from 60 to 30 pixels, but at an eye-to-eye distance of 15 pixels, performance becomes severely degraded for some algorithms. Wheeler et al. [5] examined the performance of face recognition for query images with and without super-resolution at varying resolutions in terms of eye-to-eye distance (note that this study used limited query sets containing on average only 23 subjects). Their results show that performance of face recognition improves with super-resolution compared to that without super-resolution once the eye-to-eye distance falls below 24 pixels. In general surveillance video applications, it is not uncommon for the width of the face captured by the camera to be less than 20 pixels with corresponding eye-to-eye separation of less than 11 or 12 pixels. Therefore, super-resolution may aid face recognition systems to achieve improved recognition.

The objective of this work is to comprehensively assess the performance improvement of face recognition with super-resolution using the video database of moving faces and people [1] at three subject-to-camera ranges in terms of eye-to-eye pixel distances for the query sets: (a) 5-10 pixels eye-to-eye distance, (b) 15-20 pixels, and (c) 25-30 pixels. Receiver operating characteristic curves are generated for the low-resolution original query sets and the super-resolved query sets at each range.

# 2. METHODOLOGY

## 2.1 Database

The video database of moving faces and people [1], containing both static images as well as videos, is used for this study. Specifically, the following components of the database are used: facial mug shot still images and parallel gait video. The facial mug shot still images are close-up camera acquisitions of the subjects in the database, and therefore can be used to form the high resolution (in terms of eye-to-eye pixel distance) target set for the face recognition algorithm. Only the frontal mug shots are used to form the target set because the face recognition algorithm used in this study was designed for frontal face images. The parallel gait video shows the subject moving towards the camera, enabling several different frame sequences to be selected for super-resolution that have different face resolutions (in terms of eye-to-eye distances).

Note that in order to quantify the improvement in performance achieved with super-resolution, the baseline performance must be also established by using the original low-resolution imagery as the query set. To form the baseline query set, the first frame of each sequence is used.

## 2.2 Super-resolved Query Sets

Face recognition performance is assessed at three ranges in terms of eye-to-eye distance: (a) 5-10 pixels, (b) 15-20 pixels, and (c) 25-30 pixels. For each range, three different query sets are formed: (i) original low-resolution (LR) imagery, (ii) super-resolved (SR) imagery using four consecutive frames from the video (producing a resolution improvement factor of two in the x-

and y-directions and improving the high frequency content of the imagery), and (iii) super-resolved imagery using eight consecutive frames from the video (producing a resolution improvement factor of ~2.8 in the x- and y-directions and improving the high frequency content of the imagery). Note that (iii) contained the four frames from (ii) and four additional consecutive frames. A total of nine different query sets (nomenclature specified in Table 1) each containing 80 subjects with one image per subject are generated in this study to assess performance. These query sets enable a performance assessment of face recognition as a function of subject range and image resolution.

Table 1. Query set nomenclature. Top row represents subject range from camera in terms of eye-to-eye distance.

|  | 5-10 Pixels | 15-20 Pixels | 25-30 Pixels |
|---|---|---|---|
| **Low-Resolution** | $LR_{5-10}$ | $LR_{15-20}$ | $LR_{25-30}$ |
| **Super-Resolved 4 Frames** | $SR4_{5-10}$ | $SR4_{15-20}$ | $SR4_{25-30}$ |
| **Super-Resolved 8 Frames** | $SR8_{5-10}$ | $SR8_{15-20}$ | $SR8_{25-30}$ |

## 2.3 Face Recognition Algorithm

The local region principal component analysis (LRPCA) face recognition algorithm developed by Colorado State University [6] and based on the PCA method of Bolme et al. [7] is used for this work. PCA-based methods are expected to benefit from the increased high frequency information using super-resolution image reconstruction. The LRPCA algorithm was first trained on imagery from "The Good, The Bad, and The Ugly" (GBU) subset of the Multiple Biometric Grand Challenge consisting of 522 subjects. Note that to avoid biasing the algorithm, training on a separate dataset (with respect to the query and target sets) is preferable. The parallel gait videos in the video database of moving faces and people [1] contained imagery acquired under different lighting conditions and backgrounds than the facial mug shots, so the use of the GBU for training is appropriate as the GBU database also contains imagery acquired under varying conditions, but of different subjects. Each image in the query and target datasets is first normalized to a resolution of 512×512 using manually determined eye coordinates. The query datasets are listed in Table 1, and the target dataset for each query set consists of frontal mug shots of the query subjects.

## 2.4 Measurements and Metrics

The LRPCA face recognition algorithm generates a similarity matrix which contains the distances between the query and target images, with a larger similarity score indicating higher similarity. The algorithm then scores the similarity matrices to generate receiver operating characteristic (ROC) curves, plotting the correct verification rate as a function of the false accept rate (also known as the false alarm rate, FAR). In the verification model, the face recognition system attempts to make the determination whether a person $q_i$ in the query set $Q$ matches a person $t_j$ in the target set $T$ at some threshold $c$ using the similarity matrix [9]. By varying the threshold $c$ and using a round robin evaluation procedure for the entire target set, probabilities of verification with corresponding false alarm rates are produced, enabling an ROC curve to be plotted. Note that since nine query sets are used in this work, nine ROC curves are generated and the area under the ROC curves are tabulated to assess overall performance. To visualize performance with respect to range, the correct verification rate is also plotted as a function of range at false alarm rate of 0.01, 0.05, and 0.10.

# 3. RESULTS AND DISCUSSION
## 3.1 Super-Resolved Imagery

referred to as the far range, 15-20 as the mid-range, and 25-30 as the close range.

For the far range, the LR image is highly pixilated and distorted by JPEG compression, yielding a coarse facial outline and few facial features. Super-resolution with four frames enhances the facial outline significantly along with some facial details, and

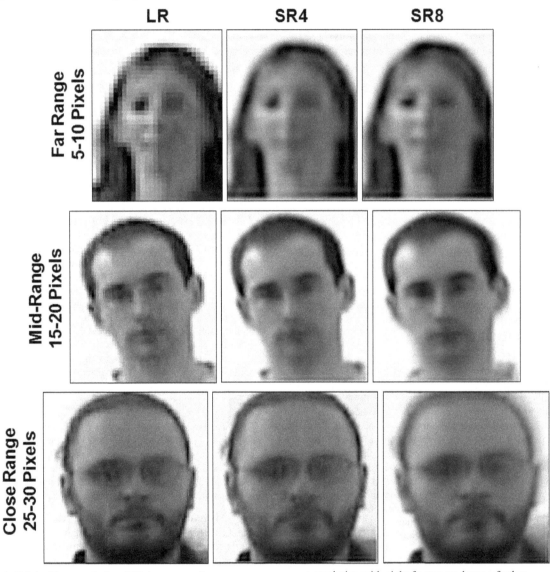

Figure 1. Original low-resolution (LR) imagery and super-resolved imagery (4 frames – SR4, 8 frames – SR8) for three subjects at three eye-to-eye distances: 5-10 pixels, 15-20 pixels, and 25-30 pixels.

Super-resolved imagery using four and eight frames are shown in Figure 1, along with original low-resolution imagery for three subjects at 5-10, 15-20, and 25-30 pixels eye-to-eye distances. Note that the native sizes of the LR, SR4, and SR8 images are different, but have been normalized for display and comparison purposes in Figure 1. The 5-10 pixels distance will also be

super-resolution with eight frames produces a further improvement in terms of visible quality at the far range. For some subjects at the far range, the long subject-to-camera distance and compression artifacts almost completely eliminated facial details in LR imagery so that super-resolution yield little benefit; super-resolution does not create information where there was none to begin with. For the mid-range, super-resolution consistently produced improved imagery with finer facial features as seen in Figure 1 (outline of glasses is even visible in the SR8 image).

As range decreases, the camera can capture finer details; decreasing range also lessens the detrimental impact of compression on facial features. Therefore, the LR imagery already contains finer details at closer ranges, and super-resolution benefit decreases causing the close range LR image in Figure 1 to appear visually comparable to the close range SR images. Note that the SR8 close range image exhibits blurring, since scale changes are much more pronounced between frames at close ranges. Although the close range SR images may not appear visually enhanced, facial recognition algorithms may still benefit from super-resolution as these algorithms operate on different principles than the human visual system.

## 3.2 Receiver Operating Characteristic Curves

Receiver operating characteristic curves at the 5-10 pixel eye-to-eye distance (red), 15-20 pixel eye-to-eye distance (green), and 25-30 eye-to-eye distance (blue) are shown in Figures 2, 3, and 4, respectively. Each figure contains three ROC curves corresponding to the low-resolution imagery and super-resolved imagery using four and eight frames. The area under the curve (AUC) for each ROC curve is tabulated in Table 2. At the far range, $SR4_{5-10}$ exhibits a slightly but consistently higher performance than LR, resulting in AUC of 0.6230 compared to AUC of 0.6028 for $LR_{5-10}$. Interestingly, $SR8_{5-10}$ has a slightly lower AUC than $LR_{5-10}$. At the mid-range, face recognition using the super-resolved imagery resulted in significantly and consistently higher performance than using the low-resolution imagery, yielding AUC improvement of 6.7% for $SR4_{15-20}$, and 10.6% for $SR8_{15-20}$. At the close range, although the benefit provided by super-resolution was not as great as at the mid-range, face recognition using the super-resolved imagery still yielded AUC improvement of 3.7% for $SR4_{25-30}$, and 4.6% for $SR8_{25-30}$. Note that AUC is a measure of the overall performance; performance is also commonly given for low false alarm rates, as addressed in Section 3.3.

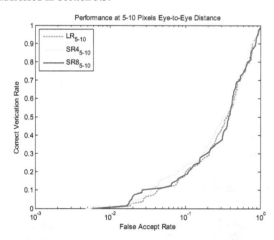

Figure 2. ROC curves at 5-10 pixels eye-to-eye distance for the original low-resolution (LR) query set and the corresponding super-resolved query sets using four frames ($SR4_{5-10}$) and eight frames ($SR8_{5-10}$).

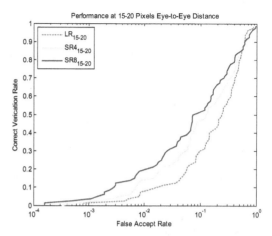

Figure 3. ROC curves at 15-20 pixels eye-to-eye distance for the original low-resolution (LR) query set and the corresponding super-resolved query sets using four frames ($SR4_{15-20}$) and eight frames ($SR8_{15-20}$).

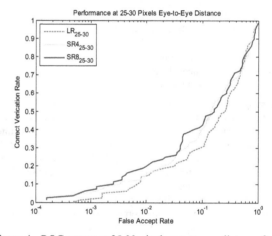

Figure 4. ROC curves at 25-30 pixels eye-to-eye distance for the original low-resolution (LR) query set and the corresponding super-resolved query sets using four frames ($SR4_{25-30}$) and eight frames ($SR8_{25-30}$).

Table 2. Area under the ROC curve. Top row represents range in terms of eye-to-eye distance.

|  | 5-10 Pixels | 15-20 Pixels | 25-30 Pixels |
|---|---|---|---|
| **Low-Resolution** | 0.6028 | 0.7150 | 0.6914 |
| **Super-Resolved 4 Frames** | 0.6230 | 0.7630 | 0.7172 |
| **Super-Resolved 8 Frames** | 0.6002 | 0.7912 | 0.7235 |

## 3.3 Performance versus Range

To visualize how performance varies with respect to distance, the correct verification rate is plotted in Figure 5 as a function of range for three commonly used false alarm rates: (a) 0.01, (b)

0.01, and (c) 0.10. Note that performance results at FAR of 0.001 are often reported for face recognition algorithms, but FAR of 0.001 was not used here due to the smaller subject sample size. At FAR = 0.01, although the change in performance is roughly linear for LR, a sharp knee is observed for SR4 and SR8, signifying that performance is flattening for ranges closer than the mid-range (15-20 pixels eye-to-eye distance). At the far range, using more frames may accentuate facial artifacts from compression effects and negatively impact the PCA-based algorithm; therefore, SR8 is observed to produce a lower verification rate than SR4, especially for higher FAR. At the mid-range where the knee occurs, the correct verification rate is 14.0% for SR4$_{15-20}$ and 19.6% for SR8$_{15-20}$ compared to 8.0% for LR$_{15-20}$, resulting in an improvement by 75% and 145%, respectively. A similar trend is observed at FAR = 0.05 with the knee also occurring at the mid-range where the correct verification rate is 29.0% for SR4$_{15-20}$ and 38.0% for SR8$_{15-20}$ compared to 16.3% for LR$_{15-20}$, resulting in an improvement by 78% and 133%, respectively. These results are consistent with the findings of [3-5]. For 5-10, 15-20, 25-30 pixel eye-to-eye distances, SR4 produced "effective" eye-to-eye distances of 10-20, 30-40, and 50-60 pixels, respectively (since the resolution improvement factor for SR4 is two in the x- and y-directions). Blackburn et al. [4] observed that face recognition performance is similar for eye-to-eye distances from 30 to 60, which would correspond to the effective eye-to-eye distances of the mid and close ranges of this study for SR4. Once the effective eye-to-eye distances falls below 30 pixels, performance changes drastically as observed in this study for SR4 as well as SR8 and in [4].

Interestingly, at FAR = 0.10, performance of SR4 and SR8 at the close range is lower than for the mid-range, suggesting that super-resolution image reconstruction is most effective for the mid-range where eye-to-eye distance is between 15-20 pixels. At the close range, the correct verification rate is 46.9% for SR4$_{25-30}$ and 40.5% for SR8$_{25-30}$ compared to 30.3% for LR$_{25-30}$, resulting in an improvement by 55% and 70%, respectively. For the investigated mid and close ranges of this study, super-resolution produced a significant improvement in the correct verification rate over the original low-resolution imagery at all false alarm rates below 0.40.

### 3.4 Absolute Verification Rates

Although super-resolution produced significant benefits for the LRPCA face recognition algorithm at the mid and close ranges relative to the performance using low-resolution imagery, the maximum achieved correct verification was below 20% at FAR of 0.01. This should not be surprising, as the verification rate achieved by an advanced fusion algorithm for face recognition on the Ugly partition of the MBGC/GBU data was slightly above 45% at a false alarm rate of 0.01 (http://face.nist.gov/mbgc/MBGCFuture/FutureChallengesMBGC.html). The target and query sets extracted from the video database [1] used in this study exhibited differences in lighting conditions, facial expressions, distance of subject to camera as well as slight differences in facial aspect angle. The variations exhibited between the query and target sets of this study are expected to be possibly more extreme than the variations in the Ugly partition of the GBU database. In addition, whereas the GBU images are high resolution (3008 × 2000), imagery from the video database is 720 × 480. The imagery used in this work is therefore a close approximation to typical surveillance imagery, and the benefits of super-resolution for face recognition shown

here suggest that super-resolution image reconstruction will be effective in practical applications.

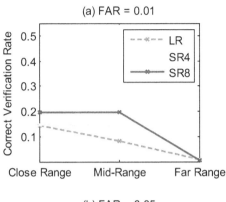

(a) FAR = 0.01

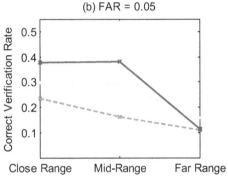

(b) FAR = 0.05

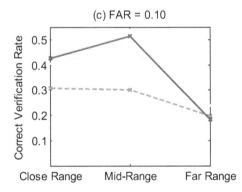

(c) FAR = 0.10

Figure 5. Performance as a function of range at three false alarm rates: (a) 0.01, (b) 0.05, and (c) 0.10.

## 4. CONCLUSION

Super-resolution has been shown to provide significant benefits for the LRPCA face recognition algorithm, especially for the mid-range where the eye-to-eye distance of the subjects is between 15-20 pixels. Performance of the LRPCA algorithm at the mid-range increased from a verification rate of 16.3% using the original low-resolution query set to 38% using the super-resolved imagery, showing that significant benefits can be achieved with super-resolution for face recognition.

In surveillance applications, lower resolution cameras are commonly used, typically acquiring images of individuals at a distance. The limited number of face pixels severely impact face recognition performance. Super-resolution image reconstruction improves the resolution and enhances the frequency content of low-resolution imagery, benefitting face recognition systems and potentially aiding the law enforcement community and homeland security.

# 5. REFERENCES

[1] O'Toole, A.J., Harms, J., Snow, S.L., Hurst, D.R., Pappas, M.R., Ayyad, J.H., and Abdi, H. 2005. A video data of moving faces and people. *IEEE Transactions on Pattern Analysis and Machine* Intelligence 27, 5 (May 2005).

[2] Young, S.S., and Driggers, R.G. 2006. Super-resolution image reconstruction from a sequence of aliased imagery. *Applied Optics* 45.

[3] Boom, B.J., Beumer, G.M., Spreeuwers, L.J., and Veldhuis, N.J. 2006. The effect of image resolution on the performance of face recognition system. In *Proceedings of the 7th International Conference on Control, Automation, Robotics, and Vision* (Singapore, December 05-08, 2006).

[4] Blackburn, D.M., Bone, M., and Phillips, P.J. 2000. Facial Recognition Vendor Test 2000.

[5] Wheeler, F.W., Liu, X., and Tu, P.H. 2007. Multi-frame super-resolution for face recognition. In *Proc. of IEEE First International Conference on Biometrics: Theory, Applications and Systems* (Washington, D.C., USA, September 27-29, 2007).

[6] Bolme, D.S., Beveridge, J.R. 2010. CSU Face Recognition Resources. *http://www.cs.colostate.edu/facerec/algorithms/lrpca2010.php.*

[7] Bolme, D.S., Beveridge, J.R., Teixeria, M., Draper, B.A. 2003. The CSU face identification evaluation system: Its purpose, features, and structure. In *Proc. of 3rd Int. Conf. on Vision Systems* (Graz, Austria, April 1-3, 2003).

[8] Grother, O., Micheals, R., and Phillips, P.J. 2003. Face Recognition Vendor Test 2002 Performance Metrics. In *NIST IR* 6982.

[9] Rizvi, S.A., Phillips, J.P., Moon, H. 1998. The FERET Verification Testing Protocol for Face Recognition Algorithms. In *NIST IR* 6281.

# Inexpensive Ground Truth and Performance Evaluation for Human Tracking using multiple Laser Measurement Sensors

William Shackleford
shackle@nist.gov

Tsai Hong
Tsai.Hong@nist.gov

Tommy Chang
Tommy.Chang@nist.gov

National Institute of Standards and Technology(NIST)
100 Bureau Dr.
Gaithersburg, MD 20899

## ABSTRACT

This paper will describe a flexible and inexpensive method of obtaining ground truth for the evaluation of Human Tracking systems. It is expected to be appropriate for evaluating systems used to allow robots and/or autonomous vehicles to operate safely around humans. It is currently focused on tracking people as they stand still or walk. It relies on multiple Laser Measurement Sensors(LMS) also called laser line scanners. The LMS's are mounted to scan in a horizontal plane. A method for quickly calibrating the relative position and orientation of each of the sensors to each other is described. A basic human tracking algorithm using the LMS's is described along with how the algorithm can be combined with a priori knowledge of the walkers intended path during the test. A graphical user interface(GUI) displays both the data obtained directly from the LMS and the output of the tracking algorithm. The GUI allows the user to verify and adjust the tracking algorithm without needing to annotate every frame, and therefore at a lower cost than systems that require extensive annotation. Tests were performed with people walking or running though several patterns, while data was simultaniously recorded by a more expensive system require individual receivers on each participant for comparison.

## Categories and Subject Descriptors

I.2.10 [**Vision and Scene Understanding**]: 3D/stereo scene analysis

## General Terms

Performance, Measurement

## Keywords

Human Tracking, Laser Measurement Sensor(LMS),Ground Truth

This paper is authored by employees of the United States Government and is in the public domain.
PerMIS'10, September 28-30, 2010, Baltimore, MD, USA.
ACM 978-1-4503-0290-6-9/28/10.

## 1. INTRODUCTION

While robots and autonomous vehicles have found applications in numerous extreme environments from Mars to the bottom of the ocean, one of the most difficult environments for robots to work in are those where the safety of people moving within the environment needs to be addressed. In an industrial setting, robots are usually required to be fenced off from people and shutdown completely when people need to breach the fence. [7] [6] In order for robots and autonomous vehicles to operate in closer proximity to people, tests of their perception systems need to be devised that will thoroughly prove the system's safety. The evaluation of these tests requires ground truth knowledge of the location of all humans in the environment during the test. In [15], thermal imaging is used to track humans for real-time mobile robot applications. In [5], laser scanners are combined with video to track humans in a scene. Ultra-WideBand (UWB) technology is used in [4]. However most of these systems were designed to be used within a fully autonomous system while others require expensive support infrastructure. Our approach is to employ multiple LMS's mounted to scan horizontally at a fixed height between the foot and knee with a Graphical User Interface(GUI) for annotation and post-processing to develop ground truth data to be used in the evaluation of other systems.

## 2. LMS MOUNTING

Figure 1 shows our apparatus for mounting each LMS. The roll and pitch can be adjusted to level by adjusting the height of each of the three feet. It is light weight enough for one person to carry easily. The height of the sensor is adjustable.

The height may be a crucial factor for which future research may be needed to provide additional guidance. The following factors should be considered in selecting the height.

- Occlusions – At very low heights, grass may occlude the sensor.

- Size of a person in the horizontal plane – At longer distances it will be more important to use a height where the person is wider in order to get more data points on the person.

- Person to person variability – People are expected to have more similarly shaped scans at ankle height than

**Figure 1: Adjustable and portable apparatus for mounting the LMS**

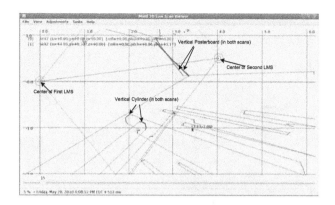

**Figure 2: Screenshot of Graphical User Interface(GUI) for Manual Calibration before calibration. Points from LMS1 are in red. Points from LMS2 are in blue.**

at a height that might correspond with one persons shoulders and another persons chest.

- Separation between people – People might be more likely to brush shoulder to shoulder than ankle to ankle.

## 3. DATA COLLECTION

Each LMS sensor was read using tools in the Mobile Open Architecture Simulation and Tools(MOAST) framework. [3] [1] [2] This provides a real-time live connection for the new programs for display and analysis described in this paper via the Neutral Messaging Language(NML) [13] [9] [10] as well as offline access through NML Packed Message Files corresponding to the MOAST defined SensorData1D data structure recorded by the MOAST Data Logger. [8] The advantages of this approach have already been tested in [12] and [11]. [1]

## 4. MANUAL VISUAL CALIBRATION

We prefer to be able to combine the output of multiple sensors. This allows us to see both sides of a person's legs, provides redundancy in case one sensors view is obstructed, and allows us to extend the area in which the experiments may be conducted. One of the first tasks to be performed before the output of multiple sensors can be combined is to determine the relative position and orientation of each of the sensors so that data can be represented in a common coordinate system. One simple approach is to use a graphical interface that allows the output of one scan to be overlaid on another and dragged into position while recording the position and orientation offset needed for alignment. A screen shot of this graphical interface is shown in Figure 2. The display shows an overhead view of the scene. While Z values are carried along in the computation, they have no effect on the display. In this figure the data from one sensor is plotted in blue while the data from the other sensor is plotted in red. Two items in this scene are useful for doing the calibration, a poster board held up by the corner of a table and a cylinder.

The GUI has a mode for adjusting each degree of freedom independently. In each mode, the point the mouse is pressed down on is dragged with the mouse position by adjusting the degree of freedom associated with that mode. When the user presses the mouse down, the screen coordinates of the mouse pointer are recorded ( $D_{screen} = \{D_{ScreenX}, D_{ScreenY}\}$ ) as well as the current offsets of the selected sensor ( $O = \{x_o, y_o, z_o, roll_o, pitch_o, yaw_o\}$ ). While dragging the position offset x,y and orientation offset roll,pitch,yaw are updated from the current mouse position ( $U_{screen} = \{U_{ScreenX}, U_{ScreenY}\}$ ). Both the mouse down position and mouse up position are converted from screen to world coordinates using Equations (1) and (2). The scale depends on the zoom level and is the ratio of meters to pixels on the display. The XOffset and YOffset variables are determined by the amount the user has scrolled the view. The corresponding sensor coordinates of the mouse down and up positions are converted from world coordinates to the selected sensor's coordinate by multiplying by the inverse of the pose created from ( $O^{-1} = Posemath.inv(\{x_o, y_o, z_0, roll_o, pitch_o, yaw_o\})$ ) using the Real-Time Control System(RCS) Posemath Library.[14] Updating the x and y offsets is trivial as seen in Equations (3) and (4). $roll_f$ and $pitch_f$ are the roll and pitch fractions, temporary variables to reduce the complexity of Equations (5) and (6) used to update roll and pitch. Equation (7) updates the yaw value.

$$x_{world} = Scale * (x_{screen}) + XOffset \quad (1)$$

$$y_{world} = Scale * (y_{screen}) + YOffset \quad (2)$$

$$x = x_o + (U_{WorldX} - D_{WorldX}) \quad (3)$$

$$y = y_o + (U_{WorldY} - D_{WorldY}) \quad (4)$$

$$D_{Sensor} = \{D_{SensorX}, D_{SensorY}\}$$
$$= Posemath.multiply(O^{-1}, D_{World})$$

---

[1] All the source code for the programs described in this paper are also now available from the MOAST repository. http://sourceforge.net/projects/moast/

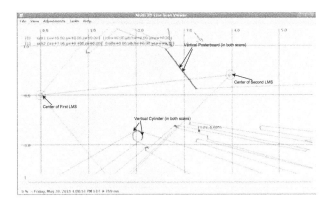

**Figure 3:** Screenshot of Graphical User Interface(GUI) for Manual Calibration after calibration. Points from LMS1 are in red. Points from LMS2 are in blue.

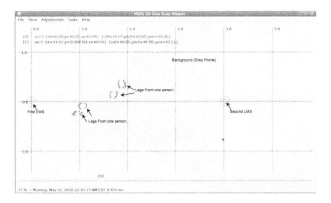

**Figure 4:** Screenshot of Graphical User Interface(GUI) showing the use of Background Subtration. Points in grey are part of the background and not processed further.

$$U_{Sensor} = \{U_{SensorX}, U_{SensorY}\}$$
$$= Posemath.multiply(O^{-1}, U_{World})$$

$$roll_f = cos(roll_0) * \frac{U_{SensorY}}{D_{SensorY}}$$

$$roll = \begin{cases} \pi & \text{if } roll_f \leq -1 \\ acos(roll_f) & \text{if } -1 < roll_f < 1 \\ 0 & \text{if } roll_f \geq 1 \end{cases} \quad (5)$$

$$pitch_f = cos(pitch_0) * \frac{U_{SensorX}}{D_{SensorX}}$$

$$pitch = \begin{cases} \pi & \text{if } pitch_f \leq -1 \\ acos(pitch_f) & \text{if } -1 < pitch_f < 1 \\ 0 & \text{if } pitch_f \geq 1 \end{cases} \quad (6)$$

$$yaw = atan(\frac{U_{SensorX}}{U_{SensorY}}) - atan(\frac{D_{SensorX}}{D_{SensorY}}) + yaw_o \quad (7)$$

The advantage of manual visual calibration is that no automatic algorithm is needed to segment the data to find points of correlation in the two or more line scan data sets. No particular calibration target is needed although simple objects with flat or circular vertical surfaces make identifying them in the display easier. The sensors were mounted on adjustable and portable frames which provides flexibility in collecting data but means that frequent calibrations are required. The GUI was intuitive enough that recalibrations could be completed in only a couple of minutes. Figure 3 shows the result of one such recalibration.

## 5. BACKGROUND SUBTRACTION

After the relative positions of each of the sensors have been calibrated, the next step is to separate possible humans from the background objects such as walls and furniture. One approach to doing this is to collect scans that will only contain the relatively fixed objects in the scene. The sensor values are collected over some period of time and the minimum range value from each sensor at each angle is stored in a background file. The background is then removed from the data by removing any point whose range is greater than the minimum recorded when establishing the background minus a threshold(10cm). This is shown in Figure 4.

## 6. LEG AND HUMAN GROUPING

Each frame of data whether read from the live sensor or from data logs contains the same SensorData1D data structure. It contains the field of view, angular resolution, a time stamp and an array with a series of range values. The sensor has different modes that can change the field of view and angular resolution. Each range value is tested against the background and values within 10cm of the background are removed from further processing. The 10cm tolerance was found to reliably remove the background. If detecting people deliberately pressing themselves up against a wall or other background object were necessary, the tolerance could be reduced. Range values that differ from the previous or next by more than 10cm are also removed. Range values of the edges of objects may have a range that represents an averaging over the beam width of the object and the farther off background. This is sometimes called the mixed-pixel effect. Eliminating points before and after changes eliminates points likely to be on edges. This tolerance can also be adjusted. The program maintains a list of humans being tracked. For each human being tracked, the program keeps a history of that person's positon over time, the current centroid of the points associated with each leg, the centroid of the two leg centroids and a list of data points from the current frame associated with each leg. Each range value is converted to a 2D cartesian point using the calibrated offset for that sensor. An object for all possible pairs of points less than twice leg tolerance apart is created and the set of pairs sorted based on the distance between pairs. Each pair is evaluated in order starting with the closest.

There are three cases:

- If neither point in the pair belongs to a leg group then create a new group and add both points.

- If exactly one of the two points belongs to a leg group

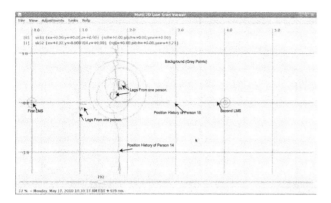

**Figure 5: Screenshot of Graphical User Interface(GUI) showing the grouping of each person and the track of that person's movement.**

check if the unassociated point can be added to the other points group.

- If both points belong to different groups check to see if the two groups can be merged. (If both points belong to the same group there is nothing to do.)

Once the points have been grouped into leg groups, the legs are associated with humans. Each leg group is tested against the set of human groups created from the previous frame of data in order based on the distance to the closest leg. The leg is associated with that human group if all of the following are true.

- The human does not already have two legs associated with it from the current frame.

- The leg is not farther than the tolerance in the expected path of that human.

- The leg is not farther than the leg tolerance away from the leg positions of the human in the previous frame.

If the leg is not closer to any human from the previous frame than the configurable threshold then a new human is added to the set.

This is shown in Figure 5.

## 7. TEST SETUP

In order to evaluate the effectiveness of this system a series of tests were performed where the tracks of humans were simultaneously recorded with this system and a system that uses four laser transmitters on tripods in each corner of the room and battery powered receivers mounted on hard hats to be worn by each participant. The transmitter/receiver system is a more expensive system that was expected to also have higher fidelity. Since each receiver has a unique identifier it is not as subject to errors where two people coming close together may be mistaken for one person or each other. The test consisted of seven patterns.

- One person walking in a circle.

- One person walking in a zigzag pattern with sharp turns.

- Two people walking side by side parallel to an imaginary line between the laser measurement sensors.

- Two people walking side by side parallel to a line orthogonal to an imaginary line between the laser measurement sensors.

- Two people crossing the center of the test area from opposite sides parallel to an imaginary line between the laser measurement sensors.

- Two people crossing the center of the test area from opposite sides parallel to a line orthogonal to an imaginary line between the laser measurement sensors.

- Two people crossing the center of the test area from corners ninety degrees apart.

Each pattern was repeated at fast and slow speeds and with the height of the laser scanners at 0.14 m (0.45 ft ), 0.4m (1.3 ft ), and 0.6 m (1.96 ft ). At the lowest height we also collected data a medium speed.

## 8. TEST RESULTS

Figure 6 shows overlapped plots of 2D overhead positions of each person in each test scenario showing both the data from the transmitter/receiver system and from the laser measurement scanners. In Figure 7 the maximum and average error for each test is plotted along with variables affecting/identifying the test. Although the computer controlling the laser scanner and the computer controlling the transmitter/receiver system were synchronized using the Network Time Protocol(NTP), analysis showed strong evidence that the transmitter/receiver system had delays up to 3 seconds that varied even during the course of a single test. Therefore errors were computed by finding the distance between each position reported by the transmitter/receiver system and the closest point reported by the human tracking algorithm using the line scanner data taken in the previous three seconds. In addition some data reported by the transmitter/receiver system was ignored due to large temporary jumps in position. The maximum error between the two systems over the test as shown in the top plot of Figure 7 varied between 0.10 m ( 0.32 ft ) and 0.76 m ( 2.49 ft ). The mean error as shown in the second to top plot of Figure 7 varied between 0.04 m ( 0.13 ft ) and 0.23 m ( 0.75 ft ). Both the mean and maximum errors peaked during the fast circle tests. There are two theories for the large errors during the fast circle tests. The first is that as a person runs around a circle they lean into the circle such that the receiver on a person's head travels a smaller radius circle than a system detecting their feet. The other theory is that the transmitter/receiver system may be doing time averaging that also might tend to reduce the size of the circle traveled. Some tuning was required after the data were collected. The default human threshold of 0.9 was chosen but was raised for two of the tests and lowered for four of them as shown in the second to bottom plot of Figure 7. When people are walking faster, especially when the sensor was mounted at the lowest height, their legs tended to move farther away from each other, which led the algorithm to mistake one person for two. This was corrected by increasing the threshold for human radius. Tests where people are closer to each other caused one leg of one person to be grouped with the wrong person. This was corrected by reducing the threshold for the human radius. For four of the tests the tracking algorithm was provided with a priori expected paths, which prevented the algorithm from associating a leg with the person on the other track in error. While the software supports expected paths of any number of line segments the expected paths provided for this test only consisted of a single line segment for each person. This meant the effort to provide the expected path was minimal. The paths were only needed for the tests where two people crossed paths at right angles and there was a potential to swap paths.

## 9. CONCLUSIONS

While some ground-truth systems are costly because they require expensive hardware and infrastructure and others require extensive hand segmentation, it is possible to produce ground-truth from less expensive systems. The key is that the ground-truth system does not need to be perfect, it only needs to be much less subject to the types of errors expected from the system under test in the particular experiment. For example while the system under test might only have views available from a moving autonomous vehicle, the ground truth system has multiple views available from fixed locations. The system under test may be required to handle occlusions while the experiment is designed to ensure the ground truth system is never occluded.

Specifications of the error range for systems for human tracking require a better definition of the position of a human. While some systems specify millimeter accuracy or better, this is typically for the position of a target on a human. The relationship of the target to the person's center of mass or a bounding volume containing the human is left unknown. The range of errors on each data point are easily obtainable from the manufacturer of the laser measurement scanner. These errors are typically only a centimeter or two and may even be in the millimeter range. However the error introduced by assuming a person's center of mass or that the center of their head is directly above the center of the cluster of points on the legs or ankles is likely greater than this. For robot safety applications, even knowing the center of mass to millimeter accuracy is not useful. To avoid hurting a person, the robot must either have the full bounding volume of the person including things that they are carrying, or assume a radius large enough to include these.

Further work will be done to determine the suitability of this system outdoors and at much larger ranges.

## 10. REFERENCES

[1] S. Balakirsky. MOAST on sourceforge.net.
https://sourceforge.net/projects/moast/.

[2] S. Balakirsky. MOAST wiki.
http://tinyurl.com/2ahr2qg.

[3] S. Balakirsky, F. Proctor, C. S. Jr, and T. Kramer. A mobile robot control framework: From simulation to reality. In *International Conference on Simulation, Modeling, and Programming for Autonomous Robots (SIMPAR 2008)*, November 2008.
http://tinyurl.com/28925aw.

[4] J. A. Corrales, J. A. Corrales, F. A. Candelas, and F. Torres. Hybrid tracking of human operators using imu/uwb data fusion by a kalman filter. In *Proceedings of the 3rd ACM/IEEE international conference on*

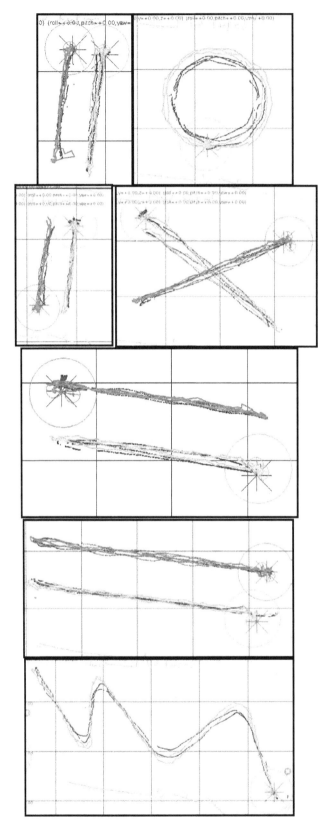

Figure 6: Results for the 0.14m height fast tests for each walking pattern. data points from the transmitter/receiver system in dark blue, background range scanner data in grey, track from person 1 in as detected by laser scanners in green, track from person 2 in purple. The light grid marks 4 m ( 13.1ft) squares. The darker lines border each test plot. Each test has three laps back and forth or around.

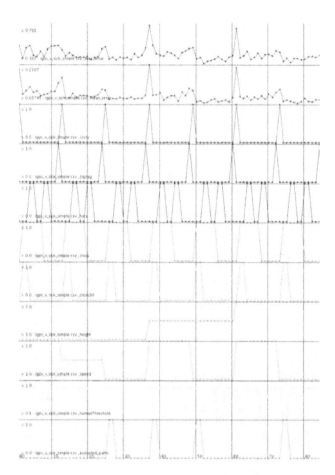

**Figure 7: Plots of the summary results for each test. X axis is the test number, each variable is plotted with a different min and max scale shown.**

*Human robot interaction*, 2008. `http://portal.acm.org/citation.cfm?id=1349822.1349848`.

[5] J. Cui, H. Zha, H. Zhao, and R. Shibasaki. Multi-modal tracking of people using laser scanners and video camera. *Image and Vision Computing*, February 2008. `http://tinyurl.com/24u2crn`.

[6] I. T. S. D. F. (ITSDF). Itsdf b56.5 safety standard for guided industrial vehicles and automated functions of manned industrial vehicles. `http://www.itsdf.org`.

[7] R. I. A. (RIA). *ANSI/RIA R15.06-1999 American National Standard for Industrial Robots and Robot Systems - Safety Requirements (revision of ANSI/RIA R15.06-1992)*. Robotic Industries Association (RIA), 1999.

[8] W. Shackleford. NML message files. `http://www.isd.mel.nist.gov/projects/rcslib/message_files.html`.

[9] W. Shackleford. The NML programmer's guide (c++ version). `http://www.isd.mel.nist.gov/projects/rcslib/NMLcpp.html`.

[10] W. Shackleford. The NML programmer's guide (java version). `http://www.isd.mel.nist.gov/projects/rcslib/NMLjava.html`.

[11] W. Shackleford. Performance evaluation of the primitive mobility execution of an automated guided vehicle within the mobility open architecture simulation and tools environment. In *Proceedings of the 14th World Multi-Conference on Systemics, Cybernetics and Informatics: WMSCI 2010 Orlando, FL, United States*, June 2010.

[12] W. Shackleford and R. Bostelman. Data collection test-bed for the evaluation of range imaging sensors for ANSI/ITSDF b56.5 safety standard for guided industrial vehicles. In *Proceedings of the Performance Metrics for Intelligent Systems Workshop*, October 2009. `http://tinyurl.com/26w96wd`.

[13] W. Shackleford, F. Proctor, and J. Michaloski. The neutral message language: A model and method for message passing in heterogeneous environments. In *Proceedings of the World Automation Conference*, June 2000. `http://tinyurl.com/2bwokte`.

[14] W. Shackleford, F. Proctor, and K. Murphy. RCS pose mathematics library. `http://www.isd.mel.nist.gov/projects/rcslib/posemathdoc/`.

[15] A. Treptowa, G. Cielniakb, and T. Duckett. Real-time people tracking for mobile robots using thermal vision. *Robotics and Autonomous Systems*, September 2006.

# Development of Performance Metrics and Test Methods for First Responder Location and Tracking Systems

Francine Amon
Building and Fire Research Lab
NIST
100 Bureau Dr
Gaithersburg MD, 20899
+011 301-975-4913
francine.amon@nist.gov

Camillo Gentile
Information Technology Lab
NIST
100 Bureau Dr
Gaithersburg MD, 20899
+011 301-975-3685
camillo.gentile@nist.gov

Kate A. Remley
Electronics and Electrical Engineering Lab
NIST
325 Broadway St
Boulder CO, 80305
+011 303-497-3672
kate.remley@nist.gov

## Categories and Subject Descriptors

D.3.3 [**Programming Languages**]: N/A

## General Terms

Measurement, Documentation, Performance, Design, Reliability, Experimentation, Security, Standardization, Verification.

## Keywords

First responder, firefighter, evaluation, test methods, location, tracking, test methods

## 1. EXTENDED ABSTRACT

The need for the development of performance requirements, metrics and test methods for evaluation of location and tracking systems is increasing as these systems begin to become commercially available for use by emergency responders. A working group was recently formed at the 5th Annual PPL Workshop[1] consisting of members of the various emergency responder communities, representatives of government agencies, and location and tracking system manufacturers with plans to collect and share information about their ongoing efforts that have bearing on this effort. The goal of the working group is to develop baseline *performance requirements* for reliable and interoperable indoor location systems for emergency responders and develop *test procedures* to validate vendor systems against those requirements. The final deliverable will be a proposed draft document in acceptable format to be presented to appropriate standards developing organization(s). The following text describes in broad terms the steps by which the draft document will be created.

## 1.1 Information Collection

Information about past and current activity in the development of performance evaluations of location/tracking systems for first responders will be collected for as many efforts as possible. This serves two main purposes: to learn from the successes and failures of others, and to foster a spirit of cooperation amongst interested parties. This work was begun last year as part of an internally funded NIST project within BFRL. Pertinent information collection items include:

- Thorough literature search on existing solution technologies and manufacturers which offer mature solutions.

- Thorough literature search on existing standards documents and user requirements, including all emergency responder communities.

- Contact key people from government agencies that are involved in or might have an interest in development of performance standards for location and tracking systems (LTS) for first responders.

- Contact emergency responders and manufacturers that are interested in LTS evaluations and invite them to contribute to this effort.

## 1.2 User Community Input

A very important aspect of this work is to maintain a close relationship with the various LTS user groups so that their requirements and desires are met to the fullest extent possible. The three main user groups are fire fighters, police, and EMS personnel. Other user groups may include the National Guard, the Coast Guard, hazmat, and USAR (technical rescue). In addition to gaining an understanding of the users' needs, information about their operating environments is also essential to design test methods that will ensure the LTS under test will perform adequately in the field. For fire fighters, the LTS must be robust enough to function in a hot, smoke-filled building, regardless of the location technology being used. The input desired from user groups includes:

- Preferred performance requirements: location accuracy, communications reliability, equipment form factor, etc.;

- Description of operation scenarios: building materials, number of floors, number of users, etc.

- Preferred user interface: voice-activated, handheld device, visual display, etc.

- Technical barriers that challenge/prohibit the use of LTS: radio frequency interference, access to building maps, etc.

- Non-technical barriers that challenge/prohibit the use of LTS: lack of resources, political climate, receptiveness of users, etc.

## 1.3 Roles of Working Group

As this information is collected and questions are answered, the scope of the current project will take shape and reveal new roles for NIST and other stakeholders in the working group. A Steering Group at the PPL Workshop was appointed to provide guidance and order to the efforts of the working group. Some important steps towards achieving the goal of the working group and facilitating the flow of activities are listed below:

- Each stakeholder will provide enough information about their respective activities to allow others to plan their work in a constructive way that may or may not involve collaborations.

- Proceed in the areas that are common among all applications while specific interest groups can work in parallel to develop test methods for the applications with which they are most concerned, with guidance from the Steering Team.

- Leverage as much as possible existing standards for performance requirements and test methods which apply generally to the ruggedness of fire equipment.

- Assign a task group the responsibility for correlating the pieces and assembling them into a cohesive document that can then be channeled to standards developing organizations (SDOs) when the latter are ready to start working on formal standards documents.

## 1.4 Related Activities at NIST

In the interest of sharing Information about past and current activity in the development of performance evaluations of location/tracking systems for first responders, relevant work at NIST includes:

- The Building and Fire Research Laboratory is compiling a prioritized list of fire scenarios that are important to the fire service with respect to LTS.

- The Building and Fire Research Laboratory is currently developing ground-truth measurement science with which to verify LTS location performance. Future work will incorporate testing of existing LTS in real-scale environments to validate the test methods. The feasibility of using small-scale test facilities for ground-truth measurements and rough-duty ruggedness testing will be explored.

- The Electrical and Electronic Engineering Laboratory is developing an understanding of the way RF signals are attenuated by building materials, reflected and redirected by building surfaces, and how interference from other wireless devices can impact RF signal quality. A measurement campaign will be conducted to characterize RF links in various structure types with respect to time-of-arrival, angle-of-arrival, received-signal-strength, etc.

- The Electrical and Electronic Engineering Laboratory will validate the use of a reduced-scale reverberation chamber in which "virtual" RF signals are generated as a method by which the performance of RF-based, and possibly other types of LTS, is measured.

- The Information Technology Laboratory will develop a computer simulator to extrapolate the tested small-scale performance of actual location/tracking systems to large-scale networks and in fire scenarios in order to validate their performance in realistic deployments.

- The Information Technology Laboratory has been involved in the development and evaluation of many different LTS technologies.

- The Manufacturing Engineering Laboratory is active in the development of standards and guidance documents for search and rescue robots, which involves LTS for certain performance tests included in the suite of requirements for some applications.

## 2. ACKNOWLEDGMENTS

While this project is just beginning, it would not have gained momentum without financial assistance from the Standards and Technology Directorate of DHS. Also, David Cyganski, Jim Duckworth, and John Orr of Worcester Polytechnic Institute helped considerably by including a session on standards development in their 5th annual Precision Indoor Personnel Location and Tracking for Emergency Responders Workshop. Lastly, our student intern, Adam Kopp's enthusiasm is infectious and much appreciated.

## 3. REFERENCES

[1]    Fifth Annual Workshop, "Precision Indoor Personnel Location and Tracking for Emergency Responders Workshop", http://www.wpi.edu/academics/ece/ppl/

# Automated Gross and Sub-pixel Registration Accuracy of Visible and Thermal Imagery

Stephen Won
Army Research Laboratory
2800 Powder Mill Rd
Adelphi, MD 20783
1-240-883-8902

stephen.won@arl.army.mil

S. Susan Young
Army Research Laboratory
2800 Powder Mill Rd
Adelphi, MD 20783
1-301-394-0230

ssyoung@arl.army.mil

Gunasekaran Seetharaman
Air Force Research Laboratory
26 Electronic Parkway
Rome, NY 13441
1-315-225-0685

gunasekaran.seetharaman@rl.af.mil

## ABSTRACT

Tracking or improving resolution of images requires that objects of interests are aligned at every frame through registration. Three motion segmentation algorithms utilizing the image gradient and five motion estimation algorithms were tested to see which would produce the best registration process at the gross and subpixel level. To test the motion segmentation, a qualitative study was performed using visible and thermal imagery to see how accurately the area of motion could be identified without producing noise. Gross shift estimation accuracy was accessed by comparing estimated shifts against a ground truth. Sub-pixel shift estimation accuracy was assessed by a series of synthetically downsampled images. The initial evaluation of segmentation revealed that the flux tensor method performed the best with a fixed threshold. For gross-shift estimation accuracy on images with well-defined objects, feature correspondence yielded the most accurate results. For images with objects that are not well-defined, optical flow methods produce more accurate results. The sub-pixel shift estimation test revealed that correlation was the only method out of the four tested that could accurately estimate motion at the sub-pixel level.

## Categories and Subject Descriptors

D.3.3 [**Image Processing and Computer Vision**]: Enhancement
– *Filtering, Registration.*

## General Terms

Algorithms, Performance

## Keywords

Super-resolution, image registration, optical flow, Horn-Schunck, Lucas-Kanade, flux tensor, SIFT

## 1. INTRODUCTION

Devices for navigation or surveillance often employ visual instruments as a means of sensing. Images from these devices can then be used for object recognition and obstacle avoidance. While not discussed in this paper, the instrument is an important part in the sensing quality provided. High resolution of details is essential to effective application in these tasks. However, resolution may be sacrificed for better capture rates, resilience in environmental conditions, or cost. Effectiveness of the instrument is reduced once the sampling rate is below the Nyquist frequency. The drawback of a lower resolution can be lessened by the application of super-resolution image reconstruction.

Super-resolution algorithms use low-resolution frames containing sub-pixel shifts to generate a high-resolution image. The algorithm splits into two processes: image registration and reconstruction. In registration, the gross- and sub-pixel shifts of an image are calculated with respect to a reference frame using image registration algorithms. Reconstruction then interpolates the low-resolution frames based on the registration shifts onto a higher resolution grid. Quality of the super-resolved image improves with the accuracy and number of different sub-pixel shifts in the frame set [1]. As a result, an accurate image registration at the sub-pixel level is necessary for an effective implementation of the super-resolution algorithm.

With surveillance images, the area of interest is often smaller than the entire frame. To reduce the amount of computation, motion segmentation has to be performed. This allows local motion estimation methods to be more accurate. In this work, segmentation methods that take advantage of the gradient of the image are compared: the product of the image differences [2], the flux tensor [3], and the squared sum of the derivatives. Although computation time is an important factor, this article focuses only on the accuracy of the gross and sub-pixel shift estimation. As a result, only a qualitative evaluation of how well the segmentation yields a box that bounds that region of motion is performed.

Once the region of motion was isolated by segmentation, the performance of four methods of image registration were evaluated: the correlation method from Young et al. [4], Horn-Schunck optical flow [5], Lucas-Kanade optical flow [6], and feature correspondence utilizing the scale-invariant feature transform (SIFT) [7]. Their performance will be quantified by their accuracy in determining the gross- and sub-pixel shift in grayscale images captured from stationary, charge-coupled device and long-wave infrared cameras [2]. Similar and extensive works of motion estimation algorithm comparisons have been done by Barron, et al. [8] and Baker, et al. [9]. For greater detail on the comparison between modern image registration methods based on optical flow for each pixel in an image, the reader is directed to those works. This work focuses on the performance of spatiotemporal and frequency methods in determining an overall image translation shift in a series of low-resolution images with automatic selection of regions of motion determined by image segmentation methods.

After segmentation and registration, performance of each registration method is assessed by comparing the calculated gross- and sub-pixel translation vector against known values of shift to assess their accuracy in determination of translation for the moving object. Visible and thermal imagery contained ground truths for gross shift translation of moving objects [2]. Sub-pixel shift accuracy was determined through a generated image set produced by sub-sampling a higher resolution image. Results show that it's best to consider both segmentation and motion estimation when trying to assess registration performance. For segmentation with a fixed threshold, the flux tensor method seems to work the best out of the three tested methods despite its partial detection of motion for low signal-to-noise ratio. For motion estimation, the SIFT method had the best gross shift estimation accuracy on frames with high signal-to-noise ratio, but with the low signal-to-noise ratio in the thermal images tested, optical flow provided the greatest accuracy. For sub-pixel shift estimation, the correlation method was the only method to reliably estimate the sub-pixel shift accurately.

# 2. METHODOLOGY

## 2.1 Motion Segmentation

The purpose of a motion segmentation phase is to identify regions of movement with minimal input from the human user, improve accuracy of the image registration, and reduce computation runtime. With all of the methods, there is a segmentation image derived from the gradient of the image set. Then, the image is thresholded before drawing a bounding box around regions of motion. To avoid small or intersecting regions, the segmentation image is also repeatedly filtered with median and Gaussian filters until there is no change in the size and number of bounding boxes. These boxes would then be processed by image registration algorithms. Each of the three motion segmentation processes are described in the following sections.

### 2.1.1 Difference Product of an Image Set

Taking the difference between two images indicates any changes that occurred assuming that the images are relatively noise free. Under this assumption, the difference of each image with a reference image would highlight the changes that occur between the two frames. With more than two frames, the product of these differences can indicate where motion occurs in the entire image set since pixel values at the moving location would be nonzero:

$$I_s = \prod_t |I_t - I_{ref}|$$

Afterwards, the segmentation image, $I_s$, is thresholded at certain levels to create the binary image for the bounding boxes [2].

### 2.1.2 Flux Tensor

The method used in this work involves the use of flux tensors to identify moving structures [3]. Flux tensors use the images' partial derivative information to extrapolate the orientation estimation and temporal changes. Their main advantage to methods utilizing similar tensors is the low computational complexity, where only the trace to the following matrix of a flux tensor is needed to isolate regions of motions:

$$J_F = \begin{vmatrix} \int_{\Omega} \left(\frac{\partial^2 I}{\partial x \partial t}\right)^2 d\vec{y} & \int_{\Omega} \frac{\partial^2 I}{\partial x \partial t}\frac{\partial^2 I}{\partial y \partial t} d\vec{y} & \int_{\Omega} \frac{\partial^2 I}{\partial x \partial t}\frac{\partial^2 I}{\partial t^2} d\vec{y} \\ \int_{\Omega} \frac{\partial^2 I}{\partial y \partial t}\frac{\partial^2 I}{\partial x \partial t} d\vec{y} & \int_{\Omega} \left(\frac{\partial^2 I}{\partial y \partial t}\right)^2 d\vec{y} & \int_{\Omega} \frac{\partial^2 I}{\partial y \partial t}\frac{\partial^2 I}{\partial t^2} d\vec{y} \\ \int_{\Omega} \frac{\partial^2 I}{\partial t^2}\frac{\partial^2 I}{\partial x \partial t} d\vec{y} & \int_{\Omega} \frac{\partial^2 I}{\partial t^2}\frac{\partial^2 I}{\partial y \partial t} d\vec{y} & \int_{\Omega} \left(\frac{\partial^2 I}{\partial t^2}\right)^2 d\vec{y} \end{vmatrix}$$

Afterwards, the segmentation image produced by the trace of the flux tensor is thresholded at 1% of the maximum value.

### 2.1.3 Change in Gradient Over Time

Similar to the flux tensor, this method takes advantage of the information provided by derivatives in each direction. However, the difference between this method and the flux tensor method is that the neighboring pixel values are not accounted for in this method. This produces segmentation values that are more prone to changes in pixel intensity in the equation:

$$I_s = \left[\sum_t \left(\frac{\partial}{\partial t}\nabla I\right)\right]^2$$

This method is also thresholded at 1% of the maximum value.

## 2.2 Image Registration

After image segmentation, each pair of images in a set is run through a image registration algorithm. After calculating the gross-shift, the images are re-aligned together using the gross-shift flow vectors. Then the images are up-sampled before the motion estimation algorithm is performed again in order to calculate the sub-pixel shift. Each motion estimation algorithm under investigation is described briefly in the subsections.

### 2.2.1 Horn-Schunck Global Smoothness Flow

Assuming that the brightness is constant in the region of motion, this process aims to minimize the error for the rate of change of the image brightness. To do this, a flow velocity is calculated for every pixel. Since this creates a large matrix, the flow vectors can be calculated through the Gauss-Seidel method, where the flow vector $(u, v)$ for the pixel can be calculated based on the average flow velocity $(\bar{u}, \bar{v})$ from the previous computation [5]:

$$u^{n+1} = \bar{u}^n - I_x[I_x\bar{u}^n + I_y\bar{v}^n + I_t]/(\alpha^2 + I_x^2 + I_y^2)$$
$$v^{n+1} = \bar{v}^n - I_x[I_x\bar{u}^n + I_y\bar{v}^n + I_t]/(\alpha^2 + I_x^2 + I_y^2)$$

where $\alpha$ is a smoothness term ($\alpha = 0.01$). This calculation is performed 100 times in order to minimize the error, similar to the work by Barron et al. [8]. After the optical flow has been calculated for the region, the average is taken for the vector components above a certain threshold under the assumption that the motion is uniform for all of the averaged pixels. To accelerate this process and to improve estimations for a fixed number of iterations, the entire process is repeated for each layer of the Gaussian pyramid representation of each image. Without the

Gaussian pyramid, the number of iterations needed to compute the optical flow field would need to equal the image size [5].

### 2.2.2 Lucas-Kanade Local Constant Flow

Like the Horn-Schunck method, the Lucas-Kanade method aims to minimize the error between two images. It does this under the assumption that the flow is constant for all pixels in a local neighborhood [6]. Because this is a local method, the process only works with a pyramidal data structure. Otherwise, it would be unable to detect medium movements since the method only looks for small changes in the image. For each layer of the pyramid, a Hessian matrix is calculated where the partial derivative of the image is taken in both spatial directions. Afterwards, the optical flow is calculated in an iterative fashion by calculating the image error and then calculating a new flow vector through matrix inversion between the Hessian and a mismatch vector [10]:

### 2.2.3 Correlation Method

Unlike the spatiotemporal methods of Horn-Schunck and Lucas-Kanade, the correlation theorem is based on the correlation and shift properties of the discrete Fourier transform (DFT) theorem. Because the method is not an iterative process, there is no need to use pyramid data structures to calculate the translation.

### 2.2.4 Scale Invariant Feature Transform (SIFT) Correspondence

The scale invariant feature transform (SIFT) is a method developed by Lowe for object recognition purposes. Like other feature detection methods, it finds features through scale-space by taking the Laplacian of two images. It improves upon this by identifying high contrast points at probable locations. Afterwards, it then calculates the orientation for each feature's gradient. A histogram containing the orientation of each feature is then produced [7], which makes the feature more robust against affine transformations unlike the previous three methods. In this work, the features identified by the SIFT algorithm are corresponded across the image set. Given a reference image, the translation vector can then be computed by taking the difference of the feature location between two time intervals.

## 2.3 Data Collection

Data was comprised of frames captured from color charge-coupled device (CCD) and forward-looking infrared (FLIR) cameras [2]. One image sequence was generated by sub-sampling an up-sampled picture in order to measure sub-pixel translation shift accuracy. Gross-shift translation accuracy was determined by the difference in the position of image features (i.e. corners, region centers, etc.). Segmentation accuracy was qualitatively assessed by making sure the bounding box included the entire range of motion in the image set. Samples of the visible, thermal, and sub-sampled test images are shown in Figure 1.

## 3. RESULTS AND DISCUSSION
## 3.1 Accuracy of Segmentation Methods

A good segmentation method would isolate the area of motion from the entire frame. This is important as many of the motion estimation algorithms only work when the image is analyzed locally; it can only work if it is analyzing only the area of motion.

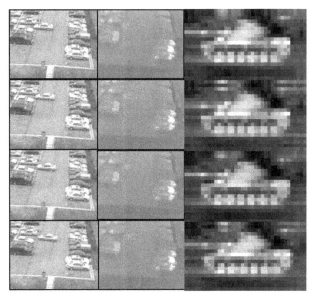

**Figure 1. Image test sets: Left column represents the visible images, middle column represents the thermal images, and the right column represents the sub-sampled images**

Each image segmentation method was evaluated on whether or not it could identify the region of motion to an approximate box in the set of visible and thermal frames shown in Figure 1. The segmentation and resulting bounding boxes for the visible and thermal images are shown in Figure 2 and 3, respectively.

With the color imagery, all three segmentation methods are able to identify the car reversing from the parking spot. However, in terms of the quality of the segmentation, it is clear that the flux tensor method provides the best segmentation since there is a low amount of noise in the segmentation image. It should also be noted that the difference product method needed the highest possible threshold setting in order to achieve that segmentation image. The segmentation and bounding box images for the color image set are shown in Figure 2. With the thermal imagery, all of the methods do not perform well when the threshold was left unchanged from the color images. The difference product and squared sum of the image derivatives fail to detect any motion. The flux tensor method was able to detect the motion, but in multiple parts along with some noise. However, if the threshold was changed to epsilon for the difference product method, it is able to effectively box the majority of the motion with one extraneous box as shown in Figure 3. Because the threshold had to be changed to the other extreme, there is a need for adaptive thresholding to more effectively filter the motion out from the segmentation image.

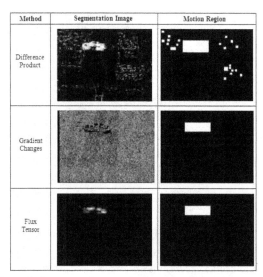

**Figure 2. Segmentation results from the visible image set. Note how the reversing car is clearly seen in all frames, but the difference product is fairly noisy.**

| Method | Segmentation Image | Motion Region |
|---|---|---|
| Difference Product | | |
| Gradient Changes | | |
| Flux Tensor | | |

**Figure 3. Segmentation results from the thermal image set. The flux tensor method has a lot of noise. The difference product could see the car, but a different threshold was needed.**

## 3.2 Accuracy of Image Registration Methods

Accuracy of each method in gross shift estimation was assessed by comparing calculated translation vectors for each moving object in each image set against the ground truth. There is an assumption that the segmentation worked and the input data for this analysis contained the bounding box location for the area of motion in each image. Image sets were selected from data that displayed no affine transformations (i.e. rotation and scaling) from [2]. Without any modification to the image segmentation method, translation vectors for a set of 16 visible frames of a car reversing are shown in Table 1. These vectors represent the total calculated shift in the images. Errors in the accepted values vary by a pixel.

**Table 1. Calculated pixel translation from each method for the visible image set**

| Image | Accepted | Corr | HS | LK | SIFT |
|---|---|---|---|---|---|
| 2 | 1 | 2 | 1 | 0 | 2 |
| 3 | 3 | 2 | 2 | 0 | 4 |
| 4 | 6 | 5 | 3 | -2 | 6 |
| 5 | 10 | 7 | 5 | 4 | 8 |
| 6 | 11 | 9 | 7 | 1 | 10 |
| 7 | 12 | 11 | 9 | 9 | 13 |
| 8 | 14 | 13 | 13 | 12 | 14 |
| 9 | 17 | 15 | 17 | 14 | 16 |
| 10 | 20 | 17 | 10 | 16 | 18 |
| 11 | 20 | 19 | 10 | 17 | 20 |
| 12 | 22 | 21 | 13 | 20 | 22 |
| 13 | 25 | 23 | 11 | 21 | 24 |
| 14 | 25 | 25 | 12 | 26 | 26 |
| 15 | 27 | 27 | 12 | 28 | 28 |
| 16 | 30 | 29 | 11 | 30 | 30 |
| Sum of Squared Errors | | 38 | 1293 | 279 | 16 |

The feature correspondence method using SIFT outperforms other methods for this image set. The correlation method is close to the performance of SIFT. However, the two optical flow methods clearly do not perform as well. Also, in terms of relative runtime, the optical flow methods ran in terms of hours while the correlation and feature correspondence methods ran in terms of minutes. As a result, the two better methods for visible images or well-defined objects are feature correspondence using SIFT and the correlation method.

With the thermal version of the same set of images, motion estimation algorithms perform different from the visible images. Optical flow methods start to produce the lowest sum of squared errors. Feature correspondence is unable to detect any motion because the low signal-to-noise ratio prevents SIFT from detecting any features. Compared to SIFT, correlation performs better. If runtime is a factor, correlation may be used despite the more accurate performance by optical flow. However, if runtime is not a factor, optical flow should be used since it is more sensitive to the slight changes in the pixel values, which is needed for ill-defined objects. The results from the tests are shown in Table 2. The best motion estimation for ill-defined images then depends on the situation: if runtime is not a factor, a method based on the image gradient should be used. Otherwise, the correlation method should be used to provide an accurate estimation while maintaining a low runtime.

It should be noted that in both gross shift estimation tests, the sub-pixel shift was also calculated. However, because there is no ground truth in the estimation, these values were rounded to the nearest pixel and added to the overall gross shift.

**Table 2. Calculated pixel translation from each method for the thermal, LWIR image set**

| Image | Accepted | Corr | HS | LK | SIFT |
|---|---|---|---|---|---|
| 2 | 0 | 2 | 0 | 0 | 0 |
| 3 | 2 | 2 | 5 | 2 | 0 |
| 4 | 2 | 6 | 7 | 5 | 0 |
| 5 | 3 | 8 | 8 | 6 | 0 |
| 6 | 5 | 10 | 9 | 9 | 0 |
| 7 | 7 | 12 | 12 | 11 | 0 |
| 8 | 8 | 14 | 12 | 13 | 0 |
| 9 | 9 | 16 | 12 | 15 | 0 |
| 10 | 9 | 18 | 11 | 16 | 0 |
| 11 | 11 | 20 | 13 | 18 | 0 |
| 12 | 15 | 22 | 15 | 21 | 0 |
| 13 | 18 | 24 | 12 | 27 | 0 |
| 14 | 18 | 26 | 16 | 28 | 0 |
| 15 | 20 | 28 | 9 | 27 | 0 |
| 16 | 22 | 30 | 9 | 25 | 0 |
| Sum of Squared Errors | | 619 | 463 | 484 | 2195 |

Sub-pixel shift accuracy could be determined by running each motion estimation algorithm on the series of down-sampled images. Because the rate and offset of the sampling was known, there is a ground truth for the sub-pixel shift of the image. With the image sub-sampled every eighth pixel on each row and each column, there were 64 sub-pixel shifts to test. Some of the results are shown on the graph in Figure 4. It is clear that feature correspondence using SIFT depends on well-defined objects since a down-sampled image would not possess any clear features. As a result, it was unable to detect any sub-pixel shift. The optical flow methods were able to detect sub-pixel shift, but not accurately. Only correlation is able to correctly estimate the sub-pixel shift with reliable accuracy.

## 4. CONCLUSIONS

Automated super-resolution image registration yields reliable results when the correlation method is combined with an effective image segmentation that isolates the region of movement. The flux tensor segmentation method is the best method to use when using only one threshold. However, to effectively evaluate segmentation, a test set of images to assess segmentation accuracy should be available. In addition, adaptive threshold could be utilized to provide better thresholding for all segmentation methods. For motion estimation for good signal-to-noise ratio objects, feature correspondence combined with correlation should be utilized for gross and sub-pixel shift estimation, respectively. However, for ill-defined images, optical flow may need to be used for gross-shift estimation. In future studies, registration accuracy should be assessed for objects with affine transformations.

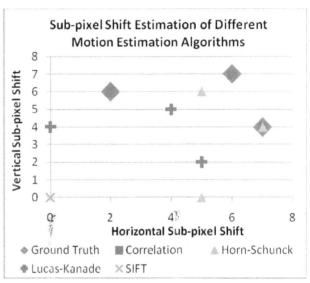

**Figure 4. Comparison of each motion estimation algorithm in sub-pixel shift estimation accuracy. Better methods are closer to the ground truth points.**

## 5. ACKNOWLEDGMENTS

The authors would like to thank Dr. Kannappan Palaniappan and the US Air Force Research Laboratory for the demonstration of flux tensors as a method of image segmentation.

## 6. REFERENCES

[1] Young, S. S., Driggers, R. G., Jacobs, E. L. 2008. Signal Processing and Performance Analysis for Imaging Systems. Artech House, Norwood, MA.

[2] Chan, A. L., 2007. A Description on the Second Dataset of the U.S. Army Research Laboratory Force Protection Surveillance System. ARL-MR-0670

[3] Bunyak, F., Palaniappan, K., Nath, S. K., Seetharaman, G. Flux tensor constrained geodesic active contours with sensor fusion for persistent object tracking. J Multimedia. 2007 August;2:20–33.

[4] Young, S. S., Driggers, R. G., 2006. Super-resolution image reconstruction from a sequence of aliased imagery. Applied Optics, Vol. 45, 5073-5085

[5] Horn, B. K. P., Schunck, B. G., 1981. Determining optical flow. Artificial Intelligence, Vol. 17, 185-203

[6] Lucas, B. D., Kanade, T., 1981, An iterative image registration technique with an application to stereo vision. In Proceedings of Imaging Understanding Workshop, 121-130

[7] Lowe, D. G., 2004. Distinctive image features from scale-invariant keypoints. International Journal of Computer Vision, 60, 2, 91-110.

[8] Barron, J.L., Fleet, D. J., Beauchemin, S. S., 1994. Performance of optical flow techniques. International Journal of Computer Vision, Vol. 12, n. 1, pp. 43-77

[9] Baker, S., Scharstein, D., Lewis, J.P., Roth S., Black, M.J., and Szeliski, R. 2007. A database and evaluation methodology for optical flow. In Proc. IEEE Int. Conf. Computer Vision. 1--8.

[10] Bouguet, J.Y. 2000. Pyramidal implementation of the Lucas-Kanade feature tracker: description of the algorithm. Technical Report, Intel Microprocessor Research

# An Indoor Study to Evaluate A Mixed-Reality Interface For Unmanned Aerial Vehicle Operations in Near Earth Environments

James T. Hing
Drexel Autonomous Systems
Lab, Drexel University
3141 Chestnut Street, MEM
Department
Philadelphia, Pennsylvania,
19104
jtoshiroh@gmail.com

Justin Menda & Kurtulus
Izzetoglu
School of Biomedical
Engineering, Drexel University
Philadelphia, Pennsylvania,
19104
jm973@drexel.edu,
ki25@drexel.edu

Paul Y. Oh[†]
Drexel Autonomous Systems
Lab, Drexel University
3141 Chestnut Street, MEM
Department
Philadelphia, Pennsylvania,
19104
paul@coe.drexel.edu

## ABSTRACT

As the appeal and proliferation of UAVs increase, they are beginning to encounter environments and scenarios for which they were not initially designed. As such, changes to the way UAVs are operated, specifically the operator interface, are being developed to address the newly emerging challenges. Efforts to increase pilot situational awareness led to the development of a mixed reality chase view piloting interface. Chase view is similar to a view of being towed behind the aircraft. It combines real world onboard camera images with a virtual representation of the vehicle and the surrounding operating environment. A series of UAV piloting experiments were performed using a flight simulation package, UAV sensor suite, and an indoor, six degree of freedom, robotic gantry. Subjects' behavioral performance while using an onboard camera view and a mixed reality chase view interface during missions was analyzed. Subjects' cognitive workload during missions was also assessed using subjective measures such as NASA task load index and non-subjective brain activity measurements using a functional Infrared Spectroscopy (fNIR) system. Behavioral analysis showed that the chase view interface improved pilot performance in near Earth flights and increased their situational awareness. fNIR analysis showed that a subjects cognitive workload was significantly less while using the chase view interface.

## Keywords

UAV, pilot training, mixed reality, near Earth environments

## 1. INTRODUCTION

Systems like the Predator and Reaper have an incredible success rate conducting medium to high altitude long endurance missions that include surveillance, targeting, and strike missions [3]. However, UAVs are evolving and quickly expanding their role beyond the traditional higher altitude surveillance. Due to advances in technology, small, lightweight UAVs, such as the Raven and Wasp, are now capable of carrying complete avionics packages and camera systems, giving them the capability to fly in environments much too cluttered for the proven large scale systems [3]. As such, changes to the way UAVs are operated, specifically the operator interface, are being developed to address the newly emerging applications.

There are many challenges to face when designing new UAV interfaces and trying to incorporate high situation awareness and telepresence for a UAV pilot. For one, the pilot is not present in the remote vehicle and therefore has no direct sensory contact (kinesthetic/vestibular, auditory, smell, etc.) with the remote environment. The visual information relayed to the UAV pilot is usually of a degraded quality when compared to direct visualization of the environment. This has been shown to directly affect a pilot's performance [10]. The UAV pilot's field of view is restricted due to the limitations of the onboard camera. The limited field of view also causes difficulty in scanning the visual environment surrounding the vehicle and can lead to disorientation [4]. Colors in the image can also be degraded which can hinder tasks such as search and targeting. Different focal lengths of the cameras can cause distortion in the periphery of images and lower image resolution, affecting the pilot's telepresence [5]. Other aspects causing difficulties in operations are large motions in the display due to the camera rotating with the UAV and little sense of the vehicle's size in the operating environment. This knowledge is highly important when operating in cluttered environments.

*The U.S. Army Medical Research Acquisition Activity, 820 Chandler Street, Fort Detrick, MD 21702-5014 is the awarding and administering acquisition office. This investigation was funded under a U.S. Army Medical Research Acquisition Activity; Cooperative Agreement W81XWH-08-2-0573. The content of the information herein does not necessarily reflect the position or the policy of the U.S. Government or the U.S. Army and no official endorsement should be inferred.
†corresponding author

Prior research from the authors [7] has introduced a mixed-reality chase view interface for UAV operations in near Earth environments to address many of these issues. Near Earth in this work represents low flying areas typically cluttered with obstacles such as trees, buldings, powerlines, etc. The chase view interface is similar to a view from behind the aircraft. It combines a real world onboard camera view with a virtual representation of the vehicle and the surrounding operating environment. The authors' prior research in [7] also presented the development of an indoor gantry system that can be used to evaluate UAV operations in near Earth environments. The 6 degree of freedom indoor robotic gantry was used to safely test and evaluate the chase view interface using different pilots and mission scenarios without the risk of costly crashes. Inside the gantry workspace is a recreation of a real world flight environment. The dynamics of the gantry end effector (holding the UAV sensor suite) is driven by the output from a flight simulation program. The author's prior results of indoor gantry trials showed an observed improvement in pilot control and precision positioning of an aircraft using the chase view interface as compared with a standard onboard camera view. These results supported the efforts toward a more extensive human factor study to validate the early claims.

Not previously studied was the cognitive workload of the subjects while using the chase view system. Data about operator cognitive workload and situational awareness are very important aspects of safe UAV operation. Low situational awareness requires higher cognitive activity to compensate for the lack of intuitive cues. Complex mission scenarios also inherently involve high cognitive workload. If a pilot can perform well using the interface but requires a high level of mental processing to do so, they may not have a suitable level of mental resources available during the flight to safely handle unexpected events such as faults or warnings. Current techniques in UAV training and pilot evaluation can be somewhat challenging for cognitive workload assessment. Many of these types of studies rely partly on self reporting surveys, such as the NASA Task Load Index (NASA-TLX) [6]. However, this is still susceptible to inconsistencies in the subject responses over a series of tests.

The use of functional near-infrared (fNIR) brain imaging in these studies enables an objective assessment of the cognitive workload of each subject that can be compared more easily. The Drexel Optical Brain Imaging Lab's fNIR sensor uses specific wavelengths of light introduced at the scalp. This sensor enables the noninvasive measurement of changes in the relative ratios of de-oxygenated hemoglobin (deoxy-Hb) and oxygenated hemoglobin (oxy-Hb) in the capillary beds during brain activity. Supporting research has shown that these ratios are related to the amount of brain activity occurring while a subject is conducting various tasks [8]. By measuring the intensity of brain activity in the prefrontal cortex, one can obtain a measure of the cognitive workload experienced by the subject [12, 11]. The results can also be used to enhance the self reported (subjective) workload results.

## 2. HYPOTHESES

Based on previous results found in [7], the following hypotheses are formulated:

### 2.1 Behavioral Hypothesis

Figure 1: fNIR sensor showing the flexible sensor housing containing 4 LED sources and 10 photodetectors.

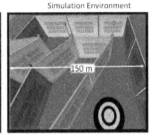

Figure 2: Left: Flight environment inside the gantry built at 1:43.5 scale. Highlighted in the image are the colored markers for the second level of the environment. Right: Simulated full scale environment.

*The chase view interface will improve a pilot's understanding of the 3D spatial relationship of the aircraft and its surroundings. It will also help pilots to produce more efficient flight paths (ie. tighter turns around obstacles).*

### 2.2 Cognitive Hypothesis

*Cognitive workload of the pilot will decrease using chase view. This is due to the stabilized camera image (horizon remaining level) and more of the environment displayed in the image. fNIR will detect a change in blood oxygenation (ie. cognitive workload) for onboard camera view subjects that is higher than chase view subjects due to the increased mental mapping and prediction of aircraft position required while using the onboard camera perspective.*

## 3. EXPERIMENTAL SETUP

A majority of the experimental setup is the same as the setup described in [7]. Integration of the fNIR system, changes to the gantry environment, and changes to the chase view interface as well as the onboard camera interface are highlighted.

### 3.1 fNIR

The fNIR sensor consists of four low power infrared emitters and ten photodetectors, dividing the forehead into 16 voxels. The emitters and detectors are set into a highly flexible rectangular foam pad, held across the forehead by hypoallergenic two-sided tape. Wires attached to each side carry the information from the sensor to the data collection computer. The components of the fNIR systems are seen in Figure 1.

### 3.2 Flight Environment

The gantry environment (Figure 2) consists of two flight levels. The lower level contains corridors and two tall pole

Onboard Camera Interface

**Figure 3:** Left: Onboard camera view with virtual instruments positioned below the image to relay information about the vehicle state. Right: Chase view with alpha blended borders.

obstacles. The upper level contains a series of colored spherical fiducials attached to the top of the corridor walls and obstacles. The physical workspace of the gantry environment is the same as in [7] however this environment is built to 1:43.5 scale to allow for accurate representation of the UAV wingspan with the width of the gantry end effector. For this study, a model of a Mako UAV with a 13 foot wingspan was used. Due to the temporal resolution of the fNIR sensor on the order of seconds, the environment was designed to continually require the pilot to update their path planning. The close quarters and multiple obstacles help to extract metrics during flights to test the hypotheses.

## 3.3 Interface Modifications

Discussions with subjects from earlier work raised an issue about the border between the rotated onboard camera and the surrounding virtual image for the chase view interface. At times there was a high contrast between the border which distracted subjects and drew their attention away from the center of the interface. The new design for the chase view interface, shown in Figure 3, addressed this issue with an added alpha blended border between the previous border of the rotated camera image and the surrounding virtual view. This helped to dramatically reduce the border contrast as well as increase subject immersion into the environment.

The onboard camera interface was modified to give a better representation of the information currently available to internal UAV pilots. Predator pilots have a heads up display superimposed onto the onboard camera images. This heads up display gives them a sense of the aircraft relative to the artificial horizon, bearing angle, and altitude. For lower computer proccessing load, the heads up display was replaced with virtual instruments as seen in Figure 3, similar to the instruments used on manned aircraft. These virtual instruments were placed directly below the onboard camera image, in clear view of the subject. The instruments displayed the aircraft relative to the artificial horizon, bearing angle, and altitude.

## 4. PROCEDURE

To assess the efficacy of the two interfaces, eleven laboratory personnel volunteered to test the conditions and to finalize the methodology; 1 female and 10 males. Differently from [7], for these tests, the subjects were separated

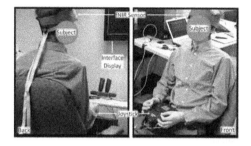

**Figure 4:** Subject operating environment. The fNIR sensor is shown strapped to the forehead of the subject with a blue felt cover to block ambient light.

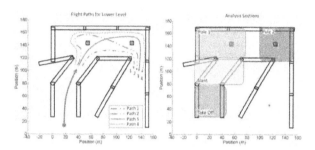

**Figure 5:** Left: Top down view of the environment with the 4 flight paths through the lower level highlighted with different patterns. Right: Analysis sections of the environment

into two groups. Six subjects operated the aircraft using only the chase view interface (chase view) and five subjects operated the aircraft using only the onboard camera interface (onboard view). One chase view and two onboard view subjects had over 200 hours of flight sim experience. These same subjects also had prior remote control aircraft training. Only one subject (chase view) had no flight sim experience at all. The rest of the subjects fell in between 1 to 200 hours of flight sim training.

There were a total of nine sessions, of which eight were recorded flight sessions. The fNIR sensor was placed on the participant's forehead during all eight flight sessions as seen in Figure 4. In all, 374 flights through the environment were recorded.

Before the beginning of each flight, an individual's cognitive baseline was recorded. This was a 20 second period of rest while the fNIR recorded oxygenation levels.

## 4.1 Session One

The subjects had a fifteen-minute introduction and free-flight session to get familiar with the dynamics of the aircraft and the flight controller.

## 4.2 Sessions Two through Nine

During each of these sessions, the subjects conducted four flight trials. Each trial represented a different flight path to follow through the environment as well as a different marker setup for the second level. The four flight paths can be seen in Figure 5. An example of the marker setup can be seen in Figure 2 where the subject is required to fly over the blue marker, then the red marker and finally the green marker. All four paths were flown during each session but were presented to the subject in random order. The marker setup was also presented in random order, however there was a total of 20 possible marker combinations.

During the flight sessions, subjects had four goals. The first goal was to fly through the test environment while maintaining a safe distance from the corridor walls and obstacles. The second goal was to correctly fly in the appropriate path around obstacles placed inside the environment. For the third goal, there was a ground target located near the end of the flight environment. The goal was to trigger a switch on the joystick when the subject felt that they were directly over the target. After the target is reached, the aircraft is automatically raised to the second level of the environment, above the corridor walls. The final goal was to fly directly over the center of the colored targets in the correct order supplied to them prior to flight. At the completion of each session (four flights in a session), the subject completed the NASA-TLX.

Starting with session seven, subjects were shown a top down view of their flight trajectory and target triggering location. This was introduced because it was noticed that most subjects' performance were saturated after six sessions. For session one through six, there was no feedback given to the subjects about their performance other than the visuals received from the interface itself.

## 4.3 Session Ten

The final session (session ten) was performed immediately after session nine was completed. The subjects were asked to fly through the gantry environment using the interface from the group they were not a part of (e.g. onboard view group used chase view interface). Every subject flew the same path (Path 2). Distance to pole objects during turns was recorded for each flight. After the two flights, the subjects were asked to fill out a multiple choice questionnaire on their thoughts about the interface they just used.

## 5. DATA ANALYSIS

## 5.1 Behavioral Data

The data analysis focused mostly on the assessment of a subject's behavioral data obtained through the measurement of aircraft positions (distances from the obstacles and targets of interest), accelerations, and operator inputs during each flight.

The environment was sectioned into four Locations(take off, slant, pole1, pole2) as seen in Figure 5. The flight variables [mean obstacle distance (ObDistance), mean magnitude angular acceleration(MagA), mean magnitude joystick velocities(jMagV)] were assessed for each flight path (1, 2, 3 and 4). The effects of View (onboard, chase) and Location (take off, slant, pole1, pole2) for each variable were evaluated using a Standard Least Squares model that evaluated each factor as well as the interaction between these factors using a full factorial design. In the event that significance was detected for location, multiple comparison Tukey tests were conducted ($\alpha = 0.05$).

In addition to the flight variables, the error variables [target error, marker error] were analyzed. The error variables contain the magnitude of the planar distance from the center of the target when the target switch is pulled (TargetError) and the magnitude of the planar distance from the nearest

Table 1: Significant effects and interactions for Paths (1,2,3,4) using Standard Least Squares Model

| Eff. or Int. | ObDist | MagA | jMagV |
|---|---|---|---|
| View | 3 | 1,2,3,4 | 2,4 |
| Location | 1,2,3,4 | 1,2,3,4 | 2,3,4 |
| View*Location | 1,2,3,4 | 1,2,3,4 | |

point on the flight path to the center of the markers (MarkerError). Chase and onboard view groups were compared for each of the error variables using a Wilcoxon nonparametric test (p<0.05 for significance). For all flight and error variables, a Spearman correlation was used to evaluate the relationship between the variable and session number for both chase view and onboard view. JMP Statistical Software (Version 8, SAS Institute, Cary, NC) and p<0.05 was taken as significant for all statistical tests.

## 5.2 Subject Workload Data

Chase and onboard view subjects NASA-TLX data was compared for each of the variables [adjusted weight rating, mental demand] using a Wilcoxon nonparametric test (p<0.05 for significance).

The hemodynamic response features from the fNIR measures (i.e., mean and peak oxy-Hb, deoxy-Hb, oxygenation) were analyzed by the Optical Brain Imaging Laboratory [9]. Analysis was run on all subjects and flights for session two through session six. It is believed that the change in session seven through session nine (showing the subjects their results) would alter the fNIR analysis so these three sections were excluded from the current fNIR analysis. A repeated measures ANOVA was run across all flights, sessions two through six, and views for each voxel. If needed, then a *Tukey-Kramer Multiple-Comparison test* was used to determine any significant differences between chase view and onboard view subjects ($\alpha = 0.05$).

## 6. RESULTS AND DISCUSSION

## 6.1 Behavioral Data

The results of the flight path analysis described earlier are shown in Figure 6, 8, 10 and the results of the Standard Least Squares Model are shown in Table 1.

### 6.1.1 Mean Angular Acceleration (MagA)

The results of mean magnitude angular acceleration for each path are shown in Figure 6. For all flight paths, the main effects of view (all p< 0.0001) and location (all p< 0.0001) were significant as shown in Table 1. In addition, at a given view and location, significant interactions were observed (p=0.001, p<0.0001, p=0.007, p=0.004 for Path 1 to Path 4 respectively) as shown in Figure 6. All paths showed a significantly higher angular acceleration at the locations of Pole 1 and Pole 2. Each of these locations requires a sharp turn which leads to an increase in the angular velocity. The higher accelerations can be explained by visual observations of the subjects' behavior during the flights. Onboard camera subjects would make very large sweeping roll maneuvers with a high amplitude in the angle. As a side result, they would overshoot their desired angle and would then proceed

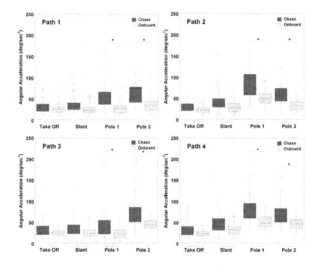

Figure 6: **Mean Magnitude Angular Acceleration for locations Take Off, Slant, Pole 1, and Pole 2. Significance, if any are, highlighted by an asterix with a line leading to the significant sets.**

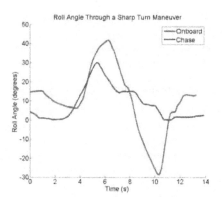

Figure 7: **Example roll angle through a sharp turn for an onboard view subject (red) and a chase view subject (blue).**

to make large and long roll maneuvers back to stabilize the aircraft. This occurred in a number of onboard view subjects because most relied on optic flow to gain awareness of the aircraft roll angle rather than the artificial horizon instrument gage. The reliance on optic flow required a relatively large roll motion before the optic flow was large enough to gather awareness from. Chase view subjects on the other hand could easily see their aircraft angle as they rolled and more easily predicted their approach to the desired angle. This allowed for much faster and more minute motions to control the roll angle. An example plot (Figure 7) shows the larger sweeping roll angles by an onboard camera subject and the smaller and minute angle corrections of a chase view subject through a sharp turn.

For all Flight Paths combined, a Spearman correlation indicated a significant negative relationship with Session for (chase view) subjects 3 ($\rho$ = -0.19, p = 0.03), 9 ($\rho$ = -0.29, p = 0.00), and 12 ($\rho$ = -0.19, p = 0.04) and (onboard

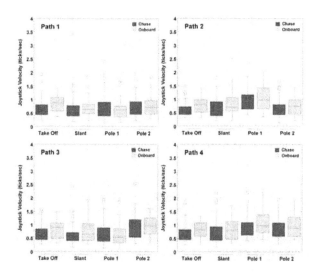

Figure 8: **Mean Magnitude Joystick Velocities for locations Take Off, Slant, Pole 1, and Pole 2. Significance, if any are, highlighted by an asterix with a line leading to the significant sets. Top:Path 1 Results Bottom: Path 2 Results**

view) subjects 4 ($\rho$ = -0.39, p = 0.00), 6 ($\rho$ = -0.35, p = 0.00), and 8 ($\rho$ = -0.38, p = 0.00). (chase view) Subject 10, however showed a significant positive relationship ($\rho$ = 0.85, p = 0.02) with session however the values of Angular Acceleration are relatively consistent. This also helps to demonstrates an improvement in control over sessions.

### 6.1.2 Mean Joystick Velocity (jMagV)

The results of mean magnitude joystick velocity for each path are shown in Figure 8. For all flights, no significant interaction was observed (p=0.32, p=0.58, p=0.34, p=0.98 for Path 1 to Path 4 respectively) (Table 1). For Path 2 and Path 4, the main effects of View (p=0.03, p=0.02 respectively) and Location(p<0.0001 for both paths) were significant while Path 3 only showed the main effect of Location as significant (p<0.001). Path 1 had none (p=0.36) for both View and Location. Observing Figure 8, while not significantly different, the onboard view subjects mean magnitude joystick velocities were higher across all paths. This leads to the conclusion that onboard view subjects were manipulating the joystick controls more than chase view subjects. This supports the claim that onboard view subjects had lower awareness of the vehicle state and stablility, thereby requiring more joystick corrections.

A Spearman correlation for Mean Joystick Velocity and session number did not show a significant relationship with session. This demonstrates that subjects did not significantly change how they manipulated the joystick across sessions.

### 6.1.3 Pole 1 and Pole 2

Figure 9 shows the phenomenon where a chase view subject flew tighter to the pole but the onboard view subject flew closer to the walls around the actual Pole 1 and the actual Pole 2. This shows that onboard view subjects tended to take wider turns to go around the obstacle which ended up

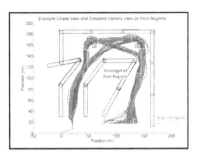

Figure 9: Top down view of the environment with the pole locations highlighted. The red line shows all the trajectories around the poles for an example onboard view subject, the blue line shows all the trajectories around the poles for an example chase view subject.

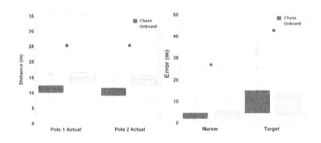

Figure 10: Left: Mean obstacle distance values to the pole obstacles during turning maneuvers. Right: Magnitude error distance of the aircraft from the Target center and center of the Markers. Significant differences are highlighted by the asterix.

taking them closer to the wall. The pole 1 and pole 2 areas were further sectioned as highlighted by yellow boxes in Figure 9. The mean obstacle distance was calculated from the aircraft to the pole itself in these sections. Figure 10 shows that in all flight paths that go around the poles (Flight Path 2,3,4), chase view has a statistically significant closer value (p<0.0001 for pole 1 actual, p<0.0001 for pole 2 actual). The data supports the behavior hypothesis, stated earlier in Section 2, that chase view enhances awareness of the vehicle's extremities by allowing the subjects to visually see when the aircraft wing tips had safely passed the obstacle. This allowed for more efficient turn paths.

### 6.1.4 Target and Marker Error

Shown in Figure 10 are chase view and onboard view results of the Target Error and Marker Error. According to the behavior hypothesis, one would expect significantly lower error with chase view versus onboard view. The chase view would give a better 3D spatial awareness of the vehicle with respect to the surrounding environment. Only the data for Marker Error supports this. The Marker Error was significantly higher (p=0.02) for the onboard view subjects when compared to the chase view subjects. The opposite was true for Target Error where the chase view group was significantly higher (p=0.006). This result can be explained by perceptual error and perspective.

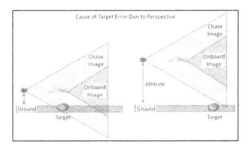

Figure 11: Left:Demonstration of how the target can be out of the onboard camera view but still in the chase view when under the aircraft. Right: Demonstration of how the target can be out of both views and still be ahead of the aircraft.

Figure 12: Screenshot showing potential perspective error.

As shown in Figure 11 when the object of interest passes out of the onboard camera image, onboard view subjects predict how long they have to wait until the aircraft is over the object. The higher up the aircraft, the longer they have to wait. Chase view subjects have the same requirement, however the object stays in view longer due to added virtual view. When low enough, the object can still be seen as it passes under the vehicle. However when higher, chase view subjects still have to wait after the target has exited even the chase view image. In early tests, chase view subjects did not understand this perspective issue and tended to trigger over the target when the virtual image appeared under the the aircraft avatar, well before the actual target area. The problem lies in that the chase view is trying to represent three dimensional information (aircraft pose in the environment) on a two dimensional display. Without proper training to account for the loss of depth perception, errors can occur. This can be seen in Figure 12 which shows a screen shot of the target task where the target appears below the aircraft avatar but due to the altitude, is well ahead of the aircraft. In early tests, not a single chase view subject triggered after the target had already passed which supports the perspective claim. During the second level flights, all subjects were closer to the height of the markers, lessening the perspective error, and thereby improving the chase view subject's results. Increased training can compensate for the potential perspective error however, using a three dimensional display for the interface would alleviate this problem.

For both Target Error and Marker Error, a Spearman

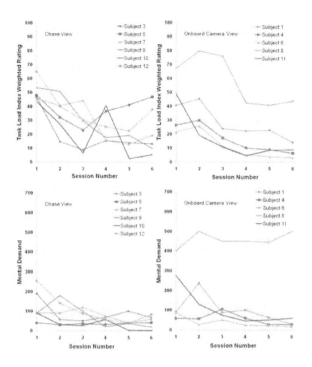

Figure 13: Task Load Index Weighted Rating across sessions. Left:chase view subjects Right:onboard view subjects

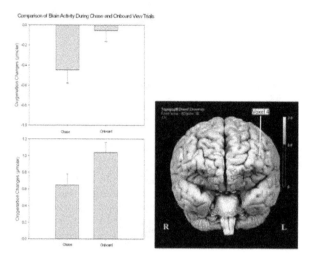

Figure 14: Average Oxygenation Changes for chase view and onboard view Subjects. For comparison of the oxygenation changes, signal level is important. Top: Average Oxygenation changes for chase view and onboard view group. Plot shows onboard view group's levels are higher. Bottom: Maximum Oxygenation changes for chase view and onboard view groups. Plot shows onboard view group's levels are higher. Right: Voxel 4 location highlighted on the brain.

correlation indicated a significant negative relationship with session for both chase view ($\rho$ = -0.49, p < 0.001) and onboard view ($\rho$ = -0.36, p < 0.001). As expected, a decrease in the amount of error is seen, after Session six, when the subjects were able to see their performance.

### 6.1.5 Workload Data

The cognitive hypothesis would suggest that the task load of the subject, specifically the mental demand of the subject, would be statistically lower for chase view. The NASA-TLX results are shown in Figure 13. When comparing the task load and mental demand were not found to be statistically significant (p=0.103, p=0.395, respectively) between chase view and onboard view. Further tests with more subjects as well as tasks that focus more on mental stimulation may help to support this hypothesis.

While the subjective tests showed no significance, the fNIR analysis showed otherwise. The difference of average oxygenation changes for all chase view and onboard view groups were found to be significant ($F_{1,361} = 6.47, p < 0.012$). These results are shown in the top of Figure 14.

The difference of maximum oxygenation changes for chase view and onboard view groups were found to be significant ($F_{1,361} = 5.94, p < 0.016$). Figure 14, bottom, shows that onboard view group had higher maximum oxygenation change when compared with the chase view group.

These comparisons were on voxel four. The location of the fourth voxel measurement registered on the brain surface is shown in Figure 14 [1]. Activation in the brain area corresponding to voxel four has been found to be sensitive during completion of standardized cognitive tasks dealing with concentration, attention, and working memory [2]. Higher oxy-

genation in this area is related to higher mental workload of the subject. Chase view subjects' average oxygenation levels for voxel four was lower than onboard view subjects, revealing that subjects using the onboard camera view were using more mental resources to conduct the flights. This result is most likely attributable to the narrower viewable angle and rolling of the environment in the onboard view, which require more cognitive processing by the subject. These results support the cognitive hypothesis.

For the Mental Demand and Overall Task Load (Weighted Rating) measures in the NASA-TLX, a Spearman correlation indicated a significant negative relationship with session for both chase view($\rho$ = -0.30, p = 0.03) and onboard view($\rho$ = -0.45, p = 0.00). Displaying results after session six, does not show a clear change in this negative trend. These results indicate that subjects became familiar and comfortable with the environment and tasks as the sessions progressed. In other words, workload seemed to decrease for all subjects as they learned what to expect and how to respond.

### 6.1.6 Session Ten

In session 10 the subjects performed two flights using the other view (ie. subjects in the chase view group used the onboard view interface). The main purpose of this session was to gather opinions about the alternate view point. It was expected that performance would decrease for each subject because they were used to operating the aircraft with their specific view point. Two flights is not enough to run a statistical analysis, however, the data showed an interesting trend. As Figure 15 shows, 4 out of 5 subjects who switched from an onboard camera view to a chase view produced a tighter more efficient turn around the obstacle. All of the

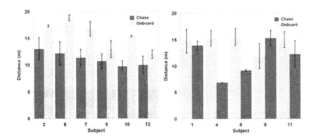

Figure 15: Mean distance from Pole 1 obstacle. The left bar is the mean distance (during a turn around the pole) for the 8 trials using the normal view, the right bar represents the mean of the 2 flights using the alternate view. Left: Chase view subjects Right: onboard view subjects

chase view subjects when switching to onboard camera view produced a much larger turn radius around the pole. This can be attributed to a lower awareness of the vehicle extremities and provides further support of the hypothesis.

After the tenth session, subjects filled out a survey about their thoughts on the view used during the session. In summary, the majority of the subjects felt that the chase view produced better awareness of the aircraft extremities and a better awareness of obstacles in the surrounding environment. Eight out of the eleven subjects preferred the chase view interface. Two of the subjects who preferred the onboard camera view stated that they would prefer the chase view interface if it was further enhanced with similar instrumentation like the onboard camera interface had. They would also have preferred the chase view if they had more flights to get used to the change in perspective.

## 7. CONCLUSIONS

The main hypothesis for the chase view interface is that it enhances a pilot's awareness of the vehicle's extremities and three dimensional spatial location in the flight environment. This will be very important during future UAV operations in near Earth environments. A series of human performance experiments were developed to test the hypothesis. Results of the studies show a significant difference between the flight paths taken by pilots using the chase view and those using the onboard camera view. The enhanced awareness allowed pilots to fly a more efficient path in a near Earth environment. Self reported preferences showed that the majority of subjects preferred the chase view interface over the traditional onboard camera perspective. All subjects reported that chase view gives a better awareness of the aircraft extremities in the flight environment and the majority report a greater awareness in the aircraft pose.

Included in these studies was a collaboration with the Drexel Brain Optical Imaging Laboratory that introduced the fNIR sensor into the evaluation and analysis of pilot performance. During the study, the fNIR sensor measured a subject's brain activity and produced an objective assessment of the subject's cognitive workload. Analysis of the fNIR data found that chase view subjects' average oxygenation levels for voxel four was significantly lower than onboard view subjects, revealing that subjects using the on-

board camera view were using more mental resources to conduct the flights. This result is most likely attributable to the narrower viewable angle and rolling of the environment in the onboard view. This requires more cognitive processing by the subject to construct an accurate working mental model of the environment and the aircraft's position in it. The benefit of a lower cognitive workload while using the chase view interface is that a pilot would have more mental resources available to handle any warnings, system faults, or other unexpected events that might occur during the flight.

The resulting designs presented serve as test beds for studying UAV pilot performance, creating training programs, and developing tools to augment UAV operations and minimize UAV accidents during operations in near Earth environments.

## 8. REFERENCES

[1] H. Ayaz, M. Izzetoglu, S. Platek, S. Bunce, K. Izzetoglu, and K. Pourrezaei. Registering fnir data to brain surface image using MRI templates. In *IEEE Eng Med Biol Soc*, volume 1, pages 2671–2674, 2006.

[2] H. Ayaz, P. Shewokis, S. Bunce, M. Schultheis, and B. Onaral. Assessment of cognitive neural correlates for a functional near infrared-based brain computer interface system. *Foundations of Augmented Cognition. Neuroergonomics and Operational Neuroscience*, pages 699–708, 2009.

[3] Department of Defense. Unmanned systems roadmap 2007-2032. Technical report, 2007.

[4] J. B. v. Erp. Controlling unmanned vehicles: the human factors solution, April 2000.

[5] M. Glumm, P. Kilduff, and A. Masley. A study on the effects of lens focal length on remote driver performance. Technical report, Army Research Laboratory, 1992.

[6] S. G. Hart. NASA-task load index (NASA-TLX); 20 years later. Technical report, NASA-Ames Research Center, 2006.

[7] J. T. Hing and P. Y. Oh. Development of an unmanned aerial vehicle piloting system with integrated motion cueing for training and pilot evaluation. *Journal of Intelligent and Robotic Systems*, 54:3–19, 2009.

[8] K. Izzetoglu. Neural correlates of cognitive workload and anesthetic depth: fnir spectroscopy investigation in humans. *Drexel University, Philadelphia, PA*, 2008.

[9] K. Izzetoglu, S. Bunce, B. Onaral, K. Pourrezaei, and B. Chance. Functional optical brain imaging using near-infrared during cognitive tasks. *International Journal of Human-Comptuer Interaction*, 17(2):211–227, 2004.

[10] D. B. Kaber, E. Onal, and M. R. Endley. Design of automation for telerobots and the effect on performance, operator situation awareness, and subjective workload. *Human Factors and Ergonomics in Manufacturing*, 10(4):409–430, 2000.

[11] A. Kelly and H. Garavan. Human functional neuroimaging of brain changes associated with practice. *Cerebral Cortex*, 15:1089–1102, 2005.

[12] J. Milton, S. Small, and A. Solodkin. On the road to automatic: Dynamic aspects in the development of expertise. *Clinical Neurophysiology*, 21:134–143, 2004.

# A Network-based Approach for Assessing Co-Operating Manned and Unmanned Systems (MUMS)

**Dr. Lora G. Weiss**
Georgia Tech Research Institute
250 14th St. NW
Atlanta, GA 30334-0822
404-407-7611, Lora.Weiss@gtri.gatech.edu

## ABSTRACT

Traditionally, robots have been programmed to do precisely what their human operators instruct them to do, but more recently, they have become more sophisticated, intelligent, and autonomous. Once they reach a sufficiently high level of intelligent autonomy, they can support more collaborative interactions with each other and with people. As robots become more and more intelligent, we will begin designing systems where robots interact with humans, rather than designing robots that are commanded by people with continual oversight. One approach to assessing how humans and robots will interact in the future is to frame the problem as a collection of intelligent nodes. Multiple, collaborating, and interacting manned and robotic systems can be represented as a collection of dynamic, interacting nodes. This paper develops preliminary metrics to support understanding the extent of preferential attachment that would arise in a system of co-operating manned and unmanned systems (MUMS). The metrics seek to help explain if attachments are localized to specific situations or if they are more pervasive throughout a MUMS society.

## General Terms

Algorithms, Measurement, Performance, Design.

## Keywords

Robotics. Clustering. Dynamic Metrics.

## 1. INTRODUCTION

MUMS is an acronym for Manned and Un-Manned Systems. Unmanned Systems may include unmanned ground vehicles (robots), unmanned air vehicles, unmanned undersea vehicles, and unmanned sea surface vehicles. We often use the terms robots and unmanned vehicles interchangeably. Co-Operating MUMS is the concept of people and machines cohabitating, cooperating, or

interacting in a shared or common environment. See Figure 1. This paper develops preliminary metrics to assess MUMS interactions in a meaningful way from an overall network and system perspective.

**Figure 1. Graphical Concept of Many Co-Operating Manned and Unmanned Systems**

These methods support analyzing dynamic MUMS interactions, where mobile robots interact and co-operate with people, but without continual oversight by an operator commanding the robots, and with multiple levels of interaction between the manned and unmanned systems. The levels of interaction include: assistance of unmanned systems to humans, independence of humans and unmanned systems (separate tasks in shared spaces), and voluntary, un-commanded assistance between humans and unmanned systems.

Our approach treats MUMS as a dynamic network of dynamic nodes, where the nodes are a mix of people, computers, and robots. Both the nodes and the edges are dynamic. The nodes are dynamic since some of them change or move in space and time, while the edges are dynamic since the connections between the nodes change as a function of time (e.g., the location of an individual, information on their activities, identification of their normal modes of behaviors, etc.). Describing these dynamic interactions poses several challenges that traditional static network architectures do not fully address.

Social robotics is an expanding research area [GT]. Kiesler and Hinds [Kie] have identified that people seem to perceive autonomous robots differently than most other computer technologies. People's mental models of robots are usually more anthropomorphic than systems being developed. They also confirm that autonomous robots are becoming more and more able to make their own decisions. Hinds, et al. [Hin] evaluate the effects of robot appearance on human-robot collaborations. They also evaluate status (e.g., subordinate, peer, and supervisor) on human-robot relationships. Breazeal [Bre] describes how to design robots to interact with people, where they learn in the human environment and learn to become social partners.

An equally impressive amount of research has been conducted in the area of understanding social and technical networks [New]. Research spans areas such as random graph theory from early on [Erd], to understanding the small world problem [Tra], and modeling the author-chain of scientific papers [deS]. Structures have emerged of the world-wide web [Bro], massive graphs [Aie], small-world networks [Wat], and scale-free networks [Bar]. Newman [New2] provides a reflective account of various networks, including social, information, technological, and biological networks in the real world. Capturing properties and creating models of the interactive nodes and the associated dynamics is an ever growing research area. The coupling of social-technical systems, as with MUMS, is yet one more application of the need for a robust capability to analyze these collections of nodes.

This research on social robotics and system networks leads to the need to start evaluating how robots will be operating in the context of a social system. We wonder how they will operate within our society, beyond one-on-one interactions with people. Will they exhibit preferential attachment or cluster by type? Are these behaviors more pervasive throughout a MUMS societal network? It is natural to expect that such attachments will result, since in social networks, certain individuals acquire more social links, e.g., if a person is older, famous, or just more personable, this person will have more connections. It will be interesting to learn if older robots will increase their connectivity to people or other robots as they age. Another question is whether or not the robots will "socialize" to become more knowledgeable and increase their situational awareness. People call this business networking, but will robots learn to do this?

Sociological networks support many dynamic interactions, yet are laden with numerous uncertainties. For example, in social networks, individuals can find relatively short paths to other individuals. This is despite having limited information about the structure of the network. Individuals also categorize themselves and each other into socially meaningful groups, often because they have the same occupation, interest, or geographical location. Without a means to estimate social distance or relationships, individuals are often unable to move information, such as a message, closer to a remote place or contact. By making social groupings, social distance feeds back into the structure of the social network, and the result is that messages, for example, make successively more precise jumps as they near their destination.

From a sociological perspective, network interactions fall into three main categories. See Table 1. Although these are worded from a sociological perspective, they apply to Co-operating MUMS networks as well. A key rationale for this research is the need to capture these notions with a rigorous approach, where metrics can be computed for these interacting systems and where

performance can be quantitatively assessed across the dynamic network of nodes.

**Table 1. Interactions within Complex Systems, from a Sociological Perspective**

| |
|---|
| • Identify conditions for a sustainable society |
|     – Design policy actions to achieve a stable system |
|     – Evaluate population growth (migration, famine, epidemics) |
|     – Incorporate trade (economic development) |
|     – Evaluate roles of conflict, trust, social groupings, and decision making |
| • Identify interactions among individuals |
|     – Evaluate creation of groups and group dynamics |
|     – Assess effects of differential rewards and differential success rates |
| • Capture elements of organizational theory |
|     – Identify the selection process |
|     – Realize that communication is an enabler (e.g., shared visions) |
|     – Integrate into effective organizations |
| *Need to capture these notions in a rigorous approach, applicable to MUMS networks and to which metrics can be applied.* |

In contrast to social networks, mathematical graphs are networks of well defined nodes whose connections are often similar and known. Capturing the dynamics of Co-operating MUMS networks poses several challenges that traditional network architectures currently do not. Traditional approaches to understanding networks of nodes often involve graph theory, lattice analysis, and centralized/decentralized analyses. Elements of current approaches also include static analyses, empirical analyses, qualitative assessments, limiting assumptions, and non-integrated approaches. For MUMS applications, the dynamic network is evolving in-situ in an unplanned and decentralized manner, so that an integrated framework that enables analysis of more complex interactions is necessary.

For interacting manned and unmanned systems that are collaborating in an un-commanded environment, these systems assemble, interact, process information, and separate from one another. For networks with large numbers of nodes, there can be thousands of such interactions. These interactions, in some ways, parallel biochemical interactions within cellular transcription networks more so than traditional mathematical or social networks. Because biological networks have evolved to perform specific functions, they are far from random [Alo]. As evolution continually adjusts these networks, they converge to a set of nodal interactions that obey general design principles.

Some of the biological design principles directly relate to MUMS networks and support the development of an initial framework for modeling, assessing, and understanding the dynamic interactions [Wei]. The features of biological transcription networks that are applicable to networks of manned and unmanned systems include the reuse of a small set of network motifs (patterns of node interactions), robustness to component tolerances, constrained interactions, and modularity. Although communications between genes may be different than for MUMS, information is conveyed between nodes and a response is generated depending on the strength or content of a stimulating signal which is the input function that triggers parts of the network into action.

A key to the understanding how to measure smaller motifs within larger collections of robotic interactions is to define and develop metrics that are reflective of interactions within a dynamic network. This paper presents a first look at expanding mathematical, sociological, and biological network analysis methods to measure and understand issues such as whether or not nodes exhibit preferential attachment to other nodes (as in society), or if preferential attachment is better than diverse attachment for robots, or if will nodes compete for links at the expense of other nodes (robots).

## 2. MUMS NETWORKS – The Components

A MUMS network consists of a collection of multiple, interacting nodes (people and robots). Each node can accomplish several tasks, but not every node can do everything. Its capabilities are determined by its sensing systems (e.g., eyes and ears for humans, lasers and radars for robots), its assets (e.g., feet and arms for humans, power and wheels for robots), its functionality, and its dynamics.

The nodes are assumed to be intelligent and autonomous and can interact in a complex external environment. They can measure internal and external states. For example, their internal state includes knowledge of their remaining fuel (or hunger for humans) or damaged components (a cracked gear for robots, a broken arm for humans). External states include physical parameters such as temperature, current position, physical contact, or communications. Communications (both overt and inferred) are extremely important for these networked systems. The information content relayed between MUMS nodes provides the stimulus for a node to react differently than in its current state. Nodes respond to these signals and act upon them. To understand a MUMS network, it is important to understand these interactions.

A *Co-Operating MUMS Network* consists of a collection of **nodes** and **edges**. Each node (person or robot) is different and has its own dynamics. Nodes interact with other nodes in different ways and across different time-scales. Not all nodes interact with each other. When nodes interact, they may do so only once or quite often, and their interactions may be different each time. For MUMS networks, the nodes are the people and the unmanned, robotic systems.

The edges in a MUMS network are the interactions between nodes, where one node directly influences another node. Edges can be directed or non-directed. Directed edges originate at one node and terminate at another node with the information flowing in one direction. Two nodes can be connected with a directed edge or with a bi-directional edge, e.g., human can ask a robot for directions, and the robot can respond with information to the person. For MUMS networks, we assume all edges are directed and that the direction of the edge indicates the direction of influence. However, not all nodes are connected to all other nodes, i.e., this is not a fully connected network. See Figure 2.

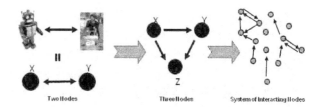

**Figure 2. Nodal Representations of Co-Operating Manned and Unmanned Systems**

## 3. MEASURES OF NODAL INTERACTION

### 3.1 General Metrics

The approach to MUMS analysis investigates relationships within dynamically evolving networks based on concepts in Table 1. A key to the success of this approach is development of concepts that enable robust interactions to be quantitatively measured and behavioral concepts to be analytically assessed. This section discusses several metrics that are reflective of interactions within a dynamic network.

***Bow-Tie Diagrams*** - "Bow-tie" diagrams [Bro, et al.] were initially developed for world-wide-web applications, but have been shown to be applicable to areas such as metabolic networks, food webs, and email networks [New]. The "bow-tie" diagram represents a central, connected component (e.g., a subway station or city center) and integrates disconnected components (e.g., robots or individuals) that link into and out of the system as a function of time. There are other external components, called tendrils, which affect the system dynamics (e.g., a street vendor) and are involved in the interplay of the network. Such a diagrammatic representation of entities is indicative of MUMS behaviors and may provide a useful for analysis.

***Scale-Free Networks*** - To capture the relationship between the complexity of the system, notions such as emergence and uncertainty must be considered. The computer science community recently identified the internet as a scale-free network. This roughly means that as entities are added to the network, the probability that they will interact with others is the same as for existing entities. From a MUMS analysis perspective, this is important. If connectedness is a measure of behavioral interactions, then introducing an additional robot to the network may not necessarily increase complexity. Understanding these dynamics may yield valuable insights into the large-scale structure needed for effective MUMS operations and parallels similar research in areas such as metabolic networks of organisms and biochemistry.

***Clustering Coefficient and Nodal Affinity*** - Nodal affinity aims to determine if entities within a network will migrate to or be attracted to other entities in the network (e.g., will Fed Ex robots interact with UPS robots). In social networks, certain nodes prefer to attach themselves to the more popular nodes. This is termed preferential attachment or nodal affinity. Capturing nodal relationships and connectivity can reveal unique behaviors within a dynamical network of systems, and would be highly applicable MUMS relationships. To capture the connectivity, a clustering coefficient can be computed [Wat]. High clustering means there is a higher chance that two nodes will interact with each other if there is another node near each of them (i.e., they have a common friend). However, too much interaction may be inefficient and may be detectable. For example, if all the Fed Ex robotic delivery trucks clustered together, they would not efficiently deliver packages. A clustering coefficient is one approach to mathematically measure interactions between nodes.

*Clustering and Complexity* - The clustering phenomenon limits a system from becoming computationally complex, in that similar nodes may group together. The probability that a new node will connect to an existing node may not be uniform, but there may possibly be a higher probability that it will be linked to a node with several other connections.

*Social Groupings* - In social networks, individuals find the shortest paths to others. This is despite having limited information about the structure of the network. If a person wants to deliver a message by having it handed from one person to the next, it turns out that each person will hand it to someone with whom they are connected. Without a means to estimate social distance, individuals are unable to move a message closer to the target. By making social groupings, social distance feeds back into the structure of the network. The result is that messages make more precise jumps as they near their target. A mathematical notion of social distance can be equally applied to MUMS networks, but where the robots are provided means to measure distances and as such progress to their destination.

*Random Networks:* For a network with $N$ nodes and $E$ edges, then there are $N(N-1)/2$ possible pairs of nodes that can be connected by an edge. Each edge can point in one of two directions, for a total of $N(N-1)$ possible directed edges between nodes. If $E$ edges are place at random in the $N(N-1)/2$ possible positions, then the probability that there is an edge between two nodes is

$$Prob(E\ Edges\ for\ N\ Nodes) = \frac{E}{N(N-1)/2}$$

For MUMS networks, the time dependant edge metric is:

$$E(t) = number\ of\ edges\ at\ time\ t$$

To assess if a MUMS network (at any given time) has a significant difference in the number of edges, one can then compute the number of standard deviations by which the network under consideration deviates from random at time $t$.

## 3.2 Specific Metrics

The metrics presented in Section 3.1 can be expanded and quantified so as to provide more specific metrics associated with MUMS networks. An initial collection of such metrics is presented in Table 2. Also provided in Table 2 is a list of questions that the metrics are intended to assess. By developing such metrics, an initial step results in attempting to quantify future manned and unmanned systems interactions.

## 4. CONCLUSIONS

This paper presented preliminary metrics to support understanding the extent of interactions that would arise in a system of co-operating manned and unmanned systems (MUMS). The metrics seek to help explain if attachments are localized to specific situations or if they are more pervasive throughout a MUMS society. Such metrics can be applied to multiple, collaborating, and interacting manned and robotic systems when they are represented as a collection of dynamic, interacting nodes. As robots become more and more intelligent, they will be able to support increased collaborative interactions with each other and with people, where rather than being commanded by people with continual oversight, they will truly interact. This paper provides an initial approach and quantifying such interactions.

## 5. REFERENCES

[Aie] W. Aiello, F. Chung, and L. Lu, "A Random Graph Model for Massive Graphs," in [New], p259-268.

[Alo] U. Alon, An Introduction to Systems Biology, Design Principles of Biological Circuits, Chapman & Hall/CRC, 2007.

[Bro] A. Broder, et al., "Graph Structure in the Web," Computer Networks, 33 (2000) 309-320.

[Bre] C. Breazeal, "Social Interactions in HRI: The Robot View," IEEE Trans. on Man, Cybernetics, and Sys – Part C, 2003.

[deS] D.de Solla Price, "Networks of Scientific Papers," Science vol. 149, in [New], p. 129-154.

[Erd] P. Erdos and A. Renyi, "On the Evolution of Random Graphs," A Mathematickai Kutato Intezet Kozlemenyei, in [New], p38-61.

[GT] Georgia Tech Research Horizons Magazine, June 8, 2007, From Science Fiction to Reality: Personal Robots Emerge to Improve Quality of Life at Work, Home, and School.

[Hin] P. Hinds, T. Roberts, H. Jones, "Whose Job Is It Anyway? A Study of Human-Robot Interaction in a Collaborative Task," Human-Computer Interaction, 2004, Vol 19, pp. 151-181, 2004.

[Kie] S. Kiesler and P. Hinds, "Introduction to This Special Issue of Human-Robot Interaction", Human-Computer Interaction, 2004, Vol 19, pp. 1-8, 2004.

[New] M. Newman, A-L Barabasi, D.J. Watts (eds), The Structure and Dynamics of Networks, Princeton Univ. Press, 2006.

[New2] M. Newman, "The Structure and Function of Complex Networks," SIAM Review, Vol. 54, No 2, p167-256, 2003.

[Tra] J. Travers, and S. Milgram, " An Experimental Study of the Small World Problem," in [New], p 130-148.

[Wat] D. J. Watts, S. H. Strogatz, "Collective Dynamics of 'Small-World' Networks," Nature, vol. 393, 4 Jun 1998.

[Wei] L.G. Weiss, "A Framework for Co-operating Manned and Unmanned Systems, Part I – Framework Description," (draft)

**Table 2. Specific MUMS Metrics**

| Metric / Method | Description | Question it Answers |
|---|---|---|
| Collaborative Filtering | <ul><li>Technique To Predict New Likes/Dislikes Based On An Individual's Other Preferences (Captures Preferential Attachment)</li><li>Used In Targeted Advertising (person who bought $x$ also bought $y$)</li><li>Build an item-item matrix determining relationships between nodes</li><li>Using the matrix, and data on the current node, predict its future state</li></ul> | Is Preferential Attachment Better than Diverse Attachment? |
| Clustering Coefficient | <ul><li>Probability That Two Nodes That Are Connected To The Same Node Will Be Connected (Probability That A Friend Of A Friend Is A Friend)</li><li>At Node $i$, $C_i = \dfrac{\text{\# Connected Nbr Pairs,}}{\frac{1}{2} k(k-1)}$ where $k$ = degree of node $i$</li><li>$C$ = Average of $C_i$</li><li>Social Networks, $C = O(1)$, Large n</li><li>Random Graphs, $C = O(1/n)$, Large n</li></ul> | Does Clustering Occur in Dynamic MUMS Networks? |
| Assortive Mixing | <ul><li>Which Nodes Pair Up With Others (e.g., mating choices, geography)</li><li>Let $E_{ij}$ = # edges that connect nodes of type $i$ to nodes of type $j$</li><li>$E = [E_{ij}]$, $e = E / \|E\|$ = normalized mixing matrix</li><li>$e_{ij}$ = fraction of edges that fall between nodes of type $i$ and $j$</li><li>$P(j \mid i)$ = Conditional Probability that Node of Type $j$ is a Neighbor of a Node of Type $i$</li><li>Let $r = \dfrac{Tr\, e - \|e2\|}{1 - \|e2\|}$</li><li>If r = 1, every edge connects to same type of node</li><li>If $r$ = 0, randomly mixed network</li><li>Otherwise, some level of mixing exists</li></ul> | Can We Calculate $r$ for a MUMS Network? |
| Degree Correlations | <ul><li>Mixing According to the Degree, $k$, of the Node</li><li>Can Give Rise to Interesting Network Structures</li><li>If Correlation Increases with $k$ => Assortive Mixing</li><li>If Correlation Decreases with $k$ => Disassortive Mixing</li><li>Social Networks are Assortive</li><li>Info, Tech, and Bio Networks are Disassortive</li></ul> | Are MUMS Environments Assortive or Disassortive? |
| Degree Distributions | <ul><li>$P(k)$ = Probability That A Node Chosen At Random Has Degree $k$</li><li>Random Graphs Have Poisson/Binomial Distributions, large $n$</li><li>Social Networks Are Right Skewed</li><li>When $P(k) = k^{-\alpha}$, System Follows a Power Law</li><li>$\alpha$ Constant => Scale-free Network Results</li></ul> | Do MUMS Environments Attain a Scale-Free Network? |
| Network Resilience, Large n | <ul><li>Node Removal – May Loose Robustness but Not Functionality</li><li>Random Node Removal => Little Effect</li><li>Targeted Node Removal => Large Effect</li></ul> | How Do Node Failures Affect MUMS Networks? |
| Network Navigation | <ul><li>The 6 Degree of Separation Model Showed Short Paths Exists</li><li>It Also Showed that People are Good at Finding Them Without Knowledge of the Network or Connectivity</li><li>Not True for Random Graphs</li><li>Without A Means To Estimate Social Distance, Individuals Are Unable To Move A Message Closer To A Remote Target</li></ul> | Can We Merge Artificial and Social Networks to Enable Efficient Navigation within MUMS Networks? |
| Models of Network Growth | <ul><li>Growth is Typically Via Adding/Removing Nodes – Too Static for Dynamic MUMS Networks</li><li>Correlation Between Age of Nodes and Degree</li><li>Older Nodes Have a Higher Mean Degree</li><li>$P_k(a) = \left(\sqrt{1-\dfrac{a}{n}}\right)\left(1-\sqrt{1-\dfrac{a}{n}}\right)^k$, for age $a$</li><li>Can Capture Age Within a Fitness Measure or Fitness Distribution</li><li>$\eta_i$ = fitness, attractiveness, or propensity to accrue new links</li><li>$\rho(\eta)$ = Distribution of $\eta_i$</li><li>$P$ (new node will attach to others) $\sim \eta_i k_i$</li></ul> | What Patterns or Statistical Regularities May Result in MUMS Networks? |

# Lessons Learned in Evaluating DARPA Advanced Military Technologies

**Craig Schlenoff**
NIST
100 Bureau Drive, Stop 8230
Gaithersburg, MD 20899
301-975-3456

craig.schlenoff@nist.gov

**Brian Weiss**
NIST
100 Bureau Drive, Stop 8230
Gaithersburg, MD 20899
301-975-4373

brian.weiss@nist.gov

**Michelle Potts Steves**
NIST
100 Bureau Drive, Stop 8940
Gaithersburg, MD 20899
301-975-3537

michelle.steves@nist.gov

## ABSTRACT

For the past six years, personnel from the National Institute of Standards and Technology (NIST) have served as the Independent Evaluation Team (IET) for two major DARPA programs. DARPA ASSIST (Advanced Soldier Sensor Information System and Technology) is an advanced technology research and development program whose objective is to exploit soldier-worn sensors to augment a Soldier's situational awareness, mission recall and reporting capability to enhance situational knowledge during and following military operations in urban terrain (MOUT) environments. This program stresses passive collection and automated activity/object recognition that output algorithms, software, and tools that will undergo system integration in future efforts. TRANSTAC (Spoken Language Communication and Translation System for Tactical Use) is another DARPA advanced technology and research program whose goal is to demonstrate capabilities to rapidly develop and field free-form, two-way speech-to-speech translation systems enabling English and foreign language speakers to communicate with one another in real-world tactical situations where an interpreter is unavailable. Several prototype systems have been developed under this program for numerous military applications including force protection, medical screening and civil affairs. Both of these efforts are concluding and as such this paper will focus on overall lessons learned in evaluating these types of technologies.

## Categories and Subject Descriptors

D.2.8. [**Software**]: Metrics – *Performance Measures*

## General Terms

Measurement, Performance, Experimentation, Human Factors, Languages

## Keywords

DARPA, ASSIST, TRANSTAC, performance evaluation, lessons learned, advanced military technology, speech translation, soldier-worn sensors

## 1. INTRODUCTION

Over the past six years, the National Institute of Standards and Technology has served as the Independent Evaluation Team (IET) for two DARPA efforts. The first effort, called ASSIST (Advanced Soldier Sensor Information System and Technology) has the objective of exploiting soldier-worn sensors to augment a Soldier's situational awareness, mission recall and reporting capability to enhance situational knowledge during and following military operations. The second program, called TRANSTAC (Spoken Language Communication and Translation System for Tactical Use) has the objective of rapidly developing and fielding free-form, two-way speech-to-speech translation systems enabling English and foreign language speakers to communicate with one another in real-world tactical situations where an interpreter is unavailable. Between these two efforts, NIST has orchestrated thirteen live evaluations involving over 100 military personnel and foreign language speakers at locations varying from Military Operations in Urban Terrains (MOUT) sites to hotel conference rooms.

In this paper, we will give a brief description of each of these two DARPA efforts and describe some of the overall lessons learned from our experiences. Section 2 describes the DARPA ASSIST and TRANSTAC efforts at a high level and the evaluation approach that was developed to assess the performance of the technologies being developed. Section 3 describes 11 lessons that were learned during the evaluations and give brief background about each. Section 4 concludes the paper.

## 2. DARPA ASSIST AND TRANSTAC EFFORTS

This section gives a brief overview of the DARPA ASSIST and TRANSTAC efforts as well at the SCORE (System, Component, and Operationally Relevant Evaluations) evaluation approach.

## 2.1 ASSIST

Soldiers are often asked to perform missions that can take many hours. Examples of missions include presence patrols (where soldiers are tasked to make their presence known in an environment for a variety of reasons), search and reconnaissance missions, apprehending suspected insurgents, etc. After a mission is complete, the Soldiers are typically asked to provide a report to their commanding officer describing the most important things that happened during the mission. This report is used to gather intelligence about the environment to allow for more informed planning for future missions. Soldiers usually provide this report based solely on their memory, still pictures, handwritten notes and/or grid coordinates that were collected during the mission, provided these tools are available to the Soldier. These missions are often very stressful for the Soldier and thus there are undoubtedly many instances in which important information is not made available in the report and thus not available for the planning of future missions.

The ASSIST program [1] addressed this challenge by instrumenting soldiers with sensors that they can wear directly on their uniform. These sensors include still cameras, video cameras, Global Positioning Systems (GPS), Inertial Navigation Systems (INS), microphones, and accelerometers. These sensors continuously record what is going on around the Soldier while on a mission. When Soldiers return from their mission, the sensor data is run through a series of software systems which index the data and create an electronic chronicle of the events that happen throughout the time that the ASSIST system was recording (as shown in Figure 1). The electronic chronicle includes times that certain sounds or keywords were heard, the times when certain types of objects were seen, and times that the Soldiers were in a specific location or performing certain actions.

With this information, Soldiers can give reports without relying solely on their memory. The electronic chronicle will help jog the Soldier's memory on activities that happened that he did not recall during the reporting period, or possibly even make him aware of an important activity that he did not notice when out on the mission. On top of this, the multimedia information that is available in the electronic chronicle is available to the Soldier to include in the report, which will provide substantially more information to the recipient of the report than the text alone.

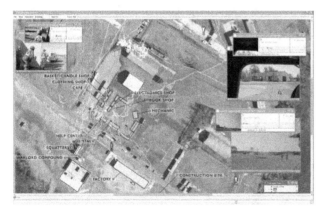

**Figure 1: User Interface for ASSIST System**

Specific technologies being developed include:

- Object Detection / Image Classification – the ability to recognize and identify objects in the environment
- Arabic Text Translation – the ability to detect, recognize and translate written Arabic text
- Sound Recognition / Speech Recognition – the ability to identify sound events (e.g. explosions, gunshots, vehicles, etc.) and recognize speech
- Shooter Localization / Shooter Classification – the ability to identify gunshots in the environment

- Soldier State Identification / Soldier Localization – the ability to identify a soldier's path of movement around an environment and characterize the actions taken by the soldier

## 2.2 TRANSTAC

The goal of the TRANSTAC program [2] is to demonstrate capabilities to rapidly develop and field free-form, two-way translation systems that enable speakers of different languages to communicate with one another in real-world tactical situations without an interpreter.

Several prototype systems have been developed under this program for numerous military applications including force protection and medical screening. The technology has been demonstrated on smartphone and laptop platforms. NIST was asked to assess the usability of the overall translation system and to individually assess each component of the system (the speech recognition, the machine translation, and the text-to-speech).

All of the TRANSTAC systems work fundamentally the same. Either English speech or an audio file is fed into the system. Automatic Speech Recognition (ASR) processes the speech to recognize what was said and generates a text file of the speech. That text file is then translated to another language using Machine Translation (MT) technology. The resulting text file is then spoken to the foreign language speaker using Text-To-Speech (TTS) technology. This same process then happens in reverse when the foreign language speaker speaks. This is shown in Figure 2.

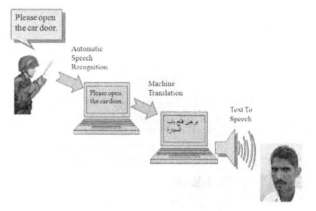

**Figure 2: How Speech Translation Works**

## 2.3 SCORE

While designing the ASSIST and TRANSTAC evaluations, the IET formulated an evaluation approach to comprehensively assess the performance of the systems. The resulting effort is known as the SCORE (System, Component, and Operationally Relevant Evaluations) [3].

SCORE is a unified set of criteria and software tools for defining a performance evaluation approach for complex intelligent systems. It provides a comprehensive evaluation blueprint that assesses the technical performance of a system and its components through isolating and changing variables as well as capturing end-user utility of the system in realistic use-case environments. SCORE is built around the premise that, in order to get a comprehensive picture of how a system performs in its actual use-case environment, technical performance should be evaluated at the component and system levels [2].

The SCORE framework advocates identifying evaluation goals and user requirements, and then identifying evaluation methodologies that support those test parameters. Once the set of evaluation methodologies that can support the evaluation have been identified, then method selection can be further refined by other logistical parameters such as availability of qualified personnel to design and conduct the assessment, what type of testing environment is needed to execute the test, what mechanisms are needed to collect the data, data analysis considerations, e.g., if time and resources exist to code many hours of video data.

SCORE takes a tiered approach to measuring the performance of intelligent systems. At the lowest level, SCORE uses elemental tests to isolate specific components and then systematically modifies variables that could affect the performance of that component to determine those variables' impact. Typically, this is performed for each relevant component with the system. At the next level, the overall system is tested in a highly structured environment to understand the performance of individual variables on the system as a whole. Then, individual capabilities of the system are isolated and tested for both their technical performance and their utility using task tests. Lastly, the technology is immersed in a longer scenario that evokes typical situations and surroundings in which the end-user is asked to perform an overall mission or procedure in a highly-relevant environment which stresses the overall system's capabilities. Formal surveys and semi-structured interviews are used to assess the usefulness of the technology to the end-user.

SCORE is unique in that:

- It is applicable to a wide range of technologies, from manufacturing to defense systems
- Elements of SCORE can be decoupled and customized based upon evaluation goals
- It has the ability to evaluate a technology at various stages of development, from conceptual to full maturation
- It combines the results of targeted evaluations to produce an extensive picture of a systems' capabilities and utility

## 3. LESSONS LEARNED

The rest of this paper will focus on the overall lessons learned while implementing the evaluations on the technologies described above. Listed below are 11 lessons, each with brief explanatory text.

### 3.1 Designing an effective evaluation can be as much of a research issue as the technology development

To truly design and implement a comprehensive evaluation plan, one must have a deep understanding of the details of the technology under test, including:

- How the technology works
- What the variables are that affect the technologies' performance

- How the technology is expected to be used by the target users including how it will be physically interacted with, in which scenarios it is most appropriate, how it will be carried around, etc.

Understandably, these are the same issues that the developers of the technology are wrestling with. However, in addition to knowing all of these factors, the people that are assessing the capabilities of the technology must also understand:

- How to develop a testing environment that can exercise the full capabilities of the system and understand the shortcomings
- How to ensure that the results obtained are statistically significant and indicative of the performance that will be experienced in the field
- How to identify and train test subjects that are representative of the targeted end users
- How to identify and instrument an environment that is representative of where the technology is expected to be used
- How to determine the metrics and measures that should be used to evaluate the systems and how to properly analyze the results of the evaluations.

These last items are key research challenges that the evaluation team has to face but the development teams rarely have to examine. Any of these factors, if not strongly considered and addressed appropriately, can detrimentally affect the validity of the evaluation results. Many of these factors are described in further detail throughout the remainder of this paper.

For the reasons stated above, it the firm belief of the authors the design of successful evaluation can be as much of a research challenge as is the design of the technology itself. This is primarily due to the number of additional factors and design constraints that must be considered to truly get a comprehensive and accurate assessment of the capabilities of the systems under test.

### 3.2 Keep your eye on the ball (the ultimate objective of the evaluation) and make sure your decisions along the way reflect that goal

As evaluation planning proceeds and new approaches and constraints are uncovered, it is often easy to get caught up in the minutia and lose sight of the big picture. Decisions are often made that solve an immediate challenge but take you further away from the goals that are trying to be accomplished.

As an example, in the DARPA TRANSTAC program, there was much discussion regarding the Soldiers' and Marines' ability to look at the screen of the TRANSTAC system while it was being used. The screens of the TRANSTAC systems contain the textual version of spoken translations. One camp felt that by looking at the screen, the Soldier/Marine was losing situation awareness of what was going on around them which could be dangerous. The other camp felt that the information was available and the Soldier/Marine should be able to look at it if they so desired. After much discussion, it was determined that the Soldiers/Marines would often be protected when using the system so they should be permitted to look at the screen.

Once this was determined, a member of the research team asked, "If the user can see the screen, why do we need to speak out the translations at all. Let's just let them look at the screen." Even though this was a logical next step, it defeated the goal of the program, namely, to create a speech-to-speech translation system. If we started to go down that path, we would be driving the technology in a direction that was contradictory to its intended purpose. Thus, we would have lost sight of the ultimate goal.

As another example in the TRANSTAC effort, one of the metrics that was used to measure the performance of the systems was a high-level concept transfer metric that gauged how many concepts could be exchanged between the speakers using the system in a ten minute period. Once the development teams understood this metric, they started making their systems faster at the expense of accuracy. The English and the foreign language speech sometimes spoke over one another, which would have been highly impractical in a fielded environment but helped them to get though more concepts quicker. They determined that they could maximize their score using this approach even though it is not how they envisioned their fielded systems operating.

The evaluation team identified this issue and is now reconsidering using that metric at all. The test subjects in previous evaluations have consistently stated that they would happily sacrifice some translation time for greater accuracy. If this metric were continued, the TRANSTAC systems would progress in a way that was not aligned with the goals of the program as a whole.

## 3.3 Deeply understand the needs and wants of the technology end users

It is usually a straightforward process to understand the exact needs and wants of technology end users in the case of testing systems that already have been fielded where end users can categorically state what they like, what they don't like, and what they would improve. Extracting end user needs and wants is non-trivial when it comes to testing emerging technologies whose end-user group(s) has yet to be specifically determined, the technologies' exact use-cases have yet to be finalized, and the precise usage procedures are unclear. During the evaluation design process, it is critical for evaluation team members to speak with representatives of the intended end-user population to thoroughly understand the related challenges they face without the technology and the constraints they are bound when presented with a new piece of equipment to carry into the field.

NIST TRANSTAC evaluation team members met with Soldiers and Marines on many occasions to deeply understand the challenges they faced when communicating with foreign language-speaking personnel without a machine translation technology. One of the most significant communication challenges currently faced is unreliable interpreters including those that either don't show up for work on time, are limited in their translation skills or have ulterior motives when facilitating dialogue between US and foreign forces. Other significant challenges include general unavailability of interpreters. This leads to Soldiers and Marines attempting to have conversations with foreign speakers using extremely limited vocabularies. All of these challenges can lead to misunderstandings, damaged relationships, and in some instances, injuries and/or loss of life.

Besides understanding the current challenges faced without machine translation technologies, it was important to understand

Soldiers' and Marines' constraints if provided with this new technology. In order to create a relevant and appropriate TRANSTAC evaluation design, it was critical to gather information from Soldiers and Marines to identify numerous elements that would ultimately feed into the evaluation including:

- The relevant dialogues for which a machine translation technology would be viable and/or most useful. Specifically, Soldiers and Marines identified six tactical domains that would lend well to machine translation either because interpreters were scarce for these tasks and/or the conversations took place in relatively secure areas. These domains were (1) Traffic Control Points/Vehicle Checkpoints, (2) Facilities Inspections, (3) Civil Affairs, (4) Medical, (5) Combined Training, and (6) Combined Operations.

- The potential operating environments that would support the use of machine translation technology. These environments aligned themselves with the above six domains. This area also includes their operating constraints or liberties available to them. For example, a Marine may have the ability to sit down with a local police official within a secure base and have a somewhat relaxed conversation about working together. On the other hand, a Soldier may be conducting census operations in a neutral village where he could encounter some unfriendly citizens.

- Criteria for success. It is important for Soldiers and Marines to accomplish their missions in timely and accurate manners without incident. For example, this correlated into the evaluation team's development of high level concept transfer metrics. These metrics included accuracy scores of the technology's ability to translate the English and foreign language concepts and the time it took each speaker to convey an utterance using the technology.

This information was also complemented by the clear statements from Soldiers and Marines that they wanted a communication tool that was easy-to-use, fast and accurate with translations, small in form factor, lightweight and durable enough to stand up to the frequent use in harsh environments. This insight provided the evaluation team with a clear idea of the Soldiers' and Marines' needs and wants.

## 3.4 Utility and technical performance assessments are both very important perspectives. Each requires different means to gather and process assessment data and yield different types of analyses.

Technology evaluations can take many forms yielding varying types and amounts of data. Data output can yield two unique types of information which are quantitative technical performance and qualitative utility assessments. Each piece of data offers unique insight into a technology's overall behavior, individual functionality and benefit to the end user. Quantitative evaluations can offer detailed information about a system's overall functionality along with specific performance metrics related to inherent components and capabilities. Determining a technology's means of failure at the system level can be a non-trivial process. Overall failures can lead to individual component and/or capabilities testing to identify the point of failure and determine which variables and/or parameters are responsible for this failure. Quantitative metrics also provide a basis of comparison among multiple evaluations and technologies. Likewise, qualitative metrics enable the evaluation team to assess the perceived worth and value the technology has to the test subjects representative of the target user population. This type of insight complements the quantitative data. For example, a technology could be 100% accurate in its function, yet if it's too heavy for the user to carry, then they will seldom use it and therefore place a low value on it. Individually, both of these data types paint very contrasting pictures. It is important the data be viewed together to get a complete understanding.

NIST's evaluations of advanced technologies have demonstrated a need to collect both types of data. In both the ASSIST and TRANSTAC programs, evaluations were conducted of technologies that had yet to be finalized and deployed to actual end users. This means that the evaluation team's analysis of the collected quantitative and qualitative data was crucial to inform the technology developers and program sponsors on the current state of the systems including specific successes and areas for improvement. Across both programs, quantitative data was captured that assessed individual technology components, capabilities, and systems. For example, component level evaluations of the TRANSTAC systems' ASR, MT, and TTS demonstrated specifically which of these components produced errors ultimately leading to system errors. Also, both programs captured qualitative data at the capability and system levels. For example, capability level evaluations of the ASSIST technologies enabled the evaluation team to capture specific feedback from Soldiers about which technology capabilities (e.g. real-time data sharing, image annotation, etc) were of the most value, easiest to use, etc. Likewise, this specific information, coupled with the other collected data enabled the evaluation team to paint a clear picture of the technologies' current state.

The NIST evaluation teams have employed an evaluation approach that captures a range of quantitative and qualitative data. This allows a definitive picture to be created of the technologies' current successes, shortcomings, and areas that must be improved.

## 3.5 There are often multiple approaches to evaluating a technology where it's crucial to identify those which will achieve the overall evaluation goals given the test constraint.

There are many approaches for evaluating systems. For any particular evaluation effort there are also various constraints that much be considered, e.g., logistical, budgetary, and programmatic concerns. Method selection must consider these concerns otherwise the assessment effort and results may be compromised in undesirable ways. The SCORE framework advocates identifying evaluation goals and user requirements, and then identifying evaluation methodologies that support those test parameters. Once the set of evaluation methodologies that can support the evaluation have been identified, then method selection can be further refined by other logistical parameters such as availability of qualified personnel to design and conduct the assessment, what type of testing environment is needed to execute the test, what mechanisms are needed to collect the data, data analysis considerations, e.g., if time and resources exist to code

many hours of video data. Approaches that do not have contingency avenues for high risk elements should be avoided if possible. For example, if an approach calls for a specific test environment , e.g., a MOUT site, but there is a high probably the test will be bumped from the site, a feasible fallback location is needed. If no reasonable fallback location is available, alternate approaches should be considered or a determination should be made that test delays are acceptable.

## 3.6 System training data and/or extensive background scenario information may be needed to perform some assessments. This must be accounted for within the test plan.

A critical element in technology development is the training data provided to the developer that will be used to 'teach' the technology how to act/behave/function appropriately during a given scenario and/or instance. Systems will only perform as effectively as their input models. Similarly, evaluation scenarios that are representative of the training data will yield performance data more indicative of the technology's actual performance as compared to those scenarios not aligned with the training data.

This lesson is visible within the design of the TRANSTAC evaluations. In addition to being responsible for creating and implementing the tests, NIST personnel were also tasked with gathering appropriate and relevant conversational training audio data. This data, composed of English and foreign language speakers conducting tactically-relevant conversations, was based upon real-world military situations and directly motivated the design of the evaluation scenarios.

Creating both the training data scenarios and the evaluation scenarios relied extensively on knowledge collected from Soldiers and Marines who have a detailed understanding of their operating environments and the types of situations the technologies would be viable (refer back to Section 3.3). The evaluation scenarios were significantly modeled after the training data scenarios to not only include realistic elements gathered from Soldiers and Marines, but to also ensure that the evaluation was representative of the data the technologies were trained.

The collection of training data was a non-trivial, multi-month process that impacted the entire evaluation schedule. This process began with IET personnel meeting with Soldiers and Marines so the necessary information could be gathered to create appropriate and current tactical scenarios. Once the information was collected and the scenarios were developed, the IET conducted weekend data collections at a recording studio where English-speaking Marines (or Soldiers) conducted conversations with foreign language speakers (of the upcoming evaluation's target language) through an interpreter based upon these tactical scenarios. Each weekend produced between 30 to 40 hours of audio data which was transcribed and translated by a separate organization. Once the data was ready for distribution, a majority was sent out to the technology developers so it could be used for training data. Only a small amount of data was held back so it could be used for the evaluations. The technology developers required at least several months to work with the data before their technologies would be ready for testing.

Under ideal conditions where only a single weekend of data is collected, this process can occur in as little as four months. Under normal conditions and uncertainties with multiple data collection events, this process takes between seven to eight months. It was crucial that this time be accounted for in the test plan.

## 3.7 Understand the interactions of the technology with the test environment and the test personnel to be mindful of the technology's ideal operating conditions and its boundaries.

The performance of the system under test is greatly and directly related to the environment in which it is being tested and the personnel that are using the system. Slight changes to either one of these factors can often have a significant effect on how well the system performs. For example, the competency of the end user in operating systems similar to the ones being tested can be the difference between success and failure. In addition, their experience being in scenarios where the technology would be useful and understanding how it can be best applied is also a critical factor.

Apart from the user itself, many other variables can play a significant role in how well a system performs. In the case of the TRANSTAC systems, these variables may include background noise, how close the microphone is to the speaker, glare issues, how dusty the environment is, wind conditions, dialect of the speakers, etc. Almost all of these variables are not true or false … there are various levels that must be understood.

No matter how familiar one gets with a type of technology, nobody knows a specific system better that its developer. The developer is best prepared to have detailed understanding of what is happening underneath the hood and understand how fundamental evaluation design procedures and variables will affect the performance of the system. However, the developer also has a vested interest in ensuring that their system works as well as possible. There is often a balancing act between setting up the evaluation environment in a way that shows the system in the best possible light vs. having an environment that is as realistic as possible to how it is expected to be used.

For both the DARPA TRANSTAC and ASSIST efforts, regular interaction occurred between the evaluation team and the developers of the technologies. In every case, the developers provided suggestions as to the best way to test the systems and what variables would be most appropriate to vary. In parallel with this, the evaluation team always spoke with the end users of the technologies (primarily military personnel) to better understand the environments in which the technology was expected to be used, including variables such as background noise, temperature and weather conditions, etc. Understanding that the technologies were still under development and not yet ready to be fielded, the evaluation team took both sides into consideration and tried to find the proper balance between realism and the known shortfalls of the systems. Often, the final evaluation procedures and environments could not take all concerns into account, but it is important that both sides understood that there were often competing goals and all parties' opinions had to be considered.

## 3.8 The background and experience of the test subjects can greatly affect their impression of the systems under test.

Test subjects, referring to those individuals using a technology during an evaluation where qualitative and/or quantitative data is collected, greatly impact data quality by their actions during the test. Their actions are dictated both by the technology training they receive prior to the evaluation and their specific backgrounds and experiences. The latter may include experiences with similar technologies and/or experiences within the operating environments the technologies under test are envisioned to be used within.

NIST's involvement in six TRANSTAC technology evaluations from 2007 to 2010 has highlighted the fact that the impressions of the Soldiers and Marines selected as test subject are greatly influenced by their specific backgrounds and experiences. A specific example of this can be seen in assigning evaluation scenarios to Marines and Soldiers. The evaluation team goes to great lengths to assign each test subject scenarios that they have intimate knowledge based upon their own deployment experiences and interactions with foreign personnel. Since the evaluation scenarios are categorized within six domains, the Soldiers and Marines are queried to see how their experiences correlate. For example, a Civil Affairs Marine would reasonably be assigned the Civil Affairs scenarios and could also be paired with some of the Facilities Inspections scenarios based upon their experiences. Conversely, an Infantry Officer would most likely be suited for the Vehicle Checkpoint/Traffic Control Point, Combined Training and Combined Operations scenarios given their backgrounds. Allowing these test subjects to use the TRANSTAC systems to facilitate dialogues they are intimately familiar supports the capture of targeted feedback. The test subjects will have high confidence in stating what worked well and what needs to be remedied with the technology in order for the system to be successful in an actual situation. Likewise, if test subjects are paired with scenarios that they have little familiarity then their dialogue struggles have great potential to negatively influence their perception of the technology.

Another background influence on the test subjects' perceptions of the technologies is if they've had prior experiences with comparable or similar systems. TRANSTAC is one of the very first programs to employ two-way, free-form, speech-to-speech translation technologies. However, several one-way speech translation systems have been previously deployed receiving mixed reviews from the Soldiers and Marines using them. During the course of the TRANSTAC test events, the evaluation team has encountered several test subjects who have used these similar, yet different technologies. To avoid their perceptions of these earlier systems from bleeding over to their TRANSTAC feedback, the evaluation team has had to make it very clear that these are two entirely separate technologies and they should 'forget' everything they know about the earlier systems.

## 3.9 The structure and content of the technology training and the feedback requests of the test subjects greatly influences the test subjects' perceptions.

Any training provided to subjects on the technology to be tested will have an impact on their interaction with the system and subsequently on their perceptions of the technology. Decisions regarding the amount and type of training required to achieve the test objectives need to be determined. Complex systems can present additional challenges when attempting to train participants. Some questions to be addressed are: How much training is needed? How long will it take and what is the schedule impact? Where will training take place? If conducted in the test environment, will that impact the test results in undesired ways? What training materials are needed, e.g., scenario content or task content? Are the training materials different or similar to the test materials and what is the impact of that? Who can provide appropriate, unbiased training? The developers know their systems the best, but they are not unbiased. Testing personnel may not be qualified to conduct training for complex systems.

Removing interactions between system developer personnel and the test subjects can help with controlling those influences on the test subjects, however, there may be advantages of system developer involvement that lead the evaluation designers to consider having the developers involved during the evaluation period. For example, it may be beneficial to the sponsoring program to have its developers see and learn first-hand how their systems are received and hear subjects' concerns. Also, as mentioned above, the systems may be sufficiently complex that only the system developer can provide adequate training or are so prototypical in nature that only the developer can set some configuration options because these controls may not yet have been exposed at the user interface. For off-the-desktop systems, various physical configurations may need to be fitted to each test subject each time the system is deployed. In any of these cases, a simple inquiry of, "So, how was it?" and the resulting discussion can have an impact on what the subject ultimately reports in their official assessment feedback. When system developers have access to the test subjects during the testing period, appropriate ground rules need to specified and enforced to control the effect of these influences.

While controlling "unofficial" feedback and subject interactions, official feedback requests need to be carefully tailored to collect data that will inform the metrics selected that meet the test objectives. How and when official subject feedback of system performance is requested will also have an impact on what is reported. For example, if subjects perceive a heavy emphasis regarding their perceptions of speed and accuracy, they will tend to focus their attention on those aspects of system performance and possibly under report other aspects of their experience with the system. Feedback solicitation always needs to be tailored to what the test was intended to collect while leaving opportunities for open-ended responses to garner feedback that might not have been anticipated. Overall, it is the test design team's responsibility to explore all of these options, consider the impacts, and make choices that meet the test and program objectives.

## 3.10 There are often multiple options available to assess specific metrics so it's critical to identify those options which are optimal to produce the desired assessments.

There are typically quite a few measures that can be collected for use in assessing any particular metric. Which measures or assessors are selected may have an impact on what is collected and reported, therefore careful attention should be paid to these choices. Additionally, as mention earlier, some measures are more or less difficult to collect, some are more costly to collect than others in terms of resources needed, some are logistically more difficult to put in place, and so on. Choices here can impact the cost of the assessments as well as the logistical feasibility of completing the data collection and analysis for assessment, therefore careful attention to these considerations during the measure selection process is prudent.

For example, when obtaining feedback from subjects, two examples of assessments could be free-form and likert-type survey responses. Free-form responses typically consist of open-ended responses that need to be coded or categorized for analysis. Likert-type responses to well-formed queries allow quantitative assessment of the data. Assessments for the latter type of data can be often much faster to perform than analysis of free-form responses, however can give a quite different perspectives of the same experience interaction.

A case in point was documented in [4]. In the early stages of the TRANSTAC evaluations, utility data was collected solely via survey instruments. Although a combination of Likert-like response questions and free-form inquiries were used, the free-form responses became repetitive and sparse over the course of the evaluation period. Adding semi-structured interviews and the resulting gathered data provided very rich insights into the survey-based data and the user experience overall. However, the cost to collect and analyze the additional data was definitely greater.

## 3.11 Be mindful that your metrics and evaluation approach may need to evolve over time.

It is typical for evaluation requirements and concerns to evolve over time, especially if the time span in which the assessments are performed is long or if there are a large number of unknowns at the beginning of the design phase. As more is learned about the system and user requirements, initially envisioned approaches may need to be modified to provide useful assessment of the system. For example, when testing a prototype system, the initial assessment goals may include user testing, but as more is learned, it may be determined that the user interface is not sufficiently developed for 'users'. In this case, another approach could be used, such as expert review, to provide some formative feedback for developers regarding how to move forward to support their eventual users effectively. Understanding of the system, its requirements, state of development, and user requirements may impact the initial assessment vision, as it may not have had the benefit of the understanding gained during the initial design phase.

For example, in both projects, the systems were evolving over time. Improvements to existing capabilities were made and new features added between evaluations. This required that changes in what was assessed be made and at times how they were assessed also changed. In particular, an early TRANSTAC platform was a laptop; in the field, it was a laptop in a backpack, where the screen could not be viewed and the systems would overheat easily. In the last evaluations, the platform was a smart phone. This meant that field evaluations could be more realistically situated in later evaluations.

Keep the high level objective of the evaluation in mind and be flexible as modifications need to be made.

## 4. DISCUSSION

In this paper, we describe the evaluation approach that has been applied to two DARPA-funded efforts over the past five years and focus on 11 lessons that have been learned during that time. This is not meant to be a comprehensive list of all the factors that should be considered when evaluating these types of systems, but instead represent some of the most critical ones as determined by the authors.

The main lesson described in this paper is that additional effort put into the design and logistic planning of the evaluation up front, can pay off quite a bit as the evaluation progresses. The design stage of the evaluation is critical and decisions made during that time have a huge effect on how successful the evaluation will be. Bad decision in the design can be very difficult to fix later on. This can be compared to the manufacturing product development cycle. Problems that are identified and resolved in the design stage of a product can cost orders of magnitude less to fix that if those same problems are not identified until the manufacturing or distribution phases.

The SCORE effort described in Section 2 of this paper evolved over the past five years to address many of the lessons described in this document. Almost all of the enhancements focused on the design state of the evaluation, including determining more well-defined approaches to characterizing the all of the evaluation participants, characterizing the variables the affected the system performance of identifying ways to control them, and assuring the

metrics that were used to assess the performance of the systems under test truly addressed the overall goal of the programs.

## 5. ACKNOWLEDGMENTS

This work was supported by the Defense Advanced Research Projects Agency (DARPA) ASSIST and TRANSTAC programs (Program Manager: Mari Maeda).

## 6. DARPA DISCLAIMER

The views, opinions, and/or findings contained in this article are those of the authors and should not be interpreted as representing the official views or policies, either expressed or implied, of the Defense Advanced Research Projects Agency or the Department of Defense.

## BIBLIOGRAPHY

[1]  C. Schlenoff, "ASSIST: Overview of the First Advanced Technology Evaluations," in *Proceedings of the 2006 Performance Metrics for Intelligent Systems (PerMIS) Conference* Gaithersburg, MD: 2006.

[2]  C. Schlenoff, B. Weiss, M. Steves, G. Sanders, F. Proctor, and A. Virts, "Evaluating Speech Translation Systems: Applying SCORE to TRANSTAC Technologies," in *Proceedings of the 2009 Performance Metrics for Intelligent Systems (PerMIS) Conference* 2009.

[3]  C. Schlenoff, "Applying the Systems, Component and Operationally-Relevant Evaluations (SCORE) Framework to Evaluate Advanced Military Technologies," *ITEA Journal of Test and Evaluation*, vol. 31, no. 1 Feb. 2010.

[4]  M. Steves and E. Morse, "Utility Assessment in TRANSTAC: Using a set of complementary methods," in *Proceedings of the 2009 Performance Metrics for Intelligent Systems Conference* Gaithersburg, MD: 2009.

# Modified Cooper Harper Scales for Assessing Unmanned Vehicle Displays

**Birsen Donmez**
University of Toronto
Dept. of Mech. and Ind. Engineering
Toronto, ON, Canada
1 (416) 978 7399

donmez@mie.utoronto.ca

**M. L. Cummings**
MIT
Dept. of Aero-Astro
Cambridge, MA, USA
1 (617) 252 1512

missyc@mit.edu

**Amy S. Brzezinski**
NASA Johnson Space Center
Expedition Vehicle Division
Houston, TX, USA
1 (281) 244 5780

amy.s.brzezinski@nasa.gov

**Hudson D. Graham**
MIT
Dept. of Aero-Astro
Cambridge, MA, USA
1 (617) 258 5046

hgraham@mit.edu

## ABSTRACT

Unmanned vehicle (UV) displays are often the only information link between operators and vehicles, so their design is critical to mission success. However, there is currently no standardized methodology for operators to subjectively assess a display's support of mission tasks. This paper proposes a subjective UV display evaluation tool: the Modified Cooper-Harper for Unmanned Vehicle Displays (MCH-UVD). The MCH-UVD is adapted from the Cooper-Harper aircraft handling scale by shifting focus to support of operator information processing. An experiment was conducted to evaluate and refine the MCH-UVD, as well as assess the need for mission-specific versus general versions. Participants (86%) thought that MCH-UVD helped them identify display deficiencies, and 32% said that they could not have identified the deficiencies without the tool. No major additional benefits were observed with mission-specific versions over the general scale.

## Categories and Subject Descriptors

C.4 [**Performance of Systems**]: Measurement Techniques
H.1.2 [**User/Machine Systems**]: Human Factors
H.5.2 [**User Interfaces**]: Evaluation/methodology

## General Terms

Measurement, Performance, Experimentation, Human Factors, Standardization.

## Keywords

Unmanned Vehicles, Display Design, Subjective Assessment, Rating Scale.

## 1. INTRODUCTION

Most of today's unmanned vehicle (UV) systems require supervision from human operators, who use displays to monitor and command UVs. Because UV operations are and will be conducted with operators physically separated from the UVs, interfaces often do and will provide the only link between the operators and the UVs. It is imperative that these interfaces effectively support the UV operator's higher level cognitive processes.

Given the rapid development and deployment of UV systems [1], a relatively simple but diagnostic display evaluation tool can provide substantial benefits to the design and implementation of UV interfaces. Such a tool should help diagnose potential interface issues, address specific deficiencies, and suggest potential remedies to improve the interfaces early in the design process, for relatively low cost and effort.

Although a general scale could provide a universal way to assess UV displays and is an attractive option due to simplicity in both administration and analysis, the increasing diversity and specificity of UV missions may require specific scales for UV display assessment. Thus, one question that needs to be addressed in the development of a standardized UV display assessment tool is whether a tool tailored to a specific mission or vehicle provides more useful and accurate results. By using a UV/mission specific scale, developers may be able to pinpoint what UV and mission-specific elements the display is not supporting. However, such an approach could be more costly in terms of time and resources.

This paper presents a subjective evaluation tool, called the Modified Cooper-Harper for Unmanned Vehicle Displays (MCH-UVD), which aims to identify and diagnose specific areas where UV displays might not support operator cognitive processes. The MCH-UVD scale is designed to be presented to UV operators immediately after display use in order to quickly gather operators' judgments on how well an interface supports UV supervision and the overall mission. The aviation industry has long relied on a standardized measurement tool, called the Cooper-Harper scale [2], for subjective evaluation of aircraft handling characteristics by pilots. The Cooper-Harper scale provides a standardized method to compare handling qualities across aircraft and help test pilots articulate specific aircraft handling problems. The MCH-UVD was modeled after the Cooper-Harper scale by adopting its flowchart format, but the focus was changed from manual aircraft handling to higher-level cognitive processes such as information analysis and decision making.

The paper also presents a preliminary experiment conducted to evaluate and refine the MCH-UVD, as well as to determine if creating a mission-specific MCH-UVD is necessary, or if the general form of the MCH-UVD is sufficient for different UV display evaluation.

## 2. MODIFIED COOPER-HARPER SCALE FOR UNMANNED VEHICLE DISPLAYS

An initial MCH-UVD adaptation was conducted by Cummings et al. [3]. Ten ratings were separated into four distinct blocks, three of which addressed a different stage of the human information processing model [4] (acquisition, analysis, and decision making), and one which represented acceptable display designs. Mandatory redesign was suggested for deficiencies in information acquisition or perception, and deficiencies in decision-making warranted improvement. The 10 categories were selected after a comprehensive usability literature review [5, 6], detailed UAV accident analyses, and extensive testing [3, 7].

This initial scale had some shortcomings. First, the scale used technical human factors terminology, with which UV operators are generally not familiar. Also, the scale did not address the action stage of the human information processing model [4], thus neglecting the effectiveness of display affordances in supporting operator tasks, which is a major consideration affecting control of UVs. Moreover, the information processing stages which were addressed by the scale were not completely divided between their representative three blocks, thus causing some overlap. Further, by prioritizing the scale strictly along the information processing model, some validity of the display deficiency severity was lost. Critical deficiencies threatening mission success can occur in any of the processing stages.

The general MCH-UVD diagnosis tool shown in Figure 1 represents a major redesign of the initial MCH-UVD. This redesign includes the use of more common language for descriptions. Like the Cooper-Harper scale that rated aircraft controllability on a scale of severity, the intent was to scale severity to reflect display support for safe mission completion. At the same time, the concept of addressing the human information processing model was maintained, as this is a critical component to UV display designs. The redesign also includes a specific UVD deficiency defined for each rating.

The diamond block questions on the left of the scale ask an operator 1) if the mission can be completed safely, 2) if the UV display aids in mission completion, and for applicable cases, 3) whether it aids in mission re-planning. Based upon the operator's answer; the tool guides the user to another question querying about display support of the mission. Within the individual diamond groups, the human information processing model is applied on a severity scale, from information acquisition to information analysis to decision-making and finally action-taking tasks. The deficiencies are deemed to be more severe for tasks earlier in the human information processing model, because if the display is flawed in supporting an earlier stage, it does not matter

how good the display supports the later phase because the operator could be acting upon a flawed input.

When operators are directed to the right of the diamond block questions, they examine a set of descriptions pertaining to potential issues. Within each diamond block, operators choose between two to four different descriptions, each of which corresponds to a MCH-UVD rating.

### 2.1 Cannot Complete Mission Task Safely

#### 2.1.1 Flawed Information Retrieval – Rating 10
A display is considered to be flawed in information retrieval when it is missing critical information, essential information cannot be located, or information becomes outdated because of long retrieval times. A display that requires extensive multi-layered search could receive a rating of 10 if searching results in long retrieval times. Generally, under this diagnosis displays do not provide operators with the necessary information they need for tasks, making higher-level information processing virtually impossible and increasing the likelihood of UV mission failure.

For example, among the major causes of the Three Mile Island disaster was the lack of display indications of the coolant level in the core and a relief valve failure [8]. The operators did not realize that the core was experiencing loss of coolant and implemented a series of incorrect actions that led to catastrophic consequences.

#### 2.1.2 Action Confusion – Rating 9
UV displays that do not provide straightforward or intuitive ways to act upon decisions are classified as having confusing action implementation. These displays may have display affordances [9] that are difficult to find or use, or that are easy to incorrectly use, thus making operator tasks hard to perform or easy to erroneously execute. Mode confusion, which occurs when operators do not understand or confuse the mode they are in [10], is another possible outcome of this rating. Incorrect task performance because of poor affordances could threaten mission success, even when information acquisition, analysis, and decision-making have been efficiently and properly performed.

For example, in 2006 a MQ-9 Predator B UAV impacted the terrain in Arizona during a nighttime border patrol mission and destroyed the aircraft. Mode confusion was identified as one of the major factors [11]. For this flight, there were two nearly physically identical consoles for the pilot and the payload operator, with the ability to transfer control from one console to the other. The functionality differed vastly depending on the mode of operation. The throttle quadrant on the pilot's console provided UAV airspeed control, but for the payload operator's console, this same quadrant controlled the camera. Before transferring control from one console to the other, the condition lever position on the payload operator's console had to be matched to the current positioning on the pilot's console. When the pilot and payload operator swapped seats, the pilot forgot to match the controls, which led to mode confusion, and ultimately, the loss of the UAV.

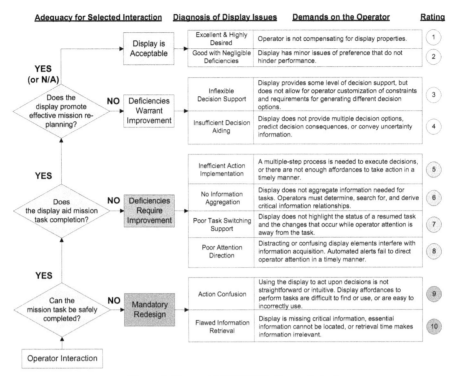

Figure 1. General MCH-UVD diagnosis tool.

## 2.2 Display does not Aid Mission Task Completion

### 2.2.1 Poor attention direction – Rating 8
These displays provide operators with the information they need, but contain distracting display elements or clutter, which could interfere with efficient information acquisition. Additionally, if the displays use automated alerting, these alerts do not attract operator attention in a timely manner. Under rating 8, information acquisition is hindered, but is still possible.

An illustrative case is the 1995 cruise ship Royal Majesty accident. After about 35 hours in transit from Bermuda to Boston, the ship grounded on the Nantucket shoals [12]. Shortly after departure, the GPS switched to dead-reckoning mode as it was no longer receiving satellite signals. None of the crew members were aware that GPS was in dead reckoning for the duration of the trip. There was a very small visual indicator on the GPS representing dead reckoning operations, but it was cluttered by other visual information. Moreover, the aural alarm indicating the switch to dead reckoning sounded only for a brief time in the chart room, but not on the bridge's central console where the watch officer stood. Thus, neither the visual display nor the auditory alert directed crew attention to the change in the system state.

### 2.2.2 Poor Task Switching Support – Rating 7
When the operator intentionally or unintentionally moves attention to one task to another, switching to the new task and switching back to the previous task comes with a cost [13-15]. UV displays receiving a rating of 7 have issues with supporting task switching. Although these displays, in part, support information analysis tasks, they do not clearly highlight the status of the resumed task and any changes that may have occurred while the operator's attention shifted. Display issues with task switching support could cause operators to make decisions and take actions based upon incorrect information, and may increase the time operators spend on analysis tasks. A classic human factors example of this problem is checklist interruption. A number of aircraft accidents have occurred due to such interruptions, particularly in the takeoff configuration when pilots are interrupted in the takeoff checklist process and forget to lower the flaps, resulting in stall and crash of the aircraft [16].

### 2.2.3 No Information Aggregation – Rating 6
UV displays that do not amass task information collectively or require operators to determine, search for, and derive critical information relationships are considered deficient in information aggregation. These displays do not suggest what information to analyze and do not co-locate different pieces of information related to a specific task, which is critical for effective decision making in dynamic environments [17]. Thus, the cognitive load of the operators increases as they have to determine what information to analyze, where the information is, and how to analyze it. These problems are exacerbated under time-pressure and dynamic settings, inherent characteristics of UV domains. For example, the poorly designed status display of Apollo 13, which lacked data history and a reference frame for oxygen tank pressure, did not aid the controllers to detect the imminent failure of a tank, leading to an emergency recovery of the spacecraft [18].

### 2.2.4 Inefficient Action Implementation – Rating 5
These displays either require unnecessary multiple step processes to execute actions, or do not provide enough affordances to take action. In these cases, displays generally support operator actions, but not efficiently, which could have negative effects on a UV

mission, particularly under time-critical situations. An illustrative example for this rating is the early version of BMW iDrive®, where drivers had to interact with a joystick and navigate through several screens for simple tasks such as changing the interior temperature.

## 2.3 Display does not Promote Effective Mission Re-planning

Re-planning decision support is not necessary in all UV missions. The N/A option allows the evaluator to bypass the question in cases where this functionality is not required such as in the case of small, handheld UAVs that are providing local imagery. UV decision support tools are generally supplemental tools, which could enhance the operator's interaction with the display [19, 20].

### 2.3.1 Insufficient Decision Aiding – Rating 4

These displays do not provide multiple decision options or predict the potential consequences of decisions. Additionally, these displays do not convey uncertainty information about decision alternatives, their potential consequences or about decision-making in general. Insufficient decision aiding might increase the likelihood of error, and potentially jeopardize mission success.

### 2.3.2 Inflexible Decision Support – Rating 3

Operators who rate a UV display as a 3 believe that it provides some level of decision-making support, but the display does not allow for operator customization of constraints and requirements to narrow down decision options. This inflexible decision support, as subjectively deemed by operators, is useful to the decision-making process but may not help operators make optimal decisions, which could potentially negatively affect a UV mission, particularly in time-critical situations.

## 2.4 Acceptable Displays

Acceptable displays include two ratings: good displays with negligible deficiencies (rating 2), excellent and highly desired displays (rating 1). A UV display receives a rating of 1 when the operator is not compensating for any deficient display properties. UV displays that receive a rating of 2 support human information processing through all four stages, but have very minor issues of preference that do not hinder operator performance. Example issues include preference of font style or size, display colors, or display element arrangement or sizing.

## 3. EVALUATING THE MODIFIED COOPER-HARPER SCALE

A human subject experiment was conducted to evaluate both general and UV/mission specific scales using two different UV displays. In addition to comparing general and specific scales, this experiment helped us better define the ratings. The MCH-UVD, presented in its general or specific form, was administered to participants as a post-test survey for evaluating two types of unmanned vehicles displays: UAV or UGV.

Figure 2 illustrates how the general MCH-UVD was modified to represent the specific unmanned ground vehicle (UGV) search mission utilized in the experiment. Defining the mission is a critical step for generating a specific MCH-UVD as the specific scale addresses the particular aspects of the UV/mission explicitly. Some of these aspects include the mission tasks that need to be safely completed by the UV, the critical information needed for the mission, the tasks/actions operators should perform, the system elements that require operator attention, the

tasks that may require re-planning, and the uncertainties in decision-making.

## 3.1 Participants

Sixty participants completed the study. The participants consisted of 24 female and 36 male MIT students, ages ranging from 18 to 45 years (mean = 20.7, SD = 4.01). The experiment lasted 1 to 1.5 hours. The participants were compensated $10/hour and were eligible to win a $50 gift card based on their performance.

## 3.2 Apparatus

The UAV condition utilized the displays created for the Onboard Planning System for UAVs in Support of Expeditionary Reconnaissance and Surveillance (OPS-USERS) simulator, developed by Aurora Flight Sciences. OPS-USERS simulates UVs conducting search and tracking operations. The UGV condition was carried out on Urban Search and Rescue Simulator (USARSim), an open source, high fidelity simulation of urban search and rescue robots and environments [21].

The OPS-USERS display was presented on a 17-inch desktop screen, in 1600 x 1024 pixels and 32-bit resolution. The display for USARSim [22] was presented on a 17-inch desktop screen, in 1280 x 1024 pixels and 32-bit resolution. Participants controlled the simulators through a generic corded computer mouse.

## 3.3 Experimental design

The experiment was a 2x2 completely randomized design. The independent variables were UVD type (UAV, UGV), and MCH-UVD type (general, specific). Equal number of participants was assigned to each of the four conditions. Each condition lasted 15 minutes.

## 3.4 Experimental tasks

Participants supervised one UAV or four UGVs. One UV and one operator is representative of many current operations, whereas the supervision of multiple UVs by one operator is the direction that UV operations are headed towards [23]. Our intent was not to compare performance across the two UV displays per se, but to compare how well the MCH-UVD scales helped identify deficiencies in different displays. Thus, experimental results were not compared across the two UV displays.

### 3.4.1 UAV Mission/Display

The UAV condition was a dynamic search and target acquisition mission. OPS-USERS allowed the participants to search for and track targets with a single UAV while monitoring the UAV's flight path and event timeline. The UAV was designed to search for targets and then track the targets upon target identification. Participants were instructed to monitor a water canal for passing ships. The objective was to maximize the number of ships found and the amount of time the ships were tracked.

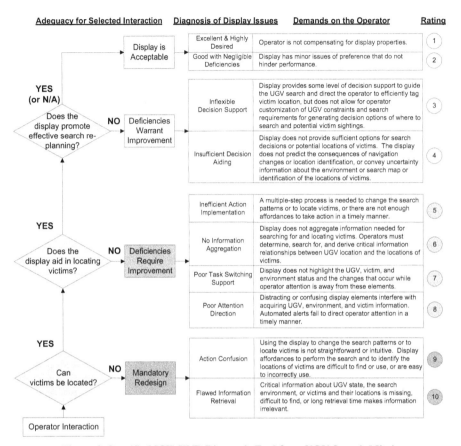

| Adequacy for Selected Interaction | Diagnosis of Display Issues | Demands on the Operator | Rating |

**Figure 2. Specific MCH-UVD Diagnosis Tool for a UGV Search Mission.**

The display (Figure 3) provided a map for tracking the UAV on its present flight path, along with an interaction control panel (bottom) for making UAV control inputs, and a panel for accepting or rejecting automation plans (left). Control inputs included creating a search or tracking task for the UAV, setting task start and end times, and creating task duration. For the purposes of this experiment, the operators were allowed to assign the UAV one task at a time. Thus, both the task value and the delay penalty seen in Figure 3 were always set to high. The operator could also modify and delete tasks using the control panel. The flight time and range of the UAV was limited by fuel, so the operator had to be aware of the fuel quantity indicated by a fuel gauge above the UAV icon. The operator had to periodically allow the UAV to return to base to refuel.

To search the canal for a target, the operator had to select a location in the canal and create a search task, and then had to accept the plan presented by the automation. Once the operator accepted the plan, a thin green line appeared showing the projected flight path from the current location of the UAV to the task, and the UAV flew to the task. Once the UAV flew over a ship (target) in the canal, the ship appeared on the map and an initial tracking task was automatically presented to the operator. The operator then had to accept the initial tracking task and the UAV tracked the ship for the duration specified by the operator.

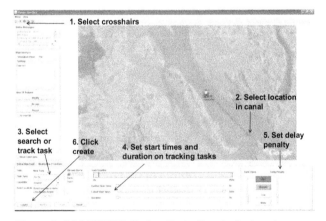

**Figure 3. OPS-USERS display (Including the instructions on creating a search task).**

### 3.4.2 UGV Mission/Display

Participants supervised four UGVs conducting a search mission for victims in a warehouse (Figure 4). The objective of the mission was to find and mark the location of as many victims as possible. The Robot List (upper left) showed each robot's camera view, whereas the Image Viewer (middle left) displayed the selected robot's camera view. Robots could be controlled by either setting way-points on the Mission panel (upper right), or by teleoperation (lower left). The Mission panel allowed operators to create, clear, and modify waypoints. Panoramic images were taken at the terminal point of waypoint sequences, which were displayed on the Image Viewer (middle left) with operator's request. Through the teleoperation panel, it was also possible to pan and tilt the cameras. After victims were spotted in the UGV's video or in the panoramic images, operators were responsible for marking the victim's location on the Map Data Viewer (lower right frame) using a pop-up frame.

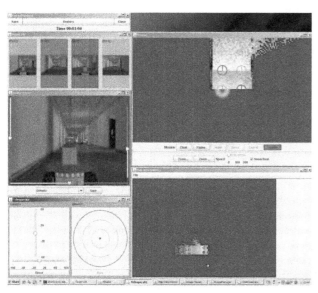

**Figure 4. USARSim display.**

### 3.4.3 Post-Mission Tasks

Following the test scenario, participants rated their workload on a Likert scale ranging from 1 to 5. Then, the test proctor showed the participants the general or specific MCH-UVD, dependent on the assigned condition, and gave a brief explanation of how to use the MCH-UVD. Participants then reported their MCH-UVD rating with an explanation for why they chose that rating and if they found any additional display deficiencies. The participants were instructed to examine all the MCH-UVD ratings before indicating these additional problems. Before compensating the participant, the test proctor asked a set of pre-determined post-test questions aimed to assess participant attitudes towards MCH-UVD.

## 4. RESULTS
## 4.1 MCH-UVD Ratings

An ordered logit model, specifically proportional odds, was developed to compare the four general groupings of ratings (i.e., display is acceptable, deficiencies warrant improvement, deficiencies require improvement, and mandatory redesign) between different displays (UAV and UGV) and MCH-UVD types (general and specific). The model was adjusted for individual differences (age and gender), subjective workload, and experimenter ratings of the operator (level of mission success, and level of display misuse). Only level of display misuse was significant and was kept in the model ($\alpha$=.05).

Level of mission success and level of display misuse were assessed by the experimenter. The alternatives for level of mission success were very poor, poor, well, and very well. The experimenter followed a set of pre-determined criteria while

rating mission success (e.g., focusing only on a small region of the canal while searching for ships received a "very poor" rating). The experimenter recorded any incorrect user input to the display as a misuse. The alternatives for the level of display misuse were: no, a few, some, and many misuses. Because there were only a few data points in each of the four levels, these levels were combined and collapsed into two: many or some misuses, and few or no misuses.

UVD type, MCH type, and UVD x MCH interaction were not significant. In the general MCH setting, five participants rated the UAV display to be acceptable, whereas in the specific MCH setting, there was only one participant who did the same. While not statistically significant, there is a trend that suggests that the general scale can lead to more optimistic ratings. None of the participants thought that a redesign was mandatory (ratings 9, 10).

The level of display misuse had a significant effect on MCH-UVD rating ($\chi^2(1)$=9.08, p=.003) (Table 1). Compared to having many or some misuses, having a few or no misuses increased the odds of selecting a better rating by an estimated 516% (Odds-Ratio: 6.16, 95% CI: 1.89, 20.09). This provides preliminary evidence for the validity of the scale suggesting that the order of severity indicated in the MCH-UVD is directly proportional to the level of display misuse. That is, displays that induce more operator misuses are also rated more severely in the MCH-UVD.

**Table 1. Number of observations in MCH-UVD categories by level of misuse**

| Level of Misuse | MCH-UVD Rating | | |
| --- | --- | --- | --- |
| | Display is acceptable | Deficiencies warrant improvement | Deficiencies require improvement |
| Few or None | 9 | 25 | 10 |
| Some or Many | 0 | 6 | 10 |

The participant ratings helped us refine MCH-UVD. The scales evaluated in the experiment were earlier versions and slightly different than the scales previously discussed. Rating number seven was initially "change blindness". The experimental data showed that there were no responses in this rating level. The lack of responses for "change blindness" can be explained in part by its large overlap with rating eight, "poor attention direction", and the term "poor attention direction" being easier to understand, and thus potentially leading participants to select it rather than "change blindness". Based on this finding, rating number seven was modified from "change blindness" to "poor task switching support", which also relates to attention allocation but is more distinctive from other ratings.

## 4.2 Display Deficiencies Identified

This section presents the total number of UV display deficiencies that were identified by each participant across the general and specific scales. This analysis is then followed by a comparison of the total number of unique display deficiencies collectively identified by all the participants in each UVD type.

### 4.2.1 UAV Display

Although only marginally significant, it appeared that participants were likely to identify more UAV display deficiencies with the specific scale compared to the general scale ($\chi^2(1)$=3.13, p=.08). A large number of deficiencies identified by all participants in the general scale condition were identical to the deficiencies identified by all participants in the specific scale condition. Four participants (27%) in each MCH condition identified a lack of display support for search guidance. A few participants indicated that better information on the remaining fuel level was necessary ($N_G^1$=2, $N_S$=1). Participants also identified deficiencies related to path planning and re-planning. In particular, the participants indicated that time delays with respect to control inputs, automatic updating, and accepting and prioritizing tasks made it harder to use the display ($N_G$=5, $N_S$=7). One participant pointed out that the automated plan merely mirrored the route input by the operator, creating unnecessary time delays. Four participants (27%) in each MCH condition indicated that imprecise UAV paths were a problem. Participants indicated that it was difficult to change the UAV flight path ($N_G$=3, $N_S$=4).

Only one unique UAV display deficiency was identified with the general scale, which was the lack of information provided on the consequences of selected actions (N=1). There were a total of four deficiencies uniquely identified with the specific scale: the lack of information on UAV flight parameters (i.e., direction, speed), obscured duration settings, difficult target detection, and the large number of steps required to change the search patterns as well as to track targets (each by one participant).

### 4.2.2 UGV Display

The number of UGV display deficiencies individually identified by the participants was not significantly different between general and specific scales. Similar to the UAV display, a large number of deficiencies identified for the UGV display with the general scale were identical to the deficiencies identified with the specific scale. Out of the 15 participants in each MCH condition, the majority identified time delays to be problematic, especially the delays associated with manual control of the vehicles and the cameras, as well as the slow UV movement in general ($N_G$=10, $N_S$=7). Participants suggested having multiple cameras on a vehicle to avoid rotating the camera. One participant in each MCH type indicated that robots did not always move smoothly and follow waypoints exactly. One participant in each condition indicated that the additional step of clearing UGV paths was difficult and unnecessary. Obstacles not displayed on UGVs' paths was another deficiency identified with both the general ($N_G$=2) and specific scales ($N_S$=4). Participants thought the two maps were confusing and unnecessary (one participant in each condition). Clutter was also deemed to be a problem ($N_G$=1, $N_S$=2).

There were a total of six deficiencies uniquely identified with the general scale. These problems included the blue background (N=1), the pop-up distractions (N=1), the lack of alerts before two UGVs collided (N=1), the lack of UV idle indication (N=1), and the lack of display customizability (N=1).

There were three uniquely identified deficiencies with the specific scale. These deficiencies included the difficulty in switching between the four robots views (N=1), as well as the issues related to UGV orientation and depth perception. Specifically, the camera angle made it difficult to know how UGVs were oriented (N=3), and it was hard for participants to estimate distances on the map based on the video feed depth perception (N=6). Therefore, participants had to place several markers to get to a desired location. This display deficiency (inaccurate goal assignment) was identified by a large number (N=9) of participants with the

specific scale and by no participants with the general scale, and is critical since it can significantly interfere with UV control. Thus in this case, the specific scale helped a larger number of operators identify a major display deficiency, which was not captured by the general scale.

### 4.3 Feedback on MCH-UVD

Out of the 57 participants who identified display deficiencies, 49, that is, 86% ($N_G$=23, $N_S$=26) thought that MCH-UVD helped them identify these display problems. 32% (NG=10, $N_S$=8) of the 57 participants said that they could not have recognized these deficiencies without the help of MCH-UVD. Fourteen percent ($N_G$=4, $N_S$=4) said that they could have identified deficiencies but would not be able to indicate the severity. An additional 12% ($N_G$=4, $N_S$=2) also indicated that they could have identified deficiencies but would not be able to describe them accurately.

There were mixed responses with respect to the design of the scales. The aspects of MCH-UVD categorized as being most useful included the detailed descriptions of display issues ($N_G$=7, $N_S$=14), flowchart ($N_G$=16, $N_S$=11), severity scale ($N_G$=1, $N_S$=2), and color coding ($N_G$=2, $N_S$=4). The aspects of MCH-UVD categorized as being least useful included the flowchart ($N_G$=9, $N_S$=10), technical terms ($N_G$=13, $N_S$=13), and wording being too long ($N_G$=3, $N_S$=16). Overall, the views on the usefulness of the flowchart format were split about in half. Some participants categorized the flowchart to be the most useful aspect guiding them in their ratings, whereas others thought that the flowchart questions were too broad, and led them to the wrong ratings. Nine participants (15%) suggested using checklists rather than picking one specific rating. Forty three percent (general: 21.5%, specific: 21.5%) found the language to be too technical and difficult to understand at times, and 32% (general: 6%, specific: 26%) found the wording to be too long. Twenty three percent (general: 6%, specific: 17%) suggested having more ratings for more display issues.

### 5. DISCUSSION

A standardized subjective display evaluation tool is an inexpensive and easy way to identify UV display improvements, as developers and testers can receive quick feedback. We proposed one such scale, MCH-UVD, in two forms: general or mission/UV specific. We also conducted a preliminary evaluation of the scale through an experiment. Participants who had more misuses with a display gave it a worse rating. Moreover, almost all of the participants (86%) thought that MCH-UVD helped them identify display deficiencies, and some (32%) said that they could not have identified the deficiencies otherwise. Although these findings are promising, it is not clear if MCH-UVD is better than other subjective methods, such as heuristic usability testing or expert evaluations. Future research should compare MCH-UVD to these existing methods.

The experiment compared the general and the UV/mission-specific scales. Although only marginally significant, individuals appeared to identify more deficiencies with the specific scale as compared to the general one. Given the limited experimental sample size, this is an important finding which has implications for the use of MCH-UVD in practice. When there are only a few operators available to rate a UV display, these results show that more deficiencies can be identified with the specific MCH-UVD.

While more unique deficiencies were identified with the general scale, these occurrences were not clustered around any clear

---

[1] Response number for general scale: $N_G$, for specific scale: $N_S$

problems. The unique deficiencies identified with the specific scale were clustered around a major design flaw not identified with the general scale. Thus, the likelihood that the specific scale could identify a major display deficiency is higher than with the general scale. Longitudinal data from actual practice with the scales could provide more insight on how much additional benefit the specific scale provides, and if this additional benefit is worth the effort. The amount of time required generating the specific scale and the additional benefit it may provide creates a trade-off.

About half of the participants considered the specific scale to be too wordy whereas there were only a few participants who thought the same for the general scale. An equal number of participants (43% of the total) evaluating specific and general scales indicated that some of the technical language was confusing. The level of technicality and the number of words needed to identify technical terms is a tradeoff, which has to be decided upon by the practitioners. Even if some participants considered the specific scale to be too wordy, others thought that the detailed descriptions were helpful. If operators are familiar with the technical terms, the amount of words used to explain them can be reduced.

In current operations, UVs are often designed to perform multiple missions, either singly or concurrently. An advantage of the specific scale is that it can be custom designed to consider more than one mission. Display developers can choose to administer multiple single-mission specific scales for each mission type, or combine the information of multiple missions into one specific scale to evaluate how a display supports all missions at once.

Because MCH-UVD diagnosis tools only provide one subjective measure of operator-UV interaction, other objective metrics should be collected to get a more comprehensive picture of how a UV display supports an operator in supervising a UV mission.

## 6. ACKNOWLEDGMENTS

This research is funded by the US Army Aberdeen Test Center (ATC). We would like to acknowledge Brooke Abounader (ATC), who provided valuable technical support and comments. Thanks to Ryne Barry and Javier Garcia for their help in data collection. Special thanks to the following persons for providing their UV displays and support: Olivier Toupet (Aurora Flight Sciences), Paul Scerri and Prasanna Velagapudi (Carnegie Mellon U.), Michael Lewis (U. of Pittsburgh), and Cameron Fraser (MIT).

## 7. REFERENCES

[1] DOD 2007. *Unmanned systems roadmap.* 2007-2032, Office of the Secretary of Defense, Washington, D.C.

[2] Harper, R. P. and Cooper, G. E. 1986. Handling qualities and pilot evaluation. *Journal of Guidance, Control, and Dynamics,* 9, 5, 515-529.

[3] Cummings, M. L., Myers, K. and Scott, S. D. 2006. Modified Cooper Harper evaluation tool for unmanned vehicle displays. In *Proceedings of UVS Canada: Conference on Unmanned Vehicle Systems Canada,* Montebello, PQ, Canada.

[4] Parasuraman, R., Sheridan, T. and Wickens, C. D. 2000. A model for types and levels of human interaction with automation. *IEEE Transactions on Systems, Man and Cybernetics - Part A: Systems and Humans,* 30, 3, 286-297.

[5] Shneiderman, B. 1998. *Designing the User-Interface: Strategies for Effective Human-Computer Interaction.* Addison Wesley Longman, Reading, MA.

[6] Nielsen, J. 1993. *Usability Engineering.* Morgan Kaufmann, San Francisco.

[7] Brzezinski, A. S. *StarVis: A Configural Decision Support Tool for Schedule Management of Multiple Unmanned Aerial Vehicles.* Master of Science, Massachusetts Institute of Technology, Cambridge, MA, 2008.

[8] Rubinstein, T. and Mason, A. F. 1979. The accident that shouldn't have happened: an analysis of the Three Mile Island. *IEEE Spectrum,* November, 33-57.

[9] Norman, D. A. 2002. *The Design of Everyday Things.* Basic Books, New York.

[10] Billings, C. E. 1997. *Aviation Automation: The Search for a Human Centered Approach.* Lawrence Erlbaum Associates, Mahwah, NJ.

[11] Carrigan, G. P., Long, D., Cummings, M. L. and Duffner, J. 2008. Human factors analysis of predator B crash. In *Proceedings of AUVSI: Unmanned Systems North America,* San Diego, CA.

[12] NTSB 1995. *Marine Accident Report, Grounding of the Panamian Passenger Ship Royal Majesty on Rose and Crown Shoal near Nantucket, Massachusetts.* NTSB/MAR-97/01, National Transportation Safety Board.

[13] Sheridan, T. B. 1972. On how often the operator supervisor should sample. *IEEE Transactions on Systems, Science, and Cybernetics,* SSC-6, 140-145.

[14] Rogers, R. D. and Monsell, S. 1995. Costs of a predictable switch between simple cognitive tasks. *Journal of Experimental Psychology: General,* 124, 2, 207-231.

[15] McFarlane, D. C. 2002. Comparison of four primary methods for coordinating the interruption of people in human-computer interaction. *Human-Computer Interaction,* 17, 1, 63-139.

[16] Degani, A. and Wiener, E. L. 1990. *Human factors of flight-deck checklists: the normal checklist.* NASA Contractor Report 177549, NASA Ames Research Center.

[17] Wickens, C. D. and Carswell, C. M. 1995. The proximity compatibility principle: Its psychological foundation and its relevance to display design. *Human Factors,* 37, 3, 473-494.

[18] Woods, D. D. 1995. Toward a theoretical base for representation design in the computer medium: Ecological perception and aiding human cognition. In J. M. Flach, P. A. Hancock, J. Caird and K. J. Vicente (Eds.), *An Ecological Approach to Human-Machine Systems I: A Global Perspective.* Lawrence Erlbaum Associates, Hillsdale, N.J., 157-188.

[19] Cummings, M. L. and Mitchell, P. J. 2006. Automated scheduling decision support for supervisory control of multiple UAVs. *AIAA Journal of Aerospace Computing, Information, and Communication,* 3, 6, 294-308.

[20] Cummings, M. L., Brzezinski, A. S. and Lee, J. D. 2007. The impact of intelligent aiding for multiple unmanned aerial vehicle schedule management. *IEEE Intelligent Systems: Special Issue on Interacting with Autonomy,* 22, 2, 52-59.

[21] Lewis, M., Wang, J. and Hughes, S. 2007. USARsim: Simulation for the study of human-robot interaction. *Journal of Cognitive Engineering and Decision Making,* 1, 1, 98-120.

[22] Wang, J. and Lewis, M. 2007. Human control of cooperating robot teams. In *Proceedings of the ACM/IEEE International Conference on Human-Robot Interaction,* Arlington, VA.

[23] Cummings, M. L., Bruni, S., Mercier, S. and Mitchell, P. J. 2007. Automation architecture for single operator, multiple UAV command and control. *The International Command and Control Journal,* 1, 2, 1-24.

# Using the "Negative Attitude Toward Robots Scale" with Telepresence Robots

Katherine M. Tsui
Computer Science Dept.
UMass Lowell
1 University Avenue
Lowell, MA 01854
ktsui@cs.uml.edu

Munjal Desai
Computer Science Dept.
UMass Lowell
1 University Avenue
Lowell, MA 01854
mdesai@cs.uml.edu

Holly A. Yanco
Computer Science Dept.
UMass Lowell
1 University Avenue
Lowell, MA 01854
holly@cs.uml.edu

Henriette Cramer[1]
SICS & Mobile Life Centre
Stockholm, Sweden
henriette@mobilelifecentre.org

Nicander Kemper
KZA b.v.
Baarn, The Netherlands
nkemper@kza.nl

## ABSTRACT

Nomura et al. designed and piloted the Negative Attitude toward Robots Scale (NARS) in 2003 [18]. NARS has been used by researchers to understand the attitudes of different people towards robots under different circumstances. To our knowledge, NARS has only been used with robots perceived to be autonomous. Our goal was to evaluate if NARS could be extended to robots that were known to have a human in the loop. Towards this end, we verified the validity of the scale with telepresence robots using an online video survey. We found differences across different cultures and gender much like other researcher in the past. Once the consistency of the scale was verified, we used NARS in our second study that involved the use of telepresence robots.

## Categories and Subject Descriptors

H.4 [**Information Systems Applications**]: Miscellaneous; D.2.8 [**Software Engineering**]: Metrics—*complexity measures, performance measures*

## General Terms

Validation

## Keywords

Telepresence robots, NARS, Validation of metrics

## 1. INTRODUCTION

As robots become more commonplace in society, it is important to understand how people feel about these robots,

---

[1] Cramer's contribution to this paper was carried out during the tenure of an ERCIM "Alain Bensoussan" Fellowship Programme.

including how they look, how they behave, and their purpose. For robots to be accepted by the masses, they must be designed in a fashion that would facilitate easier adoption. One of the initial steps is to find and understand any preconceived notions or biases that people might have against robots so that they can then be addressed. In Japan, Nomura et al. have been actively creating scales to help understand the attitudes ("Negative Attitude toward Robots Scale" [18]), anxieties ("Robot Anxiety Scale" [17]), and assumptions [13] people have towards robots.

In this paper, we summarize the development of the NARS metric and its prior uses for understanding people's attitudes towards robots, including its cross-cultural usage. In the literature, the NARS metric has only been applied to robots that are (or appear to be) autonomous. Our work extends NARS to telepresence robots that are controlled by a person. We first validated the use of the scale for telepresence robots in an online survey and then applied the scale to a study of people who were teleoperating the telepresence robots.

## 2. NEGATIVE ATTITUDE TOWARD ROBOTS SCALE (NARS)

In 2003, Nomura et al. developed a psychological tool to measure people's anxiety towards robots which evolved into the "Negative Attitude toward Robots Scale" (NARS) [18]. Nomura et al. hypothesized that people with high levels of communication apprehension towards people might also have communication apprehension with robots since people do not discriminate between humans and agents with respect to communication. The result was three subscales of negative attitudes towards "situations of interaction with robots" (NARS-S1), "social influence of robots" (NARS-S2), and "emotions in interaction with robots" (NARS-S3).

When using NARS, participants are asked to rate the items shown in Table 1 on a scale from 1 (I strongly disagree) to 5 (I strongly agree) with 3 as "undecided." A higher score for NARS-S1 and NARS-S2 indicates a more negative attitude towards robots; conversely, a lower score indicates a more positive attitude. NARS-S3 is an inverse scale and a higher score indicates a more positive attitude; conversely, a lower score indicates a more negative attitude.

### 2.1 Development of the Scale

In the beginning of 2003, Nomura et al. [18] conducted

**Table 1: Negative Attitude toward Robots Scale (NARS)**

| Subscale | Items |
|---|---|
| S1: interaction | • I would feel uneasy if I was given a job where I had to use robots.<br>• The word "robot" means nothing to me.<br>• I would feel nervous operating a robot in front of other people.<br>• I would hate the idea that robots or artificial intelligences were making judgements about things.<br>• I would feel very nervous just standing in front of a robot.<br>• I would feel paranoid talking with a robot. |
| S2: social | • I would feel uneasy if robots really had emotions.<br>• Something bad might happen if robots developed into living beings.<br>• I feel that if I depend on robots too much, something bad might happen.<br>• I am concerned that robot would be a bad influence on children.<br>• I feel that in the future society will be dominated by robots.<br>• I feel that in the future, robots will be commonplace in society.* |
| S3: emotion (inverse) | • I would feel relaxed talking with robots.<br>• If robots had emotions, I would be able to make friends with them.<br>• I feel that I could make friends with robots.**<br>• I feel comforted being with robots that have emotions.<br>• I feel comfortable being with robots.** |

Original items from Nomura et al. [18] translated by Bartneck and team. * indicates modification presented in Section 3.1; ** indicates suggestions presented in [4,5].

a pilot survey of 39 participants. The survey was a series of free response questions from which the researchers extracted 13 sentences relating to emotions and attitudes towards robots and situations in which these emotions and attitudes may occur. The survey was conducted in Japanese. The researchers also identified 16 items from the ACAS (Aikyodai's Computer Anxiety Scale in Japanese [9]) and four items from the PRCA-24 translated to Japanese (Personal Report of Communication Apprehension Scale in English [10]); these items were made robot-centric. A subset of these questions was selected as the basis for NARS.

During the summer of 2003, the preliminary NARS was administered to 263 participants from four universities and one research corporation in the Kansai area of Japan [18]. Four subscales were identified based on analysis of the results. S1 consisted of 6 items relating to anxieties toward operation and social influence; it measured "situations of interaction with robots." S2 had 5 items and measured "social influence of robots." S3 had 3 items and measured "emotions in interaction with robots." S4 had 3 items but was discarded due to a low consistency rating. NARS included subscales S1, S2, and S3.

Towards the end of 2003, Nomura et al. validated NARS with 240 participants from three universities in the Kansai and Kanto areas of Japan [18]. NARS and STAI (State-Trait Anxiety Inventory provided in Japanese [8]) were administered and then again 4 to 5 weeks later. Analysis of the ratings for the three subscales showed good reliability [18]. The English translation of the NARS items are shown in Table 1.

## 2.2 The Use of NARS

Since its creation, NARS has been used several times in the human-robot interaction (HRI) community both as a primary and supplementary performance measure (Table 2). It has been successfully used to explain the differences in participants' interactions with robots and also to highlight the effects of cultural differences on NARS.

### 2.2.1 NARS as a primary performance measure

In 2004, Nomura et al. [12] conducted a study with 240 Japanese students of whom 146 were male and 92 were female. The participants were asked to interact with a robot that was perceived to be autonomous. The robot used for the task was Robovie, and the interaction involved talking to the robot. The authors performed a two-way ANOVA and found differences in scores for subscale S1 based on gender and prior experience with robots. The results of the study suggested that there might be differences based on age. The authors also found that participants with higher S1 scores took longer to initially talk to the robot than those participants that had lower S1 scores. This finding indicated that participants with more negative attitude towards robots on the interaction subscale took longer to initiate their interaction with the robots. These results provided preliminary evidence of the usefulness of NARS in predicting user interaction based on their negative attitudes towards robots.

Also in 2004, Nomura et al. [13] conducted another study with 106 participants, 46 of whom were male and 33 female. The participants were from two different sets: university students and employees of a research corporation. The participant pool from the research corporation had an average age of 22.9 years. Age data for the university students was not provided. The participants were Japanese. This study involved finding the assumptions that people might have about robots. Although NARS was not used in this study, the authors stated that "through the development of this scale [NARS], it was found that individuals' experiences of actually seeing robots influence their negative attitudes toward robots. However, this analysis did not take into account which types of robots respondents experienced" [13]. The type of robot is one of three assumption categories that NARS does not directly address. The authors had two engineers and two psychologists debate and create a list of items for a survey to assess people's assumptions about robots. They classified the items into three categories: assumptions about type (noted above), situation, and tasks. The authors then presented this survey in Japanese to the participants

Table 2: Studies using NARS as a performance measure

| Study | Year | $n$ | Language | Robot | Description |
|---|---|---|---|---|---|
| Nomura et al. [18] | 2003 | 263 | Japanese | - | Initial efforts to create a psychological scale for NARS |
| Nomura et al. [12] | 2004 | 240 | Japanese | Robovie | Investigated gender and prior experience differences from NARS |
| Bartneck et al. [2] | 2005 | 96 | English | - | Investigated effects of cultural differences from NARS |
| Nomura et al. [11] | 2006 | 53 | Japanese | Robovie | Investigated the relationship between peoples' negative attitudes and their interaction with robots |
| Nomura et al. [16] | 2006 | 400 | Japanese | - | Attempted to find the relationship between the participants assumptions and attitudes towards robots |
| Bartneck et al. [3] | 2007 | 467 | English | Aibo | Investigated effects of cultural differences and prior robot experience |
| Nomura et al. [15] | 2007 | 17 | Japanese | Robovie-M | Investigated the relationship between peoples' attitudes towards and the distance maintained during interaction |
| Nomura et al. [14] | 2008 | 38 | Japanese | Robovie | Investigated any relationship between peoples' attitudes and their behavior towards robots |
| Cramer et al. [4, 5] | 2009 | 119 | English | Robosapien | Investigated the relationship between the robot's behavior involving contact with a person and people's attitudes. |
| Syrdal et al. [22] | 2009 | 28 | English | Peoplebot | Used NARS to explain the participants' behaviors |
| Riek et al. [20] | 2010 | 16 | English | BERTI | Examined videos of humanoid gestures (beckon, give, and handshake) |

and analyzed the data collected. This study is note-worthy because it was a preliminary attempt at creating a survey tool to gauge people's assumptions about robots.

Bartneck et al. [2] used NARS with a cross-cultural population in 2005. The authors recruited 24 Dutch participants, 19 Chinese participants living in the Netherlands, and 53 Japanese participants for their study. While the authors did not provide information about the language in which NARS was administered to the different populations, we know that NARS was translated into English by one of the authors from [12]. The authors mentioned that the Chinese participants were living in the Netherlands; however, no information about the Japanese participants was provided. This omission leads us to believe that the Japanese participants were living in Japan and were administered NARS in Japanese, while the Dutch and Chinese participants were provided NARS in English. Also, we do not have any information on whether the English translation was back translated to Japanese. For this study, no robot was used. This study was intended to highlight the differences, if any, that could be observed across different cultures. Interestingly, Bartneck et al. found that Japanese participants had significantly higher scores on the social subscale (S2) than Chinese and Dutch participants. This result indicated a more negative attitude towards robots from the Japanese participants, which they found to be surprising. The authors posited that the Japanese population in general had a wider range of exposure of robots and hence was better aware of their limitations.

In 2006, Nomura et al. [11] conducted an experiment with 53 students, 22 of whom were female and 31 male. Through this experiment, the authors were trying to investigate the relationship between negative attitudes and behaviors towards robots. The participants were all Japanese and the task involved interacting with Robovie. Like their 2004 study [12], the participants were asked to enter a room and talk with the robot and at the end the robot asked the participants to touch it. Prior to the interaction, the participants were asked to answer NARS and were also asked if they had prior experience with communicating robots. The authors noticed differences in the behavior of participants based on their NARS scores. The authors divided the participants into 2 groups based on their NARS score. The time before

which participants talked to the robots was less for participants that had lower S1 (interaction) scores than those that had higher score. This finding indicated that the tendency to avoid interacting with robots could be predicted based on NARS. The authors also found that female participants had less negative attitude than male participants on the S3 (emotion) subscale. Interestingly, they also found that the male participants stood further away than female participants.

Also in 2006, Nomura et al. [16] conducted a large scale study with 400 Japanese students, 197 of whom were male and 199 female. As part of this experiment, the authors asked the participants about their assumptions about robots using a survey similar to [13]. The authors found based on the assumptions described by the participants, most of the participants had a bias towards humanoid type robots. The authors also found that novel robot types and robots in situations involving battle evoked more negative attitudes towards robots. Since the authors only had Japanese participants, they warned against generalizing these results to people from other countries. However, it provides a compelling evidence to further investigate the assumptions of people from different countries and communities.

Bartneck et al. [3] conducted a larger cross-cultural study with a total of 467 participants from China, Germany, Japan, Mexico, Netherlands, United Kingdom, and United States in 2007. For this study, the authors used back-translation to translate NARS to the six languages. Their entire participant population was divided into two different groups: 237 participants from universities and 230 from the Aibo community. Like Nomura et al. [12], the authors found a significant gender difference on the social subscale (S2). The authors reported that "female participants were more positive on social than male participants." The authors also found that the Aibo community was significantly more positive on all three subscales compared to the other group. Finally, the authors found significant differences between participants of different countries. Although they found differences between the Aibo community participants and the other group, it was unclear as to the reasons for the differences. According to the authors, the less negative scores could have been the result of the participants' experiences with the robots. However, they also opined that the participants had robots because of their positive attitudes towards robots.

Nomura et al. [15] conducted an experiment to investigate the relationship between negative attitudes towards robots and the allowable interaction distance to robots in 2007. The authors recruited 17 Japanese students, 12 of whom were male and 5 female. The experiment was conducted using Robovie-M. The robot would move towards the participant until the participants asked the experimenters to stop the robot. Due to the low number of participants, the authors were unable to find statistically significant results with respect to NARS, but they did find a trend between the allowable distance and the NARS S2 (social) subscale.

Nomura et al. [14] conducted another study with 38 participants (22 males and 16 females) in 2008. The participants were Japanese students, and the subscales were in Japanese. The study's aim was to see if the participants' behaviors could be predicted based on the scores of NARS. Participants entered a room that had only the robot (Robovie) and then verbally interacted with and touched the robot. The authors found that the time difference from the participants being initially encouraged to touch the robot and actually touching the robot was reflected by the NARS-S2 subscale. They also found a positive correlation between the time that male participants took to talk to the robot after entering the room and the NARS-S1 subscale. The study found some differences for the female participants. They found that the distance at which the female participants stood from the robot was positively correlated by the NARS-S1 subscale and negatively by the S2 subscale.

### 2.2.2 NARS as a supplementary performance measure

Since NARS has been validated many times and across different cultures, HRI researchers have started using NARS in their experiments as a supplemental scale to help explain some of the differences that they observe. In 2009, Syrdal et al. [22] conducted an experiment with 28 participants from the University of Hertfordshire. The participants included both students and staff, with 14 female and 14 male participants. The robot, a PeopleBot from MobileRobots, had two different behaviors: socially ignorant and socially interactive. For the task, participants were required to physically interact with the co-located robot. The room that was made to resemble a living room. The tasks included moving around the room and interacting with the robot to get a pen. The robot had 2 sets of pre-defined behaviors with respect to the path that it took, the way it moved around the participant, and its speed. The participants were asked to evaluate the behavior of the robots. The authors found that NARS was useful in explaining the differences in behavior of the participants. Also in 2009, Cramer et al. [4, 5] used NARS in a video study with a Robosapien (described in the next section).

In 2010, Riek et al. [20] recruited 16 participants from a university in the United Kingdom. Of the 16 participants, 9 were female and 7 male. Riek et al. conducted a within subjects study to determine how people react to gestures made by BERTI, a humanoid torso robot. They used NARS in their experiment since NARS had been verified with British participants, particularly from universities. (See Riek et al. [20] for full details about the participants' highly varied backgrounds.) The authors showed the participants 12 different videos where the gesture types, style, and orientations were different. With respect to NARS, partici-

pants with negative attitudes towards robots were found to be less adept at understanding gestures.

### 2.3 Consistency Analysis of NARS (in English)

In 2009, Cramer et al. conducted an experiment in which they examined how people perceived a robot when physical contact and help style were factors [4, 5]. In the between subjects online survey, participants were asked to watch one of four videos featuring a Robosapien helping a woman using a word processing application on a computer. The woman has a computer problem, and the robot gives advice as to what she should do to recover her work. In the condition with physical contact, the woman tapped the Robosapien to get its attention for help, while the Robosapien touched the woman on the shoulder. The video also showed woman and the Robosapien sharing a hug and high-fiving each other at the end of the video. In the condition without the physical contact, the woman and the Robosapien only conversed. The style of the Robosapien helping the woman was also manipulated; the robot either helped when asked (reactive) or offered advice (proactive).

The participants then answered questions relating to how familiar they were with the robot in the video, to what extent they thought the person in the video should follow the robot's advice, and to what extent they would follow the robot's advice if they were the person in the video. At the end of the survey, participants were asked a subset of the NARS-S1 subscale questions with the original wording from [15] and modified S3 subscale questions in which two of the questions were altered from their original wording (Table 1). The participants rated each statement on a modified Likert scale from 1 (strongly disagree) to 7 (strongly agree) with 4 as "neither agree nor disagree."

Participants were divided into those having a positive attitude towards robots (NARS score below $\bar{x}=3.4$, $SD=1.0$) and those with negative attitudes (NARS score above $\bar{x}$). As reported in [4, 5], participants with a more negative attitude towards robots perceived the robot in the video as more machine-like and less human-like. They also thought the robot had less empathic abilities, was less dependable and less credible. They assessed the human-robot relationship as less close. Attitudes towards robots did not interact with effects of empathic accuracy or situational valence.

To establish the reliability of the English version of NARS, we computed the Cronbach alpha values for the two subscales used in this study. The Chronbach's alpha value measures the internal consistency of related questions [6].[2] We computed the Cronbach alpha to be 0.76 for NARS-S1 and 0.67 for the modified NARS-S3 subscale given the participants' responses to this survey. This result shows that the English translation of the NARS-S1 subscale can be used with people who speak English. Further, people are able to provide consistent ratings with NARS for interactions with robots shown in videos, as opposed to in person.

### 2.4 Discussion

NARS has been successfully validated and used in a range of different circumstances since its creation in 2004. NARS

---

[2]Nunnaly established that $\alpha > 0.7$ as a sufficient reliability coefficient [19]. George and Mallory categorize alpha values of 1.00-0.90 as "excellent," 0.89-0.80 as "good," 0.79-0.70 as "acceptable," 0.69-0.60 as "questionable," 0.59-0.50 as "poor," and 0.49-0.00 as "unacceptable" [7].

has been used with populations from several countries and with different robots (e.g., Robovie, Robosapien, PeopleBot, Aibo, BERTI). Recently, NARS has started to gain wider acceptance. However, as pointed out by Nomura et al. [13], NARS must be used in conjunction with a tool that also looks at how people perceive robots. Participants' perceptions about robots can be useful in explaining some of the variations that have been observed including cross cultural differences. For example, Bartneck et al. [2] suggested that the Japanese participants had a longer and richer exposure to robots and hence had a different perspective that led them to not rate as positively as the Dutch and Chinese participants. These differences could have been better explained if the assumptions that those participants made about the robots were known. The work done by Nomura et al. [13] in which they piloted a survey about people's assumptions regarding the types of robots, situations in which robots would be used, and the tasks that robots would perform needs to be refined and validated much like NARS.

In 2005, Bartneck et al. found that the Japanese participants had higher scores (and therefore had a negative attitude) than other participants. They hypothesized that because the participants were exposed to the robots for a longer period of time, they knew the limitations better. Yet in 2007, the same research group [3] found that participants who owned robots (Aibos) scored more positively on NARS compared to those participants who did not. This result seems at odds with the opinion expressed earlier in 2005. However, it should be noted that the Japanese participants who owned robots rated more positively than Japanese participants who did not in the 2007 study [3].

## 3. CASE STUDY: TELEPRESENCE ROBOTS

In all of the studies in Table 2, the participants perceived the robots to be autonomous, independent agents. In this paper, we examine if NARS can also be used for robots which clearly have a human involved in the operation of the robot. For example, telepresence robots can be thought of as mobile embodied video conferencing systems with live video and audio communication. In a sense, the person operating the telepresence robot is using it as a physical robot avatar. In the state of the art telepresence robots, an operator must log into a robot and manually drive the robot around. To this end, we conducted an online video survey of five telepresence robots and an in-person study of people operating two telepresence robots.

### 3.1 Study 1: Online survey validation

Using Amazon's Mechanical Turk [1], we conducted an online video survey of five telepresence robots in a between subjects experiment with 80 participants. We used a slightly modified version of NARS presented in English in [18]. We inserted one duplicate question in the S2 subscale. The duplicate question rephrased "I feel that in the future society will be dominated by robots" to "I feel that in the future, robots will be commonplace in society." As per the original Likert scale from [15], participants were asked to rate the NARS statements on a scale from 1 (I strongly disagree) to 5 (I strongly agree) with 3 as "undecided."

### 3.1.1 Experimental Design

In the survey, participants were asked to provide their demographic information, including age, gender, occupation,

Figure 1: Telepresence robots shown in videos (left to right): Willow Garage's Texai, SuperDroid's RP2W, Anybots' QB, RoboDynamics' Tilr, and Vgo Communications' Vgo. (Not to scale)

country of citizenship, and pet ownership. They then completed a baseline NARS rating. We also solicited information about their prior robot experience and their video game usage in the last 12 months.

Participants were asked to view three videos and answer the NARS questions after each video. In the first video, participants saw one of four of the Robosapien videos (chosen at random) used in Cramer et al.'s study [4, 5]. The second video was of the Anybots' QB robot.[3] The remaining video showed one of four telepresence robots: Willow Garage's Texai,[4] Vgo Communications' Vgo,[5] RoboDynamics' TiLR,[6] or SuperDroid's RP2W.[7] We created four versions of the survey for each of the remaining telepresence robots; twenty participants saw each video. We randomized whether the participants saw the QB robot as the second or third video. All videos of the telepresence robots demonstrated communication capabilities through the robot. All videos except RP2W showed people interacting with the operator through the robot; if the operator's live video was not shown on the robot, the operator view was also shown.

The average time spent on this survey was 1 hour 59 minutes (SD=3 hours 24 minutes). The median time was 52 minutes. It should be noted that due to the length of the survey, we allowed participants to take up to 24 hours to complete the survey but asked that they complete the survey in a single session. Participants were compensated $1.50 for completing the survey.

### 3.1.2 Participants

Seventy participants provided usable data. We discarded 10 participants' data due to submission of duplicate surveys, exiting the survey before completion, or incorrectly answering validation questions. Participants' ages ranged from 18 to 59 years ($\bar{x}$=28.66 years, SD=8.73); forty-one participants were male and twenty-nine female.

### 3.1.3 Results

For all seventy responses, we computed the Chronbach alpha values of the NARS responses in three places (shown

---

[3]http://www.youtube.com/watch?v=oN1lQcJHpO8

[4]http://www.youtube.com/user/WillowGaragevideo#p/search/4/UkG-OysZM6o

[5]http://multimedia.boston.com/m/31419836/vgo-the-videoconferencing-robot.htm

[6]http://www.youtube.com/user/robodynamics#p/u/3/RL3SKdHzF2M

[7]http://www.youtube.com/user/SDRRobots#p/u/6/zcmP57ibLYI

**Table 3: Study 1: Chronbach alpha values of NARS-Subscales** ($n_{female} = 29$, $n_{male} = 41$) **(Grey indicates "poor" or "unacceptable.")**

| | Baseline | | | After Robosapien video | | | After telepresence robot videos | | |
|---|---|---|---|---|---|---|---|---|---|
| | overall | female | male | overall | female | male | overall | female | male |
| S1 | 0.61 | 0.58 | 0.63 | 0.69 | 0.64 | 0.71 | 0.77 | 0.71 | 0.80 |
| S2 (original) | 0.63 | 0.64 | 0.61 | 0.70 | 0.69 | 0.72 | 0.78 | 0.83 | 0.75 |
| S2 (modified) | 0.56 | 0.50 | 0.58 | 0.62 | 0.61 | 0.64 | 0.69 | 0.76 | 0.63 |
| S3 | 0.80 | 0.82 | 0.79 | 0.81 | 0.87 | 0.73 | 0.80 | 0.82 | 0.78 |

in Table 3). First, participants were asked for their ratings in the demographic information section. They were asked for their ratings again in the replication of the Robosapien videos. Lastly, we aggregated the scores for all of the telepresence robots. We found that the participants had the least consistent scores for the NARS-S1 and S2 subscales in the baseline section before a robot was presented to them; this finding is not unexpected because the participants could provide scores based only on their experience or inexperience with real and fictional robots. However, after viewing the Robosapien video, the participants' scores for the S1 and S2 subscales moved from a borderline acceptable alpha value and then to a solid acceptable value after viewing the telepresence robot videos. For the NARS-S3 subscale, the Cronbach alpha values would be classified as good to excellent reliability according to George and Mallory [7].

Given the Chronbach alpha values in Table 3, we believe that the English translation of NARS is suitable for use with English speakers. In the demographic portion of the survey, we asked the participants for their current country or countries of citizenship and the country in which they have spent the most time residing. Twenty-nine participants reported the United States as their country of citizenship. Thirty-one participants were citizens of India, and the remaining were citizens of Australia (1 participant), Canada (2), Greece (1), Honduras (1), Russia (1), Singapore (1), Switzerland (1), and United Kingdom (1). There were no instances of dual citizenship. All participants reported spending the most time residing in their country of citizenship.

We found that participants responded significantly more positively to our question modification. In the baseline NARS rating, "commonplace" averaged 3.96 (SD=0.76) and "dominate" averaged 2.73 (SD=1.25) ($p<0.01$, $t(69)=7.45$). After seeing the Robosapien video, "commonplace" averaged 3.87 (SD=0.87) and "dominate" averaged 2.85 (SD=1.35) ($p<0.01$, $t(69)=5.42$). After seeing the telepresence robot videos, "commonplace" averaged 3.93 (SD=0.99) and "dominate" averaged 2.87 (SD=1.35) ($p<0.01$, $t(139)=7.63$). However, we computed the Cronbach alpha value for the S2 subscale with the "commonplace" question phrasing replacing the "dominate" phrasing and found that in all cases, the alpha value was lower as shown in Table 3. Interestingly, it appears that the "commonplace" question modification is somewhat consistent for the participants from the US and much less consistent for the participants from India ($\bar{x}_{US}=0.71$, $\bar{x}_{India}=0.20$,). However, there is no statistical difference in the NARS-S2 (modified) ratings between US and Indian participants overall or by gender.

## 3.2 Study 2: Controlling telepresence robots

From Study 1, we found that NARS can be used as a performance measure for videos of robots, which is consistent with prior research (e.g., [4, 20]). Further, we have shown that NARS can be used with videos of teleoperated robots by people. Our next step was to conduct an experiment to validate NARS with people who were operating telepresence robots. It should be noted that we used the original NARS, removing the modified NARS-S2 subscale question given the reduced overall consistency.

### 3.2.1 Experimental Design

We conducted a between subjects, in-person lab study in which participants were asked for their initial impressions of a telepresence robot. Participants were provided with an overview of the study and an informed consent form. After providing their consent, participants completed a demographic survey including age, gender, occupation, and computer usage and expertise. They then completed a baseline NARS rating. We also solicited information about their prior robot experience and their video game usage in the last 12 months.

Participants then operated one of two telepresence robots: an Anybots' QB or a Vgo Communication's Vgo (shown in Figure 1). The robot and associated interface was described by a test administrator, and the participants learned how to remotely operate the robot in a hands-on training session. Training ended when the participant felt comfortable operating the robot.

There were three tasks in this experiment. The first task was a navigation task through an office environment. The robot was placed at a starting location inside of a group cubicle, away from the participant. The participant was instructed to meet the second test administrator in a specified conference room. The second task was a communication task. Once inside the conference room, the participant engaged in a conversation with the test administrator who was sitting at a table. The third task involved viewing a dry erase board. A map of a sub-section of campus was drawn on a 4 foot high by 8 foot wide dry erase board. The participant was asked to provide instruction on how to drive the robot between two buildings (not connected or adjacent to each other).

After completing these tasks, the participant completed a post-experiment survey which included a NARS rating. The participant was debriefed by the test administrator and was shown the robot. The average length of a session from the overview of the experiment through debriefing was 1 hour.

### 3.2.2 Participants

Forty-one people participated in this experiment. Thirty-three participants successfully operated the robot. The remaining participants experienced technical difficulties and therefore did not complete the post-experiment survey; for the purposes of this analysis, we exclude their data.

Of the thirty-three participants who successfully drove the robot, twenty-three were male and ten were female.

Table 4: Study 2: Chronbach alpha values of NARS-Subscales (Grey indicates "poor" or "unacceptable.")

| | Baseline | | | After telepresence robot | | |
|---|---|---|---|---|---|---|
| | overall | G1 | G2 | overall | G1 (QB) | G2 (Vgo) |
| S1 | 0.72 | 0.79 | 0.67 | 0.65 | 0.80 | 0.64 |
| S2 | 0.62 | 0.66 | 0.63 | 0.74 | 0.62 | 0.76 |
| S3 | 0.58 | 0.70 | 0.48 | 0.66 | 0.67 | 0.65 |

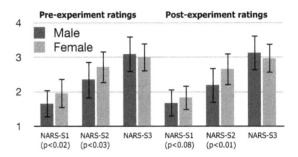

Figure 2: NARS ratings by gender ($n_{female}$=10, $n_{male}$=23). P-values are provided for significant differences found.

Eighteen participants reported their occupation as an engineer. Occupations of the fifteen remaining participants included program manager, financial analyst, product marketing manager, researcher, system administrator, researcher, and customer support. The average age of the participants was 30.6 years (SD=6.5) with a range of 23 to 49.

All participants had extensive experience with computers. Participants reported using a computer at work on average 44.3 hours per week (SD=7.9) and 19.7 hours per week (SD=13.0) in their free time. Seven participants reported moderate computer expertise, ten as experts, and thirteen as gurus. Participants reported using several different computer platforms: Macintosh (24 participants), PC (17), and Unix or Linux (21). Thirteen of thirty-three participants reported prior experience with robots.

Twenty participants reported that they played video games on average 3.3 hours per week. Thirteen played real time strategy games, and nine played shooter style video games.

### 3.2.3 Results

For the thirty-three participants, we computed the Chronbach alpha values for their baseline NARS responses from the pre-experiment survey and also for their responses provided in the post-experiment survey after having driven a telepresence robot (shown in Table 4). Fourteen participants used the QB robot (Group 1, or G1), and nineteen used the Vgo (Group 2, or G2). Using a two-tailed unpaired $t$-test with unequal variance, we found that there was no statistical difference between the baseline NARS ratings of the participants in G1 and G2.

As shown in Table 4, we notice that the NARS-S3 subscales borders on the edge of the "questionable" category with respect to consistency ($\alpha$=0.58). We further looked at G1 versus G2 and found that G1 has an acceptable level of consistency with $\alpha$=0.70, and G2's $\alpha$=0.48 falls into the "unacceptable" category. The inconsistency in G2's NARS-S3 ratings revealed a more interesting discrepancy.

Participants overall rated the statement "I would feel relaxed talking with robots" (NARS.S3.1) significantly higher ($\bar{x}$=3.61, SD=0.97) than the other two statements in the NARS-S3 subscale. The statements "if robots had emotions, I would be able to make friends with them" (NARS.S3.2) averaged 3.00 (SD=0.94), and "I feel comforted being with robots that have emotions" (NARS.S3.3) averaged 2.58 (SD=0.83). Using two-tailed paired $t$-tests, we found this difference to be significant ($p<0.01$ with $t(32)$=2.63 and 5.83 respectively). We hypothesize that this higher average rating for the statement "I would feel relaxed talking with robots" (NARS.S3.1) may be enhanced by the participants' extreme familiarity with technology including robots.

Aside from the NARS-S3 subscale being more inconsistent than expected, the remaining NARS subscale ratings from the pre-experiment survey appear to be somewhat consistent despite the fact that the participants likely provided ratings based on their experience and inexperience with real and fictional robots.

Using two-tailed unpaired $t$-tests with unequal variance on the NARS ratings after using the telepresence robot, we did not find any significant differences in the population overall between the two types of robots. However, like Bartneck et al. [3], we also found a gender difference between males and females. Bartneck et al. found that females were more positive than males in the NARS-S2 subscale (social); however, gender specific data was not directly reported [3]. In our study, we found that that females provided higher ratings (and therefore were more negative) than males for all of the NARS subscales for both the baseline and post-experiment survey (Figure 2). The female participants had more negative ratings for all of the NARS subscales with the exception NARS-S3 (emotion) for the baseline. After using the telepresence robots, the female participants had higher ratings for NARS-S1 and NARS-S2 subscales than the male participants. It should be noted that there was a small sample size for females ($n$=10) in this study with five using the QB robot and five using the Vgo robot.

## 4. CONCLUSIONS AND FUTURE WORK

We have shown the different uses of NARS by researchers (Table 2), which already shows some repetition of populations by country in these past 6 years. As the use of NARS increases, there will be more overlap and hopefully convergence to inform HRI researchers as to people's attitude towards robots by gender (which has already been seen), prior robot experience (already seen), age, and experience over time as suggested by Nomura et al. in [12]. While more data would further validate NARS, it is also important to understand the circumstances of its use. To this extent, the pilot study to investigate the assumptions by Nomura et al. [13] must be incorporated going forward.

The current version of NARS used in most studies is based on a translation from Japanese [18]. As seen in Cramer et al. [4, 5] and in our Study 1 (online video study of telepresence robots), alternative interpretations of NARS may provide items that read more naturally to native English speakers. We believe that it would be helpful to the HRI community to have a version of NARS written specifically in English and then back-translated to Japanese and validated in both languages. This basis would make it easier to translate NARS to other languages and reduce the chances of misrepresentation.

Based on our studies in which people watched videos of telepresence robots (Study 1) and in which people drove the telepresence robots (Study 2), we believe that NARS can be used in the genre of telepresence robots. We note that the consistency of NARS overall for Study 1 (all $\alpha > 0.77$) was higher than in Study 2 ($\alpha > 0.65$). We believe that this difference is due partly due to sample size (Study 1: $n=70$, Study 2: $n=33$). We also believe that the reliability between videos of robots and interactions with live robots impacted the consistency. As with any study with live robots as opposed to Wizard of Oz studies, our participants were exposed to the variance of the robot working correctly or not.

The work presented in this paper is different than almost all of the research conducted so far with NARS because telepresence robots inherently have a person in the loop. The results indicated that NARS could be applied to telepresence robots, an important finding given the rapid development of the telepresence robot industry. Because the genre of telepresence robots is in its infancy, now is the right time to figure out what people's attitudes towards these robots are and take corrective action, if needed. Work still needs to be done to validate NARS from the perspective of the people interacting with the operator through the robot.

## 5. ACKNOWLEDGMENTS

This research was funded in part by the National Science Foundation (IIS-0546309, IIS-0905228) at the University of Massachusetts Lowell and the ICIS project (BSIK03024) at the University of Amsterdam by the Dutch Ministry of Economical Affairs. The authors would like to thank Dr. Chris Uhlik of Google Engineering Research as well as Anybots and Vgo Communications for the use of their beta stage robots. The authors would also like to acknowledge Alia Amin of CWI, Vanessa Evers of the University of Amsterdam, and Bob Wielinga of the University of Amsterdam for their contributions to the Robosapien study. We thank Del Siegle of the University of Connecticut for use of his reliability calculator [21].

## 6. REFERENCES

[1] Amazon. Amazon Mechanical Turk: Artificial Artificial Intelligence, 2009. http://www.mturk.com. Accessed Dec. 2009.

[2] C. Bartneck, T. Nomura, T. Kanda, T. Suzuki, and K. Kennsuke. A Cross-Cultural Study on Attitudes Towards Robots. In *Proc. of the HCI Intl.*, 2005.

[3] C. Bartneck, T. Suzuki, T. Kanda, and T. Nomura. The Influence of People's Culture and Prior Experiences with Aibo on Their Attitude Towards Robots. *AI & Society*, 21(1):217–230, 2007.

[4] H. Cramer, A. Amin, V. Evers, and N. Kemper. Touched by Robots: Effects of Physical Contact and Proactiveness. In *Proc. of the ACM SIGCHI Conf. Workshop on "The Reign of Catz and Dogz"*, 2009.

[5] H. Cramer, N. Kemper, A. Amin, B. Wielinga, and V. Evers. 'Give me a hug': The Effects of Touch and Autonomy on People's Responses to Embodied Social Agents. *Computer Animation and Virtual Worlds*, 20(2-3):437–445, 2009.

[6] L. Cronbach. Coefficient Alpha and the Internal Structure of Tests. *Psychometrika*, 16(3):297–334, 1951.

[7] D. George and P. Mallery. *SPSS for Windows Step by Step: A Simple Guide and Reference, 11.0 update.* Allyn & Bacon, 2003.

[8] T. Hidano, M. Fukushima, M. Iwasaki, S. Soga, and C. Speilberger. STAI Manual, 2000. Tokyo: Jitsumu Kyoiku Shuppan. (In Japanese).

[9] K. Hirata. The Concept of Computer Anxiety and Measurement of It. *Bulletin of Aichi University of Education*, 39:203–212, 1990.

[10] J. McCroskey. *An Introduction to Rhetorical Communication.* Prentice-Hall Englewood Cliffs, NJ, 1982.

[11] T. Nomura, T. Kanda, and T. Suzuki. Experimental Investigation into Influence of Negative Attitudes toward Robots on Human-robot Interaction. *AI & Society*, 20(2):138–150, 2006.

[12] T. Nomura, T. Kanda, T. Suzuki, and K. Kato. Psychology in Human-robot Communication: An Attempt through Investigation of Negative Attitudes and Anxiety toward Robots. In *Proc. of the 13th IEEE Intl. Workshop on Robot and Human Interactive Communication*, pages 35–40, 2004.

[13] T. Nomura, T. Kanda, T. Suzuki, and K. Kato. People's Assumptions about Robots: Investigation of their Relationships with Attitudes and Emotions Toward Robots. In *Proc. of IEEE Intl. Workshop on Robots and Human Interactive Communication*, pages 125–130, 2005.

[14] T. Nomura, T. Kanda, T. Suzuki, and K. Kato. Prediction of Human Behavior in Human-Robot Interaction Using Psychological Scales for Anxiety and Negative Attitudes Toward Robots. *IEEE Transactions on Robotics*, 24(2):442–451, 2008.

[15] T. Nomura, T. Shintani, K. Fujii, and K. Hokabe. Experimental Investigation of Relationships between Anxiety, Negative Attitudes, and Allowable Distance of Robots. In *Proc. of the 2nd IASTED Intl. Conf. on Human Computer Interaction*, pages 13–18. ACTA Press, 2007.

[16] T. Nomura, T. Suzuki, T. Kanda, and K. Kato. Altered Attitudes of People Toward Robots: Investigation through the Negative Attitudes toward Robots Scale. In *Proc. AAAI Workshop on Human Implications of Human-Robot Interaction*, pages 29–35, 2006.

[17] T. Nomura, T. Suzuki, T. Kanda, and K. Kato. Measurement of Anxiety toward Robots. In *Proc. of the 15th IEEE Intl. Symp. on Robot and Human Interactive Communication at ROMAN*, pages 372–377, 2006.

[18] T. Nomura, T. Suzuki, T. Kanda, and K. Kato. Measurement of Negative Attitudes toward Robots. *Interaction Studies*, 7(3):437–454, 2006.

[19] J. Nunnaly. *Psychometric Theory.* McGraw-Hill, New York, 1978.

[20] L. Riek, T. Rabinowitch, P. Bremner, A. Pipe, M. Fraser, and P. Robinson. Cooperative Gestures: Effective Signaling for Humanoid Robots. In *Proc. of the 5th ACM/IEEE Intl. Conf. on Human-robot Interaction*, pages 61–68, 2010.

[21] D. Siegle. Reliability Calculator, 2000. Available at http://www.gifted.uconn.edu/siegle/research/Instrument%20Reliability%20and%20Validity/Reliability.htm. Accessed Aug. 2010.

[22] D. Syrdal, K. Dautenhahn, K. Koay, and M. Walters. The Negative Attitudes towards Robots Scale and Reactions to Robot Behaviour in a Live Human-robot Interaction Study. In *In Proc. of the AISB Symp. on New Frontiers in Human-Robot Interaction*, 2009.

# Teams Organization and Performance Analysis in Autonomous Human-Robot Teams

Huadong Wang
School of Information Sciences
University of Pittsburgh
Pittsburgh, PA 15260 U.S.A.
+1 (412) 624-9426

huw16@pitt.edu

Michael Lewis
School of Information Sciences
University of Pittsburgh
Pittsburgh, PA 15260 U.S.A.
+1 (412) 624-9426

ml@sis.pitt.edu

Shih-Yi Chien
School of Information Sciences
University of Pittsburgh
Pittsburgh, PA 15260 U.S.A.
+1 (412) 624-9426

shc56@pitt.edu

## ABSTRACT

This paper proposes a theory of human control of robot teams based on considering how people coordinate across different task allocations. Our current work focuses on domains such as foraging in which robots perform largely independent tasks. The present study addresses the interaction between automation and organization of human teams in controlling large robot teams performing an Urban Search and Rescue (USAR) task. We identify three subtasks: perceptual search-visual search for victims, assistance-teleoperation to assist robot, and navigation-path planning and coordination. For the studies reported here, navigation was selected for automation because it involves weak dependencies among robots making it more complex and because it was shown in an earlier experiment to be the most difficult. This paper reports an extended analysis of the two conditions from a larger four condition study. In these two "shared pool" conditions Twenty four simulated robots were controlled by teams of 2 participants. Sixty paid participants (30 teams) were recruited to perform the shared pool tasks in which participants shared control of the 24 UGVs and viewed the same screens. Groups in the manual control condition issued waypoints to navigate their robots. In the autonomy condition robots generated their own waypoints using distributed path planning. We identify three self-organizing team strategies in the shared pool condition: joint control operators share full authority over robots, mixed control in which one operator takes primary control while the other acts as an assistant, and split control in which operators divide the robots with each controlling a sub-team. Automating path planning improved system performance. Effects of team organization favored operator teams who shared authority for the pool of robots.

## Categories and Subject Descriptors

I.2.9 [**Artificial Intelligence**]: Robotics—*operator interfaces*

## General Terms

Human Factors, Measurement, Experimentation

## Keywords

Human-robot interaction, metrics, evaluation, multi-robot system, autonomy, team organization

## 1. INTRODUCTION

Unmanned vehicle systems (UVSs), whether in the air or ground, are intrinsically complex systems and rely on remote operator guidance to accomplish different missions. Specifically, applications for multi-robot systems (MRS) such as interplanetary construction or cooperating uninhabited aerial vehicles will require close coordination and control between human operator(s) and teams of robots in uncertain environments. Human supervision will be needed because humans must supply the perhaps changing, goals that direct MRS activity. Robot autonomy will be needed because the aggregate decision making demands of a MRS are likely to exceed the cognitive capabilities of a human operator. Envisioned missions such as search and rescue or underwater construction, however, will require multiple UV operators to work as teams to control a much larger team of UVs. For example, the Predator requires a team made up of three operators to be operational [1].

Controlling multiple robots substantially increases the complexity of the operator's task because attention must be shared among robots in order to maintain situation awareness (SA) and exert control. In the simplest case an operator controls multiple independent robots interacting with each as needed. A foraging task [2] in which each robot searches its own region would be of this category although minimal coordination might be required to avoid overlaps and prevent gaps in coverage especially if robots are in close proximity. Control performance at such tasks can be characterized by the average demand of each robot on human attention [3]. Because robots are operated independently an additional robot imposes only an additive demand on cognitive resources. Under these conditions increasing autonomy for individual robots should allow them to be neglected for longer periods of time making it possible for a single operator to control more robots.

For dependent tasks the round-robin control strategy used for controlling individual robots would force an operator to plan and predict actions needed for multiple joint activities and be highly susceptible to errors in prediction, synchronization or execution. For highly dependent tasks such as teleoperating robots to push a box, coordination demand for even two robots completely occupies an operator's attention excluding any other task [4]. A multi-UV, multi-operator discrete event simulation model has shown a similar steep increase in difficulty when teams of operators must control interacting robots as a team. [5]

If robots are not rigidly assigned to small teams under the control of a single operator, then each event requiring cooperation will either occupy more of an operator's attention than corresponding independent tasks or require the operator to find the controller of another robot and assume the communication and coordination overhead needed to coordinate with him. These interaction times are likely to be highly variable making it difficult to schedule interactions without introducing excessive idle times. Since even moderate variability in neglect time (NT) has been shown [6] capable of having an operator spending 90% of the time waiting, avoiding such bottlenecks is crucial.

We are developing a general architecture for controlling robot teams based on these observations. We begin by considering how operators self-organize to control robot teams and the effects of the different strategies they adopt. Two possible ways to impose organization on operators are through assigning a subset of robots to each or through a Shared Pool [7] in which operators service robots from the full population as needed. Robot assignment has the advantage of reducing the number of robots the operator must monitor and control. The shared pool offers the scheduling advantage of load balancing in that a pool of operators are available as robots need servicing eliminating situations in which one operator is overloaded and the other idle. Efficiencies such as improved SA that might result from controlling a dedicated team at a particular locale, however, must be sacrificed if operator attention is switched among robots following FIFO (first in first out) or similar discipline.

For monitoring, shared pool offers the redundant observer advantage in that a second observer with partially overlapping perceptual judgments may detect things missed by the first. We expect the effects of these advantages to interact with the types of autonomy possessed by the controlled robots. If navigation and path planning were fully autonomous, we would expect benefits to accrue to shared pool operators due to both scheduling and redundant observer advantages. Autonomous path planning should additionally lessen the effects of loss of SA due to switching between robots because only the victim-marking subtask would be affected. If robots were able to self-reflect and report when they need assistance we might expect to see a stronger scheduling advantage for shared pool. We would additionally expect to see substantial differences between types of autonomy in the numbers of robots that could be adequately controlled.

The present experiment compares performance of robot teams navigating either autonomously or using operator supplied waypoints. The teams were controlled by pairs of operators organized through assigned robots or as a shared pool. In recent experiments [10] we have found that participants performing an Urban Search And Rescue (USAR) foraging task using waypoint control were at or over their limits when controlling 12 robots each. Participants who were asked merely to explore showed very similar performance in area covered and reported similar levels of

workload on the NASA-TLX. Participants in a perceptual search condition in which the foraging task was performed without the requirement to navigate found twice the victims when monitoring 12 robots and reported substantially lower workload.

This paper continues this line of research by allowing robots to autonomously explore, while operators focus purely on the perceptual task. Specifically, we use autonomous path planning for 24 robots and require operators to focus on the perceptual task. Operators can also teleoperate robots that become stuck. There are distinct qualitative differences between the paths taken by autonomous robots and those laid out by human operators. Humans are able to use camera feedback and an intuitive understanding of the environment to reason about angles and perspectives that will give them the most information. The autonomous planning on the other hand, relied exclusively on occupancy grids generated from laser scan data. However, robots have the advantage of being able to focus exclusively on their path planning and work cooperatively to provide the most coverage. One of the question asked in this paper is whether the gain in search efficiency due to autonomous path planning outweighs the less natural paths and, presumably, poorer video angles that result.

The present study uses the same robots and environment but with teams of two operators assigned to control 24 robots. These operators controlled teams of 12 robots in the assigned robots condition. In the shared pool condition operators shared control of the 24 robots. Robots were navigated by operator assigned waypoints as in [10] in the manual condition and by an autonomous path planner in the autonomy condition. Participants were told they were a team and would share a joint score for the experiment. Because team organization was not dictated by the experimenter, operators were free to choose their own strategies for accomplishing their tasks. Strategies could vary over the course of the task. Operators might act with relative independence in the initial path planning phase, for example, while dividing monitoring duties later on. One of the goals of our experiment was to identify the coordination strategies that emerged and find the relationship between these strategies and performance.

## 2. Methods
### 2.1 USARSim and MrCS
The experiment reported in this paper was conducted using the USARSim robotic simulation with 24 simulated Pioneer P2-AT robots performing Urban Search and Rescue (USAR) foraging tasks. USARSim is a high-fidelity simulation of urban search and rescue (USAR) robots and environments developed as a research tool for the study of human-robot interaction (HRI) and multi-robot coordination. USARSim supports HRI by accurately rendering user interface elements (particularly camera video), accurately representing robot automation and behavior, and accurately representing the remote environment that links the operator's awareness with the robot's behaviors. USARSim uses Epic Games' UnrealEngine2 [11] to provide a high fidelity simulator at low cost and also serves as the basis for the Virtual Robots Competition of the RoboCup Rescue League. Other sensors including sonar and audio are also accurately modeled. Validation data showing close agreement in detection of walls and associated Hough transforms for a simulated Hokuyo laser range

finder are described in [13]. The current UnrealEngine2 integrates MathEngine's Karma physics engine [14] to support high fidelity rigid body simulation. Validation studies showing close agreement in behavior between USARSim models and real robots being modeled are reported in [15,16,17,18,19] as well as agreement for a variety of feature extraction techniques between USARSim images and camera video are reported in Carpin et al. [12]. MrCS (Multi-robot Control System), a multi-robot communications and control infrastructure with accompanying user interface, developed for experiments in multirobot control and RoboCup competition [20] was used in many experiments. MrCS provides facilities for starting and controlling robots in the simulation, displaying multiple camera and laser output, and supporting inter-robot communication through Machinetta which is a distributed multi-agent coordination infrastructure.

**Figure 1. The MrCS user interface with 24 robots for shared pool condition of both autonomy and manual groups.**

Figure 1 shows the elements of the MrCS. The operator selects the robot to be controlled from the colored thumbnails at the top of the screen. To view more of the selected scene shown in the large video window the operator uses pan/tilt sliders to control the camera. The current locations and paths of the robots are shown on the Map Data Viewer (bottom right). Under manual control, robots are tasked by assigning waypoints on a heading-up map on the Map Viewer (bottom right) or through a teleoperation widget (upper right). In the autonomous condition robots were equipped with autonomous path planning and could explore autonomously. In the shared pool condition the participants have equal authority to control every robot and modify marked victims.

## 2.2 Path Planning

Autonomous path planning was performed by a deterministic roadmap planner [20] developed using the Carnegie Mellon Robot Navigation Toolkit (CARMEN) [21] for these experiments. As input, the planner used the current occupancy grid representing the joint robot team knowledge of the environment and available information about the planned paths of other robots. Possible locations are generated and accepted or rejected based on the expected information gain for being at that location. The expected information gain was a function of the uncertainty in the occupancy grid around that point and whether or not another robot was known to be planning to go near that point. Edges were generated between nodes if the occupancy grid indicated a sufficiently high probability of being able to move between the locations. Finally, a branch-and-bound search was performed across the network of locations and edges for the path that maximized the expected information gain. Plans were allowed to backtrack, but no additional value was received for visiting a location multiple times. When a robot finished planning, it shared its planned path with some nearby robots to allow them to both avoid collisions and search distinct areas.

Figure 2 shows a screenshot of the path planning debugging interface. Green background shows unexplored areas, which brighter green representing higher uncertainty. Red background is the proposed path of another robot. Blue lines connecting blue circles show the possible locations and edges. The yellow line shows the planned path from the center of the window.

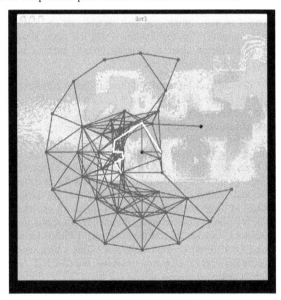

**Figure 2. Screen shot for path planning debugging interface**

## 2.3 Experimental Conditions

A large USAR environment previously used in the 2006 RoboCup Rescue Virtual Robots competition [20] was selected for use in the experiment. The environment was an office like hall with many rooms and full of obstacles like chairs, desks, and bricks. Victims were evenly distributed within the environment. The experiment followed a between groups design with 24 robots. Each task was performed by a team of 2 participants. The teams of participants in the autonomous condition were assigned 24 robots with autonomous path planning capability but they could also control one robot each time via teleoperation. Participants were instructed to use teleoperation only for helping stuck robots, not for exploration. The teams of participants in the manual control condition were assigned 24 robots, for which participants could issue sequences of waypoints as well as teleoperate any robot.

The users were seated at separate interfaces, were able to control the same robots and watch the same video and were able to communicate freely with one another. They were not given any specific instructions on how to coordinate, although they were told it was a cooperative task. Generally, the participants informally either divided the area or the robots between them. No difference was noticed in the different modalities.

## 2.4 Participants

60 paid participants (30 teams) were recruited from the University of Pittsburgh community balanced among conditions for genders. None had prior experience with robot control although most were frequent computer users.

## 2.5 Procedure

After providing demographic data participants read standard instructions on how to control robots via MrCS. In the following 30 minute training session, participants in all conditions practiced control operations. Participants were encouraged to find and mark at least one victim in the training environment under the guidance of the experimenter. After the training session, participants then began the experimental session (25 minutes) in which they performed the search task controlling 24 robots in teams. After the task, the participants were asked to complete the NASA-TLX workload survey.

Table 1 Performance Measures

| Variables | Autonomy (N=15) | | Manual (N=15) | | T-value | P |
|---|---|---|---|---|---|---|
| | $\overline{x}$ | SD | $\overline{x}$ | SD | | |
| Victim Found | 15.86 | 2.538 | 12.33 | 3.200 | 3.270 | .003 |
| Region Explored | 729.69 | 69.404 | 638.89 | 105.433 | 4.603 | .000 |
| Victim/Region ratio | 0.020 | 0.0026 | 0.193 | 0.0046 | 0.473 | .640 |
| RMS Errors | 0.521 | 0.1341 | 0.670 | 0.0988 | -3.424 | .002 |
| Missing Sequence | 69.71 | 18.898 | 43.07 | 15.714 | 4.140 | .000 |
| Select to Mark Time | 31.35 | 11.593 | 18.58 | 9.196 | 3.298 | .003 |

## 3. Result

### 3.1 Performance Measures

Table 1 shows the T-test results of performance measures between autonomy and manual conditions. Overall participants were successful in searching the environment in both conditions finding as many as 21 victims per team on a trial. The average number of victims found was 15.86 in the autonomous condition but only 12.33 for the manual control condition. A T-test showed that there was a significant difference for victims found in the two conditions (t (28) = 3.270; p= .003).

The region explored also showed a significant advantage (t (28) = 4.603; p < .001) for the autonomous condition. The extra exploration was likely due to the autonomous robots moving almost constantly, while in the manual case, an average of 7.66 robots were left after being given a single set of waypoints, with an average of 4.26 receiving no waypoints at all. It is clear from this result that taking the cognitively and time demanding task of exploration away from the operator and automating it helped overall system performance.

While participants enjoying automated path planning found more victims for which areas explored were comparable, their overall advantage in finding victims might have resulted simply from the greater opportunity afforded by exploring larger areas. To examine this possibility we tested the adjusted measure victims/region explored. A T-test was used to test the difference in the Victim/Region ratio among the autonomous and manual control conditions. The victims found per square meter had no significant difference across the two conditions (t(28) = 0.473; p = .640). This suggests that the difference in the number of victims found was exclusively due to the larger area searched.

Operator actions, robot states, and artifacts such as laser generated maps were collected throughout the experiment. Later, measures of operator behavior linked to victim observations were annotated in the data. After the user has successfully selected a robot, a series of actions need to be performed to develop sufficient situation awareness to perform the victim marking task, such as stopping the robot, viewing the map and locating the robot which may cost a certain period of time. Otherwise, when the victim passed out of the field of view (FOV) of a robot's camera, it was counted as a missed victim. T-tests showed participants in the Autonomy condition missed more victims, t(28)=4.140, p<.001. The select to mark time showed a similar pattern, t(28)=3.298, p=.003, with participants following manual control marking victims more quickly. However, the related issue of accuracy in marking victims on the laser generated map favored the autonomy conditions. T-tests showed smaller RMS errors in marking for autonomy participants, t(28)=-3.424, p=.002.

### 3.2 Team Organization

Since participants shared control of the 24 UGVs and viewed the same screens in the shared pool conditions, a responsibility allocation procedure was a necessary part of the task. In this study we observed three patterns of self-organization in the shared pool condition. Some of the participants practiced joint control controlling all 24 robots together, while others followed a Split control strategy by splitting the robots with each controlling a sub-team. A third group of mixed strategy teams failed to settle on an identifiable strategy and instead alternated between strategies suggesting joint or split control. As a result, the shared pool conditions in both autonomy and manual condition could be divided into subgroups according to the way the robots were controlled. (Table 2)

Table 2. Team Organization for shared Pool

| Condition | Split | Mixed | Joint |
|-----------|-------|-------|-------|
| Auto | 3 | 4 | 8 |
| Manual | 9 | 3 | 3 |

A chi-square test of independence was performed to examine the relation between autonomy and team organization (Figure 3). The relation between these variables was significant, $X^2_{(2, N = 23)} = 5.239$, p =.022, Manual condition participants were less likely to choose joint control than were Autonomy participants.

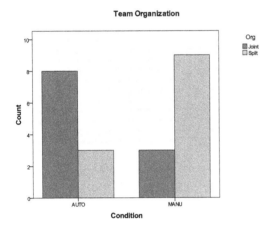

**Figure 3. Team Organization Counts**

A two-way ANOVA was conducted comparing strategies (joint, mixed, split) and the level of autonomy (auto vs. manual) for all the performance measures. A main effect for team organization was found for victim found per region explored, $F_{1, 26} = 3.627$, p= .042 (Figure 4).

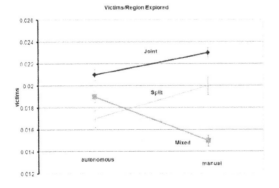

**Figure 4. Victims per Region Explored for shared pool**

Considering only teams with clearly discernible strategies (joint vs. split) T-tests show joint control participants found more victims, t(21)=-2.764, p=.012 (Figure 5). RMS error showed a similar pattern, t(21)=2.134, p=.045, with teams following joint strategies marking victims more accurately (Figure 6). However, joint control participants also missed more victims, t(21)=-3.836, p=.001.

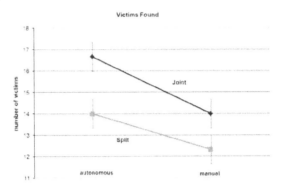

Figure 5. Victims Found for shared pool

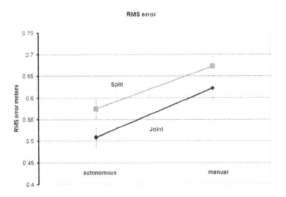

Figure6. RMS for shared pool

## 4. Discussion

### 4.1 Performance Measures

The current experiment with teams of two operators replicates the effects of automated path planning found in an earlier single operator experiment [10]. In both experiments, relieving operators of the need to perform path planning and manually controlling robots led to finding more victims and marking their locations more accurately. A deterministic roadmap planner using a distributed information gain algorithm was used in the current experiment to drive the robots unlike the previous study in which paths were played back from those generated by earlier participants. Operators appeared to have little difficulty in following these algorithmically generated paths and identified approximately the same numbers of victims as in [10] following human generated paths.

The extra exploration appears principally due to autonomous robots being able to move more or less continuously with only brief pauses. In the manual condition, by contrast, an average of 6.19 robots were left after being given a single set of waypoints, while an average of 3.13 received no waypoints at all.

Replication of the accuracy advantage for automated path planning was also reassuring because studies such as [23] suggested that this advantage might go in the other direction. Peruch et al. [23] demonstrated that self-controlled viewers tended to develop a rich survey knowledge more quickly than passive observers. Because operators in the manual control condition needed to match landmarks between camera views and the laser map, the active exposure to the environment offered by path planning and entering waypoints might have been expected to provide them a more detailed knowledge of the environment and hence greater accuracy in marking victims. Our replicated finding that automated path planning improves accuracy suggests that either the advantage in reduced cognitive load masks poorer survey knowledge in the autonomous condition or that the frequent switching between robots and viewpoints common to the two conditions allows autonomous participants to develop equivalent or superior survey knowledge.

Since avoiding missed targets is crucial to many foraging tasks such as de-mining or search and rescue, thoroughness may be more important than other performance gains such as widening the search area. The analysis of victims per region explored shows that in the assigned robot condition participants using automated path planning found twenty-two percent more victims. This gain is particularly significant because this group was exploring 67% of the map and coming close to matching the actual density of victims of .029/m2. Similar improvements in RMS error and reduction in reported workload suggest that substantial cognitive resources were required for navigation and became available for other subtasks improving overall performance when navigation was automated.

The process measures provide a somewhat different account. Operators in the autonomous conditions found more victims, explored regions more thoroughly, and marked victims more accurately, superiorities in performance of the sort often attributed to better SA. An examination of process measures, however, show the opposite may be true. Autonomous operators, however, miss almost twice as many of the victims that appear in their cameras, perhaps the result of attempting to monitor continuously moving robots which may have multiple victims in view. Select-to-mark time is much shorter in the manual conditions going as low as 18 seconds, approximately half of the 31 seconds required for autonomous operators controlling dedicated robots. These data suggest that operators in the autonomous path planning condition had, in fact, poorer SA than those choosing paths themselves. Although missing fewer of the victims appearing in their thumbnails operators in the manual condition had fewer opportunities as their robots were often idle at terminal waypoints while those in the autonomous condition moved continuously explaining their advantage on the overall performance measures. This account supports our earlier conjecture that reduced cognitive load may mask poorer survey knowledge (SA) in the autonomous condition. Confusions in marking in the shared pool condition are an additional finding with nearly half of the

markings in the shared pool condition leading to deletions while only ~16% did so when controlling dedicated robots.

## 4.2 Team Organization

A premise of our research is that if the supervisory control task can be made more similar to conventional alarm driven control, teams of operators will be able to control increasing numbers of robots due to advantages in load balancing and redundant observations. An overall advantage for Area Explored was not observed. We attribute this lack of effect to the weak contribution the assistance subtask made to team performance. While we had expected the office environment to provide many opportunities in which robots would require human assistance our results show that the robots (autonomous) managed to explore an equivalent area without any human assistance. Because the assistance subtask was the task we expected to benefit most from load balancing, its effects were muted. Suggestions of such effects, however, were found within the shared pool conditions. We hypothesized that increasing automation would improve shared pool performance which allows load balancing and redundant observations to a greater extent than assigned robot performance which does not.

This shared pool advantage was found but only for teams choosing the joint control strategy which allowed it. Joint control teams performance bettered in accuracy as well finding .021 and .023 victims/m$^2$ respectively in auto and manual conditions. A similar advantage for joint control participants was found in locating victims more accurately (Low RMS error).

These results add to a growing picture of the complex problem of controlling multiple robots with human teams. Such tasks are invariably a mixture of subtasks of varying difficulties and contributions. In this experiment the difficulty of the monitoring task dominated and human interventions of the sort described by the neglect tolerance model had little impact. In future studies we hope to examine a range of task/autonomy combinations to develop a more comprehensive theory of team for teams HRI.

## 5. ACKNOWLEDGMENTS

This research has been sponsored in part by AFOSR FA955008-10356 and ONR Grant N0001409-10680.

## 6. REFERENCES

[1] Cummings, M.L., Brzezinski, A.S. and J.D. Lee. 2007. The impact of intelligent aiding for multiple unmanned aerial vehicle schedule management. *IEEE Intelligent Systems: Special Issue on Interacting with Autonomy* 22(2): 52-59.

[2] Cao, Y., Fukunaga, A. and Kahng, A. 1997. Cooperative mobile robotics: Antecedents and directions. *Autonomous Robots*, 4, 1-23.

[3] Crandall, J., Goodrich, M., Olsen, D. and Nielsen, C. 2005. Validating human-robot interaction schemes in multitasking environments. *IEEE Transactions on Systems, Man, and Cybernetics*, Part A, 35(4):438-449.

[4] Wang, J. and Lewis, M. 2007. Assessing coordination overhead in control of robot teams. *Proceedings of 2007 IEEE International Conference on Systems, Man, and Cybernetics*, 2645-2649.

[5] Mekdeci, B. and Cummings, M.L. 2009. Modeling Multiple Human Operators in the Supervisory Control of Heterogeneous Unmanned Vehicles. *9th Conference on Performance Metrics for Intelligent Systems (PerMIS'09)*, Gaithersburg, MD.

[6] Goodrich, M., Morse, B., Engh, C., Cooper, J. and Adams, J. 2009. Towards Using UAVs in Wilderness Search and Rescue: Lessons from Field Trials. *Interaction Studies, Special Issue on Robots in the Wild: Exploring Human-Robot Interaction in Naturalistic Environments*.

[7] Lewis, M., Polvichai, J., Sycara, K. and Scerri, P. 2006. Scaling-up Human Control for Large UAV Teams. *Human Factors of Remotely Operated Vehicles, Advances in Human Performance and Cognitive Engineering Research*, Volume 7, 237-250.

[8] Gerkey, B. and Mataric, M. 2004. A formal framework for the study of task allocation in multi-robot systems. *International Journal of Robotics Research*, 23(9):939-954.

[9] Harchol-Balter, M., Crovella, M. and Murta, C. 1998. On Choosing a Task Assignment Policy for a Distributed Server System. *Proceedings of the 10th International Conference on Computer Performance Evaluation: Modelling Techniques and Tools*, 231-242.

[10] Wang, H., Lewis, M., Velagapudi, P., Scerri, P. and Sycara, K. 2009. How search and its subtasks scale in N robots. *Human Robot Interaction Conference, ACM*.

[11] (UE 2) UnrealEngine2. 2008. http://udn.epicgames.com/Two/rsrc/Two/KarmaReference/KarmaUserGuide.pdf.

[12] Carpin, S., Stoyanov, T., Nevatia, Y., Lewis, M. and Wang, J. 2006. Quantitative assessments of USARSim accuracy. *Proceedings of PerMIS*.

[13] Carpin, S., Wang, J., Lewis, M., Birk, A. and Jacoff, A. 2005. High fidelity tools for rescue robotics: Results and perspectives. *Robocup 2005 Symposium*.

[14] MathEngine Karma User Guide. 2005. http://udn.epicgames.com/Two/KarmaReference/KarmaUserGuide.pdf.

[15] Carpin, S., Lewis, M., Wang, J., Balakirsky, S. and Scrapper, C. 2006. Bridging the gap between simulation and reality in urban search and rescue. *Robocup 2006: Robot Soccer World Cup X,* Springer, Lecture Notes in Artificial Intelligence.

[16] Lewis, M., Hughes, S., Wang, J., Koes, M. and Carpin, S. 2005. Validating USARsim for use in HRI research. *Proceedings of the 49th Annual Meeting of the Human Factors and Ergonomics Society*, Orlando, FL.

[17] Pepper, C., Balakirsky, S. and Scrapper, C. 2007. Robot Simulation Physics Validation. *Proceedings of PerMIS'07*.

[18] Taylor, B., Balakirsky, S., Messina, E. and Quinn, R. 2007. Design and Validation of a Whegs Robot in USARSim. *Proceedings of PerMIS'07*.

[19] Zaratti, M., Fratarcangeli, M. and Iocchi, L. 2006. A 3D Simulator of Multiple Legged Robots based on USARSim. *Robocup 2006: Robot Soccer World Cup X*, Springer, LNAI.

[20] Balakirsky, S., Carpin, S., Kleiner, A., Lewis, M., Visser, A., Wang, J. and Zipara, V. 2007. Toward hetereogeneous robot teams for disaster mitigation: Results and performance metrics from RoboCup Rescue. *Journal of Field Robotics*.

[21] Latombe, J.C. 1991. *Robot motion planning*. Springer.

[22] Montemerlo, M., Roy, N. and Thrun, S. 2003. Perspectives on standardization in mobile robot programming: the carnegie mellon navigation (carmen) toolkit. *In Proc. of IROS*.

[23] Peruch, P., Vercher, J. and Guthier, G. 1995. Acquisition of Spatial Knowledge through Visual Exploration of Simulated Environments. *Ecological Psychology* 7(1): 1-20.

[24] Montemerlo, M., Roy, N. and Thrun, S. 2003. Perspectives on standardization in mobile robot programming: the carnegie mellon navigation (carmen) toolkit. *In Proc. of IROS*, Vol. 3, 2436- 2441.

[25] Lewis, M., Wang, H., Chien, S., Scerri, P., Velagapudi, P., Sycara, K. and Kane, B. (to appear). Teams for teams: Performance in multi-human/multi-robot teams, *Proceedings of the 54th Annual Meeting of the Human Factors and Ergonomics Society*.

# Intentions and Intention Recognition in Intelligent Agents

Dr. Gary Berg-Cross
Knowledge Strategies
gbergcross@gmail.com

Dr. Christopher Crick
Brown University
chriscrick@cs.brown.edu

## 1. INTRODUCTION

PerMIS 2009 included a special session that explored R&D work using the Theory of Mind (ToM) concept. Simply stated the ToM hypothesis is that intelligent agents attribute mental states to other agents in order to reason in a theory-like fashion about the causal relation between these unobservable mental states and the agents' subsequent behavior [53]. Such theories grow in part out of the consideration of the richness and complexity of primate social interactions, which have long been seen as a driver for the evolution of primate intelligence [34, 33]. Child research also suggests that as human infants develop they use knowledge of their own mental function as a model for how other agents function. When infants see others acting 'like me,' they construct and test a representational correspondence hypothesis that others have the same mental experience generating their behavior [44]. This is enhanced by the regularities of perceptions and actions of social interaction, where others act as if they are governed by a similar type of mind. Having a ToM is readily useful because it affords the possibility of profitably applying judgments, originally made about one's self, to others. The PerMIS session explored whether the ToM hypothesis can be testing and if the concept is useful to the goal of highly competent systems able to achieve goals in a relatively autonomous way [6].

The use of constructs like ToM follows a broad direction of research for intelligent systems (IS) and robotics. Over time we have seen a movement from deliberative robots, rooted in an early AI model, to one of reactive robots, followed by behavior-based robots and more recently intentional and motivational robots [42]. It is the potential of this latest thrust into intentionality and "intentional robots" that are discussed in this paper. Intentional plans and intentionality in the everyday sense of pursuit of plans and goals has long played a key role in "the folk ontology of mind". Starting with a vaguer formulation serving goal satisfaction, the concept of intention has matured through its long application in robotics, AI, cybernetics and IS. In part because of its clarified role in rational behavior, intentionality becomes a key concept in a wide range of disciplines from cognitive science to psychological theory. Indeed within the last ten years the development of intentional action and its understanding provided an integrative element to research as diverse as: imitation, early understanding of mental states and their properties, ToM and the recognition of others' intentions. Other work includes studies of goal-directed behavior in nonhuman animals, executive function, language acquisition, play and narrative understanding [68]. A good example of intention understanding within a ToM in animal cognition is Clayton et al's [15] study of scrub jay hiding and stealing cached food. In their study one group of scrub-jays sees another bird caching food and then is given an opportunity to make off with those caches. A second group is allowed to observe food caching, but has no opportunity to pilfer the caches. Several months later, the same 2 groups of scrub-jays are given the opportunity to cache food themselves under 2 conditions – either when observed or when alone after which they are allowed recover their cached food. Clayton et al. [15] report that only the birds with pilfering experience re-hid their caches in new sites. Such hiding would function to prevent future theft, and a parsimonious explanation for why only those birds with pilfering experience do this is because they exhibit a theory of other jay intentions and project (as in a ToM) this experience onto other scrub jays. This amounts to predicting future behavior based on their "knowledge" of likely intentions.

This paper reviews some of the thinking on, and evidence for, the importance of intentionality in cognitive agents. The remaining paper is organized into 4 following sections. First we provide a baseline review of developmental and primate work on intentions and intention recognition. These provide a firmer basis for understanding the role of intentions in cognition and why it is important for an IS. Following this we discuss some of the psychophysics of intentionality. The next section discusses intentionality involved in cognitive-social robots. A particular applied and practical focus is how to better understand the current and projected application of theories and models of biological intention to build intelligent adaptive systems that afford intention. Within this we discuss how useful intentions and their recognition appear in agent social interactions. As part of a developmental robotics approach, we sketch out a development architecture that incorporates intentions and protoplans. A final section sums up the discussion and provides some thoughts on the direction of future work.

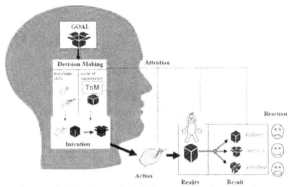

Figure 1 Simple model of Human intentional action
(adapted from Tomasello et al 2005).

Figure 1: Simple model of human intentional action
(adapted from Tomasello et al 2005)

## 2. REVIEW OF PRIMATE AND DEVELOPMENTAL WORK ON INTENTIONS AND INTENTION RECOGNITION

We start with a simple model in Figure 1 showing a central role of intentions integrating human perception, actions and problem solving (from [61]. Depicted cybernetically there, intentions support integrated perception, actions and decision making (e.g. choosing proper sub-goals from alternatives) which use models of current reality (e.g. environmental constraints) and goals (part of the mental constraints). At its extreme such models would include a ToM which could help orchestrate social interactions. This is shown as ToM ibeing used inside the Decision making process as a model of the current reality of an external person who is the subject of attentional focus. An agent's goal is shown an open (meaning extendable or modifiable in the future) box; reality is a closed (unchanging) box.

The actor chooses a means (plan), depicted as small hands doing things, which forms an intention. The resulting action (now the big hand) causes a change to reality, which leads to a reaction from the actor (shown as emotion icons). What Figure 1 depicts is an expansion of Bratman's [10] commonsense interpretation of human reasoning that an intention is a form of a plan – one of action that an organism chooses and commits itself to in pursuit of a goal. An intention thus includes both a means (action plan) as well as a goal. This idea of intentions was concretized as part of Bratman's belief-desire-intention (BDI) paradigm. The BDI framework has inspired designing in intentions as part of intelligent agents in an effort to achieve some balance between deliberative processes (deciding what to do) and means-ends reasoning (working out how to do things). In such BDI architectures, however, a relatively simple interpretation of intentions for traditional, directed problem solving domains must be hardwired in. A more dynamic model is represented in Figure 1. In this conceptualization things labeled (internal) goal, action, and attention (aka perceptual monitoring) are all seen as components within a larger, recursive cybernetic/adaptive system that serves to regulate an agent's behavioral interactions with the environment. Such a model allows intentions to play a central organizing role which pro-

vides a basis for a range of things form parsing perceptual input, understanding language, making moral judgments, interpretation linking external states and actions with internal ones, and predicting the future behavior of agents [4]. This is useful, for example, in the social-perceptual sphere since without intention recognition it is not evident how the exact same agent movements may be understood as "moving", "giving" or "loaning" an object. This recognition depends on the goals and the intention model which an agent consults along with its stored knowledge/skills and its mental model of current reality. This entire cognitive complex is "relevant" to recognizing the goals of action. A common example of misunderstanding goals occurs with young children where a caretaker may see a child's orientation to something like a box and think that the child desires something in the box. If the caretaker opens the box to give the child the contents, a negative reaction of the child may indicate that opening the box itself was the goal or part of the goal. In this and other cases the agent's chosen action is internally "rational" to the extent that it effectively accommodates the complex of knowledge, skills, and model of current reality.[1]

Taken as a whole then it seems plausible that we have a broad role for intentions in meaningful, social thought and motivated behavior that is beyond its use as simple tool for goal satisfaction. Two ways to investigate and understand intentional ability better are to investigate its evolutionary/phylogenetic development and how it develops in children ontogentically. Each of these research areas includes methods that do not rely on language expression, although those that do obviously show significant difference between verbal children and non-human animals. Early work relied on verbal reports and anecdotes, which were used to capture intuitions on intentional hypotheses [51]. More recently tight non-verbal, behavioral measures, such as gaze, have firmed up a converging, empirical and conceptual basis for intentionality. Likewise intention's relations to other concepts have come into sharper focus through its role in social cognition and the interpretation of everyday events [61]. Thus at least some intentions result in typical concrete behavioral action (represented by the large hand icon in Fig. 1) which are often accompanied by signifiers of persistent, purposive effort and/or evidence of attention [61]. This is usually clearest in social events involving agents that routinely engage objects and other agents. Such experimental results support a commonsense view that social cognition and what we know about others – the ability to perceive, interpret, and explain the actions of others – relies on the use of intention and intentionality to structure agent interactions which are understood as purposeful.

Increasingly studies directed at understanding intentionality compare the behavior of non-human primates with that of human children [64]. As previously noted, principle reasons to investigate intentions and intention recognition in non-human animals is to better understand its evolutionary

---

[1]Tomasello et al (2005) notes that 3 types of engagement emerge sequentially:

1. Dyadic action engagement: Sharing behavior and emotions.

2. Triadic engagement: Sharing goals and perception.

3. Collaborative engagement: All of the above plus joint intentions and attention.

roots and to check specific ideas and hypotheses. Generally speaking, an evolutionary argument for the emergence of animal cognition provides that a richer mental or inner world allows those animals so endowed to simulate a number of different actions ahead of time in order to test out possible consequences and evaluate them [3, 32, 29]. It is, for example, a tool for future-directed cooperation which involves dynamically generated, new goals that lack fixed values. Looked at this way the representation of intentions may serve as a bridge from the present to future possibilities as it embodies a form of symbolic, independent representations the coordinates means and goals [11]. On the whole, however, opinions remain divided on the question of whether non-human primates have a full, working theory of intentionality [24]. The chimp Sarah's success at solving problems after watching videos of a person solving various problem (getting out of a locked cage) lead Premack and Woodruff [54] to interpret this at evidence that she understood the objectives of the human in the films. The alternate explanation is that Sarah was less aware and just stored associations between the pictures and the problematic situations without having an understanding of human intentions.

The previously cited work of Tomasello et al [61], however, is illustrative of subsequent work on these issues, suggesting a degree of continuity in higher processes between humans and non-human primates. The rational "imitation" ability of agents' behavior seen by Gergely et al. [26] in young children is apparently shared to a large extent by chimpanzees [12]. Both children and non-human primates can be tested in naturalistic social settings with subjects being nonverbally requested to help the experimenter achieve goals, such as picking up a dropped sponge or opening a box. Earlier studies by Call et al. demonstrate that chimpanzees, like children, are able to distinguish between a person unwilling to perform a task, from one who is unable to help [13]. Tomasello et al. [61] advanced this work by a chimpanzees study using a food test for intention recognition. In the procedure a human began giving food to an ape through a hole in a transparent wall, but sometimes refusing to give it to the ape and sometimes attempting to give it to the ape but "failing" in the attempt. The chimpanzees gestured more and left the area earlier for humans in the unwilling situations than the unable. In the unable situation chimps tended to wait patiently throughout the unsuccessful attempts. The interpretation of these results supports the hypothesis that chimpanzees have some representation of the intentions of others – they understood the intention behind the human's failure behavior. Chimps also imitate human behavior on acts when they are successful in achieving a goal and not when they fail [49] . However, as Gardenfors [24] points out a limitation of the experiment is that what was tested was whether an action is intentional or not. It does not directly test show that the chimps had a mental representation of the contents of a specific intention. Such representations, Gardenfors believes, are a capability characteristic of human children but not of apes. As he notes it remains "for the development of new experimental paradigms before it can be judged to what extent other species understand the intentions of others." Interest in such better measures is consistent with the theme of PerMIS in pursuing a more rigorous definition of intentions and how they are recognized.

One limitation of apes seems to be some aspect of language involved in shared or social intentions. Warneken &

Tomasello [64] have been able to show that chimpanzees, like 18 month-old children, recognize the intent of simple requests (e.g. picking up a dropped object) about equally. But children are able to respond to more complex language-like requests. This limits the full range of collaborative activities to human children. Shared intentions (important for games) may emerge when individuals, who understand one another as intentional agents and interact socially. These may become collaborative interactions where participants have a shared goal (such as building towers with blocks) and coordinated action (such as one child taking the block-gatherer role as a help to pursue the overall shared goal of building a tower).

Methodologically both the child and animal studies have expanded ways in which we can identify both intention-in-action [58] and well as intention recognition through performance. Intention-in-action roughly corresponds to judging the biological plausibility of observed self-executed motor sequences (e.g. an effector tracing a continuous spatiotemporal path towards the object to be manipulated) to decide they are evidence for agent intentions. Early studies by Newtson & Engquist [50] demonstrate that human adults watching videoed action show a high degree of inter-rater agreement as to the beginnings and endings of intentional actions. Subsequently this finding, supported by child studies using infant looking times as evidence for perceived boundaries in a behavior stream, shows that they have similar boundaries to those rated by adults [1]. And we now know that even young children (18 months) readily distinguish between such intentional and unintentional behavior; identify the intentions underlying others' behavior; explain completed actions with reference to intentions, beliefs, and desires; and evaluate the social worth of actions using the concepts of intentionality and responsibility [41]. Developmentally there is now a large amount of evidence for a theory of infant development reflecting the type of inter-subjective behavior (i.e. inter-affective, inter-attentional, and inter-intentional) afforded by the cognitive architecture shown in Figure 1 [60]. There is evidence for a natural sequence to these. For example, communicative intentions can be recognized in others' behavior before the content of these intentions is accessed or inferred [20]. Intention recognition uses all of the processes shown in Figure 1 starting with an infant's recognitions that others as agents are capable of spontaneous actions – i.e. acting animatedly [67]. This is followed in 9-12 month olds who infants understand the basics of goal-directed action. They recognize that others are pursuing goals and that they will persistent upon failure, accidents or around obstacles. They seem to understand that goal success means that directed actions will stop. Later they understand that others are rationally choosing between which of various plans to implementat, and that this is an intentional act that fits with perceived reality as depicted in Figure 1. Intentionality thus provides the interpretive framework to explain why we perceive agent behavior as humans do. Children, for example, are skillful in social discernment of what others are perceiving, intending, desiring, what they know and believe. There are a wide range of phenomena to consider, but developmentally it can be argued that the foundational skill is that of understanding intentions.

Intention recognition (IR) is the process by which an agent becomes aware of the intent of others. IR is clearly important because as connected devices and intelligent agents advance and multiply we face an increasing coordination challenge. IR will be necessary for truly smart agents that anticipate needs to help agents negotiate over perceived reality and action plans.

Simple psychophysical processes that underlie the detection of others' intentional states appear to be irrepressible instincts that develop quickly in children, around the age of 9 months [55]. Through habituation studies of infants watching animated circles moving about on blank screens, Rochat, Striano and Morgan found that "infants do appear to become increasingly sensitive to subtle changes potentially specifying intentional roles" in abstract, low-context displays. When shown a video in which one circle chased another, the older (8-10 month) children were more likely than the younger ones to notice when the circles' roles (chasing vs. fleeing) suddenly switched.

This low-level processing skill develops early in children, and is accompanied by the development of other social skills [21, 27, 22], such as the attribution of agency and intentionality. Csibra found that children (again, at nine months but not at six) were able to interpret goal-directed behavior appropriately. An experimental group was shown a small circle proceeding across the visual field toward another circle, making a detour around an interposing rectangle. When the rectangle disappeared, the infants expected to see the circle move straight at the other, and were surprised when the circle moved in the same detour path that it took around the obstacle.

Csibra and his group conducted several other experiments to control for various confounds, such as the possibility that infants merely preferred the circle's straight-line approach, all else being equal. For example, by habituating the children to a circle that did not take a direct line toward a goal when one was available, they found that the differential dishabituation noted above disappeared. This, they reasoned, was because the infants no longer believed the behavior of the circle to be rational and goal-oriented. The social cognition undertaken by these children depends entirely upon their interpretation of the relative motion of these simple figures.

Attempting to determine and to model when and how typical children develop the social skills that these animations demonstrate is one avenue of research; another emerges when one looks at what happens to people whose ability to do so is impaired. Heberlein and Adolphs [30] investigated the performance of one such person, a victim of the rare Urbach-Weithe disease, which causes calcifications in the anteromedial temporal lobes [59] and completely ravaged the subject's amygdala and adjacent anterior endorhinal cortex. Asked to describe a simple animation similar to those used by Heider and Simmel [31], she used language that almost completely ignored any of the social or intentional implications that control subjects invariably mentioned, treating it entirely in terms of the abstract motion of abstract shapes. However, her inability to anthropomorphize reflexively in this way was not due to a general social deficit – she was able to describe social scenes involving dogs and children perfectly well. The authors conjecture that her amygdala damage impaired a deep automatic social-attribution reflex, while leaving intact her ability to reason and deliberately retrieve declarative social knowledge.

Researchers working with individuals on the autism spectrum have used Heider and Simmel animations to uncover similar social attribution deficits. Ami Klin [36] presented the animation to twenty each of autistic, Asperger's and normally developing adolescents and adults, and gave them each the opportunity to describe and answer questions about their interpretation of the shapes' activity. He found a marked difference between the tendency of the clinical groups and the controls to attribute agency and intentionality to the shapes, and to situate the scenario in a social milieu. For example, a typical narrative from a normally developing adolescent: "The smaller triangle more like stood up for himself and protected the little one. The big triangle got jealous of them, came out and started to pick on the smaller triangle." In contrast, an autistic adolescent with comparable verbal IQ: "The small triangle and the circle went around each other a few times. They were kind of oscillating around each other, maybe because of a magnetic field." In all, Klin found that the clinical groups noticed only about a quarter of the social elements usually identified by the controls.

## 3. THE PSYCHOPHYSICS OF INTENTIONALITY

The study of intention recognition draws from and contributes to investigations of the fundamental cognitive processing modules underpinning perception and interpretation of motion. Sixty years ago, the Belgian psychologist Albert Michotte performed hundreds of experiments investigating our tendency to attribute causality to low-context motion [46, 47]. Using a primitive animation apparatus consisting of a rotating disc, some number of colored lines painted in various swirls, and a slit which caused the lines to appear as points to the observer, he found and characterized a number of irresistible perceptual effects. For example, when one animated circle approaches another, stationary, circle, and upon reaching it stops its motion while the previously fixed one begins to move, observers invariably perceive the second circle's motion to caused by the impact of the first, an effect Michotte named "launching".

We appear to possess special-purpose perceptual modules responsible for our rapid and irresistable computation of physics-based causality. Gelman [25] and Tremoulet [62] showed that trajectories alone are enough to stimulate the perception of animacy or inanimacy. When shown small particles moving about, subjects reported greater animacy from objects that made large speed or direction changes, especially if such changes violated our physical intuitions about Newtonian mechanics. True, context has an effect – when subjects had access to orientation information as well as trajectories, they made somewhat different determinations. In later work, Tremoulet attempted to investigate the role of context more thoroughly [63]. Subjects watched a particle move along an angled trajectory, while another object was also present. That object's location affected the perception of the particle's animacy: if the particle's trajectory appeared to turn either toward or away from the object, the event looked much more animate and intentional.

Cognitive neuroscientists have looked for evidence of these animacy processing modules in the brain. Blakemore [7] conducted an fMRI experiment where subjects watched an animation where two objects interacted. One object colliding with another, causing a Michottean launching effect, activated the middle temporal gyrus. When the objects changed direction of their own accord, consistent with animacy perception, subjects' right lingual gyrus lit up. And one object orienting itself towards the other's motion, interpreted as attention, involved the superior parietal lobe. These results lend additional credence to the idea that these sorts of perceptions are the result of localized, bottom-up neural processing.

Another demonstration of animacy processing in the brain comes from an fMRI experiment by Wheatley [65]. Her subjects watched an object move on a cartoon background with recognizable features. A simple triangular object moved in a figure-8 pattern, in front of a background that looked either like a frozen lake or a tabletop strewn with toys. The idea was for the same motion to be taken as animate in one context (an ice skater on a pond) and inanimate in another (a spinning top). And indeed, nearly all of the subjects reported the expected bias, given the background. Strikingly, the whole suite of brain regions that have been identified as contributing to social cognition, from the amygdala to the medial frontal gyrus, was much more active when the stimulus was taken to be animate. The authors speculate that animacy perception primes the whole apparatus of social cognition.

If this is true, a deficit in perceiving animacy may disrupt all manner of social development. Rutherford [56] reports on experiments with autistic children that suggest that animacy perception in individuals with social deficits is less reflexive and automatic than for typically developing children and those with non-social developmental disorders. Rutherford presented these three categories of children (typically-developing, socially-unimpaired but developmentally disabled, and autism spectrum) with animations of moving circles. In the control condition, the children were asked to determine which of two balls was heavier, using Michottean stimuli such as one ball rolling towards another at high speed and hitting another, which rolls away slowly. All three groups of children learned to distinguish the heavier from the lighter ball at about the same rate. In the experimental condition, where, for example, one circle moves out of the way of another, the children were rewarded for picking the circle that moved in animate fashion. The autistic children took, on average, twice as many trials as the typically developing children to learn to distinguish animate from inanimate. Interestingly, though autistic children had a harder time with the animacy task than the weight task, typical ones picked up on animacy much faster. However, once the children had learned to distinguish animate from inanimate motion appropriately, there was no difference in the performance of the various groups when faced with previously-unseen test data. Thus, these animacy cues are available to perception, and can be learned, even by autistic children. Modeling the interpretation of these perceptual cues, as our system does, may help illuminate both the initial difficulties and the learned compensatory mechanisms observed in autistic individuals.

These modules appear responsible for our rapid and irresistable computation of physics-based causality [14], as well as facile, subconscious individuation of objects in motion independently of any association with specific contextual features [39] [57] [48]. Furthermore, different processing modules appear to attend to different levels of detail in a scene, including global, low-context motion [40].

## 4. INTENTIONS IN COGNITIVE-SOCIAL ROBOTS

These psychophysical results are immediately useful in designing computational models of intentionality. Pantelis and Feldman [52] designed artificial agents governed by simple interaction rules, and present behaviors to test subjects for evaluation. They thereby determine how humans assign intentions and personality to behaviors under explicit programmatic control. For example, perceptions of hostility vs. friendliness depended very much upon the agents' behavior with respect to others at a very specific and narrow radius of interaction.

Peter Todd and his colleagues have used simple animations of the Heider and Simmel variety for testing simple social classification heuristics [28, 2]. They asked subjects to generate animations via a game: two people sat at computers and controlled two insect-like icons using a mouse, producing simple socially significant scenarios such as "pursuit and evasion", "play" or "courting and being courted". Using these animations, they tested the ability of adults and children to categorize the interactions properly. They discovered that three-year-old children are able to distinguish, say, chasing from fighting, at rates above chance, and four- and five-year-olds perform better still. A sample of German adults was able to distinguish the six different tested intention regimes around 75% of the time, significantly better than children. Furthermore, the authors performed a cross-cultural study, looking at the categorization performance among Amazonian hunter-gatherer tribespeople. Their scores were nearly identical to those of the German adults, suggesting that the ability to intuit intention from this low-context data is not merely a cultural artifact.

Crick and Scassellati [16, 17, 18, 19] investigated intention recognition in real-world scenarios of actual playgraound games. Their system generated genuine narratives to explain the roles, goals, intentions and rules to in-progress playground games. In addition, the simplicity of the stimuli and their computational tractability enabled them to implement an intention-recogntion system as a robot controller, enabling them to explore the relationship between *watching* a game and *participating*. When taking an active part, the system was able to probe uncertainties in its learning, collapse ambiguity by performing experiments, and explore how motor control relates to social interaction [66].

Computational intentional models such as these are an active area of development. Whether with real robots such as Crick's, or in simulated worlds such as Kerr and Cohen's CAVE model [35], a fundamental question is how intentions develop within a cognitive architecture. Recently the development and use of intentions has been investigated by ontogenetic developmental robotic (DR) approaches. A DR approach takes its inspiration from developmental psychology and developmental neuroscience as opposed to the earlier behavior-based robots whose design includes fixed "motivations" that are hardwired in their structure. DR work includes studying prolonged epigenetic development to elucidate general mechanisms of intelligence development, starting with proposed cognitive development mechanisms such as motivation, shared attention, intention recognition etc. Taken as a whole DR work provides a potentially interesting and useful perspective on how to build an artificial adaptive agent, as well as to better test particular developmental the-

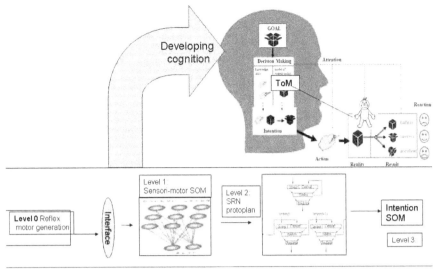

## Figure 2 Blank et al (2005) Developmental Architecture in Intentional Context

Figure 2: After Blank et al (2005)

ories including intentions. Typically work involves embedding a suitably adaptive[2] and developmentally capable IS within an ecological context so it can learn in a dynamically changing environment filled with multiple streams of raw, uninterpreted sensory information. Developmental agents are endowed with general abilities such as hierarchies of abstraction capabilities that over time enable it to control its actions and focus its attention on the most relevant features of its environment. Based on these abstractions, the robot will be able to predict how its environment will change over time, and go beyond simple reflex behavior to more purposeful behavior. DR sees this as a natural part of a developmental process driven by internally-generated motivations and instrumental tools such as ToM. These push and pull a developing agent toward ever higher-level abstractions and more complex predictions. The idea is that, as an ongoing ontogenetic development of an agent's control structure proceeds, it constrains and simplifies learning enough be make them tractable [45]. Just this idea of an agent's ongoing emergence and continued refinement of its skills has been featured at previous PerMIS workshops [5, 8]. While the role of intentions was not a specific focus it is easily incorporated into the existing architecture vision. What this work fleshes out is how a hierarchical, "developmental architecture" (Figure 2) embodies related algorithms and bottom up processes, generating abstract intentional plans from interactions with the environment. As shown in the figure, the agent starts out at Level 0 with just reflex endowments that are analogs of Piaget's first sensory-motor circular reactions, as well as some specific higher levels that look down on the lower levels and recursively learn from their activity as the

agent engages with the environment. The robot is driven by two competing motivations – to avoid boredom and achieve control over its actions. Over time these are afforded by the higher levels. Level 1 is made of a self-organizing map (SOM) which maps a "high"-dimensional input vector to a cell in a lower-dimensional matrix [37]. In this architecture the SOM "observes" the sensor and motor values that are produced as Level 0 controls the robot. Through this observation, Level 1 begins to form associations between sensors and motors and abstractions about sensors and motors within its self-organizing map. Eventually, when Level 1 has successfully captured the control information from agent interactions, these more effectively control the developing robot. A Level 2 structure observes the sensor/motor associations developed within the self-organizing map of Level 1. This structure allows the robot to anticipate events, enabling the robot agent to predict its own future. Level 2 uses a simple recurrent network (SRN) architecture [23] to recognize sequences of sensor-motor associations through time, enabling prediction what the next Level 1 state will be given its current state.

Previous work [43] has shown that this type of simple recurrent network develops representations of multi-step behaviors that might be termed protoplans. One nice thing about this architecture is that engagement with other agents allows the developmental architecture to create protoplans that reflect the actions and others. This in turn is built on by Level 3 which observes the protoplans developed by Level 2 and uses algorithms to categorize them, forming abstract version of plans. Driven by the need to master interactions with other intelligent agents these could include other agent intentions to predict agent behavior, and could leverage models of their own behavior to do this. Taken as a whole the developmental architecture of Blank et al [8] provides a parsimonious, if preliminary, model by which

---

[2]E.g. an intelligent agent should be motivationally autonomous and include adaptive control structures that manage dynamic interactions with its environment.

intentions recognition may be formed developmentally in a robot. It also provides insight into a cognitive architecture that can support and generate a ToM.

## 5. SUMMARY AND DISCUSSION

This final section sums up the discussion and provides some thoughts on the direction of future work. In this paper we argued for a central role of intentions and intention recognition in IS work. In the first section, we discussed some of baseline work on primate and child cognition studies that provide a basis for this role. In the second section we outlined studies on the neurological, psychological, and physiological foundations of intentions and IR. Follwing this we discussed some efforts to apply these ideas to cognitive robots and sketched out one developmental architecture that indicates how such a capability may emerge. We are still early in the work of development of computational models of intention-recognition. However Bello et al [4] has already shown how consideration of intentionality requirements focuses principled design choices for the construction of IS. E.g.:

- The relation of intention to other mental concepts self reflection, joint attention, communication, imitation

- Modular vs. explanatory theory formulations of intentional robots.

It should be noted that Kozma et al. [38] also provide some initial, dynamic models as ideas for how a ToM and intentions may emerge in human cognition and be implementable in intentional robots.

Questions that remain are how important is intention to levels of autonomy and other basic issues in robotics. These await formal testing and are obviously subject to clarification of autonomy levels which is not represented in either of the architectures of Figure 1 or 2. Autonomy and even several levels of autonomy is implied, however, since such an agent's behavior is directed based on initial learning experiences in specific aspects of their environment. It can be expected that work in DR will provide some useful data on this issue. Of particular use would be an applied and practical focus showing how to better understand the current and projected application of theories and models of biological intention to build intelligent adaptive systems that afford intention.

Consistent with the theme of PerMIS, research and development on intentions needs to pursue more rigorous definition of intentions and how they are recognized. A start on this has been made, but much more development is needed. We believe that development of more rigorous metrics to quantify, and indeed to detect and recognize, intent in manmade devices would be an important step towards the benchmarking progress. An obvious challenge is that measures of such rationality may not be obvious to an outside observer because they are not observable, at least before actions. This makes intention-centered systems a challenge to naive performance models and thus a very interesting topic for PerMIS consideration. Boesch [9], for example, addressed the methodological problem in many study comparisons between humans and other apes. He notes that in tests of social cognition, humans are used as stimuli and caregivers are present when during testing human infants.

Boesch concludes that we still need more studies on the cognitive capacities of humans applying the same conditions as those used for animals before we conclude on "evidence" for the absence of cognitive abilities.

## 6. REFERENCES

[1] D. Baldwin and A. Baird. Action analysis: a gateway to intentional inference. In P. Rochat, editor, *Early Social Cognition*, pages 215–240. Lawrence Erlbaum Associates, 1999.

[2] H. Clark Barrett, Peter M. Todd, Geoffrey F. Miller, and Philip W. Blythe. Accurate judgments of intention from motion cues alone: A cross-cultural study. *Evolution and Human Behavior*, 26:313–331, 2005.

[3] L. W. Barsalou. Perceptual symbol systems. *Behavioral and Brain Sciences*, 22:577–609, 1999.

[4] Paul Bello, Nicholas Cassimatis, and Kyle McDonald. Some computational desiderata for recognizing and reasoning about the intentions of others. In *Proceedings of the AAAI 2007 Spring Symposium on Intentions in Intelligent Systems*, 2007.

[5] Gary Berg-Cross. Developing knowledge for intelligent agents: exploring parallels in ontological analysis and epigenetic robotics. In *Performance Metrics for Intelligent Systems (PerMIS)*, 2006.

[6] Gary Berg-Cross. Is an agent theory of mind (tom) valuable for adaptive, intelligent systems? In *Performance Metrics for Intelligent Systems (PerMIS)*, 2009.

[7] S.-J. Blakemore, P. Boyer, M. Pachot-Clouard, A. Meltzoff, C. Segebarth, and J. Decety. The detection of contingency and animacy from simple animations in the human brain. *Cerebral Cortex*, 13:837–844, 2003.

[8] D. Blank, D. Kumar, L. Meeden, and J. Marshall. Bringing up robot: fundamental mechanisms for creating a self-motivated, self-organizing architecture. *Cybernetics and Systems*, 36:125–150, 2005.

[9] C. Boesch. What makes us human (homo sapiens)? the challenge of cognitive crossspecies comparison. *Journal of Comparative Psychology*, 121:227–240, 2007.

[10] M. E. Bratman. *Intentions, plans and practical reason*. Harvard University Press, 1987.

[11] I. Brink and P. Gardenfors. Co-operation and communication in apes and humans. *Mind and Language*, 18:484–501, 2003.

[12] D. Buttelmann, M. Carpenter, J. Call, and M. Tomasello. Enculturated chimpanzees imitate rationally. *Developmental Science*, 10:31–38, 2007.

[13] J. Call. Inferences about the location of food in the great apes (pan paniscus, pan troglodytes, gorilla gorilla, and pongo pygmaeus). *Journal of Comparative Psychology*, 118:232–241, 2004.

[14] Hoon Choi and Brian J. Scholl. Perceiving causality after the fact: Postdiction in the temporal dynamics of causal perception. *Perception*, 35:385–399, 2006.

[15] N. S. Clayton, J.M. Dally, and N. J. Emery. Social cognition by food-caching corvides: the western scrub-jay as a natural psychologist. *Philosophical Transactions of the Royal Society (Biological Sciences)*, 362:507–522, 2007.

[16] Christopher Crick, Marek Doniec, and Brian Scassellati. Who is it? inferring role and intent from agent motion. In *Proceedings of the 11th IEEE Conference on Development and Learning*, London UK, 2007. IEEE Computational Intelligence Society.

[17] Christopher Crick and Brian Scassellati. Inferring narrative and intention from playground games. In *Proceedings of the 12th IEEE Conference on Development and Learning*, Monterey CA, 2008. IEEE Computational Intelligence Society.

[18] Christopher Crick and Brian Scassellati. Intention-based robot control in social games. In *Proceedings of the Cognitive Science Society Annual Meeting*, 2009.

[19] Christopher Crick and Brian Scassellati. Controlling a robot with intention derived from motion. *Topics in Cognitive Science*, 2:114–126, 2010.

[20] G. Csibra. Recognizing communicative intentions in infancy. *Mind and Language*, 25:141–168, 2010.

[21] Gergely Csibra, Gyorgy Gergely, Szilvia Biro, Orsolya Koos, and Margaret Brockbank. Goal attribution without agency cues: the perception of 'pure reason' in infancy. *Cognition*, 72:237–267, 1999.

[22] Verena Dasser, Ib Ulbaek, and David Premack. The perception of intention. *Science*, 243:365–367, 1989.

[23] J. L. Elman. Finding structure in time. *Cognitive Science*, 14:179–211, 1990.

[24] P. Gardenfors. *Consciousness transitions: phylogenetic, ontogenetic and physiological aspects*, chapter Evolutionary and developmental aspects of intersubjectivity, pages 281–305. Elsevier, 2007.

[25] R. Gelman, F. Durgin, and L. Kaufman. *Causal cognition: A multidisciplinary debate*, chapter Distinguishing between animates and inanimates: Not by motion alone, pages 150–184. Clarendon Press, Oxford, 1995.

[26] G. Gergely, H. Bekkering, and I. Kiraly. Rational imitation in preverbal infants. *Nature*, 415:755, 2002.

[27] Gyorgy Gergely, Zoltan Nadasdy, Gergely Csibra, and Szilvia Biro. Taking the intentional stance at 12 months of age. *Cognition*, 56:165–193, 1995.

[28] Gerd Gigerenzer and Peter M. Todd. *Simple heuristics that make us smart*. Oxford University Press, New York NY, 1999.

[29] R. Grush. The emulator theory of representation: motor control, imagery and perception. *Behavioral and Brain Sciences*, 27:377–442, 2004.

[30] Andrea S. Heberlein and Ralph Adolphs. Impaired spontaneous anthropomorphizing despite intact perception and social knowledge. *Proceedings of the National Academy of Sciences*, 101:7487–7491, 2004.

[31] F. Heider and M. Simmel. An experimental study of apparent behavior. *American Journal of Psychology*, 57:243–259, 1944.

[32] G. Hesslow. Conscious thought as simulation of behaviour and perception. *Trends in Cognitive Sciences*, 6:242–247, 2002.

[33] N. K. Humphrey. *Growing points in ethology*, chapter The social function of intellect. Cambridge University Press, 1976.

[34] A. Jolly. *The evolution of primate behaviour.*

Macmillan, 1985.

[35] Wesley Kerr and Paul Cohen. Recognizing behaviors and the internal state of the participants. In *Proceedings of the IEEE 9th International Conference on Development and Learning*, 2010.

[36] Ami Klin. Attributing social meaning to ambiguous visual stimuli in higher functioning autism and asperger syndrome: The social attribution task. *Journal of Child Psychology and Psychiatry*, 41:831–846, 2000.

[37] T. Kohonen. *Self-organizing maps*. Springer, 2001.

[38] R. Kozma, T. Hunstberger, and H. Aghazarian. Implementing intentional robotics principles using ssr2k platform. In *Proceedings of the 2007 IEEE/RSJ International Conference on Intelligent Robots and Systems*, 2007.

[39] Alan M. Leslie, Fei Xu, Patrice D. Tremoulet, and Brian J. Scholl. Indexing and the object concept: developing 'what' and 'where' systems. *Trends in Cognitive Sciences*, 2(1):10–18, 1998.

[40] Jeff Loucks and Dare Baldwin. Sources of information in human action. In *Proceedings of the 30th Annual Conference of the Cognitive Science Society*, pages 121–126, Austin TX, 2008. Cognitive Science Society.

[41] Bertram F. Malle, Louis J. Moses, and Dare A. Baldwin. *Intentions and intentionality: foundations of social cognition*. MIT Press, 2001.

[42] R. Manzotti and V. Tagliasco. From "behavior-based" robots to "motivations-based" robots. *Robotics and Autonomous Systems*, 51:175–200, 2005.

[43] L. Meeden. *Towards planning: incremental investigations into adaptive robot control*. PhD thesis, Indiana University, Bloomington, 1994.

[44] A. Meltzoff. *Perspectives on imitation: from neuroscience to social science*, chapter Imitation and other minds: the like me hypothesis, pages 55–77. MIT Press, 2005.

[45] G. Metta, F. Panerai, R. Manzotti, and G. Sandini. Babybot: an artificially developing robotic agent. In *From Animals to Animats: the Sixth Conference on Simulation of Adaptive Behavior*, 2000.

[46] A. Michotte. *La perception de la causalite*. Institut Superior de Philosophie, Louvain, 1946.

[47] A. Michotte. *Feelings and emotions: The Mooseheart symposium*, chapter The emotions regarded as functional connections, pages 114–125. McGraw-Hill, New York, 1950.

[48] Stephen R. Mitroff and Brian J. Scholl. Forming and updating object representations without awareness: evidence from motion-induced blindness. *Vision Research*, 45:961–967, 2004.

[49] M. Myowa-Yamakoshi and T. Matsuzawa. Imitation of intentional manipulatory actions in chimpanzees (pan troglodytes). *Journal of Comparative Psychology*, 114:381–391, 2000.

[50] D. Newtson and G. Engquist. The perceptual organization of ongoing behavior. *Journal of Personality and Social Psychology*, 12:436–450, 1976.

[51] Richard E. Nisbett and Timothy D. Wilson. The halo effect: evidence for unconscious alteration of judgments. *Journal of Personality and Social*

*Psychology*, 35:250–256, 1977.

[52] Peter C. Pantelis and Jacob Feldman. Exploring the mental space of autonomous intentional agents. In *Proceedings of the Cognitive Science Society Annual Meeting*, 2010.

[53] D. C. Penn and D. J Povinelli. Causal cognition in human and nonhuman shape and material. *Animal Learning and Behavior*, 15:423–432, 2007.

[54] D. Premack and G. Woodruff. Does the chimpanzee have a theory of mind? *Behavioral and Brain Sciences*, 4:515–526, 1978.

[55] Philippe Rochat, Tricia Striano, and Rachel Morgan. Who is doing what to whom? young infants' developing sense of social causality in animated displays. *Perception*, 33:355–369, 2004.

[56] M. D. Rutherford, Bruce F. Pennington, and Sally J. Rogers. The perception of animacy in young children with autism. *Journal of Autism and Developmental Disorders*, 36:983–992, 2006.

[57] Brian J. Scholl. Can infants' object concepts be trained? *Trends in Cognitive Sciences*, 8(2):49–51, 2004.

[58] J. Searle. *Intentionality: an essay in the philosophy of mind.* Cambridge University Press, 1983.

[59] Claudio C V Staut and Thomas P Naidich. Urbach-wiethe disease (lipoid proteinosis). *Pediatric Neurosurgery*, 28:212–214, 1998.

[60] D. Stern. *The interpersonal world of the infant.* Basic Books, 1985.

[61] Michael Tomasello, Malinda Carpenter, Josep Call, Tanya Behne, and Henrike Moll. Understanding and sharing intentions: the origins of cultural cognition. *Behavioral and Brain Sciences*, 28:675–735, 2005.

[62] Patrice D. Tremoulet and Jacob Feldman. Perception of animacy from the motion of a single object. *Perception*, 29:943–951, 2000.

[63] Patrice D. Tremoulet and Jacob Feldman. The influence of spatial context and the role of intentionality in the interpretation of animacy from motion. *Perception & Psychophysics*, 68(6):1047–1058, 2006.

[64] F. Warneken, F. Chen, and M. Tomasello. Cooperative activities in young children and chimpanzees. *Child Development*, 3:640–663, 2006.

[65] Thalia Wheatley, Shawn C. Milleville, and Alex Martin. Understanding animate agents: Distinct roles for the social network and mirror system. *Psychological Science*, 18:469–474, 2007.

[66] Daniel M Wolpert, Kenji Doya, and Mitsuo Kawato. A unifying computational framework for motor control and social interaction. *Philisophical Transactions of the Royal Society B*, 358(1431):593–602, March 2003.

[67] A. L. Woodward. Infants selectively encode the goal object of an actor's reach. *Cognition*, 69:1–34, 1998.

[68] P. D. Zelazo, J. W. Astington, and D. R. Olson, editors. *Developing theories of intention: social understanding and self-control.* Erlbaum, 1999.

# 6-DOF Pose Estimation:
# The Need for Standardization in Industrial Applications

Shaun M. Edwards
Southwest Research Institute
6220 Culebra Road
San Antonio, Texas 78212
(210) 522-3277

Shaun.Edwards@swri.org

William C. Flannigan
Southwest Research Institute
6220 Culebra Road
San Antonio, Texas 78212
(210) 522-6805

Clay.Flannigan@swri.org

Paul T. Evans
Southwest Research Institute
6220 Culebra Road
San Antonio, Texas 78212
(210) 522-2994

Paul.Evans@swri.org

## ABSTRACT

To maintain competitiveness in the global economy, US manufacturers must innovate to enable intelligent manufacturing solutions that dramatically improve productivity and competitiveness. Advances in robots and automation utilizing high-fidelity sensors capable of characterizing dynamic and unconstrained environments represent one crucial area for development. Robots with the ability to perceive their surroundings can adapt to variable manufacturing conditions and even cooperate with human partners.

2D video-based computer vision has been the standard for robot perception for over two decades. Recent advances in 6-Degree-Of-Freedom (DOF) metrology and 3D optical sensing methods have created the potential for high-accuracy, high-resolution, real-time sensing of dynamic environments. This capability will revolutionize automated manufacturing by enabling systems to perform flexible and complex tasks that previously required human perception and dexterity.

The enabling 3D sensors and the perception software behind them are rapidly evolving. There are several fundamental sensing technologies and many software approaches to make practical use of the data. Unfortunately, standard evaluation methods have not kept pace with the development of this new sensing technology. The selection of a sensing system cannot therefore be made objectively using manufacturer provided specifications alone. This lack of standardization has slowed the acceptance of this potentially transformative technology. Measurement standards and performance metrics, specifically those that are relevant to industrial applications, are required to spur innovation and to hasten the adoption of these advanced technologies.

## Categories and Subject Descriptors

C.4 [**Performance of Systems**]: *Measurement techniques, Performance attributes;* I.4 [**Image Processing and Computer Vision**]

## General Terms

Performance

## Keywords

Sensing, Range, Pose, Industrial, Robot, 3D

## 1. INTRODUCTION

Traditional automated manufacturing systems are purpose-specific and are costly to modify for changes in production demands and product designs. The widespread use of programmable automation solutions such as industrial robots has advanced flexibility in many manufacturing environments; these solutions enable the reuse of the hardware (robot), but significant investment is still required in the application-specific sub-systems including the software, part fixturing, and end-effectors (robot tooling). In order to make step-changes in manufacturing productivity, more intelligent and flexible solutions are required.

One primary impediment for intelligent manufacturing systems is the ability to perceive and respond to dynamic and changing environments. Significant productivity improvements can be had with automation solutions that are able to sense their environment, the work object(s), and interact with humans performing supporting tasks. Such systems will enable highly flexible manufacturing that is able to respond to variations in production demands and tasks. This level of intelligence requires advanced sensors to quickly and accurately detect the surroundings as well as intelligent software architectures to make decisions and perform actions based on the sensor data.

For most flexible manufacturing tasks, a 3D spatial awareness is required. Automation solutions must be able to detect the location and velocity of work objects, other production systems, and people within the environment. For more than two decades, 2D computer vision methods have been the primary solution for spatial sensing. Many inspection and guidance applications have been successfully treated using the high resolution 2D data that cameras provide. But, many constraints are often required to enable the effective use of 2D data, and many applications, for example those that require human interaction, must have three dimensional feedback.

For these reasons, many 3D sensing technologies are being rapidly developed. The first applications were mostly for the metrology field for reverse engineering and dimensional quality. But, recent developments have advanced the sensing technologies in the areas of cost, reliability, and speed such that they are becoming appropriate for real-time applications in manufacturing environments.

However, there are obstacles for the implementation of these new sensing technologies. Many of the solutions are rapidly evolving and there are several competing technologies. Today, typical applications of 3D sensing technology require significant effort to validate a particular solution for a specific task. The cost of this validation effort overshadows the hardware investment. In addition, standardized methods for using the data provided by the sensors are in their infancy. Consequently, each application of the technology requires significant development which limits adoption.

In order to spur adoption, standard methods are required to evaluate the performance of 3D sensing systems. Measurement standards can dramatically reduce the development effort required for manufacturers to implement these advanced technologies by providing objective, comprehensive, and relevant metrics and methods for evaluating sensing system performance. In addition, performance standards will stimulate innovation within the technology providers by creating evaluation metrics for comparison of disparate systems.

This paper seeks to address the needs of 6-DOF pose (position and orientation) estimation for industrial automation. While other markets may benefit from standardization, industrial automation would arguably be one of the first beneficiaries. First, a discussion of sensing technologies will be used to demonstrate the obstacles to the adoption and the need for standardization. Next, the standardization requirements will be discussed, both in terms of low-level sensor attributes as well as higher level pose attributes. Finally, application examples demonstrate how standardization would enable large leaps in efficiency, quality, and reduction in costs for industrial processes, many of which are not automatable today.

## 2. INDUSTRIAL SENSING TECHNOLOGIES

### 2.1 2D Computer Vision

For more than two decades, 2D computer vision techniques have been the standard for pose estimation in industrial environments. Cell or robot mounted cameras provide high resolution spatial information to resolve up to 3-DOF of location and orientation. Sophisticated calibration methods were developed to eliminate intrinsic sources of optical distortion and extrinsic pose information of the camera. In addition, standards such as NTSC for analog video transmission and VGA for display formats drove commonality among sensing systems. Finally, standard libraries of image processing routines such as OpenCV were developed, standardizing processing approaches.

Because of video/camera standards, calibration methods, and standard image processing algorithms, 2D computer vision performance is well understood for many common robotic applications related to industrial automation. Indeed, the selection of an appropriate computer vision system is primarily a design exercise with little uncertainty for a wide range of applications.

### 2.2 3D Sensing

One of the challenges presented to an industrial automation engineer is the broad selection of potential sensing technologies available and the limited tools available to compare competing technologies. While certainly not exhaustive, a taxonomy of sensing modalities capable of producing high resolution, near real-time point clouds might include:

- Time of Flight
  - Scanning LIDAR
  - Flash LIDAR
- Triangulation
  - Structured Light
    - Laser Line
    - Scanning Spot
    - Projected Patterns
  - Stereo Vision

Each of these modalities has different performance characteristics and none are optimal for all applications. In addition, there is significant innovation occurring in 3D sensing that requires an up-to-date knowledge of the technologies. Most importantly, there is no formalized approach to select and evaluate a particular technology for an industrial application. In many cases, the system integrator must perform time-consuming and expensive testing just to prove feasibility, which inhibits adoption in manufacturing environments that require known reliability and return on the investment.

## 3. STANDARDIZATION REQUIREMENTS

The 3D sensors required to support workcells of the future, will need to operate over a range of distances, ambient conditions, and with varying degrees of speed and precision.

### 3.1 Raw Sensor Performance

In some cases, the raw sensor performance can be provided by the manufacturer on a datasheet, similar to a computer vision camera, for example. Characteristics such as frame rate, field of view, spatial resolution, range, repeatability, and accuracy may be provided. Depending on the sensor, some of these characteristics are easy to provide, but some may have ambiguity. For example, consider a flash LIDAR system. Repeatabilty and accuracy will be dependent on frame rate since the sensors typically average many readings over time to improve precision. In addition, ambient lighting may play a role since the ambient light can affect the signal to noise ratio of the sensor; many active laser sensors cannot function outside due to interference from direct sunlight. Similarly, temperature will often affect sensor precision and accuracy. Finally, the optical characteristics of the target may impact precision and range. Characteristics such as roughness, specularity, and color can affect the precision and range of an active sensor.

Passive sensors such as stereo vision have their own factors that affect the raw performance. Stereo vision relies on determining a correlation between two images to calculate the disparity. In scenes with little texture or repeating features, the correlation analysis may fail, giving no data or large errors.

A final factor important to the characterization of 3D sensors is variation over the field of view. For many sensors, especially those with optics, the accuracy will not be constant everywhere in the field of view. Optical distortion, typically near the extents, must be characterized.

For many classical industrial applications, the ambient conditions (lighting, temperature, dust etc.) are controlled or at least consistent and the sensing targets are known so that sensor selection can be made based on sensor specifications or limited testing alone. But, for applications that have many or complex targets, varying environmental conditions, or dynamic objects, simple sensor specifications are not sufficient.

## 3.2 Static Pose Estimation

For truly flexible industrial robot applications, the sensing system should be capable of providing the full 6-DOF pose of the workpiece without constraints on initial orientation. This possibility eliminates the workcell paradigm, where rigid tooling presents the part in a known position and orientation. Robust pose estimation allows the possibility of the automation being brought to the part or being moved to help eliminate production bottlenecks. It also moves closer to flexible automation where the same system operates on many different parts without reprogramming.

The important sensor metric for these flexible manufacturing environments is not necessarily the precision of any data point, but rather the sensor's ability to provide a pose estimate for the object. The pose estimation provides the spatial context for manipulation of the object. However, this metric is often difficult to directly asses. The ground truth pose can be very difficult to determine. Objects that have complex geometry, without reference surfaces such as planes, holes, or tooling features, may not have an easily definable "true" pose. This is often the case for cast parts, for example. In addition, manufacturing tolerances can cause deviations in the as-built parts that make existing references less useful. Sheet metal or welded parts are good examples where the as-built geometry can vary significantly from part-to-part or part-to-design. Finally, deformable objects such as fabric are even more complex since there may be no consistent geometry.

One approach towards standardization is to develop methods and objects that are repeatable and that have easily measurable pose. For example, one could envision as set of standard test objects that have known geometry such as a plane or a sphere. In addition, the objects could be created to have nominal optical characteristics of color, roughness, and reflectance. With a geometry model of the test objects, one could use standard software approaches such at the Iterative Closest Point (ICP) algorithm to obtain a convergent estimate for pose of the object. Under controlled ambient conditions (light, temperature), ground truth measurements could be provided by a laser tracker or other metrology system.

## 3.3 Dynamic Pose Estimation

Pose estimation of dynamic objects has all of the complexity of the static situation, with additional difficulties in providing ground truth state (velocity, pose) of the moving object. For rigid bodies, the static sensor characterization could be extended by fixturing the test objects to motion control devices. The simplest approach may be a linear rail or rotational stage that constrains the rigid body motion to a single degree of freedom. High accuracy positional and/or velocity information is easy to collect, but care must be taken to characterize the phase lag in the system.

One important application of dynamic pose estimation is that of human pose estimation. In industrial environments, this problem is of critical importance towards enabling tight coordination of automation systems and their human counterparts. Significant research has been done in this area and significant work is still necessary; humans are dynamic, deformable, and lacking in natural reference features. Discussion of this topic is beyond the scope of this paper, but one could imagine using a reference object for standardized testing here too. This object might be a mechanized, anatomically and kinematically accurate human form with instrumentation to provide ground truth.

It is important to point out that in applications where accurate models of the sensed object are not available, the software algorithms can be just as important as the sensor performance in determining pose estimation performance. More often than not, this is the case in real-world applications where the exact object geometry is not known a priori and the pose estimation algorithm must approximate its solution based on an assumed model. This is demonstrated in the following application examples.

## 4. APPLICATION EXAMPLES

What follows are descriptions of several applications of 3D sensing for industrial robotic applications that Southwest Research Institute® (SwRI®) is currently researching.

### 4.1 Cast Part Material Handling

In this application, SwRI was challenged with performing a material handling and assembly task for a cast part. The casting had both dimensional inaccuracies with respect to the as-design part and also no registration features to easily extract the part pose. A multi-imaging method was developed to simultaneously locate features of interest and estimate the pose of the object. Pose estimate evaluation is complicated by the fact that no reliable ground truth exists. Figure 1 shows the imaging process.

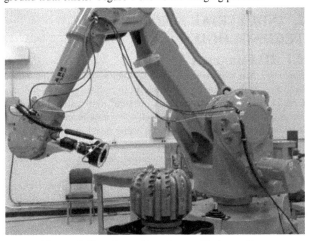

**Figure 1: Imaging a Cast Part to Estimate Pose**

## 4.2 Tube Painting

In this application, the customer has an extremely large number of unique tubular parts to be robotically painted. The number of parts is too large to consider developing fixturing methods for each variation. Even if universal tooling could be developed, the burden of creating and maintaining unique robot programs for each part is not economically viable. SwRI's approach uses a laser-line triangulation scanner to generate a 3D point cloud of the part. This point cloud is then either matched to a model of the part to generate a pose estimation, or used directly to generate robot programs automatically. Figure 2 and Figure 3 show the part scanning and robotic painting respectively.

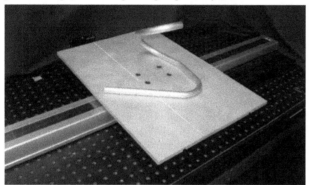

**Figure 2: Laser Line Scanning of Tube Parts**

**Figure 3: Robotic Painting of Scanned Tubes**

## 4.3 Random Package Material Handling

The challenge in this application is to robotically handle a wide range of objects which are not known a priori, but are constrained by characteristics of size and geometry. 6-DOF pose estimates of the objects are necessary to plan robot paths and gripping. A fusion of 2D imagery and 3D time-of-flight range data is utilized. Features of the objects are extracted and assumptions of geometry allow for pose estimation. Figure 4 shows some of the intermediate results.

**Figure 4: a) Camera and Range Sensor b) 2D Image of Objects c) Edge Detection d) Colorized Range Data Overlaid**

## 5. SUMMARY

The problem of 6-DOF pose estimation of objects in industrial environments has been presented. Robust sensing and perception is a key enabling technology for next generation robotic systems that are capable of handling complex and dynamic work environments. Significant advancements in productivity, quality, and safety are possible with the application of 3D sensing technologies combined with robotics and automation. The rapid advancement of 3D sensing technologies along with the variety of techniques available require standardization of performance measures to spur adoption of these methods. Further research is required to develop these performance measures, especially for dynamic and deformable challenges such as human pose estimation.

# Flexible Robotic Assembly in Dynamic Environments

Jane Shi
GM Global R&D Center
30500 Mound Road
Warren, MI 48090-9055
248-807-4212

Jane.Shi@gm.com

Roland Menassa
GM Global R&D Center
30500 Mound Road
Warren, MI 48090-9055
586-986-3890

Roland.Menassa@gm.com

## ABSTRACT

While robotic automation has played a key role in the automotive industry and specifically in stamping, welding, material handling and painting over the last 30 years, currently there are no robotic assembly applications in the final assembly of a vehicle on a moving line in domestic automotive manufacturing plants. In order for the U.S. automotive base to improve its global manufacturing competitiveness, new robotic technologies are required to enable the installation of parts on a moving assembly line. In this paper we will describe GM's comprehensive effort in achieving robotic flexible assembly on moving assembly lines, from initial moving assembly line motion characterization and robotic line tracking performance evaluation, to GM specific application development such as robotic wheel and tire load. We will then highlight three types of assembly methods in automotive general assembly, and examine assembly alignment as well as assembly manipulation motion characteristics in each type of the assembly methods. Finally we will discuss key enablers to achieve robust and flexible robotic assembly in an unfixtured and dynamic manufacturing environment.

## Categories and Subject Descriptors

C.3 [**Special-Purpose and Application-Based Systems**]: Process control systems; robotics, flexible automation

## General Terms

Flexible Robotic Assembly, Factory Automation, Automotive General Assembly

## Keywords

Flexible Robotic Assembly, Industrial Robots, Automotive Assembly

## 1. Introduction

In the automotive market of the 21st Century, with sophisticated

consumers demanding highly customized features at mass production costs, and with fuel efficiency requirements yielding a wider array of vehicle powertrains and body types, efficient manufacturing operations in the future will be characterized by their flexibility and agility in producing diverse product mixes, while also maintaining high throughput and consistently high quality. While robotic automation has played a key role in stamping, welding, material handling and painting over the last 30 years, currently there are no robotic assembly applications in the final assembly of a vehicle, as illustrated by Figure 1.

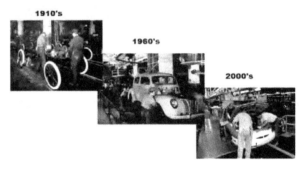

**Figure 1 Automotive Final Assembly**

In order for the U.S. automotive base to improve its global manufacturing competitiveness, new robotic technologies have to be advanced to enable the installation of parts on a moving assembly line. Past research has been conducted in utilizing visual servo techniques to track a part on a moving assembly line in US [1, 2, 3]. Recently new technology development has been undertaken to automatically load automobile tires and wheels onto moving vehicle bodies in both US [4] and in Europe [5]. In addition to the visual servo technique to track part motion, compliant force control [4, 5] and predictive modeling [6] play a key role in active assembly contact phase in order to successfully assemble the tire and wheel onto the hub in motion.

General Motors continues to conduct research and development projects to robotically automate GA assembly tasks on moving assembly lines since 2007. The research and development activities in this area include two investigative projects and several application development projects as illustrated in Figure 2. First, we have characterized the dynamic motion of six conveyance mechanisms commonly used in automotive general assembly. The conveyor motion ranges from stable and smooth motion of automated guidance vehicles (AGVs) to jerky bouncy motion of chain driven power and free conveyors. The motion profiles and their vibration frequency have been analyzed and reported [8]. Second, we have quantified several robotic line tracking solutions using three types of tracking methods: encoder, encoder plus static vision, and analog laser. The tracking performance is dependent on the dynamic motion of the conveyor. For the most stable conveyor motion, robotic position tracking accuracy is within +/- 0.5 inches in the direction of main travel but for unstable and dynamic conveyor motion, robotic position tracking performance can be off target as much as 4 inches in the direction of main travel [9].

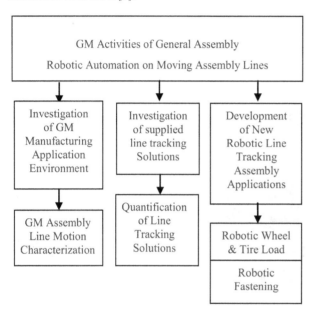

**Figure 2 GM Activities of General Assembly Robotic Automation on Moving Assembly Lines**

Currently, GM is developing robotic assembly automation applications on a moving line for applications such as wheel & tire load, and robotic fastening. Figure 3 shows the robotic line tracking development station at GM's manufacturing laboratory. An automatic guided vehicle (AGV) is a conveyor that carries vehicle bodies through the robotic automation station. For the robotic wheel & tire load, two wheel hubs, instead of an entire vehicle body, are mounted on the moving AGV to emulate the actual production environment. The AGV travels through the straight line segment inside the robotic cell at a constant speed. Two 6-axis FANUC robots are moving on a linear rail to track the AGV smooth motion to create a "moving stop station" so that all robot programming can be done without considering the line tracking speed. The linear rail is driven by a motor that is being commanded by external vision sensor inputs so that the robots on the linear rail will be able to track the AGV motion. When the steady tracking of the AGV motion is achieved, the robot automatically loads the wheel and tire onto the moving hub. In later sections, we will discuss critical assembly requirements in the wheel and tire load and discuss key enablers to achieve robust, adaptable, and highly flexible robotic assembly in an unfixtured and dynamic manufacturing environment.

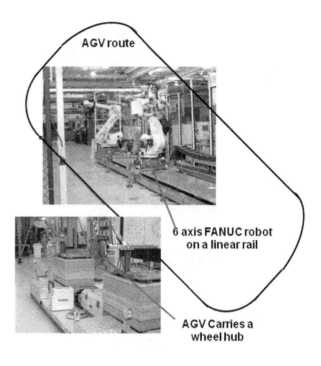

**Figure 3 The Robotic Wheel & Tire Load and Fastening Development Station on Moving Assembly Lines at GM's manufacturing laboratory**

## 2.  GM Robotic Wheel and Tire Load on a Moving Assembly Line

In automotive general assembly, key assembly steps of a wheel and hub assembly are:

1.  Align the holes on the wheel with the threaded studs on the hub,
2.  Place the wheel through the holes onto the studs against the hub flange,
3.  Place the lug nuts onto the threads,
4.  Run the lug nuts to the specified toque level.

Figure 4 illustrates these key assembly elements. The assembly tolerance between the wheel and the hub is product specific: it depends on the pattern of holes and their position tolerance as well as the hub studs location and their tolerance. Most products require the assembly tolerance to be within +/- 1 mm.

Hub

Hub flange          Threaded studs

**Figure 4 Wheel & Tire Load Assembly**

The robotic wheel & tire load on a moving assembly line utilizes several key technologies to achieve the assembly automation:

1. Coarse tracking of AGV motion - overhead vision systems above the automation station track gross motion of AGV so that the control system is able to align the linear rail system with the rough motion of the AGV.
2. Fine tracking of AGV motion – close range vision will locate features on the AGV so that the linear rail is able to track the AGV motion precisely to create a "moving stop station" for assembly automation.
3. Precision locating of hub studs – Robot end of arm tool (EOAT) has a vision camera that locates studs' location precisely and the vision offsets are used for the robots to place the wheel onto the studs. A single nut runner on the EOAT, as shown in the left image of Figure 8, picks up a single lug nut before the wheel. The nut runner tightens the lug nut automatically after the wheel is loaded on to the hub securely by the robot.
4. Robot EOAT is designed to center the wheel automatically for repeatable wheel position. This repeatability ensures that the lug nut can be placed onto the studs.
5. Robot EOAT is also designed to provide compliance when the wheel is engaged with the hub and the flange.
6. A single nut runner on the EOAT picks up a single lug nut before the wheel load. The nut runner tightens the lug nut

automatically after the wheel is loaded on to the hub securely by the robot.

Successful robotic wheel & tire load is critically dependent on a responsive linear rail control system as well as three sets of vision systems: one set for coarse AGV tracking, one set for fine AGV tracking, and one EOAT 3D vision for final precision location of assembly studs. Only after the *stable* AGV tracking is achieved with the linear rail system, i.e. the robot has no relative motion to the vehicle body; the robot program will be able to utilize the EOAT 3D vision offset to load the wheel onto the hub studs automatically and successfully, as shown in Figure 5.

**Figure 5 Automatic Robotic Wheel & Tire Load**

While the system performance of such an automation cell is currently under investigation, Cheng et al [10] has analyzed the potential system performance based on both force and visual feedback controls and Chang et al [11] has experimentally validated visual servoing performance for dynamic part tracking. Eastman et al [12] has highlighted performance evaluation and metrics for perception in intelligent systems that are applicable to this automation cell.

## 3. Flexible Robotic Assembly Automation on Moving Assembly Lines

Human operators perform complex assembly operations in automotive general assembly efficiently and effectively with inherent flexibility. Three significant characteristics of human assembly capabilities are: (1) Contacts between assembly parts are manipulated in a naturally flexible manner; (2) Multi-modal sensing signals are blended seamlessly to anticipate next steps in the assembly tasks, and (3) Reactive and adaptive actions and decisions are rendered in real-time to accomplish the assembly.

In order for robots to perform complex assembly as flexibly and adaptively as a human, we believe, some of the above human flexible assembly characteristics have to be duplicated by robots. In addition, the general assembly application domain is characterized by widely varying assembly methods and tolerances, varying part location uncertainty due to the stacked up parts to be assembled, and "dynamic uncertainty" introduced by vehicle body movement on moving assembly lines. In this section, we will examine a variety of assembly methods and their challenges for robotic automation.

## 3.1 Three Assembly Methods and the Challenge of Robotic Manipulation Skills

The first key challenge in achieving the flexible robotic assembly is the robotic manipulation skill. The robot's motion has to adapt to the actual part location with its uncertainty before and after the assembly parts are in contact with each other. In order to understand the required robotic manipulation skills needed in the robotic assembly, we will examine assembly alignment as well as assembly manipulation motion characteristics in three types of the assembly methods:

1. peg-in-a-hole assembly in 3D space, as shown in Fig. 6a,
2. contour match assembly in 3D space, as shown in Fig. 6b,
3. surface match assembly in 3D space, as shown in Fig. 6c.

**Peg-in-a-hole assembly in 3D space:** Here, the peg-in-a-hole assembly term refers to one part that is placed inside the hole of another part. One example is a wiring harness (a peg) that is pushed into a hole of a vehicle body panel as shown in Figure 6a. This type of assembly requires an alignment, generally to a plane surface, at a specific 3D point. Once the required alignment is achieved, the assembly manipulation is a linear motion in the direction of alignment. Several aspects of achieving alignment have been studies. This is a widely studied assembly [13-18]. The key enabler is the compliance control technique that allows the robotic control system to react to the contact assembly forces in real time to achieve a successful assembly.

**Contour match assembly in 3D space:** Here, the contour match assembly term refers to the assembled parts mating along a general curve contour in 3D space. One example is the weather strip that is assembled onto a door frame contour as shown in Figure 6b. This type of assembly requires an alignment along a 3D linear contour in 3D space. The required alignment could be gradually shifting along the 3D linear contour. And the assembly manipulation motion is along a general curve on the required contour with proper alignment. This class of assembly tasks requires a higher degree of accurate robotic path execution as well as force adaptation along the actual path. This class of robotic assembly has been rarely studied.

**Surface match assembly in 3D space:** Here the surface match assembly term refers to the parts that are assembled by stacking their 3D surfaces together. One example is the carpet that is placed on the vehicle body panel as shown in Figure 6c. This type of assembly requires an alignment along the surface normal in 3D space. This class of assembly may have a similar assembly path as in peg-in-hole assembly, but the contact force signature will be different. This class of robotic assembly has not yet been studied.

## 3.2 Assembly Parts in Motion and the Challenge of Robotic Perception Skills

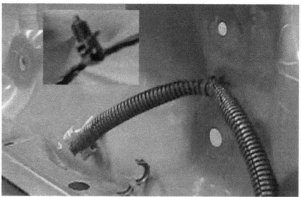

**Figure 6a Peg-in-a-Hole Assembly**

**Figure 6b Contour Match Assembly**

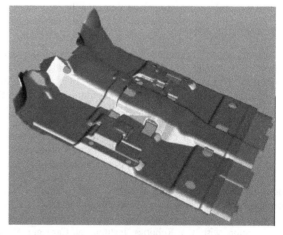

**Figure 6c Surface Match Assembly**

The second challenge is the development of new sensor fusion methods for multi-modal sensing signals, including multiple visual images, tactile sensing, and contact forces in order to anticipate next dynamic action in the assembly process.

Traditional machine vision has been utilized in robotic automation since the early days of robotics. [24, 25] Classical 2D object pose estimation techniques in visual images, from filtering, edge detection, segmentation, to final model matching and pose estimation, have matured to today's commercial products. [26] Recent products of 2+1/2D object pose estimation utilize a laser system to gain the dimensional estimation along the camera Z axis. Full 3D object pose estimation depends heavily on redundant geometry features on the parts or specialized 3D laser scanners or range sensors. There is however assembly scenarios where the vision sensors become occluded, especially during the grasp of parts, and in these cases more sensor fusion technologies with other sensors such as touch sensing are being developed. The early use of sensor fusion technology in autonomous driving has been successfully demonstrated in recent years with the DARPA Urban Grand Challenge [23].

Most of the above described object pose estimation techniques apply to static cases where the part or the environment viewed is motionless. In dynamic cases where parts are in motion, object pose estimation is always lagging behind the actual object pose. In order to use the object pose successfully in the control loop of the robotic motion, the prediction techniques are critically important. The ultimate goal of such predictive techniques is to bring the part held by the robot EOAT in contact with its mating part in an appropriate contact neighborhood so that the robotic compliant control techniques utilizing contact forces can be successfully used for the part assembly.

## 3.3 Assembly Tolerance/Dynamic Uncertainty and the Challenge of Robotic Assembly Robustness

The third and most difficult challenge is to develop necessary error recovery and retry techniques so that the robustness of robotic assembly can be improved dramatically. Without robust retrial technique, the robotic assembly often fails unexpectedly in real applications on the manufacturing assembly plant floor.

System robustness of robotic assembly is the measure of a robot's ability to continue to function despite unanticipated error conditions in its component subsystems. Here we are only referring to software error conditions rather than hardware failures. Critical robotic assembly should be fundamentally robust. Effective ways to dramatically improve system robustness are built-in robust system control methods [6,7,8] and systematic error recovery methods [42,43,44] and re-trial processes. An error recovery and retrial technique has only been investigated by B.R. Donald [19] and M.A. Peshkin [20] in order to improve robustness for a peg-in-hole assembly. Only recently a mobile manipulator [21, 22] has been developed by GM R&D to achieve this class of assembly in an autonomous and robust manner in collaboration with the Robotics Institute at Carnegie Mellon University. A force controlled spiral search technique on a planar surface was utilized to overcome the positioning uncertainty of the mobile manipulator relative to the assembly environment. One of the key learning from the project is that the robust re-trial technique under exception conditions is directly related to the alignment requirement of the assembly.

## 4. Summary

In this paper, we first highlighted GM's comprehensive effort in achieving robotic flexible assembly on moving assembly lines, from initial moving assembly line motion characterization, robotic line tracking performance evaluation, to specific application development results. GM's robotic wheel and tire load application development was described in detail to illustrate the challenges and the potential technology solutions in robotic automatic assembly.

We then described three types of assembly methods in automotive general assembly: peg-in-a-hole assembly, contour match assembly, surface match assembly, all in 3D space. We examined assembly alignment as well as assembly manipulation motion characteristics in each type of assembly methods. We presented insights and discussed challenges in robotic manipulation skills, robotic perception skills, and robotic assembly system robustness.

While robotic automation has played a key role in stamping, welding, material handling and painting over the last 30 years, currently there are no robotic assembly applications in the final assembly of a vehicle in dynamic environments in the domestic automotive manufacturing plants. In order for the U.S. automotive base to improve its global manufacturing competitiveness, new robotic technologies, robotic perception and sensor fusion algorithms, robotic manipulation control, and inherent system robustness, have to come together to advance the state of the art in flexible robotic assembly on moving assembly lines.

## 5. Acknowledgement

We would like to acknowledge the collaboration from GM colleagues David Groll, Pete Tavora, Rick Rourke and Robert Scheuerman in all activities of general assembly robotic automation on moving assembly lines.

## 6. References

[1] G. DeSouza, "A Subsumptive, Hierarchical, and Distributed Vision-based Architecture for Smart Robotics", Ph.D. Dissertation, School of Electrical and Computer Engineering, Purdue University, May 2002

[2] Y. Yoon, G. DeSouza, A. Kak, "Real-time Tracking and Pose Estimation for Industrial Objects using Geometric Features", Proceedings of the 2003 IEEE International Conference on Robotics and Automation, Sept. 14-19, Taiwan, 2003

[3] Y. Yoon, G. DeSouza, A. Kak, "A Heterogeneous Distributed Visual Servoing System for Real-time Robotic Assembly Applications", Proceedings of the 2006 IEEE International Conference on Robotics and Automation, Orlando, Florida, 2006

[4] H. Chen, W. Eakins, J. Wang, G. Zhang, T. Fuhlbrigge, "Robotic wheel loading process in automotive manufacturing

automation", Proc. of the 2009 IEEE/RSJ international conference on Intelligent robots and systems, St. Louis, MO pages. 3814-3819, Oct. 2009

[5] F. Lange, J. Werner, J. Schaerer, G. Hirzinger, "Assembling Wheels to Continuously Conveyed Car Bodies Using a Standard Industrial Robot", Proceedings of the 2010 IEEE International Conference on Robotics and Automation, Anchorage, Alaska, May 2010

[6] F. Lange, J. Scharrer, G. Hirzinger, "Classification and Prediction for Accurate Sensor-based Assembly to Moving Objects", Proceedings of the 2010 IEEE International Conference on Robotics and Automation, Anchorage, Alaska, May 2010

[7] G. Reinhart, J. Werner, "Flexible Automation for the assembly in motion", CIRP Annals - Manufacturing Technology, Volume 56, Issue 1, 2007, Pages 25-28

[8] J. Shi, "Preliminary analysis of conveyor dynamic motion for automation applications", Proceedings of the 8th Workshop on Performance Metrics for Intelligent Systems, 2008. pages 173-180

[9] J. Shi, R. F. Rourke, D. Groll, and P.W. Tavora, "Quantification of line tracking solutions for automotive applications", a book chapter in "Performance Evaluation and Benchmarking of Intelligent Systems", Eds. Raj Madhavan, Edward Tunstel, and Elena Messina, pages 311 – 338, Springer, 2009

[10] H. Chen, J. Wang, B. Zhang, G. Zhang, T. Fuhlbrigge, "Performance Analysis of Wheel Loading in automotive manufacturing", Proc. of the 6th Annual IEEE Conference on Automation Science and Engineering, Toronto, Canada, Aug. 2010

[11] T. Chang, T. Hong, M. Shneier, G. Holguin, J. Park, R.D. Eastman, "Dynamic 6DOF metrology for evaluating a visual servoing system", Proceedings of the 8th Workshop on Performance Metrics for Intelligent Systems, 2008. Pages 173-180

[12] Roger Eastman, Tsai Hong, Jane Shi, Tobias Hanning, Bala Muralikrishnan, S. Susan Yong, and Tommy Chang, "Performance Evaluation and Metrics for Perception in Intelligent Manufacturing", A book chapter in "Performance

Evaluation and Benchmarking of Intelligent Systems", Eds. Raj Madhavan, Edward Tunstel, and Elena Messina, pages 269-310, Springer, 2009

[13] Y. Xia etc al, "Dynamic analysis for peg-in-hole assembly with contact deformation", The International Journal of Avdanced Manufacturing Technology, Vol. 20, No.1-2, Aug. 2006, pp. 118-128,

[14] Y. Fei, X. Zhao, "An Assembly Process Modeling and Analysis for Robotic Multiple Peg in hole", Journal of Intelligent and Robotic Systems, Vol.36, No. 2, Feb. 2003, pp.175-189

[15] B. J. Unger et al, "Comparison of 3-D Haptic Peg-in-Hole Tasks in Real and Virtual Environments",_In *Proceedings of the Conference on Intelligent Robots and Systems (IROS 2001)*, Maui, Hawaii, October 2001

[16] H. T. Liao, M.C. Leul, "Analysis of Impact in Robotic Peg-in-Hole Assembly", Robotica, 1998, 16: 347-356

[17] J. F. Broenink, M. L.J. Tiernego, "Peg-in-Hole assembly using Impedance Control with a 6 DOF Robot" in "Simulation in Industry", Proceedings 8th European Simulation Symposium, Oct. 24-26 1996, Genoa, Italy, A. G. Bruzzone and E.H.J. Kerckhoffs (eds.)

[18] H. McCallion, G.R. Johnson, D.T. Pham, "A Compliant Device for Inserting a Peg in a Hole", International Journal of Industrial Robot, Vol. 6, No. 2, pp. 81-87, 1979

[19] B. R. Donald, *"Planning Multi-Step Error Detection and Recovery Strategies"*, The International Journal of Robotics Research, 1990 pp 892-897

[20] M.A. Peshkin: Programmed compliance for error corrective assembly, IEEE Trans. Robot. Autom. **6**, 473–482 (1990)

[21] B. Hamner, S. Koterba, J. Shi, R. Simmons. S. Singh, "An Autonomous Mobile Manipulator for Assembly Tasks", Autonomous Robots, 2010

[22] B. Hamner, S. Koterba, J. Shi, R. Simmons. S. Singh, " Mobile Robotic Dynamic Tracking for Assembly", Proc. of 2009 IEEE International Conference on Intelligent Robots and Systems (2009 IROS), St. Louis, Missouri, USA, Oct. 11 – 15, 2009

# Smart Sensing for Real-Time Pose Estimation, Assembly, and Inspection Using 3D Laser Scanning Systems

Chad English
Neptec Design Group
302 Legget Dr., Ottawa
Ontario, Canada, K2K 1Y5
1-613-599-7602

cenglish@neptec.com

## ABSTRACT

Smart sensing describes a class of sensing that uses information extracted from sensor data to automatically drive the gathering of more specific data from which more information can be gathered. This approach attempts to minimize the amount of non-relevant data gathered for the operation following a paradigm of "more information, less data" (MILD). Neptec has successfully developed a range three dimensionally intelligence (3D-i) software and sensors following this paradigm for applications in space, military, and industrial settings under dynamic environments. Applications include assembly, inspection, rendezvous & docking, and dynamic imaging. This paper discusses the approach, designs, challenges, and evaluation of these sensor systems in the context of state-of-the-art and emerging technologies.

## Categories and Subject Descriptors

I.4.8 [**Image Processing and Computer Vision**]: Scene Analysis – *motion, range data, tracking, surface fitting, time-varying imagery*

I.2.9 [**Artificial Intelligence**]: Robotics – *sensors*;

I.2.10 [**Artificial Intelligence**]: Vision and Scene Understanding – *3D/stereo scene analysis, motion, modeling and recovery of physical attributes, shape*

I.4.1 [**Image Processing and Computer Vision**]: Digitization and Image Capture - *scanning*

## General Terms

Performance, Design.

## Keywords

Pose estimate, 3D, dynamic imaging, inspection, sensor systems.

## 1. INTRODUCTION

Dynamic operations that require imaging, modeling, or assembling parts generally require real-time 6 degree-of-freedom (DOF) pose estimation (PE) to track the coordinate transformations between the sensor and objects or between multiple objects seen by the sensor. In machine vision, PE techniques generally come in two flavours: those that use fiducial targets placed on the object to be tracked and those that use natural features of the object. Fiducial targets are more invasive but traditionally have provided more robust and accurate measurements than feature-based techniques.

Over the last 20 years Neptec has developed and deployed a variety of machine vision system for PE from the camera-and-target-based Space Vision System (SVS) for assembling the International Space Station (ISS) to the laser-and-shape-based TriDAR system. Spin-off technologies have applied these technologies to space, defense, and industrial applications, including dynamic 3D imaging, 3D mapping, inspection, automatic target recogntion, metrology, GIS, helicopter landing, and rover navigation. This paper reports on Neptec's experiences, challenges, and lessons learned on these projects.

## 2. SENSORS AND SYSTEMS FOR PE

### 2.1 3D PE Sensor Technology

For high-end, robust, mid- to long-range applications based on real-time 6 DOF PE there are essentially two options: target-based systems using 2D or 3D sensors or 3D imaging sensors. The most mature 3D imaging technology is a scanning laser (triangulation or time-of-flight (TOF)). The last decade has seen the development and maturation of scannerless flash-based systems to the point where both advantages and limitations of the technology can be assessed. Recently, MEMS-based lidars have been in development. While technically a scanning lidar, the only moving part is a small oscillating mirror and hence size, weight, and power can be significantly reduced. (Close range triangulation structured light systems are not considered here due their controlled environment requirements.)

While these types of sensors are meant for different applications, their combination covers most of the performance/envelope space not currently covered by existing scanning technology (Figure 1 and Table 1). These 3D sensing techniques therefore cover most of the conceivable high-end PE applications. It is possible to combine techniques but this would not increase the coverage in terms of overall performance vs. system envelope. This approach may also retain the disadvantages of the combined techniques. For example, scanning a flash lidar creates a hybrid with high data rate and large scan volume. But it comes with the larger aperture of the flash and moving parts of the scanner, so it trades performance for footprint.

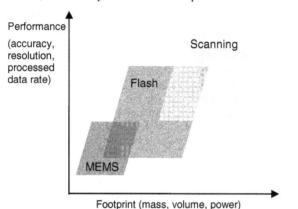

**Figure 1: Performance vs footprint of 3D sensing technologies.**

**Table 1: 3D active sensing technology comparison.**

|  | MEMS | Flash | Scanning |
|---|---|---|---|
| **FOV** | wide random access | small fixed | wide random access |
| **Data Rate** | high sequential | very high simultaneous | low sequential |
| **Accuracy** | medium | low for now | high |
| **Resolution** | high | low for now | high |
| **Reach** | short | far | far |
| **Dyn. Range** | high | low for now | high |
| **Power** | low | Medium | high |
| **Size** | small | Medium | large |
| **Mass** | small | Medium | large |
| **Moving parts** | micro mirror | no | yes |

## 2.2 AR&D Systems

In its very basic form, PE provides position (3 DOF) or position and orientation (6 DOF). Additional variables such as rates can be derived or measured. Perhaps the most basic and demanding use of PE is the rendezvous and docking of spacecraft. These craft can move relatively unconstrained in all 6 DOF, potentially at high relative rates, under harsh conditions of lighting and temperature variation, and with very high risk associated with failure.

The state-of-the-art in rendezvous & docking technology has only matured in the last decade. The Orbital Express mission of 2007 saw the first successful Autonomous Rendezvous & Docking (AR&D) system flown on-orbit [12]. This DARPA & NASA success was soon followed-up in the ESA Jules Verne ATV successful mission of 2008 [10]. Prior to these successes, rendezvous and docking and berthing systems required hands-on control by astronauts. Such systems date back to the optical cross-hairs of the 1966 Gemini 8 test docking with the unmanned Agena Target Vehicle up to Neptec's target-based Space Vision

System (SVS) for assembling the ISS [16]. It is only recently that automated systems have been attempted.

The NASA Demonstration of Autonomous Rendezvous Technology (DART) mission in April 2005 was the first attempt to perform an automated rendezvous, but with no capture or docking, without a human in the loop [24]. The mission failed when DART prematurely placed itself in a retirement phase after missing some cues and colliding with the target vehicle. The automated rendezvous system used on DART was NASA's Advanced Video Guidance Sensor (AVGS). AVGS was later successfully used on the Orbital Express mission in early 2007. The AVGS system uses cooperative retro-reflective targets on the target vehicle and applies photogrammetric algorithms to the imaged target locations in a camera, much like SVS. AVGS improves upon SVS by using two active flood lasers to image the retro targets and filters out other light frequencies, thus making it more immune to lighting conditions. AVGS shows great promise as an AR&D system, but suffers from limitations of all target-based systems: the requirement for placement of targets on the vehicle and limited views over which pose can be measured.

The Orbital Express mission actually used four sensor systems to accommodate AR&D operations: a laser rangefinder for target range information, a visible sensor for daytime pointing of the rangefinder, an IR sensor for nighttime pointing of the rangefinder, and the AVGS system for close proximity final approach and capture [15].

The ESA Jules Verne ATV mission in 2008 also used a series of sensors and instrumented to successfully rendezvous and dock with the ISS using GPS, a videometer that bounced pulsed laser beams off of passive retroreflectors, and image pattern analysis [9]. Redundant back-up LIDAR systems used pulsed TOF lasers on the retroreflectors to confirm range, but not orientation. The ATV system is similarly limited in close range operations to those of AVGS, with the additional constraint of operation using GPS for longer range operations.

Stereo-vision has been used for tele-operation during the ETS-VII mission [18][29]. This system successfully demonstrated rendezvous and docking but was operated by ground operators. Similar systems were proposed for use on the TECSAS and ConeXpress (now Smart-OLEV) missions. Stereo systems are feasible as AR&D PE sensors but are susceptible to the same problems of 2F systems such as lighting conditions, object features and contrast, and calibration of the cameras.

There have been several successful laser-based systems. The RELAVIS system developed by Optech uses 3D LIDAR data to provide PE of target vehicles [2][13]. This system is similar to Neptec's TriDAR-based tracking system in that neither system requires cooperative targets and fits measured 3D data to a reference model of the target vehicle [23]. The main differences between these systems involve the hardware design and the fitting algorithms and the subsequent accuracy and speed performance. The RELAVIS system was successfully tested on the U.S. Air Force XSS-11 mission in 2005 to provide range and bearing information. Neptec's TriDAR system successfully flew on STS-128 and STS-130 for both docking and undocking of the Space Shuttle to the International Space Station (ISS) and has been selected as baseline for several future satellite servicing and docking missions.

## 2.3 Autosynchronous Scanning Systems

Single-point flying spot scanners allow precise control and measurement. The traditional disadvantages of such systems include the mass, volume, and power required for moving parts and comparatively slow data acquisition rate.

The data rate can be mitigated by smart sensing techniques as described in Section 3. Speed, precision, and dynamic range can also be optimized using an autosynchronous scanning design. First developed by the Canadian National Research Council (NRC), Neptec licensed and adapted the autosynchronous design as the Laser Camera System (LCS) for tracking SVS targets and imaging in space [26]. After the Columbia shuttle accident in 2003, the LCS was adapted for imaging and inspecting of the shuttle Thermal Protection System (TPS) on orbit due to its high measurement precision. The autosynchronous design allows for a very narrow instantaneous field-of-view of the detector that can follow the laser spot by using the two sides of the same mirror. The high precision at standoff distances of meters makes the autosynchronous design ideal for metrology applications and Neptec has since adapted it for high-precision manufacturing applications in the Laser Metrology System (LMS) [31].

The same design was expanded to the aforementioned TriDAR AR&D sensor for long range PE. The TriDAR multiplexes a TOF pulsed lidar in the same optical path as the triangulation-based CW laser of the LCS, thereby optimizing the complementary nature of triangulation and TOF lidar [8]. PE is accomplished using real-time ICP software originally developed for automatic target recognition [7][21].

The use of a TOF lidar in the autosynchronous triangulation design also greatly increases the dynamic range of the lidar by having the laser spot "walk off" the detector at closer ranges. Such capability allows the lidar to better see through obscurants and is the basis for Neptec's Obscurant Penetrating Autosynchronous Lidar (OPAL) [32]. OPAL is essentially a TriDAR with the CW trangulation laser removed with some custom modifications to further improve obscurant penetration. It is currently used in a forward kinematic fashion using GNC information to geo-reference OPAL data to aid in landing helicopters in brown-out or white-out conditions [33]. However, in principle it can still perform PE as the TriDAR and LCS do.

## 2.4 Flash Technology

Flash imaging refers to the capability of acquiring all pixels of a 3D range image at once. For the last decade, flash 3D sensing has been perceived by many as the holy grail of 3D sensing because of its potential size and data acquisition rate. There are many ways to accomplish flash 3D imaging: CW modulation, APD array (Geiger or linear modes), and range gating. However, they all share the similar concept of flood illumination and detector array. A flash LIDAR acquires all the data at once without requiring moving parts but in doing so, it requires many times more instantaneous power. This tends to limit some combination of range, FOV, and resolution. Scanning sensors are random access which gives them an almost infinite zoom capability (limited by spot size) over a larger field of view (typically 30°) and much further range for a given laser power. By using smart sensing techniques (Section 3), a scanning LIDAR can be directed to gather only the needed data, thereby minimizing scan times and making more efficient use of the

available laser power. But that capability comes at the price of moving parts and increased power consumption. Because each point in a scanning system is acquired individually, these sensors also have much better dynamic range than flash LIDARs.

It is now clear that flash imaging will not completely replace scanning lidars but rather trade off scan volume and dynamic range for data rate, making them better suited for different applications.

## 2.5 MEMS Lidar

Microelectromechanical devices (MEMs) have the potential to improve the data rate and footprint of scanning systems [27]. A 3D sensor with similar data rate as flash LIDAR could be achieved in a much smaller package. Since the size of the achievable aperture is much less than other systems, this type of sensor is limited to short range applications. Nevertheless, this technology can enable the use of 3D sensors in applications where it was previously impossible because of the size and power consumption involved. Neptec has started development of a MEMS lidar with partners INO and CSA. Preliminary design shows promise for inexpensive short-range applications.

## 3. SMART SENSING
## 3.1 The MILD Approach

Neptec has been pursuing a new approach to three-dimensional (3D) sensing referred to as Smart Sensing. This approach applies the paradigm of "more information, less data" (MILD) with two key elements; first, intelligent algorithms, referred to as *three-dimensional intelligence* (3D-i), process the raw 3D data directly at the sensor head. Second, the output of the processing algorithms drives the 3D scanner to gather only the data necessary to compute the next set of information.

A primary example of such a 3D-i application is Neptec's tracking software primarily used on the TriDAR. The autosynchronous scanning design allows random access within the scanner FOV and hence can use arbitrary scan patterns. Figure 2 shows three typical scan patterns for the TriDAR with representative laser spot spacing at uniform time intervals. The Lissajous pattern (left) has high point density in the corners and low in the center making it useful for monitoring transitions at the edges. The Rosette pattern (center) has highest point density at the center and lowest at the periphery, much like the human eye nerves. This makes it ideal for high resolution imaging of central features while maintaining width and height in less important regions for alignment stability and monitoring purposes. The Spiral pattern (right) is uniform in angular and radial spacing and hence ideal for surface digitization, inspection, or for surfaces with uniform distribution of features.

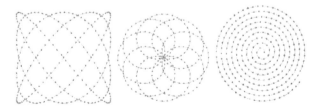

**Figure 2: Dual axes scanning patterns: 4x5 Lissajous (left), 8-petal Rosette (center), and a 9-turn Spiral (right).**

Raster scan patterns (not shown) are also typical for relatively static imaging such as LCS inspection of the Space Shuttles. Rasters have uniform spacing in horizontal and vertical directions much like the Spiral. Arbitrary patterns can also be used, limited only by the inertia of the scanning mirrors and galvo current. The three scan patterns in Figure 2 make optimal use of the natural sinusoidal inertias to cover an area in the fastest time. A single completed pattern is referred to as a *frame* of data. Frame rates depend on the chosen pattern, pattern parameters (Lissajous nodes, Rosette petals, Spiral turns), and number of points per pattern. Typically frame rates of 5-10 Hz are achievable.

Scan patterns are key to Smart Scanning real-time PE. The pattern and parameters can adapt dynamically to the PE. PE and initialization algorithms are designed around unorganized point clouds and are therefore not reliant on the details of the scan pattern or on a regular grid as with correlation operator techniques. PE is initialized using a Polygonal Aspect Hashing technique [23]. The hashing algorithm creates N-point polygons from the unorganized scan points and compares them to a reference model hash table. The cumulative matched polygons provide a limited set of pose candidates that are tested by selecting the one that best fits the scan to the database model. The key to optimum efficiency and performance of the Polygonal Aspect Hashing is to keep the reference database sparse, storing only the dominant discriminating geometric features. This provides a sufficiently accurate initial PE while keeping the number of matches manageable.

The initial PE is then used in a proprietary Iterative Closest Point (ICP) algorithm to finely align the scan data to the model. The 6 DOF tracking then uses the output PE from one data frame as the initializing PE for the next frame using ICP [22]. The PE is also used to adjust the size of the scan pattern to only gather data on the object or region as well as the position of the scan pattern within the sensor's FOV. Adaptively scanning in this manner collects only data necessary for the PE.

In this sense, Smart Scanning mitigates the slower data rate and improves efficiency of scanning sensors. Flash-based sensors can gather large datasets very quickly but do so in a brute force manner where the laser power is distributed over the whole FOV, much of which does not fall on the target region of interest. With the autosynchronous scanner, all laser power can go towards generating useful, and ultimately used, data points. Furthermore, computational power is often a limiting factor and Smart Scanning can generate enough useful points per frame to max out the processing power while providing accurate PE. The increased data rate in other systems means much of it will have to be filtered or sub-sampled to accommodate computational limitations for real-time processing. Combining these factors with the added data precision quality from autosynchronous scanning and the resulting real-time PE can be of equal or better quality over a wider range of operations given the same computing hardware.

The selective acquisition of *necessary* data is a feature of Smart Scanning that derives from the MILD paradigm. For AR&D or similar applications it is the PE that is the information of interest, not the raw data, and hence increased data rate may not be helpful. That being said, there is nothing in the Smart Sensor approach that specifically requires this type of sensor and so the 3D-i software can work with a variety of sensor technologies capable of producing 3D data. For example, the Polygonal Aspect

Hashing and real-time ICP algorithms work well with point clouds in disorganized order, semi-organized scan patterns, or organized grid patterns. The software can also filter points out of range boundaries or tracked object envelope so the only required sensor-specific pre-processing is to output 3D data in Cartesian (x,y,z) format. All of this can be run on a sensor head with embedded processing capabilities or, if not available locally, on an external processing unit.

## 3.2 Dynamic Assembly

Real-time 6 DOF PE is an application itself for a class of assembly operations that include assembly of parts such as the ISS modules, and rendezvous & docking (as described in Section 2.1). Target-based systems like SVS and AVGS can be highly accurate and reliable under controlled conditions and range of orientations where targets can be used. Targetless tracking systems such as TriDAR extend the capability and reliability to less controlled conditions such as space and subsea, but are limited to shapes that have definitive geometric features [17].

## 3.3 Dynamic Metrology

Metrology applications often require specific feature measurement rather than full digitization of parts. An example is the gap and flush of car doors in which the measurements are made at a fixed number of locations. In many such applications it is not uncommon to see sample parts fully digitized through CMM machines or part scanners. However, the ability for real-time PE can allow for direct measurement *in situ* as long as the feature of interest is visible. The use of an autosynchronous scanning system also allows arbitrary measurement patterns.

Neptec developed a demonstration of this Smart Scanning capability using the Laser Metrology System (LMS) derived from the LCS but for higher precision measurement. As a proof-of-concept, a car door mock-up was mounted on a motion control system. Full 6 DOF tracking software on the LMS, using techniques similar to those described in Section 3.1, tracked the door's motion. Four standard gap-and-flush measurement points were pre-defined in the door's frame of reference and located using the real-time PE, at which point the four gap-and-flush measurements were made by directly scanning a line across the reference points and calculating the gap-and-flush parameters directly, all while in motion and without fully digitizing the door.

## 3.4 Object Recognition

Object recognition can enhance dynamic assembly and metrology by first recognizing the objects using the same smart scanning techniques to perform the PE. Neptec's PE software first derived from real-time Automatic Target Recognition (ATR) work [7][21]. In this 3D ATR technique, scan data is compared to an a priori knowledge base of 3D objects. Rapid pruning techniques select a subset of objects and poses and the scan data is fit to the remaining cases to simultaneously select the recognized object and calculate its PE. The recognition process, including validation, can take place in <1 s on off-the-shelf processors. The technique is parallelizable and scalable for large object databases.

A key feature discovered in early ATR work is that salient features of 3D shapes can be sufficiently generated by sparse, but smart, scanning. Hence rapid scan patterns can generate the data and recognize the object in under a second. Repeated scan patterns can then generate both recognition validation and PE with each frame. Combining the multi-frame recognitions can vastly improve the recognition confidence [4]. Ultimately, by combining above techniques the sensor could recognize an object, continually increase recognition confidence, provide object PE in motion, track it, and perform metrology measurements on the object, all in real time. While this particular combination has not been demonstrated, all of the components have been tested and work modularly with each other.

## 3.5 Inspection and Digitizing

Smart Scanning and the MILD paradigm can also apply even when the data itself is the product. One class of applications that fits this circumstance is the digitization and inspections of parts or surfaces. Typically this is performed under highly controlled conditions in which 3D data is gathered from multiple views of a part and stitched together to make a full 3D model. The controlled conditions are necessary to know the coordinate transformations between the views from controlled part motion, controlled sensor motion, or multiple fixed sensors. That is, the model is assembled using the forward kinematics of known sensor and part positions.

A less controlled approach uses unknown positions but tracks fiducial targets to calculate motion between view datasets. This approach is functionally identical to SVS, except that it is data scans that are "docked" by their relative PEs to assemble a virtual 3D model rather than real object modules.

As with TriDAR to SVS, there is an even less controlled alternative that makes use of the 3D shape of the part to align multiple views via ICP or similar techniques. This is the inverse-kinematic solution in which the relative sensor positions are inferred from the multiple dataset alignments. In theory, the inverse-kinematic solutions can be less accurate than the more controlled forward-kinematic solution because they introduce a PE error. On the other hand, the forward-kinematic solution can suffer from PE error both in terms of calibrating the sensor relative locations and the amplification of small orientation errors through the moment arm between sensor and object. The latter problem is discussed in greater detail in the following section.

Neptec investigated errors due to knowledge of the sensor pose on STS-114, the Space Shuttle's 2005 return to flight after the Columbia tragedy in 2003 [6]. For inspection of the shuttle's Thermal Protection System (TPS) on orbit, Neptec's LCS is mounted at the end of a 15 m boom that is grappled and manoeuvred by the 15 m long Canadarm. Motion of the sensor within a single scan and registration of multiple scans were potential issues prior to return-to-flight on STS-114. Scans were performed of a tile bed in the cargo bay using two modes of the Canadarm. Figure 3 shows the results. The first mode, on the left, shows 3D scan results with brakes on for all joint motors. The worry for this case was that the sensor may oscillate slightly due to flexion over the 30 m structure. The second mode, on the left, was the Position and Orientation Hold Select (POHS) in which the joint motors actively attempted to hold the arm motionless. As the figure shows, the POHS results showed much greater sensor motion during scanning, creating error in the model surface.

By contrast, the inverse-kinematic solution makes use of the real-time PE from rapid scanning to align multiple scan sets. This

3D dynamic imaging technique was largely pioneered in a practical sense in the early 2000s simultaneously by Stanford's Computer Graphics Laboratory [25] and Canada's National Research Council (NRC) [3], the latter using the same auto-synchronous scanner design that is the basis for the LCS.

**Figure 3: Scans of the DTO Tile Board with Brakes on (left) and with POHS enabled (right)**

The MILD paradigm can play a particularly important role in 3D dynamic imaging. Real-time PE comes from aligning the same features in multiple scans. In that context, redundancy is inherently required. Without redundancy, there is nothing to align. But redundancy adds unnecessary data to the 3D model. One option is to throw away redundant points either by alternating patterned scans for alignment with detailed scans for imaging or through some selection process to reject points. Another option is to use the redundancy to extract a better surface measurement. The result is a smoother surface – one that more accurately represents the true object – while maintaining a minimum amount of storage space by removing redundancy. That is, more information is extracted while storing (and transmitting) less data. The efficiency from such a framework allows the model to build with linear complexity and real-time surface reconstruction [28].

## 3.6 Dynamic mapping, navigation, and GIS

A second class of applications where the 3D data itself is the product is 3D terrain mapping. Such mapping may be for a variety of purposes such as archival, civil engineering, urban planning, security, or military operations. In principle, mapping is identical to 3D object digitizing except that the object being digitized is a large area of land or urban terrain. However, there are many practical differences. The biggest difference can be seen when considering urban mapping. Large scale terrain mapping typically requires aerial imaging using a scanning lidar. This is also necessary to get the tops of buildings. Street-level mapping, including most of the data on vertical surfaces, requires mounting lidars (typically several) on ground vehicles moving at road speeds. Generating accurate cumulative data from a single data source can be challenging. Aligning the data from multiple data sources adds an additional layer of complexity.

Typically all of the data is combined by converting it to a fixed geo-reference frame. This is almost universally accomplished via the forward-kinematic method using high-end GPS and inertial navigation systems along with highly calibrated positioning and orientation of the sensors and scan angles. Achieving total accuracies comparable to the sensor accuracy requires the best available systems and calibration methods. When scanning from hundreds of meters away, even a small orientation or angular error can contribute significant positional error in the geo-referenced location of a point. Compounding this problem, ground vehicles will often lose some or all GPS signal in dense urban environments, relying solely on the inertial systems which inherently suffer from drift errors. Post-processing of collected data can often correct this error once GPS is re-established, but that can require additional detailed analysis and fine adjustments at added cost and may not be helpful in applications that require real-time mapping and localization.

As with dynamic imaging of parts, there can be benefit in the inverse-kinematic approach by extracting navigational PE information from aligning redundant data. Figure 4 shows how these two capabilities can be used to close the kinematic chain and improve the data. Closing the loop provides redundancy in both the sensor pose and the data pose. However, the redundant estimates are not equal. Figure 4 shows that the moment arm acting between the two pose sources magnifies any small errors. Small errors in the estimate of the sensor orientation (left) can result in large positional errors of the data, both relative to each other and to reality. Small errors in aligning the data sets (right) can result in large errors in estimating the sensor position.

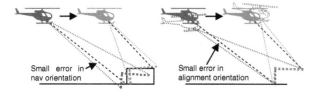

**Figure 4: Kinematic errors, forward (left), inverse (right)**

Generally speaking, the local PE will be much better than the one acting through the moment arm. The navigation data will provide a better estimate of the pose of the sensor and the ICP will provide a better estimate of the pose of the data. This does not mean that both estimates cannot be used. The navigation data can use a weighted combination of the two, such as in an Extended Kalman Filter (EKF), that weighs the local navigation data higher but can be improved slightly from the ICP PE or rely more on the ICP estimate to keep the EKF from drifting off when navigation data is unavailable, such as GPS outages. For cases with stable relative motion, an EKF may also be able to provide a sufficiently accurate PE even with the loss of both navigation data and pose information from data alignment. This principle was successfully tested by the Canadian Space Agency in partnership with Neptec and Ryerson University using Neptec's LCS and pose tracking software [1].

The general approach is the basis for the Optical IMU prototype software developed collaboratively by Neptec, Terrapoint, McGill University, and Carleton University [11]. This system applies to ground-based data collected by Terrapoint's TITAN system. It has the greatest potential for this application for two reasons: (1) TITAN is prone to occasional GPS outages during urban data collection due to the high buildings and obstructions, and (2) TITAN gathers data from all around the vehicle, putting the centroid of the collected data closer to the sensor location. This latter benefit relies on the fact that the ICP error-amplifying moment arm exists between the sensor origin and the centroid of the collected data, thus having the sensor near the data centroid minimizes this error. Figure 5 shows the misalignment of lidar data on a car from two passes with navigation drift error (top) and the corrections made by the Optical IMU software aligning the data sets (bottom).

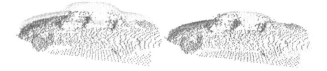

**Figure 5: Misalignment from navigation errors (left) and Optical IMU corrected (right)**

On the data side, the forward kinematic calculation from the navigation system can be used as an initial guess to seed the ICP for finer alignment and keep the alignment bounded from drifting off to an incorrect local minimum. In the case of Optical IMU, the alignment based PE was maintained by using redundancy in the multiple sensors on the TITAN system itself and hence was still prone to drift error over time, though independent from the inertial drift error. However, the approach can be applied to aligning data from TITAN during GPS loss to data gathered without GPS loss, such as from an airborne dataset or prior mapping of the area where the data can act as a GPS proxy.

Closing the kinematic loop is also the basis for Simultaneous Localization and Mapping (SLAM). In the case of SLAM, absolute knowledge of location, as in GPS, is absent. Only the inertia systems and scan data is available for generating both the map and locating the sensor (and hence the vehicle). SLAM is typically used for robotic rover navigation in unknown environments such as lunar and Martian exploration. The similarity between the requirements for the GIS mapping and rover SLAM means similar real-time PE techniques can apply. Neptec has investigated use of the technique for rovers in partnership with Carleton University [20], Carnegie Mellon University [30], and with CSA for possible implementation on the Neptec Rover Team's Juno rover [14].

# 4. SMART SENSING PERFORMANCE

Perhaps the largest challenge for Smart Sensing is the quantification of performance in any meaningful way. For the main component of PE, it seems simple enough in principle; simply measure the pose of objects with the Smart Scanning system (e.g., TriDAR) in some reference frame and compare to truth data, possibly using survey equipment. Indeed this approach is a good way to measure performance for both target-based systems and targetless systems and Neptec has done this for both SVS and TriDAR for space mission qualifications.

The problem with the approach is that PE is highly situational specific. It is reliant on the quality of sensor data, the quality of the processing algorithms, the view of the target, and perhaps most critically on the object shape itself. (In this context, the object shape of a target-based system is the arrangement of targets as seen by a given view.) In the realm of sensor data quantification there is difficulty in defining standards for 3D sensors, but the problem seems related to defining which metrics are important and which tests best measure them. Ongoing efforts at NIST and other organizations seem to be addressing this.

Quantifying performance for PE algorithms is more difficult, particularly because of the dependence on object geometry. The typical example for targetless pose is a sphere or a can. A sphere has a defined position but not orientation. A can has a single axis of symmetry along the cylinder around which the rotation angle is undefined. Even with objects that have a defined pose, generalized quantification of performance is difficult. Imagine, for instance, tracking a coffee mug. The mug itself has a well-defined true orientation in 6 DOF, but if the sensor cannot see the handle it has the same problem in defining rotation angle as with a cylinder. It is impossible to say with what accuracy a sensor system, including the PE algorithm, can estimate the pose of a coffee mug. The answer is highly dependent on whether it can see the handle or not regardless of the sensor or algorithm. Rather than being hypothetical, this is the real problem Neptec had in defining performance for the Hubble Telescope [22].

The difficulty is compounded by operational circumstances. Suppose the cylinder has unique features that can define an exact pose and the sensor has the capability to see them but simply does not. For instance, a flash 3D system may be zoomed out to capture the whole shape but misses the resolution of the small features that lock down the rotational DOF. Zoomed in it might pick up the features enough to lock down rotation angle but now cannot see the top and bottom of the cylinder to determine position along that axis. In TriDAR's case, it may be the selection of scan pattern, size of scan pattern, number of points in the scan pattern, or chosen reference point to track that affect whether the best data is collected to provide the best PE. PE accuracy can be tested on an object by object and view by view case with optimization of sensor parameters either manually for the case or automatically using some metrics, but this type of testing can be expensive.

Perhaps the best solution to the evaluation problem is through synthetic simulation. This seems counter-intuitive, especially since many computer vision journals no longer accept purely simulated results. However, a simulator allows a battery of statistical tests over a wide range of testing parameters that would be impractically expensive to perform in live testing. If the simulator is sufficiently developed and validated it can arguably provide better generalized performance metrics than live testing.

For SVS missions, NASA and Neptec used a battery of validated mission simulators. The SVS Accuracy Analysis Program (SAAP) performed Monte Carlo simulations of SVS operations to evaluate performance pre-flight and adjust mission planning; the Target Image Model (TIM) selected the optimum parameters for target tracking and validated the mission plan against certified target tracking performance; SVS Accuracy Model (SAM) provided PE sensitivity to measurement and calibration accuracy. Characterization of the input error sources and validation with full scale mission simulations in the lab were key to acceptance of these tools.

Similarly, for TriDAR missions a full sensor simulator was built into the mission planning tool [22]. TriDAR sensor characteristics were measured and included in the simulation. Lab testing using scale models of ISS modules validated the simulator performance. What is particularly interesting about the TriDAR mission planning tool is that it is the same software that runs operationally on the space shuttle. The only difference is whether the data source is the simulated TriDAR or a real one. The mission software cannot tell the difference. This feature allows the characterization of full system performance to match as closely to the real performance as possible limited only by how close the

simulated sensor performance matches that of TriDAR and how closely the CAD models of the space station match the real thing.

While synthetic simulations can provide performance metrics relevant to specific operation requirements, they do not solve the general evaluation problem. Providing generalized performance specifications seems infeasible. What may suffice is performance using a set of standard objects, perhaps ranging from easy to track pose to difficult. Ryerson University, in partnership with Neptec and CSA, developed a optimum shape for PE from 3D sensor data [5]. The resulting shape was a modified cuboctahedron that had minimal ambiguity, shown in Figure 6. A series of such shapes could vary in steps from this optimum shape towards a sphere. The performance of a PE system on such targets could provide standard metrics for comparing systems, though they could not directly provide expected performance with a different object.

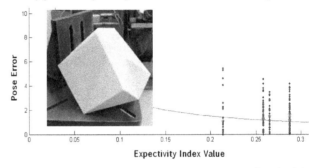

**Figure 6: Reduced-pose-ambiguity cuboctahedron (inset) with Experimental Pose Error versus Expectivity Index**

The metrics from PE evaluation generally include update rate and the precision and bias in position and orientation (or PE norm) but should include failure rate for loss of tracking. These metrics can be provided as a function of shape ambiguity (ranging from optimal to spherical) and of relative motion speed in various directions. In the case of active sensors, the standard objects might also range in surface reflectance properties.

An alternative to using standard objects for PE is to evaluate PE performance as a function of object shape properties. The modified cuboctahedron from Ryerson was developed based on Continuum-Shape Constraint Analysis (CSCA) which assigns metrics to surfaces based on the strength of their shape for self-alignment through ICP or similar algorithms. The CSCA metrics include Minimum Eigenvalue, Noise Amplification, and Expectivity Index [18]. The Minimum Eigenvalue quantifies the critical least-constrained direction in pose space; The Noise Amplification Index (NAI) adds a condition number factor to the Minimum Eigenvalue to simultaneously promote small error and isotropy in pose error space; The Expectivity Index models sensitivity to statistical noise. Figure 6 shows an example plot of experimental results for pose error as a fuction of Expectivity.

The CSCA indices are defined for a given surface and so represent object-based parameters by which different PE systems can be evaluated. Testing with individual systems can therefore generate a series of performance curves against these indices. The usefulness of this approach is that a user can measure the CSCA indices for the objects they intend to apply a PE system to and have an estimate of the pose error to expect from a specific pose system, creating an absolute performance estimate that can be compared with operational requirements.

# 5. REFERENCES

[1] Aghili, F. et al. 2010. Integrated Kalma Filter and ICP for Robust Pose Estimation. *Accepted to IEEE Sensors Journal.*

[2] Allen, A., Mak, N., and Langley, C. 2005. Development of a Scaled Ground Testbed for Lidar-based Pose Estimation, *IEEE IROS 2005* (Edmonton, AB, Aug 2). 10-15.

[3] Blais, F. et al. 2003. New Development in 3D Laser Scanners: From Static to Dynamic Multi-Modal Systems, *6th Conf Opt 3-D Meas Tech*, (Zurich, Switzerland, Sep 22-26).

[4] Bouchette, G. et al. 2007. Rapid automatic target recognition using generic 3D sensor and shape-from-motion data, *SPIE DSS* (Orlando, FL, Apr. 9-13). 6566:19.

[5] Choudhuri, A. et al. 2010. Design of Optimal Shapes for Space Docking using LIDAR-Based Vision Systems, *ASTRO 2010* (Toronto, ON, May 4-6).

[6] Deslauriers, A. et al. 2006. 3D Inspection for the Shuttle Return to Flight, *SPIE DSS* (Orlando, FL, Apr 17-20). 6220.

[7] English, C. et al. 2004. Development of a Practical 3D Automatic Target Recognition & Pose Estimation Algorithm. *SPIE DSS* (Orlando, FL, Apr 12-16). 5426:112-123.

[8] English, C. et al., 2005. Tridar: A Hybrid Sensor for Exploiting the Complimentary Nature of Triangulation and LIDAR technologies, *i-SAIRAS* (Munich, Germany, Sep 5-8). ESA SP-603, p.79.1.

[9] ESA, 2008. Rendezvous and Docking Technology, ATV Information Kit, February 2008.

[10] ESA Media Relations Office, 2008. Europe's automated ship docks to the ISS. *European Space Agency News*, April 3, 2008.

[11] Harrison, J.W., et al. 2009. Finding Anomalies in High-Density LiDAR Point Clouds, *GEOMATICA*, 63(4):397-405.

[12] Howard, R.T. et al. 2008. Orbital Express Advanced Video Guidance Sensor. In *2008 IEEE Aerospace Conference* (Big Sky, MT, March 1-8, 2008).

[13] Jasiobedzki, P., et al. 2005. Autonomous Satellite Rendezvous and Docking Using LIDAR and Model Based Vision, *SPIE DSS* (Orlando, FL, Mar 28-31). 5788:54-65.

[14] Kneisel, K. et al. 2010.Towards Vision-Based SLAM for Planet Exploration, *ASTRO 2010* (Toronto, ON, May 4–6).

[15] Leinz, M., and Chen, C. 2002. Autonomous Rendezvous and Capture Sensor System (ARCSS), *2002 Core Technologies for Space Systems* Conference (Colorado Springs, CO, Nov)

[16] MacLean, S., and Pinkney, L. 1993. Machine Vision in Space, *Can. Aeronaut. Space J.*, 39(2), 63-77.

[17] Maurelli, F. et al. 2009. Investigation of portability of space docking techniques for autonomous underwater docking, *OCEANS 2009-EUROPE* (Bremen, Germany, May 11-14).

[18] McTavish, D.J., Okouneva, G., and English, C.. 2010. Continuum Shape Constraint Analysis: A class of Integral Shape Properties Applicable for LIDAR/ICP-based Pose Estimation. *Accepted to International Journal of Shape Modeling.*

[19] Ohkami, Y., and Oda, M. 1999. NASDA's activities in space robotics, *i-SAIRAS '99* (Noordwijk, The Netherlands June 1-3). 11-18.

[20] Piechocinski, S., and Sasiadek, J. 2005. Experimental determination of relative motion measurement accuracy for an auto-synchronous triangulation scanning laser camera, *SPIE DSS* (Orlando, FL, Mar 30-Apr 2). 5791:208-217.

[21] Ruel, S. et al. 2004. Field testing of a 3D automatic target recognition and pose estimation algorithm, *SPIE DSS* (Orlando, FL, Apr 12-16). 5426:102-111.

[22] Ruel, S. et al. 2005. 3DLASSO: Real-time pose estimation from 3D data for autonomous satellite servicing, *i-SAIRAS*, (Munich, Germany, Sep 5-8). ESA SP-603.

[23] Ruel, S. et al. 2008. Target Localization from 3D data for On-Orbit Autonomous Rendezvous & Docking, *IEEE Aerospace Conference* (Big Sky, MT, March 1-8). 1-11.

[24] Rumford, T. 2002. Demonstration of Autonomous Rendezvous Technology (DART) Project Summary, *2002 Core Technologies for Space Systems Conference*, Nov.

[25] Rusinkiewicz, S., Hall-Holt, O., and Levoy, M., 2002, Real-Time 3D Model Acquisition, *SIGGRAPH 2002*, (San Antonio, TX, Jul 21). 21(3):438-446.

[26] Samson, C. et al. 2004. Neptec 3D Laser Camera System: From Space Mission STS-105 to Terrestrial Applications, *Canadian Aeronautics and Space Journal*, 50(2) 115-123.

[27] Siepmann, J.P., and Rybaltowski, A. 2005. Integrable ultra-compact, high-resolution, real-time MEMS LADAR for the individual soldier, *MILCOM 2005* (Atlantic City, NJ, Oct 17-20). 5:3073-79.

[28] Tubic, D. et al. 2004. A unified representation for interactive 3D modeling, *3DPVT 2004* (Thessaloniki, Greece, Sep 6-9). 175-182.

[29] Vergauwen, M. et al. 2000. On Satellite Vision-aided Robotics Experiment, *IEEE ICRA '00* (San Francisco, CA, Apr 24-28), 4040-4045.

[30] Wettergreen, D. et al. 2009. Design and Experimentation of a Rover Concept for Lunar Crater Resource Survey, *47th AIAA Aerospace Sciences Meeting* (Orlando, FL, Jan 5-8).

[31] Zhu, S. Smith, C., and English, C. 2005. Imaging System and Method, *Canadian patent CA 2620941*, WIPO pub no. WO/2007/025362.

[32] Zhu, X., Church, P., and Labrie, M. 2008. Lidar for obstacle detection during helicopter landing, *SPIE DSS*, (Orlando, FL, May 13). 6950:1-8.

[33] Zhu, X., Church, P., and Labrie, M. 2008. AVS Lidar for Detecting Obstacles Inside Aerosol (Chap 13), *Vision and Displays for Military and Security Applications*, ISBN 1441917225.

# Dynamic Performance Evaluation of 6D Laser Tracker Sensor

Kam Lau, Yubing Yang, Yuanqun Liu, Henry Song
Automated Precision, Inc.
15000 Johns Hopkins Dr.
Rockville, MD 20850
1-240-268-0400

## ABSTRACT

In this paper, several methods are presented for the evaluations of 6D sensor dynamic performances, including linear method and rotational method. These methods evaluate a sensor's translational and rotational characteristics under dynamic operations and have been successfully employed in the evaluations of the 3D and 6D sensor products of API. The presented methods provide a solution for accurate and systematic evaluations of general purpose 6D sensor dynamic performances.

## Categories and Subject Descriptors

D.8.2 [Performance Analysis and Design Aids]

## General Terms

Measurement, Performance

## Keywords

6D measurement, dynamic performance evaluation, laser tracker

## 1. INTRODUCTION

### 1.1 6D Measurement

Six-degree-of-freedom (6D) measurement is required when both the position and orientation of an object under measurement need to be determined, such as in robotic applications. Advancement in 6D sensor technologies and products makes possible more 6D measurement applications, and creates the need of 6D sensor evaluations. Automated Precision Inc. (API) is a pioneer of 6D sensor development and evaluations. API developed a series of laser tracker-based 6D sensor systems such as the SmartTrack System (STS) and I-360, as shown in Figure 1.

A Tracker-STS 6D measurement system is illustrated in Figure 2. A laser tracker is a 3D position measurement sensor based on spherical coordinate measurement. Its gimbal has two precision angular encoders to measure azimuth (AZ) and elevation (EL) angles, while a built-in laser interferometer (IFM) measures range (r). An STS, which is mounted on the object under measurement, is a 3D rotational measurement sensor to accomplish Pitch, Yaw and Roll measurement.

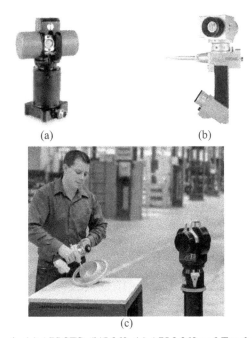

(a)  (b)

(c)

**Figure 1. (a) API STS; (b)I 360; (c) API I-360 and Tracker 6D measurement system application example**

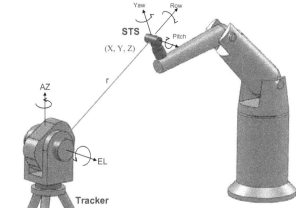

**Figure 2. Schematic illustration of 6D measurement STS and Tracker system**

### 1.2 Static vs. Dynamic

A 6D sensor is designed for both static and dynamic measurement. There is increased demand for a 6D sensor to perform under different dynamic situations. For example in robot control applications, accurate real-time 6D information of position and orientation of the robot end-effector is needed for accurate and prompt robot control feed-back. It is desired that similar accuracy obtained in dynamic measurement as in static measurement. But under many situations, dynamic measurement yields less accuracy or performance than static measurement because many sensors have dynamic performance limitations. Therefore, the static performance specifications of a 6D sensor may not be adequate to characterize a 6D sensor and its dynamic performances need to be evaluated and specified.

Dynamic performance evaluation of a 6D sensor is to find out how much the dynamic measurement results deteriorate from its static measurement results, or to explore what is the maximum speed the sensor can do while retaining acceptable accuracies. 6D sensor dynamic performance involves sensor frequency response, data stream timing and synchronization, and other sensor characteristics. How to accurately and efficiently evaluate the dynamic performances of 6D measurement sensors remains a challenging task. In this paper, we will introduce several methods in the evaluations of 6D sensor dynamic performances, including the linear method and the rotational method. These methods evaluate sensor's translational and rotational characteristics under dynamic operations and have been successfully employed in the evaluations of 3D and 6D sensor products of API. The presented methods provide a solution for accurate and systematic evaluations of general purpose 6D sensor dynamic performances.

## 2. PROBLEMS ENCOUNTERED IN DYNAMIC MEASUREMENT

Generally there are several factors that may affect dynamic performance of a 6D sensor system. The first factor is individual sensor's frequency response. This is solely depends on the individual sensor's characteristics. The second factor is the data sampling duration, especially when real-time averaging or filtering is applied to raw data. The third one is the synchronization of multiple sensor data acquisition. In API 6D sensor system, a global synchronization trigger is used to latch all sensor output simultaneously.

For some sensors, acceleration effect may also be a concern. For example, in API STS, the Roll measurement is realized by an inclinometer, which is actually a MEMS cantilever accelerometer. It is sensitive not only to rotation acceleration but also translation acceleration. Therefore, dynamic compensation is applied to the inclinometer to eliminate the translational acceleration effect on Roll measurement. The dynamic performance evaluation of STS Roll measurement can be realized by both the linear method and the rotational method, with each evaluates the sensor performance from two different perspectives.

## 3. DYNAMIC PERFORMANCE EVALUATION METHODS

Before dynamic performance evaluation, the equipment must be calibrated and verified to achieve its static accuracy. In most cases, dynamic error is superimposed on top of static error. During system dynamic performance evaluation, the measurement results from static mode test can be used as a baseline to evaluate the measurement results from dynamic mode.

In this section we introduce two 6D dynamic performance evaluation methods — linear method and rotational method.

### 3.1 Linear Method

The linear method evaluates the dynamic performance of along a specific axis of a 6D sensor. In the following discussion, we will take an API tracker as an example to evaluate its dynamic performance along X axis.

#### 3.1.1 Linear Stage Method for Tracker Evaluation

In the linear stage method, an IFM referenced linear stage is used to carry the measurement target. Using an API laser tracker as the example, a retroreflector (retro) or an SMR (spherical mounted retroreflector) is mounted on a linear stage as shown in Figure 3. The IFM and tracker are firmly fixed. The linear stage is driven by a motor, whose movement profile is programmed. Data sampling of the tracker and linear stage is synchronized by an external trigger. The measurement coordinate is defined by the tracker as illustrated in Figure 3. The moving axis of the linear stage is aligned parallel to the X axis of the tracker.

##### 3.1.1.1 Baseline Establishment

6D sensor's dynamic performance is tied to its static performance which is used as the baseline in its dynamic performance evaluations. Before dynamic performance evaluation, the tracker's static accuracy has been verified.

To obtain the baseline data in the linear stage method, the linear stage moves to a series of positions along its entire travel range. Its displacement at each position is measured by both the tracker and the IFM. The increment of Retro1 ($X_T$) measured by the tracker is mapped to the displacement of Retro2 ($D_{IFM}$) as shown in the plotted curve in Figure 4 (left).

In the $X_T$ vs. $D_{IFM}$ figure, the dashed (blue) line represents the line obtained with perfect alignment, i.e. the X axis of the tracker is aligned parallel to the stage moving axis. With perfect alignment $X_T$ is equal to $D_{IFM}$ at each point along the linear stage travel range, and the corresponding line is the reference line. The solid (red) line represents the measured data in static mode. This line deviates from the reference line because the alignment is not perfect. The difference between the measured line and the reference line is shown in Figure 4 (right). The difference represents misalignment induced error. The static measured line provides a baseline for dynamic error evaluation.

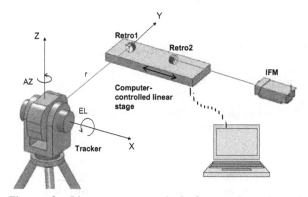

**Figure 3. Linear stage method for tracker dynamic performance evaluation**

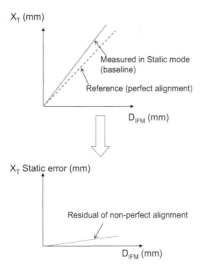

Figure 4. Obtain baseline from X-Tracker static measurement

### 3.1.1.2  Dynamic Performance Evaluation

The movement of the linear stage may be programmed to be a sinusoidal profile, linear profile or customized profile. In Figure 5 (left), the red line represents static baseline and the two green curves represent dynamic data from bidirectional travel of the linear stage. The difference between dynamic data and static baseline is shown in Figure 5 at right. This relative error provides enough information to show how well the system performs under dynamic situations.

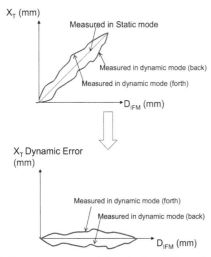

Figure 5. Compare measured data in dynamic mode and measured data in static mode to get the dynamic error

Given the measured displacement and time stamp, the speed and acceleration of the linear stage can be calculated. Therefore, the relationship of dynamic error vs. speed, and dynamic error vs. acceleration can be easily obtained. With different linear stage movement profiles, the dynamic error corresponding to different speed and acceleration profiles can be thoroughly studied.

The above discussion focuses on the X axis only. The tracker and the linear stage may be re-positioned to get the best sensitivity along other interested axes. Y axis evaluation could be done by setting up tracker Y axis parallel to the linear stage moving axis and Z axis evaluation can be done by orientating the linear stage vertically. Orientating the linear stage diagonally to the Tracker 3D coordinate will evaluate three axes at the same time.

### 3.1.2  Linear Stage Method for STS Roll Angle Measurement Evaluation

In API STS 6D sensor, Pitch and Yaw measurement are realized by encoders, their dynamic evaluation method is similar to that for the tracker, because tracker's AZ and EL angle measurement are encoder-based also. The Roll angle measurement in STS is different from the other two. As mentioned previously, the Roll measurement is realized by an inclinometer, which is actually a MEMS cantilever accelerometer. Acceleration effect influences its dynamic performance.

The linear stage method can be used to evaluate the acceleration effect for STS Roll measurement, with a slight modification of the setup in Figure 3. To test STS Roll angle measurement, Retro2 in Figure 3 is replaced with the STS under evaluation, as shown in Figure 6. As mentioned previously, acceleration effect is an important factor that affects the dynamic performance of STS Roll sensor. The inclinometer for Roll angle measurement is sensitive to both rotation acceleration and translation acceleration. While the linear stage is oscillating, the STS is not rotating around its Roll axis. Because of its sensitivity to translation acceleration, there will be an apparent oscillating roll angle output. Therefore, dynamic compensation is applied to the Roll sensor to cancel out the translation acceleration effect. With linear stage method, it is easy to evaluate whether the dynamic compensation is successful or the remaining accelerate effect influences the dynamic performance of Roll angle measurement. The evaluation step is similar to the linear stage method for tracker evaluation. First measure the Roll angle at positions along the stage travel range in static mode to establish a baseline. Next measure the roll angle in dynamic mode and compare the result with the baseline to get dynamic error.

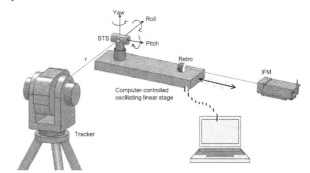

Figure 6. Oscillating linear stage method for STS Roll angle measurement evaluation

Figure 7 shows an example of the dynamically measured roll angle compared with baseline from the linear oscillating stage test.

The linear stage method helps engineers to evaluate and understand the dynamic performance of each individual axis. It is helpful for trouble shooting and development.

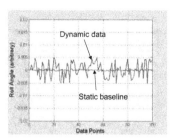

**Figure 7. The roll angle measured in dynamic mode compared with base line**

## 3.2 Rotational Method

Compared with linear method, the rotational method evaluates a 6D sensor with more complex dynamic movement, including both translation and rotation, and it does not require a reference IFM.

### 3.2.1 Rotary Bar Method for Tracker Evaluation

As shown in Figure 8, a Retro is fixed on the balanced rotary bar. The tracker is positioned at a distance of interest. The Y axis of tracker coordinate system is pointing to the center point of the rotary bar, and the rotation plane of the rotary bar is perpendicular to the Y axis of the tracker. Make sure the laser-SMR incident angle within the valid SMR incident angle at any position of the circle. In this setup, the tracker measured range is not sensitive to the retro movement with the rotary bar, and the test focus on dynamic performance evaluation of the AZ and EL encoder in the tracker. The bearing system of the rotary bar is well tuned and the rotation eccentricity is far better than the precision of the tracker.

Similar to the linear method, the static baseline needs to be established by measuring certain amount (8-12) of points around the circle statically, and fit the circle in the 3D coordinate frame, which yields the static baseline for dynamic measurement. The reference circle shown in Figure 9 is a perfect circle that ideally will be obtained with perfect alignment. Comparing the static baseline with the reference circle gives the misalignment error. Then dynamically measure the trajectory of Retro with the bar rotating. Compare the dynamic trajectory with the baseline, the difference shows the dynamic error vs. position. Figure 9 shows the trajectory from perfect alignment case (reference), static mode (baseline) and dynamic mode respectively.

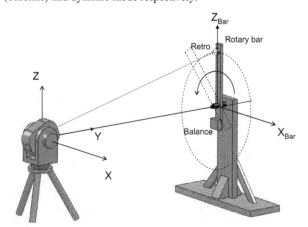

**Figure 8. Rotary bar method for tracker dynamic performance evaluation**

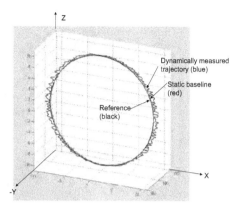

**Figure 9. The 3D trajectory measured in static mode and dynamic mode, compared with base line**

Among the three 3D coordinate axis, X, Y and Z, the Y axis have the least sensitivity to rotation depending on the rotary bar orientation in Tracker frame. The dynamic error can be further decomposed into dynamic error in X axis (DynErr-X), Y axis(DynErr-Y), and Z axis(DynErr-Z). We can focus on the relationship of DynErr-X vs. Position-X, and DynErr-Z vs. Position-Z.

Furthermore, from the measured Retro position information, it is easy to acquire Retro speed and acceleration information. Therefore, the dynamic error vs. speed, and dynamic error vs. acceleration relationship can be studied. It can further be decomposed into X, Y, Z acceleration components. By adjusting the Retro position (radius of rotation), the test may focus on error vs. speed or error vs. acceleration. Locating the Retro closer to the rotating center point, the test focuses more on acceleration; locating it further away from the center point, the test focuses more on speed. The rotary bar method is a quick and simple approach but may not provides detailed information as the linear stage method.

### 3.2.2 Rotary Table Method for STS Roll Angle Measurement Evaluation

To evaluate the STS Roll angle measurement, the rotary bar is replaced with a rotary table. The rotary table is motorized and the rotating angle is measured by an encoder. The STS is mounted on the rotary table as shown in Figure 10. The rotary table rotates around the center within a certain range, which is determined by the STS Roll sensor's working range. While the table is rotating, the inclinometer will experience both translational acceleration and rotational acceleration, in this manner Roll sensor's dynamic performance can be evaluated. With STS moves closer to the center point, it experiences less translation. And the test can focus more on rotational acceleration.

The test procedure is similar to the test of rotary bar for tracker evaluation. The reference is obtained by the rotary table encoder. The STS Roll angle with perfect alignment can be calculated from encoder angle. Next establish the baseline by measuring the roll angle along the trajectory in static mode. Then measure the roll angle in dynamic mode to find out dynamic error. Figure 12 schematically shows the data from this rotary table method for roll angle measurement evaluation.

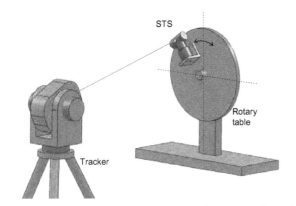

**Figure 10. Rotary table method for 6D sensor dynamic performance evaluation**

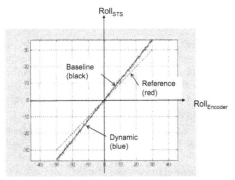

**Figure 11. The measured Roll angle in static mode and dynamic mode plotted around the 2D trajectory compared with base line**

# 4. TEST RESULTS OF API I-360 BEFORE AND AFTER DYNAMIC COMPENSATION

The Roll angle measurement of API's I-360 is also realized by an inclinometer. Therefore, it is also subjected to translational acceleration effect. The computer-controlled oscillating linear stage method has been employed to evaluate the dynamic performance of API's laser tracker based I-360 6D sensor system before and after the dynamic compensation technique has been applied to the Roll angle sensor of I-360. The setup is similar to that in Figure 6, only with STS replaced by an I-360.

The test results of the inclinometer evaluation are shown in Figure 12. The solid black line (———) represents the true linear acceleration measured by IFM; the dotted blue line (▪ ▪ ▪) represents the raw data of measured acceleration by inclinometer sensor in I-360; and the dotted red line (━━ ▪) represents the measured acceleration by inclinometer after digital recovery.

It's seen in Figure 12 that the raw data of the measured acceleration by inclinometer has a phase delay from the true acceleration measured by IFM, and it also loses some high frequency feature which is observed in the true acceleration. Therefore, digital signal processing technique is applied to the raw acceleration to get the recovered acceleration. It is obvious that

the recovered acceleration greatly compensates the phase delay and also recovers most of the high frequency feature in the acceleration.

But as address previously, the roll angle is actually not changing during the translation movement of the oscillating stage. Dynamic compensation technique is used here to compensate linear translation induced acceleration which is picked up by the inclinometer undesirably. Figure 13 shows the measured Roll angle by inclinometer before and after dynamic compensation. It is observed that dynamic compensation successfully suppresses the influence of translational acceleration on inclinometer, and this will substantially improve the dynamic performance of the inclinometer.

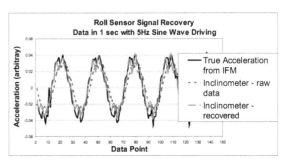

**Figure 12. Test results of level sensor reading recovery after digital recovery**

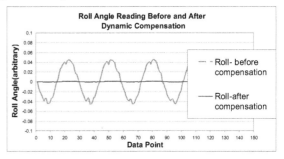

**Figure 13. Measured Roll angle from level sensor before and after dynamic compensation**

# 5. SUMMARY

This paper presented two genetic methods for dynamic performance evaluation for both 3D and 6D sensor system, the linear method and rotational method. The dynamic evaluation test with I-360 6D system shows that these methods are simple but effective for 6D sensor dynamic evaluation. Although the methods discussed are based on API's laser tracker 6D sensor system dynamic performance evaluation, they provide a systematic and accurate method for dynamic evaluation of general purpose 6D measurement technologies, including single-point, surface scanning, non-contact, and photo geometry method.

# Methodology for Evaluating Static Six-Degree-of-Freedom (6DoF) Perception Systems

Tommy Chang, Tsai Hong,
Joe Falco, Michael Shneier
National Institute of Standard and Technology
Gaithersburg, Maryland
{tchang,hongt,falco,shneier}@nist.gov

Mili Shah, Roger Eastman
Loyola University Maryland
Baltimore, Maryland
{mishah,reastman}@loyola.edu

## ABSTRACT

In this paper, we apply two fundamental approaches toward evaluating a static, vision based, six-degree-of-freedom (6DoF) pose determination system that measures the position and orientation of a part. The first approach uses groundtruth carefully obtained from a laser tracker and the second approach doesn't use any external groundtruth. The evaluation procedure focuses on characterizing both the system's accuracy and precision as well as the effect of object viewpoints.

For the groundtruth method, we first use a laser tracker for system calibration and then compare the calibrated output with the surveyed pose. In the method without external groundtruth, we evaluate the effect of viewpoint factors on the system's performance.

## Categories and Subject Descriptors

C.4 [**Performance of Systems**]: Performance attributes; B.8.2 [**Performance and Reliability**]: Performance Analysis and Design Aids

## General Terms

Performance, Measurement, Standardization, Experimentation

## Keywords

Laser Tracker, Ground Truth, 6DOF metrology, Performance Evaluation

## 1. INTRODUCTION

As part of the ongoing effort to standardize characterization and evaluation of 6DoF (six-degree-of-freedom) pose determination systems, we present a performance evaluation of a static, vision-based 6DoF system that measures the position and orientation of a part, also referred to as an object in this paper.

In general, performance evaluation methods can be grouped into two categories: with and without external groundtruth. We adopt the typical definition of external groundtruth as measurements obtained independently and simultaneously by an accurate system having better precision by more than one order of magnitude. Laser tracker, industrial robot arm, and computer graphics simulation are some examples of external groundtruth used for evaluating vision-based 6DoF systems [3, 14, 17].

Regardless of whether external groundtruth is employed or not, the goal is to obtain a quantitative understanding of the performance. "[The task of performance characterization] can be understood as an entirely statistical task." [16]

In this paper, we employ methods with and without external groundtruth to quantitatively determine the system's accuracy and precision and the effect of different viewpoints on its precision. For the groundtruth method, we first use a laser tracker for system calibration and then compare the calibrated result to the surveyed pose. For the method without using any external groundtruth, we estimate the system precision under various object viewpoints.

## 2. RELATED WORK

Here we review some common methods applied to performance characterization and evaluation of pose determination systems and algorithms [9, 3, 19, 18, 14, 13]. Other relevant work includes evaluation and characterization of ranging sensors such as LADAR (LAser Detection And Ranging) [8, 23, 1] and stereo vision [11, 17, 22], as well as algorithms including image registration [21, 5, 20, 10, 7], segmentation, and classification [2, 4]. The majority of these articles conduct experimental studies to characterize the performance under a set of controlled conditions.

In typical groundtruth methods, external groundtruth is used to compute errors, which are then used to infer the unknown parameters in the error population/distribution. A statistic such as mean, standard deviation, min, and max, is computed from an error sample.

The system under test can be thought of as an estimator of the true quantity measured independently and simultaneously by the external groundtruth system. In statistics, an estimator has two properties: bias and variance. The bias measures the average *accuracy* while the variance measures the *precision* or *reliability* of the estimator [15].

One way to determine the bias of a pose determination system is to first transform data both from the groundtruth and the system under test to a common coordinate frame.

Then, the bias is the averaged differences between the two transformed data sets. However, in most cases, the transformation between the two coordinate frames is not known exactly and any error in the transformation will contribute to the overall bias estimate. A robust calibration system [12] is needed to estimate the transformation.

Approaches without external groundtruth typically compute variance from the data. These variances are used to characterize and infer the effect of system's *precision* under different conditions, or levels of the experimental factor. In [17], a dynamic 6DoF system's performance was characterized by the standard deviation of the regression residual; although no external groundtruth was used, the motion model of the object was known. [23] and [8] characterized a LADAR system's precision (as well as accuracy) under experimental factors including target distance, surface property, and incident angle. Statistical inference could be used to generalize and test hypotheses about the system performance.

Another approach without external groundtruth relies on an objective metric that correlates with the system's performance. Groundtruth is still involved but only during the design and verification of the objective metric. Performance evaluation can then be done using only that objective metric alone. Examples of this approach include [22, 10, 7, 4]. In general, the objective metric is shown to vary monotonically with the amount of error, which is computed from the external groundtruth.

Unlike the previous two approaches, [9] compares the robustness of two pose estimation techniques analytically using sensitivity analysis in terms of variance amplification. [2] shows another example without the use of external groundtruth. Its idea is based on the *common agreement* metric applied to brain tissue classification: "if nine out of ten algorithms classify voxel x in subject i as white matter then one says there is a 90 % chance this voxel truly is white matter."

In this paper, we adopt the estimator approach that treats the 6DoF system under test as an estimator to the true pose. Performance of the 6DoF system can then be characterized by the estimator's bias and variance.

# 3. METHODS

In this section, we describe approaches with and without external groundtruth for characterizing a commercial static, vision-based, 6DoF pose determination system.

## 3.1 The Static 6Dof Vision-Based System

The vision system consists of a camera mounted on a robot arm (see Figure 1). The camera used in this study has a focal length of 6mm and a resolution of 782 by 582 pixels. There are four coordinate frames involved:

1. Robot Frame: A coordinate frame located and defined at the base of the robot arm.

2. Object Frame ($O$): The coordinate frame associated with the object.

3. Camera Frame ($C$): The coordinate frame associated with the camera, which is fixed on the robot arm.

4. Source Frame ($SF$): A user-defined global coordinate frame relative to the robot frame. This frame is usually

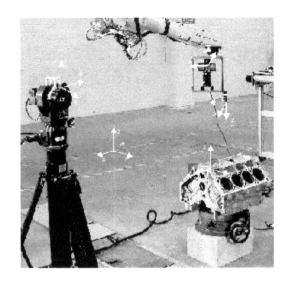

**Figure 1: The vision system and the laser tracker groundtruth system.**

conveniently aligned with the object in order for the robot to perform operations relating to the object.

The output from the vision-based system consists of object and camera poses for every measurement. Specifically, the outputs are three 4x4 homogeneous matrices:

(i) $_{SF}\mathbf{H}_O$, transformation from the object frame to the source frame. $SF$ is the source frame and $O$ is the object. $SF$ is stationary and $O$ is also stationary.

(ii) $_{SF}\mathbf{H}_C$, transformation from the camera frame to the source frame. $SF$ is the source frame and $C$ is the camera. In this case, $SF$ is stationary and $C$ is moving.

(iii) $_O\mathbf{H}_C$, transformation from the camera frame to the object frame. This is obtained by combining (i) and (ii).

Although the measurement takes $\frac{1}{30}$ of a second to acquire an image, the subsequent processing time varies. The robot arm always stop moving when taking the measurement.

## 3.2 The GroundTruth System

The groundtruth system used in our work is a calibrated 6DoF laser tracker having a precision (two sigma) of $\pm 5$ micrometer per meter. The laser tracker has two physical components: a portable active target that measures its own orientation and a base unit that measures the position of the active target. Together they provide the complete 6DoF pose of the active target.

There are two coordinate frames in the groundtruth system:

• Laser Tracker Frame ($LT$): A coordinate frame located at the base unit of the laser tracker.

• Active Target Frame ($AT$): The coordinate frame associated with the active target.

In our setup, we attached the active target next to the camera on the robot arm of the vision system. The output from the groundtruth system is the pose (represented by a 4x4 homogeneous matrix) of the active target:

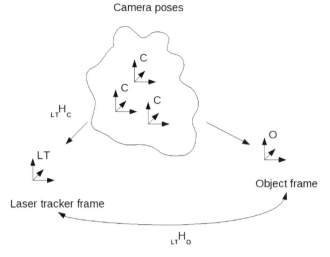

Camera poses

C
C
C

$_{LT}H_C$

LT

Laser tracker frame

O

Object frame

$_{LT}H_O$

**Figure 2:** The dynamic camera pose is independently determined by both the vision system and the laser tracker.

(iv) $_{LT}\mathbf{H}_{AT}$, transformation from the active target frame to the laser tracker frame. $AT$ is the active target and $LT$ is the laser tracker. Here $AT$ moves with the robot arm and $LT$ is stationary.

## 3.3 Using External GroundTruth

We are interested in using the groundtruth to estimate the bias of the vision system. A straight-forward way is to have the groundtruth system directly measure the camera frame of the vision system. This will provide the transformation between the two systems and allow camera pose and object pose, as measured by both systems, to be represented by a common coordinate frame.

However, it is extremely difficult to physically locate the camera frame. Even if we could physically locate the camera frame, there is still the issue of survey error due to operator skill and other human factors.

An equivalent approach is to numerically determine the best transformation (see Figure 2) between the set of correspondence data via optimization [13]. In order to carry out this equivalent approach, the vision system data and the laser tracker data (iv) are combined as

$$_{LT}\mathbf{H}_C = {}_{LT}\mathbf{H}_{AT} \times {}_{AT}\mathbf{H}_C, \qquad (1)$$

where $_{AT}\mathbf{H}_C$ was numerically determine from the robot hand-eye calibration process which included camera calibration error. Note that this transformation is constant since the active target and the camera are both rigidly mounted on the robot.

Then we construct the best-fit homogeneous matrix

$$_O\widehat{\mathbf{H}}_{LT} = \underset{\mathbf{H}}{\mathrm{argmin}} \|\mathbf{H} \, {}_{LT}\mathbf{H}_C - {}_O\mathbf{H}_C\|^2. \qquad (2)$$

This homogeneous matrix can be constructed by first calculating the optimal rotation

$$\mathbf{R} = \mathbf{VDU}^T$$

where the full Singular Value Decomposition (SVD) of the $3 \times 3$ matrix

$$\mathsf{X}\widehat{\mathsf{X}}^T = \mathbf{U\Sigma V}^T$$

and

$$\mathbf{D} = \begin{cases} \mathrm{diag}(1,1,1) & \text{if } \det(\mathbf{VU}^T) = 1, \\ \mathrm{diag}(1,1,-1) & \text{if } \det(\mathbf{VU}^T) = -1 \end{cases}.$$

Here $\mathsf{X}$ is the mean-adjusted data $_{LT}\mathbf{H}_C$ and $\widehat{\mathsf{X}}$ is the mean-adjusted data $_O\mathbf{H}_C$. Once the rotation $\mathbf{R}$ is known then the optimal translation can be calculated as

$$\mathbf{t} = \widehat{t} - \mathbf{R}t,$$

where $t$ is the mean-adjusted position data of $_{LT}\mathbf{H}_C$ and $\widehat{t}$ is the mean-adjusted position data of $_O\mathbf{H}_C$. Thus the optimal homogeneous matrix from (2) is

$$_O\widehat{\mathbf{H}}_{LT} = \begin{pmatrix} \mathbf{R} & \mathbf{t} \\ 0 & 1 \end{pmatrix}.$$

Since we also can independently survey the location of the object using the laser tracker and construct $_O\mathbf{H}_{LT}$, we can compare the results of the best-fit homogeneous matrix

$$_O\widehat{\mathbf{H}}_{LT}$$

with the groundtruth $_O\mathbf{H}_{LT}$. The difference between the best-fit matrix and the surveyed groundtruth matrix include the system bias error and the groundtruth measurement error.

## 3.4 Without using External GroundTruth

In a way, an implicit groundtruth is present in the static scenario. This implicit groundtruth is embedded into the experimental set up by having the object remain stationary. We knew the object did not move, therefore, we don't need a real external groundtruth system to measure its pose, which is just a constant by design.

### 3.4.1 Effect of object Viewpoints

We investigate the effect of different object viewpoints on the variance of the vision system. [9] studied two pose determination algorithms and showed, analytically and experimentally, that viewpoint has an effect on pose stability. In our study, instead of varying the object pose, experiments were set up to vary the camera pose. The effect of varying the camera pose is the same as varying the object pose because in both cases the camera produces the same object image. In addition, we gained an implicit groundtruth from the fact that the object remained stationary.

Four independent experiments are conducted. In each experiment, the pose of a static object is to be compared under three different measurement conditions (treatments): A, B, C. The experiments are described below:

- Exp0: scale factor
  A scale of 1.0 means that the entire object, regardless of its orientation, occupies the image as much as possible. A scale of 0.5 means that at most 2 objects can be seen simultaneously in the image, regardless of their orientations. To compute the actual scale, we first determine the minimum bounding sphere of the object and then measure the distance from camera to the object. Using the pin-hole camera model, we can then determine the scale by

$$\mathrm{scale} = \frac{\mathrm{dia}}{2 \times \mathrm{dist} \times \tan\left(\frac{\mathrm{fov}}{2}\right)},$$

where dia is the diameter of the minimum bounding sphere, dist is the distance between the camera and the object, and fov is the camera's vertical field-of-view angle.

- cond A: object seen at low-scale (computed scale = 0.37)
- cond B: object seen at mid-scale (computed scale = 0.55)
- cond C: object seen at full-scale (computed scale = 1.03)

- Exp1: position factor

  - cond A: object seen near the image border (actual camera shift = 100 mm)
  - cond B: object seen midway between center of FoV (field-of-view) and the image border (actual camera shift = 50 mm)
  - cond C: object seen at the center of FoV (0 shift)

- Exp2: azimuth factor
  Under this factor, the object is always centered in the image as the camera rotates about its optical axis.

  - cond A: object seen rotated 40 degrees
  - cond B: object seen rotated 20 degrees
  - cond C: object seen up-right

- Exp3: polar factor
  Under this factor, the object is always centered in the image as the camera rotates around the object.

  - cond A: object seen rotated 25 degrees on its side
  - cond B: object seen rotated 15 degrees on its side
  - cond C: object seen up-right

Except experiment Exp0, the object scale is fixed at 0.55 throughout the experiments.

# 4. RESULTS

This section describes the dataset obtained and their preliminary analysis.

## 4.1 Data without External Groundtruth

In each of the four viewpoint experiments, 10 runs per treatment were carried out, resulting a total of 30 runs per experiment. More runs could be used, but 10 were chosen to establish an initial preliminary study. No groundtruth data was collected in these viewpoint experiments.

We used the completely randomized design (CRD) paradigm [15] in our viewpoint experiments and identified time and robot repeatability as two nuisance factors that we have no control over. However, we did not randomize the order of runs (as to neutralize the possible timing and robot effect) for two reasons:

1. The condition/treatment order can not be changed. The commercial vision system always perform conditions A, B, C, A, B, C, ... in that cyclic order. The provided commercial software does not have an option to change the run order.

2. The robot arm was found[1] to have deterministic repeatability after warming up for 20 minutes. Therefore, the robot's performance (repeatability as specified by the manufacture) does not change with time. However, it was noted that the robot's repeatability depends on the motion as well as the initial pose at the time the motion command was issued. As a result, we always move the robot from a fixed initial pose and set the robot speed to low (as to minimize structural vibration caused by robot motion).

## 4.2 Data with External Groundtruth

Additionally, four data sets were collected together with the groundtruth. Groundtruth was obtained by matching the vision data with the corresponding laser tracker data. Since the clocks were synchronized and timestamps recorded, we can match data by their timestamp. For each data set, the camera height was measured to about 457 mm.

- For the first data set, we adjusted only the rotational motion of the camera. Specifically, we rotated the camera about the rotational axes $R_x$ and $R_y$ from $\pm 15$ degrees in increments of 5 degrees, and $R_z$ from $\pm 10$ degrees in increments of 5 degrees. (Total of 7x7x5 = 245 data; 61 have all image features detected.)

- For the second data set, we adjusted only the translational motion of the camera. Specifically, we moved the camera in the $x$ and $y$ directions from $\pm 150$ mm in increments of 50 mm. (Total of 7x7 = 49 data; 37 have all image features detected)

- For the third data set, we adjusted both the rotational and translational motion of the camera. Specifically, we rotated the camera about the rotational axes $R_y$ and $R_z$ from $\pm 5$ degrees in increments of 5 degrees, and moved the camera in the $x$ direction from $\pm 150$ mm in increments of 50 mm. (Total of 3x3x7 = 63 data; 54 have all image features detected)

- For the fourth data set, we adjusted both the rotational and translational motion of the camera. Specifically, we rotated the camera about the rotational axes $R_y$ and $R_z$ from $\pm 5$ degrees in increments of 5 degrees, and moved the camera in the $y$ direction from $\pm 150$ mm in increments of 50 mm. (Total of 3x3x7 = 63 data, 41 have all image feature detected)

## 4.3 External GroundTruth Result

Table 1 summarizes error between the optimal homogeneous matrix $_O\widehat{\mathbf{H}}_{LT}$ computed for each of the four data sets with the survey from the laser tracker $_O\mathbf{H}_{LT}$. The error shown in this table is the combined effect of survey error and the system bias. It should be noted that certain data points were ignored in the calculation of the best homogeneous matrix $_O\widehat{\mathbf{H}}_{LT}$. These points correspond to positions where all the image features could not be located by the vision system. Outliers were also removed in the construction of the optimal homogeneous matrix. These outliers were constructed using a statistical tool that identifies points as outliers if they lie outside of one and half times the interquartile range.

---

[1]We used the IS09283 robot performance standard metric and protocol describe in [6].

**Table 1: Estimates of system bias**

|  | X (mm) | y (mm) | z (mm) | Rx (deg) | Ry (deg) | Rz (deg) |
|---|---|---|---|---|---|---|
| DataSet1 | 8.696 | 2.868 | 47.191 | 0.0328 | 0.0038 | 0.2435 |
| DataSet2 | 9.272 | 3.476 | 39.755 | 0.0767 | 0.0336 | 0.1544 |
| DataSet3 | 8.946 | 6.760 | 37.092 | 0.0572 | 0.0069 | 0.0522 |
| DataSet4 | 9.569 | 4.687 | 40.551 | 0.1160 | 0.0074 | 0.1967 |

Table 1 indicates a large combined error in positional measurements. The Z-component has the largest error, and Y-component has the least error. This is not surprising, given that the image apperrance typically changes only slightly as the height of the camera changes, and the pose detection algorithm depends on only a single camera view.

Tables 2 to 6 summarize the error residual between the groundtruth data and the corresponding transformed vision data in the same coordinate. Before finding the best-fit transformation, some outlier points were removed from the groundtruth data. The points arose because the laser tracker has a problem tracking jerks in the robot's motion. Data for a short time following a jerk are incorrect. Unfortunately, this problem was only discovered after the data had been collected, and the sampling did not wait long enough for the system to settle after the camera reached its destination before collecting data. The pairs of points corresponding to these measurements were omitted from the best-fit calculations. However, the errors in the tables 2 to 6 are computed from all the collected data points that the vision system was able to detect all image features.

The requirements for most applications for which the 6DoF system were developed depends on repeatability rather than accuracy, but even here, the variation can be large. For example, in data set 4 (summarized in Table 5 and Figure 6) the system erroneously matches features. Note, however, the data set actually produced the best results when the bad matches are omitted.

Results from the four data sets are shown in Figure 3 to 6. Points were selected as outliers if they lie outside one and half times the inter-quartile range. It should be noted that there are close fits for most of the points but there are few points with a large error. These points correspond to positions where the vision system indicated a good match to the data (all features were detected) but two or more of the detected features matched to the wrong model feature.

Overall, the user would have to decide if the system was repeatable enough for a particular application. The performance data provide the necessary information to do so. The mean and standard deviation of the error, together with the maximum errors, can be compared with the tolerances of the application. They can also be used in process control; if a measured part location lies, for example, more than two standard deviations from mean, it likely indicates either a bad part or an erroneous match between the part and the model. The vision system could attempt to reacquire the part and if it failed again, the part could be rejected.

## 4.4 Result without GroundTruth

Tables 7 to 10 summarize the system variance (computed as standard deviation) among the three conditions in each of the four viewpoint experiments (see Section 3.4.1). Originally, the experiment was set up to answer the specific question: "Do pose solutions from the vision system differ significantly under different object viewpoint?" In statistics,

**Table 2: Data Set 1 — Rotation**

| 61 poses with all image features detected | | | | | | |
|---|---|---|---|---|---|---|
|  | X (mm) | y (mm) | z (mm) | Rx (deg) | Ry (deg) | Rz (deg) |
| Mean | 1.709 | 1.628 | 0.846 | 0.1824 | 0.0911 | 0.1896 |
| Median | 1.542 | 1.300 | 0.723 | 0.1621 | 0.0854 | 0.1504 |
| Std Dev | 1.109 | 1.437 | 0.537 | 0.1241 | 0.0582 | 0.1763 |
| Min | 0.043 | 0.001 | 0.008 | 0.0072 | 0.0020 | 0.0029 |
| Max | 4.391 | 5.113 | 2.551 | 0.5252 | 0.2273 | 0.9390 |

**Table 3: Data Set 2 — Translation**

| 37 poses with all image features detected | | | | | | |
|---|---|---|---|---|---|---|
|  | X (mm) | y (mm) | z (mm) | Rx (deg) | Ry (deg) | Rz (deg) |
| Mean | 1.736 | 5.848 | 1.100 | 0.1472 | 0.0332 | 0.5146 |
| Median | 1.535 | 4.397 | 0.866 | 0.1139 | 0.0234 | 0.3579 |
| Std Dev | 1.506 | 4.367 | 0.847 | 0.1316 | 0.0297 | 0.3870 |
| Min | 0.024 | 0.036 | 0.004 | 0.0023 | 0.0002 | 0.0402 |
| Max | 6.879 | 16.655 | 3.461 | 0.5660 | 0.1199 | 1.4359 |

**Table 4: Data Set 3 — Rotation and Translation**

| 54 poses with all image features detected | | | | | | |
|---|---|---|---|---|---|---|
|  | X (mm) | y (mm) | z (mm) | Rx (deg) | Ry (deg) | Rz (deg) |
| Mean | 2.454 | 8.559 | 0.730 | 0.1934 | 0.0764 | 0.7082 |
| Median | 1.678 | 5.354 | 0.676 | 0.1137 | 0.0753 | 0.4699 |
| Std Dev | 3.503 | 8.453 | 0.579 | 0.2799 | 0.0401 | 0.6907 |
| Min | 0.018 | 0.174 | 0.039 | 0.0003 | 0.0025 | 0.0106 |
| Max | 24.036 | 42.317 | 3.464 | 1.9085 | 0.1664 | 3.5107 |

**Table 5: Data Set 4 — Rotation and Translation**

| 41 poses with all image features detected | | | | | | |
|---|---|---|---|---|---|---|
|  | X (mm) | y (mm) | z (mm) | Rx (deg) | Ry (deg) | Rz (deg) |
| Mean | 20.815 | 8.260 | 46.677 | 21.9294 | 2.0078 | 3.8628 |
| Median | 1.226 | 2.464 | 0.559 | 0.0963 | 0.0872 | 0.2285 |
| Std Dev | 70.215 | 21.247 | 165.772 | 78.6847 | 8.4709 | 12.9773 |
| Min | 0.017 | 0.360 | 0.057 | 0.0015 | 0.0048 | 0.0162 |
| Max | 294.918 | 109.988 | 645.663 | 307.4627 | 51.4941 | 57.3316 |

**Table 6: Combined Data**

| Combined Data (total of 193 poses) | | | | | | |
|---|---|---|---|---|---|---|
|  | X (mm) | y (mm) | z (mm) | Rx (deg) | Ry (deg) | Rz (deg) |
| Mean | 5.941 | 5.778 | 10.498 | 4.7513 | 0.4790 | 1.1699 |
| Median | 1.461 | 2.724 | 0.686 | 0.1217 | 0.0677 | 0.2657 |
| Std Dev | 32.864 | 11.232 | 77.567 | 36.8178 | 3.9272 | 6.0726 |
| Min | 0.017 | 0.001 | 0.004 | 0.0003 | 0.0002 | 0.0029 |
| Max | 294.918 | 109.988 | 645.663 | 307.4627 | 51.4941 | 57.3316 |

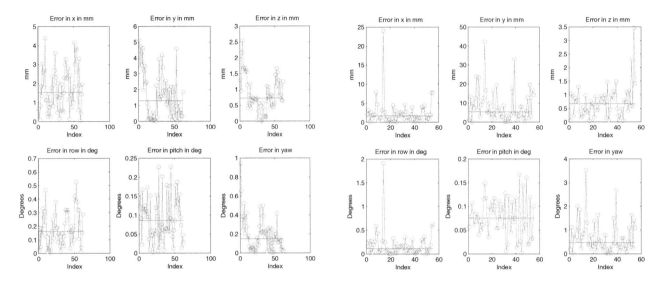

Figure 3: Data Set 1 — Rotation Only

Figure 5: Data Set 3 — Rotation and X Translation

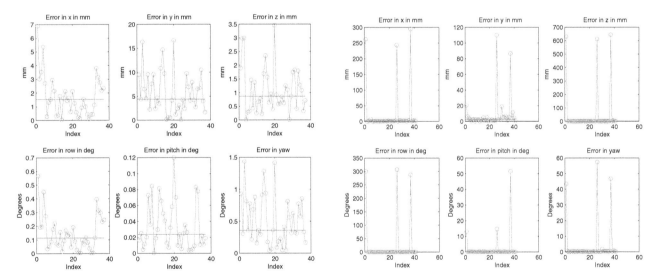

Figure 4: Data Set 2 — Translation Only

Figure 6: Data Set 4 — Rotation and Y Translation

**Table 7: Exp0 — Scale Factor**

| Std Dev | X (mm) | y (mm) | z (mm) | Rx (deg) | Ry (deg) | Rz (deg) |
|---------|--------|--------|--------|----------|----------|----------|
| CondA | 0.038 | 0.025 | 0.070 | 0.0344 | 0.0643 | 0.0096 |
| CondB | 0.046 | 0.018 | 0.078 | 0.0409 | 0.0521 | 0.0051 |
| CondC | 0.052 | 0.137 | 1.043 | 1.8300 | 0.3541 | 0.0622 |

**Table 8: Exp1 — Position Factor**

| Std Dev | X (mm) | y (mm) | z (mm) | Rx (deg) | Ry (deg) | Rz (deg) |
|---------|--------|--------|--------|----------|----------|----------|
| CondA | 0.057 | 0.021 | 0.040 | 0.1145 | 0.1445 | 0.0198 |
| CondB | 0.072 | 0.026 | 0.071 | 0.1680 | 0.1532 | 0.0164 |
| CondC | 0.087 | 0.017 | 0.073 | 0.1080 | 0.0585 | 0.0048 |

**Table 9: Exp2 — Azimuth Factor**

| Std Dev | X (mm) | y (mm) | z (mm) | Rx (deg) | Ry (deg) | Rz (deg) |
|---------|--------|--------|--------|----------|----------|----------|
| CondA | 0.010 | 0.029 | 0.032 | 0.0163 | 0.0485 | 0.0206 |
| CondB | 0.022 | 0.038 | 0.035 | 0.0245 | 0.0864 | 0.0123 |
| CondC | 0.024 | 0.026 | 0.069 | 0.0458 | 0.1092 | 0.0235 |

**Table 10: Exp3 — Polar Factor**

| Std Dev | X (mm) | y (mm) | z (mm) | Rx (deg) | Ry (deg) | Rz (deg) |
|---------|--------|--------|--------|----------|----------|----------|
| CondA | 0.097 | 0.051 | 0.294 | 0.2112 | 0.2189 | 0.0143 |
| CondB | 0.040 | 0.019 | 0.116 | 0.1191 | 0.6834 | 0.0756 |
| CondC | 0.017 | 0.032 | 0.037 | 0.1730 | 0.0387 | 0.0048 |

this type of question is commonly answered by testing the homogeneity hypothesis [15].

In our experiment, we collected just 10 measurements per each of the three conditions. Without a priori knowledge about the underlying population distributions, small samples can not be justified for use in testing the homogeneity hypothesis. Since we don't know the underlying populations, one idea is to use non-parametric approaches, which make few assumptions about the population distribution. One non-parametric approach we considered the Kruskal-Wallis test [15], which assumes the populations all have the same shape. However, since our sample size was small this assumption could not be verified.

Instead of testing the homogeneity hypothesis, another approach to answer our original question is to use statistical methods that directly compare distributions. Such methods include $\chi^2$ goodness-of-fit test, Kolmogorov-Smirnov goodness-of-fit test, and others. However, due to the small sample size and the uncertainty about our samples being representative of their populations, we did not pursue any of these methods. Nevertheless, the collected data provide some useful insights:

- From the Exp0 (scale factor) data summarized in Table 7, we observed that condition C has the largest variance compared to the two other conditions. With the exception of the X component, the variances are at least 5 times larger in condition C. Since condition C corresponds to the smallest image scale, it implies that a sudden degradation in system precision can be expected when the object in the image gets smaller than a threshold.

- With the scale set at 0.55, Tables 8 to 10 show a combined system precision that is better than $0.7°$ for orientation and 0.3 mm for position. The combined conditions encompass a viewpoint coverage of up to 100 mm shift in X position, 40 degrees in azimuth angle, and 25 degrees in polar angle.

- We noted that the physical dimension is a function of camera lens. By changing the camera lens, the vision system can be adapt to larger or smaller object. It is reasonable to think that both the accuracy and precision of the system will improve if a higher resolution camera is used.

# 5. CONCLUSION

We described and applied two common approaches for evaluating and characterizing the performance of 6DOF perception systems. External groundtruth is necessary to evaluate system accuracy in terms of its bias. System precision, in terms of its repeatability, can be evaluated with or without an external groundtruth. In both cases, the result characterizes the system under the condition in which it was operated.

For evaluating 6DoF systems, the use of an external groundtruth system is essential when the pose is dynamic or static. The mean and standard deviation of the errors, together with the maximum errors, can be compared with the tolerance of the user's requirements in their application. The user's requirements will decide if the system is repeatable enough for a particular application. However, if the external groundtruth is not available, then system uncertainty using the variance in the data may be an alternative approach for estimating the system precision.

In the case of no external groundtruth, our approach was to test whether the homogeneity hypothesis could be used to answer the question: "Do pose solutions from the vision system differ significantly under different object viewpoint?" Unfortunately, given the insufficiency of data we collected, the lack of a priori knowledge about the underlying population distributions, and the doubt about samples being representative, we were unable to justify using and applying the homogeneity hypothesis.

What performance factors to study depends on the intended application of the system. In our case, we used object viewpoint as an example. The users of 6DoF pose systems may be interested in other factors such as environmental lighting, object type, object pose, object motion, operator skill, etc.

Our long-term goal is to assist in developing a standard for performance evaluation of dynamic 6DoF measurement systems. This standard will specify quantitative, reproducible test methods to evaluate the robustness, accuracy, repeatability and other performance characteristics of dynamic 6DoF systems. The standard will also assist in the development of new applications of automation by enabling end-users to directly compare 6DoF systems as well as reducing the time spent on system evaluation, adoption and integration.

# 6. ACKNOWLEDGMENTS

We thank Dennis Murphy, Clifton Miskov, and Remus Boca for their technical support in carrying out this study.

# 7. REFERENCES

[1] D. Anderson, H. Herman, and A. Kelly. Experimental characterization of commercial flash ladar devices. In *International Conference of Sensing and Technology*, November 2005.

[2] S. Bouix, M. Martin-Fernandez, L. Ungar, M. N. M.-S. Koo, R. W. McCarley, and M. E. Shenton. On evaluating brain tissue classifiers without a ground truth. *NeuroImage*, 36:1207–1224, 2007.

[3] T. Chang, T. Hong, M. Shneier, G. Holguin, J. Park, and R. D. Eastman. Dynamic 6dof metrology for evaluating a visual servoing system. In *PerMIS '08: Proceedings of the 8th Workshop on Performance Metrics for Intelligent Systems*, pages 173–180, New York, NY, USA, 2008. ACM.

[4] C. E. Erdem, A. M. Tekalp, and B. Sankur. Metrics for performance evaluation of video object segmentation and tracking without ground-truth. *International Conference On Image Processing*, 2001.

[5] J. Fitzpatrick and J. West. A blinded evaluation and comparison of image registration methods. In *IEEE Workshop on Empirical Evaluation Methods in Computer Vision*, 1998.

[6] ISO 9283:1998. *Manipulating industrial robots — Performance criteria and related test methods. Second edition*. ISO, Geneva, Switzerland.

[7] J. Kybic. Fast no ground truth image registration accuracy evaluation: Comparison of bootstrap and hessian approaches. In *ISBI*, pages 792–795, 2008.

[8] A. M. Lytle, S. Szabo, G. Cheok, K. Saidi, and R. Norcross. Performance evaluation of a 3d imaging system for vehicle safety. In *Unmanned Systems Technology IX. Proceedings of the SPIE, Volume 6561*, 2007.

[9] C. B. Madsen. A comparative study of the robustness of two pose estimation techniques. *Machine Vision and Applications*, 9(5-6):291–303, 1997.

[10] R. Schestowitz, C. J. Twining, T. Cootes, V. Petrovic, B. Crum, and C. J. Taylor. Non-rigid registration assessment without ground truth. In *Medical Image Understanding and Analysis*, volume 2, pages 151–155, 2006.

[11] S. M. Seitz, B. Curless, J. Diebel, D. Scharstein, and R. Szeliski. A comparison and evaluation of multi-view stereo reconstruction algorithms. In *CVPR '06: Proceedings of the 2006 IEEE Computer Society Conference on Computer Vision and Pattern Recognition*, pages 519–528, Washington, DC, USA, 2006. IEEE Computer Society.

[12] M. Shah, T. Chang, and T. Hong. Mathematical metrology for evaluation a 6dof visual servoing system. In *PerMIS '09: Proceedings of the 9th Workshop on Performance Metrics for Intelligent Systems*, 2009.

[13] M. I. Shah. Six degree of freedom point correspondences. *Technical Report, Loyola University Maryland, TR2009_02.*, 2009.

[14] F. Smit and R. van Liere. A framework for performance evaluation of model-based optical trackers. *EGVE Symposium*, 6, 2008.

[15] A. C. Tamhane and D. D. Dunlop. *Statistics and Data Analysis from Elementary to Intermediate*. Prentice Hall, Upper Saddle River, NJ 07458, 2000.

[16] N. A. Thacker, A. F. Clark, J. L. Barron, J. R. Beveridge, P. Courtney, W. R. Crum, V. Ramesh, and C. Clark. Performance characterization in computer vision: A guide to best practices. *Computer Vision and Image Understanding*, 109(3):305–334, 2008.

[17] M. Tonko and H.-H. Nagel. Model-based stereo-tracking of non-polyhedral objects for automatic disassembly experiments. *International Journal of Computer Vision*, 37(1):99–118, 2000.

[18] R. van Liere and A. van Rhijn. An experimental comparison of three optical trackers for model based pose determination in virtual reality. In S. Coquillart and M. Göbel, editors, *10th Eurographics Symposium on Virtual Environments*, pages 25–34, Grenoble, France, 2004. Eurographics Association.

[19] F. Viksten, P.-E. Forssén, B. Johansson, and A. Moe. Comparison of local image descriptors for full 6 degree-of-freedom pose estimation. In *IEEE International Conference on Robotics and Automation*, Kobe, Japan, May 2009. IEEE, IEEE Robotics and Automation Society.

[20] J. B. West and J. M. Fitzpatrick. The distribution of target registration error in rigid-body, point-based registration. In *IPMI '99: Proceedings of the 16th International Conference on Information Processing in Medical Imaging*, pages 460–465, London, UK, 1999. Springer-Verlag.

[21] J. B. West, J. M. Fitzpatrick, M. Y. Wang, B. M. Dawant, C. R. M. Jr., R. M. Kessler, and R. J. Maciunas. Retrospective intermodality registration techniques for images of the head: Surface-based versus volume-based. *IEEE Trans. Med. Imaging*, 18(2):144–150, 1999.

[22] Q. Yang, R. M. Steele, D. Nister, and C. Jaynes. Learning the probability of correspondences without ground truth. In *ICCV '05: Proceedings of the Tenth IEEE International Conference on Computer Vision*, pages 1140–1147, Washington, DC, USA, 2005. IEEE Computer Society.

[23] C. Ye and J. Borenstein. Characterization of a 2-d laser scanner for mobile robot obstacle negotiation. In *Proceedings of the IEEE International Conference on Robotics and Automation*, pages 2512–2518, 2002.

# Evaluating Hierarchical Planner Performance through Field Experiments and Simulation

**Juan Pablo Gonzalez**

Autonomous Perception Research
General Dynamics Robotic Systems
1501 Ardmore Blvd

Pittsburgh, PA 15218
412-473-2164

jpgonzal@gdrs.com

**Marshal Childers**

U.S. Army Research Laboratory

Vehicle Technology Directorate
Aberdeen Proving Ground, MD
21005

410-278-7996

marshal.childers@us.army.mil

**Barry A. Bodt**

U.S. Army Research Laboratory
Computational and Informational
Sciences Directorate
Aberdeen Proving Ground, MD
21005

410-278-6659

barry.a.bodt@us.army.mil

## ABSTRACT

Most stand-alone planners have theoretical guarantees in terms of completeness, optimality and performance. However, no stand-alone planner is able to handle the complexity of real world systems accounting for kinematic and dynamic constraints while being able to operate over long ranges. This leads to hierarchical planning approaches that bring together different stand-alone planners for local and global navigation at the expense of weaker performance guarantees.

This paper presents the results of using simulation combined with field testing in order to quantify the performance of integrated hierarchical planners. While these results don't provide performance guarantees, they show clear performance differences depending on the integrated hierarchical planner used. While in general the simulated results were a good predictor of performance in the field, in some scenarios the simulated experiments did not accurately reflect the performance in the field.

## 1. INTRODUCTION

Most stand-alone planners have theoretical guarantees in terms of completeness, optimality and performance. However, no stand-alone planner is able to handle the complexity of real world systems accounting for kinematic and dynamic constraints while being able to operate over long ranges. This leads to hierarchical planning approaches that bring together different stand-alone planners for local and global navigation in order to be able to plan kinematically correct plans over long ranges [7]. Hierarchical planning approaches, however, have weaker performance guarantees, and can be affected by the difference in representations of each planner. In practice, these planners perform well in benign or somewhat complex environments, but they tend to fail in very complex environments. Recent work [9][9][10] in graduated fidelity planning and lattice-based

planning may alleviate some of these shortcomings, but is still unable to completely eliminate the need for hierarchical planning.

An integrated planner is a planner that is part of an integrated system –with sensors, actuation, etc. Because of the limitations of stand-alone planners, most integrated planners are hierarchical planners, with the added complexity of dealing with imperfect perception data, imperfect localization and system delays. Because of the complexity of the system and the integration of different subsystems, integrated planners lack most of the performance guarantees of stand-alone or even hierarchical planners.

How can integrated planners be characterized and evaluated? While recent advances in model checking [11] represent promising steps towards formal verification of such complex systems, rigorous experimentation remains the best option. However, the intractability of the problem still remains and numerous experiments in many different representative scenarios are needed to obtain meaningful data.

This paper presents the results of using simulation combined with field testing in order to quantify the performance of integrated hierarchical planners. These results were obtained during the 2009 UGV Assessment by the Army Research Lab (ARL) in Ft Indiantown Gap, PA.

While these results don't provide performance guarantees or cover all possible scenarios, they show clear performance differences depending on the planner used. While in general the simulated results were a good predictor of performance in the field, in some scenarios the simulated experiments did not accurately reflect the performance in the field.

## 2. HIERARCHICAL PLANNING

Hierarchical approaches to autonomous navigation usually divide path planning in two levels: local and global navigation. Local navigation considers the kinematic constraints of the vehicle, and has a sensor-based, high-resolution, near-field representation of the environment. Global navigation typically neglects the kinematic constraints of the vehicle and uses a lower-resolution but farther-reaching representation in order to find plans over longer distances [5].

While these two levels are complementary and can perform very well, they introduce the additional challenge of integrating them in a way that maximizes their strengths and minimizes their weaknesses. In this paper, we evaluate three different approaches to integrating global and local navigation: route-based navigation, route-based navigation with replanning, and combined navigation using the *Field Cost Interface (FCI)*.

## 2.1 Route-based navigation

In route-based navigation the global planner generates an initial route using prior map information and taking mission considerations into account. The local autonomous mobility planner (AM) then attempts to follow that route while considering the sensor information collected along the route. We use the Geometric Path Planner (GPP)[4] in order to generate global routes that consider tactical mission requirements such as travel time, mobility cost, exposure risk and coverage. The local planner is an ego-graph-based planner [8] that considers the kinematic and non-holonomic constraints of the vehicle. See Figure 1 for an example of a global route generated by the GPP.

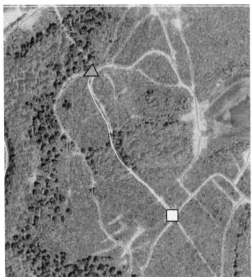

**Figure 1. Initial route (orange) planned by global planner.**

The main advantage of route-based navigation is that the route that the vehicle will follow is known in advance. However, if this route is not valid, the robot has very limited options to choose a new route. In general, the robot is given a buffer zone around the route and it is allowed to avoid obstacles and find alternate routes around this buffer zone. Figure 2 shows an example of a large blockage that invalidates the global route. In route-based navigation the global route remains the same in spite of such blockages which makes it harder for the local planner to find a viable alternative.

## 2.2 Route-based navigation with dynamic replanning

Route-based navigation with dynamic replanning follows the same scheme of route-based navigation, but the global planner updates the route periodically incorporating sensor data as the vehicle traverses the route. Because the GPP planner uses Field D* [2][3] as its planning algorithms, much of the original search performed by the GPP is reused, allowing very fast replanning in response to these changes in the environment.

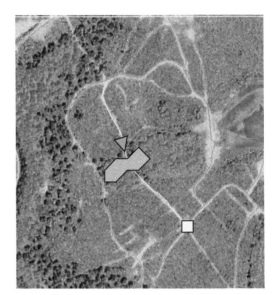

**Figure 2. Blockage on route. In route-based navigation the global route does not change in response to sensed data and the robot only uses local navigation to avoid sensed obstacles.**

If the robot encounters a blockage or a cul-de-sac, the global planner will be able to find an alternate path based on the combined prior and sensor data available. This route, however does not consider the kinematic constraints of the vehicle and the robot may not be able to follow it. When the beginning of the global route is not kinematically correct, a high maneuverability planner (HMP) is invoked in order to connect the current location of the robot to the global route. The HMP is a nonholonomic planner that models not only the position (x,y) of the XUV, but also its heading and its limited turning radius. As such,it is able to provide paths that are kinematically correct. Unlike the AM planner, the trajectories it generates are not predetermined egographs. For this reason, the HMP is able to generate much more complex trajectories that adapt to the constraints of the environment. This planner is able to automatically generate maneuvers, such as three-point turns and "k" turns. However, because of the complexity of its planning space, in a few seconds HMP can only plan trajectories within a small region near the vehicle (~20m).

Figure 3 shows an example of the dynamic replanner finding a route to avoid the blockage detected in the sensed data. Notice that the robot would have to first turn around in order to follow the route. HMP would be invoked for this maneuver, and then the AM planner would continue following the changing global route.

## 2.3 Combined navigation using FCI

When using combined navigation using the FCI the global planner continuously generates a cost field at a radius $R$ from the vehicle, using both prior data and sensor data. The local planner then attempts to plan paths to each point along this circle, thereby combining the kinematic constraints of the vehicle and the recommendations of the global planner. While planning algorithms used at the global and local level are the same as in the previous approaches, the combination through the FCI provides an interface in which the interactions between the two planners are limited to the boundary of the cost field, in a similar fashion to the approach proposed in (Lacaze, 2002).

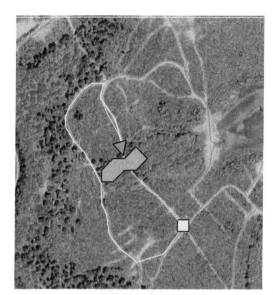

**Figure 3. Blockage on route and new route generated automatically by dynamic replanner (cyan)**

If there is only one good global route (or a global route that is much better than any alternatives) this approach would produce a similar result to the dynamic replanner, due to the relatively low cost of the single good global route. However, if there are several good global routes with comparable costs, this approach will choose the one that is cheapest from the local planner's point of view, avoiding situations where a route that is non-traversable is chosen.

The main challenge with using FCI is that it requires combining different cost metrics for the global and local planner. In order to combine these costs, the planner first scales both the global and local costs by calculating the average cost assigned to a given section of the route by both planners. This produces a cost metric that has similar scales and that adapts to different terrain types. The planner then combines the scaled costs as follows

$$C_{total} = C'_{local} + k \cdot C'_{global} \qquad (1)$$

where $C'_{local}$ and $C'_{global}$ are the scaled local and global path costs, and $k$ is a constant that is determined experimentally. This constant defines the relative weight of the global costs with respect to the local costs and is the most important parameter for the performance of the algorithm, as it compensates for any systematic differences between the local and global costs. The value of $k$ was experimentally optimized using simulations and field experiments.

Figure 4 illustrates how the FCI evaluates routes for the example from the previous figures. The cyan lines show the global paths being used to generate the field costs, and the yellow line shows the local path chosen after considering both the global and local costs.

# 3. EXPERIMENTAL SETUP
The field experimentation consisted of a series of scenarios that varied in situation and a priori data. The objective in defining scenarios was to construct challenging, diverse situations which would defeat the static route-based navigation but still allow the

potential for the Dynamic Replanner (DR) and the Field Cost Interface (FCI) planners to find an executable route to the goal without operator intervention [1].

Seven scenarios were constructed on four separate areas of terrain at Fort Indiantown Gap. In each scenario, a start point and goal were selected such that the global planner could generate an initial plan over the given terrain and with the prior terrain data provided. The planned route was physically blocked, creating scenarios that varied in difficulty from moderate to extremely difficult. Each scenario and terrain area had unique challenges which will be described below. A limited use of prior terrain information was provided to help shape the situation.

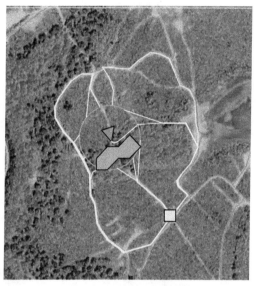

**Figure 4. Blockage on route and alternatives passed to the local planner by the FCI (cyan). The new route is selected considering the global paths and the local kinematic constrains of the vehicle.**

## 3.1 Simulation
The Robotic Interactive Visualization and Exploitation Technology (RIVET)[6] is high-fidelity simulator created under the ARL Robotics CTA. This hardware-in-the-loop platform generates real-time ladar points in a synthetic environment and provides closed-loop execution of dynamic planning algorithms and XUV mobility software. All seven scenarios were modeled in RIVET in an environment that was intended to replicate the actual location. In practice, some areas of the test site were modeled much better than others, which had an important impact on the relevance of the results obtained.

The RIVET runs were used to verify the performance of the planning algorithms as well as to validate the construction of the scenarios in accordance with the experimenter's expectations. All 63 runs were executed in RIVET. The results of the RIVET runs are included in the discussion below.

## 3.2 Field Experiments
The Field experiment was designed to replicate the RIVET parametric study but with additional replications because of expected variations in the XUV performance in the field

environment. To save time and accomplish as many useful runs as possible, all replications in each cell were not executed. For example, the baseline UGV maneuver capability was represented by using the AM Planner without interaction with other planners in the hierarchy (AM-Only). During these AM-Only runs, when it became apparent that repeated attempts to use AM-Only would produce identical results, fewer replications were done with that planner. Other cost-saving steps consisted of excluding some scenarios from the field experiment (Scenarios used in the experiment are described in the next section). Specifically, scenario #4, a variant of scenario #3 with additional prior data, was not done in the Field experiment because it was not thought to add any additional behaviors to those observed in scenario #3; and in scenarios #5 and #6, a successful solution of the cul-de-sac and subsequent plan resulted in a run of approximately 1800 m. To conserve experimental time, the runs were truncated after the XUV completely exited the cul-de-sac area and had a clear path to the goal. Several runs were re-run after events that were unrelated to the performance of the planners. For example, a steering component was broken on one run; unmapped water on the course (not near the cul-de-sac) created a mobility barrier, etc.

## 3.3  Scenarios

### 3.3.1  Scenario #1

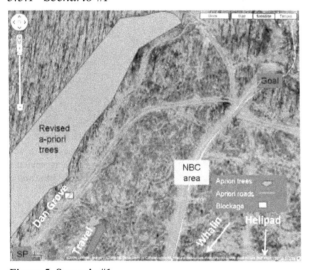

**Figure 5. Scenario #1**

In scenario #1 (Figure 5), the start point (SP) was on a trail next to a tree line. The goal was approximately 300m NE of the start. Prior data included a trail from the start point to the goal, trees to the west of the trail, a prior trail to the goal beyond the blockage, and a restricted NBC area along a possible alternate trail to the east to prevent the XUV from taking that route. The trail was blocked approx 60 m from the start point in an area surrounded by trees and high brush. There was no room for the XUV to turn around at the point of blockage. Backing up was the only possible maneuver.

### 3.3.2  Scenario# 2

In scenario #2 (Figure 6), the initial path follows the Dan Grove road, farther down than the previous scenario, and is blocked more than 30 meters after the last turning point. The intended alternate route is known through prior data and is located to the left of the main path. As in the previous run, the alternate route

requires very tight turns and goes through tall grass, which makes it difficult to find.

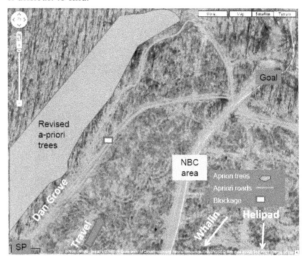

**Figure 6. Scenario #2**

### 3.3.3  Scenario #3

**Figure 7. Scenario #3**

In scenario #3 (Figure 7), the start point was on the trail at the base of a hill and the goal was on top of the hill. There was an open trail from the SP up the hill directly to the goal, but the trail was deeply rutted, steep, and surrounded by high shrubs on each side. The main path was included in the prior data. An alternate, unmarked trail existed to the right of the original path and a non-existing trail to the left of the original plan was also included in the prior data. The main path was blocked approx 80 m from the start point on the steepest part of the deeply rutted trail with high shrubs on both sides. There was no room for the XUV to turn around at the point of blockage. Backing up was the only possible maneuver. The only possible path to the goal was the unmarked trail to the west of the original plan.

### 3.3.4 Scenario #5

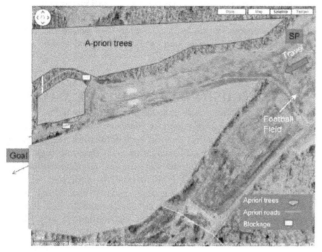

**Figure 8. Scenario #5**

In scenario #5 (Figure 8), the start point was at the opening of a large field, closed at the end except for two trails. The goal was west of the field. The initial plan was along the prior trail toward the goal which narrowed into a one lane trail for approximately 200m. Prior data included trails from the start point to the goal, trees to the north and south of the trail, an alternate prior trail at the base of the opening south of the original path, and trees between the two prior trails. The planned trail was blocked where the trail narrowed, and the alternate prior trail was also blocked where it entered the trees. This situation constituted a very large, open cul-de-sac with plenty of maneuver room for the XUV.

### 3.3.5 Scenario #6

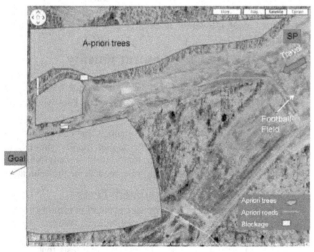

**Figure 9. Scenario #6**

Scenario #6 (Figure 9) was the same as scenario 5 except that the prior tree data was shortened by about 100m in the southern end of the field. This was done to allow the XUV to explore for alternate paths through this wooded area which had several unmarked trails.

### 3.3.6 Scenario #7

**Figure 10. Scenario #7**

Scenario #7 (Figure 10) was the intended to be the simplest of the scenarios. The start point and goal were along a tree line north of a large open area with overgrown vegetation. The main trail to the goal went between a solid tree line to the north and a small set of trees and shrubs to the south. This trail is narrow and steep but otherwise easily traversable. Both sets of trees were in the prior data. The path between the trees was blocked about 50m into the tree line. Turning around or backing up on the narrow and steep road were somewhat challenging tasks.

## 4. RESULTS

## 4.1 Route-based Navigation

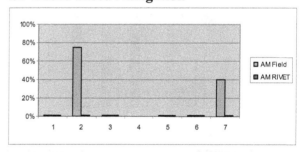

**Figure 11. Completed runs in field tests and RIVET simulations for route-based navigation**

As expected, the route-based navigation approach failed to complete most of the test scenarios. Because the experiments were designed such that the global route was invalidated by blockages, the local planner was unable to reach the goal in all but a few cases. The RIVET simulations accurately predicted the field performance in four out of the six scenarios. AM was able to find an alternate path in 3 out of 4 runs for scenario #2 in the field. This alternative path was not present in RIVET, therefore preventing the XUV from finding an alternative in simulation. In scenario #7, AM was able to backup far enough that the path was within easy reach. The simulated terrain in RIVET was significantly different in this area, providing a deeper and wider cul-de-sac that was more successful in preventing the XUV from reaching the goal.

## 4.2 Route-based Navigation with Dynamic Replanning

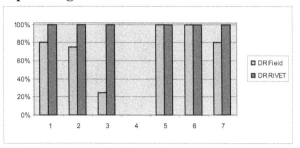

**Figure 12. Completed runs in field tests and RIVET simulations for route-based navigation with dynamic replanning**

In RIVET, route-based navigation was consistently able to reach the goal in all of the scenarios. In the field, some scenarios were consistently good, while other had varied results.

The main reason for the discrepancies between field tests and simulation was the lack of fidelity of some areas of the simulated terrain. While scenarios 5 and 6 were very close to the topology and aspect of the field, the other scenarios were not nearly as well modeled. In scenarios 1 and 2, the field tests had very tall grass and brush which was only partially modeled in simulation. Scenario #3 had a very steep and rutted trail that was modeled as a slight incline in simulation, and the alternate path had very tall grass that was not modeled either. In scenario #7 the roads were much narrower in the field than in simulation, complicating navigation significantly.

## 4.3 Combined Navigation using FCI

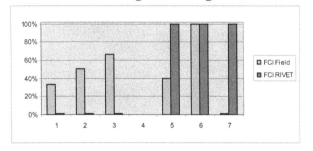

**Figure 13. Completed runs in field tests and RIVET simulations for FCI**

FCI's performance was in general inferior to that of route-based navigation with dynamic replanning. Because FCI depends on the AM planner for tight maneuvering instead of invoking HMP, its capabilities are significantly reduced in very tight scenarios such as 1,2, and 7. FCI outperformed DR in scenario #3, due to its superior ability to find paths in cluttered environments instead of just following a global route in an area where the most important information was local rather than global.

The performance of FCI was not accurately represented in RIVET. In scenarios 1, 2, and 3, the field tests results were better in the field than in RIVET. The field scenarios had more alternatives than the RIVET ones, and FCI was able to find those in several occasions. In scenario #5 the field performance was surprisingly poor, possibly because the vegetation density in the field and in RIVET was quite different and this affected the

balance between local and global navigation that needs to be achieved for successful FCI navigation. Scenario #7 is much more difficult to maneuver in the field than in RIVET. In RIVET this area was incorrectly modeled as a wide road where the vehicle was able to easily turn around, while in the field this is a very narrow road.

## 5. CONCLUSIONS AND FUTURE WORK

The results presented here indicate that although there are few theoretical guarantees in integrated planners, significant trends do show up when evaluating them in both simulation and the field. We found that route-based navigation with dynamic replanning performed better in all but one scenario, and its performance was well modeled in the RIVET simulation. As expected, we also found that static route-based navigation is of limited use when faced with blockages that render the global route invalid, and this results was also correctly modeled in simulation. FCI had a performance that was consistently worse than that of the dynamic replanner, yet better than using static route-based navigation. We also found that FCI is not well modeled in the current RIVET simulation, as the simulation does not capture local characteristics of the terrain in enough detail to replicate the complex interactions between the local and global planner.

Future work in evaluating hierarchical planner performance through field experiments and simulation includes:

## 5.1 Improving Simulation Quality

Improving the quality of the simulation should lead to better match between simulation and field testing. While it would be desirable to improve the quality of the simulation as much as possible, there is a tradeoff between the quality of the simulation and rendering speed. This tradeoff establishes limits of what can be achieved while keeping the simulation real-time. Within these limits, it would be advantageous to identify which features of the terrain are most influential in providing a more realistic UGV performance.

## 5.2 Improving Environment Fidelity

In some cases, improving the fidelity of an environment requires improving the quality of the simulation, for example when there is an environment with deep ruts that greatly affect the performance of the system.

More often, however, there are small changes that can be made to an environment that do not require higher quality simulation. These include better matching the topology of the environment, the size of open areas and the simulation models for the vehicles.

## 5.3 Developing Standardized Tests

One critical component of performance evaluation is the existence of standardized tests to measure capabilities. While creating standardized tests for outdoor environments is difficult, we should attempt to identify a small set of representative tests that can be replicated in different environments in order to properly measure the capabilities of a system, as well as progress in its development.

## REFERENCES

[1] Childers, M., Bodt, B., Hill, S., Camden, R., Gonzalez, J. P., Dean, R., Dodson, W., Kreafle, G., Lacaze, A., Sapronov, L. (2010) "Unmanned Ground Vehicle Two-Level Planning

Technology Assessment." ARL-TR (in press), U.S. Army Research Laboratory, 2010.

[2] Ferguson D. and Stentz, A. Multi-resolution Field D*, *Proceedings of the International Conference on Intelligent Autonomous Systems (IAS)*, March, 2006.

[3] Ferguson, D and Stentz, A., 2006: "Using Interpolation to Improve Path Planning: The Field D* Algorithm". Journal of Field Robotics, 2006, 23, 79-101

[4] Gonzalez, J. P.; Nagy, B. and Stentz, A., 2006: "The Geometric Path Planner for Navigating Unmanned Vehicles in Dynamic Environments". Proceedings ANS 1st Joint Emergency Preparedness and Response and Robotic and Remote Systems.

[5] Gonzalez, J.P. ; Dodson, W.; Dean, R.; Lacaze, A.; and Sapronov, L. Integrating Local and Global Navigation in Unmanned Ground Vehicles. *In Proceedings of 26th Army Science Conference*, December, 2008.

[6] Gonzalez, J.P. ; Dodson, W.; Dean, R.; Lacaze, A.; Sapronov, L; and Childers, M. Using Hardware-in-the-Loop Simulation for Parametric Analysis of Robotic Systems. *In Proceedings of the Workshop on The Role of Experiments in Robotics Research, International Conference on Robotics and Automaation (ICRA '10)*, May 2010.

[7] Lacaze, A. Hierarchical planning algorithms. *In proceedings of SPIE*, SPIE, 2002, 4715, 320

[8] Lacaze, A.; Moscovitz, Y.; DeClaris, N.; and Murphy, K. Path planning for autonomous vehicles driving over rough terrain. *In Intelligent Control (ISIC), 1998. Held jointly with IEEE International Symposium on Computational Intelligence in Robotics and Automation (CIRA), Intelligent Systems and Semiotics (ISAS), Proceedings*, 14-17 Sep 1998, 50-55

[9] Likhachev, M. and Ferguson, D. Planning Long Dynamically-Feasible Maneuvers For Autonomous Vehicles. *In Proceedings of the Robotics: Science and Systems Conference (RSS)*, 2008.

[10] Pivtoraiko, M. and Kelly, A. Differentially Constrained Motion Replanning Using State Lattices with Graduated Fidelity. *In Proceedings of the 2008 IEEE/RSJ International Conference on Intelligent Robots and Systems (IROS '08)*, September, 2008, pp. 2611-2616.

[11] Platzer, A. and Clarke, E. M.. Formal verification of curved flight collision avoidance maneuvers: A case study. *In Ana Cavalcanti and Dennis Dams, editors, 16th International Symposium on Formal Methods, FM, Eindhoven, Netherlands, Proceedings*, volume 5850 of *LNCS*, pages 547-562. Springer, 2009

# Evaluating the Performance of Unmanned Ground Vehicle Water Detection

Arturo Rankin
Jet Propulsion Laboratory
California Institute of Technology
4800 Oak Grove Drive
Pasadena, California 91109
(818) 354-9269

Arturo.Rankin@jpl.nasa.gov

Tonislav Ivanov
Jet Propulsion Laboratory
California Institute of Technology
4800 Oak Grove Drive
Pasadena, California 91109
(818) 354-5070

Tonislav.Ivanov@jpl.nasa.gov

Shane Brennan
Jet Propulsion Laboratory
California Institute of Technology
4800 Oak Grove Drive
Pasadena, California 91109
(818) 393-4146

Shane.Brennan@jpl.nasa.gov

## ABSTRACT

Water detection is a critical perception requirement for unmanned ground vehicle (UGV) autonomous navigation over cross-country terrain. Under the Robotics Collaborative Technology Alliances (RCTA) program, the Jet Propulsion Laboratory (JPL) developed a set of water detection algorithms that are used to detect, localize, and avoid water bodies large enough to be a hazard to a UGV. The JPL water detection software performs the detection and localization stages using a forward-looking stereo pair of color cameras. The 3D coordinates of water body surface points are then output to a UGV's autonomous mobility system, which is responsible for planning and executing safe paths. There are three primary methods for evaluating the performance of the water detection software. Evaluations can be performed in image space on the intermediate detection product, in map space on the final localized product, or during autonomous navigation to characterize the avoidance of a variety of water bodies. This paper describes a methodology for performing the first two types of water detection performance evaluations.

## Categories and Subject Descriptors
OpenGL, GIMP.

## General Terms
Algorithms, experimentation, performance.

## Keywords
Water detection, ground truth, stereo vision, passive perception.

## 1. INTRODUCTION

Detecting water hazards is a significant challenge to unmanned ground vehicle (UGV) autonomous navigation over cross country terrain. Traversing through deep water bodies could cause costly

damage to the electronics of UGVs. Moreover, a UGV that either breaks down due to water damage or becomes stuck in a water body during an autonomous military mission could cause further complications. These include the shifting of critical resources away from the primary mission to a rescue mission, the placing of soldiers into harm's way to support a rescue mission, the loss of advanced technology to an enemy, and mission failure.

Under the Robotics Collaborative Technology Alliances (RCTA) program, several researchers developed methods for water detection under the advanced perception technology thrust [1][2][3][4][5][6][7]. The Jet Propulsion Laboratory (JPL) participated in this effort, focusing primarily on the cues for water that can be exploited from a stereo pair of color cameras mounted to the front of a UGV. Early in the program, JPL developed an all-purpose multi-cue water detector that uses a rule base to combine water cues from color, texture, and object reflections (detectable in stereo range data) [4]. Subsequently, JPL developed three specialized stand-alone water detection algorithms (also using a forward-looking stereo pair of color cameras) to handle three general scenarios: water bodies in cluttered environments that are reflecting objects in the background (such as trees), water bodies that are out in the open and far away (where reflections of the sky dominate), and water bodies out in the open and close to the UGV (where the color coming out of the water body dominates) [6]. A summary of JPL's four water detectors is in [7].

All four water detection algorithms operate within image space during autonomous navigation and the results are fused into a single terrain classification image. Stereo range data is then used to localize detected water in a digital terrain map [5]. The 3D coordinates of water body map cells are then output to a UGV's autonomous mobility system, which is responsible for planning and executing safe paths.

There are three primary ways to evaluate the performance of the JPL water detection software. Evaluations can be performed in image space on the intermediate detection product, in map space on the final localized product, or during autonomous navigation to characterize how well detected, localized water bodies are avoided. The first two types of performance evaluations are unit-level since they characterize a single subsystem (i.e., the water detection subsystem). The last type of performance evaluation is system-level since it characterizes the combined water detection subsystem and a UGV's response to its output. All three evaluation methods have been utilized during the RCTA program. At the close of the RCTA program, the Army Research Laboratory (ARL) designed and executed a system-level experiment to test the avoidance of hazardous terrain (including water bodies) during autonomous navigation [8]. The portion of the experiment that included water body avoidance was performed on experimental unmanned vehicles (XUVs) at Fort Indiantown Gap (FITG), PA. Figure 1 shows an XUV and highlights the sensors used for water detection.

ARL has already published several papers that describe how system-level hazard avoidance evaluations were performed during RCTA [8][9]. In this paper, we focus on unit-level performance evaluations. We describe a methodology for conducting water detection performance evaluations in image space and water localization performance evaluations in map space.

**Figure 1. JPL water detection software has been integrated onboard XUVs and evaluated at Ft. Indiantown Gap, PA. A forward-looking stereo pair of color cameras provides water cues from color, texture, and object reflections.**

## 2. EVALUATION IN IMAGE SPACE
## 2.1 Ground Truthing Water Regions

The JPL water detection software detects water in image space. Therefore, the ideal place to evaluate the performance of JPL water detection is in image space. A formal evaluation of a terrain classifier is typically performed by accurately specifying the pixels that belong to the class of interest and generating a Receiver Operating Characteristic (ROC) curve which plots the true positive classification rate against the false positive classification rate.

In the past, ground truthing water pixels for image sequences (potentially containing hundreds of images) has been a very tedious process. In each image in a sequence, the perimeter of a water body was manually segmented by moving the mouse cursor around the water perimeter and "clicking" (i.e., selecting) a limited number of vertices. The vertices were then connected with straight lines and all the pixels within these N-sided polygons were labeled water. However, since water bodies are not constrained to follow straight lines, there is some inherent ground truth error with this method. Increasing the number of vertices around the perimeter of a water body will reduce the error but will also increase the time required to manually ground truth a sequence. Since the boundary of a water body expands in image space as it is approached, new vertices needed to be selected for each subsequent frame.

To automate the process of ground truthing water bodies in sequences of images, JPL has developed a software tool using Open Graphics Library (OpenGL). In the first image of a sequence, vertices still need to be manually selected. But in each

subsequent image, their 2D image coordinates are automatically updated. In the first frame, since we know the surface of a water body is horizontal, we estimate the elevation of a water body by averaging the elevation of each selected vertex using stereo range data. Given the 2D image coordinates of a vertex, it is trivial to look up its 3D coordinates since a left rectified image is registered with the corresponding stereo range image. The stereo correlator may fail to produce disparity data for some of the vertices. For vertices that have stereo 3D coordinates, their vectors are scaled so that they terminate in the estimated water surface plane. For vertices that have no stereo 3D coordinates, a left CAHV camera model [10] is used to modify the rays extending from the vertex pixels so that they also terminate in the estimated water surface plane. The new 3D coordinates of each vertex are recorded for use in subsequent frames. Each time a vertex is modified or added, the corresponding 3D coordinates are generated using the above procedure.

Since UGV position (x, y, z) and orientation data (roll, pitch, yaw) are recorded for each frame in a data set, the 3D coordinates of each vertex can be expressed in a gravity-based world coordinate frame. Given the motion of the UGV from one frame to the next, the left CAHV camera model is transformed and used to perform a linear mapping between the 3D world coordinates of the vertices and their 2D image coordinates. Since the perimeter of a water body typically has texture in visible imagery, it is unlikely that the stereo correlator would fail to produce disparity data for all vertex image coordinates. We currently do not attempt to filter out noisy stereo range measurements from the water body elevation estimate, but a random sample consensus (RANSAC) algorithm could be incorporated to do this.

Figure 2 illustrates the vertex selection process in the first frame of a sequence. Here, a large number of vertices were selected and neighbor vertices were connected with lines to label the water body. The "Action" and "View" drop down menus are shown to illustrate some of the options available to the user. Vertices can be added, moved, or deleted, and entire polygons can be moved or deleted. In addition, vertices and labeled water regions can be saved to file on a frame-by-frame basis and subsequently loaded from file to play back the results, or to further refine the labeling.

Vehicle motion causes the image coordinates of vertices along the perimeter of a water body to change. For example, as a water body is approached, it appears larger in image space. Figure 3 shows a sample result of automatically updating the image coordinates of the perimeter vertices after 47 frames of XUV motion towards the water body. The top row contains the left color image, the right color image, and the stereo range image for frame 0. The middle row contains the same images for frame 46. The bottom image contains a stereo point cloud for frame 46. Stereo was performed at full image resolution (1024x768 pixels). The ground truth region is overlaid on the left images and the stereo point cloud in yellow. In the stereo point cloud, the orange and white areas indicate where there is ground truthing error.

We implemented the following three strategies to help minimize ground truthing error:

1)   Allow the user to step through the sequence, pausing at every frame and verifying accurate labeling. If the model of the perimeter is poor, allow the user to move, add, or delete vertices.

2) Provide the option of processing the sequence in reverse order from the final image to the first image. In most of our RCTA sequences, a water body is approached from a distance and the final image contains the greatest perimeter detail. This may not be ideal for all sequences, however. In the final frame of some sequences, portions of a water body fall outside of the cameras field of view. When that occurs, additional vertices may need to be manually added as more of the water body comes into the field of view.

3) Perform non-linear segmentation between vertices to improve the modeling of the water body perimeter.

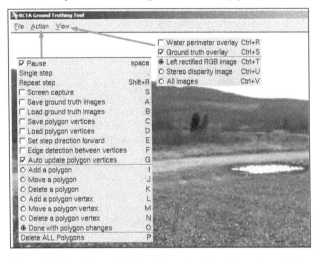

**Figure 2. A software tool has been developed to automate the process of ground truthing water bodies in sequences of images. In the first image of a sequence, vertices around the perimeter of water bodies are selected. In this example, the water body is labeled by connecting neighboring vertices with lines. Vertex selection is performed on rectified, full resolution (1024x768 pixels) imagery. Here, we are only showing a portion of the first image. The full image is shown (at a lower resolution) in the upper left image of Figure 3.**

The algorithm we selected for non-linear segmentation is called *intelligent scissors* [11]. This algorithm attempts to find the most grayscale contrast closed-loop boundary (Laplacian zero-crossing) while keeping the boundary edge smooth (gradient direction) and the texture around the boundary consistent (gradient magnitude). An optimal graph search called *live-wire boundary* is performed based on Dijkstra's [12] path finding algorithm to find a minimal cost path via dynamic programming. The open-source code for *intelligent scissors*, available under GNU Image Manipulation Program (GIMP), was adapted and integrated into the water body ground truthing tool.

For each frame in an image sequence, this code uses the automatically updated vertices from the water region segmented in the previous frame. We step around the ordered vertex list for each water body and run *intelligent scissors* between each vertex pair. *Intelligent scissors* outputs a set of connected pixels between neighbor vertices. Figure 4 illustrates the advantage of using *intelligent scissors* to model the water perimeter between vertices. In this example, only five vertices were needed along a

section of the water boundary that has a length in excess of 20 meters.

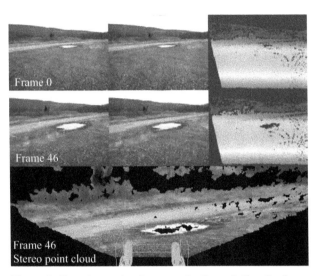

**Figure 3. Sample result of automatically updating the image coordinates of the vertices selected in Figure 2 after 47 frames. The top row contains the left rectified image, the right color image, and the stereo range image for frame 0. The middle row contains the same images for frame 46. The bottom image contains a stereo point cloud for frame 46. The ground truth region is overlaid on the left rectified images and the stereo point cloud in yellow. In the color-coded stereo range images, red corresponds to close range, blue corresponds to far range, the colors in between correspond to an intermediate range, and maroon corresponds to no stereo data.**

**Figure 4. The GIMP image viewer has an intelligent scissors tool to segment image regions along contours. We have extracted the intelligent scissors portion of GIMP and have integrated it into our ground truthing tool. In this example, only 5 vertices were needed along the cropped portion of the water boundary. Intelligent scissors is run for each pair of neighbor vertices to segment the water's edge.**

Thus far, we used the JPL water body ground truthing software tool to label one color stereo sequence of images collected at FITG on May 13, 2008. The sequence was collected while an XUV was teleoperated toward the water body partly shown in Figure 4. There is a single large water body at least partially visible in all 143 frames of the sequence. Since terrain classification and stereo range images are registered with the corresponding left camera image (after rectification), only the left rectified images are ground truthed. A binary ground truth image is saved for each left rectified image in the sequence. Figure 5 shows the results of labeling the water body in the first and last frame in the sequence. The labeling is quite good, but it is not perfect. As illustrated in the bottom row of Figure 5, it does not exclude interior objects extending out of a water body, such as sediment, vegetation, or rocks.

**Figure 5. The water perimeter (green) and labeled water region (orange) for the first and last frame of a 143 frame sequence. This sequence was ground truthed using our software tool. The labeling is quite good, but it is not perfect. For example, it does not exclude interior objects extending out of the water.**

## 2.2 Characterizing Detection Performance

The labeled sequence described in Figure 5 was processed off-line with the JPL water detection software with all three specialized detectors enabled. The water body was detected in every frame. Figure 6 shows water detection results in the form of overlapping water cues for the first and last frame in the sequence. The pixels labeled blue, magenta, and red indicate where the water body was detected by one, two, or three water detectors, respectively. The blue regions were detected based on the variation in color, the magenta regions were detected based on the variation in color and sky reflections, and the red regions were detected based on the variation in color, sky reflections, and terrain reflections.

Figure 7 shows water detection results overlaid on the labeled water body for the first and last frame in the sequence. The blue, red, and green pixels indicate true positive detection, false negative detection, and false positive detection, respectively. Note that detector labels almost the entire water body but tends to miss small portions of water on the perimeter. Along the right side of the water body, the missed detection is due to weak reflections of the grass lining the water's edge.

Figure 8 contains a graph of the true positive and false positive water detection rates for each frame in the ground truthed water sequence as a function of the minimum range to the water's leading edge. The true positive detection rate is calculated as the number of pixels correctly classified as water divided by the number of ground truth water pixels. The false positive detection rate is calculated as the number of pixels incorrectly classified as water divided by the number of ground truth water pixels.

Overall, the true positive detection rate increased as the size of the water body in image space increased. The true positive detection

rate ranged from 68% (near the beginning of the sequence) to 90% (near the end of the sequence). Note that the false positive detection rate was consistently low for the sequence. The false positive detection rate was 3.3% in one frame but remained below 0.8% in the rest of the frames. Because the false positive detection rate was fairly constant for the entire sequence, we chose the plot format in Figure 8 instead of the standard ROC format. False positive water detection only occurred around the perimeter of the labeled water body. There was substantially less false positive water detection around the perimeter of the labeled water body than false negative water detection.

**Figure 6. Overlapping water cues for the first and last frame in the ground truthed sequence. The pixels labeled blue, magenta, and red indicate where the water body was detected by one, two, or three water detectors, respectively. The blue regions were detected based on variation in color, the magenta regions were detected based on the variation in color and sky reflections, and the red regions were detected based on the variation in color, sky reflections, and terrain reflections.**

**Figure 7. Water detection results for the first and last image in the sequence. The blue, red, and green pixels indicate true positive detection, false negative detection, and false positive detection, respectively.**

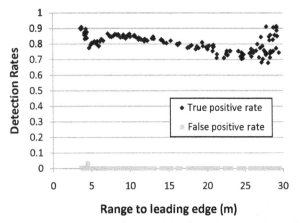

**Figure 8. The true and false positive detection rates for each frame in the ground truthed water sequence as a function of the minimum range to the water's leading edge. Each marker corresponds to an image frame.**

## 3. EVALUATION IN MAP SPACE
### 3.1 Ground Truthing Water Regions

The JPL water detection software localizes detected water in a terrain map. Therefore, the ideal place to evaluate the performance of water body localization is in map space. In order to test the accuracy of water body localization, ground truth 3D coordinates of a water body's perimeter is needed in the same coordinate frame that the vehicle's position is expressed. Ground truth water body measurements can be obtained by tracing the water's perimeter with a positioning sensor, such as differential global positioning system (DGPS), or by surveying fiducials around the water's perimeter with a total station (or other surveying instrument). The location of detected water bodies can then be compared to the ground truth data to determine its accuracy.

Stereo range data is used by the JPL water detection software to localize detected water. Stereo range data around the perimeter of a detected water body is averaged to estimate the elevation of the water body. We don't use the stereo range data corresponding to the surface of detected water bodies for two reasons. First, there may be little or no stereo range data on a water body since the surface of water bodies tend to lack texture, particularly when they are stationary. Secondly, stereo range data on reflections of objects in water has a range that corresponds to the range to the reflected object, not the surface of the water body.

Once the elevation of detected water bodies is estimated, the 3D coordinates (in the stereo range image) of the pixels classified as water are modified to correspond to the surface of water bodies. This modified 3D data are used to label cells in a terrain map as water cells for comparison against the ground truth measurements. As a water body is approached, the estimate of its elevation improves. Temporal filtering is performed in the terrain map to relocate previously detected water [5].

Water localization experiments can be performed on a ground truthed test site with or without the vehicle constrained to a predefined path. During RCTA, one of the test sites used to evaluate water localization constrained the vehicle path by using a General Dynamics Robotic Systems (GDRS) instrumented train.

The instrumented train contained a General Electric 24 volt DC motor, an Ogura Fail-Safe brake, an inertial measurement unit (IMU), a GPS receiver, three color cameras that provided narrow baseline (9.5cm), mid baseline (20.5cm), and wide baseline (30cm) stereo ranging, a GDRS ladar, and the same autonomous mobility computing hardware used on XUVs. Data from the IMU and GPS were combined with a Kalman filter to provide continuous, smoothed absolute positioning data accurate to within 0.5% of the distance traveled [13].

The instrument train was constructed to enable multiple RCTA researchers to evaluate their terrain classification algorithms in a controlled environment. The use of train tracks ensures the perception sensors always follow the same route for each test run. This type of experiment enables one to directly compare the results of multiple test runs where single or multiple factors may be varied each run, such as train speed, time of day (to evaluate the effects of lighting), and the day of year (to evaluate the effects of different environmental conditions).

Perception sensor and navigation data can be logged during test runs for offline processing with terrain classification algorithms, or terrain classification can be performed in real-time and its results logged. Figure 9 contains a picture of the instrumented train and two man-made water bodies (each approximately 1.5m x 2m) constructed adjacent to train tracks at GDRS, Westminster, Maryland. The length of the train tracks at this test site was 171 meters. JPL performed stereo data collections on this course at speed of 1, 3, and 5 m/s.

**Figure 9. A JPL passive perception system was mounted to a GDRS instrumented train. Color stereo imagery was collected on a surveyed obstacle course containing two rectangular man-made water bodies at speeds of 1, 3, and 5 m/s.**

The corners of the rectangular water bodies were surveyed using a NovAtel OEM4-G2 GPS receiver operating in RT-2 differential mode (with a base station less than 30 meters from the train starting point). The accuracy of this DGPS is 1cm +1 part per million (ppm). At the farthest end of the test course, the DPGS error due to the distance from the GPS base station was less than 2mm. At each corner, DGPS data was averaged for 10 minutes, yielding an accuracy of 1cm circular error probable (CEP), i.e., half of all the data were within 1cm of the ground truth. The standard deviation in both latitude and longitude directions was less than 1cm. DGPS land survey accuracy was verified with a

Leica TCR307 total station on six key points on the train rails. Figure 10 illustrates water detection for one frame during a 1m/s run. Note in the stereo range image that there is no range data on much of the water body, except where there is a reflection of the pole directly behind the water body.

**Figure 10. A frame showing the first man-made water body on the test course described in Figure 9 during a 1m/s run (left), water detection results overlaid on a grayscale intensity image (middle), and a wide-baseline stereo range image (right). In the color coded water detection overlay, blue, magenta, and red correspond to one, two, and three cues for water, respectively. In the stereo range image, black corresponds to no range data.**

## 3.2 Characterizing Detection Performance

The 3D coordinates of a water body localized with JPL's water detection software can be compared with the ground truth water body perimeter measurements to produce several measures of accuracy:

1) Difference in the detected and ground truth water body centroid (units: meters).
2) Percentage of the detected water body within the ground truth water body.
3) Percentage of the detected water body outside of the ground truth water body.
4) Percentage of the ground truth water body detected as water.
5) Maximum distance the detected water body perimeter strays from the ground truth water body perimeter (units: meters).

Thus far, GDRS has provided JPL with only the ground truth measurement of a single corner of the second man-made water body. JPL has processed the wide-baseline data from the 1m/s run off-line at an image resolution of 320x240 pixels using the all-purpose multi-cue based water detection algorithm [4]. (This analysis was performed before the specialized water detectors were implemented.) In Figure 11, the upper graph shows the detection and localization of both water bodies and the lower graph shows a zoom-in of the second water body. Using a 20cm resolution terrain map, the JPL water detection software localized the corner of the second man-made water body within 16cm of the ground truth position [13].

Figure 12 contains graphs of the detection range and strength of detection for both water bodies. The first water body was detected at a maximum range of 13.6 meters and the second water body was detected at a maximum range of 10.2 meters. The maximum range of detection for the second water body was slightly lower because elevated terrain near the leading edge occluded a portion of the water.

## 4. CONCLUSIONS

In this paper, we described a methodology for conducting water detection performance evaluations in image space, and water localization performance evaluations in map space. JPL has developed a software tool for ground truthing water bodies in stereo image sequences. The ground truthing tool enables users to step though a sequence of images and select a limited number of vertices (in left rectified images) around the perimeter of water bodies. We have extracted the *intelligent scissors* portion of GIMP and have integrated it into our ground truthing tool. *Intelligent scissors* is run for each pair of neighbor vertices to segment the water's edge. Stereo vision is used to update the 2D image coordinates of the vertices as the user steps from one frame to the next. At each frame, the user can add, move, or delete vertices, or move or delete entire polygons.

Typically, a water body is ground truthed in image space starting with the final image (where the water body is the largest) and ending with the first image (where the water body is the smallest). Thus far, we have used the JPL water body ground truthing software to label one color stereo sequence of images. In the 143 frame sequence, the water body was detected in every frame. The true positive detection rate ranged from 68% (at a range of 28 meters to the leading edge) to 90% (at a range of 4 meters to the leading edge). The false positive detection rate was 3.3% in one frame but remained below 0.8% in the rest of the frames.

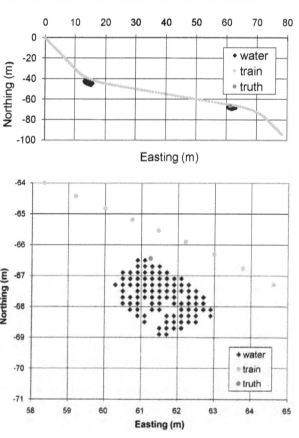

**Figure 11. Detection and localization of the two rectangular man-made water bodies shown in Figure 9. The lower graph shows a zoom-in of the second water body. The blue markers are placed at the centers of terrain map cells classified as water.**

This evaluation indicated that weak reflections of vegetation lining the edge of a water body are consistently undetected by the three specialized water detectors. In addition, the true positive water detection rate is currently underestimated when there are objects extending out of the interior of a water body, such as sediment, rocks, and vegetation. The reason for this is the water body ground truthing tool does not currently exclude these regions. Additional work is needed to enable the ground truthing tool to exclude these regions, and to filter noisy stereo range measurement during water body elevation estimation.

We also outlined several measures of accuracy for comparing the 3D coordinates of a water body localized with JPL's water detection software with 3D ground truth water body perimeter measurements. We have not experimented with any of these measures yet due to a lack of 3D ground truth water body perimeter measurements to date. More work is needed to determine the usefulness of these measures.

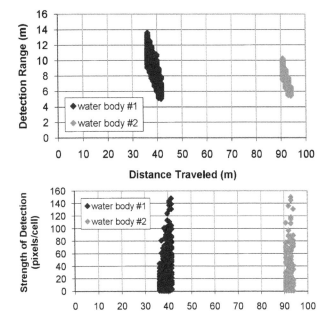

**Figure 12. Detection range and strength of detection as a function of distance traveled for the two rectangular man-made water bodies shown in Figure 9.**

## 5. ACKNOWLEDGMENTS

The research described in this paper was carried out by the Jet Propulsion Laboratory, California Institute of Technology, and was sponsored by the U.S. Army under the Robotics Collaborative Technology Alliances and Future Combat System Autonomous Navigation System programs, through agreements with the National Aeronautics and Space Administration (NASA). Reference herein to any specific commercial product, process, or service by trademark, manufacturer, or otherwise, does not constitute or imply its endorsement by the United States Government or the Jet Propulsion Laboratory, California Institute of Technology.

## 6. REFERENCES

[1] Hong, T., Rasmussen, C., Chang, T., and Shneier, M. 2002. Fusing ladar and color image information for mobile robot feature detection and tracking, *7th International Conference on Intelligent Autonomous Systems*, (Marina Del Ray, CA, Mar. 2002).

[2] Matthies, L., Bellutta, P., and McHenry, M. 2003. Detecting water hazards for autonomous off-road navigation. *Proceedings of SPIE*, Vol. 5083 (Orlando, FL, Apr. 2003), 231-242.

[3] Sarwal, A., Nett, J., and Simon, D. 2004. Detection of small water bodies. *PercepTek Robotics Technical Report*, Littleton, CO, (http://www.dtic.mil, AD# ADA433004).

[4] Rankin, A., Matthies, L., and Huertas, A. 2004. Daytime water detection by fusing multiple cues for autonomous off-road navigation. *Proceedings of the 24th Army Science Conference*, (Orlando, FL, Nov. 2004).

[5] Rankin, A. and Matthies, L. 2006. Daytime water detection and localization for unmanned vehicle autonomous navigation. *Proceedings of the 25th Army Science Conference*, (Orlando, FL, Nov. 2006).

[6] Rankin, A. and Matthies, L. 2010. Daytime water detection based on color variation. *To appear in: Proceedings of the IEEE/RSJ International Conference on Intelligent Robots and Systems*, (Taipei, Taiwan, Oct. 2010).

[7] Rankin, A., Bajracharya, M., Huertas, A., Howard, A., Moghaddam, B., Brennan, S., Ansar, A., Tang, B., Turmon, M., and Matthies, L. 2010. Stereo-vision based perception capabilities developed during the Robotics Collaborative Technology Alliances program. *Proceedings of SPIE*, Vol. 7692, (Orlando, FL, Apr. 2010), 76920C1-76920C15.

[8] Bodt, B., Childers, M., and Camden, R. 2010. A capstone experiment to assess unmanned ground vehicle tactical behaviors developed under the robotics collaborative technology alliance. *Proceedings of AUVSI*, (Denver, CO, Aug. 2010).

[9] Bodt, B. and Childers, M. 2010. A place at the table: the role of formal experimentation in the robotics collaborative technology alliance. *Proceedings of the 78th MORS Symposium*, (Quantico, VA, Jun. 2010).

[10] Yakimovsky, Y. and Cunningham, R. 1978. A system for extracting three-dimensional measurements from a stereo pair of TV cameras. *Computer Graphics and Image Processing*, 7, 195-210.

[11] Mortensen, E.N. and Barrett, W.A. 1995. Intelligent scissors for image composition. *International Conference on Computer Graphics and Interactive Techniques*, Los Angeles, CA, Aug. 1995), 191-198.

[12] Dijkstra, E.W. 1959. A note on two problems in connection with graphs, *Numerische Mathematik*, Vol. 1, 269-271.

[13] Rankin, A., Huertas, A., and Matthies, L. 2005. Evaluation of stereo vision obstacle detection algorithms for off-road autonomous navigation. *Proceedings of AUVSI*, (Baltimore, MD, Jun. 2005).

# Autonomous Mobility for Areas with Large Numbers of Pedestrians

Alberto Lacaze, Karl Murphy, Nenad Uzunovic and Joseph Putney
Robotic Research LLC
555 Quince Orchard Rd, Suite 300, Gaithersburg, MD 20878
Tel: 240-631-0008

## ABSTRACT

Autonomy for small robots is required by the military as end-users demand more uses and versatility for small robots. Unmanned ground vehicles have already proven their usefulness in IED detection and inspection; explosive ordnance disposal (EOD); reconnaissance; communications; handling hazardous materials; security; defense; and rescue. They are now being acquired in ever increasing numbers. Pure tele-operation, the method typically used to operate small robots, is a burden for the operator and does not meet demands for speed, robustness and awareness of surroundings. In addition, new types of platforms are being developed; ones that have a mission to travel close to humans, such as the LS3 (legged squadron based on Big Dog design) and the BEAR (battlefield extraction robot) as stated in the *FY2009–2034 OSD Unmanned Systems Integrated Roadmap.*

Missions are being envisioned where robots will be required to travel alongside soldiers (LS3) as companions, leaders, wing-men or followers. Additional capabilities can be easily envisioned, such as the capability of the robot to track a person, break off from their "pack" and then follow a particular person-of interest. When robots are used as companions to humans, they will require greater autonomy levels and flexible path planning, detection and prediction capabilities. As of now, robots cannot operate in crowds because the software for path planning and obstacle avoidance is not sophisticated enough to work reliably at the speeds required (e.g. the speed of a person walking). The system described in this article will provide functionality to these platforms so that missions among humans can be accomplished safely and effectively.

## Categories and Subject Descriptors

I.2.9 [**Robotics**]: Autonomous vehicles

I.2.10 [**Vision and Scene Understanding**]: Perceptual reasoning

I.2.11 [**Distributed Artificial Intelligence**]: Coherence and coordination

## General Terms

Algorithms, Measurement, Design, Security.

## Keywords

Autonomous systems, SUGVs, UGVs, safe operations, human/robot teams.

## 1. INTRODUCTION

There are several challenges to overcome before robots can safely traverse crowds of people (Figure 1). One reason this has not been accomplished before is the poor world model representation used for autonomous ground robotic systems. Most control systems for unmanned vehicles do not effectively represent or take under consideration dynamic entities in the environment in while making decisions which way to go; in other words, poor planning. Robotic systems use maps to represent the surrounding environment. Maps are an important tool to reduce the false alarms that current sensing systems provide. When the robot's sensors scan the surrounding area, they accumulate the detections, or lack of detections, in a particular cell. This makes it possible to improve the classification of static obstacles. This technique is not well suited for environments with dynamic entities – people, dogs, bikes, carts and other pedestrian-centered movers. Much of the research in detection of movers ignores the fact that the accumulation technique is no longer straight forward in dynamic environments. Representing, classifying, and tracking the moving entities will drive many of the requirements of the path planners. A system that represents movers will also have to cope with the statistical disadvantages that may be caused by not being able to simply statistically collect detections at one cell as the content of the cells can change with time.

**Figure 1. A small robot acts as a companion for a soldier while walking through a busy market.**

As the speed of a robot increases, not only are we required to detect and track movers efficiently, but we need to predict the movers' locations far enough into the future, with sufficient accuracy, so that we will have a probabilistically acceptable outcome to each of our actions. In static environments, sensing and planning are easy to decouple. In dynamics environments, the prediction of where a moving entity is going to be in the future depends, in part, on the actions of the unmanned vehicle. For example, if a person (mover) was following a robot down a hallway, and the robot stopped, then the mover would probably either stop or go around; two actions that are unlikely to occur if the robot didn't stop.

In our approach, planning in dynamic environments requires a three dimensional (3D) planning space (x,y,t) for ground vehicles. This planning space is larger than the typical 2D (x,y) spaces used for ground or, in general, for aerial vehicles where the altitude changes are mostly used as constraints rather than full dimensions of search.

## 1.1 Architecture

Robot control in a crowded area has sufficient complexity that the development and implementation of an intelligent architecture is needed. The proposed system (already tested preliminarily in simulation) will be based on a hybrid distributed/hierarchical control architecture and a matching Human Machine Interface (Figure 2). The architecture is based on 4D-RCS [1] which has already been successfully applied to a variety of ground robotic

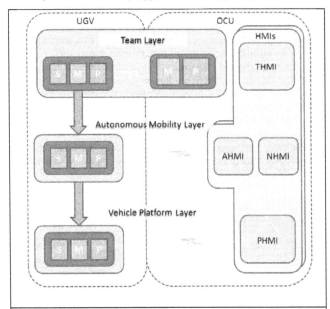

**Figure 2. The overall system diagram is a modular hybrid system that contains distributed planning elements at the coordination layer, and a hierarchical control strategy for obstacle avoidance.**

systems.

The control architecture is composed of a Team Layer, an Autonomous Mobility Layer and a Vehicle Platform Layer. Standard modules are utilized across the control hierarchy composed of Sensing, Modeling and Planning (S,M,P) modules. The Team Layer computes coarse tasks and schedules for the UGV by exploring the alpha beta expansion with the robot team for possible actions as well as the intelligent adversary possible actions. This layer is distributed between the robot and the Operator Control Unit (OCUs). A corresponding Team Human Machine Interface (THMI) provides the operators with coordination oversight. The Autonomous Mobility Layers resides

on each separate UGV. They are designed to solve the local path planning and neutralization problems. There is a corresponding Autonomy HMI (AHMI) and a Neutralization HMI (NHMI) that provide oversight for these operations.

Finally, there is a Vehicle Platform Layer in each vehicle that provides the low level control functions including: path following, communication infrastructure and e-stop facilities. As with other layers, the Platform HMI (PHMI) provides the operator with oversight of platform status.

### 1.1.1 Overall Planning System

The planning and control system will be hierarchically organized providing a group of specialized planners to solve the pursuit and chase functionalities problems. Figure 3 shows the overall planning system diagram. The top layer of the hierarchy has

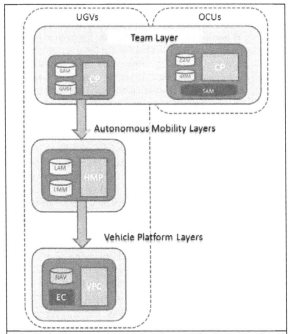

**Figure 3. The planning system is organized as a semi-distributed hierarchical architecture to minimize complexity while providing resiliency to communication outages.**

relatively courser representation and longer planning cycles, while the bottom of the hierarchy has a relatively finer representation and shorter planning cycles. At the top, the team layer plans the pursuit. It performs task allocation and rough scheduling of the robot in order to maintain proximity to the team leader. The layer is composed of a Coordination Planner (CP) which interacts with the Global Autonomous mobility Model (GAM) and the Global Mission Model (GMM).

The SUGV has an Autonomous Mobility Layer (AM). AM is composed of a local version of a layered map and exposure database (LAM and LMM). The planner at this level solves the problem of single vehicle navigation and local coordination in the case of Neutralization. This layer receives coarse plans from the Coordination Layer, and provides plans that minimize local exposure and optimize mobility constraints for the UGV. These plans are sent to the Vehicle Platform Layer where the task is to transform these plans into actuator commands. The Vehicle Platform Layer maintains the navigation solution and provides the E-stop Controller (EC).

### 1.1.2 Representation

The system provides three overlapping representations.

1. The Autonomous Mobility World Model provides traversability information that is used by the different levels to calculate the costs of the plans from a mobility standpoint.
2. The Mission Specific World Model provides information about the pedestrians, whether they are friendly, foes or team members, and their motion prediction. It is represented in the form of a probability density function (PDF) of each pedestrian being present at a location at a particular moment in time
3. The Situational Awareness World Model is designed for operator use. This representation will allow the operator to understand the environment, and intervene if necessary.

## 1.2 World Model

As presented in the architecture subsection, the world model is hierarchical in nature. The different levels of resolution provide autonomous mobility and mission specific information at different levels of resolution. The Global and Local Autonomous mobility Modules provide the classical autonomous mobility needs. This information is used by the autonomous mobility planners to find the least costly trajectories through a dynamic peopled environment, such as a marketplace. The system must be able, to not only avoid pedestrians, but to do so in the uneven terrains that the systems are likely to encounter. The following sections concentrate on what we believe is one of the most innovative parts of our research: the medium/long term pedestrian prediction.

### 1.2.1 Terrain Aware Coordination Toolbox for Intelligent Control (TACTIC)

In 2004, Robotic Research developed a system called TACTIC for predicting the opposite team's movement in structured and unstructured environments. TACTIC was successfully utilized in a tactical competition organized by the Army War College and funded by ARL. By utilizing TACTIC to predict the opposite team's locations, our team was able to outperform all other teams in the final simulated competitions.

Instead of using the Kalman filter approach for obstacle prediction, we have designed a system which considers terrain traversability in probability density function (PDF) generation. Although Kalman filters are well suited for aerial vehicle prediction, they break down in highly cluttered urban environments. TACTIC, instead, takes into consideration the probabilistic nature of the information at the core of its planning structure, borrowing from two techniques:

1) Monte Carlo approaches generate initial conditions that are assumed to be true. The planning and simulations are then performed in a deterministic fashion. Then, the process is repeated with changing initial conditions. These initial conditions are selected in a manner that matches the probabilistic profile of the variables at hand.

2) Probability grids, evidence grids, and probabilistic decision graphs propagate the probability through a graph-

based map. Most of these approaches have been used for navigational estimation or for behavior learning but they have not been robustly used for action forecasting.

The first step in developing an effective forecasting system is to create a model of the world that quickly and accurately reflects conditions and actions in the real world. The characteristics of the tracked object, in conjunction with the anticipated environmental conditions, would be part of the model. The probable location of the target would be modeled using this representation in time and space.

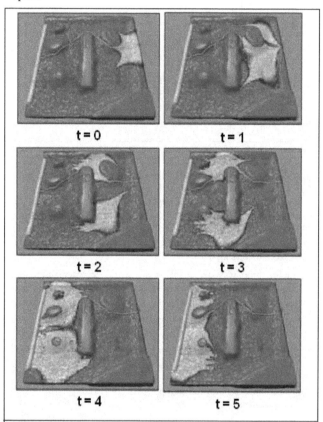

**Figure 4. PDF, over time, given a fixed starting point, terrain, target capability, and potential target's mission. Probabilities are color coded, red being the least probable and green being the most probable.**

TACTIC creates a Probability Density Function (PDF) by using a search-based modeling program. The generation of the PDF is at the core of behavioral forecasting. An example of a PDF determined by TACTIC can be seen in Figure 4.

The core of TACTIC are path planning algorithms. Given the map and movers with their approximate set of goals, we evaluate paths for each mover in the same manner as we do for planning paths for the robotic vehicle. Detected mover's size, dynamics (based on classification), velocity, and other constraining characteristics are used to calculate all possible paths that this mover could take. Since we take into consideration dynamic capabilities of the mover, knowing its exact goal does not affect short term predictions, which are in the order of a few seconds.

The precise location of the predicted goals does affect long term prediction which greatly improves planning.

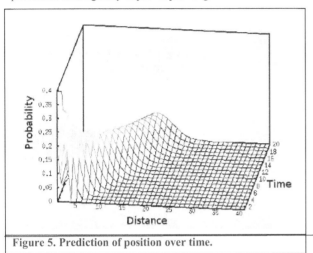

**Figure 5. Prediction of position over time.**

Figure 5 displays a simple case of probability of a mover as a function of distance and time. TACTIC predicts future occupancy of the (x,y,time) cells and represents them as a probability function. This probability function takes as inputs the current mover's classification, velocity, approximate goal, and a 2-dimensional terrain map. TACTIC assumes that movers will most likely take the easier path to achieve their goals. Therefore the likelihood of a mover taking a certain path is directly related to the cost of traversing it.

Great attention was dedicated to the world representation. We designed a flexible interface where sensing, world modeling and path planning algorithms can easily work.

Since two and a half dimensional maps have worked well for static environments, they were kept to serve the same purpose –

representing a static world. Dynamic environments add much more complexity to the problem. In order to plan in time, we have to estimate where the detected moving entities will be in the near future. Since the problem is probabilistic in nature, we decided to represent moving entities as probabilities in time. We created a 3-dimensional (x,y,t) space filled with probabilistic clouds that describe estimated future positions for movers. These probabilistic clouds are defined as a set of discrete distributions $p_m(x,y,t)$, one for each mover, that describes the probability of arrival for that particular mover into that particular cell in (x,y,t) space. Therefore, each mover has a probabilistic cloud associated with it and each cloud adds up to one for each slice in time, i.e., every mover has to be somewhere in each slice in time.

$$\sum_x \sum_y p_m(x,y,t) = 1, \text{ where } 0 < t < \max time, \text{ and}$$

$$0 < m < \max mover$$

Therefore, the new interface that represents the currently sensed world is divided into two layers for computational efficiency and the information carried is chosen to optimally represent the nature of the problem. Static objects are mapped into a 2-dimensional (x,y) space in relative coordinate system, and movers are represented in 3-dimensional space (x,y,time) due to the probabilistic nature of the problem. Figure 6 shows multiple layers in the interface. Static obstacles described in the 2-dimensional map are shown more to the left overlaid with buildings, and on the road we see many movers represented as clouds of points.

**Figure 6 – Multiple layers in the world model interface.**

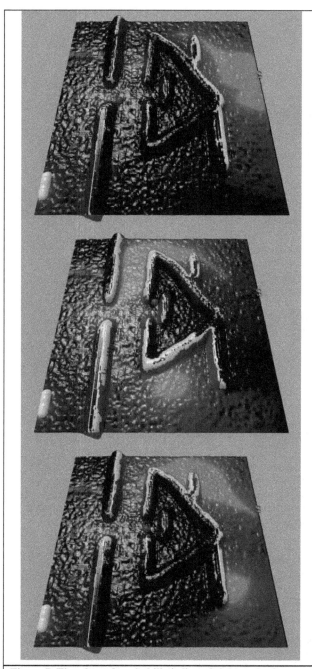

**Figure 7. Time-lapsed probabilistic line of sight and sniper locations for a moving procession. Procession starts at S, and progresses towards the yellow spheres through the choke point.**

TACTIC was successfully used to predict the motion of non-combatant pedestrians in simulation. The resulting (x,y,t) probability maps are displayed in Figure 6. In this figure, the predicted motion of each pedestrian creates a probabilistic cloud of where each pedestrian is likely to be located in the next 1-15 seconds. This prediction is affected by the terrain that the pedestrian is likely to traverse.

Since the autonomous robotic system must pursue team members through a marketplace, it will not only be necessary to predict the future location of these pedestrians, but also their predicted line of sight. Figure 7 shows the predicted line of sight of a pedestrian that was initially detected at S (left of the image). The red areas show the likely line of sight locations as the pedestrian traverses around the terrain and obstacles, going towards the left of the map (yellow balls). Green areas are "cresting" areas where, under this scenario, if the SUGV is placed in those locations, it would actually be silhouetted against the sky. The system plans towards the brighter red areas in (x,y,t) to achieve the highest likelihood of line of sight to the friend or foe.

## 1.3 Planning

The (x,y,t) planning was demonstrated in simulation. Since then, a much more simplified version of this planner (only x,y) was developed by Robotic Research for the Multi-Autonomous Ground-robotic International Challenge (MAGIC 2010) that is jointly sponsored by the Australian and US Departments of Defense. This competition has the goal to develop next-generation fully autonomous ground vehicle systems that can be deployed effectively in military operations and civilian emergency situations.

### 1.3.1 Planning strategies

Most planning systems have three common components:

*A search engine* is at the core of most planners. It is a highly optimized graph search technique. Although a very interesting theoretical problem, it was demonstrated in 1985 that given a graph with positive edges and a heuristic, there is no algorithm capable of opening less nodes than A* (A* is an algorithm used in path planning to determine the optimal path to travel). Modifications of A* (dynamic A*, D*, etc) are mostly very small changes to the algorithm that exploit particular aspects of the problem at hand. In general, this is a very well traveled road for research.

*Cost Computation* assigns a value of traversing an edge within the graph. In the proposed system, the cost computation is based on the probabilistic representation of the predicted movers. The probability of collisions is computed based on the probability of other vehicles occupying the same space as our vehicle at the same time. Cost computation is generally the most computationally intensive aspect of path planning. It is our experience that about 80% of planning cycle time is normally spent on this task.

*Graph Generation* provides the largest discriminator between the different planning systems. The artistry and know-how of planning is generally hidden in the graph generator. Systems that generate wasteful graphs will spend their computing cycles looking for solutions in parts of the space that are unlikely to be selected, while good graphs will focus the computational resources to optimizing the problem. The three planning methodologies presented in the previous section are only different on how these dynamic graphs are being generated. Many commonly used algorithms like D* and field D* utilize grid graphs that do not properly match the non-uniform nature of the world. In particular, when dealing with movers, we need to focus the search on areas surrounding the movers in time and space.

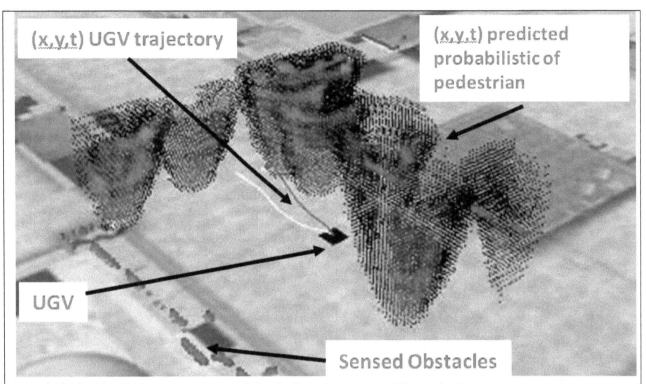

**Figure 8. Engineering display – representation of planning in unstructured world in (x,y,time)**

**Time dimension is represented as up in this image. Aerial view of the simulation scenario. The robot's current position is the black square in the middle of the screen. Yellow line shows planned path. Red line shows the same planned path in 3 dimensions (x, y, time) Black clouds show (x, y, time) locations with some probability of a mover being there. Red clouds show (x, y, time) locations with high probability of a mover being there.**

The planning system is composed of egographs and high maneuverability ego-graphs.

### 1.3.2    Ego-graphs

Ego-graphs encode kinematically and dynamically correct trajectories. They are computed offline to save time since they are computationally expensive to calculate. Current conditions in the vehicle determine a subset of these trajectories that are applicable at this point in time. These graphs are ego centric in the sense that they have the vehicle located in the middle and pointing forward. Some of the initial conditions that are encoded are wheel angle, speed, goal angle, etc. They provide a variety of connectors from the vehicle location to a relatively close goal given by the coordination layer. The vehicle location is not actually the current vehicle location; it is the predicted vehicle location at the end of the planning cycle.

### 1.3.3    High Maneuverability Ego-graphs

Although the offline computed ego-graphs provide a large enough vocabulary to deal with most situations, there are some situations that need larger vocabularies (parking lots, crowded markets, etc). Under these conditions, the offline ego-graphs are not sufficient to

find a suitable solution to the problem. On the other hand, pre-computing a huge number of ego-graphs offline would slow down the online cost evaluation of the average planning loop. High Maneuverability ego-graphs are generated online by expanding a (x,y,heading) space on the specific complex area (Figure 8).

## 2.  CONCLUSION

A system capable of traversing a busy marketplace was developed and tested in simulation. The system provides an efficient way of predicting and planning with a large number of movers. It is our plan to test the system in a SUGV platform during 2010.

## 3.  ACKNOWLEDGMENTS

Our thanks to ARL and DARPA for funding portions of this research.

## 4.  REFERENCES

[1]  J. S. Albus, et al. (2002)  4D/RCS Version 2.0: A Reference Model Architecture for Unmanned Vehicle Systems, NISTIR 6910, National Institute of Standards and Technology, Gaithersburg, MD.
http://www.isd.mel.nist.gov/documents/albus/4DRCS_ver2.pdf

# Observations on Single Operator Performance Controlling Two UGVs in a Field Assessment

Susan G. Hill
U.S. Army Research Laboratory
Human Research & Engineering Directorate
Aberdeen Proving Ground, MD 21005
410.278.6237

sghill@arl.army.mil

## ABSTRACT

The experimental assessment described in this paper looked at span of control within the context of a larger assessment of tactical behaviors. Span of control refers, generally, to the number and type of robotic assets an operator controls. This paper describes the span of control portion of the tactical behaviors assessment that took place at the U.S. Army Research Laboratory (ARL) Robotics Research Facility at Fort Indiantown Gap, PA, during the fall of 2009. Three operators controlled two unmanned ground vehicles simultaneously for a total of six runs. The assessment is briefly described. The bulk of the discussion, however, addresses experimenter observations of the assessment process gleaned from subjective ratings and post-run interviews and issues that need to be addressed to improve assessment in the future.

## Categories and Subject Descriptors

I.2.9 [Artificial Intelligence]: Robotics – *autonomous vehicles, operator interfaces*

## General Terms

Human Factors, Measurement, Experimentation

## Keywords

human-robot interaction, operator interface, operator workload, span of control, unmanned ground vehicle, UGV, XUV

## 1. INTRODUCTION

A continuing topic of interest to those studying the interaction of humans and robots is that of span of control. In essence, span of control addresses the question of how many unmanned vehicles an operator can successfully operate simultaneously. This is, of course, of interest as a means of taking advantage of the ability of autonomous unmanned systems to act on their own or to act with less than the operator's full attention.

The experimental assessment described in this paper looked at span of control within the context of a larger assessment of tactical behaviors, where various planners and algorithms were

*PerMIS '10*, September 28-30, 2010, Baltimore, MD, USA.
ACM 978-1-4503-0290-6-9/28/10

examined. The details of this large assessment will be presented in a technical report [8]. This paper is intended to discuss a subset of that large assessment examining span of control. Specifically, this paper will discuss observations that relate to the ability to assess operator span of control in a field test environment.

## 2. BACKGROUND

The larger tactical behaviors experiment is one of a series of field tests that have been performed to assess progress made on intelligent behaviors for unmanned systems during the last few years of the initial eight-year Robotics Collaborative Technology Alliance. The previous assessments are documented in a series of reports [1, 5, 6, 7].

The current study is the second time that span of control was specifically addressed in a technical assessment. Operator span of control was a highlighted topic in a field experiment in 2005 using the U.S. Army's Experimental Unmanned Vehicle (XUV) [15]. Goals of this first experiment were to examine the use of scalable interfaces and to examine operator span of control when controlling one versus two autonomous unmanned ground vehicles. Two Soldiers performed missions that included monitoring, downloading and reporting on simulated reconnaissance, surveillance, and target acquisition (RSTA) images, and responding to unplanned operator intervention requests from the XUV. Observations from that experiment suggested that the Soldiers could manage the two XUVs under the conditions presented. Also, we observed that three elements of information appeared to be of particular importance to the operators: status of connectivity with the robot; robot status; and RSTA icons indicating new images available. Not surprisingly, workload for both robots was perceived as greater than workload for one robot.

Span of control refers, generally, to the number and type of robotic assets an operator controls. Robotic assets are intended to be force multipliers, but recent practice has been one robotic asset assigned to one (or more) operator(s). As Chen *et al.* [4] point out, the number of robots that one person can control is influenced by a number of factors including robot technology capability, mission requirements, and logistics. Olsen, Goodrich and colleagues have introduced the concepts of neglect time, interaction time, and fan-out which address qualitative and quantitative aspects of human interaction with single and multiple robots [9, 13, 16, 17]. Crandall & Cummings have extended those metric concepts to an operator interacting with multiple robots [10].

It is also thought important that operators not be overburdened -- too much workload can affect performance. Span of control (the ability to control multiple robots at a time) is related to the workload for controlling each robot as well as the effects of switching between the robots. Operator workload has been explored for the XUV previously; workload was found to be affected by terrain and significantly increased during teleoperation [18]. However, this early study is not readily comparable to the present study; the autonomous tactical behaviors are considerably more advanced in the present study, as is the operator display and control interface. Also, in the previous study, workload was measured for a 1:1 human-robot ratio. Switching between robots for control, as operators experienced in this present study when controlling two robots, has costs in workload and performance [13].

This paper describes the span of control portion of the tactical behaviors assessment that took place at the U.S. Army Research Laboratory (ARL) Robotics Research Facility at Fort Indiantown Gap, PA, during the fall of 2009. A brief report of that portion of the assessment and its findings are presented. The bulk of the discussion, however, addresses observations of the assessment process and issues that need to be addressed to improve assessment in the future.

# 3. Method
## 3.1 Participants

Three civilian novice participants were recruited from within ARL. All three were male engineers, so each had a technical background. The three participants had no previous experience operating this unmanned ground vehicle (UGV). They received several hours of training on the UGV operations using the Robotics Collaborative Technology Alliance (CTA) System Integration Laboratory (SIL) simulation capability. The participants then performed a series of runs of one operator controlling one UGV. Following those trials, which served as practical, hands-on experience, the operators performed a total of six dual runs (two UGVs for each operator).

## 3.2 Equipment

### 3.2.1 Experimental Unmanned Vehicle (XUV)

The UGVs used in this field experiment were XUVs from the U.S. Army Research Laboratory's initial Robotics Collaborative Technology Alliance, a consortium of industrial, academic and government laboratory partners. The XUV is approximately 1588 kg (3500 lb), has four-wheel drive and four-wheel steering. It was equipped with a suite of advanced technology in perception and intelligent control and an operator control unit (OCU) interface. The OCU interface provides a means for operators to monitor the XUV's autonomous progress and to assist each XUV in navigating out of trouble and returning to autonomous mobility when required. The OCU was housed in a high-mobility multipurpose wheeled vehicle (HMMWV). The operator controlled the XUVs from the HMMWV workstation. During operation, a separate "safety vehicle" shadowed each XUV, prepared to activate a controlled emergency stop (e-stop) of the

XUV if deemed necessary. A photo of the XUV is shown in Figure 1.

**Figure 1. Experimental Unmanned Vehicle (XUV) from the U.S. Army Research Laboratory was used as the UGV in this field assessment.**

### 3.2.2 Operator Control Unit

The operator interface used in the field experiment was developed initially in the 2003-2005 timeframe by the first Robotics CTA and has been continually enhanced since then. The interface is called the Tactical Control Unit (TCU) and has been implemented on three sizes of hardware [11, 12]. For this experiment, the vehicle-mounted, 18-inch screen display was used initially. However, technical difficulties with the vehicle mounted display required a switch to using the 10.4-inch portable touch screen tablet display for some of the runs. The operators were able to adapt quickly as the interfaces are almost identical except for size. Please note, however, that the operators did not use a consistent OCU throughout the experiment. This did not appear to have a major impact on operator performance; however, it is unclear the degree to which this affected operator performance. Figure 2 shows a participant using the vehicle-mounted 18-inch screen display.

**Figure 2. Participant using the 18" vehicle-mounted operator control unit (OCU) within the OCU HMMWV.**

## 3.3 Course and Mission

Specific terrain courses were developed to present various levels of challenge to the tactical behaviors intelligent control algorithms. Courses (Red, Gold, Urban) were developed and used for other parts of the tactical behaviors experiment, specifically examining several intelligent planners under various conditions. The White Course was set up to investigate the issue of operator span of control. Two roughly parallel routes, called White Course #1 and White Course #2, were established. (see Figure 3). First, the operators operated one UGV on one route of the White Course. These "single" runs served as training and preparation for the "dual" runs; the dual runs consisted of one operator simultaneously controlling two UGVs, one UGV on each of the two White Course routes. Several different intelligence planners were evaluated in the overall tactical behaviors assessment [8]. However, only the Mixed planner which uses a distinct planner for each type of mobility segment (e.g., roads, off-road, high maneuverability) was used for the operator span of control White Course.

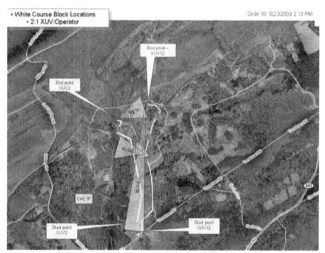

**Figure 3. The White Course is composed of two, roughly parallel, routes (shown in white), where two UGVs traveled simultaneously for the dual runs. The routes are primarily on unpaved roads.**

Each White Course presented up to six challenges to the operator and UGV going from the start point to the end goal. These challenges were of two types. There were mobility challenges where the operator and UGV had to discover the road block on the route and find an alternative path, primarily an on-road path, to the goal. An example of a road block is shown in Figure 4. The second type of challenge was to take and examine RSTA images of identified areas of interest from designated points enroute to the end goal and at the end goal. (The end goal was the designated Observation Point.) An example of the RSTA screen with images is shown in Figure 5. The operator was asked to view the image, take additional photographs as needed, in order to see if there were any targets of interest in the images and then report them. Each White Course route was about 1.2 km and each run took about 15 minutes to complete.

**Figure 4. An example of a road block that was used as a mobility challenge for the UGV and required operator attention.**

Two levels of difficulty were identified for the course runs based on the number of challenges presented. Both types of challenges (road blocks and RSTA images) required operator attention to ensure they were completed successfully. It was thought that the number of tasks requiring attention would correspond to perceived operator task loading. The two levels of difficulty are defined in Table 1.

**Table 1. Two conditions of difficulty are defined by the number of challenges.**

| Span of Control (operator:UGV ratio) | Low Difficulty | High Difficulty |
|---|---|---|
| Dual (1:2) | 2 RSTAs 0 Blocks | 4 RSTAs 2 Blocks |

**Figure 5. An example of a Reconnaissance, Surveillance, and Target Acquistion (RSTA) screen viewed by the operator.**

For each dual mission (i.e., run), the operator was seated in a stationary HMMWV with the TCU and loaded the specific mission parameters and routes for the UGV. The participant did not have line of sight to the unmanned vehicles. He then executed the mission, with both UGVs starting at (almost) the same time and proceeding along their planned paths. The participants monitored the UGVs as they encountered the road blocks; the participants also performed the RSTA tasks for each UGV enroute to the Observation Point. The challenges were location-based, not associated with any specific timing during the mission.

## 3.4 Data Collection and Results

The operators completed 22 single runs and six dual runs (runs with two UGVs) over three days; the focus here is on the six dual runs. For the dual runs, 100% (6/6) of the mobility challenges were overcome – every road block in the six runs was discovered and successfully addressed through finding alternative paths. The UGVs achieved the end goal 92% (11/12) of the time; the only time one of the UGVs did not achieve the end goal was when the UGV became high-centered on a rock and had to be towed. Otherwise, the operator was able to maneuver the UGV through teleoperation or replanning to allow the unmanned system to continue its mission and reach the end goal.

Across the six runs, the number of safety interventions for each 15-minute run ranged from 0-4, with an average of about 2 interventions per run. Task switching was an inherent component of the operator performance. The TCU required the operator to select the specific UGV of interest via a touch display in order to see the RSTA images from that UGV or perform teleoperation. For our purposes, when a specific UGV was selected, we considered that an "obvious" task switch. The "obvious" switch almost always preceded an activity involving the selected UGV. Switches were made like a toggle switch; if the current focus was on XUV2, then a switch was made to XUV12, which then remained the focus until XUV2 was selected again. The number of obvious switches ranged between a minimum of 5-10 for the dual runs, with an average of about 7 switches per 15-minute run.

Performance related to the RSTA images was not quantified; there were technical difficulties with the RSTA camera that caused the RSTA task to be inconsistent across runs. The RSTA tasks, then, were considered as a task load on the operator, contributing to the "low" and "high" difficulty conditions, but were not specifically measured. Therefore, only the system performance measures of overcoming mobility challenges (i.e., road blocks) and reaching the end goal are reported.

Workload was assessed through the use of participants' subjective ratings of workload via NASA Task Load Index (TLX) [14], using unweighted scores [2]. The average TLX scores, both overall and subscales, for the six runs are shown in Table 2. Workload ratings are similar for low and high difficulty conditions. Mental demand and Effort subscales had the relatively highest ratings. Temporal demand had a relatively high rating in the low difficulty condition and a relatively low rating in the high difficulty condition.

**Table 2. Average subjective ratings of workload (standard deviation) across difficulty conditions, using TLX on a 0-100 (low-high) scale (n=3).**

| TLX Subscale | Low Difficulty | High Difficulty |
|---|---|---|
| Mental Demand | 46 (25.1) | 43 (25.1) |
| Physical Demand | 16 (5.7) | 15 (5.0) |
| Temporal Demand | 55 (30.4) | 26 (20.8) |
| Performance* | 25 (18.0) | 15 (5.0) |
| Effort | 50 (27.8) | 43 (20.8) |
| Frustration | 25 (15.0) | 28 (27.5) |
| Overall TLX Average | 36 (17.2) | 28 (10.5) |

*low score indicates subjective rating of good performance.

## 4. OBSERVATIONS

There were a number of experimenter observations made during the operator span of control runs based on directly viewing operator performance as well as post-run interviews. Eight observations are presented, with some discussion of their significance. Each of these observations has implications for how best to assess operator, UGV, and system performance. The last two observations (Observations 7 & 8) are specifically related to the methodology used during the experiment and to the way in which the assessment was conducted. Both issues highlight problems in conducting unmanned systems experiments in a field setting when operator performance is of specific interest.

*1--Performance was a combination of operator and robot.*
It is important to note that for these runs, the system performance is a combination of both robot and operator performance. Other parts of the tactical behaviors assessment, interested in the tactical behavior planning, looked only at the algorithms implemented on the UGV and did not allow an operator to intervene or "solve" a problem that the robotic intelligence could not. The assessment challenge here is to measure performance that reflects the roles of both operator and robot, yet also provides information sufficient to diagnose weak spots and areas for improvement.

*2--There was no clear impact of level of difficulty on operator workload reports.*
Interestingly, the impact of the level of difficulty (i.e., the number of block and RSTAs) was not clearly shown in how the operator rated and discussed his workload at the end of each run. Workload seemed to have more to do with the difficulty encountered for each individual element of the run. Therefore, workload consists of more than the number of tasks that an operator must perform. This particular manipulation of level of difficulty was not as effective in changing workload levels as planned and can be improved in future assessments. The differences seen in the Temporal demand subscale for the two difficulty levels appear to result from a single rating.

*3--Operators reported low-moderate workload.*

Overall, the operators reported low to moderate workload for each level of difficulty. They did not, on the whole, feel overburdened or unable to accomplish their tasks, and in fact, thought they did pretty well. They thought they could successfully manage both robots for the amount of tasks required. Remember, though, this was their only task. They had no collateral duties. Even communicating on the radio was done by someone else in the vehicle. In future assessments, requiring the operator to have additional assigned duties would add to a more realistic task loading.

*4--Operator interface (displays and controls) were usable, but can be improved.*

The TCU (operator control unit), the displays and controls, were successfully used by the operators, but there were many specific suggestions for improvement. A general observation was that the Map Display showing the moving vehicles was important. Also important was the status of each vehicle. But the operators didn't always think they had sufficient information, or easily accessed information, on each robot. The amount of screen space given to robot status was relatively small and status messages were not always clear. Some information was available only when a specific UGV was "selected" and only the information pertaining to that particular UGV was displayed (e.g., RSTA images). Therefore, specific switching between UGVs was required. Note that this is related to the observation that operators did not always feel they had sufficient information for diagnosis of problems (discussed in Observation 6.) However, because this is a research program interface, not a fielded system, some status messages were intended more for the program software developers than for novice operators.

*5--Task switching and sequential servicing of robots both helped and hindered mission performance.*

We saw a number of instances of operator task switching – changing the focus of attention from one task to another [13]. Task switching is inherent in the control of more than one robot. But there is always a "cost" to switching – the operator must refocus and quickly understand the current situation. In some cases, while an operator was focusing on one of the UGVs, the other UGV was waiting for an operator response, (e.g., when the operator was examining the RSTA image from one UGV, the other UGV had taken a RSTA image and was waiting for the operator to issue a command to continue the mission). However, there were no critical time constraints here – if there were time constraints, the wait time would be much more significant. So, switching allowed the operator to accomplish the task, but hindered performance with a "cost" and impact of robots waiting for operator attention.

*6--When technical difficulties arose, operators did not always have sufficient information to understand or diagnose the problems.*

There were a number of comments by operators relating to their desire for more status information, and additional ways to understand the current status, activity, and reasoning of the UGVs. This was a general issue with operating remotely – the information the operator received was what the sensors provided (e.g., camera views). So, it was important to provide whatever status information was available in a cogent way. (Remember that this user interface is a research tool, not a fieldable system.) Further research is needed to determine how the robot can provide more understanding on what is happening remotely. Operators sometimes had to make a guess at an appropriate response – they took "manual" pictures when the automated RSTA camera feature did not appear to work. When they couldn't take manual pictures, the operators waited about a minute, and when nothing happened, just moved on without actually knowing why they could not accomplish the desired task. The participants kept the mission going when they felt they did not have the ability to diagnose the problems encountered. A question arises if this is the response we are looking for in the assessment and how best to direct the operator as to the priority of mission completion versus understanding of problems encountered.

*7--Safety vehicle emergency stops influenced operator performance; the operator knew that Safety would not allow the UGVs to perform unsafe acts.*

We did notice, and operators stated, that the operators were quite aware that the Safety vehicle would stop the UGVs if the operators were about to perform an unsafe action, and/or if Safety was concerned about the "well-being" of the UGV. The operators, therefore, appeared to recognize the inherent safety of the UGV; the operators knew that there was a secondary means to stop the UGV from unsafe actions in addition to their primary control. This is a general problem with the fidelity of the experiment which is also seen in human performance in simulated environments when the humans know that they won't be harmed or killed. This issue seemed more noticeable than in the previous span of control experiment [15], possibly due to the more sophisticated tactical behaviors resulting from using the various intelligence planners on the UGV (see [8] for further explanation). We need to consider ways to lessen this effect and have safety requirements be less intrusive when operators participate and operator performance (and system performance with operators) is of interest.

*8--Constraints on operator actions influenced system performance (e.g., minimize teleoperation, no-go/restricted access area.)*

There were some constraints on operator performance. One of the constraints involved the permissible operating terrain – there are areas where vehicles are not permitted to travel (no-go zones) at the field site. Therefore, the operator couldn't maneuver the UGV in all areas and was constrained in backup distance and turning radius. Another constraint was the instruction to minimize teleoperation – novice operators often just want to "drive" the UGV, but the operator had been instructed to allow the autonomy to function as much as possible. Again, this is a question of the fidelity of the experiment and its impact on operator and system performance.

## 5. DISCUSSION

There are two primary points for discussion. The first point is that the operators could manage the two robots under these conditions. There were no system performance failures due to operator control; the mobility challenges (i.e., blocks) were all overcome and the only instance of the UGV not reaching the end point was due to terrain interaction (a big rock), not operator performance. However, the conditions for this assessment did not reflect actual conditions for military operations. For example, the operators only communicated with the data collectors within the OCU HMMWV; they were not responsible for the radio communication with other (safety) vehicles. Experimenters observed some instances where both UGVs were in close proximity to each other and the operator seemed only partially aware of the exact locations of the UGVs. There were also instances where UGVs waited to be attended to; in this assessment, time to accomplish tasks was not critical. But these observations are not reflected at the system performance level. Better metrics and measures are needed to describe system performance, and the contributions of operator performance to system performance.

A second point for discussion is that there are challenges in controlling external influences on operator performance. Improvements are needed in methods for system assessment. In particular, an appropriate balance is needed between the role of the safety vehicle and the ability of the operator to be fully responsible for the UGV. The safety role is important in protecting people, property, the environment and the UGV itself from harm. However, if operators are fully aware that no catastrophic harm will come to the UGV, then there may be less vigilance, unconscious though it may be, to ensure the status and actions of the UGV are safe. Careful wording of instructions to the operators may play a part here, as well as the training and experience of the operator. For example, on the one hand, we instructed the operators to control the UGV carefully; on the other hand, we encouraged the operator to allow the UGV to proceed autonomously to as great an extent as possible and not be overly cautious with the UGV control. More hands-on experience for the operator, not just training, might provide a greater sense of the capabilities and limitations of the UGV.

Both operator and system performance measurement, metrics, and assessment methodology continue to be a challenge that needs to be addressed and continually improved.

# 6. ACKNOWLEDGMENTS

The author would like to thank Mr. Marshal Childers and Dr. Barry Bodt, U.S. ARL and Mr. Rick Camden, L3/MPRI, for their leadership in the planning and execution of this experiment. The author also thanks the contractors of General Dynamics Robotic Systems and Alion Science and Technology for their technical support during the assessment in preparing the robots and in training and data collection.

# 7. REFERENCES

[1] Bodt, B., Childers, M., and Camden, R. 2010. "*A Capstone Experiment to Assess Unmanned Ground Vehicle Tactical Behaviors Developed under the Robotics Collaborative Technology Alliance*", presented at AUVSI North America 2010 Conference, Denver, CO, 24-27 August, 2010.

[2] Byers, J.C., Bittner, Jr., A.C. and Hill, S.G. (1989). Traditional and raw Task Load Index (TLX) correlations: Are paired comparisons necessary? In *Advances in industrial ergonomics and safety I* (pp. 481-485). London: Taylor and Francis.

[3] Chen, J., Haas, E. and Barnes, M. 2007. Human Performance Issues and User Interface Design for Teleoperated Robots. *IEEE Transactions on Systems, Man and Cybernetics – Part C: Applications and Review*, 37,6 (November 2007), 1231-1245.

[4] Chen, J. Haas, E., Pillalamarri, K. and Jacobson, C. 2006. *Human-Robot Interface: Issues in Operator Performance, Interface Design, and Technologies* (ARL-TR-3834). U.S. Army Research Laboratory, Aberdeen Proving Ground, MD.

[5] Childers, M., Bodt, B., Hill, S., and Camden, R. 2008. "*The Impact of Multi-Level Path Planning on Unmanned Ground Vehicle Behavior*," poster presentation at 26th Army Science Conference, Orlando, FL, Dec 2008.

[6] Childers, M., Bodt, B., Hill, S., Dean, R., Dodson, W., and Sutton, L. 2007. *Assessing the Impact of Bi-directional Information Flow in Unmanned Ground Vehicle Operation: A Pilot Study*. Performance Metrics for Intelligent Systems Workshop (PerMIS'07), pp22-28. (Gaithersburg, MD, August 28-30, 2007).

[7] Childers, M., Bodt, B., Hill, S., Camden, R., Dean, R., Dodson, W., Sutton, L., and Sapronov, L. 2009. *Unmanned Ground Vehicle Tactical Behaviors Technology Assessment* (ARL-TR-4698). U.S. Army Research Laboratory, Aberdeen Proving Ground, MD.

[8] Childers, M., Bodt, B., Hill, S., Camden, R., Dean, R., and Gonzalez, J.P., *Robotics CTA Capstone Experiment: Unmanned Ground Vehicle (UGV) Tactical Behaviors Technology Assessment*, in preparation.

[9] Crandall, J., Goodrich, M., Olsen, D. and Nielsen, C. 2005. Validating human-robot interaction schemes in multitasking environments. *IEEE Transactions on Systems, Man, and Cybernetics—Part A: Systems and Humans*, 1-12.

[10] Crandall, J.W. and Cummings, M.L. 2007. Developing performance metrics for the supervisory control of multiple robots. In *Proceeding of the 2nd ACM SIGCHI/SIGART Conference on Human-Robot Interaction (HRI'07)*. ACM Press, New York, NY, 33-40.

[11] Dahn, D. and Gacy, M. 2006. Human control of unmanned systems under stressful conditions. In *Proceedings of the 1st Joint Response/Robotic and Remote Systems Topical Meeting,* Salt Lake City, UT.

[12] Gacy, M. and Dahn, D. 2006. Commonality of control paradigms for unmanned systems. In *Proceeding of the 1st ACM 175 SIGCHI/SIGART Conference on Human-Robot Interaction (HRI'06)*. ACM Press, New York, NY, 339-340.

[13] Goodrich, M., Quigley, M. and Cosenzo, K. 2005. Task switching and mulit-robot teams. In *Multi-robot Systems. From Swarms to Intelligent Autonomata. Vol III. Proceedings from 2005 International Workshop on Mulitple Systems* (L. Parker, F. Schneider & A. Schultz, Eds), 185-195.

[14] Hart, S. and Staveland, L. 1988. Development of NASA TLX (Task Load Index): Results of Empirical and Theoretical Research. In P. Hancock & N. Meshkati (Eds.), *Human Mental Workload*. Elsevier, Amsterdam, The Netherlands, 139-183.

[15] Hill, S. and Bodt, B. 2007. A field experiment of autonomous mobility: Operator workload for one and two robots. *Proceedings of the 2007 ACM/IEEE Conference on*

*Human-Robot Interaction*, March 8-11, Arlington, VA. (pp. 169-176).

[16] Olsen, D.R., Jr., and Goodrich, M. A. 2003. Metrics For evaluating human-robot interactions. In *Proceedings of PERMIS 2003*.

[17] Olsen, D.R., Jr., Wood, S. and Turner, J. 2004. Metrics for human driving of multiple robots. In *Proceedings of the 2004 IEEE International Conference on Robotics & Automation (ICRA'04)*. (New Orleans, LA, April 2004). IEEE, 2315-2320.

[18] Schipani, S. 2003. An evaluation of operator workload during partially-autonomous vehicle operations. In *Proceedings of PerMIS 2003,* September 2003.

[19] Steinfeld, A., Fong, T., Kaber, D., Lewis, M., Scholtz, J., Schultz, A. and Goodrich, M. 2006. Common metrics for human robot interaction. In *Proceedings of the 2006 Human Robot Interaction Conference (HRI'06)* (Salt Lake City, UT, March 2-4, 2006). ACM Press, New York, NY, 33-40.

# Assessing Unmanned Ground Vehicle Tactical Behaviors Performance

Marshal A. Childers
U.S. Army Research Laboratory
Vehicle Technology Directorate
Aberdeen Proving Ground, MD 21005
410-278-7996
marshal.childers@us.army.mil

Barry A. Bodt
U.S. Army Research Laboratory
Computational and Informational
Sciences Directorate
Aberdeen Proving Ground, MD 21005
410-278-6659
barry.a.bodt@us.army.mil

Richard Camden
L3/MPRI
RDRL-VTA
Aberdeen Proving Ground, MD 21005
410-278-2639
richard.camden@us.army.mil

## ABSTRACT

The Army Research Laboratory Robotic Collaborative Technology Alliance (RCTA) made significant advances in perception (LADAR and near and mid-term perception algorithms) and planning (global/local route planning, shared map data, and the ability to use time as a planning factor) which enabled true UGV autonomous navigation (planning and controlling the course and position of a vehicle) [1,3]. This opened the door to a myriad of operational-like capabilities which we call tactical behaviors. The purpose of this paper is to provide an overview of the assessment process with a focus on performance metrics and to foster collaboration with other investigators in order to further derive meaningful metrics for UGV autonomous navigation.

## Categories and Subject Descriptors

I.2.9 [**Robotics**]: Autonomous vehicles

## General Terms

Algorithms, Measurement, Performance, Experimentation

## Keywords

Tactical behaviors, unmanned ground vehicle, UGV, XUV, path planning, bi-directional information flow

## 1. INTRODUCTION

At the conclusion of the Demo III program [1], unmanned ground vehicle (UGV) capability could be described as semi-autonomous mobility, moving from A to B following closely spaced waypoints, following the planned path within a specified distance (~50m), and calling for operator assistance when needed. The U.S. Army Research Laboratory Robotic Collaborative Technology Alliance (RCTA) made significant advances in perception (LADAR and near and mid-term perception algorithms) and planning (global/local route planning, shared map data, and the ability to use time as a planning factor) which

enabled true autonomous navigation (planning and controlling the course and position of a vehicle). This opened the door to a myriad of operational-like capabilities which we call tactical behaviors. The Army Research Lab periodically conducted field experiments throughout the RCTA to assess the progress and readiness of RCTA developed technologies. The purpose of this paper is to provide an overview of the assessment process with a focus on performance metrics and to foster collaboration with other investigators in order to further derive meaningful metrics for UGV autonomous navigation.

## 2. TACTICAL BEHAVIORS

Over the length of the RCTA, as technology advanced, the definition of tactical behaviors expanded until it included the capability of autonomous navigation on roads, trails, cross-country and urban terrain while:

- detecting, classifying and avoiding static obstacles
- detecting, classifying and avoiding people in various sizes, postures and movements
- detecting and avoiding moving vehicles
- following the rules of the road
- achieving a designated goal point in spite of obstacles or blocks on the original planned route
- minimizing the need for operator assistance

Using a notional reconnaissance mission as a framework, autonomous navigation must be accomplished with a purpose, including the following operational-like behaviors (see Figure 1):

- avoid being observed
- observe an area of interest
- use terrain features
- understand military control measures

## 3. ASSESSMENT PROCESS

The approach taken throughout the RCTA program was to integrate developing technology and software onto the eXperimental Unmanned Vehicle (XUV) and then stress the system by exposing it to progressively difficult operational-like challenges while collecting meaningful measures of performance [2].

In early work, the focus was for the XUV to autonomously arrive at an assigned observation point, with soldier-operators determining the initial global route on the operator control unit (OCU), monitoring XUV progress, and remotely assisting the robot when it got stuck, relying only on the OCU information and teleoperation cameras. Operators would then initiate, receive, and

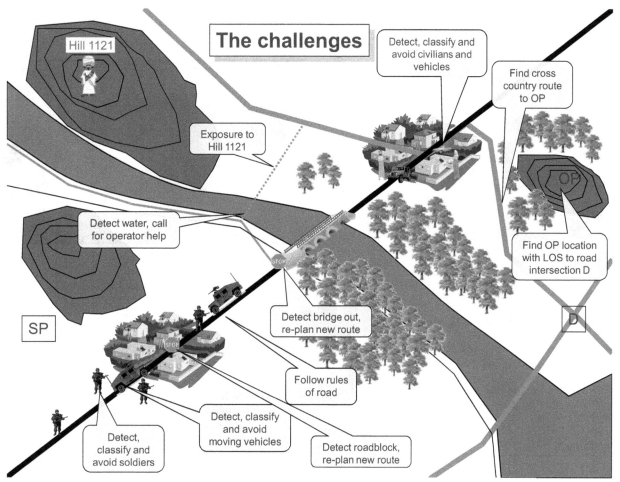

**Figure 1 Tactical Behavior challenges**

*SP (Start Point); OP (Observation Point); LOS (Line of Sight)

interpret a reconnaissance, surveillance, and target acquisition (RSTA) scan from the one *or two* robots under their direction. Operators were stressed with varying workloads and observations and XUV performance metrics were collected, the results of which contributed to changes in the OCU/RSTA control to enable more effective and efficient soldier control [8].

Follow-on experiments examined the XUV capability to find and maneuver to the specified Observation Post (OP) with a threshold visibility to a named area of interest (NAI) as determined by the local sensors. When at the OP, the XUV visibility to the NAI was frequently blocked by local vegetation which led to the development of the OP Finder.

A common cause of failure for autonomous navigation was the vegetated cul-de-sac. The XUV would enter a cul-de-sac and, finding no direct way toward the goal, would try to navigate out by backing up a limited distance along its path to gain a different perspective on potential local routes. This approach was only successful if the cul-de-sac was shallow enough that the new perspective would show a path out that would be within the deviation tolerance of the global route; otherwise, the operator was called for help. Detecting and solving a cul-de-sac or

roadblock became a major metric of autonomous navigation success.

A further shortfall was the inability to navigate on roads following the normal rules of the road and avoiding moving vehicles and pedestrians. The Demo III planner was incapable of handling moving obstacles because the obstacle persisted in the local map along its perceived route, thus appearing as a large obstacle. Successfully detecting and avoiding dynamic obstacles (vehicles and pedestrians) became another significant metric.

## 4. ENABLING TECHNOLOGIES

### 4.1 Platform and Sensors

The platform used throughout the experiments was the XUV, shown in Figure 2. Sensors mounted on the XUV over the course of the RCTA program included: Gen II and Gen IV LADARs, front and rear SICK LADAR, monocular teleoperation camera, stereo cameras for obstacle detection and classification, and a RSTA suite. The Operator Control Unit (OCU - Figure 3.) was mounted in the HMMWV, which served as the control vehicle. The OCU provided a large map for situational awareness and interfaces for planning/monitoring of unmanned assets, teleoperation, and control of RSTA sensors [2].

predicting future locations in time. This enabled the XUV to maneuver correctly in the vicinity of dynamic objects.

**Figure 2. Experimental Unmannrd Vehicle (XUV)**

**Figure 3. Operator Control Unit (OCU)**

## 4.2 Navigation (Planning) Algorithms

Tactical behaviors were enabled by advances in sharing sensed data among levels in the planning hierarchy and by increased capability in navigation planning algorithms.

A High Maneuverability Planner (HMP) capable of maneuvering the XUV in tight spaces, such as an OP, and an OP Finder, that used local perception to find a location with maximum visibility to the area of interest, were developed after the early OP experiments.

The most significant solution advanced consisted of bi-directional information flow (BIP) and a hybrid global/local planner [4-6]. Local data sensed by the XUV was used locally while simultaneously updating the global map. When called upon, the global planner would incorporate this new information, often leading to a feasible route opportunity to which the XUV could return. Prior to this improvement the XUV would not have been able to return to that opportunity because it was limited in by a prescribed back-up procedure and by a specified maximum deviation from the initial route plan. To this latter concern, the XUV was untethered from the initial global route through a new planner that balanced costs from the local route (within sensor view) with global costs from the initial route and allowed more flexibility for the robot to advance toward the goal. Feature data was also leveraged to support the choice of a stealthy route relative to a predetermined threat location. RSTA operations were refined to include new strategies in local re-positioning of the XUV at the observation point to overcome foreground vegetation occluding the view to the area of interest. Building on this multi-level planning approach, dynamic path replanning was developed to provide several alternative routes for planner consideration each second, based on a continuous updating of the global map with locally sensed information. HMP enabled the XUV to transition to new plans which required tight initial turns [7].

Later work integrated knowledge of rules of the road into a separate traffic planner which enabled planning in time, thus placing the moving object precisely in the local map and

Finally, the integration of the Dynamic Replanner (DR) and the Traffic Planner and the ability to transition between the two via the HMP provided seamless autonomous navigation in any environment during the RCTA Capstone Experiment [2].

## 5. EXPERIMENTAL FACTORS

In each experiment the principal variable conditions were chosen to reflect the technology being assessed, the capability that it provided, and the factors likely to influence XUV performance. For example, in the OP Finder experiments, the principal conditions were OP Finder algorithm, % NAI observed, range of OP planner. In the most recent tactical behavior experiments the principle conditions were planning algorithms, a priori data, and the number and location of blocked paths.

All experiments were conducted at Fort Indiantown Gap Tactical Vehicle Maneuver Area-B seen in Figure 4. This maneuver area provided a limited but rich experimental environment, including roads, trails, trees, dense and light vegetation, and streams typical of a tactical maneuver area.

Many factors were uncontrolled by their nature. Most experiments carried over several days, hence weather varied. Time of year brought its own variations of snow, rain, and foliage. Between experiments, other military users of the terrain altered the environment by forging new trails and creating large ruts. During any single experiment, no single course was usually suitable to provide the terrain challenges necessary to examine the technologies under scrutiny; so several courses were generally laid out to provide the venue to evaluate each experimental condition. Each course was usually given a unique name for identification, such as the gold course or the black course.

## 6. EXPERIMENTAL DESIGN

The experimental conditions were usually arranged in a factorial structure with replications to be run according to a randomized schedule to the extent practicable. The factorial integrity of the

**Figure 4 Fort Indiantown Gap Tactical Vehicle Maneuver Area Bravo (TVMA-B)**

design was usually maintained; however, there was occasionally a deliberate modification based on existing knowledge and knowledge gained during experimentation. Time and resources were always constrained in the field experiment. To maximize the collection of useful information, occasionally and to save time, some replications were not completed when it was clear that additional runs would result in identical results.

For example, in the final (Capstone) experiment of the RCTA, conducted in Fall 2009, on the gold course, the progression of challenges could be considered sequential, in that the four-blockage condition was not attempted until the no-blockage and two-blockage challenges had been exhausted. In addition, the Autonomous Mobility Planner (AM), i.e. without BIP and a global/local planner, was not carried forward to the four-block condition, because its inability to solve a deep cul-de-sac problem had been established in a previous experiment.[10] The Mixed planner (combination of the DR and Traffic planners) that was concurrently performing well on the red course was substituted for AM under the four-block challenge in the principal factorial design on the gold course. Some additional runs with DR and Mixed planners under the four-block, gold course challenge were conducted with additional range time made available at the end of the test [2].

**Table 1  Experimental Design for Capstone Gold Course**

| Gold Course Experimental Design | | | | | | |
|---|---|---|---|---|---|---|
| | Basic Experiment | | | | Excursions | |
| Blocks | No blocks | | Two blocks (1 block@cul-de-sac and 1 road block) | | Four blocks (2 blocks@cul-de-sac + 2 road blocks + path to helo pad) | | |
| Planner | AM | DR | AM | DR | AM | DR | Mixed |
| Road network only apriori data | 2/2 | 2/2 | 2/2 | 2/2 | | 2/2 | 2/1 |
| SFM + road network apriori data | 2/1 | 2/2 | 2/1 | 2/1 | | 2/2 | 2/1 |
| Rmax + road network apriori data | 2/2 | 2/2 | 2/2 | 2/2 | | 2/2 | 2/5 |
| planned / actual repetitions | | | | | | | |

# 7.  RESPONSE MEASURES

Establishing meaningful response measures in an operational test is inherently difficult because the control of extraneous, potentially lurking, variables not directly under study is not possible, and the experimental unit whose performance is to be measured is the system of integrated technologies as opposed to an isolated subsystem. Indeed, terrain, which clearly drives perception and planning, can only be selected through wholesale adoption of a course; another course with similar macro terrain features may yield a different outcome because of nuances at the micro level. The presence of dust, rain, and other environmental conditions cannot be controlled, nor the malfunction of hardware not related to the technologies under study. When a system success occurs, all subsystems are credited with the achievement, but when a failure occurs, which is to blame? Toward the end of an acquisition cycle, one might not care which is to blame, but upstream in the applied research phase it is important to both gauge system promise and to provide subsystem feedback. To do this required dissection of performance within a run.

## 7.1  RESPONSE MEASURE EXAMPLES

### 7.1.1  Span of Control, TRL6 update Apr 06

In April 06 [4], an experiment was conducted that examined operator control issues and repeated a portion of the TRL-6 Black Course as run four years earlier (See Figure 5). This experiment was prior to the development of more advanced planners, so the Demo III paradigm of backing up three times before calling for operator intervention was still in effect. The metrics shown were those used in the TRL6 experiment, the purpose of which was to evaluate technology readiness. All of the major metrics applied in 2006 (average speed, kilometers between backups, and kilometers between operator interventions) showed improvements over the TRL6 results (See Table 2).

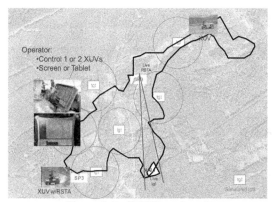

**Figure 5 April 06 Experiment**

**Table 2 TRL6 and April 2006 Experiment Rerun Results**

| TRL 6 Black Course* | | | | | |
|---|---|---|---|---|---|
| Experiment | Date | Dist (km) | Avg Speed (kph) | km/ back up | km/teleop |
| TRL-6 | Dec 02-Mar 03 | 100 | 5.2 | 0.23 | 1.5 |
| Rerun | May 06 | 54.7 | 8.1 | 0.33 | 2.5 |

\* cross country and trails

This experiment used soldiers from the Mounted Maneuver Battle Lab as operators of one or two XUVs simultaneously. Soldiers were observed and questioned at the conclusion of each RSTA/AM mission. It was observed that one operator could successfully manage two robots in the missions in this experiment. As expected, operator workload increased in two-robot missions and the HMMWV-mounted 21" OCU screen and the hand-held Tablet were both satisfactorily used by the soldiers. Numerous interface improvements were offered by the soldiers for consideration by the OCU developers [8].

### 7.1.2 OP Finder – February 2008

In this experiment [4], the XUV was tasked to move to an OP, find a location there that afforded at least 70% visibility of the NAI based on perception of local obstacles with respect to calculated lines of sight between the XUV and the NAI (See Figures 6, 7).

**Figure 6 RSTA Picture of NAI**

**Figure 7 Zoomed RSTA Picture**

The performance metric was binary: Did the OP afford visibility to 70% of the NAI? Success was determined by two means: the algorithm self-reported whether nor not the location was a Good OP and the RSTA picture taken from the location was examined to determine the number of targets seen (7 of 10 was a Good OP). The results of this experiment showed differences in algorithm performance as well as differences in the metric values depending upon the source of the measurement. (See Table 3).

**Table 3 OP Finder Algorithm Performance**

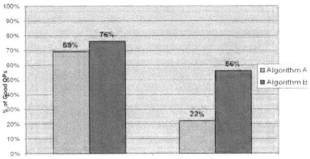

### 7.1.3 Two level planners-Capstone Oct 2009

A portion of the Capstone experiment examined the autonomous navigation performance of the XUV under various planning systems; AM Planner only, Dynamic Replanning with bi-directional information flow, Traffic Planner, and the Mixed Planner (DR+Traffic). Other experimental factors included several levels of *a priori* data and several levels of course difficulty (no blockages, two blockages, four blockages; see Table 1).

Metrics on the system performance centered on whether or not the XUV could detect a terrain blockage and plan for an alternative route around the blockage. Successful alternatives included going around the blockage, planning for a reasonably local alternative path, or replanning a drastically revised path that significantly deviated from the original plan. There was not a "single answer" to each terrain challenge. On each run, the XUV performance was closely observed from the following safety vehicle as well as remotely from the OCU control vehicle where more detailed engineering diagnostic monitoring software was tracking the progress of the XUV. Figure 8 illustrates the scoring for run 205 where the XUV detected both blockages in the deep cul-de-sac, replanned and navigated out of the cul-de-sac back to the road, detected the blockage across the road, replanned and followed an off-road detour through trees around the blockage, continued on the road until it detected the blockage under the canopy, replanned and executed a route off-road and explored the terrain until it discovered a clear path up the hill to the OP. In this run, the metric of "overcoming terrain challenges" was met in five instances.

**Figure 8 Run 205, Capstone Gold Course**

The Gold course results are summarized in Table 4 [2].

### Table 4 Gold Course Terrain Challenge Results

| Blocks | No blocks | | | Two blocks (1 block@cul-de-sac and 1 road block) | | | Four blocks (2 blocks@cul-de-sac + 2 road blocks + path to helo pad) | | |
|---|---|---|---|---|---|---|---|---|---|
| Planner | AM | DR | Mixed | AM | DR | Mixed | AM | DR | Mixed |
| Road network only apriori data | 1/2 | 2/2 | | 0/2 | 4/4 | | | 6/7 | 2/2 |
| SFM + road network apriori data | 0/1 | 1/2 | | 0/1 | 1/2 | | | 8/10 | 5/5 |
| Rmax + road network apriori data | 2/2 | 2/2 | | 3/4 | 4/4 | | | 10/10 | 23/24 |

## 8. SUMMARY OF PERTINENT ASSESSMENTS

Over the course of the RCTA, a series of experiments with increasing complexity were conducted in order to assess the advancing capabilities provided by RCTA research efforts. A summary of the experiments is given in Table 5 including the metrics used in each experiment.

## 9. CHALLENGES

Assessing the readiness of UGV technologies is a challenge in an environment where every major factor seems to be changing – technology improves, new capabilities are achieved, terrain features change with seasons and weather, and the XUV has inherent mobility limitations. Radio communications between the XUV and OCU controller, while never a controlled factor in an experiment, never-the-less, often exerted unforeseen influence on operational aspects of the experiment. Technology innovations are often on the edge of readiness when taken to a field experiment and developers are often still refining the algorithms and parameters that effect performance. This is a normal and highly useful practice for developers but creates difficulties when the objective is to assess a technology in a structured experiment where responses are measurable and attributable. Every experiment required flexibility on the part of developers and experimenters.

## 10. CONCLUSION

The metrics applied during the course of these technology assessments provided a qualitative measure of UGV integrated performance and in some instances quantitative evaluation of subsystem technologies. These results of such assessments keep

### Table 5 RCTA UGV Tactical behaviors Experiments

| Experiment | Date | Technology | Factors considered | Metrics |
|---|---|---|---|---|
| TRL-6 | 2002-2003 | AM planner | XUV speed, terrain type, terrain difficulty, length of run, operator intervention strategy | route completion; average speed; intervention frequency and duration; backup frequency |
| RSTA (canned pics) | May-05 | OCU control of RSTA | OTM** vs not OTM | # of targets correctly Identified |
| Span of Control; TRL6 rerun; OCU | Apr-06 | HMP; OP Finder; OCU control of RSTA | 1:1 or 2:1 span of control; mil operators; screen vs tablet OCU | operator workload (subjective); route completion; average speed; intervention frequency and duration; backup frequency |
| TB Pilot Study | Jun-07 | BIP, manual global planner, FCI* | Planners: AM, BIP, FCI (various weights) | mission outcome |
| OP Finder | Feb-08 | HMP, OP Finder RSTA control fm OCU | 2 OP Finders, 4 OP/NAI combos | % targets seen on RSTA scan of NAI |
| TB-RIVET*** | Apr-09 | Planners: AM, DR, FCI | scenarios; Planner | % goals achieved |
| TB-field | May-09 | Planners: AM, DR, FCI | number of blocks; scenarios; Planner | % obstacles solved; % goals achieved |
| TB-Capstone | Oct-09 | Planners: AM, DR, Traffic Planner, Mixed Planner; water detection | number of blocks, number of dynamic vehicles, scenarios, 1:1/2:1 span of control, Planner; apriori data | % obstacles solved; % goals achieved; operator workload (subjective) |

*FCI: Field Cost Interface Planner, **OTM: on the move, ***RIVET: hardware-in-the-loop simulation the Army Research Laboratory and Army leadership informed on the state-of-the-art in unmanned ground vehicle research and insure that research funds are properly invested. Considering the nature of applied research with technology at various levels of development and maturity, it is assumed that the metrics used to evaluate system performance must take into account end-to-end performance in a relevant environment if those measures are to be meaningful with respect to assessing capabilities in tactical behaviors. A goal is to derive additional metrics that can be applied across experiments so that improvements in performance can be assessed over time.

# 11. ACKNOWLEDGMENTS

The authors thank the engineers and technicians of General Dynamics Robotic Systems for their support in the field during preparation and execution of each technology assessment.

# 12. REFERENCES

[1] Bodt, B, & Camden, R (2004). "Technology Readiness Level 6 and Autonomous Mobility." SPIE Defense & Security, Unmanned Ground Vehicle Technology VI, Vol. 5422, September 2004, pp 302-313.

[2] Bodt, B., Childers, M., Camden, R., "*A Capstone Experiment to Assess Unmanned Ground Vehicle Tactical Behaviors Developed under the Robotics Collaborative Technology Alliance*", presented at AUVSI North America 2010 Conference, Denver, CO, 24-27 August, 2010.

[3] Camden, R, Bodt, B, Schipani,S., Bornstein, J., Runyon, T., French, F., Shoemaker, C., Jacoff, A., and Lytle, A., (2005), "Autonomous Mobility Technology Assessment Final Report." ARL-TR-3471[*], U.S. Army Research Laboratory.

[4] Childers, M., Bodt, B., Hill, S., Camden, R., (2008), "The Impact of Multi-Level Path Planning on Unmanned Ground Vehicle Tactical Behavior." 26th Army Science Conference, December 2008.

[5] Childers, M., Bodt, B., Hill, S., Dean, R., Dodson, W., and Sutton, L. (2007), "*Assessing the Impact of Bi-directional Information Flow in Unmanned Ground Vehicle Operation: A Pilot Study*" Performance Metrics for Intelligent Systems. PerMIS Proceedings 2007.

[6] Childers, M., Bodt, B., Hill, S., Camden, R., Dean, R., Dodson, W., Sutton, L., and Sapronov, L., *Unmanned Ground Vehicle Tactical Behaviors Technology Assessment* (ARL-TR-4698). U.S. Army Research Laboratory, Aberdeen Proving Ground, MD, January 2009.

[7] Childers, M., Bodt, B., Hill, S., Camden, R., J.P. Gonzalez,, J. P., Dean, R., Dodson, W., Kreafle, G., Lacaze, A., Sapronov, L. (2010) "Unmanned Ground Vehicle Two-Level Planning Technology Assessment." ARL-TR (in press), U.S. Army Research Laboratory, 2010.

[8] Hill, S. & Bodt, B. (2007). A field experiment of autonomous mobility: Operator workload for one and two robots. Proceedings of the 2007 ACM/IEEE Conference on Human-Robot Interaction, March 8-11, 2007, Arlington, VA. (pp. 169-176).

* ARL technical reports can be obtained from the Defense Technical Information Center via www.dtic.mil

# Evaluation criteria for appearance based maps

Gorkem Erinc, Stefano Carpin
School of Engineering
5200 N Lake Rd
University of California, Merced, USA
{gerinc,scarpin}@ucmerced.edu

## ABSTRACT

We present a set of task-based performance evaluation criteria designed to measure the quality of appearance based maps. Instead of aiming to measure a map's overall goodness, metrics defined in this paper focus on individual tasks, namely localization, planning, and navigation, and the quality of the map with respect to the their successful execution. The performance of a map in terms of localization is measured by the amount of information captured from the environment and the accuracy of this information. The planning metric favors instead maps with high connectivity and measures the validity of these connections. The navigation criterion, on the other hand, computes the robustness and stability associated with the paths that a robot will extract from the map. These metrics are tested on appearance maps created in our lab and their distinctiveness is shown.

## 1. INTRODUCTION

Perception is one of the keys to build intelligent robotic systems operating in unstructured environments. Most often robots gather information through their sensors and build a map, i.e. spatial model of the environment they operate in. By using this internal representation they can accomplish complex tasks and autonomously operate in a given environment. Therefore, not surprisingly mapping is one of the most studied problems in robotics. Up to now most of the research efforts have been devoted to metric maps, i.e. maps providing metric information about the elements in the map [18]. However, thanks to recent developments in sensor technology and computer vision algorithms, appearance based maps have recently surfaced and are gaining momentum[1]. Systems based on omni-directional [20] and monocular cameras [15, 9] work in image space and do not necessarily need metric localization for mapping or navigation purposes. In other words, localization and mapping

---

[1]For sake of completeness one should also mention a third approach, namely topological maps. These however will not be further considered in this paper

hinges on an *appearance based map*.

An appearance map[2] is an undirected weighted graph $G = (V, E)$ in which each vertex $v \in V$ represents an image captured by a camera at a certain position in the workspace. An edge $e_{ij} \in E$ connects two distinct vertices $v_i, v_j$ whenever the associated images are sufficiently similar, accordingly to a given similarity metric. A frequent way to define similarity between two images is to extract salient features from each image and count the number of common ones. The number of matching features is considered as the indication of similarity and is then set as the weight of that edge. Hence, the weight $w_{ij}$ associated with an edge measures the similarity between images assigned to vertices $v_i$ and $v_j$. An example appearance graph is shown in Fig. 1.

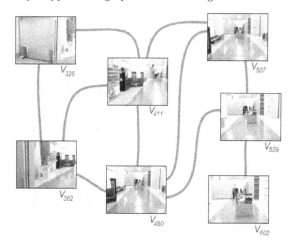

**Figure 1: The figure shows an appearance based map with 7 vertices. Edges are added between sufficiently similar images.**

Appearance based maps are gaining momentum because they can be built with the only aid of a monocular camera, thus offering a cheap alternative to solutions based on different sensors. Also, by incorporating visual elements, they may be easier to integrate into intelligent systems expected to interact with untrained human users.

In this paper we propose a set of evaluation criteria for appearance based maps. The topic of map benchmarking

---

[2]At the moment there is no universally accepted definition of appearance map, however the one we embrace in this manuscript is consistent with a significant fraction of formerly published papers on the topic.

has recently generated much interest also for metric maps. However, despite some proposals, no consensus exists yet for metric maps (see [2] and references therein). Due to their more recent introduction, no metrics have been proposed yet for appearance based maps. There are many reasons to justify the creation of metrics for appearance based maps, and for maps in general. The main one is that robotics researchers are in great need of objective quality measures to evaluate the impact of the countless ideas proposed in this quickly growing field. To date, for most problems it is impossible to compare two different solutions according to widely accepted criteria. The peculiar nature of robotics research also undermines the experimental replication of published results. However, given the recent dramatic changes in information technology, it is nowadays possible and needed to converge towards accepted performance measures, and to disseminate experimental data so that these assessments can be performed and repeated by an arbitrary third party.

The intrinsic purpose of a map evaluation metric is to measure the quality of different maps and determine which map is the best in general or in terms of some specific criteria. The maps to be evaluated can be generated by different agents using different algorithms. On the other hand, this metric can also be used to measure the effectiveness of one part of the mapping algorithm. For instance, by using the same set of images different appearance maps can be built by changing the parameters or the algorithms used in the map building procedure. In this paper, focusing on the former goal, we present evaluation criteria measuring the quality of a map independently of the algorithm used to build it. Hence, during the evaluation of a map the building blocks of the map creation algorithm are treated as black boxes, and the metric is designed in a way that minimizes the effects of these building blocks.

## 2. EVALUATION OF VISUAL MAPS

The ideal quality-assessment of a map would be performed by comparing it to the ground truth, i.e. the real value of the variable to be estimated. However, in most cases ground truth might not be easily accessible, or it may be time consuming to acquire. This is a well-known problem for any kind of map. In addition, approaches based on appearance graphs sample 3D environments with 2D images, and it is therefore impractical to generate a map serving as ground truth. In fact, the real environment is the only source which can be used as ground truth. Hence, the quality of an appearance graph can be best measured by evaluating how well it captures the desired properties of the environment it models.

A map by definition is a representation of the environment, and therefore, it may be natural to conclude that the map with most resemblance has the utmost quality. However, this point of view skips the basic motivation behind the need of a map, i.e. its utilization for the successful completion of a given task. A robot creates some form of an internal representation of the environment as a tool to successfully achieve its assigned mission. Thus, for the map to be most useful to the robot, it has to offer enough information to complete the assignment. Consider for example a robot performing inside a warehouse whose task is to quickly navigate between target locations revealed during the mission. One cannot rule out the possibility that a robot using a map with good geometric accuracy, but possibly cumbersome, may be outperformed by one using a model with an inferior geometric accuracy but easier to process.

With this motivation, we advocate that the assessment shall not be detached form the task at hand. Despite the fact that this statement may seem fairly trivial, in the context of occupancy grid maps one faces a significant amount of scholar work where maps are most often treated as images, and therefore contrasted and evaluated using algorithms and metrics that have little to do with the ultimate task the maps are needed for. On the contrary, we propose three task-centric evaluation criteria, namely localization, navigation, and planning.

### 2.1 Localization

The ability to estimate its own position is one of the very fundamental robot abilities enabling the successful completion of a variety of tasks. Hence, it is natural to evaluate a map with respect to its usefulness for localization. Unlike in metric maps, localization in appearance graphs is realized by finding within the map the image most similar to the one perceived by the robot when it needs to localize itself[3]. The robot is declared lost if it cannot localize itself to any image in the map.

The utility of the map with respect to localization is measured by the robot's localization performance using that map. A good metric should assign high utility to maps providing good localization. The goodness of localization in appearance graphs can be defined in two ways: 1) coverage 2) accuracy. The *coverage* metric measures the amount of information in the environment captured by the images in the appearance graph. To this end, we propose to collect a set of pictures captured at random locations in the environment where the map is created and use them as query images.

This method of evaluation of a map's merit based on its localization performance requires the use of an image retrieval algorithm in order to find the vertex with the most similar image in the graph. Over the years, several nearest neighbor search based approaches using kd-trees and k-means clustering have been proposed as solutions for the image retrieval problem [9, 14]. Today, SIFT features [11] and the bag-of-words image representation [17] are at the core of state-of-art large scale image retrieval systems. Hence, several versions of bag-of-words algorithm have been proposed as the basis of the localization procedure within a visual map [1, 8, 10, 19]. Nevertheless, even the most successful image retrieval algorithms have sub-perfect performances. In other words, the image retrieval algorithm used for localization can return an invalid image/feature matching resulting in wrong localization. Therefore, the erroneous localization ratio depends on the performance of the image retrieval algorithm and less on the quality of the map being evaluated. In order to minimize the effect of the image retrieval algorithm on the quality score of the map, the proposed method will ignore false image matchings and focus only on valid image correspondences.

Having set the scene, the coverage of a map is defined as

---

[3]We acknowledge this standpoint is somewhat simplified because one would likely get better results by considering not just the current image, but a sequence. This extension is subject to further investigations.

the percentage of successful localizations:

$$l_{cov} = \frac{L_{success}}{L_{total}}. \qquad (1)$$

Localization accuracy, on the other hand, describes the closeness of the estimated location to the real location of the robot. From the appearance graph perspective the robot will benefit from an accurate localization when the returned and query image look alike. Since similarity between images is encoded by the number of matched features, the accuracy has a positive correlation with the number of correct feature matches. Besides sharing features originating from the same objects in the environment, in similar images these objects should appear in close proximity in terms of image coordinates. In order to capture this idea, the accuracy error is defined as the average distance between corresponding features' image coordinates.

$$l_{acc} = \frac{\sum_{i=1}^{N} d\left(a_i, q_i\right)}{N} \qquad (2)$$

where $d(.)$ is the Euclidean distance function, $a$ and $q$ are corresponding features from the retrieved and query image respectively, and $N$ is the number of feature matches between these two images.

Then, the average localization accuracy error of all queries is assigned as the overall accuracy error of the map.

The localization accuracy metric favors appearance graphs with large number of vertices since the probability of having a similar image for a random query image increases with the number of images in the map. On the other hand, if the number of vertices in the map are limited due to the amount of data that can be stored, then a map consisting of images taken all around the environment will be preferred since it will reduce the number of times the robot gets lost. However, when the robot localizes itself, the localization will have less accuracy for a random query image since the images are spread around. Hence, for a fixed number of vertices allowed in the map, there is a balance between accuracy and coverage.

The reader should also note that neither accuracy nor coverage metrics consider the edges in the graph, but they both focus exclusively on the amount of information captured by the images encoded in the vertices.

## 2.2 Planning

In order to reach full autonomy, robots need to choose their actions by themselves. Planning can be realized using the so-called state space which provides an abstraction of the overall system. Similarly, an appearance graph with vertices corresponding to states and edges corresponding to actions can be used for path planning, i.e. finding the shortest path in the appearance space between two nodes in the graph. In the literature there are several search algorithms which work directly on undirected weighted graphs such as Dijkstra's algorithm. The time complexity of any planning algorithm working on graphs will increase with the number of vertices and edges. Hence, from the perspective of planning efficiency, maps with less vertices and edges will be preferred. Furthermore, the number of extracted features are correlated with the number of vertices and have a direct effect on the running time of the planner since most of the image matching algorithms utilize nearest neighbor search

in the high dimensional feature space. Hence, it can be concluded that the amount of data required to store the map is an indication of its performance in planning tasks, and data size comparison should be a part of the general map evaluation process.

For planning tasks, it is important that a map is well connected and contains a good representation of passages between places. Such a map will have a higher utilization rate than a map which reflects an accurate and detailed representation of the environment in general, but also includes an edge between two images of two places that are physically separated. Hence, a metric to measure the usefulness of a map with respect to path planning should consider the ability to plan paths that are valid in the real environment. Inspired from the work by Collins et. al. [5], we would like to measure the validity of the paths in a map by comparing paths generated within both the appearance graph and the actual environment.

In this test representing the *exactness* of the map, the ratio of paths that are valid in the map, but invalid the real environment will be calculated. To measure the ratio of these paths, also known as *false positives*, two connected vertices are randomly selected from the appearance graph. Then, it is tested whether two places identified from these images are actually connected in the real environment. The physical connectivity assessment can be performed either visually or by teleoperating the robot which constructed the map from one place to another. Even though one can argue that the visual inspection introduces some subjectivity into the metric, for robots with well-known kinematics and structured environments it is expected it will provide an accurate approximation. A generated path failing this test is identified as the false positive. The false positive ratio is then estimated by repeatedly generating random paths and counting the ones that fail the connectivity test.

Alternatively, as proposed in [5] to evaluate metric maps, a map can also be evaluated in terms of *completeness* by the ratio of the paths that actually exist in the environment, but are not captured in the map, i.e. so-called *false negatives*. Borrowing the same idea that we used to compute false positive paths, two images from the map are randomly selected and a graph search algorithm is used to find a path connecting these two images. If this path cannot be computed due to the fact that two images lie in disconnected components of the graph but the path exists in the real environment, the path will be declared as a false negative. The ratio of false negatives will reflect the inability of the planner to find a path using the map.

One could argue that two random images should be randomly selected from the environment instead of the map if the completeness of the map is to be measured. However, in that case, first, each random image sampled from the environment should be localized in the map. As stated in section 2.1, this localization procedure measures the coverage of the map and may result in failure either if the map has low coverage score or if the localization algorithm fails to find the valid match in the map. Therefore, to measure the utility of each task separately, query images are sampled from the images in the map. Applying this criterion in the selection of query images, this metric, however, will return zero false negative scores for any appearance graph consisting of only one connected segment since there will always be a path between any two vertices of the graph.

## 2.3 Navigation

Navigation, defined as the ability to reach an assigned target location from the robot's current position, is another fundamental level of competence that is greatly influenced by the available spatial model.

The evaluation criterion based on the planning task defined in section 2.2 punishing invalid paths generated using the map also evaluates maps with respect to the robust navigation criterion. Maps receiving high scores in this metric will be the ones representing environments that consist of physically apart places with similar appearances. Due to the computed similarity between them, the mapping algorithm may create an edge between the images of these places and since an edge encoding a similarity is interpreted as traversable, a graph search will return a path in between which is in fact invalid. Thus, a map with high false positive ratio will provide the robot a medium in which the probability of bumping into an obstacle is high. However, the contrary is not necessarily true. In a different scenario, navigation between two vertices $v_i$ and $v_k$ sharing an edge due to their similar visual signatures may not be possible. In other words, a visual similarity criterion for edge creation depends on the map building algorithm and an edge may not necessarily encode an indication of traversibility. This path will not be distinguished by the planning metric and classified as a false positive since these vertices may be indeed physically connected. However, the robot trying to follow this direct path may not be able to navigate in between.

Motivated from this idea the quality of the map should also be evaluated with respect to navigational criterion. We therefore embraced the idea of measuring the navigability of a map by computing the stability and robustness of its internal paths in terms of robot navigation. This metric is applied to the random paths generated to evaluate the planning quality. Since most of the proposed algorithms [7, 4, 13, 6, 16] base their servoing algorithm on multi-view geometry or more specifically on the fundamental matrix, we grasped the idea of measuring the quality of the fundamental matrix, $F$, for each pair of consecutive images in the path. Given two matched images their corresponding features are extracted. Then, a RANSAC algorithm as described in [12] is utilized to compute the fundamental matrix based on a number of randomly selected tentative feature matches. Based on [3], the error in the computed fundamental matrix is computed as the mean distance of points to their epipolar lines in the second image.

$$Err_F = \frac{\sum\limits_{i=1}^{N} d\left(\overline{\mathbf{x}}_i, F\mathbf{x}_i\right) + dist\left(\mathbf{x}_i, F^T\overline{\mathbf{x}}_i\right)}{2N}$$

where $(\mathbf{x}_i, \overline{\mathbf{x}}_i)$, $i = 1, \ldots, N$ are the $N$ corresponding features and $d(.)$ is the distance between a point and a line.

The average error of the fundamental matrix along the path is computed and returned as navigation error of the path. The overall navigation error of the map is then assigned as the average navigation error of all randomly created paths.

## 3. RESULTS

In this section we exemplify how the proposed metric work on a set of appearance based maps. In order to capture a broader spectrum of maps, a P3AT robot equipped with a monocular camera is teleoperated in the environment twice resulting in image sequences from two independent runs. These images are fed as the input to our map creation algorithm described in [7]. The paths followed during these runs and the test runs are shown in figure 2. A total of 1064 test images are collected by teleoperating a P3AT robot in the environment. The test image sequence is divided into three subpaths as shown in different colors in Fig. 2.

In order to increase heterogeneity, different parameters are used while building the two maps. In the first run (represented with blue circles in Fig. 2), a higher image capturing frequency is used resulting in map, $m_1$ with a larger number of images. Furthermore, comparing to the second map $m_2$, a more conservative approach is taken in the image retrieval algorithm by increasing the required number of feature matches for an image in the map to be matched with a query image. As a result two very different appearance graphs are created.

## 3.1 Localization

The core component in localization procedure in appearance graphs is the image matching function. As mentioned before, the quality of the localization results are mainly dependent on the image retrieval algorithm. Therefore, image matches should be verified for each localization test. Since no ground truth data is available stating which image matches are valid, each image match has to be visually verified by the person evaluating the map. Due to the simplicity of an image match verification task to humans, we believe at this point no subjectivity is introduced into the evaluation. This way false positives are eliminated. In order to also account for false negatives, a human should verify if a query image has actually a corresponding image in the map that the image retrieval algorithm could not locate. However, this task is not trivial and unlike comparing just two images to detect a false positive, it requires to go through all the images in the map. Hence, we choose the best possible image retrieval algorithm and think it as a black-box that behaves like an independent external source introducing this noise in terms of false negative image matches. Due to the fact that this algorithm affects both of the maps being evaluated, no bias is introduced into quality evaluation.

From each test run $n = 10$ images are chosen randomly. Each image is fed as the query image into the image retrieval algorithm and localization in the map is declared if the algorithm can match that image within the map and the user visually verifies it. For each successful localization, coverage ratio is increased and the accuracy of the match is calculated based on equation 2. Some examples of successful localizations are shown in figure 3. This procedure is repeated $m = 10$ times and the average scores are returned as the result of the evaluation of appearance maps in terms of localization task which are presented in table 1. As expected, $m_1$ with 148 vertices incurred in lower accuracy error when compared to $m_2$ with 99 vertices due to the higher probability of containing a similar image to a random image. On the other hand, in terms of localization coverage, $m_1$ scored almost the same in the first two test runs whereas $m_2$ scored almost twice as $m_1$ in the third test run. As it can be seen in Fig. 2, the two paths followed to collect images to build maps are almost identical except the small loop in the second map. The images in the third run were collected while the robot was traversing in the middle of the lab fol-

Image collection for map building

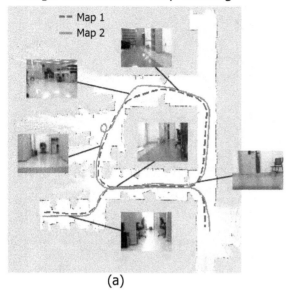

Image collection for testing

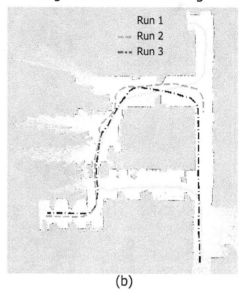

(a)            (b)

Figure 2: a) The paths followed by the robot during the map building processes are shown. b) Three paths followed to collect test images are shown.

lowing the opposite direction of the map generation runs. Therefore, as expected, images pointing the opposite direction did not match to any of the images in $m_1$, whereas they matched the images captured while the robot was making a full turn.

**Table 1: Localization quality**

|  | Run1 | | Run2 | | Run3 | |
|---|---|---|---|---|---|---|
|  | $cov$ | $err_{acc}$ | $cov$ | $err_{acc}$ | $cov$ | $err_{acc}$ |
| $m_1$ | 0.52 | 27.02 | 0.78 | 34.48 | 0.22 | 21.74 |
| $m_2$ | 0.50 | 43.47 | 0.77 | 33.32 | 0.37 | 37.03 |

### 3.2 Planning

As presented above, the first map benefits from having more vertices and obtained a higher score in localization accuracy. Theoretically, a map with infinite number of images should have the utmost accuracy. On the other hand, this map will gain high scores from one side, but will lose performance in planning tasks due to high number of vertices and associated features. Table 2 summarizes the elements of the maps and the amount of data required to store them.

**Table 2: Amount of data captured within maps**

|  | $\|V\|$ | $\|E\|$ | $\|D\|$ | dataSize(MB) |
|---|---|---|---|---|
| $m_1$ | 148 | 1396 | 24487 | 2.43 |
| $m_2$ | 99 | 408 | 15824 | 1.56 |

In order to measure the exactness and completeness of the set of paths which can be generated within a map, $n = 10$ image pairs are randomly selected from the map. Then, Dijkstra's algorithm is utilized to find a path connecting these two images where the number of matching features are used as costs. Repeating this procedure $m = 10$ times,

the total number of false negatives are counted. The ratio of the number of false negatives to the total number of path computing requests shows the connectivity of the map. Instead of counting the number of disconnected components in the map, this score considers the size of each disconnected component. For instance, failing to create an edge between second and third vertex has much less effect than failing it between two vertices from two large disconnected graphs.

The ratio of false negatives are measured for two maps being evaluated. The second map $m_2$ is fully connected and therefore gets completeness score of 1. On the other hand, $m_1$ has multiple connected components and therefore gets non-zero false negatives. In order to demonstrate how this metric behaves in the presence of only few edges, the parameter $TS$ is used to set the minimum number of feature matches required to declare two images as a match. In different tests the value of $TS$ varies and the performance is evaluated as a function of $TS$. The increase in the threshold results in a map with edges only between very similar images. Due to this decrease in connectivity the false negative ratio increases as shown in Fig. 4. The sudden jump between $TS = 30$ and $TS = 40$ is the result of losing connectivity in the middle of the path causing the map to split into two components with large number of vertices. Therefore, the probability of randomly selecting both vertices from the same connected subgraph decreases drastically.

The measure of exactness, on the other hand, captures the idea of detecting false positives, i.e. paths that do not exist in the real environment. In other words, the map should contain images captured in disconnected parts of the environment. However, a map generated from a single run will not have such images since the robot will only be able to travel between physically connected places. Hence, it will get an exactness score of 1.

The value of this metric will become apparent only when

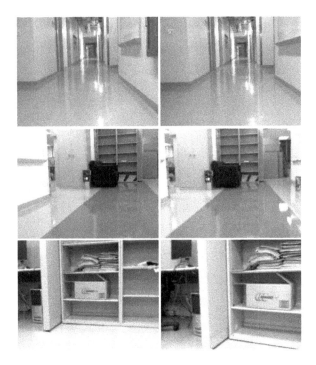

Figure 3: Sample image matches are shown. The left column contains query images whereas the retrieved images are shown in the right column. Localization accuracy errors computed for these matches are: 19.13, 50.26, 72.01 (top-down)

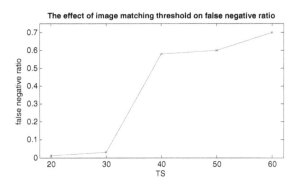

Figure 4: The effect of the number of feature correspondences to declare an image match, $TS$, on the number of false negatives of path validity test is shown.

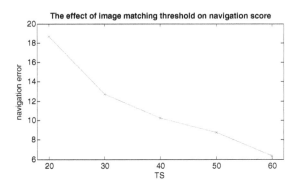

Figure 5: The effect of the number of feature correspondences to declare an image match, $TS$, on the average navigation error of randomly selected paths is shown.

evaluating maps that are the results of a multi-robot map merging process. In a scenario where robots create local maps of different floors of a building, they can exchange information wirelessly without the necessity to share the same physical environment. The merged map, on the other hand, may contain links between similar images, even though they might belong to physically disconnected parts of the environment. This metric, measuring the ratio of such paths, i.e. false positives, will evaluate the exactness of merged maps. Hence, we leave the validation of this metric for future work, since visual map merging algorithms are not currently available.

## 3.3 Navigation

The navigability score associated with an appearance map is defined as the average quality of the fundamental matrix between consecutive images of a random image sequence. By design this metric favors maps which use a more conservative approach by only creating edges between very similar images. In order to show this effect, navigability metric is applied on the maps built in the previous section by changing the threshold responsible for determining when an edge is created. Fig. 5 presents the trend of this error as the edge selection procedure gets more selective. As expected, the more similarity required to create an edge, the lower navigation error is obtained for that map.

## 4. DISCUSSION AND CONCLUSIONS

The proposed metrics measure the performance of appearance based maps with respect to different tasks. These met-

rics focusing on different aspects of the map may not agree on one final map being the best for all tasks, but will measure the map's specific task-based performance. However, these objective measures should be repeatable so that other researchers can reproduce the same experiments to compare published results with their own algorithms. Since the real environment is used as ground truth and providing access to it is not feasible, the data that is used in the computation of the performance metrics should be shared in an online public repository. First of all, images that are captured during the navigation of the robot are needed in order to generate a map of the environment. Different map creation algorithms can be tested on this image set and then evaluated by the task based measures proposed in this paper. In addition to this image set, the computation of the localization metric needs images captured at random locations in the environment. The planning metric, on the other hand, requires the information whether there is actually a physical path in the real environment between the locations encoded in the randomly selected images from the map. This information can be captured in a binary *connectivity matrix* which stores all possible image combinations. Each element in this matrix stores true if two images corresponding to this element are physically connected, and false otherwise. Similarly, in order to count false negatives to calculate the planning metric, we need to know whether random images from the environment are physically connected. In summary, in order to make visual map generation and benchmarking possible even without the privilege of accessing the real environment, the following elements should be made available to third parties: 1) the image set collected by the robot along its path; 2) random test images captured in the same environment; 3) their connectivity matrices. Only then the experiments can be repeated and the performance of map generation algorithms can be compared.

# 5. REFERENCES

[1] A. Angeli, D. Filliat, S. Doncieux, and J.-A. Meyer. Fast and incremental method for loop-closure detection using bags of visual words. *IEEE Transactions on Robotics*, 24(5):1027–1037, October 2008.

[2] B. Balaguer, S. Balakirsky, S. Carpin, and A. Visser. Evaluating maps produced by urban search and rescue robots: Lessons learned from robocup. *Autonomous Robots*, 27(4):449–464, 2009.

[3] B. Boufama and R. Mohr. Epipole and fundamental matrix estimation using the virtual parallax property. In *Proceedings of International Conference on Computer Vision*, 1995.

[4] G. Chesi, G. L. Mariottini, D. Prattichizzo, and A. Vicino. Epipole-based visual servoing for mobile robots. *Advanced Robotics*, 20(2):225–280, 2006.

[5] T. Collins, J. Collins, and C. Ryan. Occupancy grid mapping: An emprical evaluation. In *Proceedings of the Mediterranean Conference on Control and Automation*, 2007.

[6] A. Danesi, D. Fontanelli, and A. Bicchi. Visual servoing on image maps. In *Proceedings of IEEE International Symposium on Experimental Robotics (ISER06)*, 2006.

[7] G. Erinc and S. Carpin. Image-based mapping and navigation with heterogeneous robots. In *Proceedings of the 2009 IEEE International Conference on Intelligent Robots and Systems*, pages 5807–5814, 2009.

[8] D. Filliat. A visual bag of words method for interactive qualitative localization and mapping. In *Proceedings of the IEEE International Conference on Robotics and Automation (ICRA)*, 2007.

[9] F. Fraundorfer, C. Engels, and D. Nister. Topological mapping, localization and navigation using image collections. In *Proceedings of International Conference on Intelligent Robots and Systems (IROS)*, 2007.

[10] Y. Kalantidis, G. Tolias, E. Spyrou, P. Mylonas, and Y. Avrithis. Visual image retrieval and localization. In *International Workshop on Content-Based Multimedia Indexing (CBMI)*, 2009.

[11] D. G. Lowe. Distinctive image features from scale-invariant keypoints. *International Journal of Computer Vision*, 60:91–110, 2004.

[12] L. Maohai, H. Bingrong, and L. Ronghua. Novel method for monocular vision based mobile robot localization. In *Proceedings of International Conference on Computational Intelligence and Security*, 2006.

[13] G. L. Mariottini, G. Oriolo, and D. Prattichizzo. Image-based visual servoing for nonholonomic mobile robots using epipolar geometry. *IEEE Transactions on Robotics*, 23(1):87–100, 2 2007.

[14] E. Motard, B. Raducanu, V. Cadenat, and J. Vitria. Incremental on-line topological map learning for a visual homing application. In *Proceedings of the IEEE International Conference on Robotics and Automation (ICRA)*, 2007.

[15] S. Segvic, A. Remazeilles, A. Diosi, and F. Chaumette. A mapping and localization framework for scalable appearance-based navigation. *Computer Vision and Image Understanding*, 2008.

[16] A. Shademan and F. Janabi-Sharifi. Using scale-invariant feature points in visual servoing. In *Proceedings of International Society for Optical Engineering*, 2004.

[17] J. Sivic and A. Zisserman. Video google: A text retrieval approach to object matching in videos. In *Proceedings of the IEEE International Conference on Computer Vision (ICCV)*, 2007.

[18] S. Thrun. Robotic mapping: A survey. In G. Lakemeyer and B. Nebel, editors, *Exploring Artificial Intelligence in the New Millenium*. Morgan Kaufmann, 2002.

[19] Z. Wu, Q. Ke, J. Sun, and H.-Y. Shum. A multi-sample, multi-tree approach to bag-of-words image representation for image retrieval. In *Proceedings of the IEEE International Conference on Computer Vision (ICCV)*, 2009.

[20] Z. Zivkovic, O. Booij, and B. Krose. From images to rooms. *Robotics and Autonomous Systems (RAS)*, 55:411–418, 5 2007.

# Evaluation of Maps using Fixed Shapes:
# The Fiducial Map Metric

Sören Schwertfeger[*]
National Institute of Standards
and Technology
Gaithersburg, MD USA
s.schwertfeger@jacobs-
university.de

Adam Jacoff
National Institute of Standards
and Technology
Gaithersburg, MD USA
adam.jacoff@nist.gov

Chris Scrapper
The MITRE Corporation
McLean, VA, USA
cscrapper@mitre.org

Johannes Pellenz
Active Vision Group
University of Koblenz-Landau
Koblenz, Germany
johannes.pellenz@uni-
koblenz.de

Alexander Kleiner
University of Freiburg
Freiburg, Germany
kleiner@informatik.uni-
freiburg.de

## ABSTRACT

Mapping is an important task for mobile robots. Assessing the quality of those maps is an open topic. A new approach on map evaluation is presented here. It makes use of artificial objects placed in the environment named "Fiducials". Using the known ground-truth positions and the positions of the fiducials identified in the map, a number of quality attributes can be assigned to that map. Those attributes are weighed to compute a final score depending on the application domain. During the 2010 NIST Response Robot Evaluation Exercise at Disaster City an area was populated with fiducials and different mapping runs were performed. The maps generated there are assessed in this paper demonstrating the Fiducial approach. Finally this map scoring algorithm is compared to other approaches found in literature.

## Categories and Subject Descriptors

D.2.8 [**Software Engineering**]: Metrics—*Complexity measures, Performance measures*; I.2.9 [**Artificial Intelligence**]: Robotics—*Miscellaneous*

## General Terms

Performance, Algorithms

---

[*]Mr. Schwertfeger is also a PhD Student at the Jacobs University Bremen, Germany

## Keywords

Map evaluation, SLAM

## 1. INTRODUCTION

Mobile robots often generate maps. Those maps are usually used to enable the robot to perform certain tasks like, for example, autonomous navigation using path planning. Maps also assist an operator of a remotely teleoperated robot in locating the robot in the environment. They do this by providing information of features of interest like corners, hallways, rooms, objects, voids, landmarks, etc. Those features are referenced in the map in a global coordinate system defined by the application. This frame of reference can be a geographic coordinate system of the earth or a local one defined by the application (e.g., robot start pose or pose of an operator station).

Maps generated by mobile robots are abstractions of the real world which always contain inaccuracies or errors. Especially on extended missions or in rough terrain maps often contain large errors. But the usefulness of a map not only depends on its quality but also on the application. In some domains certain errors are neglectable or not so important. That is why there is not one measurement for map quality. Different attributes of a map should be measured separately and weighed according to the needs of the application. Those attributes can include:

- Coverage: How much area was traversed or visited.

- Resolution quality: To what level or detail are features visible.

- Global accuracy: Correctness of positions of features in the global reference frame.

- Relative accuracy: Correctness of feature positions after correcting (often the initial error of) the map reference frame.

- Local consistencies: Correctness of positions of different local groups of features relative to each other.

**Figure 1: Picture of the maze in which the experiments were performed. Also visible are two barrels that are used as fiducials.**

- Topological accuracy: To what level can directions (e.g. "go left at the 2nd crossing") be extracted?

Note that the resolution quality not only depends on the actual size of the gird cells of the map but is also influenced by the quality of the localization. If there are pose errors between scans of the same object its features blur or completely vanish. Depending on the groups chosen there can be multiple local accuracies.

Many factors influence the quality of a map:

- Environment: Sparse environments are difficult for most mapping approaches. These could be wide open areas or hallways with minimal features.

- Robot path: The path that a robot took to gather the sensor data could contain different amounts of loops. Furthermore, the terrain could be even or difficult to traverse, causing the robot to roll and pitch.

- Robotic platform: Features like active sensing or suspended locomotion can increase map quality. Parts of the robot in the field of view of the sensors are disadvantageous for mapping.

- Sensors: The range, field of view, structural errors, accuracy and the position of the sensor on the robot influence mapping algorithms.

- Computational power: Simultaneous Localization And Mapping (SLAM) [5] algorithms can be computationally very intensive. If the map has to be generated online to aid other tasks like path planning, processing time is often sparse on mobile robots. Then less scans can be used, or the number of particles in a particle filter is reduced, or loop closing and graph optimization algorithms are executed less frequently.

- Algorithm: The mapping algorithm itself influences the map quality to a great extent.

## 2. FIDUCIAL APPROACH

Using fiducials is a new approach to solve the problem of evaluating the quality of maps. Fiducials are artificial features placed in the environment which can be identified in the resulting map. Using the Fiducial approach, several of the above mentioned attributes can be measured to assess the quality of maps. The only information needed to score maps are the (ground-truth) positions of all fiducials in the environment. Upon scoring, each fiducial has to be identified in the map together with its position.

This approach completely abstracts from all other information contained in the map like walls, unexplored and explored areas and other features. However, given a dense enough distribution of fiducials, this method reflects the quality of those features well enough. This is because measuring the localization performance of the SLAM algorithm suffices since applying sensor data to the map given perfect localization is typically easy.

The fiducials used in this paper are cylinders placed in the environment. Those can either be cut in half and (typically) placed on either side of a wall or are separated by a short artificial wall. In the following representations, said cylinders in the actual maps will be refered to as barrels since barrels were used as cylinder approximations in the experiments (see figure 1). Fiducials are then the objects in the actual environment and its model - the ground truth map. As mentioned above there are (usually) two fiducial-parts (A and B) respectively barrel-parts (A and B).

All attributes scored by the Fiducial approach have values between 0 % and 100 % where 0 % means poorest quality while perfect results get a value of 100 %. This allows easy application of dependent weights to the attributes to come to a simple overall score for maps consisting of just one number. The coverage, resolution quality as well as global, relative and local accuracies can be determined using the Fiducial approach. However, the fiducials first have to be identified in the map. Although the Fiducial metric works in principle for 3D maps as well, 2D maps are considered for the rest of the paper.

### 2.1 Identification of Fiducials in the map

The following steps are performed to find the fiducials in the map and to register their position:

1. **Rasterize**: Render the map to a two-dimensional grid with a sufficiently high resolution (if the map is already present in a raster format this step is obviously already done).

2. **Colorization**: Remove all probabilistic entries in the grid such that there are exactly three color values left:

   - Free (typically white): No obstacle
   - Unknown (typically gray): Unobserved area (e.g. voids, also "content" of barrels)
   - Obstacle (typically black): Obstruction (e.g. walls, barrel)

3. **Identify barrel parts**: Find all obstacles which form parts of circles with the correct radius. The minimum visible angular opening of the circle has to be 2/3 of the actual opening of that part of the barrel.

4. **Assignment**: For each fiducial part, assign one or none of the barrel parts identified in the previous step.

Each of those barrel parts can be assigned to maximum one fiducial part.

5. **Determine Position**: For each barrel part assigned to a fiducial part compute the position of the center point of the circle forming the barrel. This is then the position of the barrel part. Thus the positions of two parts of a cut-in-half-barrel are just separated by the thickness of the wall.

All of the steps above could be computed by applying appropriate algorithms. For example, feature extraction methods like circular Hough transform [2] could be used to find the barrel parts. The problem of assigning barrel parts to fiducial parts could be solved by finding the mapping that resolves in the best global or relative accuracy. Since those algorithms were not implemented yet in the tools used for the experiments presented in this paper, both steps where done by hand.

The following three attributes use distances between two positions to measure the error. For those there are maximum distances $d_{max}^{attribute}$ defined which are considered to be the worst case for the attribute. The values can, but don't have to, be the same for those three attributes. Furthermore the actual distance error $d$ can be discretized to certain values, for example the barrel radius. This can be done in order to avoid differences in scoring which are caused by the inherent error of the ground truth data and to put the resulting scores in bins of similar qualities.

## 2.2 Global Accuracy

For every barrel-part assigned to a ground-truth-fiducial part calculate the distance $d$ to the (global) position of the corresponding fiducial. Distances $d$ greater than $d_{max}^{accuracy}$ are set to $d_{max}^{accuracy}$. The error $e$ is then calculated as $e = \frac{d}{d_{max}^{accuracy}}$. Average over the errors for all those barrel parts. The value for the global accuracy is then $1 - e$ such that perfect maps get a 100 % number.

## 2.3 Relative Accuracy

The error of the global accuracy is minimized (or the accuracy value maximized) by rotating, translating or even scaling the map. This can be easily done by just changing the poses of the barrel parts, thus eliminating the identification step for each iteration. Often the value for the transformation is just the error in the start pose. If there was no agreement on a global frame of reference (as in the following experiments) only the relative accuracy can be computed while there can be no score for the global accuracy.

## 2.4 Local Consistencies

For all groups calculate the distance errors between entries of a group.

In the following experiments the two parts of a fiducial form a group. Those groups are either classified as short range or long range depending on the minimum distance a robot would have to travel in order to see both barrel parts.

For each pair/group where at least one barrel part has been found:

1. Calculate the geometric distance between the positions of the two barrel parts A and B: $d_{barrel}$.

2. If one of the barrel parts was not identified in the map, set $d_{barrel}$ to a very high value.

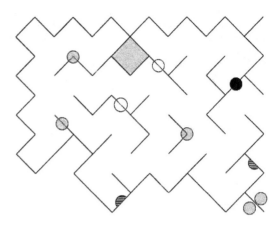

**Figure 2: The maze and the fiducials in the ground truth map. The ranges needed to traverse from one fiducial part to the other correspond to the color of the void: gray=four pallets; white=eight pallets; black=twelve pallets; striped=single barrel (no group = no distance).**

3. Get the distance between the two corresponding (ground truth) fiducial parts: $d_{fiducial}$.

4. The absolute value of the difference of the distances from step 1) and 2) is the error for this group: $e = min(d_{max}^{consistency}, |d_{barrel} - d_{fiducial}|)/d_{max}^{consistency}$.

The "short range consistency" is thus one minus the average of the error of all short range groups while the "long range consistency" is one minus the average error of the long range groups.

Using barrels or half-barrels on opposite sides of walls has two advantages. First it is very easy to judge the quality of the those pairs by just looking at the map and checking if those barrels are properly aligned and form a good circle without big gaps. This already allows a user to quickly assess a map score without any algorithmic computations.

Second, one can very easily measure the ground truth distance between those fiducial parts. Thus, even when the ground truth positions of the fiducials are unknown or their measurement contains a great error, one can still compute very accurate local consistency scores. For barrels which are simply cut in half and placed on either side of a wall their distance is equal to the thickness of the wall.

Other local consistencies are also possible, for example all fiducials in one room or area.

## 2.5 Coverage

The ratio of the number of fiducial parts assigned to a barrel part to the total number of fiducial parts. So a value of 100 % means that all fiducials have been mapped while for an error value of 0 no barrels have been found.

## 2.6 Resolution Quality

The resolution quality can be assessed by measuring the quality of the barrel voids. For each barrel part which is assigned to a fiducial part calculate the area marked as unknown. This can be done by rendering or scaling the map

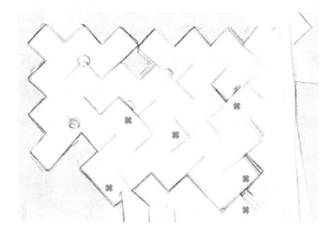

Figure 3: Map 1

and the ground truth to the same scale and simply counting unknown pixels.

The area is summed up for all those barrel parts assigned to a fiducial part. The ratio of the this sum of unknown areas to the actual (unknown) area of all according fiducial parts is the value for this attribute.

This attribute has some problems caused by sensors seeing below or above the actual barrels in the environment and is thus less accurate than the attributes mentioned earlier.

## 3. EXPERIMENTS

The data presented here has been gathered during the Response Robot Evaluation Exercise Disaster City 2010 [6]. There a maze in a building on an inclined plane has been mapped as well as an adjoining hall and the area in front of this building. Figure 2 shows the ground truth map for the maze. The two different types of fiducials described later have been applied there. Only for the maze the exact poses of the fiducials are known and thus only this part of the maps is used to evaluate their quality in this paper. The software used is a second generation of the Jacobs Map Analysis Toolkit [11].

As fiducials, barrels with a radius of thirty centimeters and a height of one meter are used. They come in two different configurations.

**Percent Fiducials** consists of two barrels and one piece of square plywood (about 1.2m x 1.2m or 4ft x 4ft). Those are mainly used outdoors where walls are less present.

**Wall Fiducials** are built by cutting one barrel in half and putting both halves on opposite sides of a wall, forming a nearly exact circle when viewed from the top. They come also in a variation where the barrel is cut into a 1/4th and a 3/4th piece which are placed on corners.

The sensors used are a Hokuyo UTM-30LX laser range finder (LRF) with a field of view of 270°, an angular resolution of 0.25° and a range of above 30 m as well as a Xsens MTi gyro and accelerometer.[1] Those were mounted on a stick and connected to a Laptop. The sensor data was col-

---

[1] Any mention of commercial products is for information only; it does not imply recommendation or endorsement by NIST.

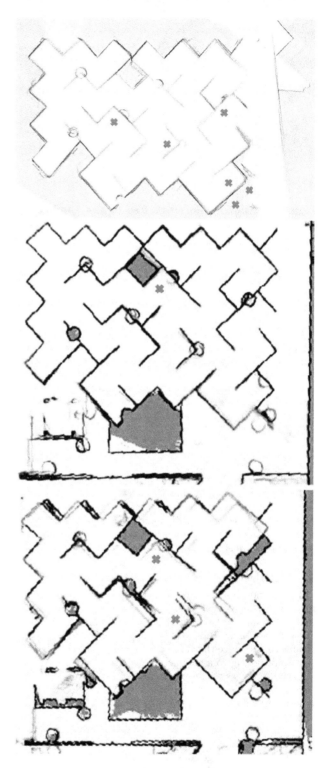

Figure 4: Maps 2, 3 and 4

Figure 5: Map 1 colored to free (white), unknown (gray) and occupied (black) according to section 2.1.

| Map | Barrel parts | Short-range pairs | Long-range pairs |
|-----|-------------|-------------------|------------------|
| 1 | 10 | 3 of 6 | 1 of 3 |
| 2 | 10 | 3 of 6 | 1 of 2 |
| 3 | 15 | 6 of 6 | 2 of 3 |
| 4 | 13 | 4 of 6 | 2 (1) of 3 |

Table 1: Count of identified barrels in the second column. Complete and found short- and long-range groups in the third and fourth column (e.g. 3 of 6 means that for 6 groups at least one barrel was found while for three groups both barrels are identified). One of the long-range groups of Map 4 has a distance $d$ bigger than $d_{max}^{consistency}$.

lected by a person holding the stick with the sensors slowly walking through the maze and the environment.

Two different mapping algorithms were tested. Since the programs did not use a common data format the data was collected repeatedly using different paths and different persons. Two maps were created for each mapping algorithm. Those maps are shown in Figures 3 and 4.

## 4. RESULTS

This section compares the results of Fiducial map scoring for the four maps gathered. In Figure 2, the ground truth map including the location of the fiducials is shown. There are a total of 16 fiducial parts present. 14 of those form seven groups (pairs) since they are on opposite sides of walls while two don't belong to a complete fiducial.

Each group was assigned a distance, measured in "pallets" (the 1.2 m square area for each element). This distance reflects the minimum number of pallets that has to be traversed to get from on part to the other in the group. The values are 12 for one fiducial, 8 pallets for two more and 4 for the other four fiducials. The 12 and 8 pallet groups are used for the long range consistency while the four four pallet groups are used for the short range consistency.

### 4.1 Coverage and Local Consistency Results

Figures 5 and 6 show the maps after the colorization step

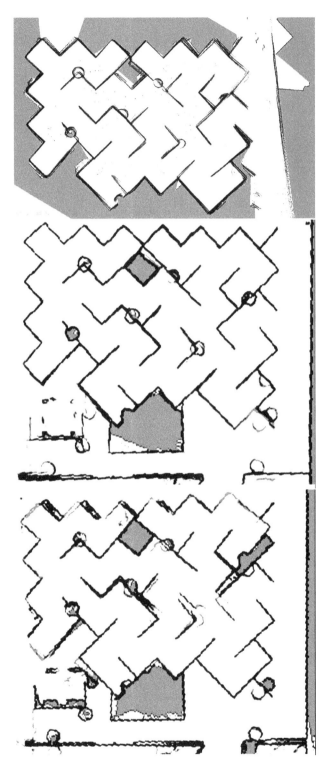

Figure 6: Maps 2, 3 and 4 colored.

| Map | Barrel parts | Total distance (barrel radii) | Average error (barrel radii) | Average error (cm) |
|---|---|---|---|---|
| 1 | 10 | 3.5 | 0.35 | 10.5 |
| 2 | 10 | 1.7 | 0.17 | 5.1 |
| 3 | 15 | 2.2 | 0.15 | 4.5 |
| 4 | 13 | 5.1 | 0.39 | 11.8 |

Table 2: Measured distances/ errors for the identified barrel parts for the relative accuracy attribute.

| Map | Barrel Count Unknown > 50 % |
|---|---|
| 1 | 20 % |
| 2 | 20 % |
| 3 | 40 % |
| 4 | 46 % |

Table 3: Unknown void areas. Barrel parts which are filled with at least 50 % unknown area are simply counted.

| Map | Coverage | Consistency | | Relative Accuracy | Average |
|---|---|---|---|---|---|
| | | Short | Long | | |
| 1 | 63 % | 50 % | 33 % | 83 % | 57 % |
| 2 | 63 % | 50 % | 50 % | 92 % | 64 % |
| 3 | 94 % | 100 % | 66 % | 93 % | 88 % |
| 4 | 81 % | 75 % | 33 % | 81 % | 68 % |

Table 4: Results of some attributes. The coverage, short-range and long-range consistencies as well as the relative accuracy are shown.

from section 2.1. In Table 1, the counts for identified barrels are provided. The crosses in Figures 3 and 4 mark the missing fiducial parts. Those are used to calculate the coverage as shown in table 4. The first table furthermore contains data for the local consistencies. For the sake of simplicity, the value for $d_{max}^{consistency}$ and for the discretization are chosen to be one barrel radius (30 cm). This way it is easy to just count all those groups/ pairs which are within said distance.

## 4.2 Relative Accuracy Results

Table 2 contains the data for the relative accuracy. The optimization step was done by hand by overlaying the maps with the ground truth map such that a best possible fit was achieved. The distances between the barrel- and fiducial parts were summed up. The chosen value of the barrel diameter (60 cm) for $d_{max}^{accuracy}$ was in no case exceeded.

Table 4 also contains the values for the relative accuracy calculated after the formula from 2.2. Global accuracy cannot be calculated because there was no global frame of reference.

## 4.3 Resolution Quality Results

Because of the problem mentioned before, where laser scans can hit the wall below or above the barrel, the results of this attribute are not satisfying. Even in the best map (Map 3), eight of the 16 barrel parts are completely white. For the sake of completeness the results of this calculation are presented in table 3.

## 4.4 Result Discussion

In this section the results of the Fiducial approach as shown in table 4 are discussed.

The $1/4^{th}$ barrels are more difficult to map and identify than the other sizes. This could be used to measure the Resolution Quality. But those might be too difficult to automatically detect, such that they should be avoided in future experiments.

The coverage values for Maps 1 and 2 are significantly lower than the other two. But the maze, the area of interest, has been explored in all mapping runs. The reason for this is, that the fiducials do not appear in a good enough quality in the first two maps. So it has to be noted that the coverage attribute of the Fiducial approach only measures the area covered with good enough map quality.

The consistency values reflect the map quality quite well. The best map in the set, Map 3, achieves the highest score. It can also be seen that the short-range consistency is always at least better than the long-range consistency, which is an expected result. The short-range consistency values for the first two maps again suffer from the unrecognizable fiducials. But Map 2 did not see any of the percent-fiducials. Those were also not counted for the long-range consistency such that the average value for the remaining two groups is better. The broken barrel in Map 4 is a long range one and has, in accordance with the algorithm, lowered the long-range consistency score.

The attributes from table 4 were averaged in the last column, giving each attribute the same weight. The average results reflect the subjective map quality quite well such that the Fiducial map scoring algorithm seems to be a viable algorithmic metric for mapping algorithms.

## 5. COMPARISON WITH PREVIOUS WORK

The analysis of robot generated maps is a relatively new field. Chandran-Ramesh and Newman [4] work in 3D on planar patches. They detect suspicious and plausible arrangements of those planes and classify the map accordingly. A 2D version of their approach could work on lines instead of planes. The algorithm does not make use of any ground truth information. Thus a map which looks nice might get a good score even if it seriously broken at some point.

Kümmerle et al. [7] proposed a method that does not compare the maps themselves but compares the robot path estimated by the SLAM algorithms with the ground truth path of the robot. This method is an excellent map metric if the preconditions that this algorithm demands are met. Instead of having to have a ground truth map now a ground truth robot path is needed. As discussed in the paper that usually implies human involvement. Especially in an event like RoboCupRescue, where the same environment is explored by different robots (using completely different paths) having a ground truth map representation is more easy to get. The second problem is that, next to the actual map, one needs to obtain the actual pose estimations from the SLAM algorithm. Wulf et al. [13] suggest a similar method. Here the groud truth path is generated using manually supervised Monte Carlo Localization of the 3D scans working on surveyed reference maps. A similarity of both algorithms with the Fiducial metric is the assumption that correct localization is a sufficient enough indicator for a good map quality.

Lakaemper and Adluru [8] use a comparison with a ground truth map. They create Virtual Scans out of the target map and measure an alignment energy as map metric. The approach makes use of line- and rectangle-detection which might not be available in unstructured environments. It measures topological correctness and can also quantify the global correctness, just like the Fiducial approach does using the Global Accuracy and the Local Consistencies.

The metric of Wagan, Godil and Li [12] is a feature based approach comparing a map to a ground truth map. A Harris corner detector, the Hough transform and Scale-Invariant Feature Transform (SIFT) are used to extract features from both maps. The features are pairwise matched based on their distance. The quality measure is the number of matched features in the map versus the number of ground truth features. The feature detectors are quite vulnerable to the actual method of rendering the LRF scans. As mentioned in the paper, already changes like noise, jagged lines and distortions pose problems to the feature detectors. This approach can thus only be applied to nearly perfect maps.

Pellenz and Paulus [9] also propose to use feature extraction. Next to using Speeded Up Robust Features (SURF) they also extract rooms as features from the gird map. The extracted rooms are matched with those from the ground truth map, taking into account the topology and the size and shape of the rooms. The average match error per feature is then the quality metric. This work and the Fiducial approach have in common, that they use few, large and easy to detect features (barrel/ room). The rooms have to be fully mapped in order to be used. Distortions could happen within one (bigger) room, potentially hindering the correct mapping to the ground truth room. The use of easy to distribute fiducials seems to be advantageous, since their density can be easily controlled and they can be concentrated in areas of interest. Barrels are small enough that they can be registered with a single scan but still big enough to show in low resolution maps. The room detection will not work in unstructured environments.

Balaguer et al. [1] presents the solution used for the problem of scoring maps in the RoboCup Rescue Virtual Robots competition. There different aspects of the map as well as additional information like features are scored. One of them is the Skeleton Quality which represents the topological structure of the rendered map. The number of false positives and false negatives determine this part of the score, where a false positive is defined as a node which cannot be accessed while a false negative is a clear topological location which is available but has not been included in the skeleton map. The Fiducial approach indirectly supports a similar topological quality measure, if Local Consistency groups with according fiducials are created.

Varsadan, Birk and Pfingsthorn [11] use an image based approach. The Ψ-similarity calculates the average Manhattan distance from the pixels of the ground truth map to the nearest pixel of the same color in the map and vice-versa. This approach only measures the global accuracy and is prone to noise and distortions and can thus only applied to very good maps.

Birk [3] computes one interesting attribute of maps as map metric - the level of brokenness. This structural error is measured by using the Ψ-similarity to find parts of the map which don't fit. This area is then cut-out and registered with the ground truth, thus finding the frame of reference. This is repeated till all of the map is registered. The count of generated sub-maps is the brokenness. This brokeness information can, to some degree, also be found in topological map attributes, for example by comparing different Local Consistencies with each other or the Relative Accuracy.

One big advantage of the Fiducial approach is the low amount of ground truth information needed in oder to compute a score. Kümmerle et al. [7] need a ground truth path while the others use a ground truth map. In the proposed approach just the fiducial positions relative to each other (for Global Accuracy in a global reference frame) have to be provided. If only the Local Consistencies are to be scored, in the proposed wall-barrel-system, the only information needed is the thickness of the walls. The metric can be fully automated while still allowing quick quantitative assessments of the map quality by just looking at the image of the map. The only part of the maps actually evaluated are the fiducials. Thus, as long as the fiducials are detectable in the map, all other mapping errors like noise or broken parts don't effect this algorithm. This metric does not rely on naturally occurring features, although those could be used if they are dense and large enough. This is also the biggest disadvantage of the Fiducial approach, meaning that only environments with such fiducials can be scored.

# 6. CONCLUSIONS

This paper introduces the problem of map evaluation and proposes a novel approach to it: the Fiducial map metric. The different attributes of this metric are presented and exercised on four maps. Those maps where gathered during the 2010 NIST Response Robot Evaluation Exercise at Disaster City in an environment populated with fiducials in the form of barrels. The resulting numbers for the different attributes and maps support the Fiducial approach. In the previous section the Fiducial metric is compared with other metrics. Demanding low efforts regarding the collection of ground truth data, being robust against many map errors and measuring many different map attributes the Fiducial Map Metric performs well in the task of map scoring, as long as fiducials are present in the environment.

Further work is planned by applying the Fiducial metric to maps from RoboCup 2010, especially in the context of the RoboCupRescue Interleague Mapping Challenge [10]. Another important task is to fully automate all steps of the algorithm. Additional work can also be done by using identified fiducials to form topological paths using ground truth information and scoring the quality of those paths.

## Acknowledgments

The Department of Homeland Security sponsored the production of this material under an Interagency Agreement with the National Institute of Standards and Technology. Thanks also to the Texas Engineering Extension Service, a member of the Texas A&M University System, for use of their Disaster City emergency responder training facility.

## 7. REFERENCES

[1] B. Balaguer, S. Balakirsky, S. Carpin, and A. Visser. Evaluating maps produced by urban search and rescue robots: lessons learned from robocup. *Autonomous Robots*, 27:449–464, 2009.

[2] D. H. Ballard. Generalizing the hough transform to detect arbitrary shapes. *Pattern Recognition*, 13(3):111–122, 1981.

[3] A. Birk. A Quantitative Assessment of Structural Errors in Grid Maps. *Autonomous Robots*, 28:187–196, 2010.

[4] M. Chandran-Ramesh and P. Newman. Assessing Map Quality using Conditional Random Fields. In C. Laugier and R. Siegwart, editors, *Field and Service Robotics, Springer Tracts in Advanced Robotics*. Springer, 2008.

[5] H. Durrant-Whyte and T. Bailey. Simultaneous localization and mapping: Part I. *IEEE Robotics and Automation Magazine*, pages 99–108, June 2006.

[6] A. Jacoff and E. Messina. DHS/NIST response robot evaluation exercises. In *IEEE International Workshop on Safety, Security and Rescue Robotics, SSRR*, Gaithersburg, MD, USA, 2006.

[7] R. Kümmerle, B. Steder, C. Dornhege, M. Ruhnke, G. Grisetti, C. Stachniss, and A. Kleiner. On measuring the accuracy of slam algorithms, 2009.

[8] R. Lakaemper and N. Adluru. Using virtual scans for improved mapping and evaluation. *Auton. Robots*, 27(4):431–448, 2009.

[9] J. Pellenz and D. Paulus. Mapping and Map Scoring at the RoboCupRescue Competition. Quantitative Performance Evaluation of Navigation Solutions for Mobile Robots (RSS 2008, Workshop CD), 2008.

[10] S. Schwertfeger. Robocuprescue interleague mapping challenge. http://robotics.jacobs-university.de/mappingChallenge/.

[11] I. Varsadan, A. Birk, and M. Pfingsthorn. Determining Map Quality through an Image Similarity Metric. In L. Iocchi, H. Matsubara, A. Weitzenfeld, and C. Zhou, editors, *RoboCup 2008: Robot WorldCup XII, Lecture Notes in Artificial Intelligence (LNAI)*. Springer, 2009.

[12] A. I. Wagan, A. Godil, and X. Li. Map quality assessment. In *PerMIS '08: Proceedings of the 8th Workshop on Performance Metrics for Intelligent Systems*, pages 278–282, New York, NY, USA, 2008. ACM.

[13] O. Wulf, A. Nuchter, J. Hertzberg, and B. Wagner. Ground truth evaluation of large urban 6d slam. pages 650 –657, oct. 2007.

# The Platform- and Hardware-in-the-loop Simulator for Multi-Robot Cooperation

Tomonari Furukawa, Lin Chi Mak, Kunjin Ryu and Xianqiao Tong
Department of Mechanical Engineering, Virginia Tech
IALR, 150 Slayton Avenue
Danville, VA 24540
{tomonari, linchi, kunjin, txq1986}@vt.edu

## ABSTRACT

This paper presents a platform- and hardware-in-the-loop simulator (PHILS), which was developed for the evaluation of cooperative performance of multiple autonomous robots and their testing in virtual environments. The simulator consists of computers each with a graphics processing unit (GPU), monitors, a network switch that links the computers, and a server-client simulation software system installed on the computers. The cooperative performance of multiple autonomous robots can be evaluated by linking computers each to be mounted on a robot to the network and running and testing autonomous robots in a virtual environment. Unlike the conventional hardware-in-the-loop simulators or multi-robot simulators, the primary advantage of the PHILS is that it can test cooperative autonomous robots and analyze their cooperative performance as well as hardware performance in a real-time virtual environment, enabling the implementation of synchronous and asynchronous communication strategies and the control of communication delay and loss.

## Categories and Subject Descriptors

H.4 [**Information Systems Applications**]: Miscellaneous; D.2.8 [**Software Engineering**]: Metrics—*complexity measures, performance measures*

## General Terms

Theory

## Keywords

Performance evaluation, multi-robot cooperation, multi-robot simulator, cooperative estimation and control

## 1. INTRODUCTION

Cooperative use of multiple robots has advantages over the use of a single robot in both efficiency and capability.

If each robot is assigned a task which does not duplicate with those of other robots, the efficiency will be multiplied by the number of robots. If multiple robots are assigned a single task, the capability is multiplied by the number of robots. As a consequence, the last few decades have seen the increasing popularity of studying multi-robot cooperation.

Despite the popularity, the cooperative behavior of multiple robots is complex. They are subject to not only the individual inter-constraints but also the cooperative intra-constraints. In addition, ineffective cooperation may simply results in an inefficient and/or incapable performance. Since the operation of the multi-robot system is also expensive, it is desirable that the performance of the system be tested in virtual environments and qualitatively and quantitatively evaluated before it starts to be tested in real environments.

The past efforts on the virtual testing of multi-robot systems can be divided into two areas. In the first, the primary focus has been directed to the modeling of a complex system including the multi-agent system, kinematics and dynamics of each robot and its environments [7, 5, 8, 12]. Object-oriented programing and visualization belong to this area. The second area has been more focused on communication and network [13, 2]. The development of a server-client system that allows the visualization of multiple robots on multiple computers belong to this. While dramatic progress has been seen in these areas, the current systems in each area are rather evolving independently without integration. In addition, the virtual testing is mostly focused on the simulation or the qualitative analysis of the cooperative estimation and control strategy where important performance criteria such as the effect of hardware and the quantitative capability of the cooperative estimation and control strategy are completely missing.

This paper presents the design and the development of a platform- and hardware-in-the-loop simulator (PHILS) proposed and implemented by the authors for the evaluation of cooperative performance of multiple autonomous robots and their testing in virtual environments. The simulator consists of computers each with a graphics processing unit (GPU), monitors, a network switch that links the computers, and a server-client simulation software system installed on the computers. Out of the computers, three computers create an environment where one computer runs a server program, and another computer calculates motion of mobile objects, and the last computer manages environmental parameters. The other computers are connected to a monitor, run a client visualizer using GPU and view the environment with static and mobile objects as well as autonomous robots where one computer is allocated to each autonomous robot to calculate its motion and show its view. The cooperative performance of multiple autonomous robots can be evaluated by linking computers each to be mounted on a robot to monitors and the network switch and running and testing autonomous robots in a virtual environment. Unlike the conventional hardware-in-the-loop simulators or multi-robot simulators, the primary advantage of the PHILS is that it can test cooperative autonomous robots and analyze their cooperative performance as well as hardware performance in a real-time virtual environment while different communication strategies and parameters are implemented.

The paper is organized as follows. Sections 2 and 3 deal with the object and sensor platform models and the enhanced cooperative Bayesian estimation and control that could be tested and evaluated by the PHILS. The design and the development of the PHILS are presented in Section 4. Section 5 investigates the efficacy of the enhanced approach with the belief fusion using the PHILS and conclusions are summarized in the final section.

## 2. OBJECT AND SENSOR PLATFORM MODELS

Consider an object $o$ of interest, the motion of which is discretely given by

$$\mathbf{x}_{k+1}^o = \mathbf{f}^o\left(\mathbf{x}_k^o, \mathbf{u}_k^o, \mathbf{w}_k^o\right), \qquad (1)$$

where $\mathbf{x}_k^o \in \mathcal{X}^o$ is the state of the object at time step $k$, $\mathbf{u}_k^o \in \mathcal{U}^o$ is the set of control inputs of the object, and $\mathbf{w}_k^o \in \mathcal{W}^o$ is the "system noise" of the object.

In order for the formulation of the cooperative estimation and control problem, this moving object is searched and tracked by a group of sensor platforms $s = \{s_1, ..., s_{n_s}\}$, the global states of which are assumed to be accurately known by the use of sensors such as GPS, a compass and an IMU. The motion model of sensor platform $s_i$ is thus given by

$$\mathbf{x}_{k+1}^{s_i} = \mathbf{f}^{s_i}\left(\mathbf{x}_k^{s_i}, \mathbf{u}_k^{s_i}\right), \qquad (2)$$

where $\mathbf{x}_k^{s_i} \in \mathcal{X}^{s_i}$ and $\mathbf{u}_k^{s_i} \in \mathcal{U}^{s_i}$ represent the state and control input of the sensor platform, respectively. The sensor platform also carries a sensor with an "observable region" as its physical limitation to observe an object. The observable region is determined not only by the properties of the sensor such as signal intensity but also the properties of the object such as the reflectivity. Defining the probability of detection (POD) $0 \le P_D\left(\mathbf{x}_k^o | \mathbf{x}_k^s\right) \le 1$ from these factors as a reliability measure for detecting the object $o$, the observable region can be expressed as $^{s_i}\mathcal{X}_O^o = \{\mathbf{x}_k^o | 0 < P_D\left(\mathbf{x}_k^o | \mathbf{x}_k^{s_i}\right) \le 1\}$. Accordingly, the object state observed from the sensor platform, $^{s_i}\mathbf{z}_k^t \in \mathcal{X}^t$, is given by

$$^{s_i}\mathbf{z}_k^o = \begin{cases} ^{s_i}\mathbf{h}^o\left(\mathbf{x}_k^o, \mathbf{x}_k^{s_i}, {}^{s_i}\mathbf{v}_k^o\right) & \mathbf{x}_k^o \in {}^{s_i}\mathcal{X}_O^o \\ \varnothing & \mathbf{x}_o^t \notin {}^{s_i}\mathcal{X}_O^o, \end{cases} \qquad (3)$$

where $^{s_i}\mathbf{v}_k^t$ represents the observation noise, and $\varnothing$ represents an "empty element", indicating that the observation contained no information on the object or that the object is unobservable when it is not within the observable region.

## 3. ENHANCED COOPERATIVE BAYESIAN ESTIMATION AND CONTROL

### 3.1 Overview

Figure 1 shows the schematic diagram of the enhanced cooperative Bayesian estimation and control, which is based on the belief fusion previously proposed by the authors. Unlike the conventional deterministic estimation and control, each sensor platform does not directly utilizes observations to determine its control action. In the Bayesian estimation and control, the sensor platform determines its control action by optimizing the quantity derived from the belief of the object of concern, such as a target. Therefore, the recursive Bayesian estimation recursively updates the belief in both measurement and time, and an observation is used to simply create an observation likelihood. In order for cooperative estimation and control, the enhanced cooperative Bayesian estimation and control further adopts the belief fusion and allows each sensor platform to update the belief with maximum accuracy.

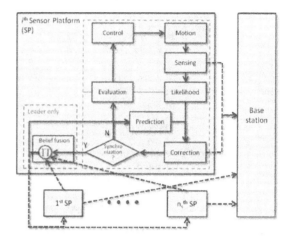

**Figure 1: Enhanced estimation and control**

### 3.2 Recursive Bayesian Estimation

Recursive Bayesian estimation (RBE) forms a basis to the maintenance of belief on a dynamically moving object [1, 14]. Given prior belief as well as knowledge on its motion and observations, RBE updates and maintains the belief using two recursive processes, prediction and correction. Let the prior belief on the object be $p\left(\tilde{\mathbf{x}}_0^o\right)$ where $p(\cdot)$ is a probability density function. Prediction uses knowledge on motion written in the form of a probabilistic Markov motion model $p\left(\mathbf{x}_{k+1}^o | \mathbf{x}_k^o\right)$ and updates the belief in time by using Chapman-Kolmogorov equation:

$$p\left(\mathbf{x}_k^o | {}^{s_i}\tilde{\mathbf{z}}_{1:k-1}, \tilde{\mathbf{x}}_{1:k-1}^{s_i}\right)$$
$$= \int_{\mathcal{X}^o} p\left(\mathbf{x}_k^o | \mathbf{x}_{k-1}^o\right) p\left(\mathbf{x}_{k-1}^o | {}^{s_i}\tilde{\mathbf{z}}_{1:k-1}, \tilde{\mathbf{x}}_{1:k-1}^{s_i}\right) d\mathbf{x}_{k-1}^o, \qquad (4)$$

where $p\left(\mathbf{x}_{k-1}^o | {}^{s_i}\tilde{\mathbf{z}}_{1:k-1}, \tilde{\mathbf{x}}_{1:k-1}^{s_i}\right) = p\left(\tilde{\mathbf{x}}_0^o\right)$ when $k = 0$, and $\tilde{\mathbf{x}}_{1:k}^{s_i} \equiv \{\tilde{\mathbf{x}}_\kappa^{s_i} | \forall \kappa \in \{1, ..., k\}\}$ and $^{s_i}\tilde{\mathbf{z}}_{1:k} \equiv \{^{s_i}\tilde{\mathbf{z}}_\kappa | \forall \kappa \in \{1, ..., k\}\}$ represent a sequence of states of the sensor platform $s_i$ and a sequence of observations by the sensor platform from time step 1 to time step $k$ respectively. Note here that $(\tilde{\cdot})$ represents an instance of variable $(\cdot)$.

Correction, on the other hand, constructs an observation likelihood $l^{s_i}\left(\mathbf{x}_k^o | {}^{s_i}\tilde{\mathbf{z}}_k, \tilde{\mathbf{x}}_k^{s_i}\right)$ from observation $^{s_i}\tilde{\mathbf{z}}_k$ and updates the belief in measurement using Bayes theorem:

$$p\left(\mathbf{x}_k^o|^{s_i}\tilde{\mathbf{z}}_{1:k},\tilde{\mathbf{x}}_{1:k}^{s_i}\right)$$
$$=\frac{l^{s_i}\left(\mathbf{x}_k^o|^{s_i}\tilde{\mathbf{z}}_k,\tilde{\mathbf{x}}_k^{s_i}\right)p\left(\mathbf{x}_k^o|^{s_i}\tilde{\mathbf{z}}_{1:k-1},\tilde{\mathbf{x}}_{1:k}^{s_i}\right)}{\int_{\mathcal{X}^o}l^{s_i}\left(\mathbf{x}_k^o|^{s_i}\tilde{\mathbf{z}}_k,\tilde{\mathbf{x}}_k^{s_i}\right)p\left(\mathbf{x}_k^o|^{s_i}\tilde{\mathbf{z}}_{1:k-1},\tilde{\mathbf{x}}_{1:k}^{s_i}\right)d\mathbf{x}_{k-1}^o},$$

$$(5)$$

or

$$p\left(\mathbf{x}_k^o|^{s_i}\tilde{\mathbf{z}}_{1:k},\tilde{\mathbf{x}}_{1:k}^{s_i}\right)=\frac{g_c\left(\mathbf{x}_k^o|^{s_i}\tilde{\mathbf{z}}_{1:k},\tilde{\mathbf{x}}_{1:k}^{s_i}\right)}{\int_{\mathcal{X}^o}g_c\left(\mathbf{x}_k^o|^{s_i}\tilde{\mathbf{z}}_{1:k},\tilde{\mathbf{x}}_{1:k}^{s_i}\right)d\mathbf{x}_{k-1}^o},\quad(6)$$

where

$$g_c\left(\mathbf{x}_k^o|^{s_i}\tilde{\mathbf{z}}_{1:k},\tilde{\mathbf{x}}_{1:k}^{s_i}\right)$$
$$=l^{s_i}\left(\mathbf{x}_k^o|^{s_i}\tilde{\mathbf{z}}_k,\tilde{\mathbf{x}}_k^{s_i}\right)p\left(\mathbf{x}_k^o|^{s_i}\tilde{\mathbf{z}}_{1:k-1},\tilde{\mathbf{x}}_{1:k}^{s_i}\right).\quad(7)$$

Note that the likelihood takes two different forms depending on the detectability of the object and is given by

$$l^{s_i}\left(\mathbf{x}_k^o|^{s_i}\tilde{\mathbf{z}}_k^o,\tilde{\mathbf{x}}_k^{s_i}\right)=\begin{cases}1-P_D\left(\mathbf{x}_k^o|\tilde{\mathbf{x}}_k^{s_i}\right)&\not\exists^{s_i}\tilde{\mathbf{z}}_k^o\in{}^{s_i}\mathcal{X}_D^o\\p\left(\mathbf{x}_k^o|^{s_i}\tilde{\mathbf{z}}_k^o,\tilde{\mathbf{x}}_k^{s_i}\right)&\exists^{s_i}\tilde{\mathbf{z}}_k^o\in{}^{s_i}\mathcal{X}_D^o\end{cases}$$

$$(8)$$

where $^{s_i}\mathcal{X}_D^o$ is the "detectable region" of the sensor platform $s_i$, which describes the region within which the sensor confidently finds the object $o$, i.e.,

$$^{s_i}\mathcal{X}_D^o=\{\mathbf{x}_k^o|\epsilon^o<P_D\left(\mathbf{x}_k^o|\mathbf{x}_k^{s_i}\right)\le1\}\subset{}^{s_i}\mathcal{X}_O^o,$$

where $\epsilon^o$ is a positive threshold value which determines the detection of the object. Depending on whether there exists an observed object within the detectable region, the upper and lower formulas provide likelihoods useful for search and tracking, respectively. If the observed object state is not within the detectable region, the observation is insignificant. As a result, the likelihood is defined in terms of the negation of the POD. If the observation is within the detectable region, the likelihood can be defined as a probability density function having its peak around the observed object state.

### 3.3 Belief fusion

Unlike the traditional observation fusion, the belief fusion collects beliefs from other sensor platforms at the lead sensor platform and synchronizes the belief of all the sensor platforms by sending the fused belief. Given the belief of the sensor platform $s_i$ as $p\left(\mathbf{x}_k^o|^{s_i}\mathbf{z}_{1:k},\mathbf{x}_{1:k}^{s_i}\right)$, the fused belief $p\left(\mathbf{x}_k^o|^s\mathbf{z}_{1:k},\mathbf{x}_{1:k}^s\right)$ is given by

$$p\left(\mathbf{x}_k^o|^s\tilde{\mathbf{z}}_{1:k},\tilde{\mathbf{x}}_{1:k}^s\right)$$
$$=\frac{\prod_{i=1}^{n_s}p\left(\mathbf{x}_k^o|^{s_i}\tilde{\mathbf{z}}_{1:k},\tilde{\mathbf{x}}_{1:k}^{s_i}\right)}{\int_{\mathcal{X}^o}\prod_{i=1}^{n_s}p\left(\mathbf{x}_k^o|^{s_i}\tilde{\mathbf{z}}_{1:k},\tilde{\mathbf{x}}_{1:k}^{s_i}\right)d\mathbf{x}_k^o}.\quad(9)$$

Note that the multiplied belief is normalized since it is not a probability density function otherwise.

### 3.4 Bayesian control

Unlike the conventional deterministic control where the control objective is given by the initial expected object state, the control objective in the RBE framework is concerned with the entire object belief and thus defined with the initial object belief as

$$J^{s_i}\left(\mathbf{u}_{k:k+n_k-1}^{s_i}|\tilde{\mathbf{x}}_k^{s_i},\tilde{p}_{\mathbf{x}_k^o|^{s_i}\tilde{\mathbf{z}}_{1:k}^o,\tilde{\mathbf{x}}_{1:k}^{s_i}}\left(\cdot\right)\right)\to\max_{\mathbf{u}_{k:k+n_k-1}^{s_i}}.\quad(10)$$

The objective function is given by

$$J^{s_i}\left(\cdot\right)=\omega p_{\mathbf{x}_{k+n_k}^o}\left(g\left(\mathbf{x}_{k+n_k}^{s_i}\right)|^{s_i}\tilde{\mathbf{z}}_{1:k}^o,\tilde{\mathbf{x}}_{1:k}^{s_i}\right)$$
$$+\quad(1-\omega)f\left(\mathbf{x}_{k+n_k}^{s_i},p_{\mathbf{x}_{k+n_k}^o}\left(\cdot\right)\right),\quad(11)$$

where the second term of the terminal objective is added to direct the sensor platform towards the location where the belief is high even when the belief is locally flat, for instance,

$$f\left(\mathbf{x}_{k+n_k}^{s_i},p_{\mathbf{x}_{k+n_k}^o}\left(\cdot\right)\right)$$
$$=\left|\mathbf{x}_{k+n_k}^{s_i}-\arg\max p_{\mathbf{x}_{k+n_k}^o}|\left(g\left(\mathbf{x}_{k+n_k}^{s_i}\right)|^{s_i}\tilde{\mathbf{z}}_{1:k}^o,\tilde{\mathbf{x}}_{1:k}^{s_i}\right)\right|,$$

$$(12)$$

which navigates the sensor platform directly towards the peak of the belief.

## 4. PLATFORM- AND HARDWARE-IN-THE-LOOP SIMULATOR

### 4.1 Concept and Design

Figure 2 shows the schematic design of the PHILS. The simulator consists of computers, monitors, a network switch that links the computers, and a server-client simulation software system installed on the computers. Out of the computers, three computers create an environment where one computer runs a server program so that client computers can share the same environment, another computer calculates motion of mobile objects in the environment, Equation (1), using GPU since the motion of multiple objects can be calculated parallelly, and the last computer with a GPU and a monitor acts as the environmental server and manages environmental parameters such as time, weather and communication speed whilst visualizing the behavior of all the autonomous robots in the environment under the support of GPU. The other computers are each equipped with a GPU and connected to a monitor, run a client visualizer using the GPU and view the environment with static and mobile objects as well as autonomous robots where one computer is allocated to each autonomous robot to calculate its motion in Equation (2) and show its view.

The cooperative performance of multiple autonomous robots can be evaluated by linking computers each to be mounted on a robot to the network switch and calculate Equations (4)-(12) and running and testing autonomous robots in a virtual environment. The PHILS provides a monitor to each on-board computer since the performance of the onboard computers, which we check at the base station can be monitored simultaneously. The computer to be used as the base station can also be connected and tested in the virtual environment. Unlike the conventional hardware-in-the-loop simulators or multi-robot simulators, the primary advantage of the PHILS is that it can test cooperative autonomous robots and analyze their cooperative performance as well as hardware performance in a real-time virtual environment, enabling the implementation of synchronous and asynchronous communication strategies and the control of communication delay and loss.

### 4.2 Development and Implementation

Figure 3 shows the PHILS developed by realizing the design whereas the detailed specifications of components of

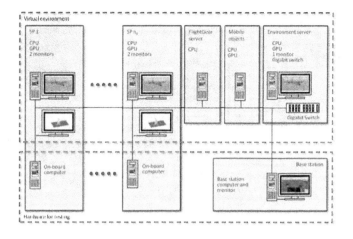

Figure 2: The platform-in-the-loop simulator

the developed PHILS are listed in Table 1. In the current setup, the PHILS has eight sets of a computer and two LCD monitors for the simulation and visualization of sensor platforms, meaning that it can accommodate the cooperation up to eight autonomous robots. The eight computers, as well as the other three computers that create an environment, are all those with the CPU of Dual Core 2.4GHz and the GPU of 32 stream processors. The eight monitors showing the views of autonomous robots are of 40 inch in size while the other eight monitors to connect to the on-board computers are of 19 inch in size. The monitor showing the global view is a LCD projector. The network switch is of Gigabit speed so that the speed of wireless communication can be controlled with delay.

The server, the client and the visualiser are all of FlightGear, which is an open-source simulator which was primarily designed for aerial vehicles but can now also incorporate ground vehicles. By accessing to the server, the FlightGear client can possess information on all the autonomous robots and mobile objects as well as the other environmental objects such as terrain and static objects and visualize them on the client computer. For the network communication, both the TCP/IP and the UDP are utilized.

Table 1: PHILS specifications

| Type | Qty | Specs |
|---|---|---|
| Computer | 11 | Shuttle XPC |
| CPU | 11 | Intel Core2Duo, 2.4GHz |
| Memory | 11 | 3.25 GB RAM |
| GPU | 10 | NVidia GeForce 8400GS |
| LCD monitor | 8 | Toshiba 40 inch |
| LCD monitor | 8 | Gateway 19 inch |
| LCD projector | 1 | Epson SVGA |
| Network switch | 1 | NETGEAR Gigabit 24 port |
| Visualizer | - | FlightGear |
| Server-client | - | FlightGear |
| Network protocol | - | TCP/IP, UDP |

## 5. NUMERICAL EXAMPLES

This section presents results of a series of qualitative and quantitative tests carried out to investigate the performance of the cooperation schemes and hardware systems using the developed PHILS. Tests 1 and 2 investigate the validity of the proposed approach through algebraic computations whereas its applicability to cooperative search and tracking (SAT) is examined in Test 3. Table 2 lists the on-board computers connected to the PHILS and investigated.

Table 2: On-board computer specifications

| Type | Qty | Specs |
|---|---|---|
| Computer | 8 | ASUS EeeBox |
| CPU | 8 | Intel Core2Duo, 1.6GHz |
| Memory | 8 | 1.0 GB RAM |
| GPU | 8 | NVidia Ion |

### 5.1 Validation

#### 5.1.1 Real-time performance of belief fusion (Test 1)

The first test was aimed at investigating the real-time performance of the belief fusion with respect to the prediction and the correction processes. Since the belief fusion is a synchronous communication effort while the prediction and the correction are carried out on each on-board computer with no communication, its real-time performance cannot be comparatively studied with those of the prediction and the correction by conventional simulators. As all the processes were implemented on GPUs, the speedup was investigated in addition to the time by solving the same problem with a CPU only.

Figures 4(b) and 4(a) show the resulting speedup and computation time with respect to different grid sizes respectively. The result of time shows the increasing influence of the belief fusion in time with the increase of the grid size. This is largely due to the increase of the number of data to communicate in the belief fusion, which does not exist in the prediction and the correction processes. The result of speedup further shows that the decreasing influence of the prediction in time is due to its increase in speedup.

#### 5.1.2 Belief fusion vs. observation fusion (Test 2)

This validation test was performed to investigate the effectiveness of the belief fusion comparatively. The compu-

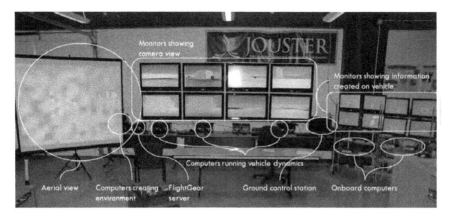

Figure 3: Developed platform-in-the-loop simulator

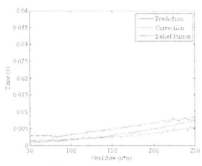

(a) Speedup vs. grid size

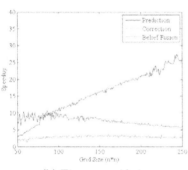

(b) Time vs. grid size

Figure 4: Performance of belief fusion (Test 1)

tation time required for one RBE using the proposed belief fusion approach was first measured and compared with that using the conventional observation fusion approach [6, 11]. As the RBE with the observation fusion requires the the observation fusion with synchronous communication in addition to the prediction and the correction process with no communication, the conventional simulators is not usable to investigate the effect of the observation fusion and its comparison to the belief fusion. Since the belief updated at each sensor platform carries past information, the belief fusion may not be performed frequently. The computation time was also investigated with respect to different frequencies of belief fusion.

Figure 5(a) shows the computation times of one RBE necessary for the belief fusion approach and the conventional observation fusion approach. Since the proposed belief fusion approach performs belief fusion outside the loop of RBE, its process simply consists of the prediction and the correction operations. As a consequence, the conventional approach is slower than the belief fusion approach. Since the observation fusion is nearly five times as long as the RBE without the observation fusion in time, the conventional approach is equivalent to losing the information of five RBEs from the other sensor platforms.

Shown in Figure 5(b) are the computation time required for 100 RBEs by the belief fusion approach with different intervals of belief fusion and that by the conventional approach with observation fusion at every RBE. Estimation with belief fusion at every RBE takes longer than the RBE with the observation fusion since the belief fusion requires the communication of the entire belief. However, it is seen that the belief fusion approach requires half the computation time of the conventional approach when the number of intervals is around five. If the accuracy of the belief can be maintained with less belief fusions, the computation time can be reduced by one order. In addition, the conventional approach may not become feasible when the communication delay due to the distance between sensor platforms is introduced to this result. This result by the PHILS strongly justifies the superiority of the belief fusion approach to the conventional approach.

## 5.2 Cooperative Search and Tracking (Test 3)

The problem described in this subsection is a simplified marine search and rescue scenario where a life raft with prior belief is drifted by the wind and current and autonomous rescue helicopters search for and track the life raft to rescue victims [3]. The life raft or the object model moves on a horizontal plane and is given by

$$
\begin{aligned}
x_k^o &= x_{k-1}^o + \Delta t \cdot v_{k-1}^o \cos \gamma_{k-1}^o \\
y_k^o &= y_{k-1}^o + \Delta t \cdot v_{k-1}^o \sin \gamma_{k-1}^o,
\end{aligned}
\tag{13}
$$

where $v^o$ and $\gamma^o$ are the velocity and direction of the object motion caused by the wind and current, each subject to a Gaussian noise, and $\Delta t$ is a time increment. The prior belief on the object is also Gaussian. The autonomous helicopters or sensor platforms are assumed to move on a horizontal

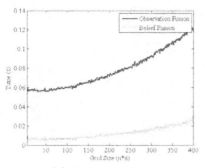

(a) Time vs. grid size

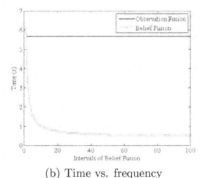

(b) Time vs. frequency

**Figure 5: Belief fusion (Test 2)**

plane and given by

$$
\begin{aligned}
x_k^{s_i} &= x_{k-1}^{s_i} + \Delta t \cdot v_{k-1}^{s_i} \cos \gamma_{k-1}^{s_i} \\
y_k^{s_i} &= y_{k-1}^{s_i} + \Delta t \cdot v_{k-1}^{s_i} \sin \gamma_{k-1}^{s_i} \\
\theta_k^{s_i} &= \theta_{k-1}^{s_i} + \Delta t \cdot \alpha^{s_i} \gamma_{k-1}^{s_i},
\end{aligned}
\tag{14}
$$

where $v^{s_i}$ and $\gamma^{s_i}$ are the velocity and turn of the sensor platform and $\alpha^{s_i}$ is a coefficient governing the rate of turn. The POD $P_D\left(\mathbf{x}_k^o | \tilde{\mathbf{x}}_k^{s_i}\right)$ is given by a Gaussian distribution, whereas the likelihood $l\left(\mathbf{x}_k^o |^{s_i} \tilde{\mathbf{z}}_k^o, \tilde{\mathbf{x}}_k^{s_i}\right)$ when the object is detected is given by a Gaussian distribution with variances proportional to the distance between the sensor platform and the object. Table 3 shows the major parameters of the cooperative SAT problem. The communication speed of 70 Mbps is a known peak performance of 802.11n in real world.

Figure 6 first shows the snapshot of the cooperative SAT and the trajectories of the helicopters with the belief on the object. These show the successful operation on the developed PHILS and the successful cooperative SAT using the proposed real-time non-Gaussian estimation approach. Figure 7 then shows the distance of each helicopter to the object and the information entropy with respect to time by both the proposed and the conventional approaches. The resulting transition of distances shows that the proposed approach outperforms the conventional approach by finding the object significantly earlier although the belief fusion was performed at every 500 RBEs. The slow performance of the conventional approach is a result of excessive communication with delay. The information entropy of the proposed approach is similarly better than that of the conventional approach due to the earlier detection of the object. Although infrequent belief fusion in the proposed approach makes the information entropy high after a certain period of time, all the helicopters could still keep detecting the object and maintain the information entropy low on average.

(a) Snapshot of cooperative SAT

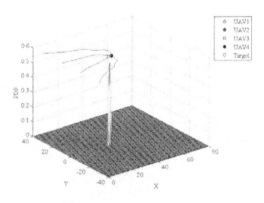

(b) Result of cooperative SAT

**Figure 6: Cooperative search and tracking (Test 3)**

## 6. CONCLUSION AND FUTURE WORK

This paper has presented the PHILS designed and developed by the authors for the evaluation of cooperative performance of multiple autonomous robots and their testing in virtual environments. The cooperative performance of multiple autonomous robots can be evaluated by linking computers each to be mounted on a robot to the network and running and testing autonomous robots in a virtual environment. The primary advantage of the PHILS is that it can test cooperative autonomous robots and analyze their cooperative performance as well as hardware performance in a real-time virtual environment while the synchronous and

**Table 3: Major parameters of the cooperative SAT problem**

|  | Parameter | Value |
|---|---|---|
| Sensor Platform | Velocity $v_k^{s_i}$ | 0.12 km/s |
|  | Turn coef. $\alpha^{s_i}$ | 0.8 |
|  | POD var. | [0.2 km, 0.2 km] |
|  | Threshold $\epsilon^o$ | 0.01 |
|  | Communication | 70 Mbps |
| Object | Velocity $v_k^o$ | N(0.1 km/s, 0.02 km/s) |
|  | Direction $\gamma_k^o$ | N(0 rad, 0.7 rad) |
|  | Prior $[x_0^o, y_0^o]$ | N([-1 km, 1 km], diag{0.3 km, 0.2 km}) |

asynchronous communication and the communication delay and loss can be implemented and controlled.

Numerical examples have first validated the performance of the belief fusion approach using the PHILS. The belief fusion approach was then applied to the cooperative SAT by autonomous helicopters, and its superiority to the conventional observation fusion approach and applicability to real-world problems have been demonstrated using the PHILS.

The current study is merely the first step for the multi-robot cooperation and the use of the PHILS, and various extensive studies are possible. In connection to the recent effort on refining the present formulations [4, 9, 10], various theoretical, numerical and experimental works are being performed.

## 7. ACKNOWLEDGMENTS

This work was primarily supported by US Army International Technology Center - Pacific (FA23896-08-1-4129) and the US Army RDECOM/TARDEC (FA2386-10-1-4017). Administrative support by the Asian Office of Aerospace Research and Development was greatly acknowledged.

## 8. REFERENCES

[1] Bergman, N. *Recursive Bayesian Estimation Navigation and Tracking Applications*, Ph.D Dissertation, Linkopings University, 1999.

[2] Carpin, S., Lewis, M., Wang, J, Balakirsky, S., Scrapper, C., "USARSim: A Robot Simulator for Research and Education," *2007 IEEE International Conference on Robotics and Automation*, Roma, April 10-14, 2007, pp. 1400-1405, 2007.

[3] Furukawa, T., Bourgault, F., Lavis, B. and Durrant-Whyte, H.F., "Bayesian Search-and-Tracking Using Coordinated UAVs for Lost Targets," *2006 IEEE International Conference on Robotics and Automation*, Orlando, May 14-18, 2006, pp. 2521-2526, 2006.

[4] Furukawa, T., Durrant-Whyte, H.F., Lavis, B., "The Element-based Method - Theory and its Application to Bayesian Search and Tracking," IEEE/RSJ International Conference on Intelligent Robots and Systems, San Diego, October 29-Nov 2, 2007, pp. 2807-2812, 2007.

[5] Gerkey, B., Vaughan, R.T., Howard, A., "The Player/Stage Project: Tools for Multi-Robot and Distributed Sensor Systems," Proceedings of the International Conference on Advanced Robotics (ICAR 2003), Coimbra, Portugal, June 30 - July 3, 2003, pp. 317-323, 2003.

[6] Grime, S., Durrant-Whyte, H.F., "Data Fusion in Decentralized Sensor Networks," Control Engineering Practice, Vol. 2, No. 5, pp.849-863, 1994.

[7] Jakobi, N., Husbands, P. Harvey, I., "Noise and the Reality gap: The Use of Simulation in Evolutionary Robotics," Advances in Artificial Life - Lecture Notes in Computer Science, pp. 704-720, 1995.

[8] Koenig, N.; Howard, A., "Design and Use Paradigms for Gazebo, An Open-source Multi-robot Simulator," IEEE/RSJ International Conference on Intelligent Robots and Systems, September 28 - October 2, 2004, pp. 2149 - 2154, 2004.

[9] Lavis, B., Furukawa, "HyPE: Hybrid Particle-Element Approach for Recursive Bayesian Searching and Tracking," Proceedings of Robotics: Science and Systems IV, June 2008, Zurich, 2008.

[10] Lavis, B., Furukawa, T. Durrant-Whyte, H.F., "Dynamic Space Reconfiguration for Bayesian Search and Tracking with Moving Targets," Autonomous Robots, Vol. 24, No. 4, pp. 387-399, 2008.

[11] Makarenko, A., Durrant-Whyte, H.F., "Decentralized Data Fusion and Control in Active Sensor Networks,' Proc. of the Seventh Conference on Information Fusion, 2004.

[12] Michel, O., "WebotsTM: Professional Mobile Robot Simulation," International Journal of Advanced Robotic Systems, Vol. 1, No. 1, pp.39-42, 2004.

[13] Scrapper, C., Balakirsky, S., Messina, E. "MOAST and USARSim - A Combined Framework for the Development and Testing of Autonomous Systems," SPIE Defense and Security Symposium, Orlando, FL, April 17-21, 2006.

[14] Tarantola, A., *Inverse Problem Theory and Methods for Model Parameter Estimation*, Society for Industrial and Applied Mathematics, Philadelphia, 2005.

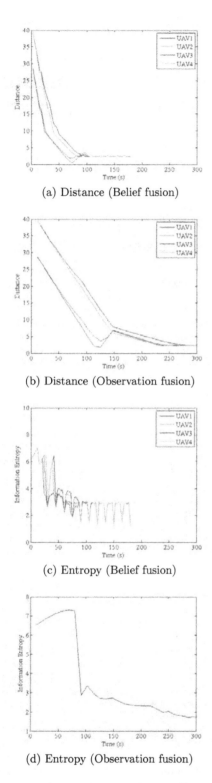

(a) Distance (Belief fusion)

(b) Distance (Observation fusion)

(c) Entropy (Belief fusion)

(d) Entropy (Observation fusion)

Figure 7: Distance to object and information entropy (Test 3)

# Towards Evaluating World Modeling for Autonomous Navigation in Unstructured and Dynamic Environments

Rolf Lakaemper
Temple University
Philadelphia, PA, USA
lakamper@temple.edu

Raj Madhavan
Institute for Systems Research
University of Maryland, College Park &
Intelligent Systems Division
National Institute of Standards and Technology
Gaithersburg, MD, USA
madhavan@umd.edu/madhavan@nist.gov

## ABSTRACT

With funding from the Commerce Department's National Institute of Standards and Technology (NIST) Measurement Science and Engineering Research Grants[1], the authors have recently embarked on a three year project to create and experimentally validate a framework by which automated guided vehicles (AGVs) can automatically generate a sufficiently accurate internal map (world model) of its surroundings. The work presented in this paper discusses challenges involved and reports on a possible extension to a previously-developed mapping technique in evaluating world models of such dynamic and unstructured environments. The paper also reports on the authors' views in bringing together the community to collectively address this problem from end-users', vendors' and developers' points of view.

## General Terms

Performance Evaluation, Benchmarking, World Modeling, Manufacturing

## Keywords

automated guided vehicles, forklifts, robot mapping and navigation, warehouses, factory floors

## 1. INTRODUCTION

Having robots sense unstructured environments and automatically generate a sufficiently accurate world model is still an unsolved problem, despite advances in computing power and sensor technologies. The solution requires a framework

---

[1]The project is jointly carried out by Temple University and the University of Maryland, College Park, under award ARRA-60NANB10D012 to "bolster U.S. scientific and technological infrastructure, increasing our nation's ability to innovate, compete, and solve scientific and technological problems".

for generating accurate representations that takes into account the dynamic nature of the operational domain. For example, Automated Guided Vehicles (AGVs) are widely used on factory floors and warehouses to transport goods. Currently they require highly structured environments and reference markers installed throughout the intended domain of operation, which, apart from carrying prohibitively high maintenance and installation costs, are not able to cope with dynamic changes in the environment. This has widespread implications for the applicability of AGVs, and also drastically limits the way modern warehouses and manufacturing floors can be designed. A breakthrough will be achieved if AGVs could cope with unstructured, dynamic environments and adapt to human-centered collaboration. A similar analogy can be extended to various domains.

Measuring the performance of such navigation systems requires scientifically sound and statistically significant metrics, measurement, and evaluation methodologies for quantifying their performance. With funding from the Commerce Department's National Institute of Standards and Technology[2] Measurement Science and Engineering Research Grants, the authors have recently embarked on a three year project to create and experimentally validate a framework by which AGVs can automatically generate a sufficiently accurate internal map (world model) of its surroundings. In addition, the authors are also interested in designing experiments and test methods to enable performance evaluation and benchmarking towards characterizing constituent components of navigation and world modeling systems that provide statistically significant results and quantifiable performance data. The work presented in this paper discusses challenges involved in evaluating world models of such dynamic and unstructured environments.

This paper is structured as follows: Section 2 discusses AGVs and their acceptance within the manufacturing industry. Sections 3 and 4 discuss world modeling and challenges associated with evaluating such models. Section 5 presents our ideas on how to evaluate robot-generated world models. Section 6 concludes the paper by summarizing remaining issues and our continuing work.

---

[2]Certain commercial equipment, instruments, or materials are identified in this document. Such identification does not imply recommendation or endorsement by the National Institute of Standards and Technology nor does it imply that the products identified are necessarily the best available for the purpose.

## 2. AGV: INTEREST AND ACCEPTANCE

Robotics and automation holds immense promise as a key transformative technology to positively impact U.S. manufacturing. From traditional and well-established applications in the automotive industry to emerging applications such as material handling, palletizing, and logistics in warehouses, the use of robots can increase productivity whilst ensuring personnel safety. Automated Guided Vehicles (AGVs) represent an integral component of today's manufacturing processes. They are widely used on factory floors for intrafactory transport of goods between conveyors and assembly sections, parts and frame movements, and truck-trailer loading and unloading. To offset prohibitively expensive maintenance and installation costs, and thus expand the AGV's markets and utility beyond what is possible today, it is evident that the dependency on infrastructure is to be minimized (if not eliminated).

A survey on adoption of AGVs conducted in July 2009 by RMT Robotics and Modern Materials Handling Magazine offers some interesting insight into the end-user's opinion about AGVs (see Figures 1, 2). The survey asked end-users about AGV related topics for e.g. desired characteristics of AGVs. While most of the desired characteristics such as durability, low maintenance and adaptability are to be expected, topics related to improved navigation were given a comparably significant attention: open path navigation (78%), obstacle avoidance (91%), no external path guides/sensors (67%). At the same time, the consideration to use AGVs is enormous, see Figure 2. Putting these two results together surely shows that an improvement in navigation capabilities will open up a huge market.

**Figure 1: Adapted from an RMT Robotics and Modern Materials Handling Magazine survey. See text for more details.**

However, the same survey shows a strong contrast to the interest in AGVs when it comes to familiarity with AGVs. Nearly 50% of the users admitted to be not very/not at all familiar; even 86% have not used or even evaluated the use of AGVs. This discrepancy strongly suggests that the current state of AGVs does not match the needs of end-users. Dependable and robust navigation on factory floors is an important factor to remedy this situation.

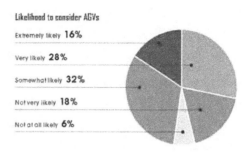

**Figure 2: Adapted from an RMT Robotics and Modern Materials Handling Magazine survey. See text for more details.**

## 3. WORLD MODELING

Sensing unstructured environments and automatically generating a sufficiently accurate world model without re- engineering the operating environment is still an unsolved problem despite advances in sensor systems and computing power. To create useful man-machine collaborative systems and to provide continual situational awareness, a framework for generating accurate representations of the operational domain is imperative. Even in the well-established industrial robotics area, it is telling that only five percent of those robots employ sensors as part of their feedback loop [2]. The science of robot vision has gone through significant changes in the past decades. Limitations of purely geometry driven approaches necessitated the need for statistical methods. Although these methods, like Iterative Closest Point (ICP) [1] or Particle Filters [6], generated excellent results in many applications, limitations still exist, e.g. the necessity for a high sampling density, the dependency on odometry, and the utilization of low-level features (pixels/reflection points) only.

These limitations might partially explain the reluctance and hesitation of many AGV vendors to work towards an improvement of the heavily constrained (virtual) track- and marker-based AGV systems. The recently held North American Material Handling Logistics Tradeshow [7], a premier handling event with participation of major AGV and forklift vendors, provided ample testimony to the fact that the majority of AGV developers are reluctant to abandon the track or marker guided paradigm. While only a few companies are beginning to present approaches of track and marker free navigation, most indulge in little engineering improvements like invisible (chemical) tracks, markers with improved visibility, more sophisticated pattern markers, etc. None of the latter approaches are solutions to the previously-mentioned navigation capabilities, demanded by the end-users.

The employment of AGVs is driven by a single parameter: productivity. Only if the application of new technology offers a clear advantage in terms of productivity it will be applied. An interesting example is the application of current AGVs in warehouses: even if (again: mostly track or marker based) solutions of automated vehicles inside warehouses are implemented, there is, in general, no solution for 'the last five meters', the task of loading pallets into trucks.

Compared to the low increase in productivity, the technical challenge and the needed investment into research and development is too high to be appealing as 'low hanging fruit'.

Looking at promising solutions for robot navigation tasks that exist in theoretical publications and, at an academic level, in implementation, robot navigation in constrained unstructured and dynamic environments like factories and warehouses seems within reach. That begs the question: Why aren't we seeing AGVs freely roaming in these environments? We have an interesting discrepancy between academia and industrial implementation (often referred to as the 'real world'):

- Scientists claim to have robust and fast solutions even for seemingly more challenging tasks in robotics Vs Performance is assessed by academia only (peer evaluation of journal papers with stronger emphasis on theory).

- Mapping in (static) indoor environments is often seen as a solved problem by academia Vs Industry acceptable algorithms are seldom implemented.

## 4. EVALUATION OF WORLD MODELING

Not surprisingly, the development of efficient world modeling schemes has received its due attention from roboticists. A myriad of approaches have been proposed and implemented, some with greater success than others. The capabilities and limitations of these approaches vary significantly depending not only on the operational domain, and onboard sensor suite limitations, but also on the requirements of the end-user: Will a 2D map suffice as an approximation of a 3D environment? Is a metric map really needed or is it sufficient to have a topological representation for the intended tasks or do we need a hybrid metric-topological map [13]? It is thus essential for both developers and consumers of robotic systems to understand the performance characteristics of employed methodologies which will allow them to make an informed decision.

To our knowledge, there is no accepted benchmark for quantitatively evaluating the performance of robotic mapping systems against user-defined requirements. Currently, the evaluation of robotic maps is based on qualitative analysis (i.e. visual inspection). This approach does not allow for better understanding of what errors specific systems are prone to and what systems meet the requirements. It has become common practice in the literature to compare newly developed mapping algorithms with former methods by presenting images of generated maps. This procedure turns out to be suboptimal, particularly when applied to large-scale maps.

Some researchers have recognized the need for quantitative evaluation of mapping and position estimation schemes and are attempting to address it through several programs. For example, there are initiatives to provide collections of standard robotics data sets such as Radish: The Robotics Data Set Repository [9] and RAWSEEDS: Robotics Advancement through Web-publishing of Sensorial and Elaborated Extensive Data Sets [10]) and source codes of various robotics algorithms, such as OpenSLAM [8] and the Mobile Robot Programming Toolkit [12]. While a step in the right direction, they do not address objective performance evaluation and replication of algorithms is not straightforward. NIST's Reference Test Arenas for urban search and rescue

robots have been developed to provide the research community with an efficient way to test their algorithms without having to incur the costs associated with maintaining functional robots and traveling to one of the permanent arena sites for validation and practice.

The RoboCup Rescue competitions [11] have proved to be a good forum to evaluate task-based performance of robots. An image similarity metric and a cross entropy metric are outlined in [15] to measure the quality of occupancy grid maps. The metric gives an indication of distortion of the map with respect to a ground truth map in the presence of noise and pose errors. This metric is embedded in the Jacobs Map Analysis Toolkit [14] and has been tested for comparing maps in the RoboCup context. The Jacobs Map Analysis Toolkit, recently extended to evaluate maps using fiducial markers, has major drawbacks since it is purely tailored to perform evaluation of geometric precision, which limits its versatility to be applied to evaluation of maps under different aspects, e.g. the aforementioned end-user requirements (i.e. 2D/3D, topological/geometric mapping).

We provide a different approach to mapping evaluation based on the principles of an algorithm which was originally introduced in [3] as a mapping algorithm: Force Field Simulation (FFS) with Virtual Scans (VS). Although originally created for mapping, a re-interpretation of its core principles leads to an evaluation tool (the 'evaluation mapper') for mapping evaluation with ground truth. The evaluation mapper is tailored for evaluation and not optimized to build maps. Mapping based on FFS-VS is a promising candidate to solve the evaluation task.

## 5. FFS AS AN EVALUATION TOOL

This section will give a short introduction to FFS&VS with respect to its re-interpretation as a mapping tool. Further details about FFS&VS can be found in [3]. The basic principle of FFS (see Figure 3): driven by attractive forces between features, single scans are iteratively translated/rotated. By laws of physics, such a system converges towards a (local) minimum of its potential.

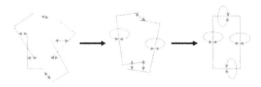

**Figure 3: Basic principle of FFS: alignment of single scans is based on attraction-forces, computed from corresponding features.**

FFS can be extended using hypotheses of expected features in the environment, so called Virtual Scans, see Figure 4. Currently, these features are mid level geometric objects, like planes, rectangles etc. These objects are detected by a module based on mid level spatial cognition (MLSC), see Figure 4. Real data and Virtual Scans are fed into the iterative Force Field Simulation (FFS) alignment approach. FFS cannot distinguish between real and virtual scans. After each iteration, the resulting global map is re-analyzed to state (new) hypotheses (=create VS).

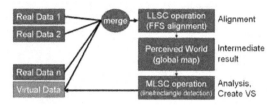

**Figure 4: FFS extended by Virtual Scans: While FFS is a Low Level Spatial Cognition (LLSC) based module, the map analysis is based on Mid Level Spatial Cognition (MLSC) principles. Virtual scans augment the data gained from sensors.**

Interestingly, FFS&VS can align a set of local maps (e.g. single scans) towards a 'ground truth'. With a little re-interpretation, this can be used for map-evaluation, making the tool an evaluation-mapper:

- Assuming a ground truth map $G$, and the result $R$ of a mapping algorithm under evaluation, proceed as follows:

- Change the role of $G$ and $R$: $R$ becomes ground truth, and is used as Virtual Scan.

- Manually split $G$ into logic (intuitive, motivation follows) parts.

- Use FFS to align $G$ towards $R$.

- Evaluate the alignment effort $G$ towards $R$, leading to a quality measure of $R$.

The split of the ground truth map and its alignment to the evaluated map is a major difference between the proposed approach and the static approach used by the Jacobs Toolkit. A more general view on map evaluation highlights the versatility gained by this step.

## 5.1 Grid-based Evaluation

In grid-based evaluation, the map to be evaluated (target map) and the ground truth map are both embedded into a common grid. The grid cells are labeled using properties like 'object', 'empty space' or 'hidden'. Tools using this approach, e.g. the Jacobs Toolkit, measure the local geometric accuracy of the map. Since only low level features (object/empty space) are incorporated, the target map must be close to the ground truth map: it is assumed that low level correspondences imply higher level correspondences. Larger errors in the global appearance of maps cannot be quantified; globally erroneous maps are classified as 'wrong' - even if they are locally correct.

Figure 5 illustrates a case where global geometric correctness might be of minor interest compared to only locally geometric, yet globally topological accuracy. This is the case for optimal path-planning algorithms for AGVs. Figure 5, left, shows the ground truth map. Figure 5, center, illustrates a mapping result with high global geometric correctness, although the bottom part is wrong in details. Figure

5, right, is an example for a map with a high global geometric error. However, all details (obstacles, target position in bottom section) are mapped correctly, the map is also topologically correct (two rooms are connected by hallways). A grid-based approach will prefer the center map to the right one. If the map is intended for AGV navigation, the right map is of higher quality: it shows correctly that the target (red dot) is reachable from the current position (black dot) using the right hallway. The center map misleads the AGV to take the left hallway, a probably expensive mistake. Grid-based approaches such as the Jacobs Toolkit aim to measure the global topographic quality of a robot map; they cannot quantify the topological qualities of a map.

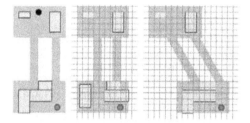

**Figure 5: Grid-based evaluation. Left: Ground truth map. Two rooms (green, top and bottom) with obstacles (gray) are connected by two hallways (green, center). The target (red dot) can only be reached from the current position (black dot) using the right hallway. Center: Mapping example with high global and low local correctness. Right: Mapping example with low global and high local correctness. A grid-based map evaluation will prefer the center map, although for AGV navigation the right map is of higher utility.**

## 5.2 Pose-based Evaluation

A different approach to mapping evaluation is pose-based map quality estimation [4]. Pose-based fitness exploits the fact that precise robot localization is dual to robot mapping: if the robot pose is precisely known in the ground truth map, the scans can be registered based on the pose estimates. Since robot pose measurements are imprecise, the scan data itself has to be taken into account to register the scans in a common coordinate system. Successful registration of scans adjusts the robot poses defined by the target map into the ground truth coordinate system.

Evaluation based on pose information compares the adjustment of robot poses; the sum of all pose errors yields the overall error. The main advantage of pose-based evaluation is its applicability in higher dimensions (for e.g. in 6D-Simultaneous Localization and Mapping schemes). The number of poses to be evaluated is dimensionality independent, whereas the memory consumption of a grid-based evaluation approach increases for 3D applications to a prohibitive cubic behavior. Hence there is high interest in gaining knowledge about pose-based evaluation. The global topological correctness is captured by the fact that only a few rotations are needed to achieve the optimal result. Pose-based approaches have certain drawbacks, mostly related to the fact that rotational and translational errors have significantly different perceptual effects, but are handled alike in the pose error computation.

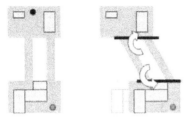

Figure 6: Pose-based evaluation. The target map (right) is transformed to match the ground truth (left). The transformation parameters (here: rotation, arrows) are used to quantify the map quality. The topological correctness of the target map is reflected by the fact that only two rotations are needed to achieve the optimal map.

## 5.3 Hybrid Evaluation

FFS&VS, if used as evaluation-mapper as described above, can be utilized for combined evaluation with respect to topographical and topological map properties, which results in a hybrid pose/grid-based evaluation methodology. Emerging from the proposed framework, Virtual Scan assisted Force Field Simulation, it is designed to eliminate the drawbacks of pure pose- or grid-based evaluation schemes while exploiting their advantages. Using the target map as a fixed virtual scan with high confidence weight, it aligns the single scans of the decomposed ground truth map to the target map, see Figure 7.

Observe that in this approach we transform the ground truth map, not the target map. There are two reasons for such an approach: first, it makes the evaluation independent of the target map's data format. Since the target map is not transformed, it can be given in any format (e.g. geotiff). Second, and perhaps more importantly, the part-decomposition of the ground truth map can reflect the task specific requirements of the world modeling framework. For example, the ground truth map of Figure 7(a) is decomposed into top room, hallways and bottom room. These three parts are required to be mapped with high geometric accuracy. The hybrid approach quantifies the map quality using pose-based parameters and grid-based parameters from additional evaluations on the single parts. Their relative pose, defines the global appearance of the map, which is captured by the transformation parameters. The importance weight of the transformation parameters can be individually determined.

## 6. CONCLUSIONS AND FUTURE WORK

This paper presented some preliminary thoughts on how to evaluate robot-generated world modeling schemes for unstructured and dynamic environments. The use of world modeling for achieving autonomous navigation of AGVs and forklifts on manufacturing floors and warehouses was elaborated. Many open questions remain: What is the indus-

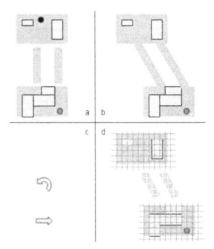

Figure 7: Hybrid evaluation methodology. (a) Decomposed ground truth map (3 parts). (b) Target map. (c) Mapping transformation of (a) to (b). (d) Grid-based evaluation on transformed parts. The final score is computed using task adjusted weights for transformation parameters and grid evaluation results.

try's view on the discrepancy between the quality assessment of algorithms of academia and industry? What are industry's requirements? What are typical cases of environments where AGVs are needed? Which of the different mapping approaches could be upgraded to live up to industry standards?

The paper also emphasized the need for objective evaluation via development of test methods to quantify the quality of world models. Our ongoing work is focused on developing benchmarking schemes and how these can be channeled towards facilitating the development of standards for the AGV industry [5].

In an effort to bring together the academic and research communities together, the authors have organized two workshops, held in early September 2010 at Temple University and at the 2010 Performance Metrics for Intelligent Systems (PerMIS) Workshop where these issues were discussed. The discussion focused on the challenges in achieving these goals. Technical presentations and open discussions centered on how to create and experimentally validate world modeling frameworks for unstructured environments amidst dynamic objects.

## 7. REFERENCES

[1] P. Besl and N. McKay. A method for Registration of 3D Shapes. *IEEE PAMI*, 14, 1992.
[2] CCC/CRA. Roadmapping for robotics. http://www.us-robotics.us.
[3] R. Lakaemper. Improving sparse laser scan alignment with virtual scans. In *International Conference on Intelligent Robots and Systems (IROS08)*, Nice, France, September 2008. IEEE.

[4] R. Lakaemper, A. Nuechter, and N. Adluru. Performance of 6d lum and ffs slam. In *Performance Metrics for Intelligent Systems (PerMIS) Workshop*, Gaithersburg, MD, 2008.

[5] R. Madhavan, R. Lakaemper, and T. Kalmar-Nagy. Benchmarking and standardization of intelligent robotic systems. In *14th International Conference on Advanced Robotics (ICAR 2009)*, Munich, Germany, June 2009.

[6] M. Montemerlo, S. Thrun, D. Koller, and B. Wegbreit. Fastslam 2.0: An improved particle filtering algorithm for simultaneous localization and mapping that provably converges. *Proc. of the Int. Conf. on Artificial Intelligence (IJCAI)*, 2003.

[7] NA. North American Material Handling Logistics Tradeshow, Cleveland, Ohio, April 2010.

[8] OpenSLAM. http://www.openslam.org.

[9] Radish. The robotics data set repository. http://radish.sourceforge.net.

[10] RAWSEEDS. Robotics advancement through web-publishing of sensorial and elaborated extensive data sets. http://www.rawseeds.org.

[11] Robocuprescue. http://www.robocuprescue.org.

[12] M. Robots. The mobile robot programming toolkit. http://babel.isa. uma.es/mrpt/.

[13] S. Thrun. Learning metric-topological maps for indoor mobile robot navigation. *Artificial Intelligence*, 1998.

[14] J. University. Jacobs map analysis toolkit. http://robotics.iu-bremen.de/datasets/mapevaluation.

[15] I. Varsadan, A. Birk, and M. Pfingsthorn. Determining map quality through an image similarity metric. In *Lecture Notes in Artificial Intelligence (LNAI): RoboCup 2008,Robot WorldCup XII*, 2008.

# Co-X Panel Discussion

**Elena Messina**
National Institute of Standards and Technology
100 Bureau Drive MS 8230
Gaithersburg, MD 20899
+1 301-975-3510

elena.messina@nist.gov

**Brian A. Weiss**
National Institute of Standards and Technology
100 Bureau Drive MS 8230
Gaithersburg, MD 20899
+1 301-975-4373

brian.weiss@nist.gov

**Raj Madhavan**
Institute for Systems Research
University of Maryland, College Park &
National Institute of Standards and Technology
100 Bureau Drive MS 8230
Gaithersburg, MD 20899
+1 301-975-2865

raj.madhavan@nist.gov

## ABSTRACT
Robots as co-protectors, co-inhabitants, co-workers, co-integrants, or more generically, "Co-X" will improve effectiveness, efficiency, safety, security, and improve quality of life in the coming years. In-keeping with the theme of PerMIS'10, which investigated the role of performance assessment in evaluating intelligent systems that co-exist with humans, a panel discussion was held focusing on the Co-X vision. This document synthesizes the discussions held during this session

## Keywords
Co-X, Performance Metrics, Standards, Human-Robot Collaboration

## 1. INTRODUCTION
Robots that work safely in collaboration with and close proximity to humans, complementing and augmenting their abilities may usher in new benefits economically and societally. Robots as co-protectors, co-inhabitants, co-workers, co-integrants, or more generically, "Co-X" will improve effectiveness, efficiency, safety, security, and improve quality of life in the coming years. This year's theme for PerMIS was investigating the key role of performance assessment in developing intelligent systems that can **co-exist** with humans towards improving the quality of our lives intertwined with automation. In-keeping with the theme, a panel discussion was held focusing on the Co-X vision. This document synthesizes the discussions held during this session.

A mix of panelists representing various domains and application perspectives were invited:

- ∞ Greg Dudek, McGill University
- ∞ Ken Goldberg University of California – Berkeley
- ∞ Helen Greiner, CyPhy Works
- ∞ Howard Harary, National Institute of Standards and Technology
- ∞ Susan Hill, Army Research Laboratory
- ∞ Paul Oh, Drexel University
- ∞ Holly Yanco, University of Massachusetts – Lowell

The PerMIS'10 panel members were given the following charge: Considering the Co-X vision, discuss the implications for research and development as well as strategies for realizing this vision.

Panelists were asked to consider questions along the following lines:

- ∞ How to achieve this Co-X vision: do you believe that there are cross-cutting common technologies underlying co-X systems that serve the diverse application domains? In other words, are there basic competences that should be the focus of initial efforts prior to adding the domain-specific capabilities?
- ∞ What are desired qualities of a Co-X system?
- ∞ What are the underlying infratechnologies (building blocks, standards, metrics, development tools)?
- ∞ What are strategies to advance this vision?
  - o Examples may include open innovation platforms, and/or competitions, ...

What role could/should performance metrics, performance evaluations, and standards play in advancing a Co-X vision?

## 2. THE CO-X VISION
Elena Messina began the discussion with an overview of the Co-X concept. Robots that are able to work side-by-side with humans will spur a growth in the robotics field. New applications and domains will be made possible, leading to robots becoming more mainstream and commonplace. Co-X robots can enable humans to transcend their limitations. They complement human abilities and also augment their capabilities. Humans and Co-X robots should be able to interact in a natural fashion, meaning forms of verbal speech and gestures should be understood by the robots.

An initial list of domains of participation for Co-X includes manufacturing and logistics, medical and healthcare, defense and security, housekeeping, mining, agriculture, and transportation. Myriad other possibilities exist, such as space exploration.

Co-X robots will work in close proximity with humans and may physically interact with humans. Therefore, safety concerns are paramount. Other cross-cutting concerns are cost and societal acceptance.

Examples of capabilities that Co-X robots require are:
- ∞ Direct Human-Robot Communication
  - o Natural language, gestural, neural
  - o Rich Semantic Understanding
- ∞ Robust functioning in complex, unstructured, dynamic environments

- ∞ Variable Levels of Autonomy
- ∞ Learning and Adaptation
  - o In situ learning for communication, behavior, preferences
- ∞ Dexterous manipulation: Human-like and beyond
- ∞ Mobility: Human-like and beyond
- ∞ Strength, accuracy, rapidity of response/execution

These capabilities are made possible by underlying infrastructural technologies, as enumerated in the CCC Robotics Roadmap [1]. Examples are perception, autonomous navigation, novel mechanisms and actuators, human-like dexterous manipulation, intuitive and safe interfaces, and skill acquisition. The Co-X vision is indeed consonant with the CCC roadmap Synthesis, as illustrated in Figure 1.

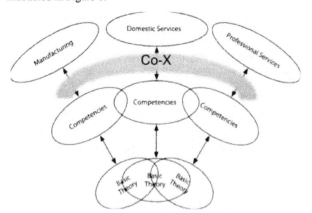

**Figure 1. Co-X Cross-cutting capabilities underlie all the application domains for the next generation robotics. Figure adapted from the Robotics Roadmap [1]. The attributes of Co-X are pre-requisites for success in the intended application domains (manufacturing, domestic, professional).**

## 3. Summary of the Panel Discussion

The discussion with the panelists was wide-ranging, with active audience participation as well. General themes emerged from the panel. They included contextual issues (general technological and societal trends), key technologies for enabling Co-X, and strategies for stimulating progress towards Co-X.

### 3.1 Contextual Issues

Technology is changing quickly, which influences the mindset of young persons. A panelist spoke of the gap between the class of 198X (the Megabyte generation) and 2015+ (the Terabyte generation). Certainly, advances in computational power, as well as sensors and mechanisms, enable much more complex algorithms and capabilities for robots. The pace of technological advancement is accelerating as well, implying that we will attain the minimum raw computation power (and storage capacity) in the next few decades for implementing general-purpose robots. Correspondingly, there has been an erosion of boundaries in the information age. For instance, the distinction between products and services is blurred in cell phones. Social media has eroded the boundary between producers of content and users, and companies like Amazon[1] straddle information technology media,

communications, and consumer electronics. It is hard to predict now how Co-X robots will be applied once they become a reality.

### 3.2 Competencies and Technologies that Underlie Co-X

One panelist suggested that we should ask for a toolbox of fundamental competencies that can be used for Co-X development. Simultaneous localization and mapping (SLAM) is an example of a fundamental competence that would be part of the toolbox. It was suggested by an audience member that the competencies that robots should have be complementary to human competencies. Perception is an example where humans have certain strengths (e.g., able to understand very complex scenes with our eyes) and weaknesses (e.g., our eyes only work within certain parts of the spectrum and have limited range/resolution).

The need for humans and robots to operate as a team was a recurring theme from the panelists, not surprising when talking about Co-X. Many roboticists have not considered the human in the loop when designing their robots; this needs to change. A seamless interaction between the human and the robot in real-world environments is desired. This interaction necessitates that robots have adjustable levels of autonomy and very flexible means of communicating with humans. The robot must know when the human needs assistance and when it needs to ask the human for help.

Handing off control between the human and robot is a particularly thorny aspect of interaction. For instance, if the robot has a failure and the human has to pick up where it left off, how does the robot convey information about itself, the environment, and the status of its assigned task? In general, successful communication will require the robot to know what to tell the human as well as when it's appropriate to tell the human – in other words the system has to have to have competent articulation capabilities in this regard.

The robot should provide feedback confirmation when it receives instructions from a human. Gestures are a natural means of communicating (and may be essential in certain domains, such as noisy factory floors or during military operations where silence may be critical). Voice recognition and natural language understanding are technologies that are being developed for non-robotics domains and could be leveraged for Co-X.

### 3.3 Strategies for Advancing the State-of-the-art to Achieve Co-X

The panel suggested various strategies for accelerating the pace of progress. A strong roadmap was suggested as a necessary tool to provide guidance to the community. The semiconductor industry created a roadmap [2] that took many years to develop, with input from many, and which is updated on a regular basis. This has served them very well as they have made steady progress towards achieving the technical goals.[2] The Robotics Roadmap is a great start, but greater detail is needed.

---

[1] Certain commercial companies, products and software are identified in this paper in order to explain our research. Such

identification does not imply recommendation or endorsement by NIST, nor does it imply that the companies, products and software identified are necessarily the best available for the purpose.

[2] "'What technical capabilities need to be developed for the industry to stay on Moore's Law and the other trends?' The ITRS assesses the principal technology needs to guide the shared

Necessary prerequisites include benchmarks and standards. One panelist framed it as physics envy. It must be very clear what is being measured. This will allow for comparing different solutions against one another.

Another strategy suggested was coming up with challenges we want to take on as a community. We could circulate ideas through a white paper and get feedback from the various stakeholders. Challenges should have verifiable, measurable goals that we agree to as a community. Some asked whether the challenge approach was a good mechanism for aiming the research and moving it ahead; in fact, there has been good progress in the past decade without these challenges. Others noted that the goals should challenges (and their goals) must be carefully chosen since failing to achieve a goal can have negative consequences. Also, a clear winner can give the false impression that the problem is solved and that no more investments should be made in an area. Therefore the challenges should have a high bar, but also include achievable goals – both short and long term. Often there is excellent research that does not make the transition into products. The panel discussed how to bridge this gap. Having industry set the challenges was one possibility.

The idea of robotics challenges is not new, of course. Many are aware of the Defense Advanced Research Projects Agency (DARPA) Grand Challenges that featured autonomous vehicles navigating multi-terrain courses (2004 and 2005) as well as within an urban, multi-vehicle environment (2007). One panel member called attention to the fact that, in 1997 Ken Goldberg, along with Howard Moraff, organized a panel discussion as part of the IEEE International Conference on Robotics and Automation on "Grand Challenges in Robotics." Attributes of a Grand Challenge were listed as

∞ broad scope or large scale
∞ requires many teams and many efforts
∞ high risk
∞ high potential impact
∞ capture the imagination

The meta-challenges that will arise as a result of achieving the goal are still perfectly relevant today:
∞ acceptance by users
∞ human augmentation
∞ human-centered end-user technology
∞ zero-fault safety
∞ robust functionality
∞ performance matched to human intuition
∞ compelling applications

As a side note, another barrier to progress is the fact that robotics is at the mercy of so many technologies (e.g., batteries or other energy sources for robots are a limiting factor).

## 3.4 What is the Nature of Robotics Research?
The panel finished with a discussion of the nature of robotics research.

∞ Are roboticists bench scientists or applied scientists?
∞ Is the university the best place to address the end goals of Co-X?
∞ Or should academics focus on fundamental science?
∞ Is robotics theory or science?

The role of the "citizen scientist" was also debated. The sensor that was the game-changer for the DARPA Urban Challenge was developed by a couple of brothers who run a stereo speaker company.[3] Thousands of smart phone applications are developed by citizens. There was no consensus on the role that citizen scientists can play in advancing the state of robotics. The sensor developers closed the gap between good fundamental research and moved it to commercialization. They did not perform the fundamental research.

## 4. CONCLUSIONS
Although there was not one hundred percent agreement, the panel generally espoused the need for fundamental competences to be developed, along with benchmarks and measures (standards) that are arrived at by the community. Having grand challenge problems can not only stimulate progress and excitement but also motivate other contributions. Detailed, well-defined roadmaps have proven to help muster progress within a major industry and should be considered for robotics as well. Ultimately, all agreed that the Co-X vision was worth trying to achieve.

## 5. REFERENCES
[1] "A Roadmap for U.S. Robotics: From Internet to Robotics," CCC and CRA (NSF-funded), 2009, http://www.us-robotics.us/

[2] Semiconductor Industry Association, The International Technology Roadmap for Semiconductors, 2009 Edition. http://www.itrs.net/Links/2009ITRS/Home2009.htm

[3] Rendleman, J., "Engines of Change," Government Computer News, August 3, 2007. http://gcn.com/articles/2007/08/03/engines-of-change.aspx

research, showing the "targets" that need to be met. These targets are as much as possible quantified and expressed in tables, showing the evolution of key parameters over time. Accompanying text explains and clarifies the numbers contained in the tables where appropriate." [2] The following are a few examples of technology areas for which target values are defined for up to 15 years into the future: System Drivers Design Test and Test Equipment Process Integration, Devices, and Structures Emerging Research Devices and Lithography.

www.ingramcontent.com/pod-product-compliance
Lightning Source LLC
Chambersburg PA
CBHW080548060326
40689CB00021B/4781